AF504013

EXHIBITIONIST

View from a moving train

rd Dorment
rred vision
man painter
chter, subject
nt exhibition
ate Gallery

lery's major autumn
til January 12, 1992)
e work of the avant-
painter **Gerhard Rich-**
the rare occasions in
when the gallery has
pective to a foreign art-
me as an odd choice.
lifficult, highly intellec-
n artist to respect, per-
t one I personally much

cident that the most illu-
ay in the exhibition cata-
ritten not by an art critic
storian but by a political
Neal Ascherson needs to
's work into the perspec-
t German history because
keys to understanding that
the story of Richter's life.
East Germany in 1932, he
craft of oil painting in the
rt Academy. From a techni-
of view that training was
Richter was taught to draw,
a canvas, to apply oil paint,
e glazes by methods which
ged little since the 19th cen-
such an education placed no
two particular qualities art-
e West then considered all-
t: spontaneity and imagina-
ial realism was the only style
ed, subjects approved by the
nist party the only content
. Though almost all of his
ork has disappeared, presum-
chter turned out portraits of
s and party officials, or else
ical scenes glorifying the
tion.
imagine such a man's half-fas-
d and half-appalied reaction
in 1959 at the Venice Biennale
t saw Jackson Pollock's drips of
int and Lucio Fontana's slashed
ases. A bigger shock was to
. When Richter finally escaped
e West to settle in Düsseldorf in
he was already 29, with 10 years
ull-time academic art training
nd him. What, then, can he have
e of the Neo-Dada art of the
xus group, or of Joseph Beuys's
lptures made of fat and felt, both
which were then flourishing in Düs-
dorf? How can he have coped with
sheer contempt in which the
ant-garde held oil painting in those
ars? Richter had just escaped from
lictatorship which told him *what to*
int; now he discovered a different
ranny, this one commercial, which
precated the act of painting at all.
In this bind Richter continued to
urn out beautifully crafted oil paint-
ngs, but he harnessed his formidable
mic technique to subjects delib-

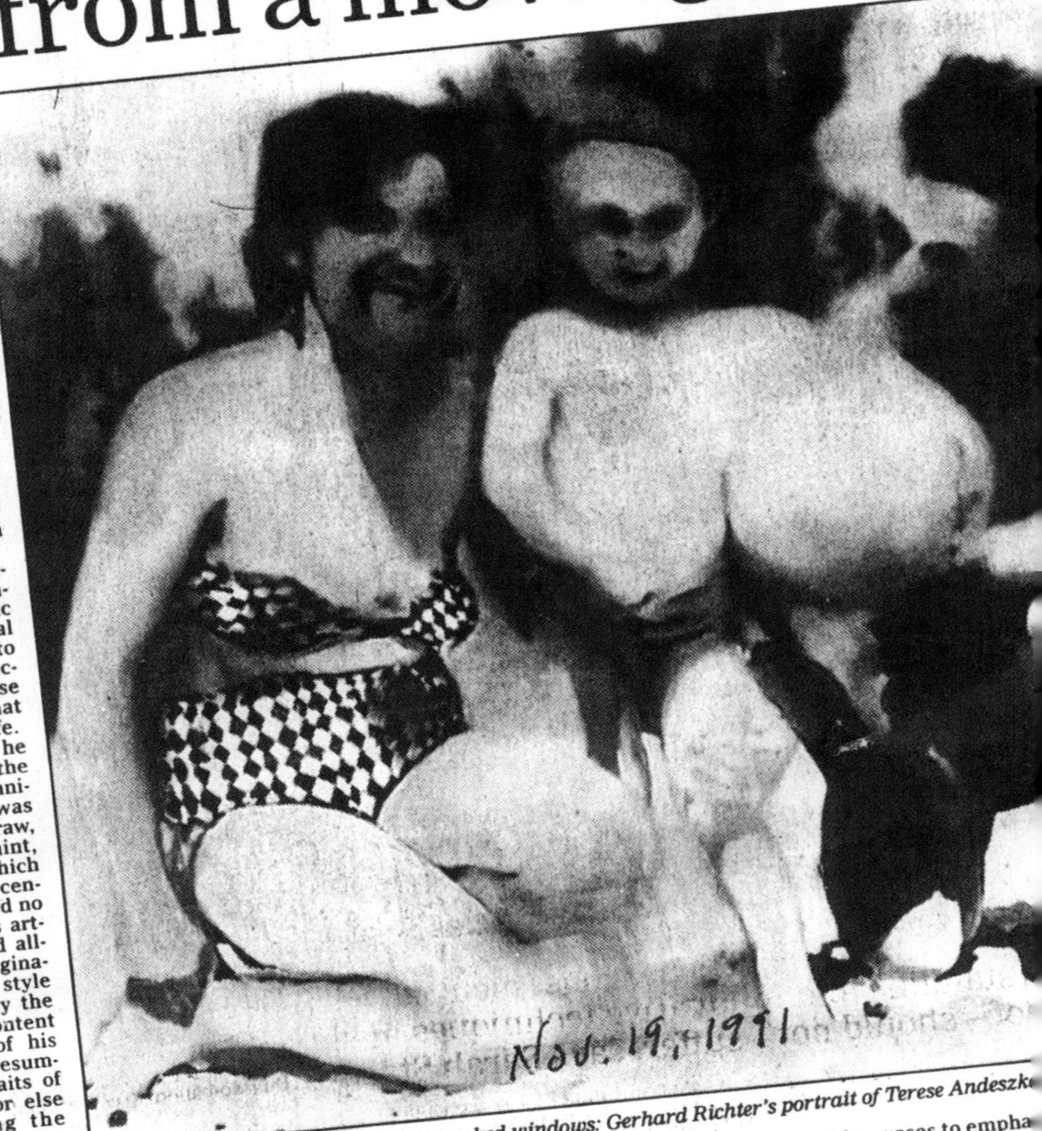

Seeing the world through rain-streaked windows: Gerhard Richter's portrait of Terese Andeszka

invisible brushstrokes. Lest the result
look too much like an actual photograph, Richter cultivated the slight
loss of focus caused by the projection
and enlargement of the photograph,
even going over the wet canvas with a
dry brush to emphasise the blurring.
The effect is reminiscent of objects
and landscapes seen from the rain-
streaked windows of a moving train:
these early pictures are all about leaving things behind, about ordinary
things that pass through our lives and
are never seen again, such as newspaper photographs or images
glimpsed on a TV screen. Occasionally, a subject like a fighter bomber or
aerial views of vulnerable cities
remind us that Richter must have
lived through the bombing of Dres-
den, but he himself presents these
subjects deadpan, with no comment,
ordinary still-lifes as banal and uninflected as anything painted by Andy
Warhol.

It was but a short step from this
photo-based work to fully abstract
paintings, but, once again, with a
twist. Instead of relying on spontaneous gesture, as did the Abstract
Expressionists, Richter again
attempted to minimise subjective
feeling, expression itself, by accent-
ing the conscious and deliberate role
the artist plays in making a work of
art. He therefore projected slides of
his own abstract watercolours on to
large-scale canvases, then painstak-

'6 All his life Richter has been desperately trying, and failing, to paint 'Nothing' 9

ingly painted the results with the precision of a 19th-century academic
master. Realism as practised in

vases to empha
what he paints.
Indeed, if ev
an aesthetic of
art that sets
Richter is its
And so in the
the Tate sho
grey, it is not
tant, but the
with the abs
absence of fe
ion. It is the
illustrating
is more or le
desperately
paint all his
I have se
in which th
forced to
every pain
how it is p
has painte
tualising a
difficulty
ings is tha
ably tedio
struck m
show of

EXHIBITIONIST

Writing about Art
in a Daily Newspaper

RICHARD DORMENT

WILMINGTON SQUARE BOOKS
AN IMPRINT OF BITTER LEMON PRESS

WILMINGTON SQUARE BOOKS
An imprint of Bitter Lemon Press

First published in 2016 by
Wilmington Square Books
47 Wilmington Square
London WC1X 0ET

www.bitterlemonpress.com

A CIP record for this book is available from the British Library

ISBN 978-1-908524-676

9 8 7 6 5 4 3 2 1

Designed and typeset by Jane Havell Associates
Printed in China

Deborah Loeb Brice

Contents

Preface

Out of the thousands of reviews I wrote for *The Daily Telegraph* I've selected only the ones that make me look good – the ones I think still read well or said something about the subject I hadn't read before. Those pieces were also the most fun to write and the ones in which I hear my own voice most distinctly. Otherwise the selection is essentially random.

The inclusion or not of an artist does not reflect my sense of his or her stature or my feelings about their work. The absence of reviews of Tony Cragg, Richard Deacon or Anish Kapoor only means that I've never written well enough about them to justify reprinting a review here. Likewise, the quality of an exhibition was irrelevant in the selection. I've omitted my review of the Leonardo exhibition at the National Gallery because the piece didn't add anything new, but I have included one devoted to a single heavily overpainted work by Pieter Bruegel the Elder.

The reviews are reprinted more or less as written. Inane final paragraphs telling readers not to miss a show have been dropped. Two reviews written years apart about Susan Hiller are spliced together because my earlier (and better) description of one of her most powerful works was too good to leave out. Describing the same artwork twice was always a problem for me; the second version never had the energy of the first. When I came to review Jackson Pollock's 1998 retrospective I found I couldn't improve on a description of his *Mural* written five years earlier for *American Art in the 20th Century*. I've condensed the wording in the original so you don't have to read the same thing twice.

My first thanks go to my publisher John Nicoll who didn't flinch when I asked him whether he'd consider bringing out a book of my old reviews. He then whittled down the 160 or so reviews I initially presented him with to the 116 we now have. Jane Havell is responsible for the snappy design and elegant layout of the book, and also for some very necessary editing and proofreading. Michael Paraskos took on the tedious job of picture researcher with patience, tact and good humour.

Sincere thanks to Richard Calvocoressi, Lily Dorment, Caroline Egremont, Andy Goldsworthy, Holly Goldsworthy, John Hatt, Ben Read and Marina Vaizey. I am indebted to Gavin Filler at the *Telegraph*'s picture archive and to the paper's librarian, Lorraine Goodspeed.

The editor of the Arts Pages is the most important person in a critic's professional life. They draw up our reviewing schedules and approve our pieces before publication, whether or not they personally edit the copy. This means that at some possibly unconscious level the tone of each review is pitched to the personality of the editor who would be its first reader. There were six art editors while I was at *The Daily Telegraph* and all were a pleasure to work with. However, 90 per cent of the reviews in this book were written under the three who served longest – and to them my gratitude is inexpressible.

As I explain in my introduction, Miriam Gross bore the brunt of the annoyance my early reviews sometimes caused. In time I learned how to say what I meant without attracting lawyers' letters, but back then I became used to telephone calls from Miriam saying my presence was required in the legal department. These occasions terrified me, but fortunately the editor Max Hastings considered threatened lawsuits a sure sign that a journalist was doing his job.

By the time Sarah Crompton inherited me I'd mellowed a lot. Fortunately, she wasn't mellow at all. Personal interest (her husband is an artist and she became the paper's dance critic) made her a redoubtable defender of the visual and performing arts. Under her the arts pages expanded and became more sophisticated. Her engagement with issues raised in my reviews and her readiness to express appreciation when she thought a review worked made me a more confident critic. Paul Gent's editing did my writing a power of good. Like all good editors he saved me from myself. By cutting out superfluities and fripperies he gave weight to my writing and accorded a degree of authority to my criticism that surprised me more than anyone.

On occasion Mark Monahan played the good cop to Paul's bad. If you find any jokes in these pages, he let them slip in. And our revered administrative secretary on the Arts Desk, Louise Dowman, made all our lives possible.

Finally, the quality and the quantity of colour reproductions in this book were made possible by a grant from the Deborah Loeb Brice Foundation. I can't begin to list the number of arts institutions in Britain that have had buildings repaired or extended or rebuilt from top to bottom thanks to her generous support. Everyone in this country who has seen a play at the National Theatre, visited one of the National Museums in London or smaller venues like the Courtauld or Watts galleries in the last 25 years has something to thank Deborah Loeb Brice for. I can only express my own thanks by dedicating this book to her.

Introduction

When I started at *The Daily Telegraph* in December 1986 exhibitions at the Tate Gallery, British Museum, Hayward Gallery and Royal Academy were every bit as ambitious as those in Paris or New York – but they were few and far between compared to what we are used to today. London galleries tended to stage one big loan exhibition at a time, several times a year. With the exception of the Royal Academy, little thought was given to exhibition design. Alone of all European capitals, London had no museum or gallery of modern art. Nor was there a dedicated space at the National Gallery big enough to stage substantial loan shows. When you talked about the art market you meant Old Master dealers within walking distance of Sotheby's and Christie's. Interest in contemporary art was intense – but limited to a relatively small, hidden group of curators and enthusiasts who didn't feel connected to a mainstream culture that still regarded modern art with suspicion.

By the time I left the *Telegraph* in June 2015, London had displaced New York as the centre of the museum and gallery world. Spectacular building projects at the National Gallery, Royal Academy, Tate, British Museum and the Queen's Gallery attracted millions of new visitors from this country and abroad. Smaller venues including the Courtauld Gallery, Dulwich Picture Gallery and Wallace Collection either instituted exhibition programmes or stepped up existing ones. Extensions at the Serpentine and Whitechapel galleries more than doubled the space available for loan exhibitions. From 1995 onwards, exhibition design in most national museums became routine, so that visitors to loan shows came to expect an element of spectacle or glamour in addition to the art.

International curators and collectors flew in for the annual Frieze Art Fair and to see exhibitions at Gagosian, White Cube and the Saatchi Gallery. In 1998 Christie's held the first major auction entirely devoted to contemporary art in London, not New York. As more galleries showing art at the cutting edge opened in the East End, habitués of the older established galleries such as Anthony d'Offay off Bond Street and the Lisson Gallery in Lisson Grove became adept at navigating the streets (or more accurately back streets) of Hackney, Shoreditch, Bethnal Green and Bermondsey. Many of the most active venues for contemporary art were outside the capital – at the Bristol Arnolfini, Oxford's MoMA and Birmingham's Ikon. Edinburgh had the Fruitmarket, and Glasgow both the Third Eye Centre and later the Transmission Gallery.

What follows is my own partial, patchy, highly personal and, I am sure, fallible account of those years.

1

Growing up in the US, I am not sure I ever heard the term 'art history' until I was in my second year reading classics at Princeton University. Unhappy with a badly taught course on the Roman poet Lucretius, I sat in on a lecture by the young art historian Robert Rosenblum. When I entered the lecture hall he was holding forth in front of a 15-foot-high image of Géricault's *Raft of the Medusa* – and I almost swooned with excitement. That same day I transferred to the art history department and didn't look back (or up) until almost ten years later when, as a graduate fellow at Columbia University, I returned from Europe with a doctorate and the intention of working in a museum.

Specifically, it was the Philadelphia Museum of Art, where from 1973 to 1976 I held the job of assistant curator in the department of European painting. This was an experience that instilled a lifelong respect for the curatorial profession, even though I came to realise that my own vocation was to write about art, not to look after it.

The next ten years were spent in London living hand-to-mouth as a freelance researcher and exhibition organiser. By 1986 I'd completed a catalogue of Philadelphia's collection of British paintings, a biography of the *fin de siècle* British sculptor Alfred Gilbert, and catalogues of exhibitions I'd curated either on my own or with colleagues.[1] For a

1. A retrospective of *James McNeill Whistler* that I co-curated with Margaret Macdonald came later. It opened at the Tate Gallery and travelled to Washington and Paris in 1994–95.

short period, I contributed fortnightly exhibition reviews to *Country Life*, but the idea of writing for a mass circulation newspaper never crossed my mind.

Then in 1986 Neil MacGregor stepped down as the editor of the *Burlington Magazine* to become director of the National Gallery of Art in Trafalgar Square. I applied for his job at the *Burlington* and was invited to come in for an interview. During our conversation something happened that would lead to a change of career: a member of the interviewing panel asked me a question I hadn't seen coming. The director of the Ashmolean Museum, Christopher White, asked whether I was aware that the editor of the *Burlington* is expected to write a monthly leader at the front of the magazine (I wasn't) and wondered whether there was any topic of current interest to scholars and curators I'd like to address in an editorial.

Was there ever.

A few months earlier I'd organised an exhibition at the Royal Academy on the art of the British sculptor Alfred Gilbert. In the days and weeks following the opening I'd had my first exposure to the vacuity of art journalism in Great Britain. The problem wasn't the range or diversity of coverage – the show had been reviewed in all the mainstream papers and the notices were generally positive. But Gilbert's was hardly a household name and at that period very few journalists who wrote about art for daily newspapers had much interest in the byways of art history. Most of those who reviewed that show did little more than rewrite the press release. They'd describe the works of art and then say something about Gilbert's life, but otherwise brought little knowledge and less curiosity to their review. I could detect no sense of personal engagement either with the art or with the highly theatrical installation designed by the architect Piers Gough.

That's what I told the interviewing panel – and added that without knowledgeable or at least responsible art critics in the popular press no conduit existed between artists and curators on the one hand and the gallery-going public on the other. I'd been used to reading John Russell in the *New York Times*, a critic who always tried to convey a sense of what the artist was trying to achieve, whether or not he thought the work successful. This is why it puzzled me that scholars who wrote for the *Burlington* didn't seem to mind when journalists

made so little effort to explain and evaluate the exhibitions they
worked so hard to create.

Like any generalisations based on one set of data, what I said was
not entirely true. There were respected and highly readable British
critics including John Golding, Lawrence Gowing and David
Sylvester, but they didn't write regularly for newspapers. Those
who did (Richard Cork, Caroline Tisdall and Paul Overy) were
good critics, but had not reviewed the Gilbert show. Even so,
my complaint was worth making: there was no reason why the
mainstream press in this country should not cover the exhibitions of
art old and new in reviews that had the depth of thought routinely
found in British book reviews and theatre criticism.

Precisely this was about to happen – and far sooner than anyone
in that room could have anticipated. In that very year, 1986, Rupert
Murdoch took on the powerful print unions when he moved his
newspapers (*The Times*, the *Sun* and the *News of the World*) to
Wapping. By putting an end to wildcat strikes, astronomical salaries,
over-manning of the workforce and the refusal of printers to accept
even basic new technologies, Murdoch rejuvenated the British press.
In the wake of Wapping, newspapers could potentially become
profitable again.

The Independent, a new quality broadsheet, was particularly
important.[2] It blew a blast of fresh air through the whole of British
journalism, noticeably in the arts pages, which were by far the best
on Fleet Street. Especially influential at the beginning was Andrew
Graham-Dixon, a young art critic who started at the *Independent*
in 1986. His reviews set a standard that rival newspapers couldn't
ignore. Writing on art became much livelier as critics reported on, and
took sides for or against contemporary art, and sometimes incited the
culture wars that raged in Britain in the early 1990s.

Released from the stranglehold of the print unions, all British
newspapers were able to increase the number of pages they printed,
which in turn meant that more space was available to cover arts,
features and sport. In time, the impact of all this on museums and
galleries would be incalculable.

2. Stephen Glover, 'The Righteous Mind', *The New Statesman*,
5–11 September 2014, pp. 27–31.

Meanwhile, Conrad Black bought *The Daily Telegraph* and the recently appointed arts editor Miriam Gross was looking for an art critic. As a former literary editor at the *Observer* Miriam didn't know any art critics, so she telephoned her friend Kate Trevelyan who worked at the *Burlington Magazine*. As I was later to learn, Kate remembered the American who'd recently been into the office for an interview – and how he'd banged on about the poor quality of art reviewing in British newspapers.

So that's how I came to write about art in the biggest-selling broadsheet in the country. In 1987 the paper sold 1,147,000 copies per day, in contrast to its nearest broadsheet rival *The Times* (442,000). For the next fifteen years the circulation never fell below one million and even by 2009 it stood at over 900,000. The number of copies actually read (as opposed to the number purchased at a newsstand or by subscription) was estimated to be double that. Of course, only a fraction of those readers looked at the art reviews. Even so, those figures inspired awe in someone whose own (admittedly book-length) publications might sell a few hundred copies at most.

From the start I was struck by the range of opinion you could read in the British press. On the day after its opening, an opera, play or art exhibition was covered by at least five daily broadsheets, the same again on Sunday, plus weekly magazines such as the *Spectator* and *New Statesman* and a weekly review on BBC Radio 3. Unlike in New York, everything in this country was up for discussion and culture was as much a part of the national debate as politics or sport.

Miriam was the ideal mentor for someone who had never written for a newspaper before. I couldn't go wrong if I pitched my reviews to her – a highly intelligent person who I could not assume had any detailed knowledge of the period or school I was covering that week. From the questions she asked about my first draughts, I learned how to take readers with me by the addition of a swift definition of a style, a school, a medium or a technique without interrupting the flow of an argument.

Most valuable to me was her scepticism. When writing about new art I knew her baloney-detector would be on high alert. That made me a much more stringent critic than I would otherwise have been. The worst critics write for small-circulation periodicals or online blogs read exclusively by fellow enthusiasts. 'To what purpose?' became

the first question I asked myself when I looked at a new work of art.
If I wasn't sure why an artist made an artwork, the chances are they
weren't either. 'To shock' or 'to disturb' are not adequate answers.

I quickly learned that the closest parallel to the arts pages in
a daily newspaper is not news or features but sport. Readers who
follow football or cricket usually know something (and often quite
a lot) about the sport. What they are looking for in sports writing is
sophisticated analysis of the play in yesterday's match. The same is
true of writing on exhibitions. As well as describing the art clearly you
have to convey as vividly as possible what it was like to walk through
a show and then say how you responded to it.

But again, you had to do it with a broad brush and you had to
hold the reader's interest until the last paragraph. You needed a
'hook' to engage the reader's attention, and it was important to get
straight to the art without a long preamble. Never ever tell your
readers the show is a turkey until near the end of the review, because
the moment you do is the moment they stop reading.

My reviews were usually much better if I knew nothing about
the subject of the exhibition. Good critical writing entails a process
of interrogation which is best done in a spirit of self-doubt. I no more
knew what I was going to say about an exhibition while I was in it
than a sports writer does the outcome of a match. For the same reason,
I found I was able to write more effectively if I didn't talk about a
review while I was working on it. I did not go to openings and knew
very few artists, critics, dealers or collectors. For about ten years I
spoke to my friend David Sylvester every day on the telephone. We
had a pact that we would not discuss my review for that week until
after it appeared in print. Otherwise I'd have become his mouthpiece.

I tried not to pre-judge an artist or an exhibition but sometimes
it couldn't be helped. Any artwork that involved diagrams and
blackboards I knew in advance I'd hate. With a few sublime
exceptions (Janet Cardiff and George Bures Miller, or Susan Hiller),
I approached sound installations requiring headphones with the
deepest suspicion.

The speed at which each review had to be turned around was new
to me and so was the vertiginous switch from writing about art made
of neon tubing one week to sixteenth-century African bronzes the
next. Art historians spend years researching and writing books and

catalogues, then enjoy their hour in the spotlight when their exhibition opens or their book appears in print. Accustomed to that sort of pace, the weekly buzz I got in journalism quickly became addictive.

2

The change in London's art scene is in large part the responsibility of a small group of energetic and media-savvy museum directors who hit their stride in the late 1980s and early '90s. Neil Macgregor at the National Gallery and then British Museum; Nicholas Serota at the Tate Gallery; Norman Rosenthal at the Royal Academy – all were in their early forties when they began the long, slow process of creating new and appreciative audiences for the visual arts. Like them, Julia Peyton-Jones at the Serpentine, Maryanne Stevens at the RA and Rosalind Savill at the Wallace Collection were so young when they started that they had 25 years or more to transform their institutions into the roaring successes they became. The same was true of Tim Clifford and Richard Calvocoressi at the National Galleries of Scotland.[3] My deepest respect was reserved for James Lingwood and Michael Morris who founded Artangel, the visionary charity that brought new art out of the gallery into public spaces. But to a degree that I do not believe has been fully recognised, a revitalised popular press played a crucial role in creating public interest in the individual artists these impresarios were showing and in the group exhibitions they were staging.

Then, too, their careers unfolded during the period when the Heritage Lottery Fund began to pour hundreds of millions of pounds into the infrastructure of our museums and galleries. Building projects on this scale had not happened in this country since the development of the South Kensington museums sector in the mid-nineteenth century. Lottery money and the Art Fund also made possible the acquisition for the nation of individual paintings and sometimes entire collections that would otherwise have gone abroad or been dispersed.[4]

3. Some of the most significant acquisitions to UK national collections, of both British and foreign art, were made during Tim Clifford's directorship of the National Gallery of Scotland (1984–2006).

4. The expansion was nationwide – and included new galleries at Gateshead, Wakefield, Margate, Walsall, Chichester and Nottingham.

All this was happening at a time when fortunes were being made in the City. The boom made possible by Mrs Thatcher's economic policies created a distinct new social class of collectors and potential patrons. In a way that Britain hadn't seen before, glamorous openings and dinners became an integral part of major exhibitions. Occasions like the Serpentine Gallery's summer party were covered by *Tatler* and *Hello! Magazine*. Princess Diana showed up. Art had not been this fashionable since the opening of the Grosvenor Gallery in 1877.

A decade after I started at the *Telegraph*, hardly a week went by when an important exhibition wasn't opening somewhere in London.[5] I loved being part of all that, even if only to comment on it. Though I continued to curate exhibitions and contribute to catalogues, I started to identify myself as a journalist, not as an art historian.

3

I had a lot of time for most of the broadsheet critics who arrived in the wake of Wapping. But in those days there was also a kind of critic who you don't come across much any more: the ones who were permanently, professionally angry. When anyone wrote appreciatively about modern art (and in those days at *The Daily Telegraph* 'modern' meant after the Franco-Prussian War), it was against a background of shrill mockery and unrelenting opposition. Journalists such as Peter Fuller at the *Sunday Telegraph,* Giles Auty at the *Spectator* and Brian Sewell at the *Evening Standard* routinely told their readers that modern art was a con, an offence to the eye, an affront to civilised values. They were joined in their efforts to make time stand still by enraged newspaper editors and furious columnists, including the absurd Paul Johnson, author of *I Hate Picasso*.

At a time when most people in this country had so little interest in new art that you had to go out of your way to find it, they wrote hysterical articles about the 'peril' of modernity threatening the nation. I was still enough of a New Yorker to find this unbelievable.

The lightning rod towards which hostile critics hurled their thunderbolts was the Turner Prize. Their non-stop vilification unintentionally became the magic ingredient that made the prize world-famous. Carefully coordinated public protests by failed artists

5. 'How not to prize art', *Sunday Telegraph,* 7 November 1993.

such as the *Stuckists* and the *K Foundation* became something of a ritual on the night the prize was awarded. The camera crews they summoned to film them picketing on the steps of the Tate Gallery ensured a mention of the prize on the *Ten o'Clock News*, and so added to the combustible mixture of art, money, celebrity and mass media which would turn London into the centre for seeing, showing and selling art that it is today.

There is a myth still in circulation that these critics were somehow brave to speak out against photo-based, video and installation art. In this fictional version of what happened, these few good men courageously stood up to a sinister cultural dictator, Nicholas Serota – whom they depicted as a megalomaniac bent on foisting his uniquely perverse and obscure vision of art on the British people. They, self-appointed guardians of traditional values, dared to say what everyone secretly thought: the emperor was wearing no clothes.

In fact, there was nothing secret about the British public's dislike of modern art and nothing courageous about telling readers of the *Evening Standard*, *Spectator*, *Daily Telegraph* and *Sunday Telegraph* what most of them already thought. Week after week the same bully-boys informed the public that good art was a matter of drawing correctly and getting the perspective right. They never considered that art might have something to do with ideas, imagination, originality, insight or universality. I'm not saying they didn't believe what they wrote, only that there was nothing audacious about saying it.

Judging by their reviews, they were unaware of the art on view at the great museums of the world – MoMA, the Pompidou, the Stedelijk and the Reina Sophia. If they had visited those collections they might have realised that Serota was an eloquent representative of Britain at the top table of international cultural activity and one who, as it happened, took every opportunity to promote painting not only at the Tate but also at the international Biennales.

Unfortunately for me, *The Daily Telegraph* and *Sunday Telegraph* were conservative, culturally as well as politically. They began to publish articles and leaders attacking new art in general and my reviews of new art in particular. I'd write about Gilbert and George; the next day a leader would appear advising readers to pay no attention to what the paper's art critic had just said.

When the Turner Prize rolled round every year, I braced myself for another skirmish with my employers. One example, written by the editor of the *Sunday Telegraph*, Charles Moore, just after Rachel Whiteread won the Turner Prize in 1993, will serve to give an idea of what this entailed. It began by informing readers that J. M. W. Turner himself would not have won the Turner Prize. That was because Turner was really a *conservative* (my italics) painter and not, as most art historians had always believed, the most radically innovative British artist of the nineteenth century.[6] When I replied to his piece in an article a few weeks later, I made a point of adding that throughout his career J. M. W. Turner encountered the same sort of hostility the editor of the *Sunday Telegraph* was then dishing out to young artists.

It was fair enough that the paper should be able to state its viewpoint alongside mine, but also obvious that it didn't lead to a sense of job security. When I was offered the job of chief art critic on the *Guardian* I jumped in a taxi straight from Alan Rusbridger's office and handed in my notice. To my amazement, I was asked to stay on – and if at this point you are wondering why my resignation was not accepted with jubilation, so was I.

The explanation, as far as I could make out, was this: the paper had been haemorrhaging readers and sales were decreasing. This was not because subscribers were switching to *The Times* or *Daily Mail* but because they were dying. Consultants were hired to advise on how the paper might appeal to younger readers. As described to me by an eye-witness, the editorial team met the consultants in the editor's office to discuss their conclusions. Spread out on a large table was a copy of that morning's *Telegraph*. As the consultants turned each page they let rip with their criticisms, pointing out the old-fashioned layout and gloomy typography while wondering aloud who on earth read the *hang 'em and flog 'em* articles the paper was famous for – apart, that is, from choleric colonels in the Home Counties and shires.

And then they came to the arts pages.

By sheer chance, my review of the Tate Gallery's *Gerhard Richter* exhibition had been published that morning. It was illustrated with one of the artist's most haunting paintings – of a blurred black-and-white snapshot showing a young family at a beach. For the first time that morning the consultants were ecstatic. They were adamant that

6. 'Turner: most radical of the lot', *Daily Telegraph*, 23 November 1993.

this was the kind of article the *Telegraph* needed if it wanted to change its geriatric image and appeal to a more curious, open-minded readership.[7] That was the turning point. From then on I was in theory free to write whatever I wished.

And so my reviews stayed on – for about two more decades. One reason is that I believed our arts pages were now the best in Fleet Street. Then, too, I knew I had a visibility on a conservative newspaper I would not have had in one on the left. At the *Telegraph* I looked edgy and transgressive, when in reality my taste in art was fairly cautious. Though I regularly made the rounds of the East End galleries, restrictions on space meant that I could only cover an emerging artist's work when he or she appeared in a group show at the Saatchi Gallery or on the Turner Prize shortlist.

Yet because I wrote with sympathy about a few prominent artists I became associated with what Brian Sewell termed the 'Serota Tendency' – an intended insult which meant anyone who made, exhibited, countenanced or wrote about conceptual, video, performance or installation art.[8] I didn't care. Looking back, *Telegraph* readers who were interested enough to read my reviews were given a reasonably comprehensive overview of what was happening in contemporary art – not at the rock face of the avant-garde, but when that art entered mainstream British culture.

Public attitudes towards art changed over time – not because of anything art critics wrote but because of the art itself. A turning point was the exhibition in the autumn of 1993 of Rachel Whiteread's *House*, a concrete cast of the empty interior of an ordinary terraced house of a sort Londoners passed every day without looking at twice. Because it stood in a public space on the edge of a park in east London, *House* broke through some invisible psychological barrier to touch the hearts of people who may not have taken an interest in modern art before.

7. This was also the moment when the *Telegraph* hired its first-ever rock critic, although the term they used was 'pop'.

8. During the twelve years Serota was in sole charge of the Tate Gallery he used his enormous influence to promote painting at every possible opportunity. There were no major video or photographic shows at the Tate while he was there. The exhibitions of painting for which he was personally responsible included Ellsworth Kelly, Robert Ryman, Leon Kossoff, Patrick Heron, Jackson Pollock, Lovis Corinth and Ben Nicholson.

They could see for themselves what this extraordinary young artist had created – as opposed to reading what critics wrote about it.

Projects sponsored by Artangel, as well as the Unilever series of installations in the Turbine Hall of Tate Modern and the changing artworks on the fourth plinth in Trafalgar Square were hugely important, as was Anthony d'Offay's inspired idea to circulate exhibitions of blue-chip modern art to museums and galleries all over the country. All these programmes allowed members of the public to make up their own minds – and that was fatal to the enemies of progressive art.

In 1997 the newly elected Labour government deliberately used modern British art as a way of branding itself as young and forward-looking. Tate Modern opened in 2000 and a year later the government introduced a policy of free admission to all national museums. That opened the floodgates. Attendance figures at the V&A and other museums doubled. Damian Hirst and Tracey Emin became media celebrities in a way that had not been seen in this country since Whistler, Wilde and Ruskin in the late nineteenth century. At the Royal Academy, exhibitions by Anish Kapoor and David Hockney attracted visitor numbers that Burlington House last experienced when protective barriers had to be erected to keep the crowds from damaging William Powell Frith's *Derby Day*.

4

Every critic carries a gold standard in his head against which we judge new art. For me it was the American Pop Art and Minimalism I'd seen as a young graduate student in New York of the early 1970s: Jasper Johns, Robert Rauschenberg, Cy Twombly, Frank Stella, Brice Marden, Andy Warhol, Donald Judd, Carl Andre, Dan Flavin and Richard Serra. I was lucky that when I started writing art criticism, British sculpture (but not painting) measured up to that high standard. The generation of British artists ascendant or fully established in the late '80s included Richard Long, Anish Kapoor, Tony Cragg, Richard Deacon and Richard Wentworth.

In their work I felt the same sense I'd had in New York of artists breaking free from the traditions and conventions of their medium, rethinking everything about what sculpture was and how it could be made. In their hands it might be monumental or ephemeral and created out of anything – stone, metal, wood, photographs, powdered dyes, paper, found objects. It could be riveted, bent, stacked, carved, screwed, glued or scattered on the floor or wall.

Close on their heels came the Young British Artists. The best known – Damian Hirst, Tracey Emin, Sarah Lucas and Angus Fairhurst – were a joyless lot, obsessed with death, sex, masturbation, alcohol and drugs to the exclusion of all other human experience except greed. I could acknowledge the ferocious humour of Lucas's early sculptures and thought that every so often Hirst could come up with an artwork of audacious brilliance, but I had no natural sympathy for what they were doing. As happens all the time in daily life, I could see the point of them, but they weren't my type.

Contrast that to the heartfelt response I had to the pathos and nuance in films and installations by Mark Wallinger or Douglas Gordon – the two most significant artists associated with the YBAs. Gordon couldn't make an artwork that didn't feel intensely personal to me, whether it was unspooling in slow motion the small-town America of my childhood in the backgrounds of Hitchcock's *Psycho* or filming a football match in which the mesmerised cameras only follow one astonishing player, Zinedine Zidane.

Installation and conceptual art by Francis Alÿs, Dinos and Jake Chapman, Robert Gober, Christian Marclay and Giuseppe Pennone (among others) all engaged my attention in a way that painting in the 1990s did not. The one British painter I came to like a lot was Chris Ofili, particularly his immersive series of thirteen colour-drenched canvases *The Upstairs Room* (though, come to think of it, that too is an installation). I saw an awful lot of video art over the years and most of it left me cold. Special mention must be made of Tacita Dean's 63-minute film showing a herd of cows ambling from an enclosure to an open field during an eclipse of the sun. It ranks as the single worst viewing experience of my life.[9]

Every so often I wished I could re-write a review. It wasn't until after I'd already written about Doris Salcedo's *Shibboleth* in Tate Modern's Turbine Hall that I realised it had two parts – visual and written – and that I'd only written about the first. The part you saw

9. The title of my review of her retrospective was 'Mind-numbing home movies that seem to last for an eternity.'

consisted of a deep, ominous crack in the flooring that ran down the length of that vast hall. A few days later it struck me that there was another aspect to the work: the press release and the wall label, both written by the artist. Most conceptual artists allow viewers to project their own thoughts and feelings on to an artwork. They leave the interpretation up to us. Salcedo didn't do that. She told us in words exactly what the crack symbolised: racism. That transformed the meaning of the work from vague and arty to precise and political. Racism – and only racism – was undermining the foundations of society.

Most of the time, my background in traditional art history is an advantage when looking at new art. But it can also be an impediment when I am confronted with an artwork that I can't place in my mental rolodex of styles, schools, traditions, influences and artistic pedigrees. Inconveniently (if you are an art critic), that is most likely to happen when I come across truly original work. For example, on my encounter with the first of Matthew Barney's *Cremaster* series of films I found the imagery so strange and the subject so unclassifiable that I made the mistake of dismissing it. Then I saw more of the films, read other critics, and in my next review wrote a grovelling apology. (That doesn't mean I've become an uncritical fan.)

5

When it came time to step down from the *Telegraph*, of course I asked myself whether anything I wrote was in any way important. Apart from their possible educational value, did my reviews make the slightest difference to anyone other than a handful of rich artists, manipulative museum directors or spoiled art collectors? The answer is no. Critics mostly perform a simple service. We direct readers to exhibitions worth seeing and explain why. Whenever I commented on what I considered reprehensible behaviour (the sacking of good curators to save money or the government's appointment of an unqualified individual to head a cultural body) it was energy wasted.

The pieces in this book collected under the heading 'Art Politics' provide some idea of the kinds of issues that concerned me enough to devote my weekly allotment of 1,200 words to writing. Still, the most effective commentaries in that section are basically reviews. The best way for critics to put our ideas across is not to tackle abuses or cock-

ups directly but to do our jobs well and let readers draw their own
conclusions. You have to trust museum directors to take note when
criticism is serious and hope that arts ministers can tell the difference
between a knee-jerk whinge and justified censure.

I felt I was doing something actively worthwhile when I sat
on boards and committees including the Wallace Collection, Watts
Gallery, British Council and Government Art Collection. I loved
the sense that for once my input might be having some practical
effect – whether it was acquiring pictures for a British embassy or a
government building, helping to choose the British representative at
the Venice Biennale or raising money to make an institution stronger
or to extend its life into the next century. But of course the only reason
I was asked to help in each of those cases was because my day job at
the *Telegraph* allowed me to see so much and meet so many of those
responsible for doing so much so right for so long.

It was a privilege.

1

ANCIENT AND NON-EUROPEAN ART

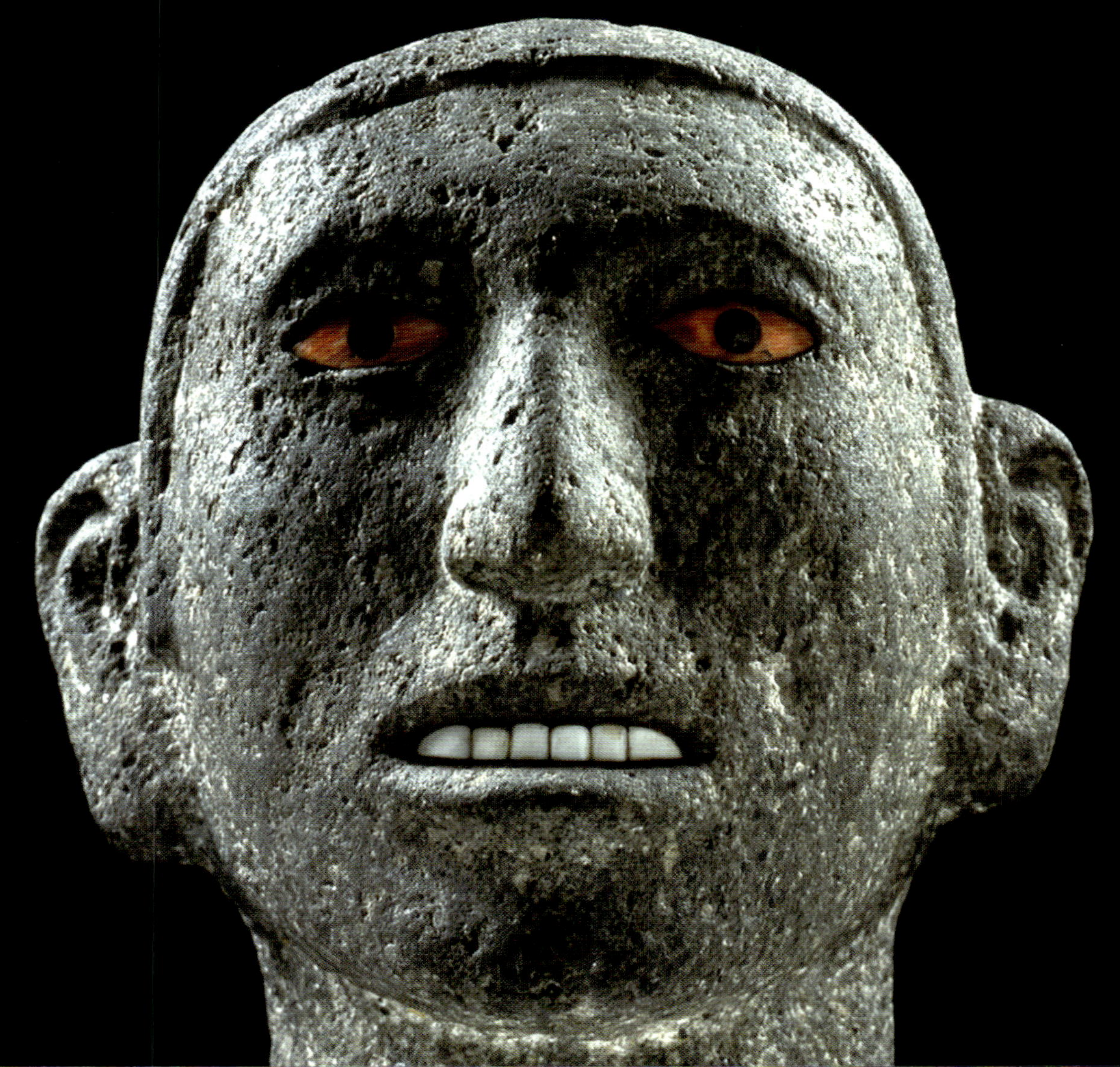

Ice Age Art

Dolni Vestonice Female Figure (*also called* **The Venus of Dolni Vestonice**), *29,000–20,000 BC Moravske Zemske Museum, Brno*

How many exhibitions have you been to that can claim to show the oldest known figurative art? Have you ever read an exhibition label that described an object as the 'oldest known portrait of a woman' or the 'oldest known ceramic figure'? When the curator of the British Museum's *Ice Age Art* uses the term 'deep history' to characterise the show, she really means it. Most of the material in it was made in Europe and Central Asia between 40,000 and 12,000 years ago.

The measurements of time we encounter in the catalogue and labels are almost impossible for those of us accustomed to think in terms of years and centuries to grasp. Delicate carvings in bone, stone, antler or ivory are dated to within the closest couple of thousand years. That in turn means that the questions you ask are different from the usual ones. Since no individual 'hands' or schools associated with particular times or places can be identified, the whole concept of artistic style is problematic. The presence of a carved puppet and a wooden flute speak of a civilisation that included story-telling and music as well as visual art, but in general we can only speculate as to why most of these objects and images were made or how they were used.

Until well into the twentieth century, the carvings and drawings we see at the British Museum were normally exhibited in natural history and ethnographic museums where they were dehumanised by labels identifying them as artefacts made by primitive people. That is why it was important for the British Museum to make it crystal clear that what visitors see is art. Most of the objects on display had no practical use or else are embellished in ways that go far beyond utilitarian necessity.

Take for example the tiny ceramic figure of an obese woman with pendulous breasts, wide hips and a roll of fat around her middle which was made of baked clay between 31,000 and 27,000 years ago.

5 February 2013

Ice Age Art: The Arrival of the Modern Mind

British Museum, London

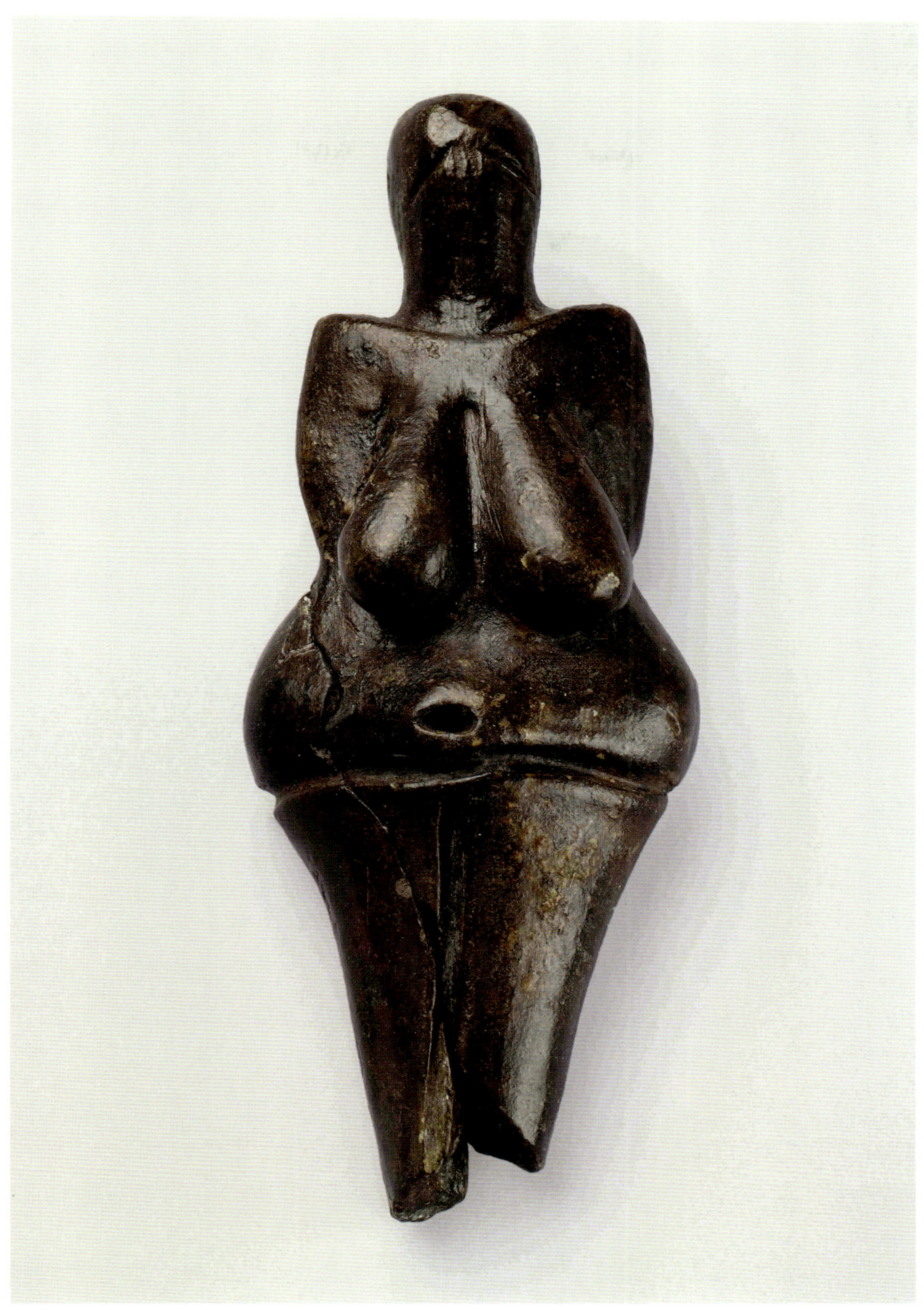

Whoever created it made decisions that can have had no other purpose than to enhance its beauty or add to its aesthetic perfection.

We will never know whether it was made as a fetish or talisman or as a representation of a supernatural being. What we do know is what we can see: that the head is as perfect an oval as anything by Brancusì, that the stylised shoulders and breasts are symmetrically balanced and that the line of body fat below the navel is shaped to 'rhyme' with the inverted arc of the shoulder blades.

What is less obvious, at least to me, is the significance of the figure's nudity. Because we grow up with the idea that art began with the Greeks, we take the nude figure for granted. But the Ice Age got its name for a reason.

People went around wrapped in skins and furs, which means that the representation of nudity, like the exaggeration and stylisation of the body parts, was either an artistic convention or had some symbolic meaning. But this degree of abstraction is confined to the representation of the human figure. Animals are depicted naturalistically by artists who were careful to show just how a hairy wolverine lifts one big padded paw as it moves through snow, or what it looks like when a bison lifts its head to bellow.

The sophistication of the artistic techniques used in the great majority of works on view is self-evident. In an incised drawing on bone showing two female deer estimated to date between 14,000 and 12,000 years ago, the artist first drew the contours of the bodies in outline, and then used finely shaded lines to create volume and the texture of fur. The mouth, eyes, gills and fins in an incised drawing of a fish are so precisely described that it can be identified as a sole. And an incised drawing on a fragment of rib found in the La Vache cave in France depicts three lions in motion, necks and tails extended as if closing in on their prey. Several of these sculptures are pierced, either to be worn as decoration or suspended in space. At the British Museum they are lit to show how their shadows would have danced over the fire-lit surfaces of caves or tents.

I can't remember the last time I saw a show with so many rare and beautiful objects on loan from museums in Germany, France, the Czech Republic and Siberia. My one hesitation about it is summed up by the subtitle, 'The Arrival of the Modern Mind'. It seems to me that the modern mind, like the middle class, is always arriving, in every century since time began. And in this case I'm not sure what it means. As my earlier reference to Brancusì reveals, it is by seeing this art through the prism of twentieth-century art that we came to appreciate its aesthetic dimensions. But that doesn't make it 'modern'. In fact what I like most about it is that it is mysterious and strange and like nothing else in our experience. Any idea that the people who made these objects are just like us is contradicted by the complete absence of representations of love or affection between men and women or mothers and children.

In terms of the syntax of art, the depiction of movement is highly selective since animals are shown in motion, but not humans. One of the show's highlights is the superbly carved ivory figure with the head of a lion and the torso of a man made about 40,000 years ago. It certainly proves that the imaginative faculty existed, and one of the surprises of the show is the absence of representations of imaginary and mythical creatures such as the dragons you find in some aboriginal cave paintings from 40,000 years ago.

While it is inevitable that we bring our knowledge of twentieth-century art to our perception of this work, that is very different from projecting modern ideas about art on to the distant past. The star object you'll see reproduced in every review of the show is the female figure carved from mammoth ivory found in the Lespugue Cave in 1922. Picasso was fascinated by its faceted breasts, hips and buttocks, which resemble the pre-Cubist and Cubist pictures of female figures he made from 1906 onwards. But Cubism is about taking the human figure apart and then putting it back together again. The planes and facets in the Lespugue figure have nothing to do with that kind of abstraction.

But that's a small point, and I can well understand why the British Museum needs to put a period that is so unfamiliar to most visitors into a context we can recognise. Both in the show and in the first-rate catalogue, Jill Cook has achieved the difficult feat of making art made in the mists of time feel almost familiar.

The Painted Tomb-Chapel of Nebamun

It is only January, but I don't expect to see an exhibition in the next twelve months more moving than what is on view in the British Museum's new gallery of ancient Egyptian art. Beautifully designed, lit and labelled, it is devoted to one of the best-loved works of art in the museum – the wall paintings from the tomb-chapel of Nebamun, an obscure accountant attached to the Temple of Amun in Thebes (present-day Karnak) who died around 1350 BC.

Relatively little painting of any kind survives from the ancient world, so it is hard to overestimate the historical importance of these famous fragments showing scenes from the life of an ordinary man who lived for a flickering moment at the dawn of history.

But, equally, recent conservation confirms that these are works of art of the highest aesthetic quality. They were painted not by jobbing artisans but by true artists who made conscious aesthetic decisions, and were sometimes willing to break with the pictorial conventions of Egyptian art to achieve a surprising degree of naturalism.

One explanation for their appeal, I think, is that, unlike a lot of Egyptian art, they were intended to be seen by the living, not the dead. They come not from a sealed burial chamber (like the treasures of Tutankhamun) but from a chapel with an entrance at ground level which was accessible to the public.

Visitors who came to pray or to make offerings would have admired the murals for qualities that would make any work of art from any historical period exceptional – the confident draughtsmanship, the wonderful sense of colour, the intensity of the observation, the ability to convey human foibles and, not least, the sense of fun. These scenes of everyday life in ancient Egypt show us how rich and poor dressed, moved, spoke, dined, made music, hunted, planted and gardened.

They were executed by a team of no more than six anonymous

20 January 2009

The Painted Tomb-Chapel of Nebamun

British Museum, London

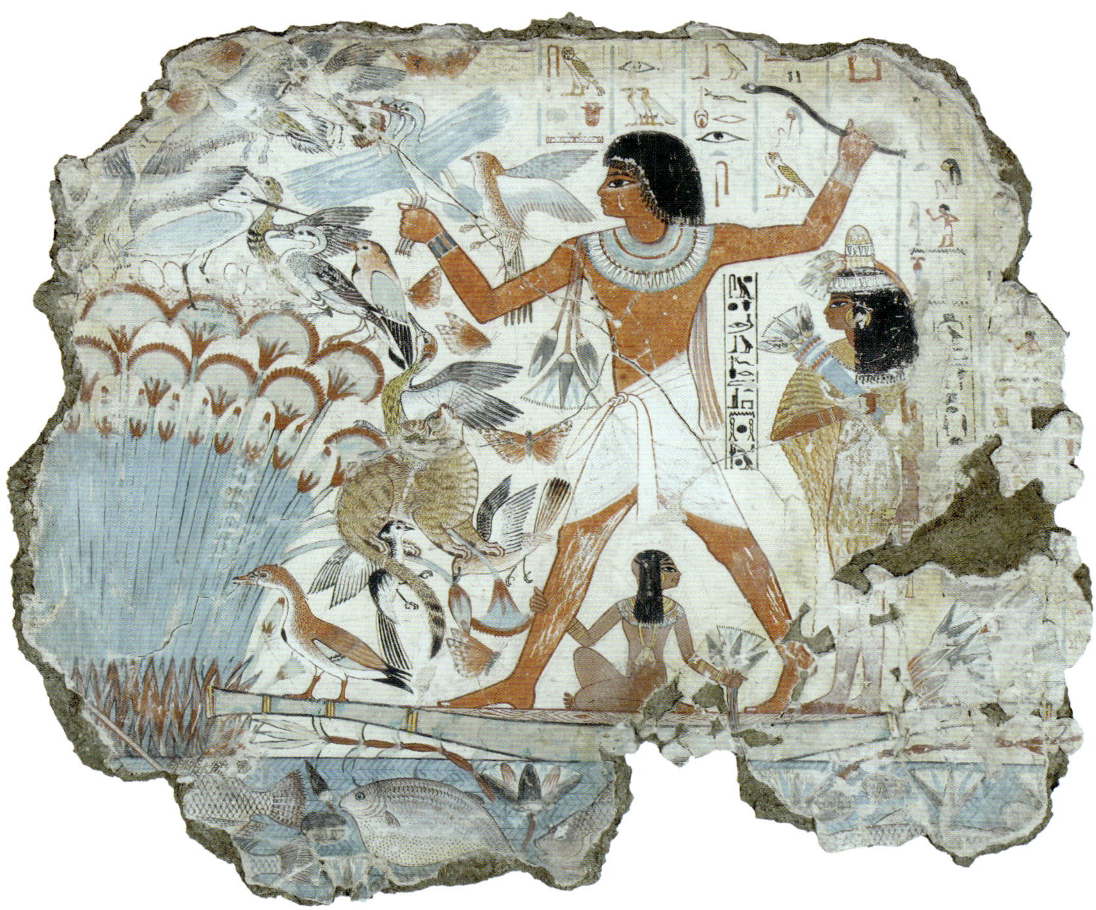

Nebamun Hunting in the Marshes, c. 1350 BC
British Museum, London

painters belonging to the workshop overseen by a master. Scholars don't know why Nebamun, who occupied a relatively modest place in the social hierarchy, rated so splendid a memorial, but their best guess is that the artist in charge of the project was a friend, relative or neighbour who knew the deceased personally and – you'd like to think – remembered him with affection.

And so, in the scene where Nebamun is shown hunting wildfowl from a skiff in marshland along the Nile, the artist adheres to the conventions of Egyptian art by showing the accountant in profile and making him much bigger than the figures of his wife and young daughter who accompany him. But this artist goes further – he makes sure that Nebamun stands out by painting his flesh using impastoed white under paint covered with a layer of red. Seen within the dark interior of the chapel, the figure would have appeared to glow.

The same artist (or another artist from the workshop, assuming that one specialised in figures, another in still life, a third in birds and animals) didn't actually need to show the marshes as alive with birds, butterflies, flowers and fish. One or two schematically drawn examples of each species would have served to symbolise the hunt. But the air is loud with the beating of wings as a havoc of startled birds rises up from the clump of papyrus at the hunter's approach, each so carefully delineated that a lepidopterist could identify the species of butterfly fluttering in front of Nebamun, and you don't need to be an ornithologist to spot the geese, wagtails, shrikes, ducks, egrets and herons.

Among the fish in the rippling blue water under the skiff you find a poisonous puffer fish, and a mullet delicately dappled using a stippling technique to suggest the shimmering, silvery quality of its scales. The point is that this level of detail is unnecessary, which is precisely why it belongs in the realm of art, not craft or decoration.

Likewise, in the scenes where Nebamun's servants and scribes herd cattle and geese for the annual inventory of his possessions, the artist is careful to differentiate between each creature's appearance and even personality. He takes enormous pleasure in showing big fat geese next to tiny goslings, and delights in the way a few geese have turned in the opposite direction from the gaggle, or flap their wings, or seem to look up curiously as one of their number is placed in a straw basket. Above these scenes, the hieroglyphic speech bubbles tell us that the herdsmen argue among themselves and remind each other to conduct themselves with decorum in front of their master.

The draughtsmanship, too, is of a high order. Look at how the long sinuous line of one steer's back is 'rhymed' with the extended arm of the drover behind it, or how the head of the bald cowman at the front of the herd adds to the strong leftward flow of the composition.

And, finally, it is the attention to detail that makes these scenes so accessible to us today. Look at the way three female musicians clap in time to the music of a flute played by a fourth musician, with the words of their song spelled out in a hieroglyphic speech bubble above their heads. Surprisingly, two of the seated musicians are shown not in profile, as we expect in Egyptian art, but full face. The artist felt able to break the rules because the women he was depicting were foreign and of low status, but in doing so this anonymous artist gives

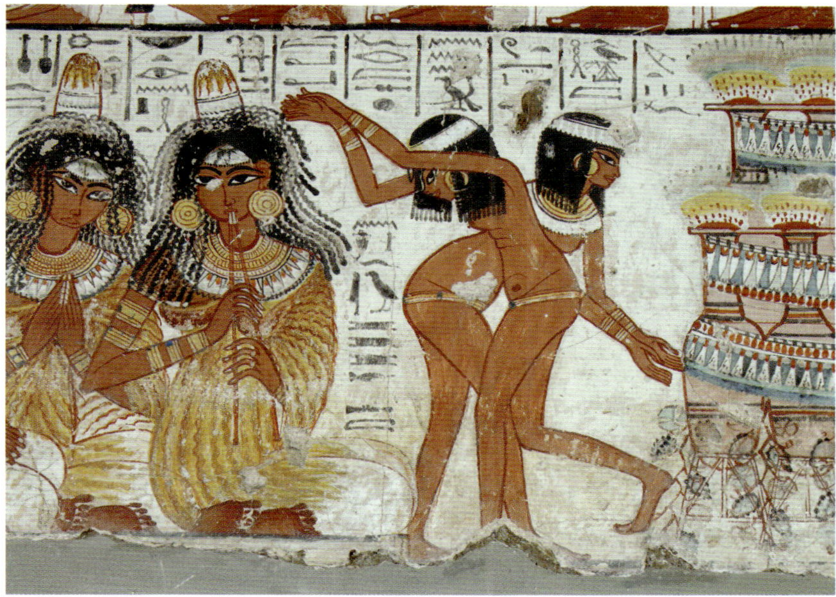

us a glimpse of his artistic personality. For an instant, time has stood still, and across three millennia he gives us a little wink.

Though the captions and wall labels give you just the right amount of information to enhance your understanding of each scene, it's a measure of the greatness of the Nebamun paintings that they aren't really needed. Even young children will enjoy the wonderfully whiskery hares, and will appreciate the scene where the tawny cat catches a plump bird in its mouth. In floor-to-ceiling cases facing the paintings, the curator Richard Parkinson has placed ancient Egyptian chairs, cosmetics jars, jewellery and implements for hunting and fishing similar to those that appear in the pictures.

The whole gallery brings ancient Egypt to life in a peculiarly intimate and touching way, and, because it is a permanent gallery, its opening is an infinitely more important event than any temporary exhibition. What a gift!

Fragment of an Egyptian Queen's Face, c. 1353–1336 BC
Metropolitan Museum of Art, New York

Egypt's Dazzling Sun

It finally happened. The thing I dreaded. Walking through an exhibition at the Grand Palais in Paris last week, I was seized with an irresistible desire to kiss a work of art. Or at least to press my lips passionately against a glass exhibition case. The work in question was the fragmentary face of Queen Tiy, a sensual sliver of exquisitely carved yellow jasper showing the lusciously full lips of the consort of Pharaoh Amenhotep III. And although I restrained myself, I was not alone in my osculatory urge. Queen Tiy's lips, infinitesimally up-turned at one corner as though about to curve into a mocking smile, also mesmerised a knot of French journalists who seemed unable to tear themselves away from *les lèvres*.

That the sense of intimacy we all felt for a woman who lived for a brief moment at the dawn of history was so tactile is the achievement of *Egypt's Dazzling Sun: Amenhotep III and his World*. This unforgettable show is that rare thing, an exhibition built on a daringly original premise: that by studying the statues and objects known to have been made during one pharaoh's 38-year reign (about 1391–1353 BC) we can approach the art of ancient Egypt exactly as we would that of any cultural period – the reign of Louis XIV, let us say, or the Second Empire.

Why is this so innovative? Because from the day of our first school outing to the British Museum we are taught to look at Egyptian art in terms of its function in daily life and religious ritual – as though aesthetic considerations were of secondary interest to the craftsmen who made it. The organisers of this show are art historians, not archaeologists. Concerned with stylistic analysis and aesthetic discrimination, they have identified different sculptural ateliers associated with identifiable stone quarries and even recognised the 'hands' of separate (though of course anonymous) artistic personalities.

10 March 1993

Egypt's Dazzling Sun: Amenhotep III and his World

Grand Palais, Paris

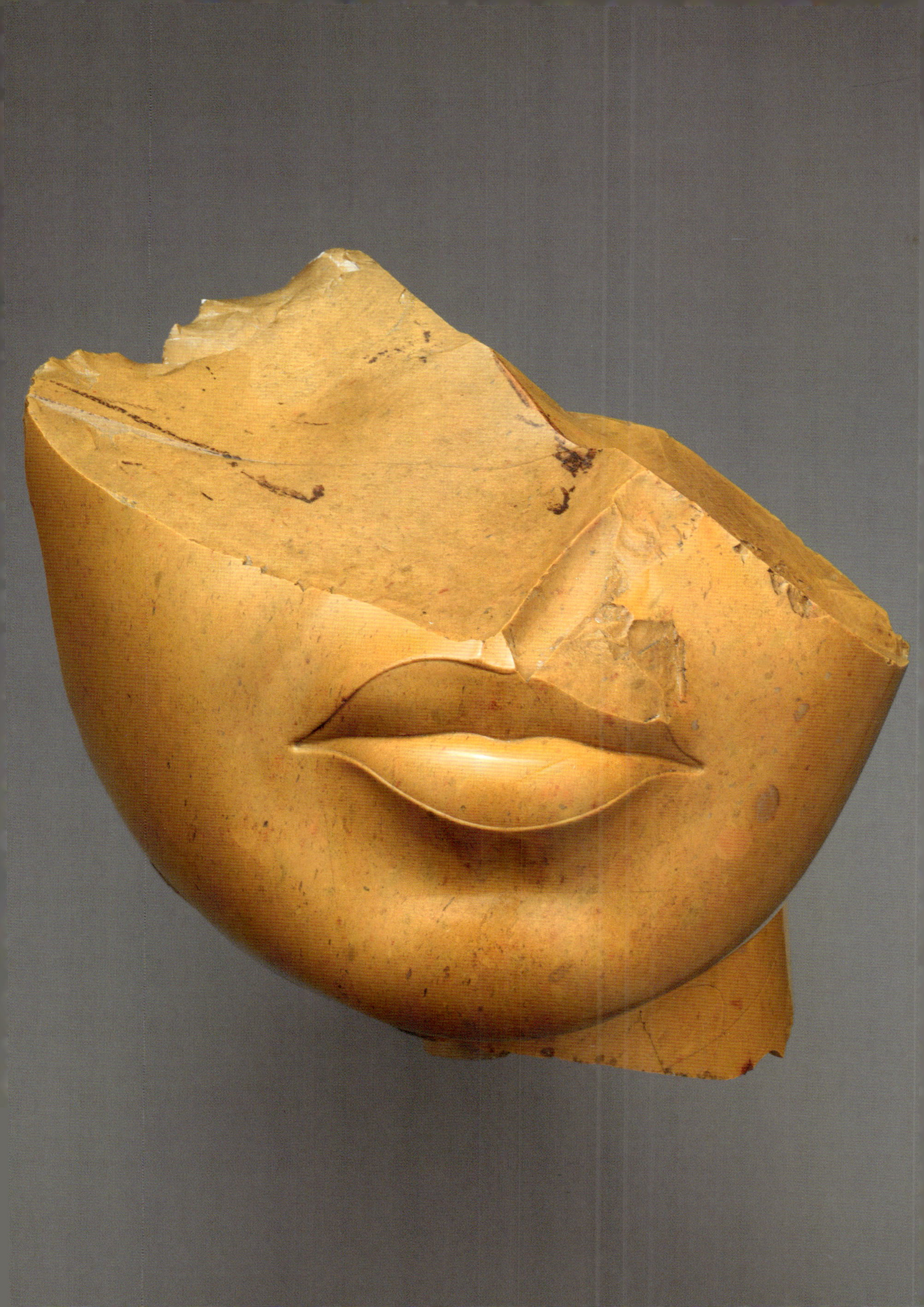

Everything has been chosen solely for its artistic quality. We become aware not only of a statue's status as a votive offering but also of the way the artist has suggested a torso's sagging flesh through parallel rows of lightly incised undulating lines, or of how one portraitist makes us conscious of the king's humanity, while another deliberately suppresses it. At the end, subtle differences in carving, or variations in accepted proportions, betray the hand of the fine artist as opposed to the mere artisan.

The dramatic entrance to the exhibition is guarded by a recumbent lioness made of red granite, symbol of the pharaoh himself, from the Temple of Soleb in the Sudan. As we draw close to examine the severely stylised curves of head and haunch, we realise that the animal's ears are pricked back, alert to our footstep. A lion only holds its ears in this way for an instant before it attacks. The statue's meaning is therefore clear: as guardian of the temple and protector of the deity, the pharaoh is vigilant – we approach at our peril.

And beyond, looming up out of the darkness, we glimpse a series of colossal heads of Amenhotep III. This long face and its distinctive features soon become instantly recognisable, with those almond-shaped eyes outlined with kohl, and that fleshy, slightly overhung upper lip. One of the most spectacular examples, from the British Museum, must have belonged to a statue 25 or 30 feet high. It is made of polished brown quartzite, a dark stone embedded with yellow and brown sand which makes the statue glisten as though moist. The sculptors who made this head carefully contrasted the softly modelled face with the rougher texture of lips, eyebrows, crown, beard strap and head band.

The mood of the show changes from room to room, as we move from temple and tomb to marshland and desert. In one darkened gallery a divine baboon squats on its haunches, a ferocious funeral deity whose wild cries the Egyptians interpreted as a secret language known only to the pharaoh. This superbly carved statue seems to sit watch over the rounded Canopic jars with their distinctive human-headed stoppers, which would have contained the perishable entrails of the deceased.

Nearby we become aware of the sinister presence of three black granodiorite effigies showing the lion-headed goddess Sekhmet seated on their thrones, a merciless jury of grim widows. Erected in their hundreds by Amenhotep III, such statues guaranteed divine protection against floods and pestilence.

In fact, Amenhotep III (father of the more famous Akhenaten and the presumed grandfather of Tutankhamun) seems to have done an excellent job as a living intermediary between the gods and his people. His reign saw a golden age of peace and incredible plenty for the Egyptian people. Amenhotep used his army for vast building projects and kept a second army of glassmakers, potters, jewellers, ceramicists, carvers and painters in full-time occupation, like Louis XIV with his factories at Sèvres and tapestry works at Gobelin.

The second half of this classic exhibition focuses on the pharaoh's family. Through their portraits we come to know the king and his royal consort, his one surviving son and four daughters, his in-laws and the prominent members of his court. From museums all over the world the organisers have borrowed objects these people might have owned and used – bronzes and jewels, brightly painted limestone reliefs and terracotta jars, bowls made of faience (a glazed earthenware), intricately carved combs and spoons in wood and ivory.

This is a courtly art, an art made for refined and sophisticated palates. Two objects stand out: a tiny glass bottle in the shape of a goggle-eyed fish striped in swirls of blue, yellow and white, which must be one of the finest pieces of ancient glass in existence, and a jewel-like faience sphinx in turquoise blue, only a few inches high, which might bear comparison with the finest Chinese porcelain.

Perhaps best of all, the exhibition brings Egyptian art to life in a peculiarly touching way. We learn, for example, that the king's favourite colour was a fierce cobalt blue with turquoise trim, but that his wife preferred white or yellow. We watch the royal family change and grow old in front of our eyes – not in the great public monuments, of course, but in the intimate, private works of sculpture such as the exquisite *Head of the Aged Queen Tiy*, a masterpiece showing the ravaged beauty a few years after the death of her husband.

Kingdom of Ife:
Sculptures from West Africa

Seated Figure
from Tada, Ife, late
13th–early 14th
centuries
Nigerian National
Commission for
Museums and
Monuments

About half-way through the British Museum's astounding *Kingdom of Ife: Sculptures from West Africa* we come across two small freestanding terracotta heads, each representing a victim of human sacrifice. Made near the Atlantic coast of what is today Nigeria between 1100 and about 1400 AD, they are only around six inches in length and by no means the most sophisticated or refined works on view.

But look at them up close. The scarification marks on one head indicate that it represents a stranger, presumably a warrior captured in battle. Yet the artist has gone to great lengths to show the victim's physical suffering and mental anguish. Both victims are gagged with a rope pulled so tightly through their mouth that their eyes bulge. On each face the artist conveys the terror and violent struggle of a human being fully conscious that he is about to face ritual execution. These West African sculptors reveal an empathy with the 'other' that you only find in the art of highly advanced cultures. It is a quality unknown (as far as I know) in the art of Mesoamerica or Central Africa, where captives are represented not as human beings but as generic types.

The Yoruba-speaking city state of Ife flourished as a cosmopolitan centre of trade and industry in the three centuries after 1100, its situation on the banks of the River Niger providing access to the busy trade routes that made it wealthy. Three hundred years before the arrival of Europeans at the end of the fifteenth century, Ife was importing the copper and brass that enabled its artisans to cast bronze using the lost wax process.

The artist who in the early fourteenth century created the naturalistic bronze seated figure found in the village of Tada had an understanding of the musculature of the human body that would not be seen in European sculpture until Donatello and Lorenzo Ghiberti more than a century later. With a patterned sarong wrapped around

2 March 2010

Kingdom of Ife:
Sculptures from
West Africa

British Museum,
London

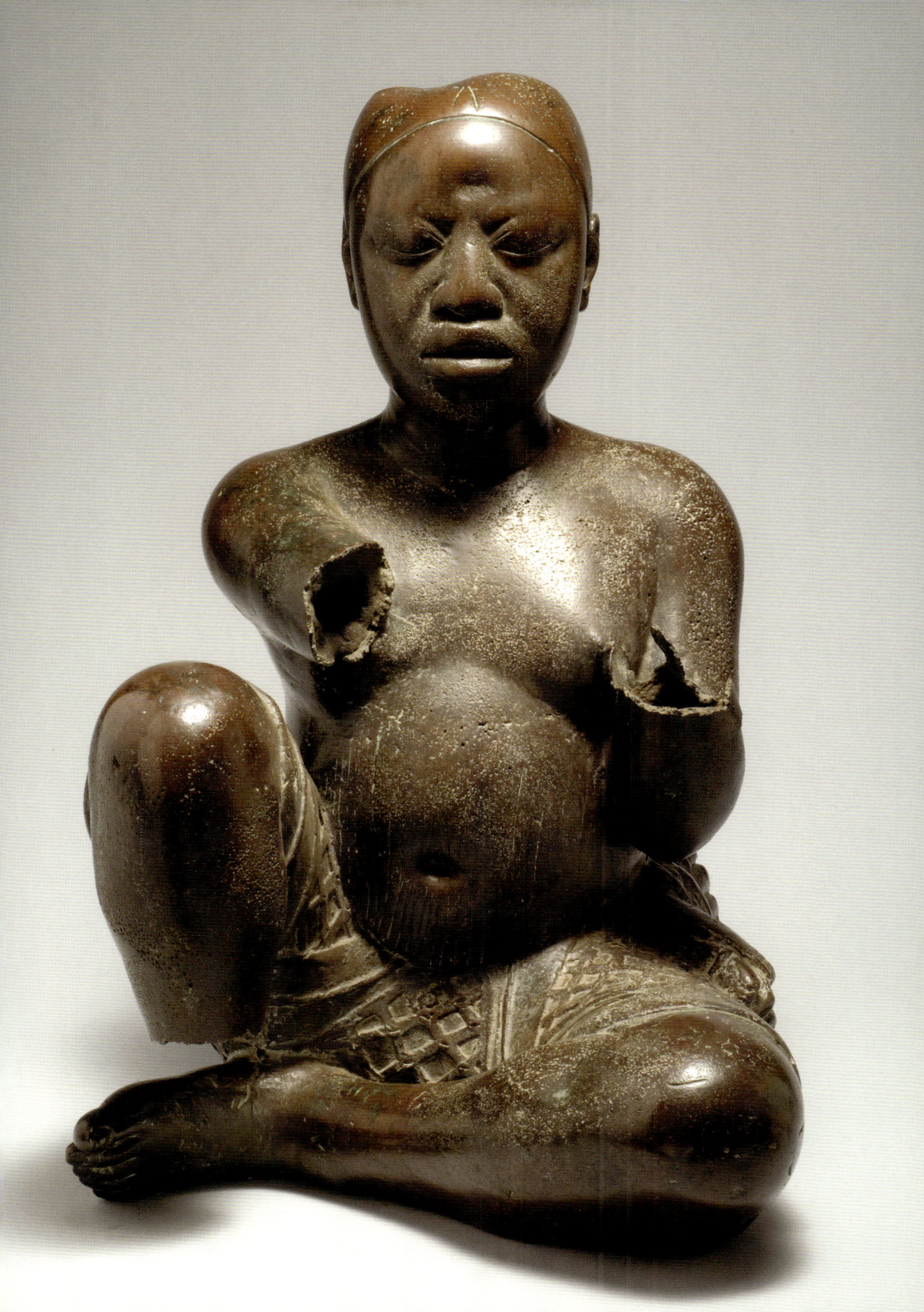

his waist and tied with a tasselled sash, the plump figure is shown sitting with his left leg tucked under his raised right thigh. The complex pose presents the sculptor with the challenge of representing a heavy man who has shifted most of his weight on to his left hip, throwing his body slightly off balance. When the sculptor had finished modelling the figure, it was then cast in pure copper. The result is a technical *tour de force* in which the smooth surface of the soft and sagging flesh is contrasted with the intricate detail of the textured cloth.

In the absence of written records, scholars can only guess why such works were made or what purpose they served. Many of the life-size copper alloy heads in this show represent the *oomi* (king) wearing a crown or diadem covered with beads. All date from the end of the fourteenth or early fifteenth century and each one is so different from the others in bone structure and features that they must be portraits. Most appear to be male, but others, like a crowned head in which striations from forehead to chin follow the contours of the face, look like either women or boys. Some were once polychromed, others retain traces of gold. Those without crowns have holes at the forehead to attach real crowns of fibre and feathers to the head; in others the holes are at the mouth and jawline to attach beaded veils that symbolised the ruler's power to bless or curse.

In the early fifteenth century metal workers from Ife taught artisans working for the king of their country's vassal state, Benin, the secrets of lost wax bronze casting. A few late bronzes in this show remind us that Benin bronze sculpture was primarily associated with the court and royal palace. Benin figures tend to be highly stylised and are limited in subject matter to representations of the king, his warriors, messengers, and the animals sacred to them. One of the most spectacular objects in the show, a full-length standing figure of a bowman, feels to me closer in spirit to Benin than to Ife, for the pose is stiff and hieratic and the artist has made no attempt to animate or individualise the crudely scarified face. But the crisply cast details of his costume – the knife buried in his quilted tunic, the quiver on his back, the heavy anklets and amazing braided headdress – give the figure a precious, jewel-like quality I associate with courtly art, whether of Benin or Fabergé. By contrast, Ife sculpture tends to be more naturalistic and to show people from every level of society, including the old and the sick.

Several terracotta fragments clearly represent limbs of those suffering from rickets or elephantiasis. Many of the female heads are so regal in bearing and serene in expression they must represent either queens or goddesses. Even the scarification marks produced by chasing the surface of the bronze faces with a sharp tool enhances their mysterious beauty.

This is the first show ever devoted to the sculpture of Ife anywhere in the world. The quality of the full-length statues, portrait heads, ritual objects and vessels loaned by Nigeria's National Commission for Museums and Monuments is flabbergasting.

Mictlantecuhtli
(Lord of Death),
c. 1480
Templo Mayor
Museum, Mexico City

Aztecs

It has been many years since London has seen a show as powerful as
Aztecs, the Royal Academy's autumn blockbuster. But the exhibition is
not for the chicken-hearted or the lily-livered. If in the Aztec mentality
there was any concept of love, tenderness, mercy or pity, it is not
reflected in their art. Alone among world cultures, Aztec art contains
no representation of a mother with her child, no depiction of one
human being extending kindness or affection towards another, no
recognition of the erotic or sexual side of human nature. What is more,
as far as I can see, no Aztec artist tried to suggest the idea of man's
interior or spiritual life.

What the Aztecs did possess was an imaginative genius for giving
form to man's deepest terrors. Aztec gods were not loved but feared,
terrifying beings to be propitiated with rivers of blood. Deities like
the dreadful Huehueteotl, the old, old god with an evil wrinkled face,
glare out at us in gallery after gallery, until, by the time we reach the
end of the show, we feel oppressed, weighed down by their glowering
presence. Though the religion brought to Mexico by the Spanish
conquerors at the beginning of the sixteenth century was in its effects
even crueller than that practised by the Aztecs, the few Christian
symbols from the colonial period at the very end of this exhibition
at least represent ideals utterly absent from the Aztec world view:
forgiveness, humility and hope.

For eyes accustomed to twentieth-century art, there is nothing
remarkable about the depiction of brutality. How much grace or
sweetness do we find, for example, in Picasso's *Demoiselles d'Avignon*?
The difference is that there were other sides to Picasso's work,
whereas, from first to last, Aztec stone carving has only one purpose,
to scare the wits out of the viewer. Even a god such as Xochipilli,
lord of flowers, dance and poetry, who wears elaborate bracelets,
headdress and arm bands, has a face as cruel as the blade of an axe.

13 November 2002

Aztecs

Royal Academy,
London

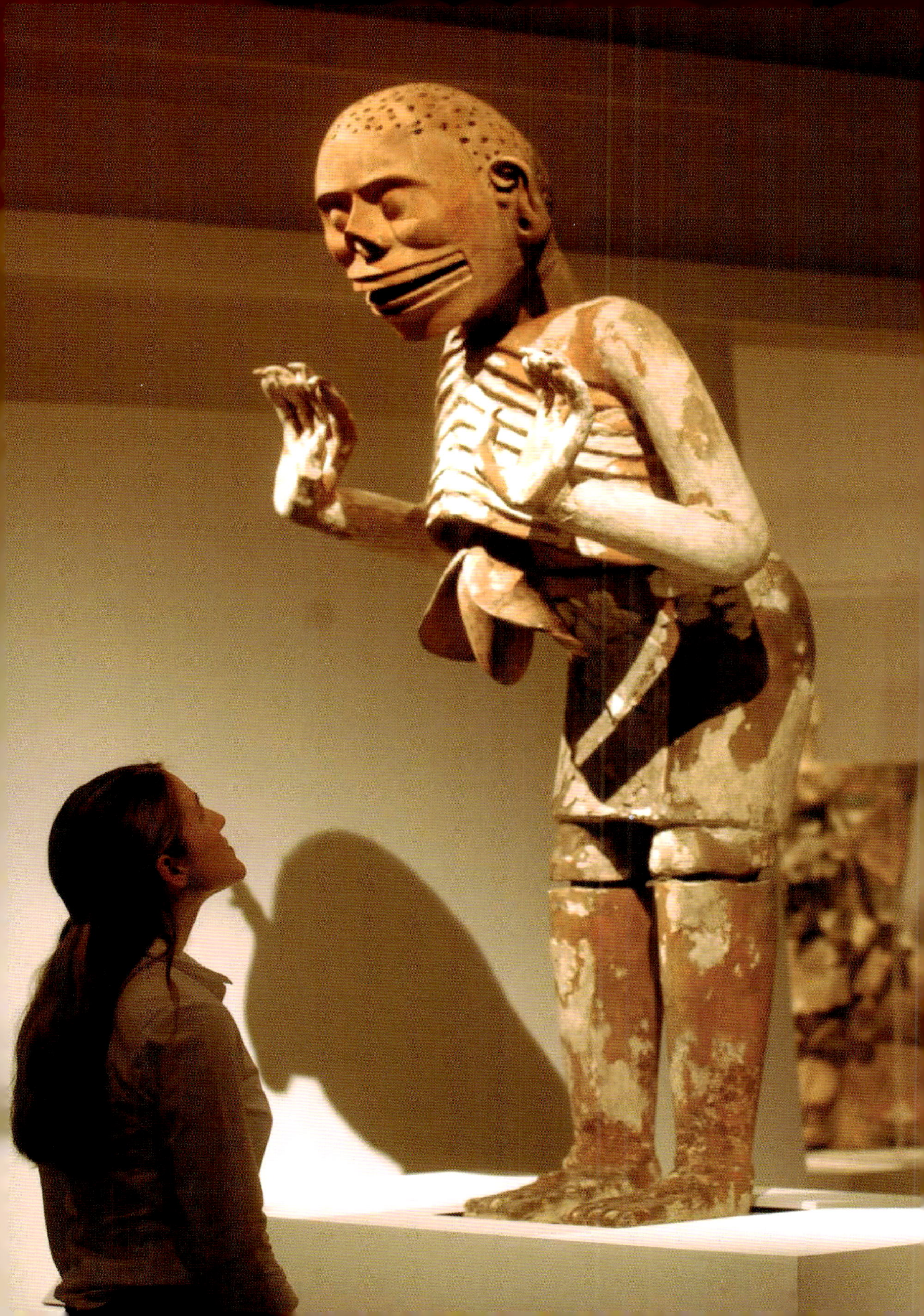

After walking through this exhibition, you may well conclude that Aztec culture basically consisted of an elaborate cult of death. For, as we all know, Aztec religion involved human sacrifice on an unimaginable scale. Their priests ritually offered to the gods the blood and hearts not only of warriors captured in battle, but of their own people. Nothing dreamed up by the set designers for *Indiana Jones and the Temple of Doom* begins to match the fearful reality of the great full-length statues actually found in the Templo Mayor in the heart of modern Mexico City.

The truly terrifying Mictlantecuhtli (Lord of Death) is shown in an over-life-size statue made of fired clay and stucco as a creature half-flayed, with his rib cage exposed and his liver hanging out. Dramatically installed on a high plinth at the Royal Academy, the god's great, clawed hands seem to reach out greedily as he bends over a new victim. We can easily imagine the terror of the person laid before his altar, his back arched so that a flint knife can easily pierce the living flesh to tear out his still beating heart. And since the Aztecs were also cannibals, the victim knew that after his death his flesh would be eaten, accompanied by a delicious chocolate sauce.

Certainly, there are moments of light relief, as in the wonderful representations of animals, birds, fish and insects (actually gods who have taken animal form), including a monumental coiled rattlesnake in granite, and an adorable stone dog that sits up begging on its hind legs. A truly low-down, plug-ugly toad shows that the Aztecs at least had a sense of humour. But, almost as soon as you have decided the Aztecs really weren't so bad, in the very next gallery you come across what must be the single nastiest object ever displayed in the Royal Academy.

This is a clay container made for the flayed skin of sacrificial victims. It is perfectly preserved, complete with a tight-fitting lid to prevent the stench from escaping. According to the label, the knobbly pustules on the surface of this repulsive vessel are intended to replicate the bobbles of fat found inside human skin. And that's another thing: as you contemplate the objects in this show, try to remember that the temples they were found in must have smelled like abattoirs.

Blood-soaked as Aztec culture was, theirs was an art of enormous formal sophistication and refinement. It takes some time in front of a massive brazier of fired clay to realise the complexity of its construction in the form of a dead warrior held in the open mouth of a giant eagle, still holding his shield and a quiver full of arrows. Easier for the eye to grasp is the semi-abstract simplicity of a triangular face mask of green stone, with oval eyes made of shell and obsidian, and round ear plugs of jade.

Two great votive vessels in the form of two relatively benign deities in the Aztec pantheon, Chicomecoatl and Xilonen, show the goddesses wearing heavy beads and enormous headdresses, and holding up delicately carved ears of maize and corn. A round shield made of feathers and embroidered with gold is an incredible survival that gives us a glimpse of the luxury and colour that were also part of this civilisation. It reminds us, too, that the stone and clay figures we have just seen were originally cloaked with feathers and adorned with fabrics. A group of rare codices, hand-written and illustrated manuscripts showing Aztec customs (and, from the Hispanic period, episodes in the conquest of Mexico) close the exhibition.

This huge show, with more than 350 objects in it, is held together by Ivor Heal's dramatic design. Though the show covers two centuries, it was difficult for me to see any formal development or change in Aztec art until the arrival of the Spaniards. I have to come clean and say that Mesoamerican art as a whole leaves me cold. But I recognise that thanks to the ambition and scale of this show, as well as the knock-down quality of the loans the Royal Academy has wangled from Mexico's National Institute of Anthropology and History and the Museum of the Templo Mayor, this is one of the best of the year.

The *Padshahnama*

When I tell you that an imperial Mogul manuscript from the
Royal Library at Windsor Castle is on view in London, you might or
might not sit up and take notice. So let me put it another way. The
Padshahnama, or 'Chronicle of the king of the world', is to Mogul
painting what the Taj Mahal is to Mogul architecture – one of the most
sublime works of art in existence. But unlike the Taj Mahal, few
people have seen the *Padshahnama*, for it has been in the Royal Library
since 1797, when the Nawab of Oudh presented it to King George III.
Over the past hundred years the bound volume has been exhibited
on four occasions. Even then, only one or two pages were visible at
a time.

Recently the volume was unbound for conservation. This has
enabled the Queen to put all 44 of its sumptuous illustrations on
view to the public for the first time. Framed, lit and hung in an
appropriately theatrical setting, they are on show in the Queen's
Gallery at Buckingham Palace. In May the manuscript will tour
America, before being re-bound and returned to Windsor. So drop
everything, cancel appointments, rearrange schedules, book a day
off. You know what you have to do, and you have only six weeks
in which to do it.

Shah-Jahan was the fifth and most powerful of the Mogul
emperors, and is best known for having built the Taj Mahal. His
reign, from 1628 to 1658, overlapped with that of Charles I of England.
It is easy to see similarities between these two supremely cultivated
monarchs, both of whom lived to see their thrones usurped by a
fanatical religious zealot who brought an end to the visual culture
that had flourished under their patronage.

In the late 1630s Shah-Jahan commissioned an illustrated chronicle
of his reign. Writing in the court language, Persian, the scribe left
blank spaces to be filled in with paintings illustrating the darbars

19 March 1997

The *Padshahnama*

The Queen's Gallery,
Buckingham Palace,
London

(audiences or receptions), weddings, hunts, elephant fights and battles
described in the narrative. The text in the Royal Collection, which
covers the first ten years of the reign, was finished in about 1657.

It is important to realise, however, that the paintings illustrating
it were made about twenty years earlier, probably as part of a visual
archive of the emperor's reign. The explanation for the marvellous
intensity of observation is that they were painted more or less on the
spot. In the celebrated scene showing the accession ceremonies, for
example, the architectural setting is recognisable as the hall of public
audiences in the Agra fort. We even know the names of the nobles
and court officials assembled before the throne in rigidly hierarchical
order.

Sometimes a tiny detail can be explained not because it is
mentioned in the text but because it depicts something an
independent witness – an ambassador or a missionary – noted
elsewhere. In the scene showing Shah-Jahan honouring his eldest son
at his wedding, we would be hard-pressed to identify the purpose of
a row of tiny gold-painted figures in the distance had not an English
traveller described the spectacular display of fireworks in the shape
of monsters erected by the banks of the river that night.

The wealth and splendour of Shah-Jahan's court is so incredible
that no storyteller could have made it up. Page after page, our eyes
are dazzled by delicately rendered ropes of pearls, jewelled turbans,
Agra carpets and silken canopies, elephants with golden trappings
carrying ladies of the harem in elaborate covered howdahs, and
horses richly caparisoned with bridles of silver and saddle rugs
of embroidered silk and velvet. No detail is too small to escape the
painter's attention. In one scene, showing the decapitation of a rebel,
a haze of microscopic flies swarm over the severed head. Look closely
at minutely rendered medallions worn by some of the courtiers in the
darbar scenes and you see the distinctive profile of Shah-Jahan.

All fourteen painters who worked on the illustrations had joined
the imperial workshops during the reigns of Shah-Jahan's grandfather
Akbar, and father Jahangir. We are looking at the work of the most
celebrated Mogul artists at the height of their powers. Their method of
working was slow, but to understand it is to understand the jewel-like
clarity and brilliance that characterises Mogul art. First, the artist
made a preliminary sketch. This he traced on to another sheet of paper

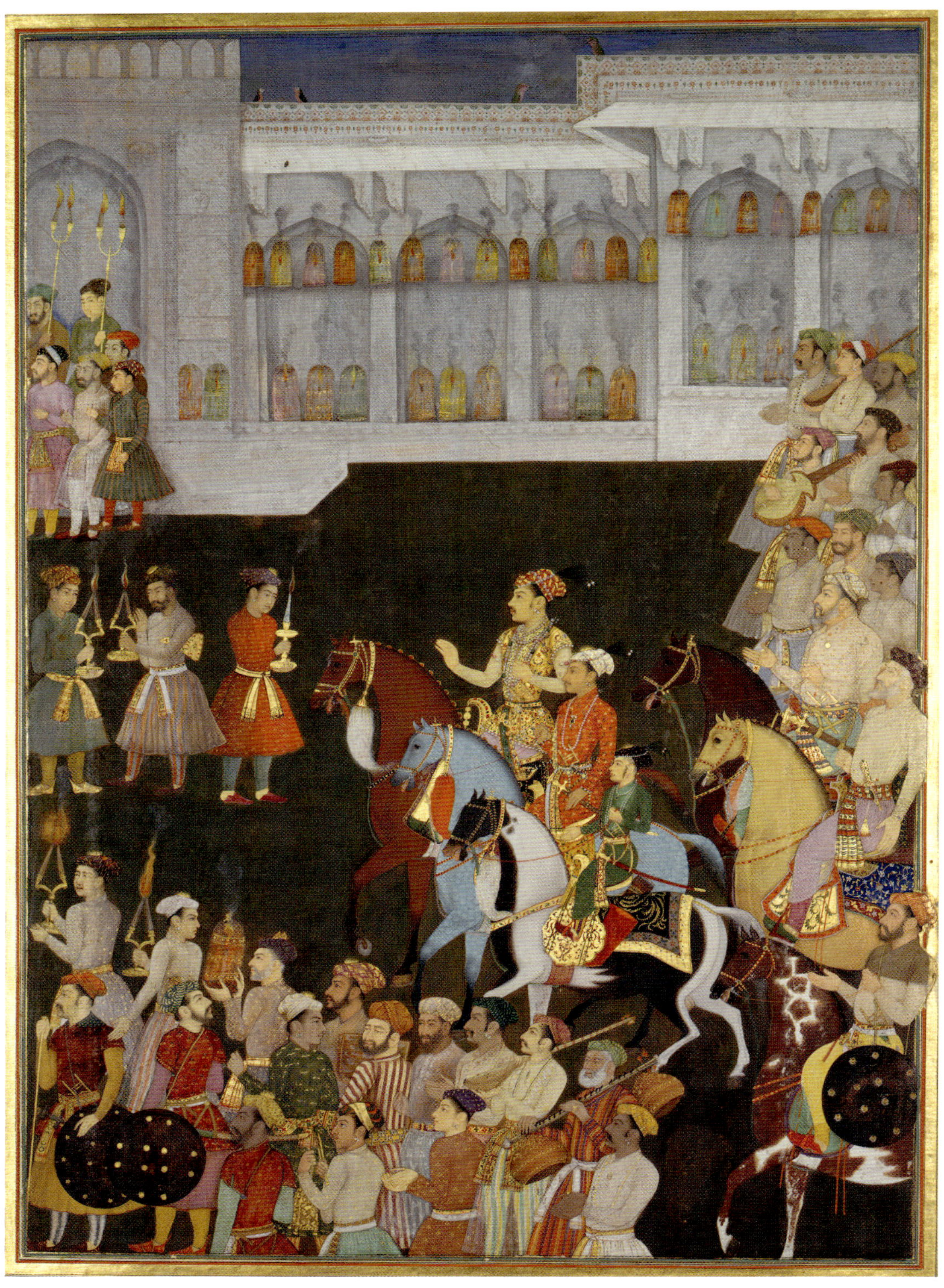

to produce an outline drawing, which was then covered with white translucent gouache.

Working with tiny brushes, he added colour – clear lemon yellows, lilacs, apple greens, mauves and scarlets made from vegetable and mineral pigments. Finally – and this is the real secret of the dazzling effect on the eye – the sheet was turned over and burnished with an agate implement to create an enamel-smooth surface which bore no trace of the artist's touch.

This working method left very little room for improvisation, and at first glance it looks as though one artist painted all the pictures. But gradually you detect different hands at work, as different styles and distinct artistic personalities begin to emerge, some influenced by European art, others not. In the depictions of court scenes, the stylised, flattened figures are rendered in profile and placed one behind the other with no attempt to represent spatial recession. Men wearing striped silk tunics stand against carpets with geometric designs and floral wall paintings in a riot of colour and pattern. But in several of the battle and hunting scenes, space opens up, and in distant vistas the artists allow themselves a sketchiness and freedom you rarely find in the scenes that show the assembled court. Because the manuscript has been preserved bound in a royal library since it was made, light has not faded the vivid, piercingly intense colours.

Abd al-Hamid Lahawri
Illustration from the
Padshahnama,
1656–57
The Royal Collection

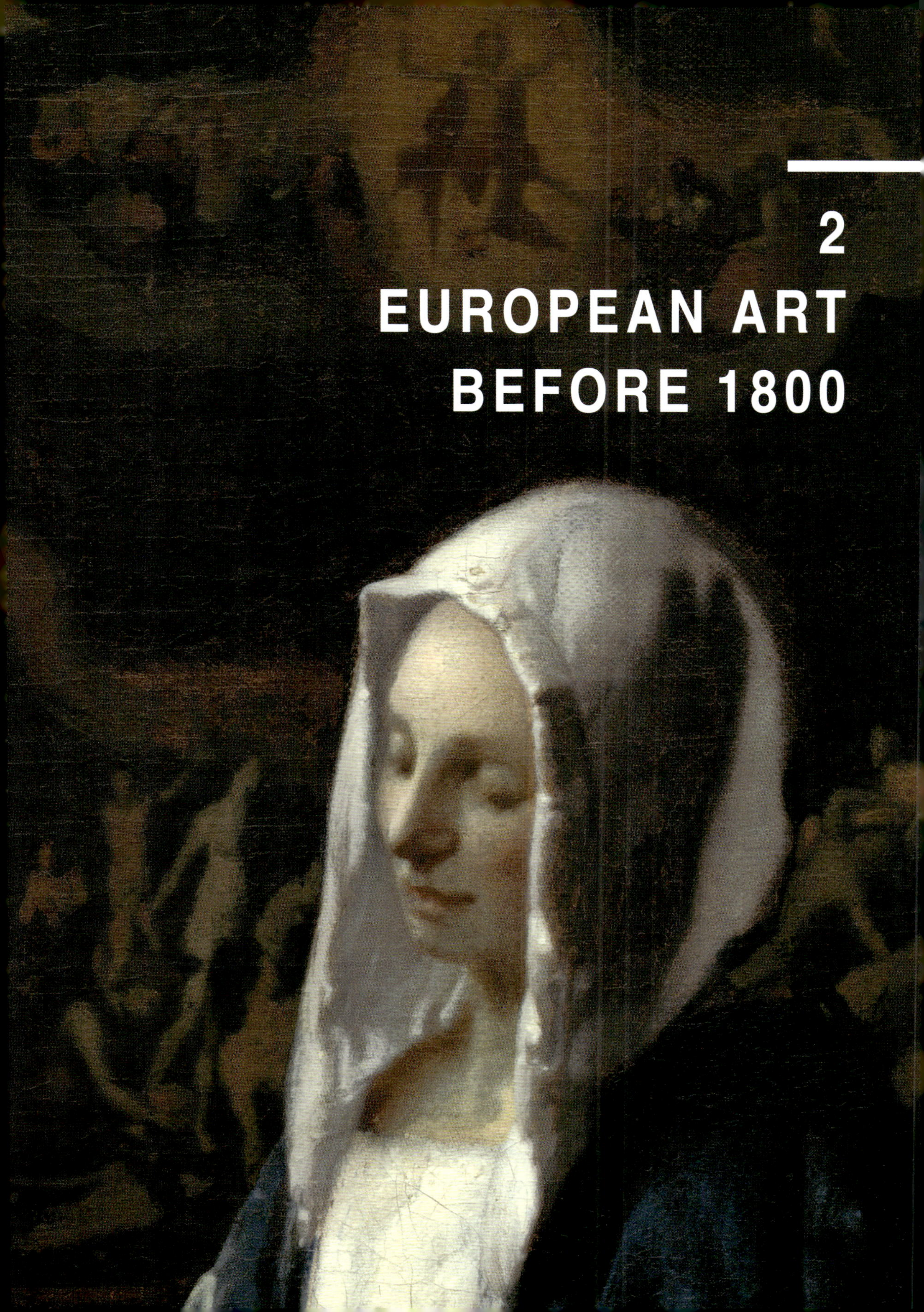
2
EUROPEAN ART
BEFORE 1800

Pieter Bruegel the Elder
**Massacre of the
Innocents**, *c. 1565–67*
The Royal Collection

Pieter Bruegel the Elder

When is a painting finished? Is it the moment when the artist lays down his or her brush? Or when the canvas is signed? Or do great pictures, as I believe, have a life of their own, continuing to evolve even after they leave the studio?

Of course, colours can fade or darken over the years, but meaning can change, too, depending on who owns a work of art, where it is displayed and how it is treated. Time itself can impinge on the reading of an image when a later generation interprets it through the prism of its own experience, often in ways that the artist may never have intended.

There could be no better example of this phenomenon than Pieter Bruegel the Elder's *Massacre of the Innocents* in the Royal Collection. Painted in 1565–67 and acquired more than a century later by Charles II, it shows a Flemish village in the dead of winter, with new-fallen snow covering pitched roofs, icicles hanging from eaves, bare branches, a frozen pond and patches of hard earth visible under trampled snow.

This bleak landscape makes a suitable backdrop for a scene of pure horror – the murder by King Herod's soldiers of all male children in Palestine under the age of two. But, instead of setting the Biblical story in a faraway land in the distant past, Bruegel shows men and women of his own time, dressed in contemporary clothing and living in a prosperous village with two-storey brick houses and a substantial church of stone.

A master of narrative invention, he steps back to give us a bird's-eye view of the carnage so that our eye must move slowly across the picture surface to examine each heart-rending episode in turn: a father falls to his knees to beg a mounted soldier to spare his child; a couple implore a killer to take their daughter instead of their son; troops use pikes, axes and a battering ram to break down doors; mounted

4 November 2008

Bruegel to Rubens:
Masters of Flemish
Painting

The Queen's Gallery,
Buckingham Palace,
London

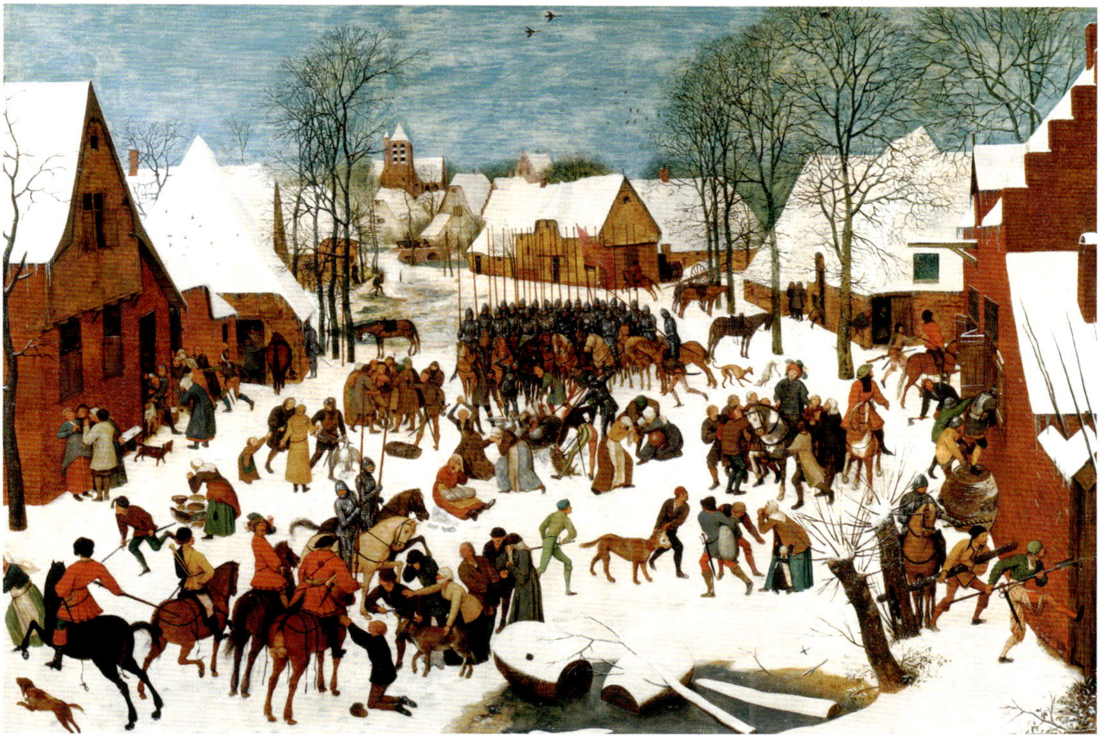

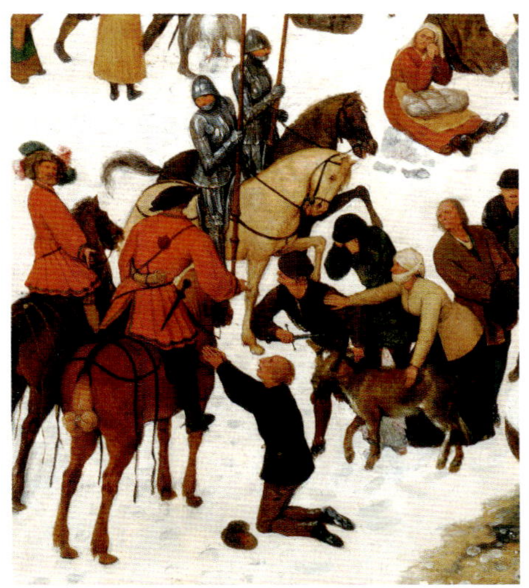

knights in armour guard the approach to the village to block the only means of escape. So beautifully painted is every detail that we can almost hear the cries of anguish carried in the cold air, the grunts of the soldiers and the methodical clink of cold steel.

If you've been looking at the reproduction of the picture as you read these words, by now you may be wondering about my eyesight. Instead of slitting the throats of infants, the soldiers are killing turkeys, a goose and a doe. Distraught mothers weep not over bloody corpses, but over hams, a cheese or nondescript bundles spread out in the snow. This is because the picture we see today looks very different from the one Bruegel painted.

The first owner, the Holy Roman Emperor Rudolph II, ordered that all the dead babies be painted out and replaced with animals, objects and foodstuffs. His intention was to turn a scene of massacre into one of mere plunder. Perhaps the subject was too distressing for a collector as cultivated as Rudolph, but more likely the Emperor did not feel comfortable with a picture showing the massacre by a king of his own subjects.

Especially troubling to Rudolph would be the figures on horseback – two sergeants in red coats on the left and the smiling young herald on the right. Unlike the thugs who only carry out their orders, they are clearly men of higher rank, representatives of the government, and so directly answerable to the ruler.

Then, too, Rudolph was a Habsburg, and Bruegel's picture was an undisguised allusion to atrocities committed in Flanders under the harsh rule of the Spanish branch of his family. By having it repainted, the Emperor sought to mitigate the cruelty of a picture that in its own time must have been as inflammatory as Picasso's *Guernica*. Rightly, modern conservationists have decided to leave the changes ordered by Rudolph intact. Not only are they now part of the picture's history, but they add new layers to its meaning.

And that is not the end of the story. Rudolph's alterations created a scene that to modern sensibilities may be even more resonant of calculated evil than the picture as originally painted.

For one thing, the absence of blood and gore creates an atmosphere of eerie stillness, as though we are watching a silent film in slow motion. Then, too, the changes somehow make the actions of the soldiers in rounding up their victims look more deliberate than frenzied. Instead of slaughtering their victims on the spot, it now looks as though the army is taking the children away to be disposed of elsewhere. Because we aren't distracted by the sight of blood in the snow, it is easy to imagine the scene after the troops have gone, when numb silence descends on the village once more, leaving these people to face their loss.

Caravaggio: The Final Years

At the heart of the National Gallery's *Caravaggio: The Final Years* the vast canvas of *The Raising of Lazarus* looms up out the darkness, a ghostly, ghastly apparition. One of the artist's most sublime figural compositions, it was painted in 1609 for the high altar of a church just outside Messina in Sicily.

The whole upper half of the canvas is empty, but in the lower half a crowded frieze of figures, fitfully lit by flickering light, extends from edge to edge. We viewers enter the picture at the extreme left, through the highlighted face of the onlooker who cranes his neck to see what is going on. Following the direction of his gaze, we are drawn by the light that travels horizontally across Christ's outstretched arm and limp index finger to the exact centre of the composition, the raised arm of the putrefying corpse, Lazarus.

The long diagonal of Lazarus's nude body fills the right-hand side of the composition, which is closed off at the right by the figures of Mary and Martha. As divine light strikes the open palm of his raised arm, infusing him with life, the fingers of both his hands stiffen and spread. We can see that the miracle of his resurrection has already occurred, but none of the onlookers yet realises what has happened, for Mary is still bending close to her brother's face with her mouth open, in a desperate effort to breathe life back into him. Only now, after we have 'read' the picture from left to right, do we see that the outflung arms of Lazarus form a cross. This is Caravaggio's way of underscoring the deeper significance of the Biblical story, which foreshadows Christ's own death and resurrection.

When Michelangelo Merisi da Caravaggio painted *The Raising of Lazarus* he was thirty-nine and had one more year to live. His career can be divided roughly into three phases. Arriving in Rome in 1591, he began as a painter of still lifes and of half-length canvases showing

23 February 2005

Caravaggio: The Final Years

National Gallery, London

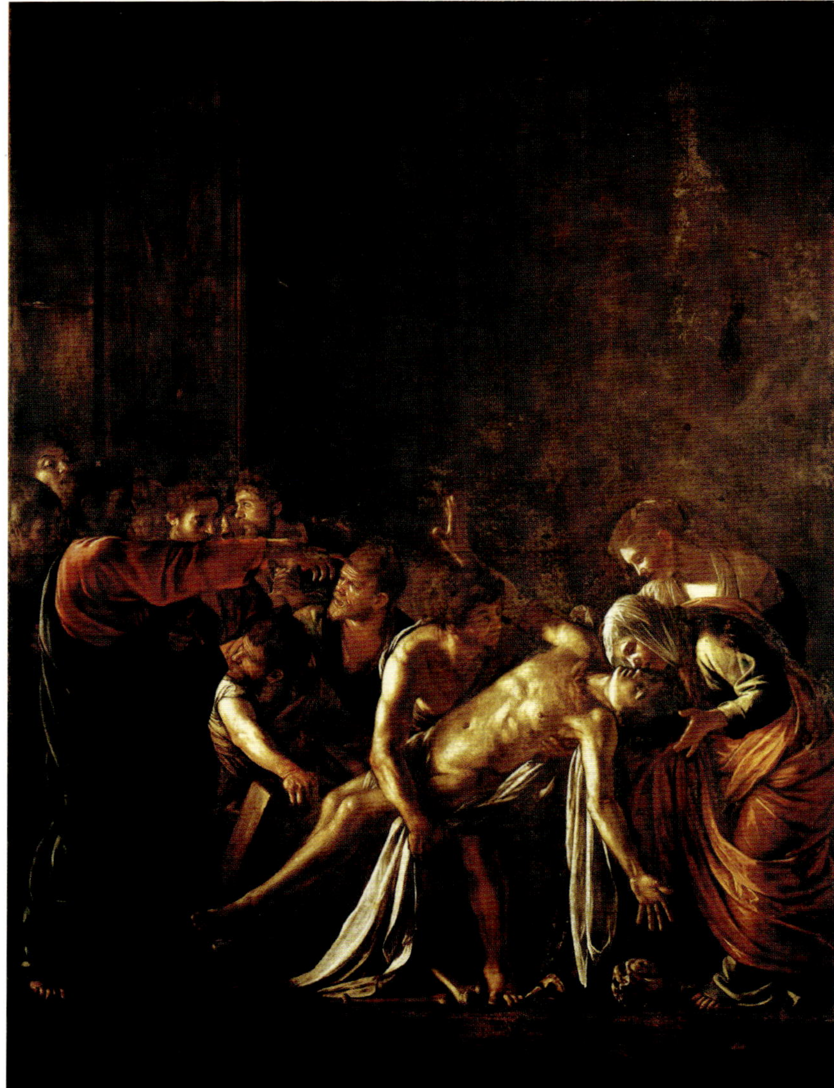

half-dressed Roman street boys, often in frankly seductive poses, which were much appreciated by his clerical patrons. Then, beginning with *The Calling of St Matthew* (1599), he matured into a painter of dramatic, large-scale religious compositions for Roman churches. This exhibition looks at the third phase in Caravaggio's career, the work he did after his flight from Rome in 1606.

On 28 May of that year Caravaggio mortally wounded a man named Ranuccio Tomassoni in a street brawl. Escaping from papal jurisdiction, he began his final four-year peregrination from Naples to Malta and from Malta to Sicily. At each stop along the way he left large religious compositions in which action is largely replaced by an ineffable atmosphere of stillness and contemplation.

This magnificent show starts with what you might call the back-story, a comparison between two versions of *The Supper at Emmaus* that succinctly sums up Caravaggio's career until 1606. The famous one in the National Gallery of 1601 shows the beardless (and therefore as yet unrecognised) Christ in the act of blessing the food on the table, as the two disciples, suddenly realising who this stranger is, react in astonishment. As a foil to their amazement, the still unenlightened innkeeper impassively looks on.

Strong, even light reveals forms and casts deep shadows on the wall behind the figures. The brilliant colours, the explosive gestures of the two disciples, and the way the powerful composition zigzags in and out of the space: all these are used to show off the painter's incredible technical skill and powers of invention.

By contrast, the version of the picture in the Brera Museum in Milan, painted five years later in 1606, is quietly introspective. Now the composition has been simplified, the lighting muted, the action focused, and the gestures contained. Stripping away all inessentials, Caravaggio sets the action in a void, thus emphasising the solemn, Eucharistic moment when Christ, now shown bearded, blesses the bread and wine. Though not nearly as audacious a picture as the first version, the Brera picture is a more spiritual, more contemplative one. What we learn through this comparison is important: that Caravaggio had begun to paint in his 'late' style even before he left Rome.

Whether Caravaggio became a devoutly religious man in his later years we will never know, but he took a form of holy orders when he became a Knight of Malta and the evidence of the late pictures themselves tells us that he thought deeply about his faith. No detail in them is unintentional or without significance.

Caravaggio had many followers, but the single quality that makes works by him more profound than those of his imitators is a pictorial intelligence born out of a profound understanding of the subjects he painted. An example occurs in the small gallery where two paintings represent the period when, after a year in Naples, Caravaggio took up residence in Malta, a military outpost occupied by the Knights of St John whose order he joined in July 1608.

In a portrait of that year thought to represent Fra Antonio Martelli, Caravaggio shows his subject wearing a crumpled silk habit emblazoned with the Grand Cross of Malta. The genius of the picture lies in the infinitesimal movement of the knight's left hand as he lifts the sword ever so slightly from its scabbard, while at the same time continuing to finger rosary beads with his right hand. The two actions epitomise the mission of the Knights of Malta, an order made up of soldiers sworn to fight for the Christian faith.

Another brawl, a gunshot, and one of the knights is seriously wounded. Caravaggio is defrocked, imprisoned, and escapes to Sicily. By the time we come to the largest gallery in the exhibition, in which the great altarpieces from Messina hang, Caravaggio is a wholly different painter from the one who had left Rome. Working in these provincial cities far from the sophisticated Roman milieu, Caravaggio was more open to local influences – from Greek icons, which are so obviously the visual source for the quarter-moon shape of the Madonna's pose in *The Adoration of the Shepherds* to the classical relief sculptures that surely inspired the shallow frieze of figures in *The Raising of Lazarus*.

Though a whiff of sensuality still lingers of the earlier period, in these last works you find a new spirituality, a mellow acceptance of man's frailty. Now, too, he brings acute psychological perception to the way he renders good and evil. Look at the composition of a half-length picture showing *Salome with the Head of John the Baptist* from Madrid. Caravaggio has crowded the three figures to the right side of the canvas, leaving a black void at the left. Salome, her cold eyes locked with ours, turns with the platter bearing the severed head away from the light and into the darkness, a damned soul.

Because so many of the late works are too fragile to travel, there are only sixteen pictures in the show. Two – a *Sleeping Cupid* from Florence and a *St John the Baptist* from Rome – are extraordinarily ugly, but no less fascinating for that. The battered condition of several others just adds to the sense that in the last pictures Caravaggio spoke of the spirit transcending the flesh. Only the wonderful *Annunciation* from Nancy is so scraped down that you can't be quite sure what you are looking at, but, even then, there is no more bravura passage in the whole of the exhibition than the Mannerist figure of the muscular angel plummeting to earth to greet a serenely unfazed Virgin Mary.

Johannes Vermeer

In Johannes Vermeer's *Woman Holding a Balance* a young woman stands perfectly still as she concentrates on balancing a pair of scales. With one hand resting gently on a table for support, she suspends the instrument between the thumb and forefinger, extending her small finger outward to steady her hand during the few seconds it takes for the two pans to level off. As the late afternoon sunlight filters through a yellow curtain at the upper left, the silence is almost palpable. The woman holds her breath. Nothing moves. Time stands still.

To move one element in the meticulously constructed composition by a fraction of an inch would be to upset its equilibrium. The strong vertical of the picture frame hanging on the wall behind the woman divides the composition into two halves, while the bottom edge of the same frame bisects it horizontally. Having subtly created four equal quarters, Vermeer then balances them diagonally, void against mass and light against dark.

At the same time, the viewer's eye is irresistibly drawn to the vanishing point in the exact centre of the canvas, just to the left of the hand holding the scales. Since Vermeer isolates those scales against a patch of empty wall, in pictorial terms they stabilise the composition like a bolt.

If this rigid underlying structure creates a sense of serenity, Vermeer's understanding of the physical properties of paint suffuses an otherwise sombre work with unexpected sensuality. Throughout, he explores delicate colour harmonies, picking up shades of blue and of yellow and letting them ripple through his composition. Using a variety of painting techniques, he contrasts areas of dense, opaque pigment with other areas where the paint is thin and transparent. The texture of the ermine trim on the woman's blue jacket, for example, is utterly different from that of the watery sunlight bathing the wall at the upper left. And the luminous glow suffusing the woman's arms

22 November 1996

Johannes Vermeer

National Gallery of Art, Washington, DC

and face is created by applying a glaze of semi-transparent light pink pigment over a layer of white.

But no amount of technical or compositional analysis can penetrate the mysterious heart of Vermeer's art. As we look at *Woman Holding a Balance*, tiny details begin to resonate with meaning. A casket overflowing with gold and pearls lies on the table before the woman, yet the balance is empty, apart from two pools of light. She herself seems to stand as if balanced between a looking glass hanging on the wall in front of her and the heavier weight of a painting of *The Last Judgement* framing her figure from behind. Most important of all, the woman is heavily pregnant.

Neither genre painting nor allegory, *Woman Holding a Balance* is something far rarer and far more profound: the depiction of a moment of spiritual illumination. Reminded by the jewels and looking-glass of the vanities of the world, and by the picture of *The Last Judgement* of her duty to live her life in the perspective of eternity, the woman is taking the measure of her own life, balancing what is good against what is bad. In this sense, the painting is simply about the virtues of moderation and self-knowledge.

But having looked at it for most of my adult life, only last week did I come fully to understand its meaning. I believe the woman in the picture realises that the child she is carrying within her is like an empty balance, capable of turning towards good or evil, the flesh or the spirit. What is more, *Woman Holding a Balance* is a painting – one wants to say a parable – about the Catholic doctrine of free will.

Born in 1632, Vermeer was brought up as a Calvinist, but converted to Catholicism in 1654 at the time of his marriage to a daughter of one of Delft's leading Catholics. His conversion meant that he meditated deeply on the irreconcilable argument between the Calvinist doctrine of the soul predestined at birth for salvation or damnation and the Catholic belief in the individual's ability to choose, with God's grace, between good and evil. What more perfect expression of the latter viewpoint than an empty balance, which has value only if capable of free movement?

Vermeer belongs to the Northern Renaissance tradition of depicting the world with clarity and brilliance, while infusing ordinary, everyday things with spiritual significance. As in the paintings of Jan van Eyck and Rogier van der Weyden, the soft,

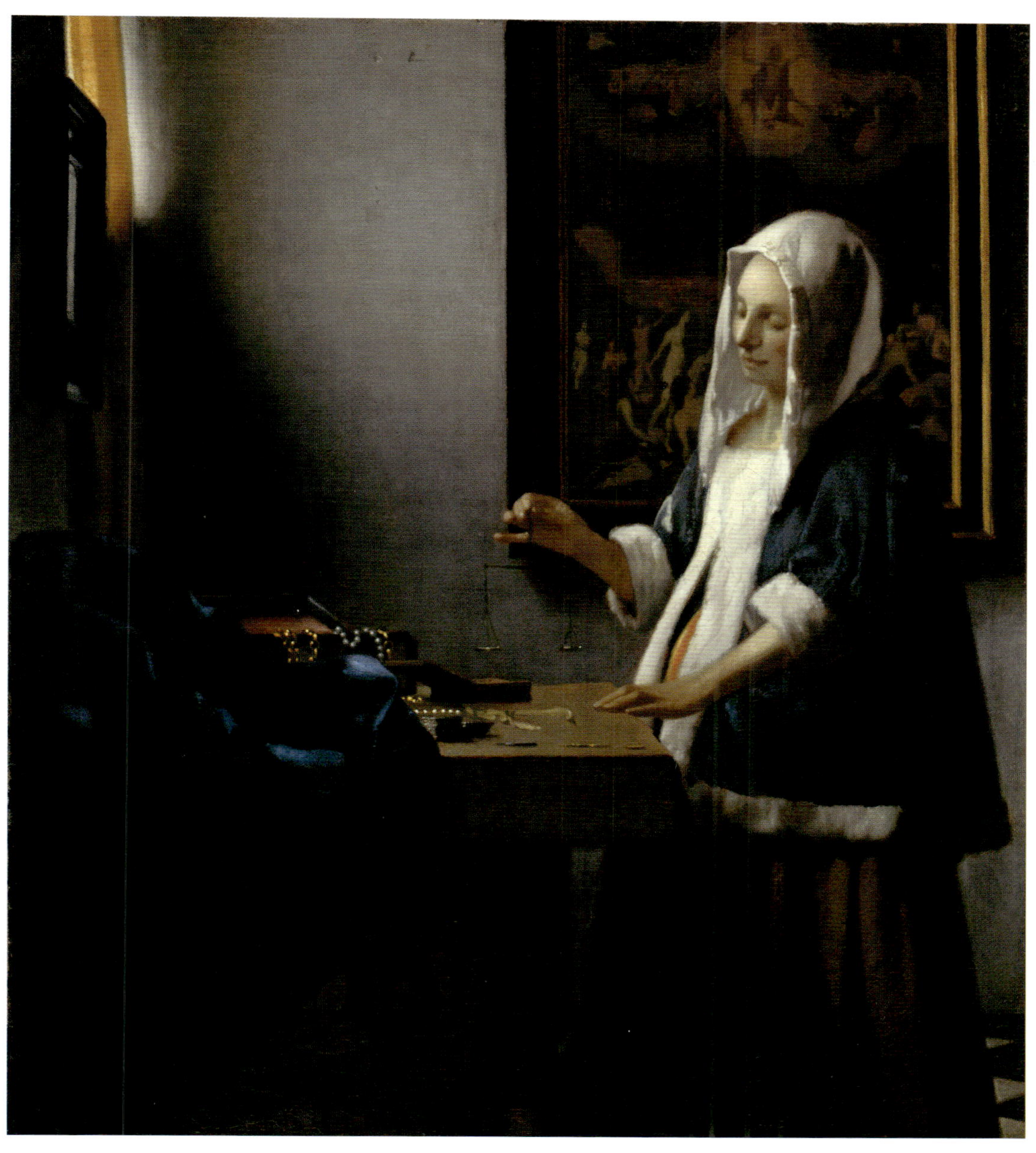

Johannes Vermeer
**Woman Holding a
Balance**, *c. 1663–64*
*National Gallery of Art,
Washington , DC*

diffused light flooding into the room in *Woman Holding a Balance* suggests gradual spiritual illumination, the gift of God which may be used to attain salvation.

As you see from my analysis of this one picture, we can't look at a work by Vermeer quickly, still less can we make generalisations about his art in a relatively short review such as this one. Whether it is the limpidly pure *Young Woman with a Water Pitcher* from the Metropolitan Museum, or the sun-drenched sensuality of the *Woman with a Pearl Necklace* from Berlin, his genius was to manipulate patterns of light and colour in order to create moods of quiet reflection. But these in turn encourage us to look within ourselves, to take stock of the moral and spiritual values by which we live our lives.

Marcel Proust illustrated this phenomenon when he had his fictional poet Bergotte expire in front of Vermeer's panoramic cityscape, the *View of Delft*. While looking at 'a little patch of yellow wall . . . so well painted that it was . . . of a beauty sufficient in itself', Bergotte realises how meretricious his own art has been. Dying, he sees a vision of a balance – in one of its scales his own life, in the other, the little patch of wall so beautifully painted in yellow. What Proust understood about Vermeer's art is its profundity. In looking at it, we learn about ourselves.

In the first exhibition ever devoted to Vermeer, the National Gallery of Art in Washington DC has brought together 21 of his paintings, three-fifths of Vermeer's 36 accepted works. Eight paintings (including, disastrously, the *View of Delft*) have been cleaned for the occasion, which will not happen again – indeed, considering the irreplaceable value of these works of art, should not happen again.

Though a crowded gallery is not the ideal way to experience the serenity and timelessness of Vermeer, I can't imagine a more beautiful show, nor one that will stay longer in my memory. Stepping out of it into the rooms containing the National Gallery's collection of seventeenth-century Dutch paintings, I tried to respond to the works of Pieter de Hooch and Gerard Ter Borch. I failed. All I could feel in front of their pictures was the busy, rushing world swallowing me up again.

Jean-Baptiste Siméon Chardin

Looking at Chardin's *Glass of Water and Coffee Pot* it is easy to understand why eighteenth-century theorists and academicians considered still-life painting inferior to historical, mythological and even genre subjects. After all, what does the picture show? Two perfectly plain vessels such as any of us might find in our own kitchens, placed on a shelf along with three heads of garlic and a sprig of some common herb, perhaps sage.

At first sight, there seems to be no particular order in their arrangement, nor any natural relationship between them. Since the colours are muted, the light even and the background neutral, it looks as though Chardin has taken a great deal of trouble to paint nothing at all.

But in that nothing he has explored a whole world of visual sensation. First, there is the invisible compositional structure that gives the picture its feeling of stability and calm. Chardin divides the rectangular canvas vertically in half, at the empty space between the glass and the jug, then divides it again horizontally at the line running from the rim of the glass to the handle of the jug. At the centre of the canvas, therefore, the two vessels form a second (inner) rectangle, within which all the picture's drama unfolds.

It may sound odd to describe as dramatic the way the eye moves from the bits of garlic and herb hanging over the shelf in the foreground to the glass of water in the middle distance and earthenware jug at the back of the ledge. But in a spatial journey of perhaps a few inches Chardin plays off light against dark, solid against void, transparency against opacity, the whole time carefully differentiating between textures that reflect light (water, glass, glazed ceramic) and those that absorb it (the dry papery skin of the garlic).

The otherwise disparate objects are knitted together by the air

8 March 2000

Chardin

Royal Academy,
London

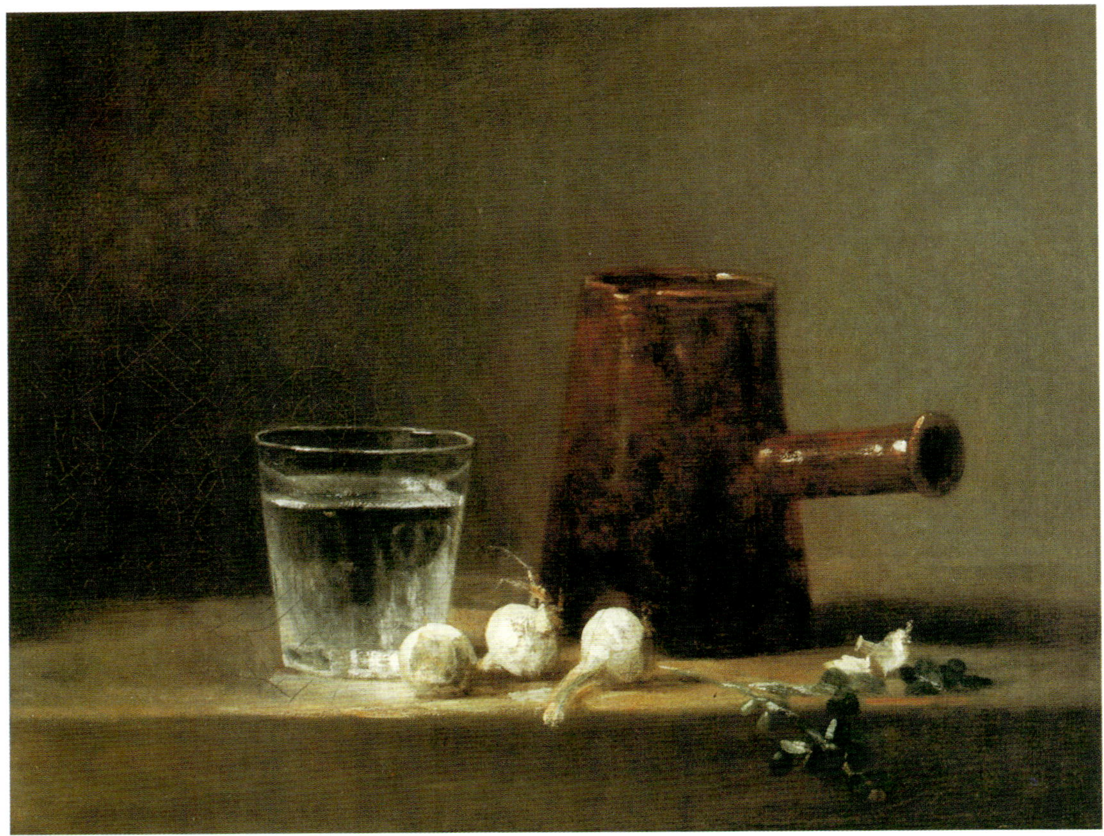

that circulates around them and by the gentle light that falls over the whole composition. As the eye adjusts to Chardin's low tones, the colours gradually emerge: the indescribably subtle range of blues, greys and whites with which he creates the reflections in the clear water, the soft pearl-white of the garlic, and the infinite modulations of brown, black and white in the coffee pot and its shadow.

It is a critical commonplace to describe Chardin's solemn and unprepossessing still lifes as the antithesis to the frivolity that characterised the prevailing rococo style in France. Just imagine, for example, the aristocratic chic with which his great contemporary Jean-Baptiste Oudry would have imbued such a subject, how he would have transformed the contents of a housewife's larder into a display of abundance fit for the eyes of the king himself.

But Chardin steps back from his own subjects, refusing to impose any non-visual values on his paintings: no narrative, no symbol, no sentiment, no dimension that could be construed as overtly political or sacred. Having taken infinite pains to achieve this utter simplicity, he refuses to manipulate our response to the reality he shows us. The most sensuous of artists, Chardin evokes in his still lifes the senses of taste, sight and touch.

But the moral heart of his work lies in his ability to paint silence. He allows us the freedom to invest the objects he depicts with our own thoughts and feelings, not his. It is as though each thing he paints is permitted to fulfil its own latent potential to be beautiful. In his genre subjects, as in his still lifes, what appears to be empty is shown to be full and what looks like nothing turns out to be everything.

When he paints a little boy who has taken a break from his homework to concentrate on a toy top spinning on his desk, his mind is for the moment fully occupied, but absolutely empty of thought. The spinning top becomes a perfect metaphor for a state of utter absorption but profound mental rest.

For Chardin, it is at empty moments such as these, when people don't know they are being observed, that they are at their most human, their most vulnerable, their most natural. The young man blowing soap bubbles is using his mind, certainly, but to concentrate on an act so trivial that it does not rise to the level of a thought. By depicting him at a moment when he is off his guard like this, Chardin chooses to paint something relatively rare in art (and otherwise unknown in a century as intrigued by physiognomy as the eighteenth), the human face when it is devoid of expression, and therefore empty of character or psychological nuance.

In the later still lifes particularly, Chardin paints another kind of emptiness: death. What is so extraordinary about his depiction of dead animals in *A Rabbit, Two Thrushes and Some Straw on a Stone Table* or *Two Rabbits, a Pheasant and a Seville Orange on a Stone Ledge* is the way in which the artist conveys the finality of death, its awesome silence.

Unlike Goya in his studies of dead game and fish, Chardin implies no sense of outrage, no anger at the fate of these animals. Instead, he looks at them with compassion, an emotion subtly different from pity because it is extended towards an equal, not an inferior.

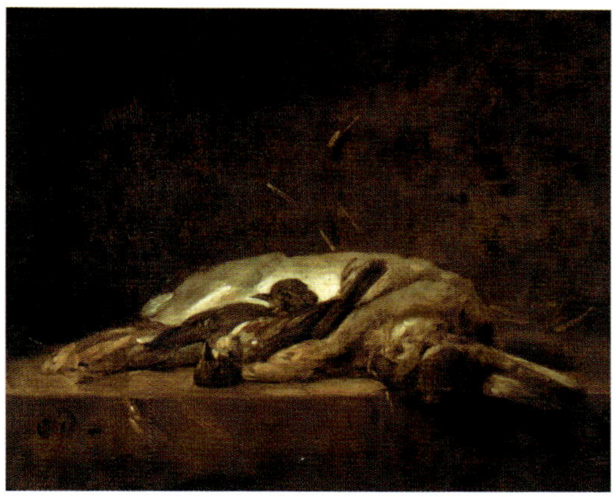

Jean-Baptiste Siméon Chardin
A Rabbit, Two Thrushes and Some Straw on a Stone Table, *1755*
Musée de la Chasse et de la Nature, Paris

By showing them nestled together like small children tucked in bed, he accords them the consolation of eternal peace, making death look almost bearable, a sort of endless sleep.

Because he delighted in faded colours, you might at first assume that Chardin is not a colourist. But just try to describe in words the colouring of the feathers in the shuttlecock held by the adorable child in *Girl with Shuttlecock*, or those in the striped skirt of the nurse in the beautiful *Meal for a Convalescent*. Grey, white, mauve, rose, taupe and light blue – all those are present, but there is also a suggestion of yellow, when, as far as I can tell, no yellow is actually used in either picture.

No less a colourist than Matisse was forced to confront the fluid, ever-changing nature of Chardin's colour when as a student working in the Louvre he copied *The Smoker's Case*. Day after day he was baffled by the elusive blue on the padded lid of the box in the centre of the picture – a blue, his biographer notes, that could look pink one day and green the next. Matisse tried everything he could think of to pin down the secret of this painting, using a magnifying glass, studying the texture, the grain of the canvas, the glazes, the objects themselves and the transitions from light to shade. To no avail.

The reason Chardin's colours look different in different lights is because he built up his pictures using thin layers of paint, beginning with an orangey-red ground followed by a thin coating of grey-beige. He would then allow each successive layer to show through the one on top of it, until he applied a final glaze of transparent paint over the finished picture. The last thing he did to the poignant, late still life *Two Rabbits with Game Bag and Powder Flask* was to dip the tip of his brush into blue-grey pigment, then pull it very lightly across the finished canvas to create a delicately textured surface. The technique, like a dusting of fine powder, is utterly at one with the ineffable tenderness, the 'reverence', with which he paints the two dead creatures.

Chardin is a painter of the Enlightenment, an artist who grounded his art on what could be experienced and observed. He cultivated a sort of detached contemplativeness and dealt in subtle distinctions. To look at his art properly you need peace.

Goya's *Portrait of the Condesa de Chinchon*

Today a masterpiece by Goya, his *Portrait of the Condesa de Chinchón*, goes on view at the National Gallery in Trafalgar Square for the next six weeks. On loan from the family of the Dukes of Sueca, the painting has only rarely left Madrid, and as one of Spain's greatest national treasures it can never permanently leave Spain.

The portrait must be a candidate for one of the most beautiful pictures in the world. Goya can create the illusion of form out of a few delicate flicks of a brush, whether in the painting of the ribbons that tie and decorate the sitter's cap, in the bravura painting of the folds of her white and cream silk dress, or in the breathtaking speed with which he sketches in the arm of the gold chair on which she sits.

In passages such as these we see how Goya provides a link between the painting of Velázquez in the seventeenth century and that of Manet in the nineteenth. But almost the most remarkable thing about the picture is how, out of an apparently neutral black background, Goya builds an endlessly fascinating modulation of light and dark, filling the painting with space and atmosphere.

María Teresa de Borbón y Vallabriga, Condesa de Chinchón, was the daughter of Dom Luis de Borbon, and a niece of King Charles III, the former King of Naples who had succeeded to the throne of Spain in 1759. Her father, the King's brother, had married the daughter of a Stuart lady and it is from this Scots grandmother that María Teresa inherited her surprising red-blonde hair. Goya had known and painted María Teresa as a child in the enchanting portrait now in the National Gallery of Art in Washington, so he was on terms of some intimacy with her and her family when she sat, at the age of twenty, for this full-length portrait of 1800.

To understand Goya's portrait, we need to know something about the intrigues at the Spanish court. In 1788 the young Countess of Chinchón's cousin, Charles IV, succeeded her uncle as King of Spain.

14 April 1988

Portrait of the Condesa de Chinchón

National Gallery, London

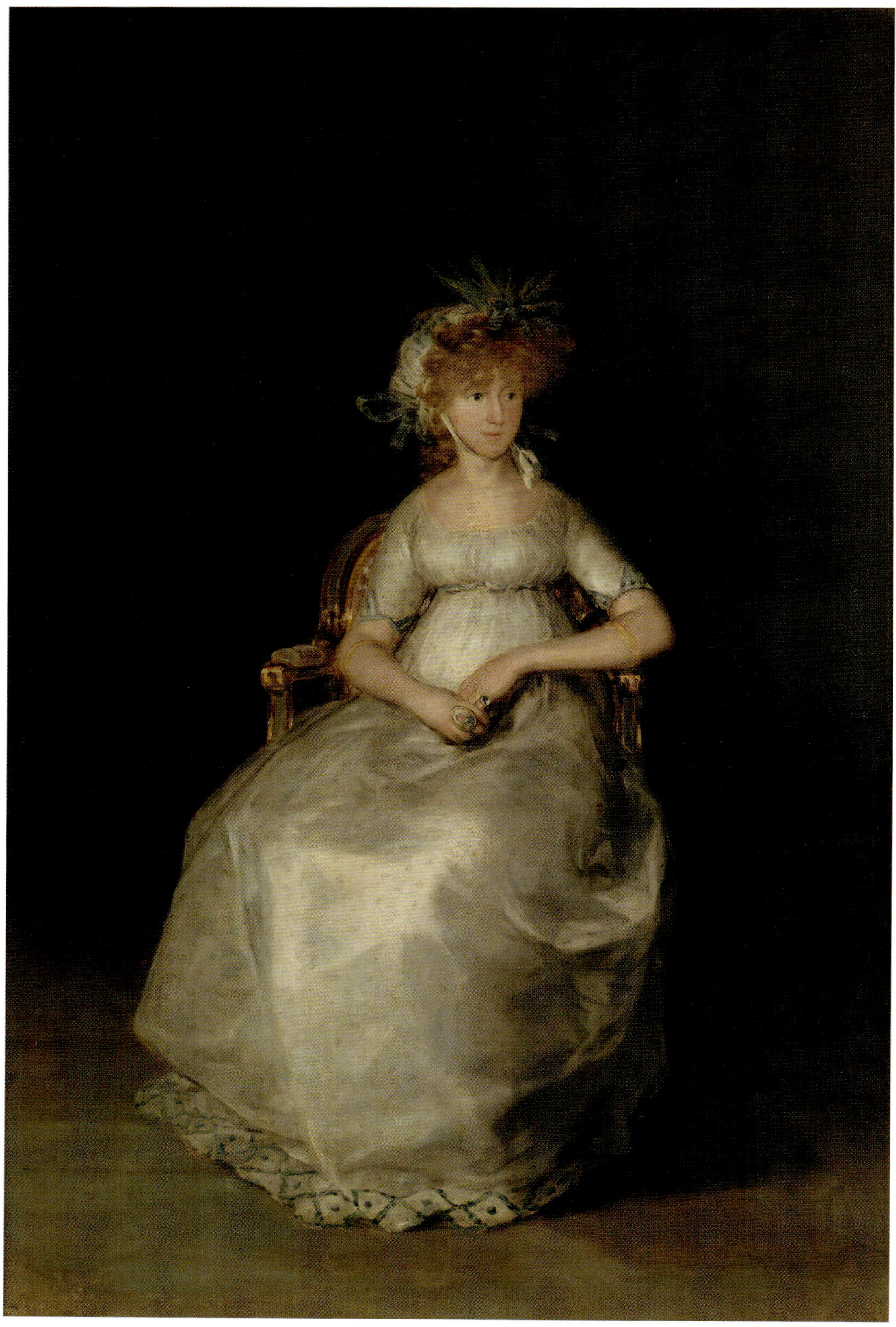

The new King was boorish and stupid; his scheming and vicious wife, Queen María Luisa, much worse. Goya painted the pair often in portraits they were too dim to realise ridiculed their pretensions as mercilessly as they exposed their physical and moral shortcomings. Enter the Queen's lover, the professional soldier Manuel Godoy, who, through a mixture of intelligence and a highly developed predatory instinct, rose at court to become Prime Minister and, with the title Prince of the Peace, the real ruler of Spain.

In order for Godoy to maintain his position at court without open scandal, the Queen needed to find him a token wife. She chose the nineteen-year-old Condesa de Chinchón. After their marriage in 1799 Godoy and his wife rarely met; he showed her little affection, and continued to be the Queen's lover. When the popular uprising of 1808 drove him into exile with the King, María Teresa went to live under the protection of her brother Don Luis, primate of Spain and Cardinal Archbishop of Toledo.

When Goya painted her, the Condesa de Chinchón was pregnant. The sheaf of green wheat in her hair symbolises her fertility, and the sketchily painted portrait miniature on her ring represents her absent husband. Goya shows her as a simple and innocent young woman, deliberately placed within the canvas so that she is surrounded by space, thus emphasising her vulnerability and isolation.

If the secret half-smile playing on her face suggests her pleasure in her pregnancy, her eyes betray bewilderment, and perhaps also a dignified acceptance of her humiliation. Comparing this image to Goya's other portraits of the Spanish royal family, it is clear that he saw María Teresa as somehow protected by her simplicity and goodness from the corruption of the court.

Francisco de Goya
Portrait of the Condesa de Chinchón, *1800*
Museo Nacional del Prado, Madrid

Citizens and Kings:
Portraits in the Age of Revolution

At one level, the Royal Academy's *Citizens and Kings* is simply about what its subtitle says it is about: *Portraits in the Age of Revolution, 1760–1830*. But it isn't simply a survey of European and American portraiture from Goya to Ingres and from Reynolds to Lawrence. It is also about the effect of the Enlightenment, and of the American and French revolutions on the men and women who lived through them. Freedom of thought and expression; the equality of man; the nature of genius; the role of the individual in society; the sanctity of the family; the value of feelings and emotions – all these ideas, disseminated in writings of Diderot, Voltaire, Rousseau, Jefferson and de Sade, entered the European bloodstream and quickly found expression in the visual arts.

Then, too, the years covered by the exhibition saw the Napoleonic Wars and their aftermath, a period not quite like any other in history. For artists and writers, the era possessed a quality of scintillation and of urgency, a sense of people living out extraordinary destinies at a time when Europe's fate hung not only on the outcome of battles and revolutions, but also on the personalities of great men such as Wellington and Napoleon. In short, we are looking at an age of profound political and psychological change, as old ways of thinking gave way to new. In this respect, the career of the British painter Thomas Lawrence is exemplary. Although he tried his hand at history painting, he soon gave it up to devote his career exclusively to portraiture, realising, I think, that contemporary events and personalities were actually more dramatic, and cast on a more heroic scale, than any subjects he could have found in ancient history or English literature.

The show starts with a spectacular *coup de théâtre*, a gallery hung with full-length portraits of European heads of state in an age of the Enlightened Despots and their successors. Both Catherine the Great

30 January 2007

Citizens and Kings:
Portraits in the Age of
Revolution, 1760–1830

Royal Academy,
London

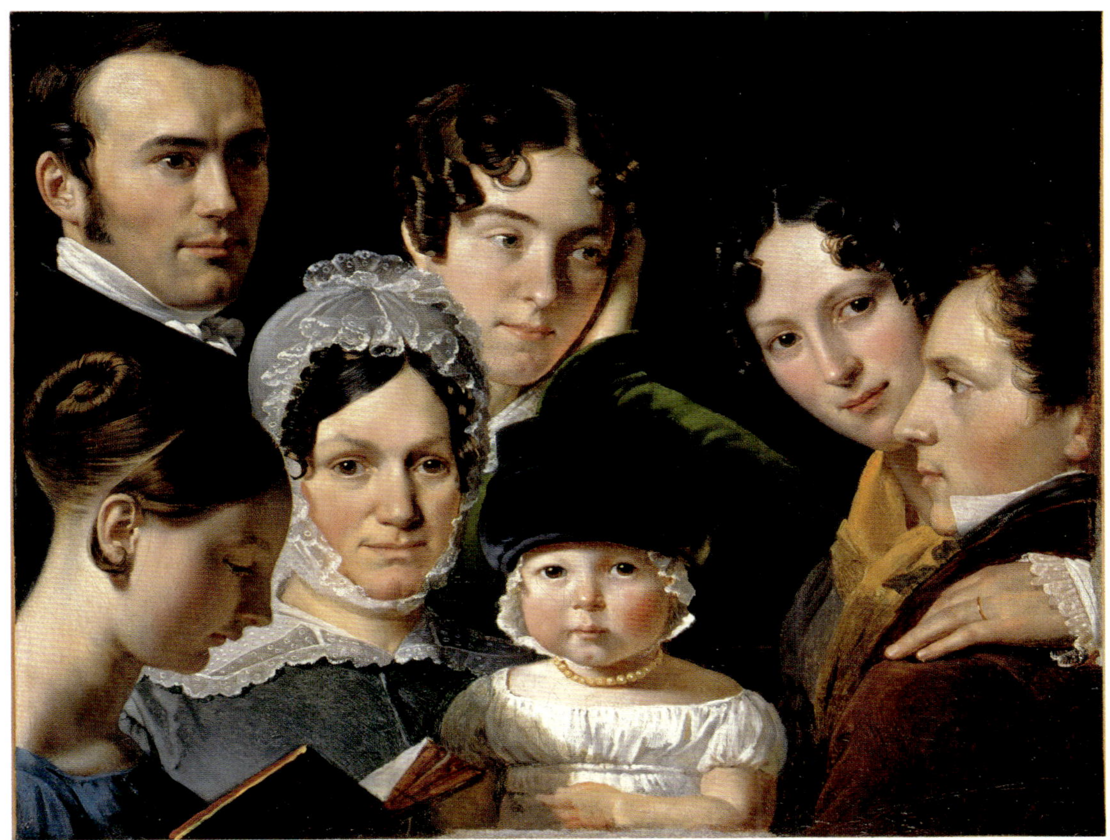

and Louis XVI are represented in magnificent state portraits showing them crowned, robed, orbed and sceptred – rulers by divine right who yet are presented as benevolent human beings. But, even in this gallery, disillusion with the idea of the divine right of kings is beginning to show. When Francisco Goya paints the ugly and suspicious King of Spain, Ferdinand VII, wearing robes of state that overwhelm his spindly frame, the artist clearly entertained no illusions about his failings as a man and as a ruler.

Even more tellingly, in his sublime 1819 portrait, Lawrence shows Pope Pius VII, the aristocratic Benedictine monk who was elected pope in 1800, not as the successor to St Peter (there is no sign of the papal attribute of the triple tiara), but as a scholar and patron of the arts. Behind him, we see a distant view of the new wing of the Vatican sculpture galleries, signalling the Pope's cultivated mind and his custodianship of classical antiquity. Lawrence ignores the Pontiff's status as a spiritual and temporal leader, transforming him instead into a symbol of the civilised values that returned to Europe with the defeat of his great enemy, Napoleon.

These early galleries are full of fascinating comparisons between portraits painted before, during and after the French Revolution. Contrast Elizabeth Vigée-Lebrun's decorous portrait of Louis XVI's minister of finance, Charles-Alexandre de Calonne, with Goya's stunning likeness of Ferdinand Guillemardet, the new French Republic's ambassador to Spain. The first, dressed in a black silk suit and wearing a powdered wig, is a man of the *ancien régime*. Though one of the most powerful men in France, his carriage is relaxed and he exudes an aura of geniality, a quality that for him is as natural as polite deportment, or good manners. The second man, although certainly no lout, casually drapes one arm over the back of his chair with the assurance of one who is unfamiliar with the concept of self-effacement – and means to get his way.

Likewise, a cultural and historical chasm separates Vigée-Lebrun's 1789 portrait of the Comtesse de la Châtre from Jacques-Louis David's austere likeness of the Marquise d'Orvilliers, painted the year after the Revolution began, in 1790. Vigée-Lebrun indicates the social milieu in which her sitter moved by the elegance of her simple white muslin frock and by a glimpse of the graceful curve of the settee behind her. What is disconcerting about David's portrait is that it has no background and, therefore, no context. We can't identify the sitter's class by her surroundings or even by her clothing. Only her political allegiance, signalled by the red sash around her waist and red ribbon in her hair, is made plain. David, a revolutionary, wants to wipe the slate clean, to start again, like Pol Pot in Year Zero.

All revolutions end in reaction. Jacques-Louis David's bone-chilling portrait of *Napoleon I on the Imperial Throne* was painted as early as 1806, and it brings us back full-circle to the image of a ruler as a semi-divine being, at the foot of whose throne it is only natural to kneel. Monarchs separate themselves from their subjects by the magnificence of their costume; politicians usually find it safer to dress down. Gilbert Stuart's great portrait of George Washington (1796) shows the American president in sober black silk suit and standing in his office, by his desk. Though hardly a man of the people, neither does he flaunt his status. But what about those who have no power? How do they present themselves to the world?

Gilbert Stuart
George Washington,
1796
National Portrait Gallery, Washington DC

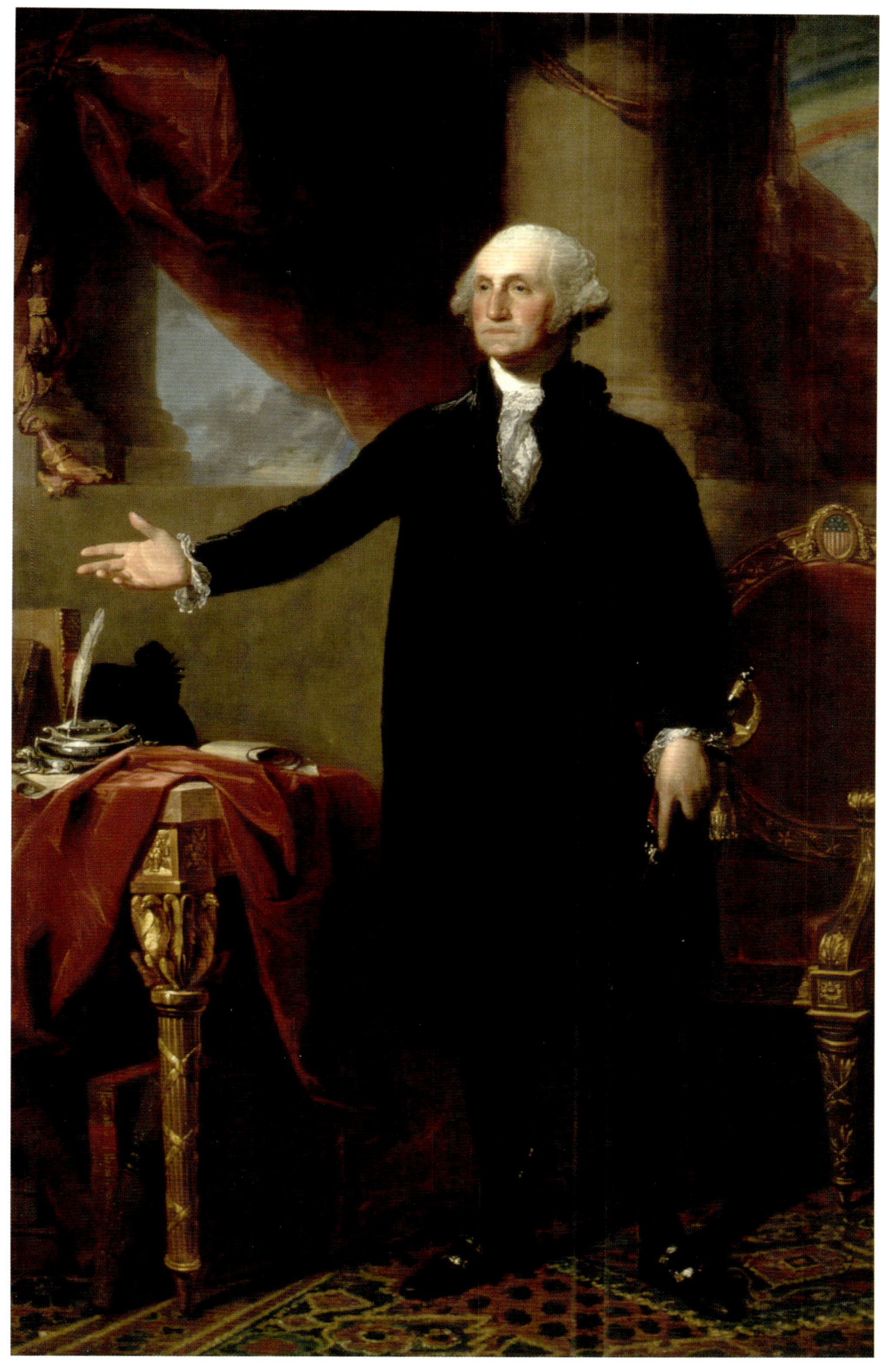

In Reynolds's wonderful portrait of the Countess of Bute walking
through the autumnal park of her Scottish estate, he catches her in
mid-stride with her little dog at her side and a parasol in her arms.
This small, grey-haired old lady is so grand that she doesn't need
ermine or a coronet to signal her social position. By contrast, just as
Napoleon re-introduced the trappings of royalty to reinforce his claim
to the throne of France, so, in François Gérard's ravishing portrait of
the Emperor's mother (*Madame Mère*), the illiterate Corsican woman
would, I suspect, strike a Reynolds or a Vigée-Lebrun as just the
tiniest bit vulgar in her richly embroidered floor-length velvet coat,
white silk dress, gauze veil spangled with golden stars and royal
diadem in her hair.

Then there are those men and women whose claim to importance
was neither birth nor power, but talent and knowledge. Even Goya's
Marques de Villafranca wants the world to see him first and foremost
as a lover of the music of Joseph Haydn. Raeburn's portrait of the
brilliant geologist James Hutton shows an unprepossessing man in an
unbuttoned brown suit who doesn't bother to turn to face the painter,
let alone wear a wig to disguise his thinning hair. His claim to our
attention rests on only one thing – his
scientific knowledge, signalled by the
samples of chalk fossils, minerals and
shells on the table in front of him. In just
the same way, the Swiss painter Jean-Pierre
Saint-Ours paints an elderly banker who is
proud not of the money he has made, but
of the collection of Flemish and Dutch
paintings he amassed after making it.

In antique and even Renaissance
portrait busts, sculptors normally ignored
a sitter's physical imperfections. But in
this show Claude-André Deseins's plaster
head-and-shoulders of the politician
and orator the Comte de Mirabeau does
nothing to minimise the sitter's hideously
pockmarked face. And, for those who
know Jacques-Louis David's famous self-
portrait, his posthumous marble bust by

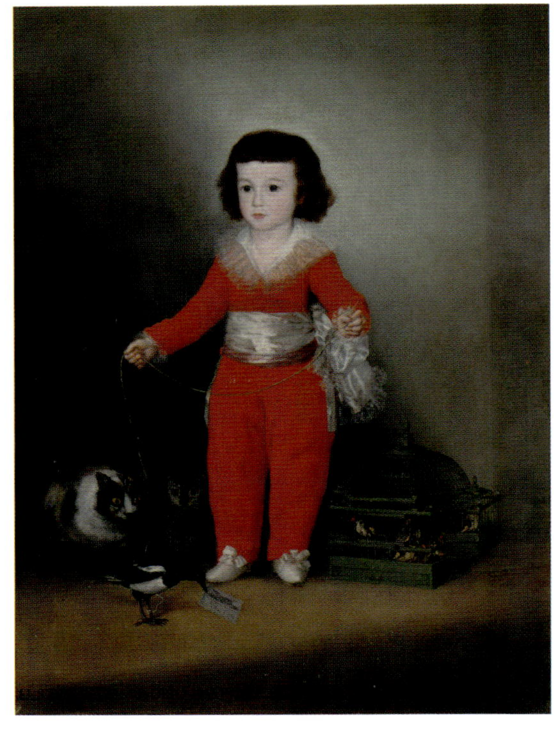

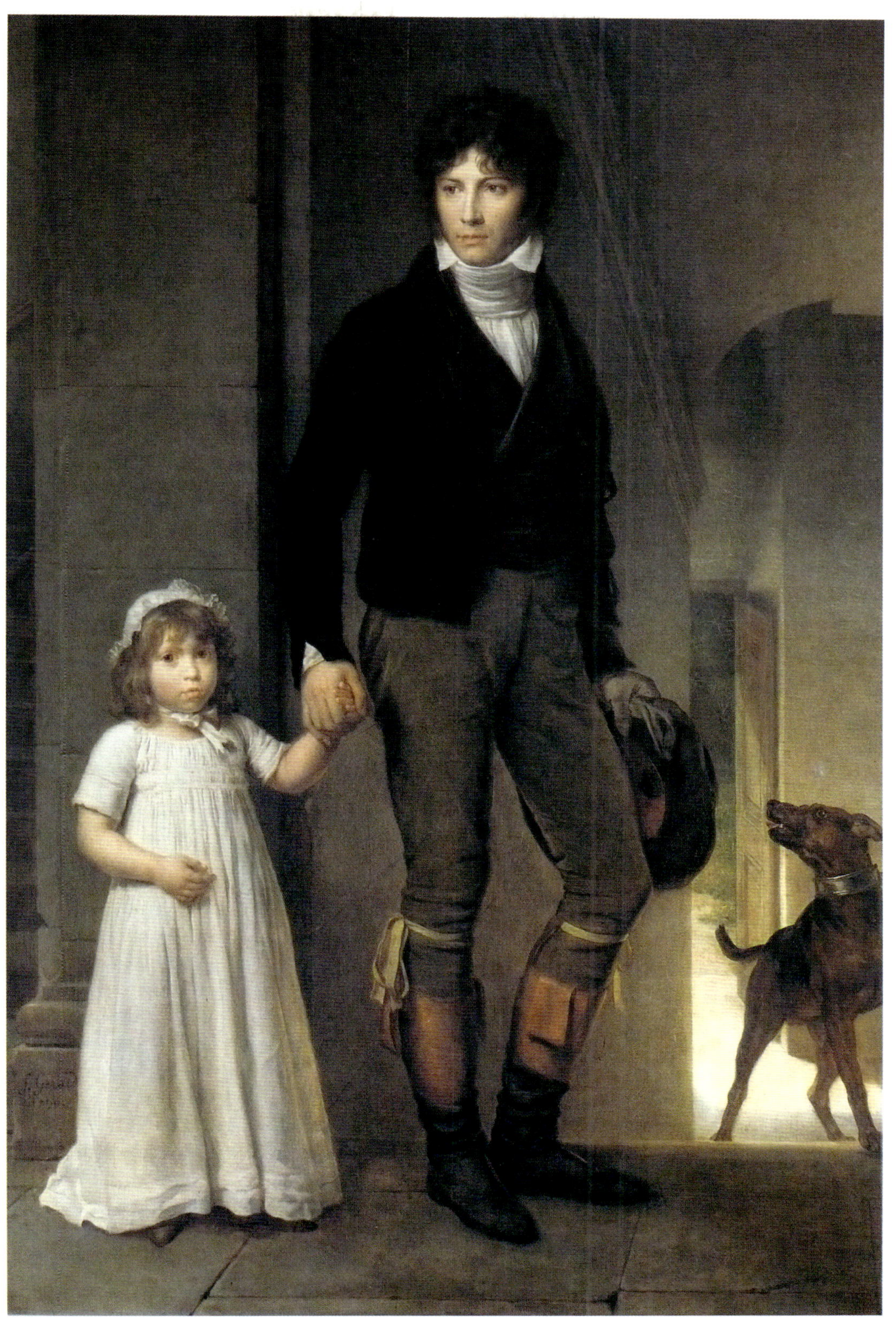

François Rude will come as a shock. The disfigurement of his left cheek by a tumour, which in the self-portrait looks like a minor blemish, is shown to have been a major deformity, distorting his entire face.

You could, I think, see the entire show as a search for this kind of truth. When the nineteenth-century Danish painter Christian Købke depicts a fellow artist, he shows him in a simple Biedermeier interior, as matter-of-fact about his calling as he would be about being an accountant. In no sphere of life is truth easier to detect than in children, which is why the purity and innocence Goya depicts in his portrait of little Don Manuel Osorio Manrique de Zuñiga and François Gérard shows in his likeness of the tiny daughter of J.-B. Isabey catch you in the throat.

The structure of the show moves back and forth in time, from one country to another. The final section, which contains late portraits that David, Lawrence and Delacroix painted after the fall of Napoleon, are among the most moving in the show because all these artists attempt the grand manner of portraiture, and just can't carry it off. The world had changed too profoundly. The poses, the grand costumes, the pretentious accessories that swept us away in the eighteenth and early nineteenth centuries no longer work because the artists no longer believe in them.

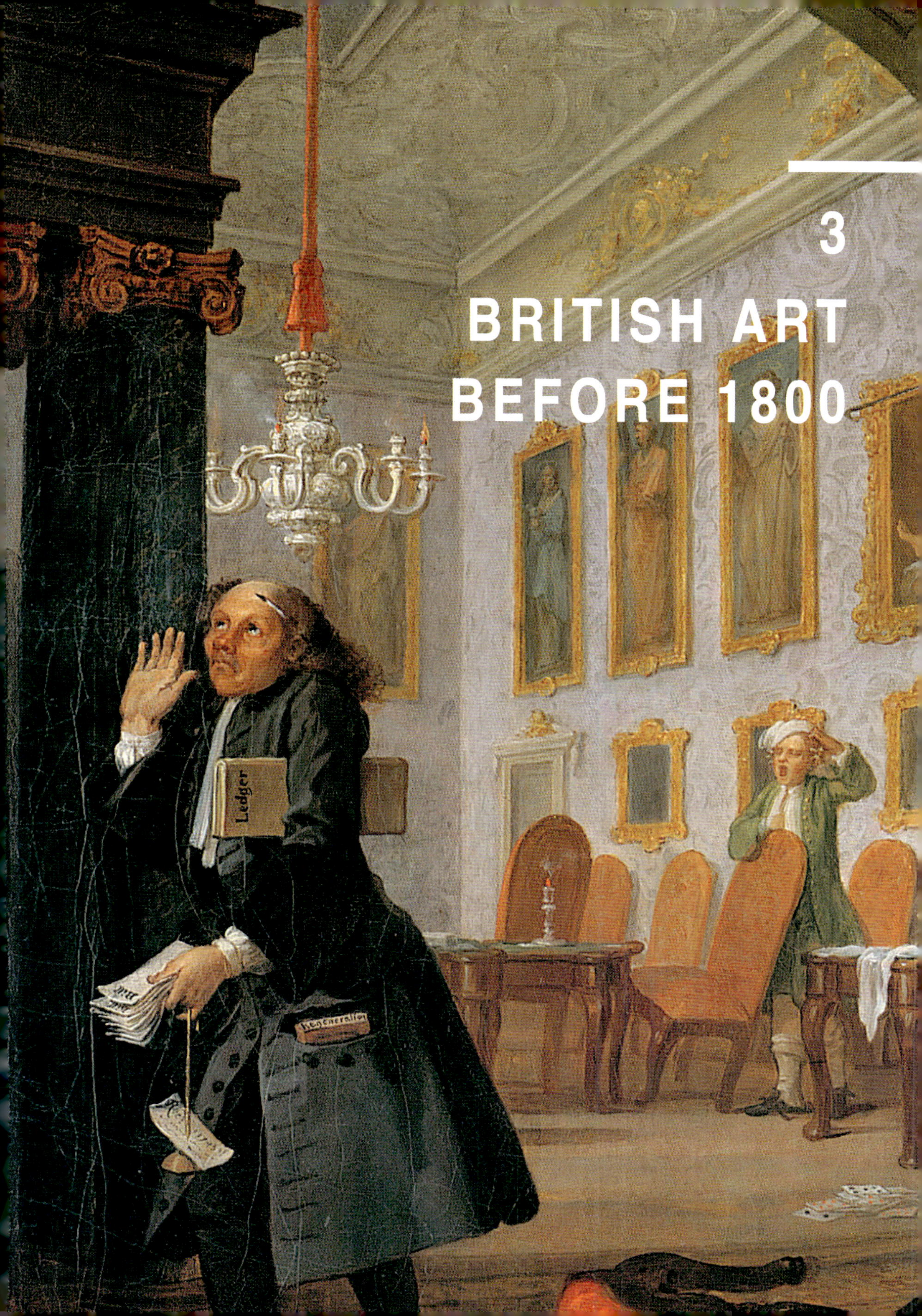

3

BRITISH ART
BEFORE 1800

Alexander Pope, François Roubiliac and the Portrait Bust

If you want to attract crowds then you might not think of staging a show around an artist no one's ever heard of, a poet who's no longer read and an art form that's deeply unfashionable. Yet *Fame and Friendship: Pope, Roubiliac and the Portrait Bust* at Waddesdon Manor is not only the most original exhibition of the year, but one of the most enjoyable.

The problem with the marble portrait bust, a form popular in eighteenth-century England, is that to someone who isn't a specialist, all of them look alike. Sure, the sitters are different but the work of Peter Scheemakers is indistinguishable from that of John Rysbrack and both look a lot like Joseph Nollekens, who was their junior by a full generation.

That's because all these sculptors tended to suppress evidence of their individual styles in order to emphasise the association of the portrait bust with precedents in the ancient world. Of course there are stylistic distinctions between them, but exhibitions devoted to single sculptors are so rare that it is difficult to see enough work by one artist to say what makes him different from all the others.

That's what makes this show so interesting. The French Huguenot sculptor Louis-François Roubiliac came to London in 1730 to escape religious persecution. France's loss was London's gain. Among the artists who arrived at around the same time as Roubiliac were the great silversmith Paul de Lamerie and the engraver Hubert-François Gravelot, who became the young Thomas Gainsborough's drawing master. A Gallic elegance, informality and lightness of touch in the work of all three helped to establish the rococo style in England.

Within a decade of his arrival Roubiliac had become the go-to sculptor for the celebrity portrait, counting William Hogarth, David Garrick and George Frederick Handel among his sitters. So when friends of the most famous poet in England wished to commission

Louis-François Roubiliac
Alexander Pope, *1760*
Rothschild Collection, Waddesdon Manor

24 June 2014

Fame and Friendship: Pope, Roubiliac and the Portrait Bust

Waddesdon Manor

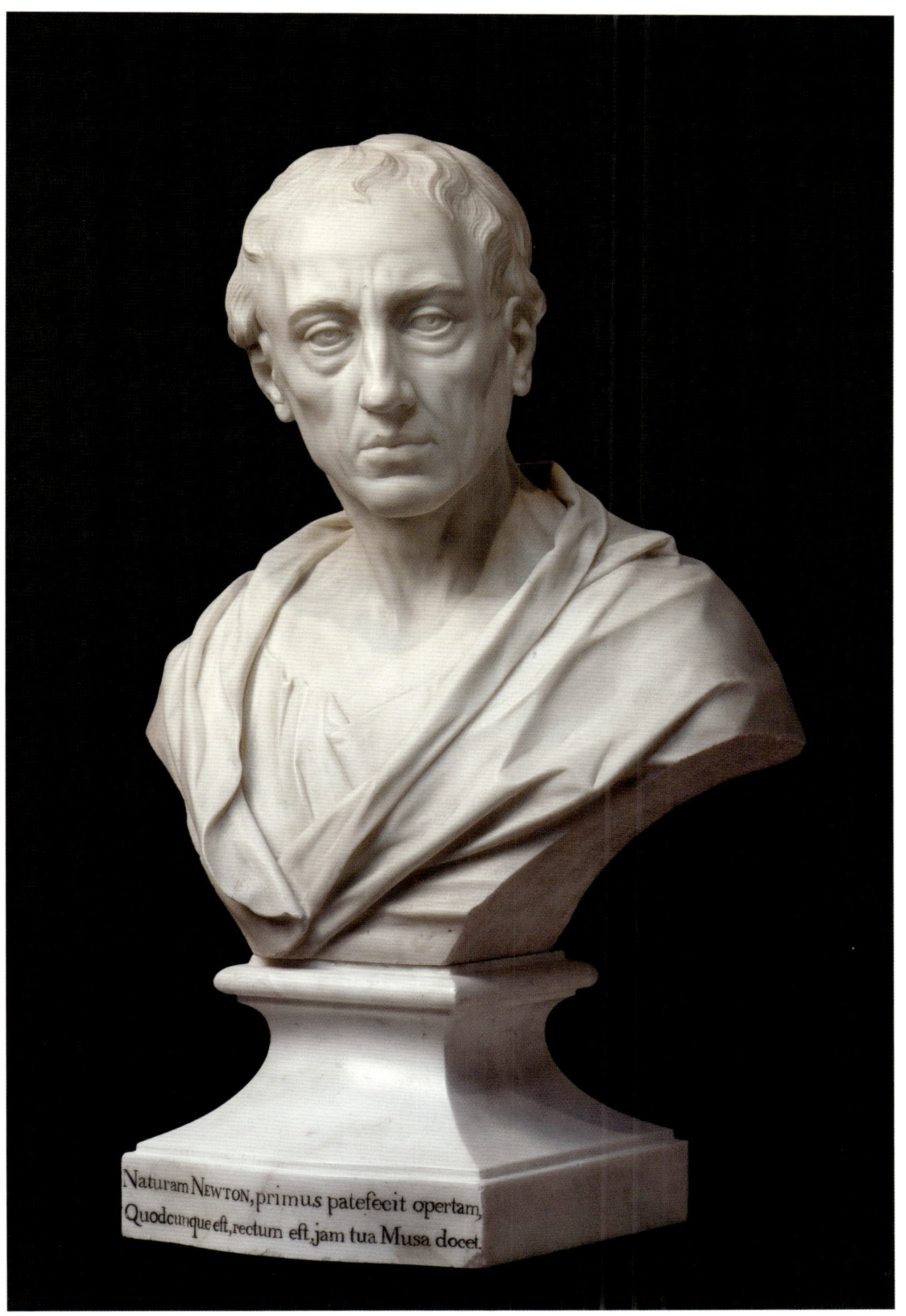
Naturam NEWTON, primus patefecit opertam,
Quodcunque eft, rectum eft, jam tua Musa docet.

his portrait bust, it was natural that they should turn to the country's most celebrated sculptor.

When Roubiliac met Alexander Pope in 1738 the poet had only six more years to live. Though not an old man, Pope had become famous in his twenties with the publication of *An Essay on Criticism*, *The Rape of the Lock* and his translation of *The Iliad*. The portrait of Pope engraved as the frontispiece of the first edition of his collected works shows the head and upper torso of a handsome twenty-seven-year-old man wearing a full-bottomed wig.

How different this carefully controlled public image is from the quick sketch in pencil made without Pope's knowledge by the minor English artist William Hoare. It shows the poet at full length, so that we can see the devastating effects of the tubercular condition that had stunted his growth, deformed his body and left him in constant pain.

What happened between the two men during the hours the artist spent modelling the poet's head from life is the focus of this exhibition. As well as their fame, the two men had much in common. Pope's Catholicism made him an outsider in England much as Roubiliac's religion counted against him in France. And just as the French sculptor was successful here, so Pope was the first English poet whose work became well known in France, where translations of *An Essay on Man* established his reputation as a poet of the Enlightenment.

On entering the larger of the two ornate rooms, what you see are eight marble busts – all by Roubiliac, all of Pope, and all, apparently, exactly alike. That 'apparently' is what the exhibition is about. It shows us how wrong this first impression is by asking us to look closely at each bust, noting small differences and making fine distinctions between superficially similar works of art.

To understand what we are seeing we have to follow the sculptor's creative process, beginning with a terracotta bust which was cast directly from that of the bust modelled in clay from the life. Far more than in any of the marbles derived from it, we find in the terracotta abundant evidence of the sculptor's hand. If you walk round to the back of the statue and look inside the hollow cast you see fingerprints pressed into the clay, and notice, too, that when he came to model that hair Roubiliac used an implement of some kind instead of his fingers.

The result has all the immediacy of a painter's sketch. You feel that it is as close as any of us can ever get to being in Pope's presence.

Some of the eight busts are of his head only, others the shoulders too – but all show the poet's gaunt, fine-boned face, full lips, and high cheekbones tilted to one side as though engaged in conversation. At a time when men wore periwigs, his hair is close-cropped in emulation of ancient Roman portraiture. The association with the antique is accentuated in the bust belonging to the Shipley Gallery in Yorkshire, which is the only one in which the eyes are left blank.

The curator Malcolm Baker makes it clear in his excellent catalogue that Pope micro-managed his public image. It was therefore his choice to present himself as a man of grave nobility – a decision that left no hint of the sparkling wit you find in his poems, still less of the malicious tongue for which he was also famous.

This exhibition asks the visitor to look closely at the subtle surface textures, the precision with which details like the thin neckline of the poet's garment are carved. And with close looking comes insight. For example, the bust from a private collection once owned by Pope's friend Lord Mansfield is very slightly smaller than the others and also the one that makes the poet look most intense and vulnerable. It may be too much to say that here the sculptor hints at the chronic pain in which Pope lived, but something about it feels deeply private. I don't think it was ever intended for public exhibition. By contrast, a highly polished bust now at Yale is much more official in feel; the prominent vein in the one at Waddesdon suggests the strain of holding his head in one position during the sitting.

With these eight busts the curator is able to do something very rare: teach us how to look.

William Hogarth

Poor William Hogarth. Only a few years after his death in 1764, the Rev. John Trusler published a commentary on Hogarth's series of engravings *A Harlot's Progress* and *A Rake's Progress* in which the good clergyman read their stories as morally instructive allegories, forgetting that the prints were more likely to hang in a gentleman's club than in a Sunday school.

What Trusler began in the eighteenth century, po-faced academics in the late twentieth continued in turgid books and catalogues that presented Hogarth largely in terms of the political, religious and social issues he satirised in his depiction of Georgian London. Of course, Hogarth did indeed comment on current events and morality, but, if we put all the emphasis on that aspect of his work, we miss a lot of its fun and all of its high spirits.

The triumph of Tate Britain's comprehensive exhibition of Hogarth's paintings and prints is that the organisers, Mark Hallett and Christine Riding, 'get' Hogarth. They revel in the seductive beauty of the oil paintings and the crispness and clarity of early impressions of the prints. Their beautifully installed exhibition makes it clear that although relatively slow to develop in terms of his painting technique, in his mature paintings Hogarth is a major European master. Nothing will ever bring me round to later history paintings such as the limp *Moses Brought to Pharaoh's Daughter*, but there aren't many of these in a show that, as far as I can tell, has most of the major works in it, apart from the large-scale murals.

Born in London in 1697, William Hogarth was the son of a scholar from the north of England whose attempt to establish a coffee house where only Latin was spoken landed him in the Fleet prison, where he spent four years as a bankrupt. Hogarth determined not to make his father's mistake but to seek financial security by courting popular success.

6 February 2007

Hogarth

Tate Britain, London

He is the first British artist to paint subjects we now take for granted: scenes from Shakespeare and Milton, middle-class portraits, and what he dubbed 'modern moral subjects' – stories of contemporary life as fresh as the morning papers told in the series of paintings and engravings like *The Rake's* and *The Harlot's Progress*, and *Marriage A-la-Mode*.

His formal schooling came to an end at the age of ten or eleven. Apprenticed in 1714 to a silver-plate engraver, his real training as an artist began in 1720, when he entered the new academy of art run by his future father-in-law, Sir James Thornhill. Here he was taught to draw from life, but also to develop a system of visual mnemonics whereby the artist chose a subject, perhaps made a quick sketch, and then returned to his studio to paint it from memory. This ability to recall a scene at will meant that Hogarth painted straight on to the canvas so that nothing stood between him and the fluent, spontaneous application of paint.

In the 1736 painting *Evening*, for example, when we ask ourselves how Hogarth could possibly have captured so perfectly the tantrum of the fat little boy whose sister tries to take away his gingerbread, the answer must be that he saw such a child in the street, memorised the contorted face and clenched fists, then went home to paint them.

Hogarth's naturalism goes hand-in-hand with a dislike for academic art and for all things foreign. Elegant without being pompous, he will start a subject with a straight face and end it with a guffaw. In the pair of paintings *Before* and *After*, for example, it looks as though he is going to ape the French fashion for painting *fêtes galantes* in the scene showing the decorous seduction of a pretty maiden by a gallant swain. But then he sends the whole genre up in the second picture, which shows the same couple after their fumbled intercourse, her hoisted skirt and his undone breeches more *Fanny Hill* than *Pamela*. Freshness like this he identified as quintessentially a British quality, like roast beef and beer.

Ironically, though, Hogarth wasn't a natural painter. In *The Christening* and *The Denunciation* of 1729, the handling of paint is still tight and his palette restricted to low tones, suggesting that his training as an engraver meant that he used his brush as though it were a pencil or engraver's tool. This sense that he is drawing in paint persists in many of the early conversation pieces (small-scale group portraits) of the late 1720s and early '30s showing families and friends interacting with each other with an air of intimacy and naturalness that flew in the face of what was then considered polite deportment.

But in the second version of *A Scene from 'The Beggar's Opera'* (1731), we can already detect the beginnings of the painterly fluency that will be characteristic of all his mature work. Here Hogarth depicts a performance of a hit play that had been written, produced and acted in by his friends. By including in our field of vision the proscenium arch that frames the stage, he turns every viewer into a member of the audience watching the dramatic climax of the story, when Polly and Lucy beg their respective fathers to spare the life of Macheath. And here, for the first time, Hogarth adds to the topicality of the subject by including portraits of the actress Lavinia Fenton and her lover the Duke of Bolton.

The instinctive sense of theatricality displayed here led to three famous narrative cycles of the 1730s and '40s, in each of which he invented a fictional character who lives in our collective imaginations as surely as do Tom Jones and Clarissa Harlow. They are the whore Moll Hackabout, the libertine Tom Rakewell, and the young couple married for convenience, the Earl and Countess of Squanderfield. Then, using narrative techniques more usual in the theatre and the novel than the visual arts, he told the stories of their descent to ruin, disease, madness and death as it unfolded from one canvas to another.

Each series is structured like a work of literature, with the equivalents of an introduction, story line, climax and epilogue. In each there are anti-heroes and villains, minor characters who unexpectedly reappear in the story, and several sub-plots. Characters develop from one canvas to the next, as for example in *Marriage A-la-Mode* when we meet the future Countess as a snivelling teenager being forced into an arranged marriage in scene one, only to find that she has matured into a satiated sex kitten in scene two. There are what we would today call 'celebrity guest appearances' as when the castrato Giovanni Carestini is shown seated among the French hairdressers and hangers-on at the Countess's morning levée.

By the mid-1730s Hogarth brings an easy fluency to the creation of complex compositions painted in bright, clear colours. And when we come to the sketch for *The Country Dance* (1745), Hogarth's touch is as light, his colours as soft, and his brushstrokes as free as Fragonard's.

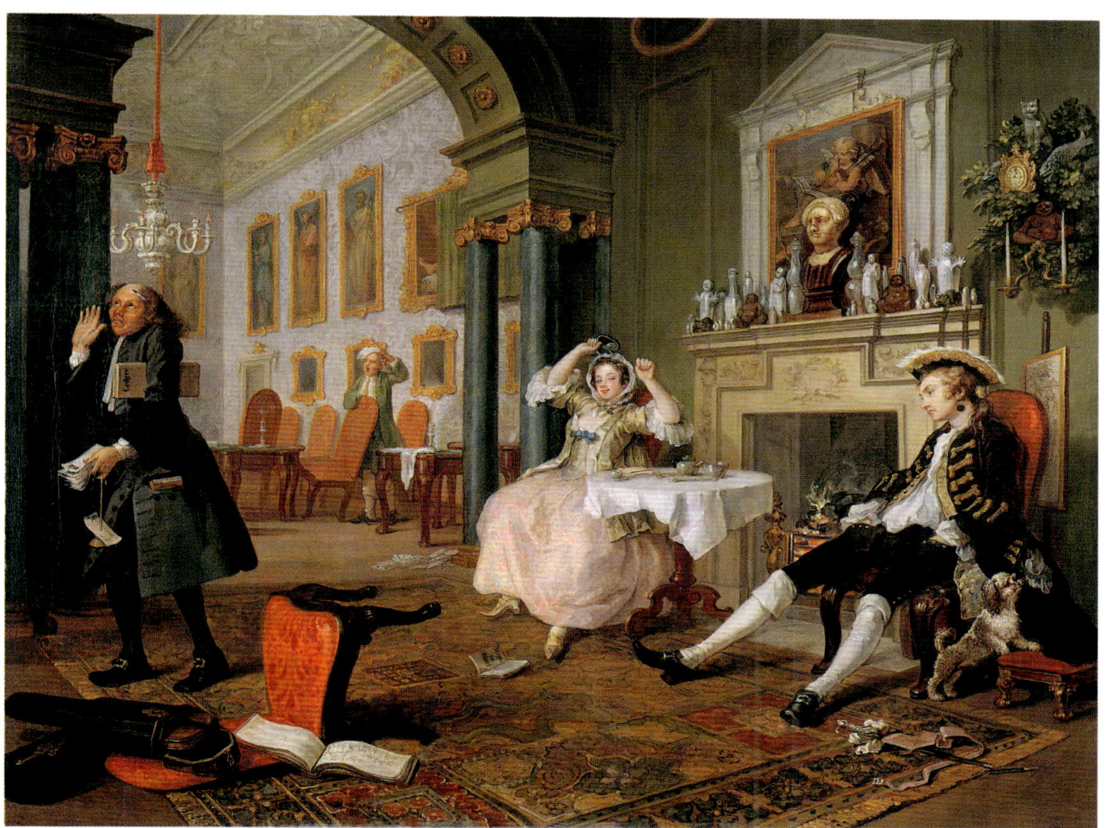

In fact, the sensuous handling of oil paint in later canvases such as *The March to Finchley* and *The Election* is curiously at odds with the puking, pissing, drooling and groping it is used to depict.

To the 1740s belong masterpieces of British portraiture such as *Captain Coram*, *Mrs Salter* and *George Arnold*, images of the British face at its most open and straightforward. From a technical point of view, Hogarth just gets better and better. In the wonderful *Thomas Herring, Archbishop of Canterbury*, he uses swirls and rivulets of white paint to conjure up the white folds in the sleeves with a freedom we haven't seen before.

Thomas Gainsborough:
The Harvest Wagon

In 1759, the thirty-two-year-old Thomas Gainsborough moved his practice in portraiture from Ipswich to Bath. One effect of the move was to expose him both to the romantic, rolling landscape of the West Country and to the Old Master paintings hanging at Bowood, Wilton, Longleat and Corsham Court.

But cosmopolitan though Bath was, Gainsborough still found himself in the provinces. In order not to cut himself out of the fiercely competitive London market, he continued to send work for exhibition in the capital each year between 1761 and 1768. Now, these were the very years when his great rival Joshua Reynolds was virtually inventing the English grand manner. Gainsborough took note. Stimulated by the example of Reynolds, no less than by his reverence for Rubens and van Dyck, he attempted his own version of the grand manner.

We can see one result in his early masterpiece *The Harvest Wagon*, which he sent for exhibition at the Society of Artists in 1767. At first glance we might take this delightful landscape, with farm workers travelling home after a day's work, for a scene the artist actually witnessed in the countryside outside Bath. A closer look reveals that it is nothing of the sort. In *The Harvest Wagon* Gainsborough anticipated Reynolds's advice to the students of the Royal Academy when, in his Sixth Discourse, he recommended that when painting figures they borrow their poses and gestures from the Old Masters. Wishing to raise the prestige of British painting, Reynolds hoped through these visual quotations to associate the work of modern British artists with the masterpieces from the past.

Gainsborough's picture is full of such borrowings. The triangular group of figures on the wagon itself, for example, is based on the sketch for Rubens's *Descent from the Cross* (then at Corsham Court), while the rearing horse reined in by the young farmhand is taken

28 April 1995

Thomas Gainsborough:
The Harvest Wagon

Birmingham Museum
and Art Gallery

from the famous classical sculptural group known as *The Horse Tamers*. Any educated viewer in the eighteenth century would have noticed that the lad mopping his brow in the wagon pays homage to Hogarth's Rake in the asylum scene from the series *The Rake's Progress*, itself distantly based on the Roman statue *The Dying Gladiator*.

But far from being a dry compilation of visual quotations, *The Harvest Wagon* represents a supreme example of the English rococo style at its lightest and freshest. Where Reynolds sought to infuse a sort of moral grandeur into his art, Gainsborough creates a timeless but down-to-earth arcadia. The feathery trees and fluffy clouds, the palette of pale pinks, greens and blues all put one in mind of Watteau's *Embarkation for Cythera*. And there is a puppyish vitality about the young farm workers that reminds me of Boucher's or Fragonard's frolicking gods and goddesses.

Yet even more important than this rococo sense of playful elegance is the picture's erotic atmosphere. Though the day has nearly ended, the heat has hardly abated and the workers are still hot and sweaty. The young men perspire and take deep draughts from the cider keg; the girls wear their bodices low and bare their shoulders. What with the rearing stallion masterfully held in check by the young boy, this is a frisky picture, a picture about propinquity and tumescence and fecundity.

Gainsborough's Bath period came to an end in 1774. In that year he moved to London, soon invested in government securities and in due course began to work for George III. Now in his late forties and with his two daughters grown women, he was free to pursue his own interests in art and life. Notoriously, these interests did not include portraiture. 'I'm sick of Portraits,' he told a friend, 'and wish very much to . . . walk off to some sweet Village when I can paint Landskips and enjoy the fag End of Life in quietness and ease.'

In 1784 he returned to the theme of *The Harvest Wagon*. In this second version the fitful, scudding clouds and dark shelf of overhanging rock reveal a deepened understanding of Rubens's landscapes, and reflect an appreciation too of the newly fashionable aesthetic theory of the 'picturesque'. But a more profound difference between the two pictures has to do with its sexual charge – or, rather, lack of it. The second version of *The Harvest Wagon* is now full of

women and children. The only man on board decorously assists
a somewhat plain girl in a kerchief on to the cart. And whereas in
the first picture wisps of hay told us that the time of year was late
summer, now bundles of faggots foreshadow the coming winter. The
high-spirited stallion has become a broken-down cart-horse, whipped
by a man with a stoop. In short, this is an old man's picture. Its gentle
melancholy suggests that life is over, hot youth gone. Three years after
painting it, Gainsborough died from cancer, aged sixty-two.

The Birmingham Museum and Art Gallery has mounted a small
but beautiful exhibition around the two pictures (from the Barber
Institute of Fine Arts at the University of Birmingham and the Art
Gallery of Ontario, Toronto). Though narrow in focus, the show
teaches us more about the wellsprings of Gainsborough's genius
than a more comprehensive exhibition ever could.

Thomas Gainsborough
The Harvest Wagon

Top: c. 1767
Barber Institute of Fine
Arts, University of
Birmingham

Right: 1784–85
Art Gallery of Ontario,
Toronto

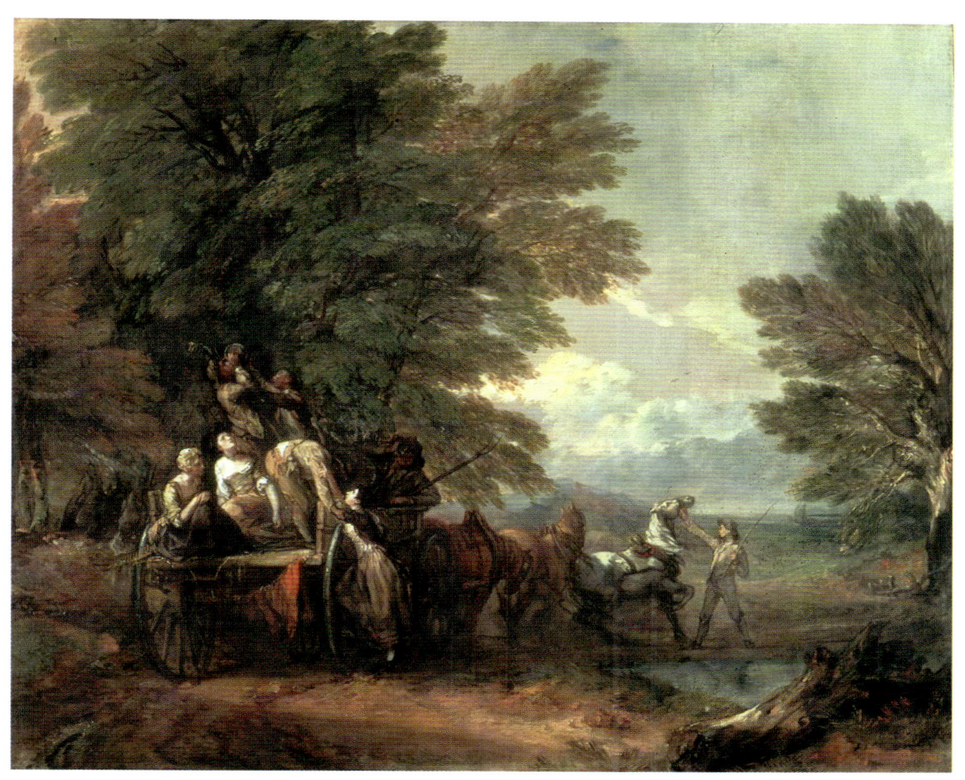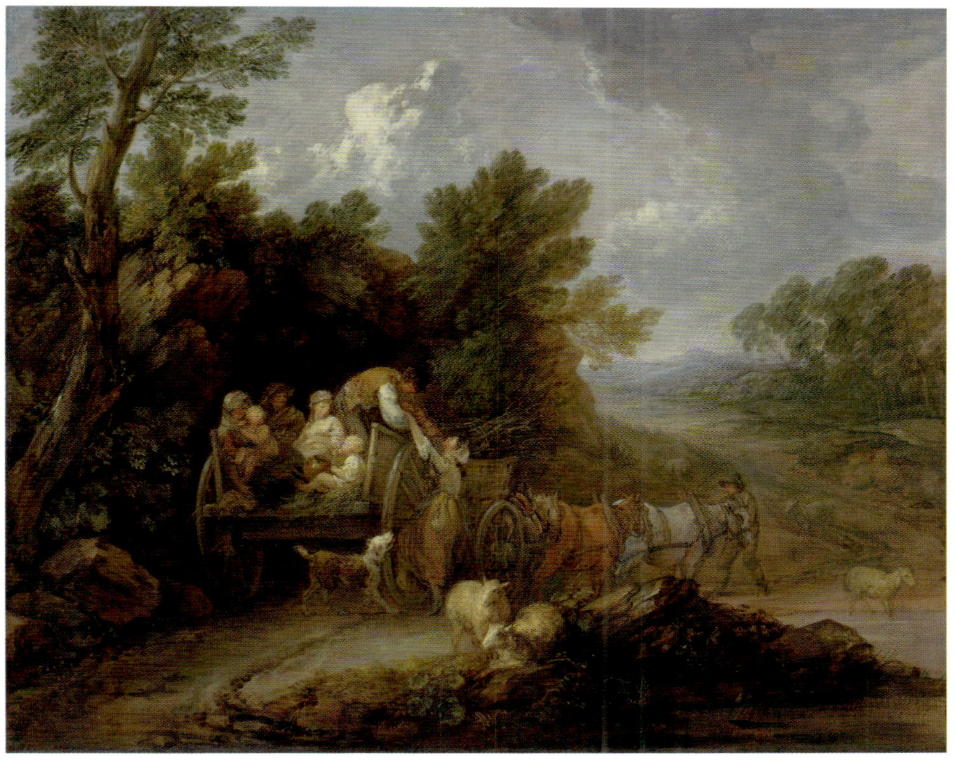

Vases and Volcanoes

You could call *Vases and Volcanoes* the British Museum's first ever 'sex and shopping' show. It is devoted to Sir William Hamilton – connoisseur, archaeologist, vulcanologist, and British Ambassador to the court of Naples for most of the second half of the eighteenth century. He distinguished himself in all these activities, but when it came to shopping Hamilton was in a league of his own. He formed not one, but two outstanding collections of Greek vases, to say nothing of the important marbles, bronzes, cameos and intaglios which he acquired during his time in Italy, and which eventually found their way into the British Museum.

But enough about shopping. On to sex. Emma Hart, later Lady Hamilton, was not exactly a prostitute, just as she was not exactly an actress. Said to have begun her career posing in the nude as Hebe Vestina, the rosy Goddess of Health, in Dr Graham's Temple of Health in the Adelphi, she might have gone on the stage had she not been taken up and kept by a string of protectors. Emma enters the history of art when her young lover Charles Greville brought her to the studio of George Romney in 1782. At that moment, life, in the dazzling form of Emma Hart, collided with art, in the shape of the shy and neurotic Romney, and resulted in one of the most fruitful partnerships in the history of British painting.

Like all eighteenth-century British portrait painters, Romney took a keen interest in how to represent the effects on the human face of pride, anger, love, envy, sorrow and fear. The problem for the painter was to find an opportunity to observe the physical manifestations of these passions long enough to record them in paint. One solution was to attend the theatre, but an even better one was to find an actor or actress to pose for you – as Reynolds had David Garrick or Mrs Kemble, and as Romney was to have Emma.

The distinction between actress, whore and artist's model was hard

17 April 1996

Vases and Volcanoes

British Museum, London

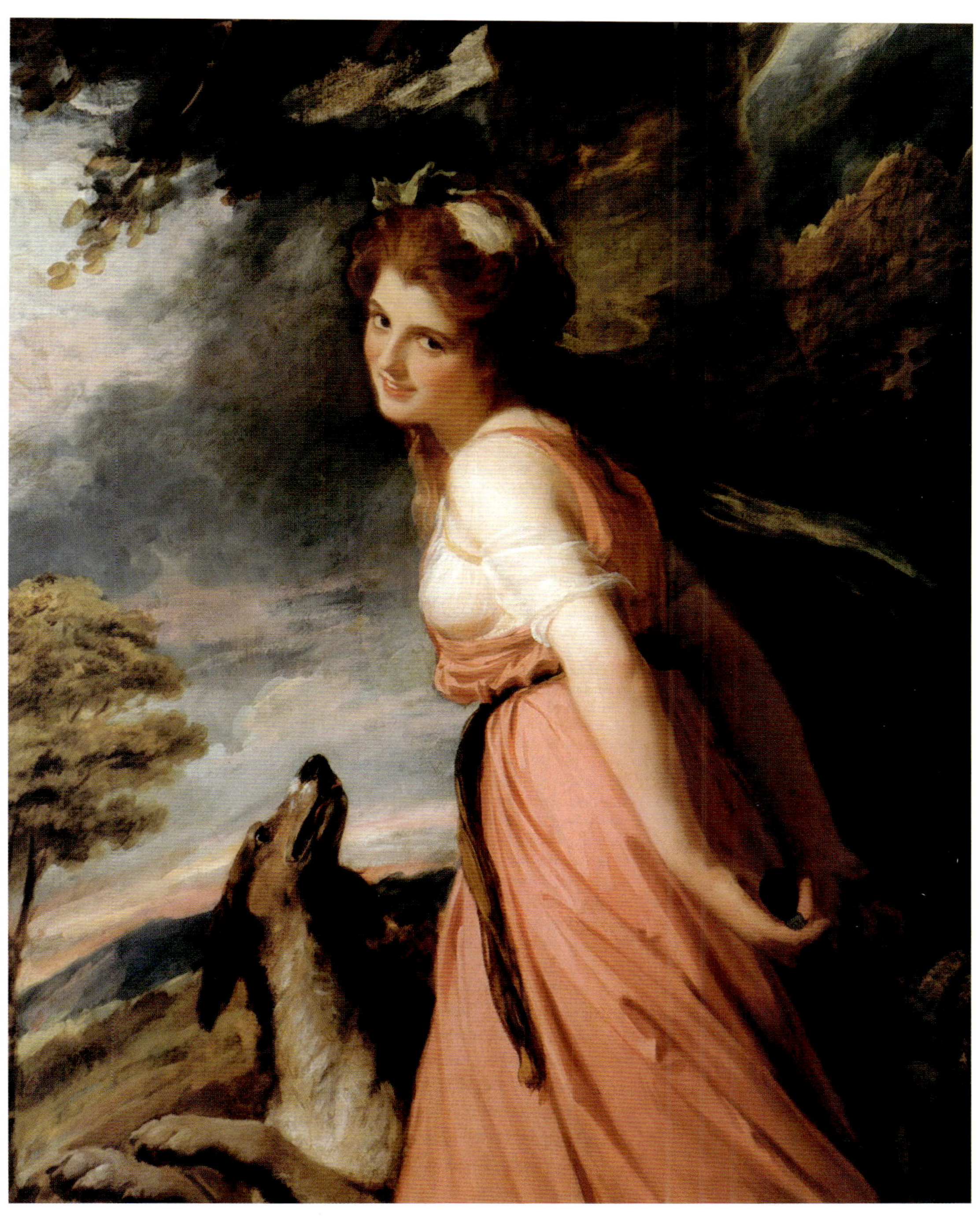

to draw in the eighteenth century. Romney seized on Emma's natural beauty and talent for acting, encouraging her to express the gamut of emotions from joy to rage, and then turned the sketches he made of her into dozens of pictures, showing her as St Cecilia, Medea, a bacchante, Circe or Shakespeare's Miranda.

Romney's pictures of Emma (and the prints after them) spread her renown as one of the most beautiful women in Europe. But in 1786, the impoverished Greville packed his young mistress off to Naples, cynically offering her to his elderly uncle Sir William Hamilton. Sir William was a kindly widower living in a palazzo overlooking the Bay of Naples, and an intimate both of Queen Maria Carolina and her near-idiot of a husband King Ferdinand IV.

When, to his family's horror, Hamilton married this sweet-natured but uneducated adventuress in 1791, he did so in order to be able to present her at court. It is at this moment that she moves into the mainstream of European history. For Emma was a remarkably effective ambassadress. As the wife of the British Ambassador to the Kingdom of the Two Sicilies during the first decade of the Napoleonic Wars, Emma became the confidante of Maria Carolina (sister of Marie Antoinette), and so helped to fan the flames of anti-French feeling at the Bourbon court.

While in Naples, Emma used the acting skills she had practised in Romney's studio to create her famous Attitudes, a cross between *tableaux vivants* and the performances that she gave in private throughout Europe and England. In them, Emma would portray the very roles in which Romney had painted her, dressed in a loose classical chemise and shawl and using only a few props such as an antique vase or a chair. When performing her Attitudes she apparently never spoke, relying instead on expression and gesture to convey her meaning. Today we would call the Attitudes performance art.

Goethe's famous description of them, written from Naples in 1787, underlines how they developed naturally from her posing sessions in Romney's studio: 'She lets down her hair, and with a few shawls gives so much variety to her poses, gestures, expressions, etc., that the spectator can hardly believe his eyes. He sees what thousands of artists would have liked to express realised before him in movements and surprising transformations, standing, kneeling, sitting, reclining, serious, sad, playful, ecstatic, contrite, alluring, threatening, anxious, one pose follows another without a break.'

It has long been obvious to me from the many pictures showing her in performance that I would have found Emma the most frightful bore. What's more, by the time of her famous love affair with Admiral Horatio Nelson (apparently condoned by Sir William) she had turned into the blowsy monster we see in Gilray's famous caricature of her as Dido lamenting the departure of Aeneas. After Nelson's death at the Battle of Trafalgar in 1805 she took to drink and died penniless in 1815.

One would have to go out of one's way to create a dull exhibition about the Hamiltons, and there isn't an object without interest in *Vases and Volcanoes*. Visually, the exhibition brings to life the worlds of culture, science and diplomacy in which Hamilton moved. A magnificent panoramic view of the Bay of Naples from Hamilton's apartments in the Palazzo Sessa by the Italian landscape painter G. B. Lusieri hangs near full-length portraits of Hamilton by Sir Joshua Reynolds and David Allan. Wilhelm Tischbein's depiction of the assembled Neapolitan court suggests something of the spectacle of the hunts at Persano and Caserta. There is a fascinating study of the slums of Naples by the incomparable Thomas Jones, and views of Vesuvius by John Robert Cozens, while the young Mozart puts in an appearance, giving a concert in the Neapolitan palace of Lord Fortrose and his cronies in an enchanting picture by Pietro Fabris. But nothing quite captures our attention like the section devoted to portraits of Emma. Before there was a word for it, she was a star.

Thomas Jones

In the whole of eighteenth-century British art there is nothing more mysterious or elusive than a group of modest oil sketches on paper painted in Naples in the early 1780s by the Welsh artist Thomas Jones. Born in Powys in 1742, the son of a great landowner, Jones must have been as stubborn as he was independent-minded. Unusually for a man in his social position, and much to his parents' initial dismay, he turned down a career in the Church to study art in London. After ten fairly successful years exhibiting conventional landscapes at the Royal Academy and Incorporated Society of Artists, he set out for Rome in 1776. By 1780, he had moved to Naples. The famous series on which his modern reputation is based was executed just before his return to Britain in 1783.

Turning his back on the tourist attractions of Vesuvius and Capri, Jones represents exactly what he could see from the roof terrace of his quarters near the Castel Nuova in the centre of the city, from the stucco facade of the house opposite his own to washing hanging out to dry on a balcony set high up in a crumbling wall. In another sketch, he looks up from his studio just outside Naples to paint the half-hidden dome of a baroque church rising above the tiled roofs of an adjacent convent. Sometimes we see a building clearly and from head-on. At others a low wall or a mass of foliage fills the foreground in such a way that it obstructs the principal motif. Often a view appears to have been cropped arbitrarily like a snapshot, and this only adds to the impression that it was painted quickly, before the light changed and the strong patterns of shadow and dark shifted.

What feels so remarkably modern about these sketches is Jones's approach to pictorial composition. In the National Museum of Wales's *Buildings in Naples*, for example, we are initially struck by the rhythmic disposition over the picture surface of his lights and darks, surfaces and voids, verticals and horizontals. The composition looks

21 May 2003

Thomas Jones: An Artist Rediscovered

National Museum and Gallery of Wales, Cardiff

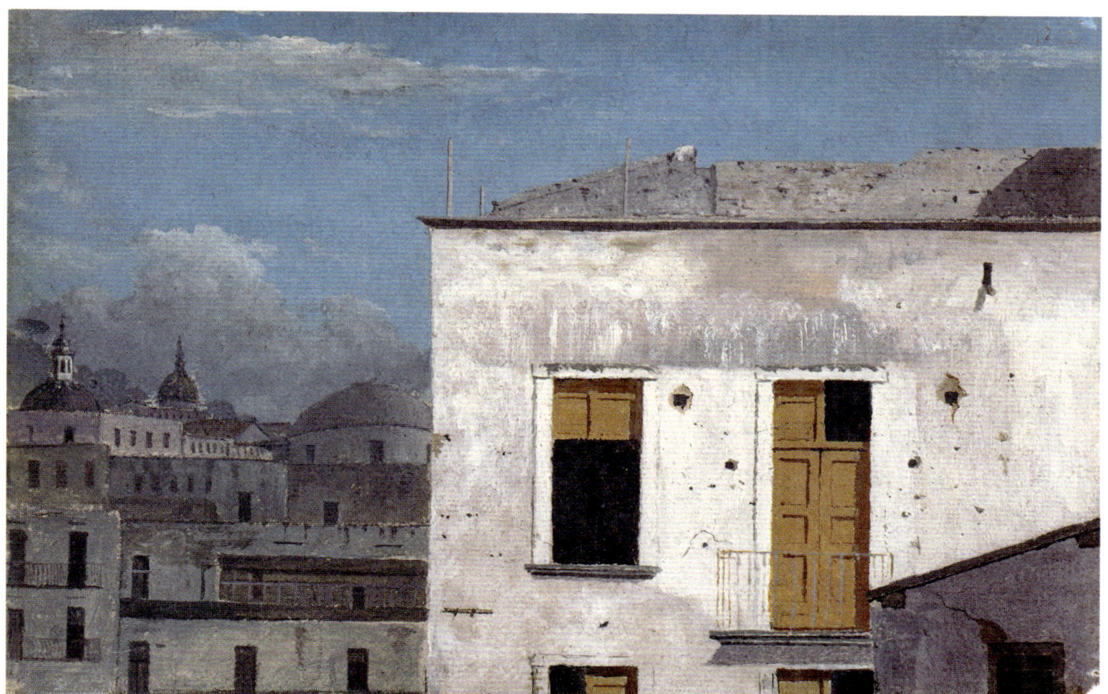

perfectly natural, but stare at this little picture for a few minutes and you begin to feel that it is built upon a hidden geometry of rectangles, squares and triangles. In the National Gallery's *A Wall in Naples*, the flat strip of blue at the top represents an empty patch of sky, but it also reads as a rectangular area of flat pigment that both stabilises the composition and echoes the accent of blue washing on the balcony.

Rather like Thomas Ruff's photographs of the facades of modern buildings, the Neapolitan sketches give nothing away. Shutters open on to blank interiors, and there are no people to animate the apparently deserted buildings. It is no wonder that these sketches have been seen as indicative of Jones's state of mind at the time he made them. For, at this point in his life, he was an unsuccessful artist who had found every window of official patronage closed to him, and who described himself as being, from childhood, of 'a melancholy turn'.

But, though I have some sympathy for this interpretation of the sketches, it is one of the tasks of art history to demystify works of art by explaining how and why they were made. The achievement of the magnificent new show of Jones's work at the National Museum and

Gallery of Wales is to place the famous series into the context both of Jones's whole career and within the practice of art in his time.

For one thing, the extensive under-drawing in the sketches shows that they are not improvised *plein-air* paintings, dashed off in a moment either of inspiration or despair. For another, contemporary artists such as the Italian view-painter Giovanni Battista Lusieri had become very successful painting panoramic views over the rooftops of Rome and Naples, while the French landscape painter Pierre-Henri Valenciennes made similarly informal outdoor sketches directly from nature.

Jones's master, the landscape painter Richard Wilson, taught Jones to study nature directly through oil sketches, and trained his pupil to a high standard of technical competence and precise observation. In several topographically accurate views of the local scenery in his native Radnorshire, painted in the early 1770s for his own personal interest, we first detect some of the freshness and informality that characterise the Neapolitan sketches. Comparing a 1772 sketch in oil on paper of Pencerrig with the far more conventional landscapes Jones painted for public exhibition and sale at the same time makes it clear that, in the former, Jones speaks in his own voice, while, in the latter, he feels he must imitate Wilson and Claude. What is more, from the moment Jones arrived in Rome he chose unusual viewpoints from which to paint the famous sites of Tivoli and the Colosseum. The Neapolitan views look a little less inexplicable when you see them alongside those made in Rome.

But what was the purpose of the 'private' sketches? One answer lies in a large finished landscape entitled *The Bay of Naples* in this show. On the right-hand side we see the very building depicted in the National Gallery sketch, complete with washing hanging from the window, and including the long strip of white fabric that scholars now identify as an infant's swaddling cloth.

Recent cleaning has uncovered a signature and the date 1786, confirming that Jones painted the work after he returned to Britain, using the National Gallery sketch as an *aide mémoire*. In other words, the probable explanation for the studies of Neapolitan rooftops and facades is that Jones intended to use them as tools of his trade, to create finished works of art back in the studio. But this didn't quite happen. On the death of his older brother, he inherited a great estate and ended his days as Lord Lieutenant of Radnorshire. Though he continued to paint, art was relegated to the status of an all-consuming hobby, not his profession.

I noticed, however, that, in the Welsh views painted after his final return to Britain, Jones concentrated exclusively on the scenery around his own home rather than recording the dramatic landscape of North Wales as his teacher Richard Wilson had done. I wonder whether this is not another clue to the lingering enigma that surrounds the Neapolitan sketches. Could it be that Jones was a bit lazy, a bit unimaginative, a man who, on those hot afternoons when all Naples was in siesta, filled in the hours between two and four by painting what happened to be right to hand, the view from his terrace?

If so, they are the visual equivalents of the fascinating journal he kept during his years in Italy, made for his own private amusement and to remember what he had seen and whom he had met when he returned home. The Jones we meet in his journals is a highly likeable fellow. I like to think of him as an old man, taking these sketches out on a winter's evening to show his two daughters: 'See, this is what it was like – on that spring day, on that afternoon, at that hour, all those years ago.'

Art On the Line

In a famous letter to the committee of artists responsible for hanging the Royal Academy's summer exhibition in 1784, Thomas Gainsborough announced that he could not possibly allow his group portrait of the three eldest daughters of George III to be hung at a height 'higher than five feet & a half'. In attempting to dictate to the authorities in this way, Gainsborough was asking for a radical breach in the academy's rules. He knew perfectly well that full- or three-quarter-length portraits were normally hung above the 'line', a wooden moulding running around the Great Room at Somerset House at a height of about seven and a half feet from the floor.

But Gainsborough explained that he had painted the picture 'in so tender a light, that notwithstanding he approves of the established Line for Strong Effects the likenesses & Work of the Picture will not be seen any higher'. The importance of the matter should not be underestimated. When the committee refused to comply with his demand, Gainsborough resigned and never again exhibited at the Royal Academy.

Art On the Line at the Courtauld Gallery makes us understand for the first time precisely what was at stake. The organiser, David Solkin, and his team have achieved something I would have thought impossible: an accurate reconstruction of a Royal Academy summer exhibition as it might have looked in the late eighteenth and early nineteenth centuries in the actual spaces in which it took place. The result is much more than an academic exercise. British artists worked in the knowledge that their pictures would be seen under the specific conditions that prevailed at Somerset House. Unless you understand the hanging system at the Royal Academy, you don't understand how desperate artists were to grab the visitor's attention with dramatic or topical subjects, bright colours and inventive compositions.

The RA summer exhibition was among the great spectacles of

24 January 2001
Art On the Line
Courtauld Gallery,
London

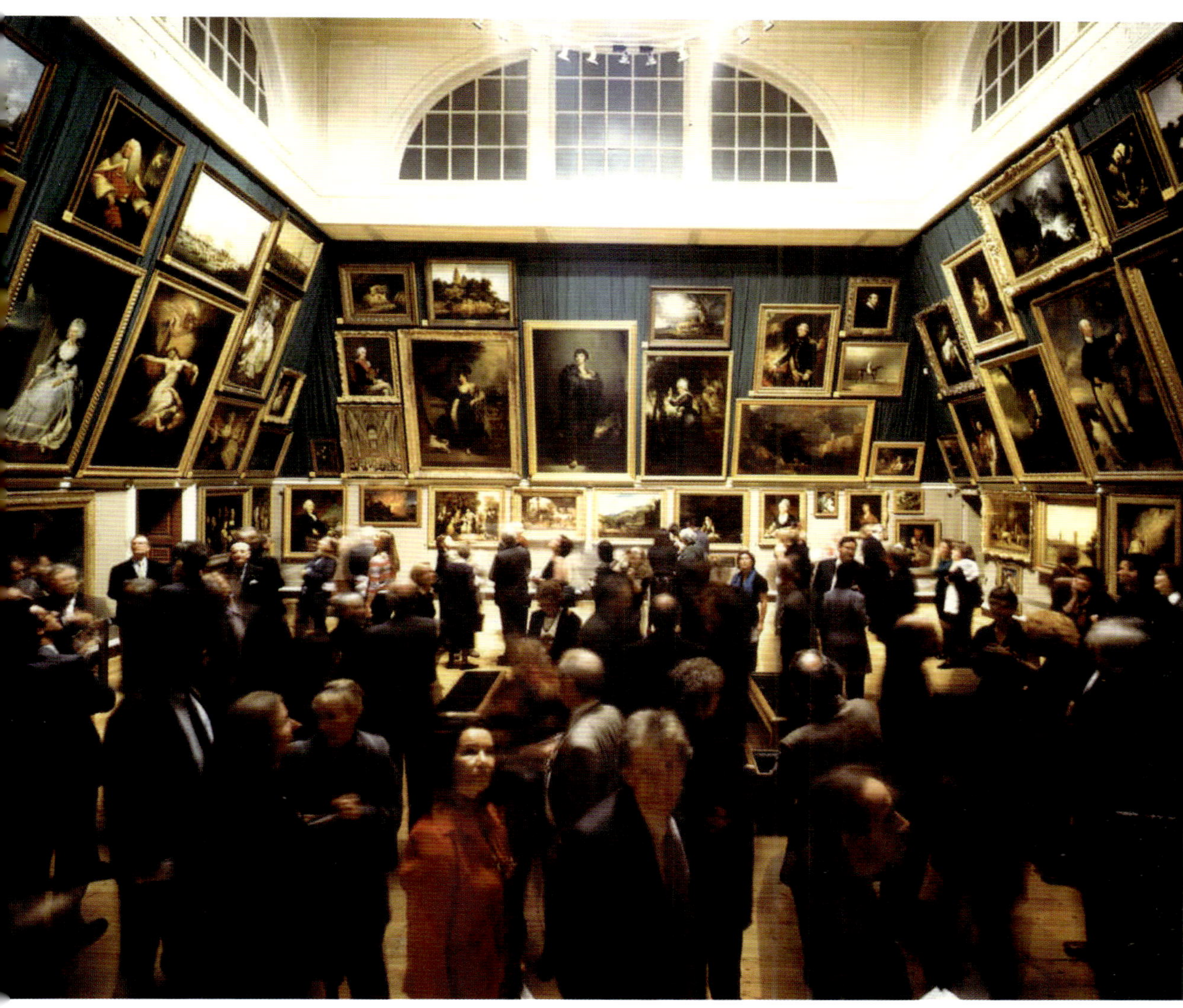

Georgian and Regency London. In the spring and early summer, people of all classes flocked to Somerset House, Sir William Chambers's long, low palace on the Thames, where they toiled up the narrow, vertiginous staircase to emerge with a whoosh of excitement at the top-lit galleries under the roof. As we follow in their footsteps, we understand for the first time what it must have been like finally to step into 'The Great Room' – the high, square, oddly proportioned chamber that was the dramatic heart of the annual exhibition. Here, all four walls were hung from floor to ceiling and frame to frame with works that were an absolute mirror of British society.

The places of honour in the centre of each wall were reserved for full-length portraits of members of the Royal Family – but also for portraits of adventuresses and courtesans, society beauties such as Georgiana Duchess of Devonshire or Lady Betty Foster, actors such as John Philip Kemble or Mrs Siddons, writers such as Dr Johnson, Byron (seen here in full Greek kit) or Sir Walter Scott. There were pictures of military heroes such as Nelson, and pictures that illustrated events such as Philip de Loutherbourg's *Battle of Alexandria* of 1805. In a world without photography or even cheap reproductive engraving, how exciting it must have been to see what the celebrities you had only read about in newspapers or gossiped about in the coffee houses actually looked like.

The walls were covered in green baize (so that artists were careful about how much green they used in their pictures, and tended to favour red). Pictures above the line were cantilevered out from the wall in order to minimize the glare on the varnished surfaces from daylight pouring through the arch-shaped windows near the ceiling.

Above all, artists were aware of the height at which their pictures hung. Looking at Reynolds's broadly painted portraits, you understand that it was essential they be hung above the line because they work best when seen from far away. By contrast, the feathery touch and pastel colours in Gainsborough's series of oval portraits of the children of George III work only from close to and, therefore, must hang below the line. Sir Thomas Lawrence's portrait of *John Philip Kemble in the role of Coriolanus* 'works' only when viewed from below. The actor seems to step forward almost on to our heads, as though we are in the pit of the theatre.

The area below the line was reserved for smaller and more detailed pictures. In fact, the visitor has to look at *Art On the Line* from two entirely different perspectives. To see the art below the line, we must move in close to the walls. To see the larger paintings above the line we step back into the centre of the room. Eighteenth-century visitors brought spyglasses and telescopes to inspect the pictures hung near the ceiling. For this show, the organisers have provided binoculars, though they aren't really necessary.

What effect did all this have on the art itself? The first thing we realise is how competitive British artists were. In this show, we come across Sir David Wilkie's *The Blind Fiddler* – a charming rustic genre scene that was one of the 'hits' of the 1807 RA show. Next to it hangs J. M. W. Turner's *The Blacksmith's Shop*, a similar rustic genre picture painted in response to Wilkie, and shown in the following year's RA. Here was a case of 'anything you can do, I can do better'. More viciously, there were cases of painters elbowing competitors out of the way, as we know from the story of Turner 'killing' the pale green Constable hanging next to his painting by adding a luscious crimson disc of pigment to his foreground.

In this show we find Reynolds's *Death of Dido* hanging near Henry Fuseli's treatment of the same subject, both of which were shown in the same Royal Academy exhibition of 1781. Fuseli must have seen Reynolds at work on his picture and decided to challenge him. As a result, one composition is horizontal, the other vertical; one shows the emotions on the faces of the protagonists, in the other all the faces are hidden. Through such stunts, unknowns and foreigners made their name in the bull-ring that was the art world in London.

Reynolds, the first president of the Royal Academy, hoped that, by giving the British public access to the best works of art, the institution would instruct and elevate the nation's taste. Instead, artists became obsessed with producing novel subjects, striking visual effects, and harsh bright colours. Either an artist became a popular and commerical entertainer, or he faced obscurity.

I can't remember seeing an exhibition of historic British painting as illuminating or as exciting as this one. The show covers the years 1780, when the Academy moved to Somerset House, to 1836, when it transferred to Trafalgar Square. The organisers have chosen pictures shown in summer exhibitions throughout this period, and eliminated the dross that (then as now) vitiated the impact of each individual exhibition. The quality of what's been borrowed is astounding – from Reynolds's swaggering portrait of George IV as Prince of Wales from the Earl of Arundel, to ravishing Gainsboroughs from the Queen.

Swagger Portraits

Thomas Lawrence
Portrait of Catherine Grey, Lady Manners, *1794*
Cleveland Musem of Art

No, no, no. The Tate Gallery has got it all wrong. In its hugely enjoyable new exhibition, *The Swagger Portrait,* the Tate misses the whole point of the Swagger. Not just any grand full-length portrait can aspire to the status of Swagger. The true Swagger is a society portrait in which the artist substitutes sheer visual panache for the revelation of character. The purpose of its existence can be summed up in three words: pure, undiluted exhibitionism. The Swagger has all the subtlety of an oncoming bus.

The Swagger Portrait belongs as much to the history of style as it does to the history of art. It is fundamental to the genre that the sitter need have no intrinsic merits or accomplishments to justify the overblown bravado with which he presents himself to the world. He or she may or may not be beautiful or talented or powerful, but it is essential that they be made to seem so. The subject of the Swagger craves publicity. I'd wager that 90 per cent of those painted after 1768 hung at some point in the Royal Academy. Long before Andy Warhol made celebrity itself the subject of his art, the Swagger was the vehicle through which the politically or socially ambitious could advertise their attractions.

The painter who aspires to paint a Swagger Portrait must start by discovering within himself a talent for outrageous flattery, a genius for the superficial. His feeling for nonchalant glamour must be matched by the sitter's aptitude for shameless strutting and preening. In this exhibition a whole roll-call of narcissists carry on in feathers and pearls, silks and chiffons, turbans and tiaras, breastplates and busbies. The rope of pearls worn by Sargent's Mrs Carl Meyer actually touches her toes.

In the true Swagger portrait, the subject doesn't appear to pose, but artfully disposes himself over a handy balustrade, or else luxuriates on the softest of divans, hardly aware that her portrait is being

28 October 1992
The Swagger Portrait
Tate Gallery, London

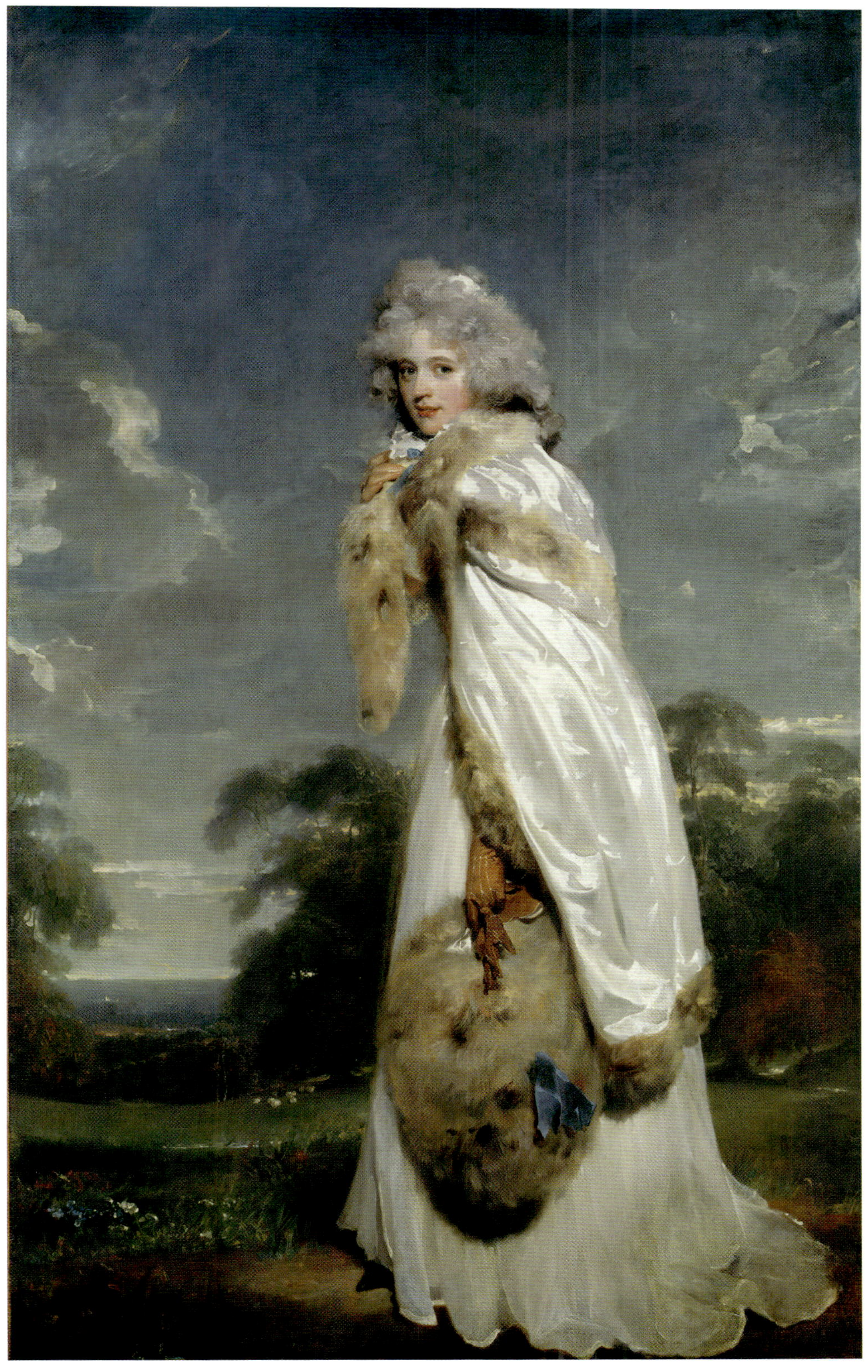

painted at all. The end product must not suggest an artist laboriously drawing a likeness and then working up the portrait, but a painting knocked off in an afternoon by a fellow guest, who happened to be an artist, at a weekend in a grand country house.

Women, of course, are invariably slim, long-necked, and impossibly graceful. Jewels drip rather than hang from ears and necks. Character is never the point. Sweet temper, modesty or diffidence may all be very well in their place, but they certainly don't belong in the Swagger Portrait. It is more important for straight-backed society beauties to exude serenity than to betray the slightest personality.

In terms of technique, the Swagger Portrait depends on the controlled application of juicy pigments through brushy brushwork, a style glimpsed in embryo in van Dyck's draperies and landscape backgrounds, and in the wonderfully baroque swirls of that greatest of English-born seventeenth-century painters, William Dobson. But true Swagger was brought to gooey perfection by the foreigners Sargent, Boldini and de Lazlo, all of whom used the brush not to explore form but to create a sense of surface excitement as a foil to the absolute self-assurance of the sitter.

Between van Dyck and Sargent came Lawrence, whose portrait of Catherine Grey, Lady Manners, is the very quintessence of Swagger. As bird-brained a beauty as ever Jane Austen cast as a foil to one of her clever heroines, she stands on the steps of her country mansion, the Mannerist sweep of her long white dress seeming to go on forever, her head topped by a dizzy millinery confection somewhere between a loosely tied turban and a veil. In case we miss the point, Lawrence juxtaposes her fan-tailed figure with that of a splendid peacock on the balustrade behind her.

Even supposing Lady Manners had any character to reveal, Lawrence contrives to tell us all about her without the slightest allusion to it. Another artist might probe her personality through a look, a smile, a turn of the head. Lawrence tells us all we need to know through costume, props, landscape and pose. And what do we learn? Well, exactly what she wanted us to know: that she is beautiful, rich, aristocratic and dresses divinely.

On the other hand, one of the secrets of the successful Swagger Portrait is for the painter to discover the most disreputable aspect of

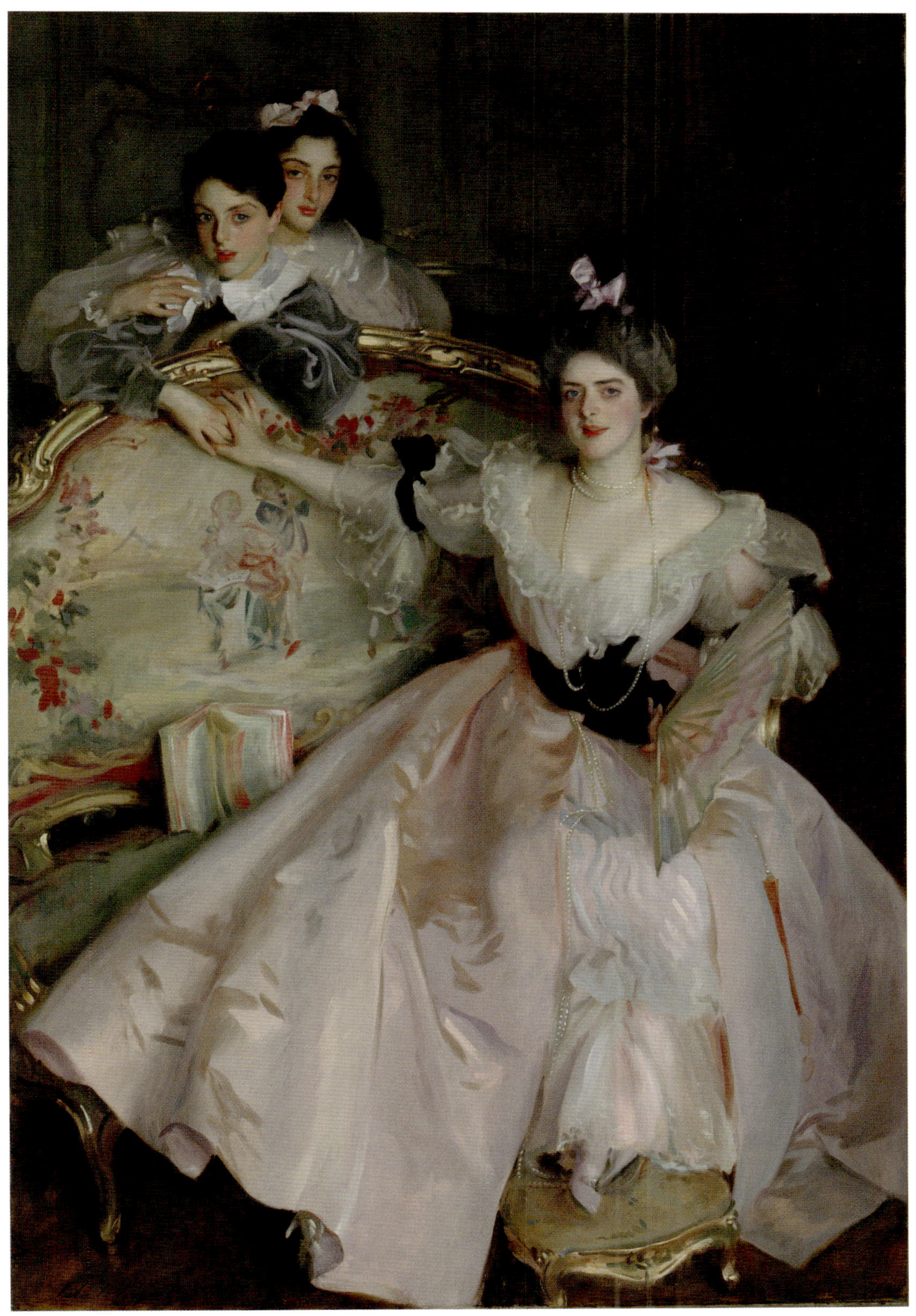

the sitter's character and then stress that very trait. That lovely
Restoration wanton Barbara Villiers, Duchess of Cleveland, poses
for Lely with her hair just slightly tousled and her melting eyes half-
closed, as though she had just left the King's bed. Sargent's Mrs Meyer
is much more interested in charming us viewers than she is in her two
neglected, cowering children.

Likewise, Lady Colin Campbell's reputation as a loose woman had
driven her from society and forced her to become, of all things, an art
critic. As though to broadcast the message that the subject didn't give
a damn what the world thought or said, Boldini turns her into a
caricature of the *femme fatale*, wearing a dress of all but indecent
decolletage and positively ogling the viewer. On her death she left
the portrait to the National Portrait Gallery. Now that's Swagger.

Not to have enjoyed this show would be like not having a good
time at a production of *Tosca* sung by Callas and Domingo. It's like a
tub of caviar – or rather a mountain of Turkish delight. Yet there are
plenty of second-rate pictures by first-rate artists here, and too many
portraits which should be here and aren't. Van Dyck's *Sir Robert and
Lady Shirley*, Kneller's *Chinese Convert*, Reynolds's *Lord Belmont* and
Sargent's *Sir Frank Swettenham*: all are sorely missed.

Then there are the pictures that do not belong in this show.
Hogarth's *Captain Coram*, for example, is notable precisely because
it so brilliantly undermines the essentially foreign tradition of
Swagger. It shows a modest, good man, a man of real virtue and true
accomplishments. Coram wears his ordinary clothes, and faces us
without pretension, but is posed in a setting that lends classical
dignity to an image Hogarth knew would hang in a very grand public
space. Reynolds's *Duke of Cumberland* is as ugly and brutal as ever we
imagined. By my definition the portrait isn't Swagger since Reynolds
goes right to the heart of his character, not flattering him but
skewering him forever in the eyes of posterity. Reynolds's *Lord
Heathfield*, Lawrence's *Queen Charlotte*, Millais's *Mrs Bischoffsheim*: each
treats the character of its subject too seriously to qualify as Swagger.
Yet who can complain when each in its own way is a masterpiece?

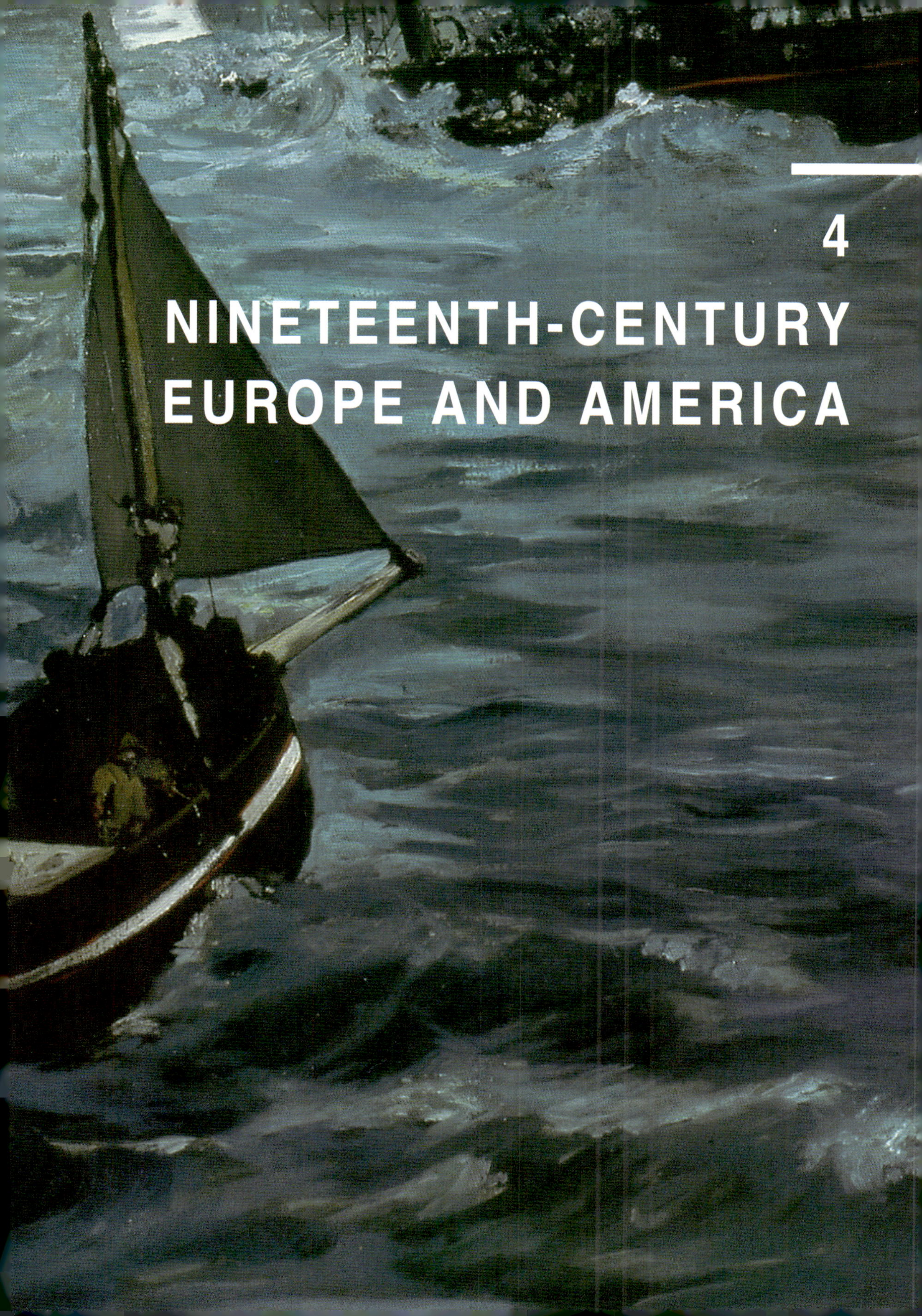
4
NINETEENTH-CENTURY
EUROPE AND AMERICA

Fierce Friends: Artists and Animals

The first picture you see in the exhibition *Fierce Friends: Artists and Animals 1750–1900* is of a giraffe – sort of. Painted in about 1785, the creature in it has the neck of a giraffe, but its back is too long, its haunches too developed, and its legs are out of proportion to its body. Like most Europeans in the eighteenth century, the anonymous French artist who painted it had never seen a real giraffe. He relied on eyewitness descriptions, and on the skin of a giraffe the scientist and adventurer François Levallard had brought back from South Africa.

Exotic animals shipped back to Europe at this time usually died soon after arrival, even supposing they survived the voyage. Until about 1900, taxidermy consisted of stuffing the carcass with straw, so the results fell apart after a few years. This meant that ordinary men and women had very few opportunities to see exotic animals at first hand until the establishment of the first zoos – in Paris in 1793, in London in 1818. For an accurate depiction of a giraffe Europeans had to wait until 1827 and the arrival of the first living specimen, when the Swiss artist Jacques-Laurent Agasse painted his lovely study of the Nubian giraffe sent to King George IV by the Ottoman Viceroy of Egypt.

For most people in the eighteenth century, animals meant farm animals, carriage horses, and food for the table. But the Enlightenment was an age both of exploration and of discovery, as more and more species of animals, birds, fish and insects were identified and brought back from the South Seas, Africa and India. In 1740 almost 600 species of animals were known to science. A hundred years later the number had risen to 2,400, including many that are familiar to most children today as a matter of course – ostrich, rhino, orang-utan and buffalo.

Kings and princes, to be sure, had their own menageries, and wealthy collectors added rare birds, fish and mammals (shown side by side with two-headed calves and fake dragons) to their cabinets of

1 November 2005

Fierce Friends:
Artists and Animals
1750–1900

Van Gogh Museum,
Amsterdam

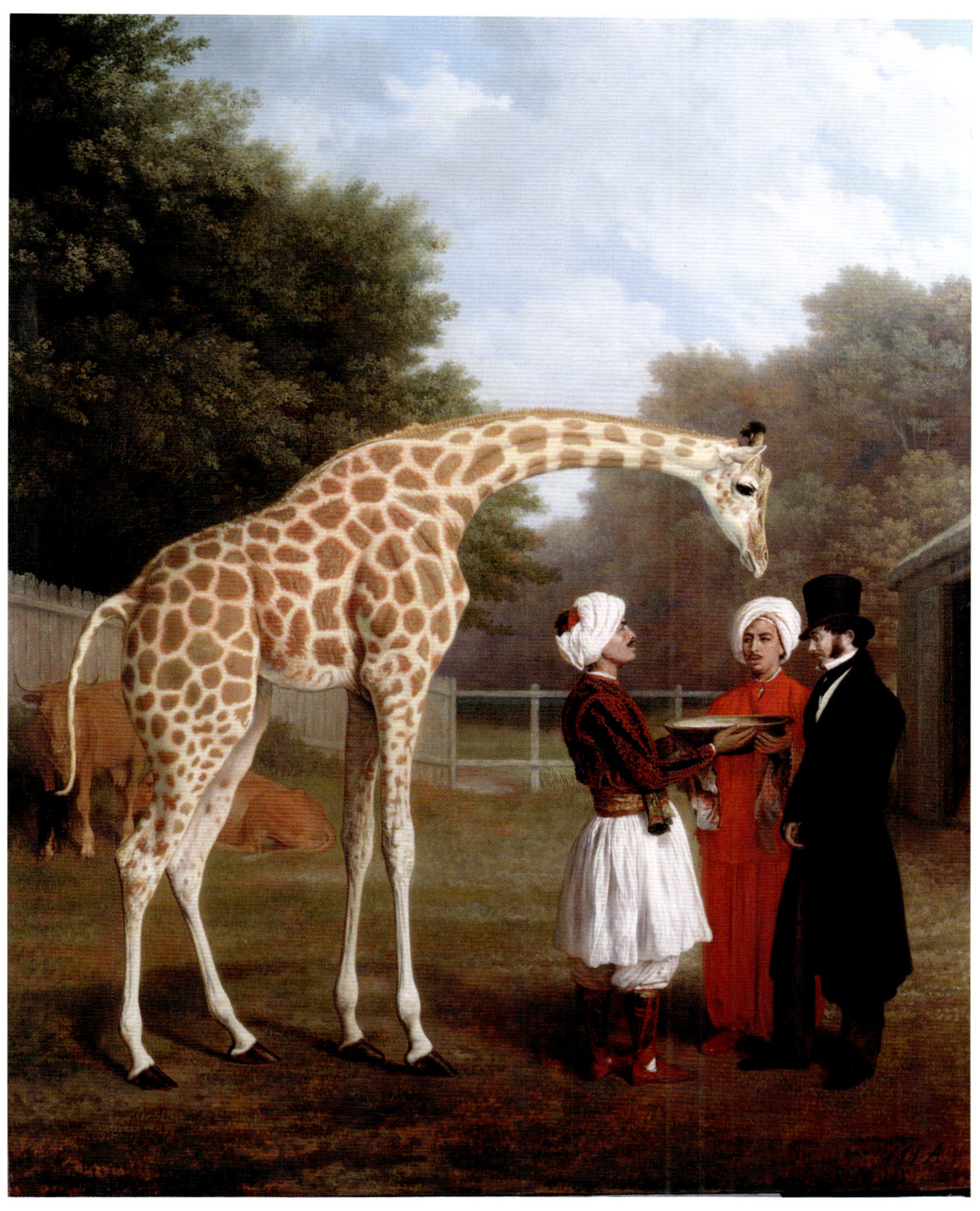

curiosities. In this way, the forerunners of modern zoos and museums developed along parallel lines. On special occasions an entrepreneur might exhibit a wild beast to the paying public, as was the case when the Venetian artist Pietro Longhi painted bored masqueraders at carnival time gawping at a pathetic rhinoceros. Out of such displays came another invention of the nineteenth century, the circus.

Wider knowledge of the animal kingdom came with the publication of George-Louis Leclerc Comte de Buffon's multi-volume *Histoire Naturelle* (1749–88). Based on specimens studied in the royal menageries, this remarkable book is still treasured – not for its scientific accuracy, but for its glorious hand-coloured engravings. Far too expensive for most people to buy, it at least helped to make men and women aware of the beauty of certain animals, as we can see in a service of Sèvres porcelain created in 1793, where the decorative motifs are taken from the birds drawn by de Buffon.

Gradually, humans began to notice that dumb creatures have feelings. Man cannot afford to feel pity for an animal bred for food. When that wonderful artist Jean-Baptise Oudry shows a display of dead game in the 1740s he is simply painting a luxury – fresh meat – available only to the well-off. Peasants ate bread. His lavish paintings were considered suitable decoration for the dining rooms of the nobility because no one then expressed the slightest ethical or moral hesitation about hunting and killing rabbit, deer and boar for the table, or about slaughtering such vermin as foxes and wolves.

Domestic animals were a different story. When Oudry depicts a hound with her newborn puppies, the simple picture has revolutionary overtones. The pretty white bitch, noticing that two of her pups have fallen asleep and are not getting the nourishment they need, is full of maternal solicitude. At a time when French noblewomen still sent their babes out to wet-nurses, even an animal is shown to display true maternal feeling. And in 1824, the year Delacroix shows two horses killed in battle, there is a new element in man's attitude towards the wanton slaughter of beautiful creatures: compassion.

Delacroix's little masterpiece pierces the heart, whereas the grotesque memorial to animals killed in war unveiled in London last year leaves the viewer cold. But the moral impulse behind the creation of both works is exactly the same.

Once animals can be loved for their innocence or good nature, it becomes more difficult to treat them cruelly. Almost fifteen years before Jean-Baptise Greuze painted a picture of a young girl mourning her pet sparrow (1765), William Hogarth published his series of prints, *The Stages of Cruelty*, showing how the mistreatment of animals, whether by torturing cats, staging cockfights, or beating a horse, leads inexorably to the devaluing of all forms of life, including human. In this show it is almost impossible to look at Emile Edouard Mouchy's horrifying depiction of the vivisection of a dog (1832) without wincing. Though such experiments represent a necessary evil, our very squeamishness represents another rung upward in the moral evolution of mankind.

This process started in the early nineteenth century, when men began to see in the animal kingdom a mirror image of their own feelings. In his portrayal of a horse frightened by lightning, Géricault lets us see the animal's tensed body, foam-flecked mouth and brow furrowed in anxiety.

In *The Jealous Lioness* of about 1880, the German artist Paul Meyerheim shows a caged lioness enraged at the attention her mate is paying to a beautiful lion tamer. Gradually artists begin to blur the distinctions between animal and human. When Edwin Landseer in *Low Life* and *High Life* contrasts a mongrel guard dog with a deer hound, the animals are surrogates for their absent masters, a butcher and a nobleman. All these artists emphasised the physical and

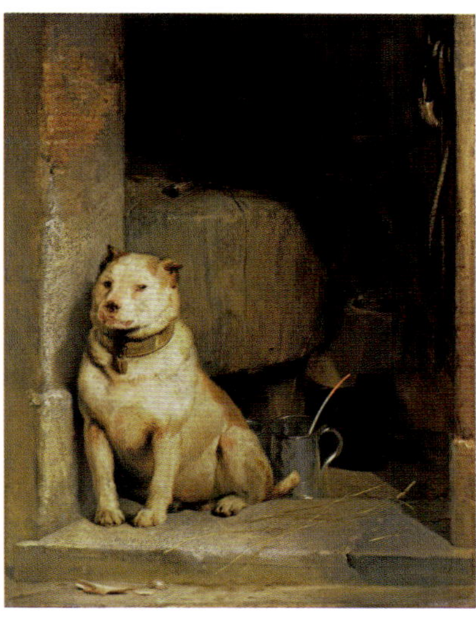
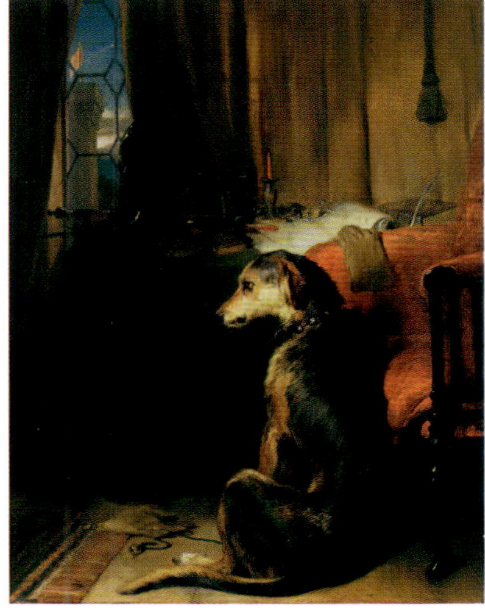

Edwin Henry Landseer
Right: **Low Life**
Far right: **High Life**, *both 1829*
Tate Gallery, London

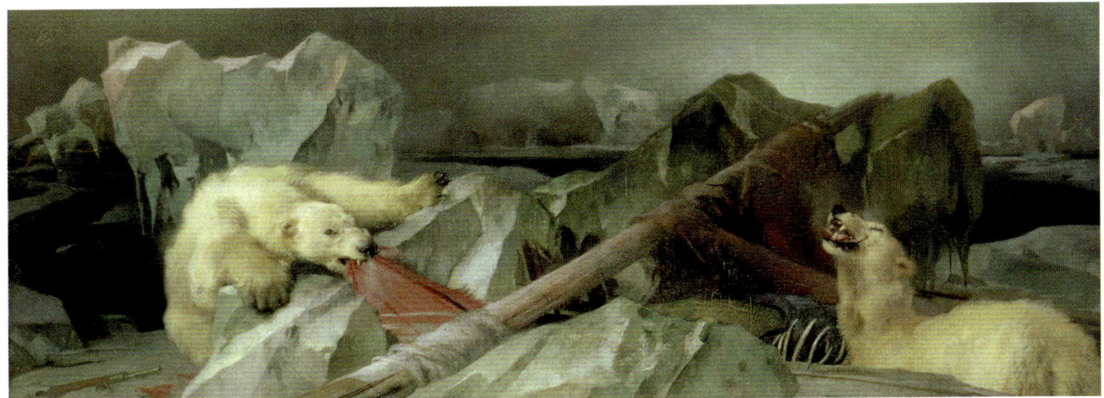

emotional resemblances between animals and human beings long
before Darwin changed our relationship to the animal world by
proving that we are descended from animals.

In one of their many original readings of familiar images, the
organisers of the show see *Man Proposes, God Disposes*, Landseer's
magnificent depiction of polar bears tearing apart the wreckage
of Sir John Franklin's doomed expedition to the North Pole, as an
illustration of Darwinism at work. The humans perished because,
unlike the bears, they were ill-adapted to the hostile environment in
which they found themselves. What is more, as those who first saw
this picture would have known, *in extremis* the explorers reverted
to their animal instincts by eating the weakest members of the crew,
one by one.

What I've written so far does not begin to suggest how rich and
complex this exhibition is. Among the rarities on view is the first work
of art painted under water, when in 1864 the Austrian diplomat and
traveller Eugen Ransonnet-Villez invented a diving bell that enabled
him to work directly from nature, recording the underwater view of
refracted light and blurred shadows, strange sea creatures and weird
corals, just as they really look. Here's a fact I bet you didn't know:
until the world's first aquarium opened in Regent's Park in 1853,
mankind had seen fish only when they were dead or dying.

For reasons that I will never understand, the Van Gogh Museum
saw this as a show for children and so pitched the labels and display
to eight-year-olds. In fact, parts of it will scare small children witless,
and the content of the show couldn't be more sophisticated. But that
is a minor irritant.

Edwin Henry Landseer
**Man Proposes,
God Disposes**, *1864*
*Royal Holloway,
University of London*

Light!

Towards the beginning of *Light!*, the impressive new show at the Van Gogh Museum in Amsterdam, we encounter a flickering black-and-white film made by no less an eminence than Thomas Edison, inventor of the electric light bulb. Its subject is the Buffalo Pan-American Exposition of 1903, and it is the first film to be shot at night entirely by artificial light.

Even today, the pavilions, miraculously outlined with twinkling electric lights against the night sky, look to us like a scene from *The Arabian Nights*. But try for a moment to put yourself in the shoes of a family who had just travelled to upstate New York from the Midwest or the prairies – and who may well have been living in a house where oil lamps were still in use. Nothing – not television, not space travel, not computers – gives us any idea of the awe our great-grandparents must have felt when they saw the world illuminated by electricity for the first time.

But then, they themselves had probably forgotten that for their ancestors all work had stopped at twilight, theatrical performances took place only in the daytime, and ships had to wait until dawn before entering harbours. Before the late eighteenth century, the best way to enhance the efficacy of candlelight was the chandelier, its faceted glass enabling one candle to do the work of half a dozen.

Everything changed in 1780 with the coming of the Argand lamp, an invention that gave a new dimension to the word 'enlightenment'. Based on the principle that the more oxygen you feed burning oil, the brighter and longer the flame will bum, this simple contraption enabled people to light their homes cheaply, artists to paint (as well as to draw) at night, and ordinary men and women to walk the streets and visit the theatre after dark.

After this, new revolutions in lighting took place every decade or so for the next hundred years. Oil, gas, petroleum, paraffin, carbon arc

22 November 2000

Light! Art & Science, Technology & Society

Van Gogh Museum, Amsterdam

lights, electric light and incandescent light: one followed the other
in quick succession. The Van Gogh Museum's *Light!* (subtitled *Art &
Science, Technology & Society*) looks at the way artists in the industrial
age, 1750–1900, responded to each new development in lighting
technology.

At the simplest level, new forms of light created new subjects for
artists to paint. By the second half of the eighteenth century, factory
owners in the Midlands had instituted night shifts, at once depriving
many of their workers of natural light and creating the pyrotechnic
spectacles that so fascinated Jacques Philippe de Loutherbourg and
Joseph Wright of Derby. Such artists discovered nightly in the coke
and iron works at Coalbrookdale the explosions of colour, heat, light
and sound that they had in the past found only in the eruptions of
Vesuvius or in displays of fireworks. More than a century later, the
American artist Winslow Homer depicted the ingenious use of light as
a weapon in his painting of an incident during the Spanish–American
War when Americans turned giant searchlights on the harbour at
Santiago de Cuba, and so prevented the Spanish fleet from slipping
away by night.

In addition to showing how light stimulated artists to paint new
subjects, this exhibition asks searching questions about the role that
new lighting technologies played in the actual creation of works of art.
The first artist to paint a picture entirely by artificial light (an Argand
lamp) was the French romantic painter Anne-Louis Girodet, whose
Pygmalion was exhibited at the Salon of 1819. When an artist paints
by day, he has limited opportunity to manipulate light. But because
artificial sources of illumination produce such varied effects of light,
and because they can be so easily controlled, they can be used to
change what the artist actually sees in front of him.

In Wilhelm Bendz's depiction of a life class at the Charlottenburg
academy of fine arts in 1826, for example, an assistant is shown
mounting a ladder to adjust a bank of Argand lamps, directing their
warm light on the nude model to produce dramatic shadows which
could be changed with each new pose. And, of course, our perception
of colour changes in different lighting conditions. When Henri de
Toulouse-Lautrec painted performers and clients mooching around
the Moulin Rouge, he was fascinated by the way the gas lamps turned
their painted faces a sickly shade of green.

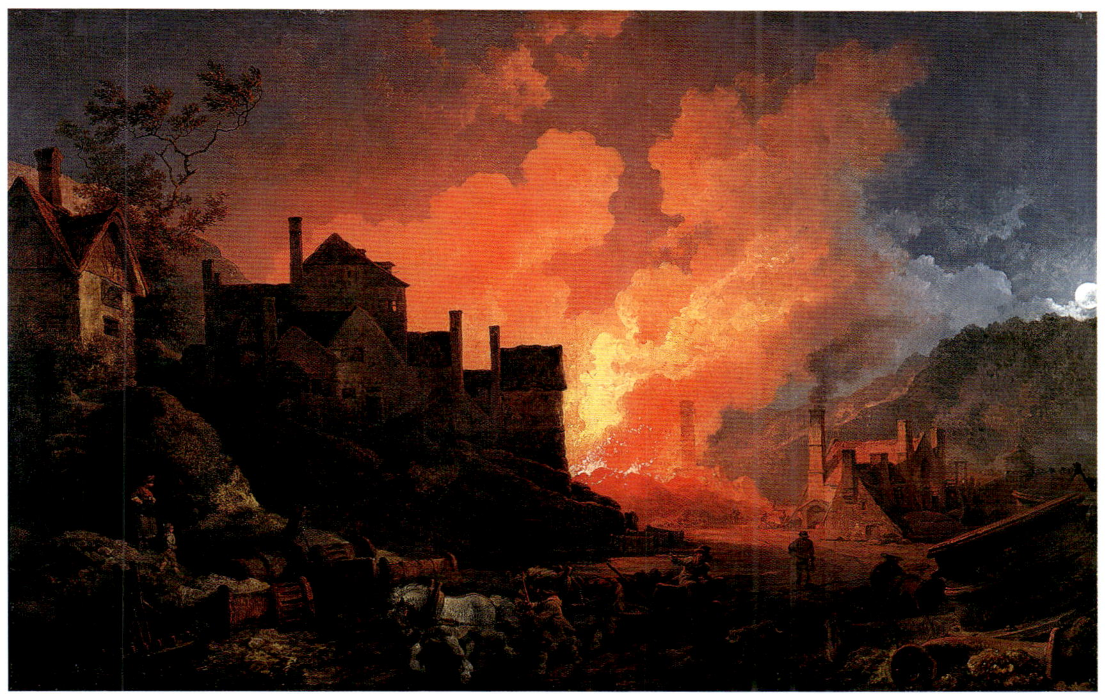

No matter how carefully the artist controlled the lighting conditions under which he worked, however, he had little control over the conditions under which the work would be exhibited. A fascinating canvas by Auguste Vinchon shows King Louise Philippe and his family visiting the sculpture gallery at Versailles by night, accompanied by a shoal of courtiers carrying enormous lamps with reflectors to direct the light on to the marble statues, thus casting them into deep relief and throwing dramatic shadows on the walls.

The Italian Symbolist Giovanni Segantini shows two of his models looking at one of his own landscapes by lamplight. The strange effect that he explores in this work is how the colours and tonal relationships in a landscape painted by natural light look totally different under artificial light. When in 1878 the French government directed that the Salon be illuminated by arc lights so that working-class people could visit the exhibition in the evening, the painters complained bitterly that the cold, new lighting drained pictures painted by oil or gaslight of colour.

That they were absolutely right can be seen in the Danish artist Peder Krøya's depiction of a reception at the Carlsberg Glyptotek.

The harsh, dead light from the newly installed electric arc lamps not only depletes the room of colour, but gives the people in it an unhealthy pallor. After seeing this picture it comes as no surprise to learn that arc lighting was considered too strong for domestic use. Edison invented the electric light bulb because he wished to find a light source as gentle and easy on the eye as oil.

All this is fascinating enough. But far from limiting enquiry to the scientific or technical effects that new forms of lighting had on art, this show probes the symbolic significance of light as well. One example will have to do. In one of Degas's most powerful genre scenes, a bearded man and half-dressed woman are shown in the privacy of a bedroom. As she turns away from him and he blocks the doorway, the atmosphere is so charged with menace that the enigmatic subject has often been described as the aftermath of a murder, or the prelude to a rape. What makes the picture so worrying is that by placing a shaded oil lamp on the table between the man and woman, Degas subverts the traditional depiction of husbands, wives and children gathered cosily around a lamp at night, and turns what should be a symbol of domestic harmony into one of seething tension.

With three hundred exhibits, this is a huge show, taking up three floors of the spectacularly renovated Van Gogh Museum. It covers such light-related topics as the silhouette, the daguerreotype, theatrical lighting, eye tests, street lighting and the excitement that men and women must once have felt when replacing a light bulb. *Light!* achieves the remarkable feat of awakening in the visitor a sense of what it must have been like to see these new light sources for the first time. Since each one utterly changed the way we lived by changing the way we saw, I don't think it is possible to overestimate the importance of what the organisers, Andreas Blühm and Louise Lippincott, have done.

Jean-Baptiste Camille Corot

In one sense Jean-Baptiste Camille Corot's small oil sketch of *The Island of San Bartolomeo* depicts nothing very special: an island in the Tiber, one of the celebrated sites of Rome, baking in the glare of the noonday sun. Corot gives us the view from head on, with no diagonal lines to guide our eye into the picture space. He sees the densely built-over island from just off-centre, flanked on either side by identical arched bridges, and sandwiched between equal areas of sky above and water below. That is all. There is no unusual viewpoint, no bravura brushwork, no sense of the artist's having laboured to achieve the perfect sense of stillness and equilibrium.

Our first reaction is to marvel at the freshness of Corot's vision. Surely this is an unpremeditated transcription in paint of exactly what the artist saw on that hot summer's afternoon in 1826. But the longer we look, the more we detect a classical monumentality and underlying geometry which suggest that this is anything but an impromptu study. Seen close to, the minute detail we would expect to find in a 'photographic' view of nature is not there. The mosaic of interlocking colours that makes up the central group of buildings has an overall unity which, when taken out of the context of the picture, is virtually abstract, like an isolated passage in a Cubist painting. Form, colour, light and space seem to be one and the same. To our eyes the picture looks forward not so much to the Impressionists as to Cézanne. But can a work painted in the early nineteenth century really be a harbinger of all that is most radical in modern art? Or are we viewing the picture through the prism of Post-Impressionism, thereby misunderstanding it and the artist who painted it?

Born in Paris in 1796, the twenty-nine-year-old Corot arrived in Rome in December 1825 to find a tradition of painting oil sketches directly from nature which had flourished there since the eighteenth century. Steeped in neo-classical theories of the hierarchies of

1 June 1991

Corot

South Bank Centre, London

painting, Corot's contemporaries divided landscape into three categories. The high moral seriousness of the *paysage historique* gave way to the less portentous *vue* and descended to the humble *étude*. The first two types of landscape would normally have been painted in the artist's studio and exhibited in the Salon. But the *étude*, the oil study painted directly from nature, had a different purpose. It was not an end in itself, but a type of *aide mémoire* designed to be consulted during the painting of a large studio landscape, or else retained as a tool for the use of students back in Paris.

In Rome, Corot found an international set of artists all busily sketching from nature. Whether German, French or English, they tended to travel in packs from one predictable classical site to another, rarely straying far from the tourist spots recommended by the guidebooks of the period. As with *The Island of San Bartolomeo*, Corot's oil sketches on the whole do not deviate from this pattern.

And so the first thing to realise about Corot is that his open-air studies are remarkable not because they are avant-garde precursors of Impressionism or Post-Impressionism, but because in choosing to work directly from nature and to record the most obvious landmarks, he was following deeply conservative conventions of neo-classical practice. The proper context in which to view Corot's landscapes is not the future they foretell, but the tradition they bring to an end.

But there are important differences between Corot's on-the-spot studies of the 1820s and those of such eighteenth-century predecessors as Pierre Henri de Valenciennes and the Welsh artist Thomas Jones. Whereas their most innovative work has the hasty look of an improvised sketch (often of exceedingly modest subjects), Corot brought with him from Paris a reverence for the classical tradition in landscape painting. To the freshness and spontaneity of his vision of nature, he added the restraint and discipline of Poussin or Gaspard Dughet. 'One must be rigorous in the face of nature,' he wrote, 'and not content oneself with a sketch made in haste.'

The bridge that linked these two apparently irreconcilable ways of looking at nature was drawing. Corot drew his scene in outline on the canvas, so that before he began to paint, his design was already 'completed'. He then filled in the picture with colour, rather like a child with a colouring book. In this way colour and drawing are kept completely separate, and the artist is in total command over both his

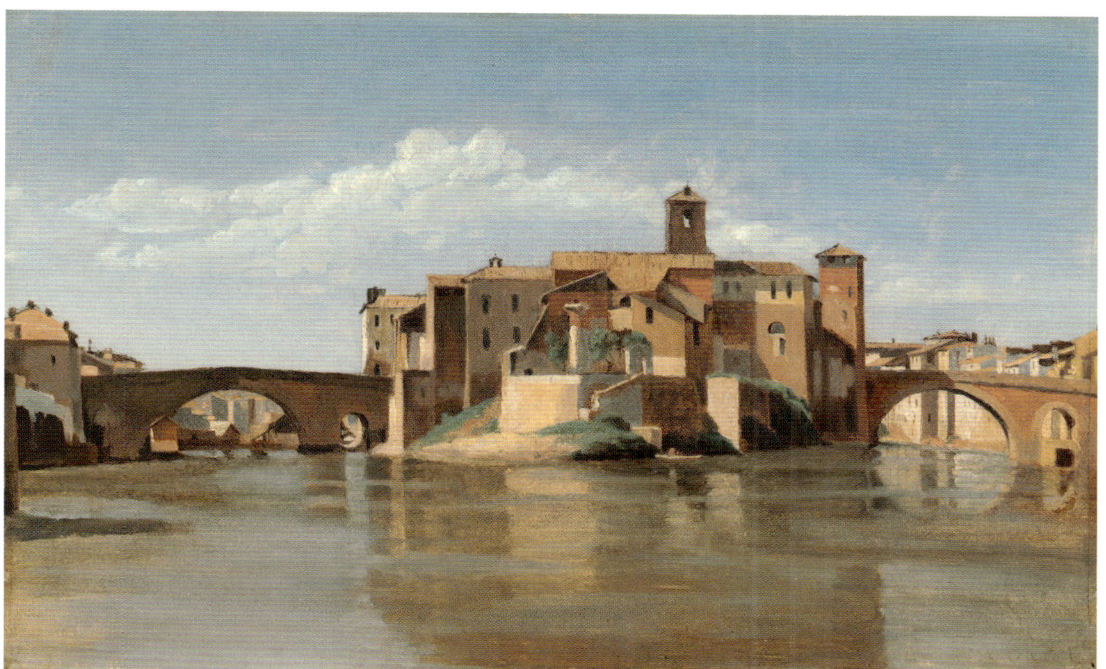

composition and his colour from the outset. Crucial to the success of this aesthetic is the small scale of the canvas. Corot applied his colours on the spot so that only with a canvas of manageable size could he create the impression of perfect unity in all the parts. In *The Island of San Bartolomeo*, the composition is based on an invisible underlying grid of horizontals and verticals, over which Corot lays a harmonious blend of subtle colours. In addition to the blue of the sky and its reflection in the water, he restricts his palette to a narrow range of ochres, browns and dull greens, which he applies with deft, unemphatic touches of the brush.

Until now Corot has been an artist waiting for a critic to make this long misunderstood and underestimated master accessible to a twentieth-century audience. Even as near perfect a little exhibition as the South Bank Centre's touring show of the landscapes, drawings and a few portraits fails to do justice to his genius because the catalogue makes no attempt to interpret his pictures for us. After seeing it, therefore, I read Peter Galassi's recently published *Corot in Italy: Open-Air Painting and the Classical Landscape Tradition*. His magnificent study transformed my understanding of Corot's art and is the source for much of the information in this review.

Christen Købke

Painted in 1838, *View from Dosseringen towards Østerbro*, by the Danish painter Christen Købke, shows nothing more interesting than two middle-class couples on a simple wooden dock. Clearly they have just returned from a sailing party to the large country house visible in the distance across the lake. Frock-coated and top-hatted, one man sees to the boat's mast, assisted by another, whose bent head is covered in a straw hat. Their wives chat with a third woman, who has perhaps been walking with her little boy on the path at the left. Judging by the quality of the light, the time is about half an hour before sunset on a fine summer's evening. Though the sky is still blue, the water reflects the mauve and orange tints in the long low bank of distant cloud.

Købke so sensitively conveys the atmosphere of absolute peace that we feel even the slightest sounds – the low murmur of ladies' voices, the hollow clink of the rigging – are unnaturally amplified in the surrounding stillness. It is a moment of no particular significance, in a place of pleasant but not outstanding natural beauty. But for one split second, time stands still.

'Sturm und Drang', 'Romantic Yearning', 'Awe before Nature', the 'Sublime': name a cliché about northern European painting, and Købke's little masterpiece contradicts it. And yet among the pictures on view at the National Gallery's exhibition *Caspar David Friedrich to Ferdinand Hodler: A Romantic Tradition* it belongs as fully to the northern painterly tradition as the more obviously romantic images of Caspar David Friedrich or Caspar Wolf.

Before attempting briefly to survey this large exhibition, which is drawn from the collection of the Oskar Reinhart Foundation at Winterthur in Switzerland, I'd like to discuss the composition and painting technique in Købke's landscape in some detail. For northern painting differs from Mediterranean in far more concrete ways than the vague (and often meaningless) categories of Romantic v. Classic.

8 June 1994

Caspar David Friedrich to Ferdinand Hodler: A Romantic Tradition

National Gallery, London

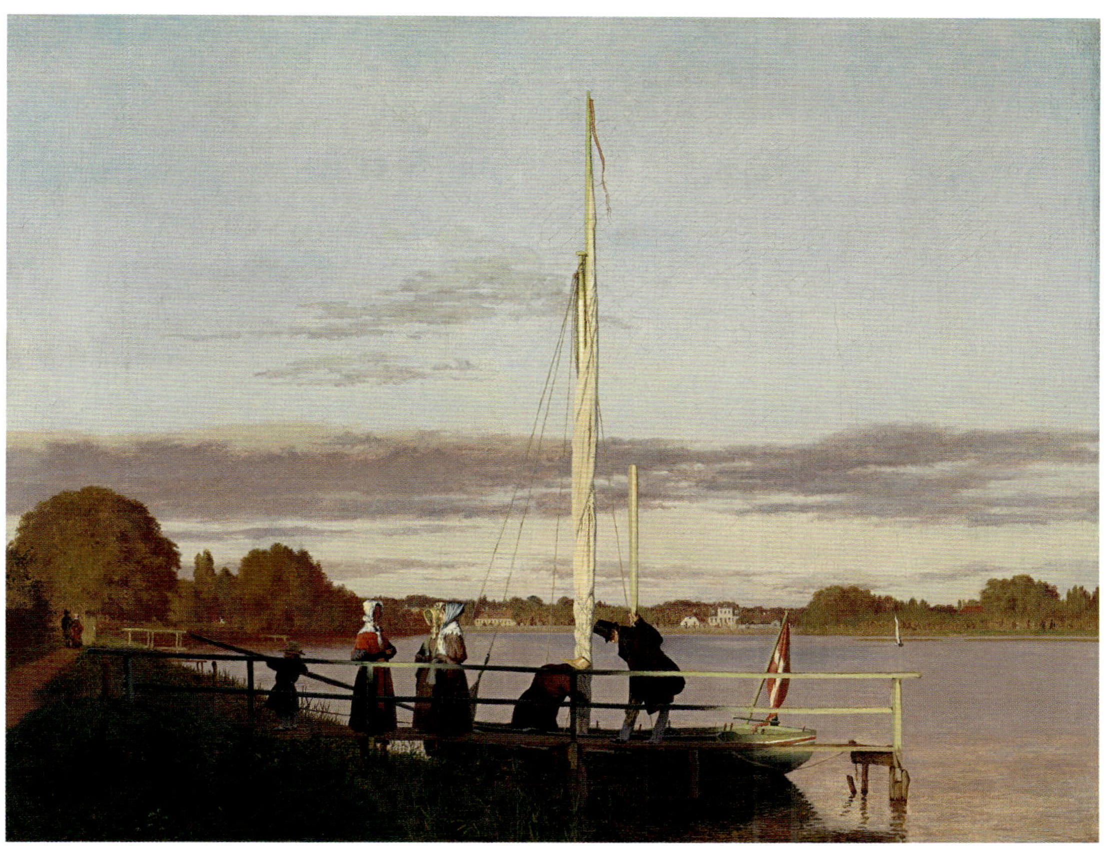

In the first place, the picture's sense of perfect equilibrium seems unforced because it has been created by an invisible geometric grid underlying the composition. Købke divides his picture in two by placing the perpendicular mast in the exact middle of the rectangular canvas. Horizontally, the wooded shoreline divides the lower third of the canvas from the sky, which occupies the upper two-thirds. In the frieze of figures in the foreground, all the women's heads (and one man's hand) just touch the tops of the trees; the men bend their heads in such a way as to stabilise the long line of the tall white mast. To move a single element in this perfectly symmetrical composition would be to risk ruining it. The red shawl of the woman on the left, to take one example, balances the red of the Danish flag on the stern of the boat to the right, as though to put the central figures in parentheses.

But a carefully constructed composition anchored in geometry is not, after all, so very unusual in nineteenth-century painting. Many landscapes by Monet, for example, are at least as meticulously thought out as the Købke, and yet Monet feels to us so much more informal, so much more 'natural' a painter than the Dane. Something about the picture disturbs the modern eye. For all its limpid clarity, why does it look and feel so little like the way we actually see the world?

The answer, I think, lies in the northern painting technique, in which the artist works from light to dark, and places exceptional importance on the pencil underdrawing. The painter first prepared a white ground, then carefully drew his composition in pencil. Unless he were like Friedrich and reinforced his pencil outlines in ink, he next filled them in with pigment, possibly working systematically from left to right, and finishing each section of the canvas before beginning on the next. It is a technique that might be compared to 'painting by numbers'.

It was not until the 1850s that the German scientist Hermann Ludwig von Helmholtz, working on the physiology of vision, discovered how the human eye actually works. It sees objects in the centre of the foreground in great detail, but blurs peripheral areas in the foreground and middle distance. Conversely, if we are looking into the distance, the eye will see the horizon clearly but blur objects in the foreground.

The importance northern artists tended to place on meticulous under-drawing meant that when it came to applying pigment, all areas of the composition tended to be painted with equal emphasis. The insistent clarity in Købke's picture feels unreal because every area of the canvas is 'in focus'. Our eyes have to move to take the canvas in bit by bit, in a way that they don't in real life.

Contrast this to advanced French painting of the 1860s and 1870s. Those artists understood that parts of the world are always in focus while others are not. Though the dab-and-dash brushstrokes and high-pitched colours of Impressionist pictures are in fact highly unnatural, they feel true to our experience of seeing the world. In this exhibition, Wilhelm Leibl's magnificent canvas *The Village Politicians* shows a scene of peasant life that should feel as earthy as a Courbet. But the obsessively refined draughtsmanship gives the work a clean, crisp hyper-clarity that, paradoxically, feels less vivid than Courbet's richly atmospheric scumbles.

This exhibition surveys such an extensive period in the history
of art, and includes so many artists from Germany, Austria and
Scandinavia, that the only true unifying factor in the show is
Reinhart's own taste. He liked idiosyncratic pictures by the great
northern masters, with a strong bias towards landscape, and against
historical or religious paintings. The show, which begins in the
mid-eighteenth century with the Swiss painters Agasse and Fuseli,
contains dozens or artists of whom I had only the haziest knowledge,
and others of whom I'd never heard at all. In the first category Leibl,
Feuerbach, Thoma, Runge and von Marées are all represented by
characteristic pictures, though not necessarily by major examples
of their work. In the second, a view of a quarry in Rome by the (to
me) unknown Giovanni Giacometti was so strong it almost leapt
off the wall.

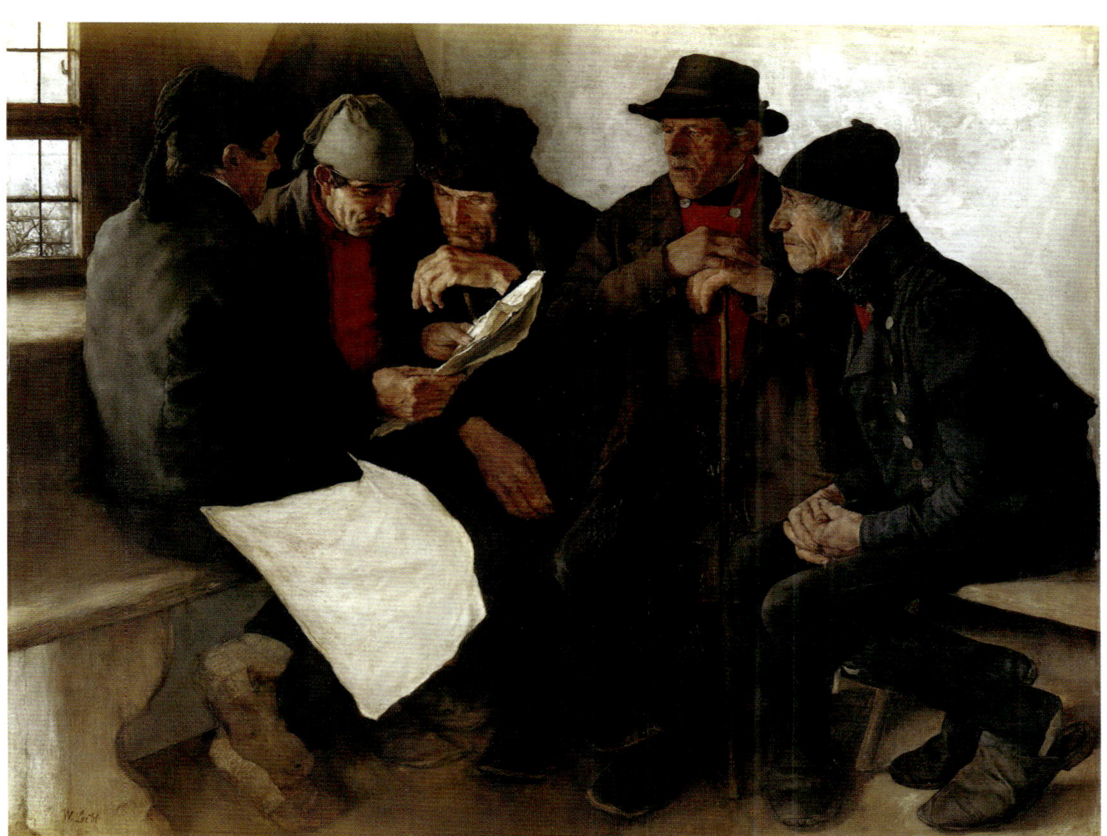

Wilhelm Leibl
**The Village
Politicians**, *1877*
*Museum Oskar
Reinhart am
Stadtgarten,
Winterthur*

American Sublime

About half-way through the exhibition *American Sublime*, Tate Britain's magisterial survey of landscape painting in the United States from 1820 to 1880, Frederic Edwin Church's monumental view of Niagara Falls looms in front of us. Standing before the nine-foot-high canvas, it takes a minute or two for a European viewer to realise that something about it feels wrong. It is not the subject or the size of the picture that is worrying – Turner, after all, painted Swiss waterfalls crashing down sheer cliff faces, and British artists from Constable to James Ward worked on this scale. Nor is the sharp intake of breath inspired by the sight of Niagara Falls an unfamiliar sensation, for the concept of the 'sublime' had been used to describe similar subjects in European paintings since the eighteenth century.

Then you see what it is that feels so strange: it has no composition. We search for a sense of recession from the foreground to the middle ground and distance, but the eye can find no orderly and rational way to enter the space and explore the scene. Instead, we are plunged straight into the roiling, lethal chasm at our feet, as though falling into the picture rather than standing outside it. We are unable to navigate through a picture in which there is no single focus of interest. The top, bottom, centre and sides of the canvas are all of equal importance, just as they will be in the paintings of later Americans such as Jackson Pollock, Barnett Newman and Clyfford Still.

At this point you discover something else that marks the painting as American and not European – there are no brushstrokes, no 'facture' or evidence of the artist's handing of the paint. It is as though, faced with a subject of such overwhelming power, Church needed to efface all evidence of his own personality by allowing the subject to speak directly to the viewer without the mediation of the artist's hand. If you don't believe me, try this experiment. When you walk through the exhibition, pick any picture at random and try to

20 February 2002
American Sublime
Tate Britain, London

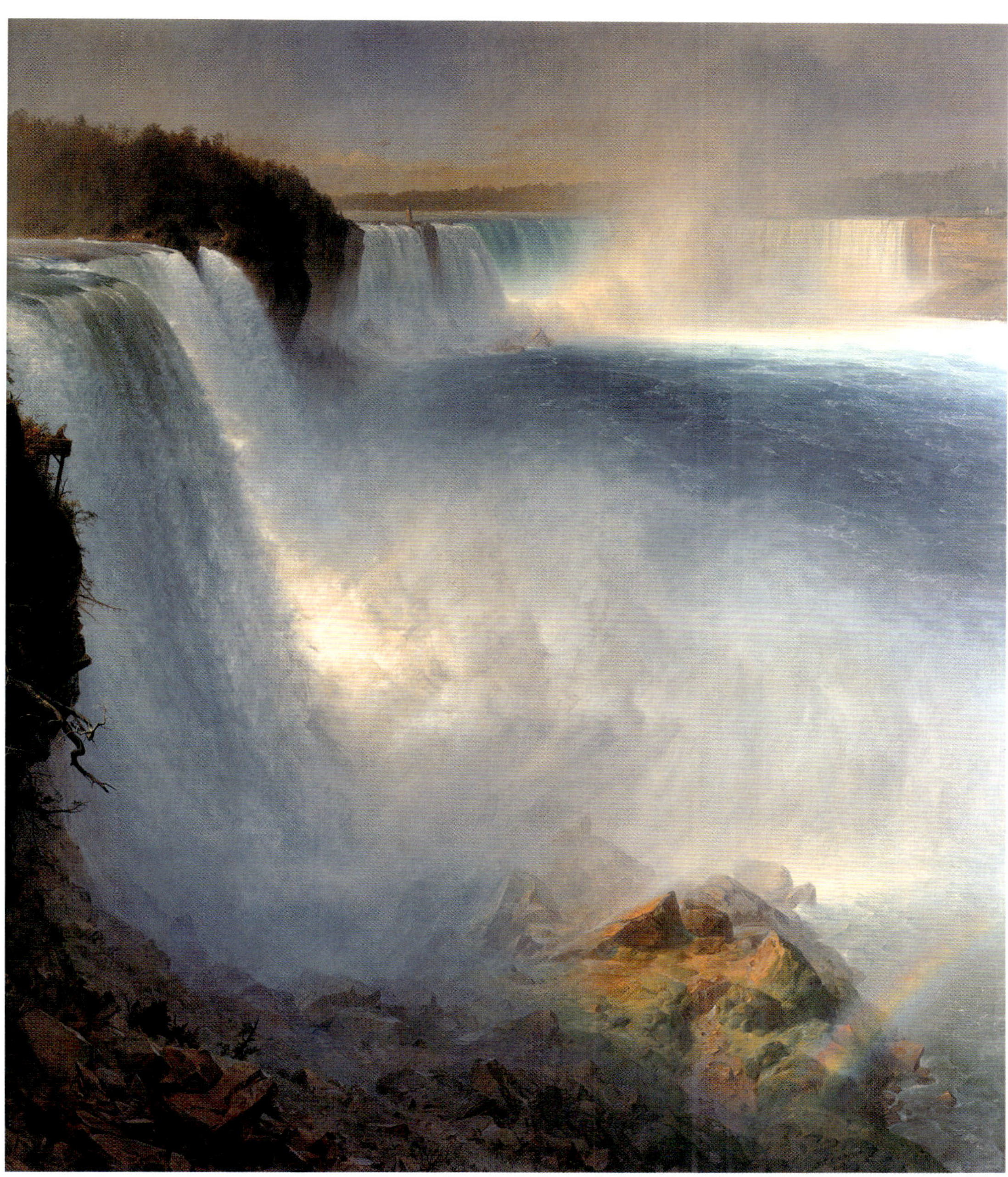

isolate a passage of 'pure' painting, and see whether you can enjoy it on its own, as you can sensuously painted details in pictures by Turner or Constable – or for that matter by Delacroix or Manet. You can't do it. With the exception of the great painter of the American West, Thomas Moran, there is no evidence in American landscape painting of what the French call '*la belle peinture*'.

American Sublime begins deceptively. In the first gallery, medium-
size landscapes by Thomas Cole, Jasper Francis Cropsey and John
Frederick Kensett look like earnest tributes to European Old Masters.
As scenic views they are pretty enough, but, as works of art, they are
not particularly interesting. The paint surface feels 'dead', making
them look like the kind of pictures you find in jigsaw puzzles. As we
move through the show, the quality of the paint surface never really
becomes more scintillating, even though from a technical point of
view Church, Albert Bierstadt, Fitz Hugh Lane or Martin Johnson
Heade were able to conjure up astounding effects of light, atmosphere
and weather. In European art, we value a quality of nonchalance, or
sketchiness. In this show, only in the gallery hung with ravishing oil
sketches from nature do the artists appear to improvise, to work at
speed.

That is because in American art there is no concept of visual
shorthand – the swift squiggle of the loaded brush that creates the
illusion of a figure or a natural form – as there is in great European art.
The function of the American artist's brush is simply and laboriously
to describe, not to fool the eye, or even to delight it. It is the whole
scene that gives aesthetic pleasure, not isolated passages of paint,
because it is the subject that is beautiful, not the way it is painted.

European visitors may or may not feel aesthetic pleasure in front
of these paintings but, in a way, aesthetic pleasure is only part of their
point. No American, standing in front of Sanford Robinson Gifford's
The Wilderness or Cropsey's huge *Autumn – on the Hudson River*
can suppress a patriotic stab at the heart and a lump in the throat.
Americans draw little distinction between the love of their country
and its landscape. Just think of the lyrics to its patriotic songs. God
doesn't bless the American people, he blesses its mountains, prairies
and shining seas.

But nothing in art is ever simple, and the American attitude
towards its landscape is full of conflict and ambiguity. This exhibition
makes us aware that Thomas Cole's five-picture sequence of canvases,
The Course of Empire, was painted during the expansionist presidency
of Andrew Jackson by a conservative artist horrified by a government
policy of unrestrained industrialisation entailing the wanton
destruction of a wilderness. He presents the country as a new Rome,
a great civilisation whose arrogance and heedlessness will bring upon

it ultimate destruction. Again, from a European perspective, this is not new. Turner in England never stopped warning his countrymen against the dangers of empire. But Cole shares with other American artists a propensity for agonising not so much about foreign conquest as about his country's destiny. These artists record the country's compulsion to expand westwards, a 'manifest destiny' in which progress went hand-in-hand with the obliteration of the natural beauty their paintings celebrate. Indeed, in the case of Moran, who was employed by the railroads to paint images that would encourage tourism in the western territories, art and commercial exploitation went hand-in-hand.

Many of the sites of natural beauty we see in this exhibition disappeared during the lifetimes of the artists who painted them. Within a generation or two, the white clapboard hotels and houses in Cropsey's *Catskill Mountain House* or Cole's *View of the White Mountains* (1839) would become resorts, villages, towns and cities. Permeating the exhibition is a sense of ineffable melancholy. Fitz Hugh Lane's small-scale and meticulously painted view of schooners on Penobscot Bay in Maine is a case in point. It is dusk. A few pink-tinged cirrus clouds are disappearing in the soft mauve sky. In the absolute stillness, an evening chill ripples the water. The moment is passing even as we watch. But look closely at the schooner, and you notice its cargo – timber being shipped to eastern cities from northern logging camps. As the cities grow, the forest disappears.

I don't mean it as a criticism when I say that such moments of intense, inner illumination are as rare in *American Sublime* as they are in American culture. As the exhibition moves towards its climax, the pictures become bigger, more elaborate and more thunderous in their effects, until in the last two galleries, devoted to Church, Moran and Bierstadt, many are almost indistinguishable from theatrical backdrops. I am thinking of mural-sized works such as Bierstadt's Wagnerian vista *Storm in the Rocky Mountains – Mt Rosalie*, or Church's awe-inspiring masterpiece, *The Icebergs*. But then the quality of the works chosen is remarkable. In one gallery alone, three of the supreme masterpieces of American art hang together: Church's *The Andes of Ecuador*, *Cotopaxi* and *Rainy Season in the Tropics*. *American Sublime* is wonderful. An exhibition I shall return to again and again.

Manet and the Sea

In June 1864, in the closing months of the American Civil War, all France was enthralled by accounts of a deadly naval skirmish between a Yankee and a Rebel warship off the coast of northern France. On the afternoon of 19 June, spectators climbed into boats or rushed to cliffs above Cherbourg, hoping to witness the historic confrontation between the Union corvette *Kearsarge* and the Confederate raider *Alabama*. It is not clear what, if anything, they could see from the land, but, when the guns fell silent, the whole world learned that the ironclad steamship *Kearsarge* had sunk the *Alabama* with the loss of several lives.

The Battle of the USS Kearsarge and the CSS Alabama was Edouard Manet's first attempt to paint the sea. Though a dedicated Parisian, he had been familiar with ships and the sea from his teenage years, when he had sailed to Brazil to gain the experience necessary to pass into the naval academy. He had not seen the exchange of fire between the two American ships, but, like everyone else in France, he had read accounts of it in the press. Working in his Paris studio from written descriptions, sketches, possibly from photographs, and above all from his imagination, he quickly completed his four-foot-square canvas. Speed was important because, by mid-July, less than a month after the battle, the picture was on public display in a shop window in Paris.

Purporting to be Manet's despatch from the front line, *The Battle of the USS Kearsarge and the CSS Alabama* is painting as journalism. As exciting as the morning headlines, it was intended to grab the attention of the man on the street with an 'eyewitness' description of an event everyone was still talking about. There hadn't been a naval engagement in European waters for more than half a century, well before the invention of the steamship. Manet, therefore, counted on the novelty of his depiction of modern warfare to attract the public's attention.

30 June 2004

Edouard Manet:
Impressions of the Sea

Van Gogh Museum,
Amsterdam

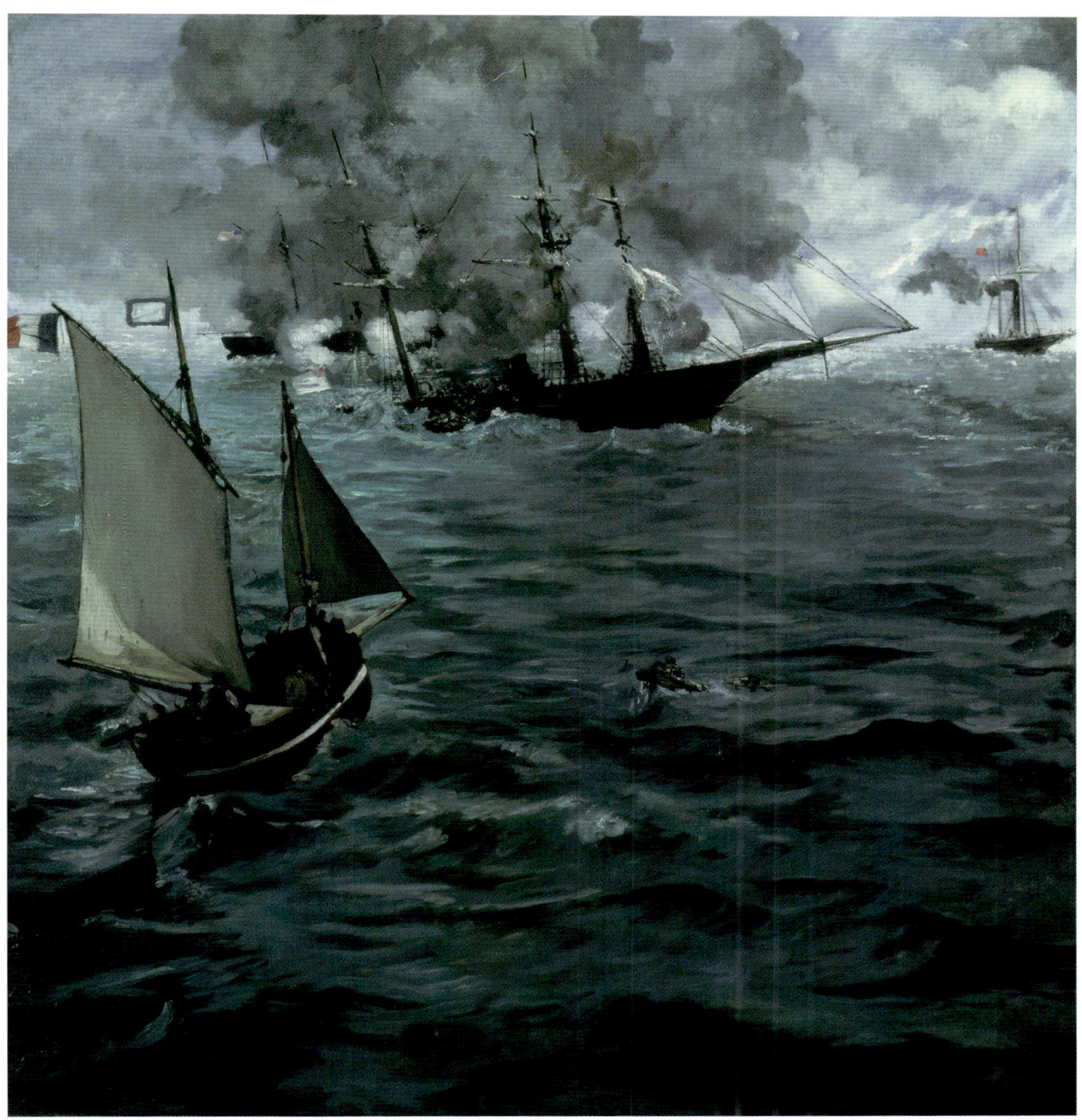

In this respect, *The Kearsarge and the Alabama* was precursor to another of Manet's crowd-pulling, up-to-the-minute illustrations of a news story that would engross all France – his *Execution of the Emperor Maximilian* of 1867. In *The Kearsarge and the Alabama*, Manet breaks with the conventions of maritime painting by establishing the horizon line near the top of the picture. This in turn tilts the picture plane upwards, and enables the painter to deploy his ships and figures over the flat field of colour used to represent the sea. The high

viewpoint conveys the sensation that we, too, are on the cliffs above
Cherbourg looking out over the disturbed sea, which Manet paints
with rhythmically repeated strokes of black and aquamarine paint,
a tapestry of colour brushed on to the canvas upwards and sideways
with a syncopated, rocky action of the hand. Look for a few minutes,
and you may begin to feel seasick.

In the tradition of depicting scenes of maritime warfare that
began in seventeenth-century Holland and was very much alive in
nineteenth-century France, it was imperative that the artist showed
clearly the insignia, design and size of the opposing ships. How else
could the viewer understand how they engaged in battle? Manet
ignores that convention, emphasising instead the confusion and
chaos that those who witness naval combat experience. Omitting a
foreground to lead our eye gradually into the picture, Manet plunges
us headlong into the action. Knocked off-balance by the vertiginous
viewpoint and confused by the clouds of cannon smoke obscuring the
combatants, we have difficulty making sense of the scene in front of
us. Which ship is the *Kearsarge*? Which the *Alabama*? After a moment
or two, we figure out that that the three-masted ship sinking stern first
at the top of the picture must be the *Alabama*, and that clouds of steam
and smoke hide the Union ship.

Depictions of naval battles tend to be static. Manet creates drama
and movement in his picture by including the little sailboat flying
the French tricolour in the foreground. Ploughing through the waves,
it races to rescue survivors of the *Alabama*, who cling to a capsized
lifeboat at the right. The dinghy towed by this sailboat, and the
American flag flying from the *Kearsarge*, help us to piece together the
unfolding drama, and help, too, to convey the impression that Manet
was actually there. Like all the best reportage, everything about the
picture is urgent and specific and says to the viewer: 'I saw this.'

The Alabama and the Kearsarge perfectly demonstrates what was
so new, so fresh, so modern about Manet's art. The flattening of the
pictorial space, the use of an aquamarine so strong it requires a black
of equal intensity to balance it, the refusal to clarify the action, the
sheer modernity of the subject: all this broke new ground in the
history of art. Yet balancing these innovations, Manet was thoroughly
conservative when it came to the accurate rendering of the masts and
rigging on a sailing ship. The boats in his pictures are real, solid, three-

dimensional forms, firmly held in place by that unearthly shade of aquamarine he invariably uses to render the sea.

No artist more perfectly conveys the smack of a salty sea breeze, fresh cold wind in your face, the exhilaration of a boat under full sail, the bustling excitement of a passenger ship's departure or arrival. It is not quite true to say that the sea is the subject of his pictures, because, unlike Courbet, Whistler or Monet, he rarely paints it on its own, untouched by a human presence.

Whether in his achingly beautiful nocturne, *Moonlight, Boulogne-sur-mer*, in which cold moonlight shines down through turbulent clouds over figures huddled on blackened docks, or in the thrilling *Escape of Rochefort*, for Manet the sea is a place that any schoolboy would recognise – a place of adventure, intrigue and romance. His closest affinities are with R. L. Stevenson and Conrad if you like, not with Whistler and Debussy. Manet painted about forty sea paintings, one tenth of his total *oeuvre*. More than thirty of these are on show alongside work by Whistler, Courbet, Monet, Renoir, Boudin and Jongkind in the Van Gogh Museum's magnificent *Edouard Manet: Impressions of the Sea*.

The intelligent, purposeful juxtapositions reveal the extraordinary interdependence of these artists. The show is like a visual fugue, with each artist in different ways and at different times in their careers borrowing ideas first explored by others. The clearest example is the give and take between Whistler and Manet, but the exceptionally beautiful installation allows us to follow Manet's creative process from picture to picture as he engages with each of the artists with whom he came into contact.

Manet's *Luncheon in the Studio*

Edouard Manet's *Luncheon in the Studio* from Munich's Neue Pinakothek is one of those pictures that are easy to look at but difficult to fathom. It's a large painting, a metre by a metre and a half – about the same size as Manet's famous *A Bar at the Folies-Bergère*, which is being shown directly opposite it in a small show at the Courtauld Gallery. Each shows a figure, close to and in sharp focus, looking out from the canvas as though the person exists in a space somewhere between the sketchily painted background of the picture and the one in which we viewers are standing. Although the tonality of *Luncheon* is more sombre than that of *A Bar at the Folies-Bergère*, it is easy to imagine the startling visual impact the pictures made when hung amid rows of brown academic paintings at the Paris Salons of 1869 and 1882.

The situation in *Luncheon* is obvious. A young man has risen from the table after lunch to pose for the artist, turning his back on the gentleman still finishing his coffee and cigar at the right, and the serving woman who comes in with a silver coffee pot at the left. The boy stands so close to the picture plane that his legs are cropped below the knees, blandly looking out of the picture, but without making eye contact with us. Like the enigmatic barmaid in *A Bar at the Folies-Bergère*, the figure is fascinating because of Manet's paradoxical ability to combine physical proximity and emotional distance, his tantalising mixture of intimacy and detachment.

But what kind of picture are we looking at? A genre subject? A narrative? A portrait? Psychologically, there is nothing particularly fraught in what is happening – a bored teenager is posing for the artist with as little enthusiasm as my nephews muster when I insist on taking their photograph at a family gathering. I'm not at all sure that knowing the identity of the sitter is necessary for understanding the picture, but it is certainly very interesting.

24 November 2004

Manet Face to Face

Courtauld Gallery, London

He is Léon Koëlla-Leenhoff, the son of Manet's wife Suzanne
Leenhoff, a Dutch woman who had entered the Manet household
to teach piano to young Edouard and his brother. The identity of the
boy's father is still a matter of speculation, but our best guess is that
it was Manet's father, a distinguished judge. In 1863, the year after the
death of the elder Manet, Edouard married Suzanne, thereby making
the eleven-year-old Léon his stepson as well as his half-brother. The
child posed often for Manet, most famously as *The Boy with a Sword*
of 1861.

What is relevant to understanding the picture is that, in the
summer of 1868, the sixteen-year-old Léon had just taken his first job,
as a runner for the banking house of Degas's father. For I believe that
he is wearing clothes purchased with his first wages. The short black
velvet coat, striped shirt and tie, straw hat, and corduroy trousers look
brand new, at least in comparison with the visibly frayed velvet coat
the barmaid wears in *A Bar at the Folies-Bergère*. I wonder whether
Manet was amused (or perhaps touched) to see Léon's new purchases,
for, to my eye, the boy is as fastidious about his appearance as only a
sixteen-year-old can be. The expression on his face has been described
as 'snobbish' and aloof, but I see something different – a sense that
this boy is not yet secure in his own identity.

We can all think of many representations of convivial lunches
in Impressionist paintings by Renoir and Monet as though we had
glimpsed a moment from real life. But the minute you start to examine
Manet's picture closely, you realise that it was formally posed, an
obvious studio concoction. Manet may be a great realist painter,
but nothing about the details of the painting are realistic. There is no
restaurant in Europe where you'd find a pile of armour like the one
at the left, and I doubt that a man in Manet's circle would keep his
hat on while dining indoors.

In fact, Manet began his canvas while staying at the Folkestone
Hotel in Boulogne during the summer of 1868, but finished it back
in his studio in Paris. X-rays reveal the figure of a woman, probably
Suzanne, standing at the left, looking across to the seated man. A large
greyhound once filled the foreground, held on a short leash by Léon.
But the presence of the mother and the family pet would instantly
have turned the picture into a conventional family group. Manet
rubbed them out because he had no wish to paint the kind of 'slice

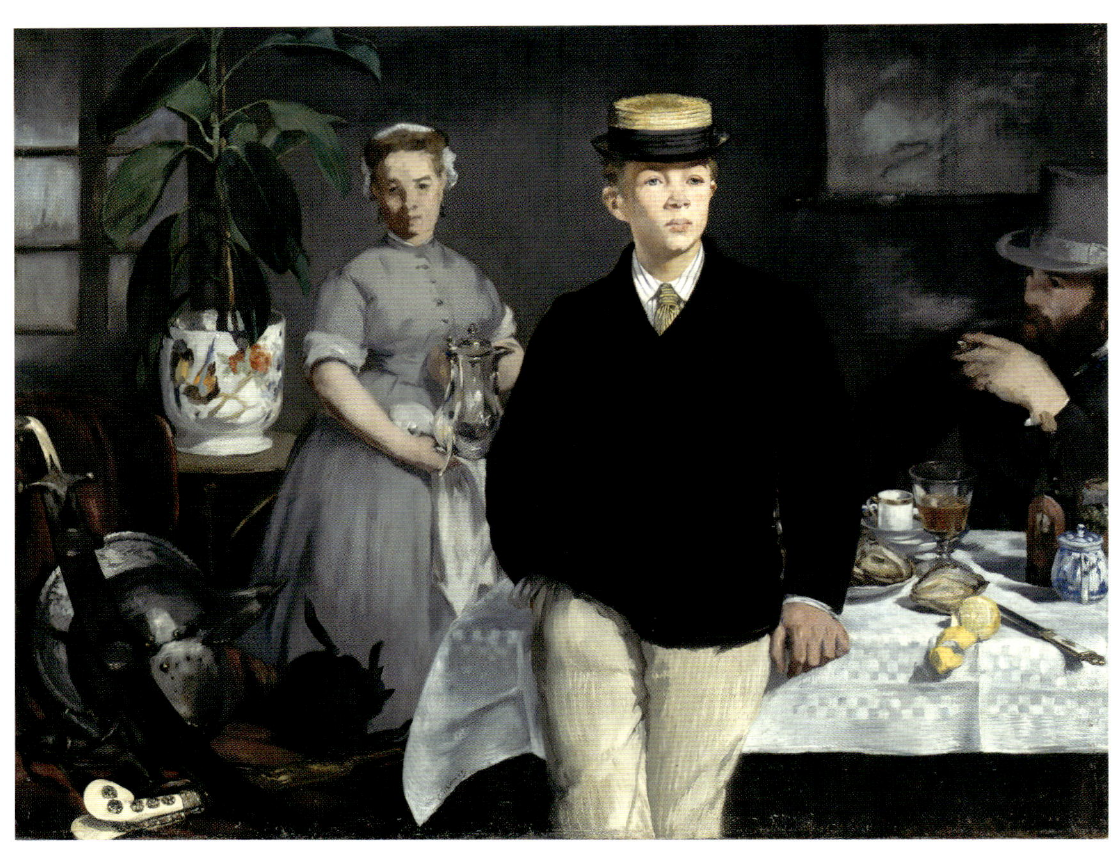

Edouard Manet
Luncheon in the Studio, *1868*
Neue Pinakothek,
Munich

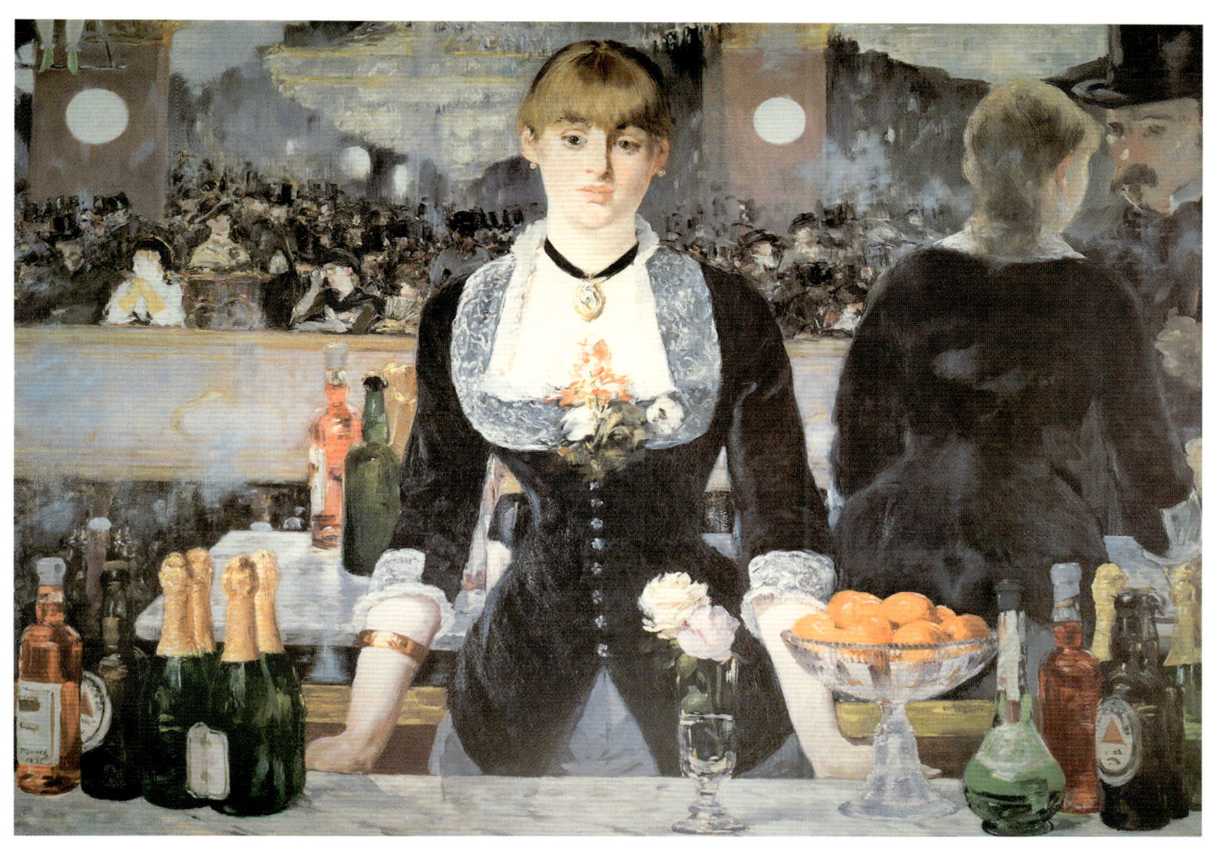

Edouard Manet
A Bar at the Folies-Bergère, *1882*
Courtauld Institute
of Art, London

of life' beloved of the Impressionists, from whom he always kept his distance. He wanted us to see three people modelling for him in a studio filled with props.

For, as with his early masterpieces *Olympia* and *Déjeuner sur l'herbe*, the subject of *Luncheon* can be explained only by reference to the Old Masters. Once you stop trying to find a narrative connecting the people in the picture, you discover that Manet has taken us on a tour through the history of art, from the delicious still life paying homage to Dutch seventeenth-century master Pieter Claesz and the wall map that evokes Vermeer, to the superbly painted Renaissance helmet, ivory-handled rifle and scimitar that would have interested both romantics and Orientalists. Manet acknowledges the craze for Japonisme in the white jardinière lusciously painted with brightly coloured flowers and birds at the left. There is also, I think, a glance across the Channel to Manet's friend and rival Whistler in the view of a smudged sailboat and steamship through the window.

As soon as our brains tell us there is no story to unravel, our eyes are free to feast on the way Manet's brush conjures up the exquisitely painted lemon, the hard texture of the twisting rind a brighter, drier yellow than that used for the pulp. We luxuriate in the way Manet conjures up the red wine in the clear glass, the gold rim of the white coffee cup, the striations in the blue-and-white sugar bowl, and the subtly repeated pattern in the tablecloth. We scan the picture not for clues as to the relationship between the boy and the seated man, but in order to marvel at the way in which the whole design of birds and flowers in the jardinière is created with flicks and touches of blue, black, yellow and red. And oh, that wonderful black cat grooming itself against the soft grey of the serving woman's skirt!

Across the gallery, *A Bar at the Folies-Bergère* contains its own enigmas, and passages of sheer visual delight, but because that picture is always here in London, it's the presence of *Luncheon* here that should encourage you to head down to Somerset House to see this little gem of a show.

Winslow Homer

Winslow Homer is the great storyteller of nineteenth-century American art. That's what he's doing in his 1884 canvas *The Life Line*, the dramatic climax of Dulwich Picture Gallery's groundbreaking exhibition *Winslow Homer: Poet of the Sea*. The picture shows the rescue of a woman from a ship that has foundered on the rocky New England coast. A fishing boat or coastguard cutter (just out of sight) has thrown a lifeline to the stricken vessel, and one of the sailors has made the perilous journey between the two boats to take the passengers to safety on a stout seat, which is suspended from rope and drawn along by a pulley.

At first we assume the woman has been taken from the water. In fact, she has fainted from sheer terror. And no wonder. The two figures are only a few feet above the waves, inching along the lifeline to the rescue vessel, when a gust of wind blows the woman's scarlet scarf up into the seaman's face. At this critical moment, halfway between the two boats, he can't see what he is doing and can't remove the scarf because he needs both arms to hold on to the woman. Nothing I saw on television last week was half as exciting.

But, unlike TV, Homer's picture attributes no romantic or sexual overtones to the sailor's desperate struggle to save the swooning woman. He undercuts such a reading by showing the woman's dress hoisted up over her stockings to expose her thighs, thus depriving her of grace as well as dignity, even as he deprives her rescuer of his identity by covering his face. Homer is a realist painter and this is real life, an incident he witnessed off the New Jersey coast. To emphasise the mortal danger of the work it depicts, Homer omits a foreground, and so we viewers look down in the lethal waves just below us.

Homer's ability to choose compelling images, coupled with his relative lack of interest in the execution of the work, are qualities you will find again and again in American art from Edward Hopper to

7 March 2006

Winslow Homer:
Poet of the Sea

Dulwich Picture Gallery,
London

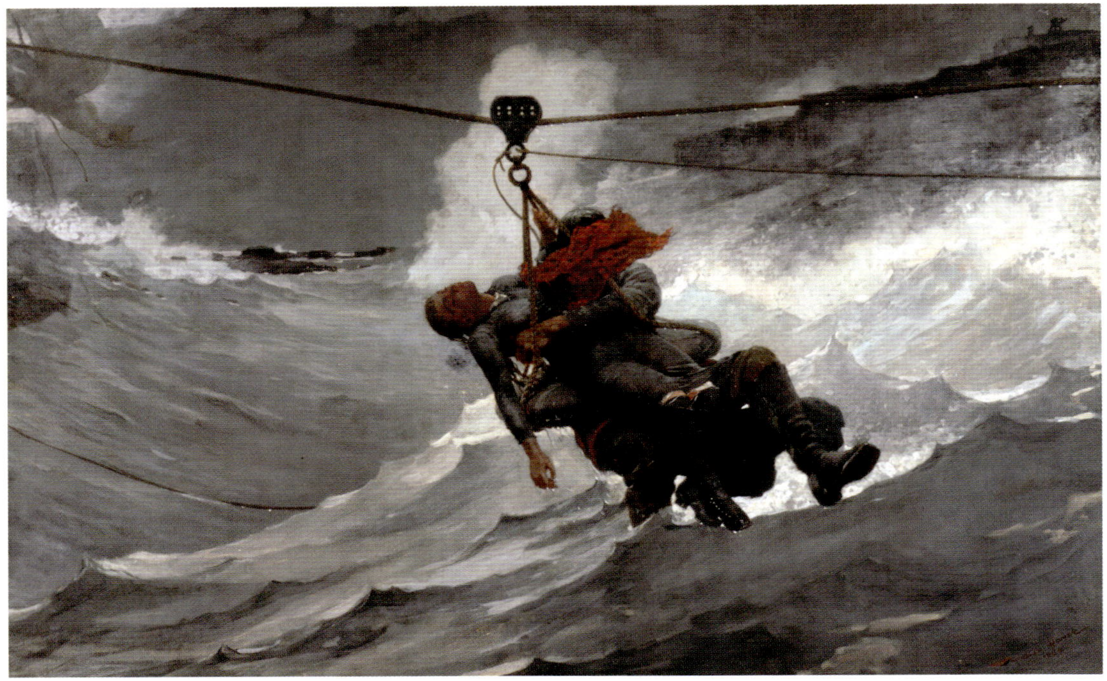

Andy Warhol. This is because all of these artists started their careers as illustrators. Homer, who was self-taught, made his name during the American Civil War, when his vivid illustrated reports from the front appeared in *Scribner's Monthly* and *Harper's Weekly* magazines.

As it happens, one of his early Civil War paintings is on view in London right now, at the National Gallery's *Americans in Paris* exhibition. Painted a year after the war ended, *Prisoners from the Front* shows a young Union officer confronting three Confederate prisoners in a Virginia landscape devastated by battle. Although Homer is a masterful draughtsman and brings both compassion and psychological insight into the depiction of these men, his actual handling of paint is uncertain. For this very reason, he spent a year in Paris between 1866 and 1867, in an attempt to learn the craft of painting. But, unlike his compatriots in Paris, he never studied with a master like Gérôme, but spent his time in the Louvre, learning directly from the Old Masters.

Perhaps this is precisely why Homer was able to preserve his imaginative response to nature and to prevent his art from being stifled by academic sterility. But it also meant that he did not master

Winslow Homer
The Life Line, *1884*
Philadelphia Museum of Art

the craft of painting until very late in his career. As a commendably honest essay in the catalogue of the Dulwich exhibition points out, his background as an illustrator taught him how to choose a compelling image, to create a powerful composition and to achieve a balance in tonal values – but only late in the day did he attain technical mastery of his medium, whether in oil or watercolour.

Homer went back to the US too soon. A few more years of European study would have equipped him with painterly skills you don't find in the great majority of pictures on view at Dulwich. In the US, Homer is considered a great watercolourist. But, when you see his work in this country, where great artists who used watercolour include Turner, Cotman and Cox, it is hard to agree. And, even if his American patrons didn't know this, Homer did.

In mid-career he sought new sources of inspiration in Europe. Unlike the majority of his contemporaries, he headed not for France but for England. Between 1881 and 1883 he lived in the fishing village of Cullercoats, in the north-east. Here he painted and drew the fishermen and their women living along this bleak coast. To Homer, they must have been as exotic as their counterparts were to French artists painting in Brittany – or for that matter Tahiti. His studies of women standing isolated against the sky or mending nets fundamentally changed the direction of his work as an artist.

After his return to America, he melded his great gifts as a reporter with his knowledge of the sea to paint some of the best-known and best-loved images in American art. Alas, the greatest of these, *The Gulf Stream*, is missing from this show. Without it, it is hard to understand why during his lifetime Americans regarded Homer as their greatest living painter. Still, you catch a whiff of greatness in wonderfully detailed watercolours such as *Sponge Fishermen, Bahamas*. And in *The Painter Eliphalet Terry Fishing* he exhibits his knack for capturing evening light in the green, white and blue reflections in the rose-tinted water.

Cézanne: *The Card Players*

Cézanne's series of paintings *The Card Players* is the cornerstone of his work between 1890 and 1895, and the prelude to the explosive creative achievement of his last years. It was a simple but inspired idea for the Courtauld Gallery to bring together three of the five versions of the picture and to display them alongside the preparatory studies in pencil, watercolour and oil. In addition, three of Cézanne's most powerful portraits, all showing one of the models Cézanne used for *The Card Players*, complete our understanding of how he worked during this crucial period.

Although it isn't a big show, we emerge more aware than ever of the complexity of Cézanne's art, but no nearer to penetrating the enigma of Cézanne himself. All we can do is to stand back and watch the artist's thought processes over a span of five years, as he casts a critical eye over a finished canvas, decides that he can do something to improve it, starts another canvas, fails again, but fails better. Moving from picture to picture, we can see how he corrects and strengthens perceived weaknesses, as in each attempt he tries to find monumentality, simplicity and pictorial unity.

The 1880s was a period of synthesis and consolidation in his art, when he moved decisively away from Impressionism to paint compositions in which he used verticals, horizontals and diagonals both to build up mass and to establish structure. In the views of Mont Sainte-Victoire, form and volume emerge out of faceted planes of colour applied with short strokes of a loaded brush.

The first question to ask ourselves is what interested Cézanne about the subject of men sitting around a table playing cards? Of all of the categories into which academic theory divided painting, genre subjects were among the least prestigious. The theme of the card players was not particularly common in art at this date, and Cézanne's treatment of it has nothing to do with the rowdy tavern

26 October 2010

Cézanne: *The Card Players*

Courtauld Gallery, London

scenes popular in seventeenth-century Dutch and French art.

Here is what I think happened. As he considered tackling a genre subject, he must have asked himself how he could show several figures interacting naturally with one another and yet retain the architectonic structure that permeates his paintings of static landscapes and inert still lifes. The answer was to show a scene from everyday life in which nobody moves – a card game. In what other subject could several men be shown sitting around a table facing each other without talking, gesturing or even looking up? In a card game, each player studies the hand he has been dealt so intently that his lack of movement and the absence of even the slightest expressive reaction to his opponents looks quite natural. The subject of a card game was as close as Cézanne could find to a human still life.

The show starts in 1890, with the first version of *The Card Players*, now in the Metropolitan Museum of Art. In it, Cézanne shows three agricultural labourers seated at a plain table, watched by a fourth figure standing behind them. Cézanne turns the men (who worked on his family estate in Aix-en-Provence and whom he knew by name) into objects of no more or less importance than a bottle or a glass in a still life. They do not move, and if they think they do not show it.

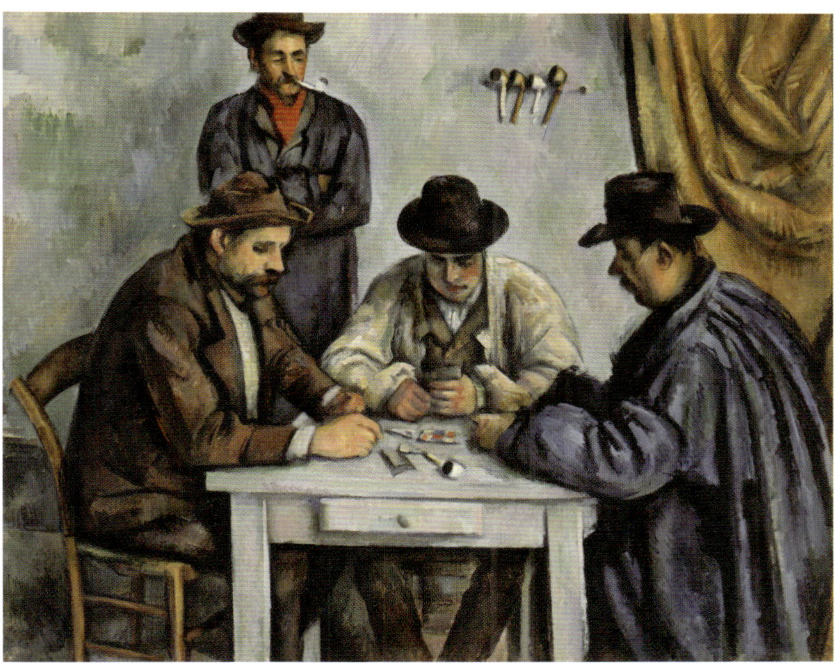

Paul Cézanne
The Card Players,
1890–92
Metropolitan Museum
of Art, New York

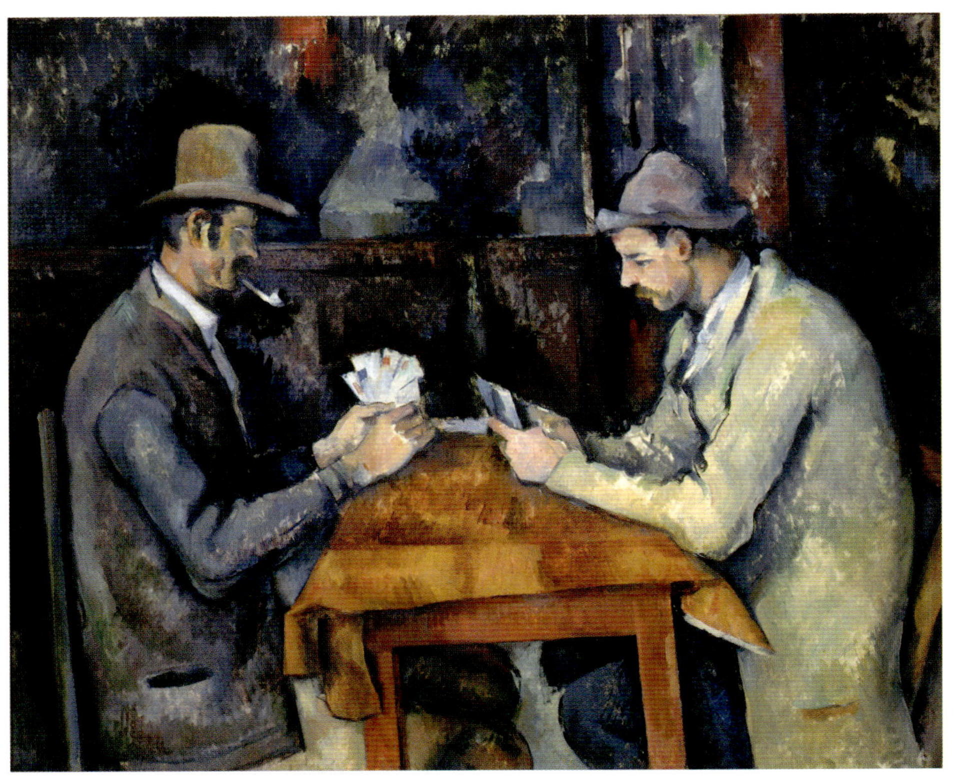

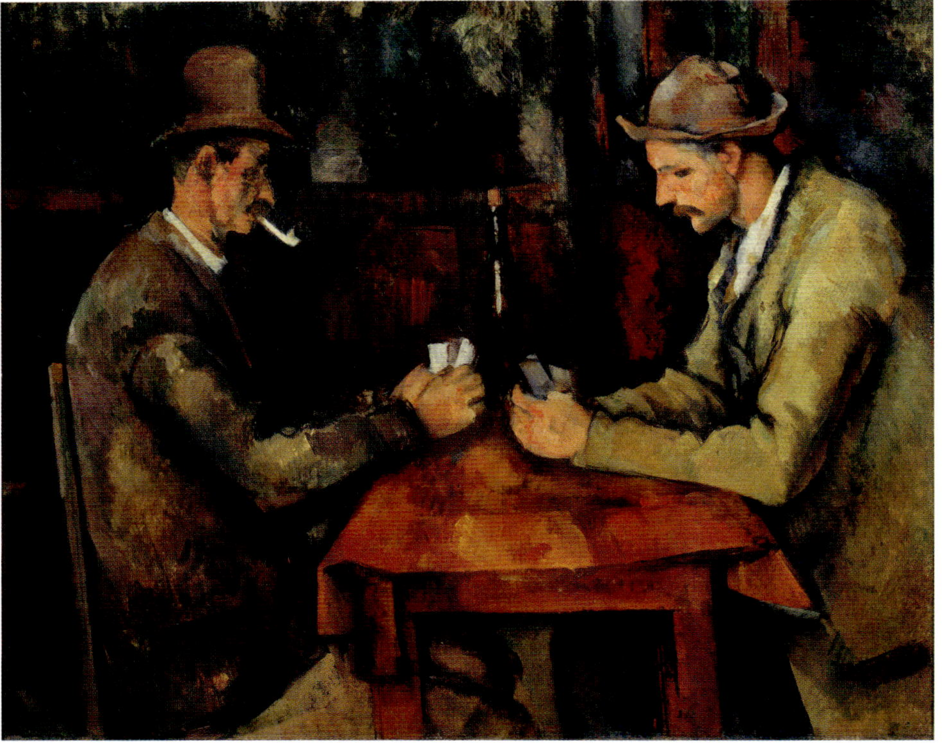

Already in place are two important elements in the composition that he would not change – the curved backs of the two monumental figures who sit like brackets on either side of the table, and the ambiguous setting – a bare room that could be a tavern, a domestic interior or the artist's studio. Recent technical examination confirms what the eye tells us: that Cézanne drew and painted each model separately, then with great difficulty combined the four figures on the canvas.

In the finished picture, the dense mass of the three men bent over their game is alleviated by playful details like the *trompe l'oeil* rack of pipes on the wall and the open drawer in the foreground. The dark tones of the men's clothing are relieved with accents of red, and in a passage of bravura painting, Cézanne adds a medley of green, blue, grey, white and yellow brushstrokes on the wall at the left. These animated washes of colours suggest Provençal light and air flooding into the room through an unseen window or door.

Yet Cézanne was right to be dissatisfied. The picture is flawed because it is too ambitious. Whereas ambiguous spatial transitions are fascinating in his still lifes and landscapes, when they occur in a figure painting they only serve to confuse and distract the viewer. Here, it is impossible to decide where the standing man is in relation either to the card players or to the far wall. What I think happened is that Cézanne realised that all of the picture's visual interest was concentrated in the lower half and in the foreground. The standing man, like the pipe rack and the swag of drapery, were added to draw the eye upward and into depth.

By the time he came to paint the versions of the picture in the Courtauld Gallery and the Musée d'Orsay, Cézanne realised that the solution to his conundrum was to reduce the number of card players from three to two. Now there are no spectators and nothing on the table apart from a single wine bottle. Like a sculptor who eliminates all extraneous detail, Cézanne freed himself to deal with formal problems such as the picture's spatial structure and compositional stability. These two later versions move painting into new realms of visual experience. Cézanne had already suppressed facial expression, gesture and anecdote. Now he minimises texture, limits the depth of field, and restricts his palette to ochre, greys, browns and blues.

The two players face each other across a plain table covered with a simple cloth, sitting at a slight angle to the picture plane. Behind them, the diagonal of the brown wainscoting tilts upward to the right, counterbalancing the table's downward slope. Not a single line in the picture is straight, including the vertical of the mirror's edge at the right, the table legs and the wine bottle. And yet we don't feel seasick, because each pull in one direction is counterbalanced by a tug in the other. Notice that one hat rim curves downward, the other up, or how the two men's jacket pockets are 'rhymed' with the diagonals formed by their arms.

The background has been reduced to a dark blur, while the figures fill the painting almost edge to edge, immeasurably increasing the mystery, tension and sense of claustrophobia. Gone are all still life details. Whereas in the early version at the Met and one in the Barnes Collection (which is not in the exhibition) we are still in a world Courbet could have painted, what Cézanne is doing in these latter canvases is unprecedented. When they were finally shown after Cézanne's death, they opened the gateway to Cubism.

Renoir at the Theatre

Why do people go to opening nights at the theatre, opera and art galleries? The answer is: to see and to be seen. That, in a nutshell, is what is happening in Pierre-Auguste Renoir's magical painting *La Loge* ('The box at the theatre'), the subject of a small, old-fashioned 'art-in-context' exhibition, focusing on this Impressionist masterpiece from the permanent collection at the Courtauld Gallery.

Painted in 1874 and shown in the first Impressionist exhibition of that year, it depicts a fashionable couple seated in the best seats at the theatre or opera. We can't know whether the curtain has already gone up because at this date house lights were not dimmed. We viewers see the anonymous man and woman from the same level across the amphitheatre and in close-up, implying that we are seated opposite and watching them through opera glasses.

Two things are happening simultaneously: one active, the other passive. The man raises his binoculars to look to the upper balconies, presumably to get a closer look at a beautiful woman. But his wife (or more probably mistress) sits perfectly still, her opera glasses in one gloved hand and her fan and handkerchief in the other, with a slight smile playing on her lips. Her gaze is unfocused, as though she is lost in thought, unaware of being observed. This last detail is important because it reinforces the idea that we are watching her from a distance through binoculars. Since she isn't conscious of our interest, we can feast our eyes on her slightly blowsy beauty, which is set off to perfection by her ravishing dress, jewels and flowers.

Parisian cartoonists had long been having fun with the subject of romantic and social carryings-on in boxes at the theatre, but Renoir was among the first artists to treat the theme, which he saw as part of the spectacle of modern life in the big city. When we look at the picture, he wants us to be intrigued by this pair and to ask ourselves who they are and what is happening between them. Though Renoir

11 March 2008

Renoir at the Theatre: Looking at *La Loge*

Courtauld Gallery, London

leaves the woman's precise social status unclear, her heavy use of cosmetics and deep décolletage suggests that she is *une demi-mondaine*. That he was acutely sensitive to social nuances of this sort is suggested by another painting in this show in which a lady who is plainly from the highest level of society is shown in a box at the opera wearing a demure black evening gown without jewels or face paint.

The woman in *La Loge* is not in her first youth. Her lover or protector has begun to look at other women, and she may not have much time left to find his successor. If (as I believe) she is meant to be seen as a courtesan, then her passive demeanour has a purpose – she is signalling her availability by displaying her charms for all to see, well aware that the eyes of every man in the theatre are on her.

And how could you not look at such a dazzling creature? As Aileen Ribeiro explains in her informative catalogue essay, the woman in the picture is dressed in the height of fashion in a silk gown of eighteenth-century inspiration called a *polonaise*. On the back of her chair we catch a glimpse of her ermine wrap, and she wears flowers in her hair and a corsage inserted into a tiny vial of water at her bosom. It is difficult to tell whether those are diamonds in her ears and pearls around her neck because Renoir handles paint so freely that they could just as easily be glass.

La Loge is candy floss, confectionery in paint. Renoir uses rivers of flowing black paint to create the bold stripes running down the silk dress, and the white of that dress isn't really white but white mixed with light blue, so that the overall effect is not, as it technically should be, a black and white painting, but a blur of blues and pinks with little zings of yellow-gold.

For all his virtuosity here, from a technical point of view Renoir is the most uneven of all the Impressionists. He painted too much and too quickly and didn't destroy works that really should never have seen the light of day. Even in this small exhibition, the quality of his painting lurches wildly between pictures that Renoir expended time and thought on, and those he didn't. Compare *La Loge*, for example, with a small-scale replica hanging next to it. It is so slapdash in its execution that the surface looks like a bar of soap that's melted in the bath.

Mary Cassatt is a much more consistent painter, who was also attracted to the subject of the theatre. Indeed, her *At the Français, a*

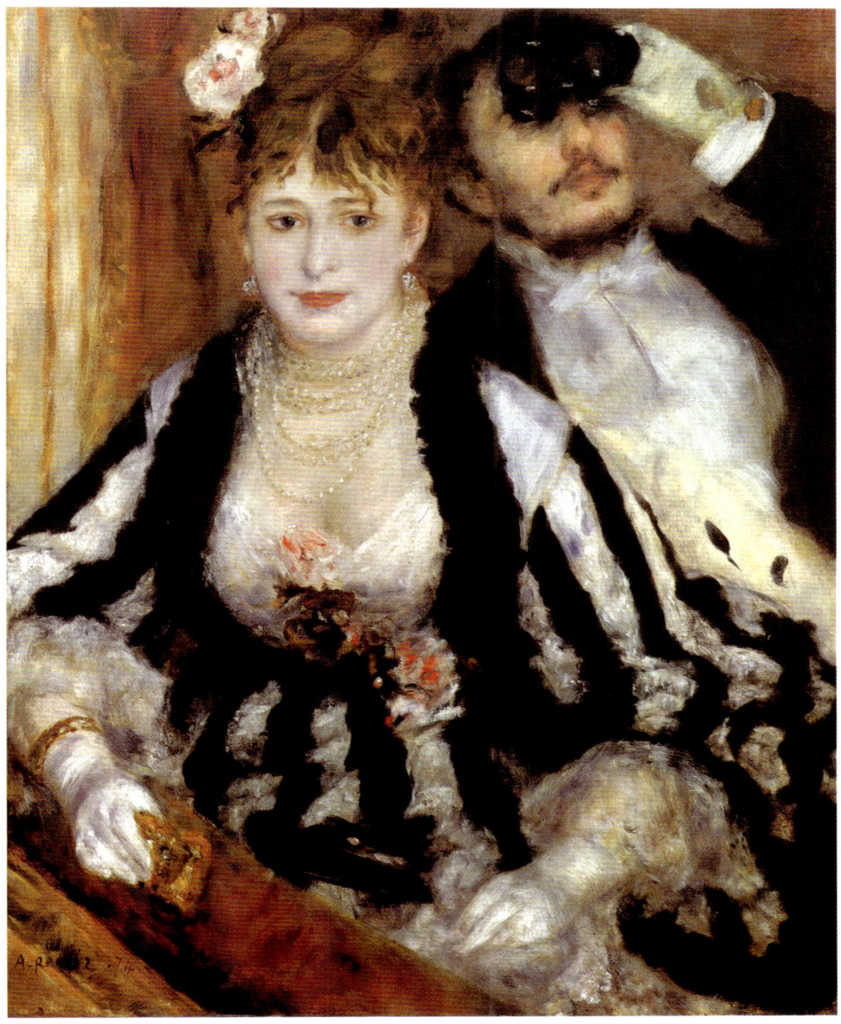

Sketch looks to me like a direct response to Renoir's *La Loge*. For here a woman (who may be a widow because she is dressed entirely in black) is seen in a theatre box on her own, assertively using her opera glasses to see what's happening on the stage, unaware that she is the object of intense scrutiny by a man in a distant box, who is so frantic to get a good look at her that he leans out over the ledge of the box with his binoculars glued to his eyes. Cassatt contrasts her intelligence and dignity with behaviour that is not just boorish but subtly threatening because, unlike the woman in *La Loge*, she is genuinely unconscious of what is happening.

Henri Rousseau

One of the more obscure delights of Paris is the Palais des Mirages, an extravagant *son et lumière* housed at the back of the Musée Grévin, the waxwork museum located on the city's once fashionable thoroughfare, the Grands Boulevards. Originally created for the Paris World's Fair of 1900 to introduce the French public to the wonders of electric lighting, it was bought intact by the museum in 1901 and transported to the 4th *arondissement*, where it has delighted adults and children ever since.

Performances (on the half hour) begin when visitors are ushered into a windowless chamber. As the room darkens, coloured lights begin to play on walls lined from floor to ceiling with distorting mirrors. At first we find ourselves in an enchanted forest surrounded by murmuring leaves and the cries of wild birds. Then, to the crash of thunder and the sound of driving rain, the scene changes to become a jungle in the monsoon. At the climax, flashes of 'lightning' illuminate the interior, and, to the squeals of children, a dozen stuffed pythons drop down from the ceiling, stopping just above our heads. It is all great fun, and utterly of its period, which was one of technological innovation coupled with colonial expansion. At the very moment when Parisians saw their first electric lamp, motor car and airship, they also experienced the frisson of contact with people and animals from Africa and the East.

I have no idea whether Henri Rousseau ever visited the Palais des Mirages, but its very existence is a clue as to how we should look at the art of this most enigmatic of French painters. For Rousseau is both innocent and knowing. The animals in his pictures are no more intended to represent real beasts than the *son et lumière* resembles an actual jungle, and yet he artfully manipulates his audience, so that images that initially make us smile eventually cause us to feel uneasy. This remarkable artist – one of the most influential of the whole

8 November 2005

Henri Rousseau: Jungles in Paris

Tate Modern, London

twentieth century – is the focus of a full-scale exhibition at Tate Modern.

Henri Rousseau was born in 1844 in a small market town in north-west France, the son of an ironmonger. In the 1870s he held down a job as a clerk in the Paris customs house (hence his nickname Le Douanier, the Customs Inspector), but for most of his life he was a reasonably successful amateur painter who lived a life of pinched semi-respectability in a suburb of Paris. In 1893 he was able to retire on a modest pension to devote the last sixteen years of his life to his art, which was admired and collected by a circle of avant-garde artists and poets that included Pablo Picasso, Robert Delaunay, Guillaume Apollinaire and Wassily Kandinsky.

Rousseau had no formal training, but learnt his technique by copying paintings in the Louvre and also by seeking the advice of successful academic artists such as Emmanuel Frémiet and Jean-Léon Gérôme. Though some critics ridiculed his faux-naïf work, from the beginning there were those who realised how sophisticated it really was. In 1886 he exhibited his *Carnival Evening* at the Salon des Indépendants, which was seen and admired by no less a critic than Félix Vallotton.

This moonlit nocturne, in which a black Pierrot, smoking a cigarette, strolls with his dusky Columbine at the edge of a forest in winter, has all the ineffable sadness of a Watteau. And yet, the longer you look at this exquisite and apparently innocent scene, the more menacing it feels. It's hard to put your finger on what is wrong, but it has to do with the isolation of the little figures, the bare branches of the trees, and a night sky irradiated by milky moonlight.

Five years later Rousseau exhibited *Tiger in a Tropical Storm (Surprised!)*, a jungle scene in which all the stylistic elements we associate with his mature paintings are already in place. A lively pattern of dense jungle foliage keeps the eye on the surface of the picture. Light falls evenly on hard, clear outlines. There are no shading, no shadows and no aerial perspective.

From a distance, the work looks like a tapestry because no part of the canvas is given greater visual emphasis than any other. Though the snarling tiger is probably copied from a Japanese scroll painting, it looks like a paper cut-out pasted on to a flat stage backdrop. This cartoon creature wouldn't scare a mouse. Like Rousseau's paper

moons and cardboard skies, it exists in a land of make-believe. What
sets Rousseau apart from the many orientalist painters who flourished
in turn-of-the-century Paris is this sense of fantasy, carried off with
absolute conviction.

In 1891 Rousseau stopped painting jungle scenes, only to resume
again in 1904. According to Christopher Green in his excellent
catalogue essay, the reason isn't hard to fathom. In 1903 Paul Gauguin
died, and the following year Parisians saw a retrospective of his work.
Stimulated by Gauguin's exotic pictures of the South Seas (and also by
the prices they were beginning to fetch), Rousseau started to paint his
own versions. But, unlike Gauguin, Rousseau had never left France,
and so found his jungles in illustrated magazines, and his wild
animals in the Jardin des Plantes and among the stuffed animals
in the Zoological Galleries. This is where he saw the 'Senegal Lion
Devouring an Antelope', a startlingly realistic taxidermy tableau
that he used for his 1906 painting *The Hungry Lion Throws Itself on
the Antelope*. Both the painting and the stuffed animals are in this
exhibition.

Typically, Rousseau set the scene in a jungle of unearthly beauty
populated by two flesh-eating birds, a jaguar in a tree, and a weird
creature with a gorilla's body and a crow's head watching the scene
from the depths of the forest. Inimitably, when he came to depict the
dying antelope, Rousseau added one beautifully painted tear. That
last detail suggests the all-important role of Rousseau's visual
imagination in his creative process. Apollinaire tells us that Rousseau
had 'such a strong sense of reality that when he painted a fantastic
subject, he was sometimes terrified and, trembling, obliged to open
the window'. Just look at the care with which each leaf in every tree
is painted, how each is given its own shade of green, black or brown.
There isn't an inch of this jungle that Rousseau hasn't pictured in his
mind's eye before lovingly delineating it.

For me Rousseau's greatness lies in the way he used detail to
evoke atmosphere in paintings such as *The Dream*. Here, the
wonderful figure of the black flute player with his rainbow-striped
loincloth is camouflaged by jungle foliage alive with fantastic blooms
and spangled with strange fruits, so that you have to look twice to
see him, like the treasure hidden in a children's picture puzzle. In
The Snake Charmer the whole left-hand side of the picture is bathed in

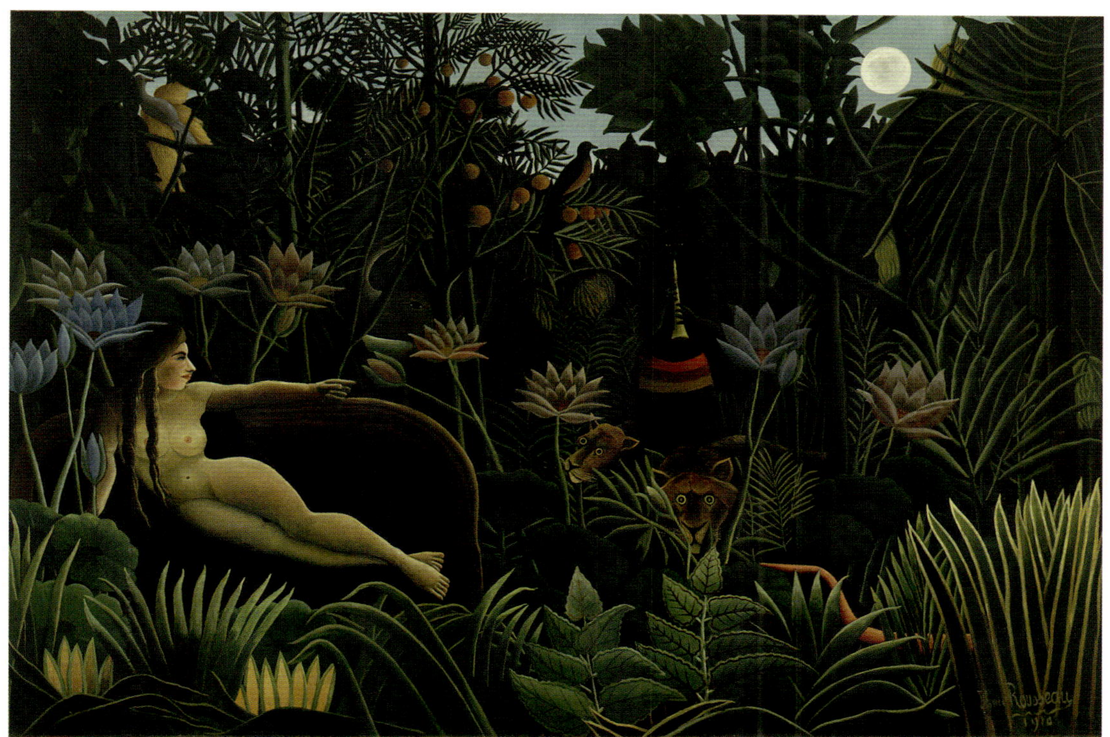

a watery moonlight. The black snake charmer, playing her flute to coax from the trees a slither of black serpents, stands at the edge of a black jungle. Seen against the light, she becomes the extension or embodiment of the jungle's darkness. The whites of her eyes hold us viewers spellbound – as fascinated as the snakes.

Except that Rousseau's small landscapes and cityscapes are far less interesting to me than the large-scale exhibition pictures, everything about this exhibition feels right, from the juxtaposition of his paintings of monkeys with those of comical football players, to a wonderful gallery filled with photos, documents and films that bring Rousseau and his world to life.

Thomas Eakins

Perhaps the best way to introduce a British audience to the American artist Thomas Eakins is to describe the city where he was born and where he worked – Philadelphia, Pennsylvania. Though in fact the fourth largest city in the United States, Philadelphia feels like a small town. Graciously situated at the confluence of the Schuylkill and Delaware rivers, its libraries, museums and orchestra are among the oldest and best in the country. The University of Pennsylvania, with its teaching hospital and medical school, contributes to the intellectual life of a city which has always prided itself on its self-sufficiency.

And yet something has always been missing from Philadelphia, some hard-to-define sense of purpose and optimism. Though pleasant enough to live in, Philadelphia's location, half-way between the government in Washington and the Stock Exchange in New York, gives it the feel of a provincial backwater. Prosperous in the colonial and federal periods, after the Civil War it began a long, slow process of economic decline. By the beginning of the twentieth century, its aristocracy had withdrawn to their suburban mansions, leaving the city to a professional class of architects, doctors and professors – and to successive waves of Irish, Italian and Polish immigrants.

Even when the city played host to the great centennial exhibition of 1876, thoughtful Philadelphians wondered uneasily whether theirs was a city with a past but no future. Oppressed by the Puritan legacy of its Quaker founders and by the work ethic of later German Mennonite settlers, Philadelphia never had a reputation for gaiety. Strict licensing laws closed the city down early. When the comedian W. C. Fields cracked that on his tombstone he wanted inscribed, 'On the whole, I'd rather be in Philadelphia,' Americans got the joke.

This is the place Thomas Eakins records in his paintings. Born in 1844, he studied in Paris under the academician Jean-Léon Gérôme, returning to America in 1870 with a craftsman-like understanding of

8 October 1993

Thomas Eakins and the Heart of American Life

National Portrait Gallery, London

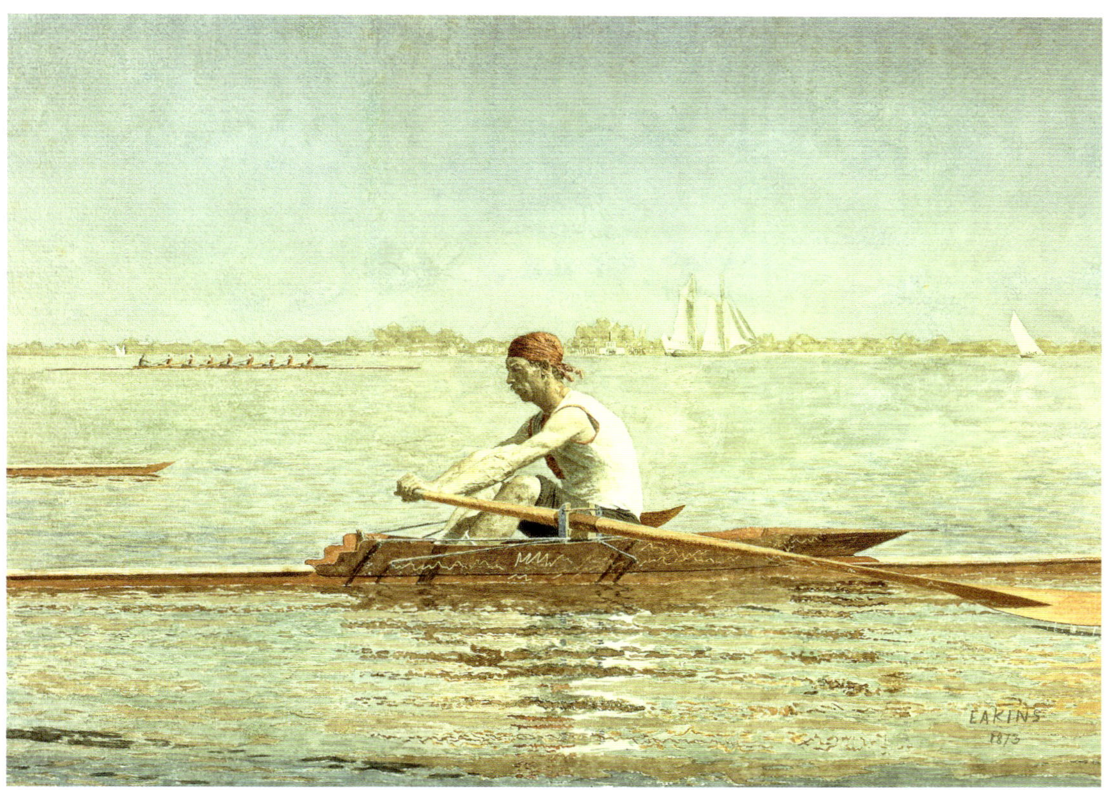

Thomas Eakins
**John Biglin in a
Single Scull**, *1873*
*Metropolitan Museum
of Art, New York*

drawing, composition and the correct rendering of anatomy and
perspective. Like the surgeon who appears in his masterpiece *The
Gross Clinic*, Eakins approached art as a science requiring knowledge,
not inspiration. Eakins mastered optics, drawing and human anatomy
before his brush touched canvas. When preparing to paint athletes
sculling on the Schuylkill River, Eakins first drew a perspective
rendering of the river view so precise that he actually measured the
intervals between ripples in the water. Before tackling the trotting
horses in his splendid painting of *The Fairman Rogers Four-in-Hand* in
1879, he first studied Eadweard Muybridge's serial photographs of
horses in rapid motion, published only a year earlier.

Walking through the marvellous Eakins exhibition at the National
Portrait Gallery, the first ever held in Europe, one is struck by the
stability and the gloom of the world Eakins depicts. When he shows
his two-and-a-half-year-old niece playing on the parlour floor with
her building blocks (*Baby at Play*, 1876), the shadow falling over the
little girl's eyes tells us that this is no vision of childhood innocence

we are witnessing. Piling one block on top of another, she proceeds
with the tense concentration of an adult. Frivolous toys like a doll
and miniature horse and cart lie untouched in the background. And
it may not be irrelevant that, when the same child grew up, she took
her own life.

Time seems to stand still in Eakins's paintings. Cultivated ladies
play the piano in dim, heavily curtained interiors; a plain young
woman sings of loss and memory; Eakins's mousey little wife poses
edgily for her husband, the rims of her eyes red from weeping. His
former student Amelia Van Buren, seemingly enveloped in a hideous,
oversized Victorian armchair, stares vacantly out of the picture, as
though lacking the energy to struggle against boredom and lassitude.
Even outdoor activity brings no relief. In one canvas, *John Biglin in a
Single Scull* (1873), the professional rowing champion is captured in
mid-stroke, his whole body straining at the oar, a sportsman grimly
determined to win.

The element that Eakins omits from his art is simply this: the joy
and pleasure of life. I want to compare him not to a painter but to a
playwright, Henrik Ibsen. As in Ibsen, a strong undertow of repressed
sexuality runs throughout Eakins's work. In one picture showing a
model posing for a sculptor, the ravishingly painted still life of the
model's discarded clothes and underclothes lends to her nudity
a deep erotic charge. And Eakins's pictures of male boxers and
swimmers can be seen as the visual equivalents of his friend Walt
Whitman's hymns to sensual manly comradeship.

Eakins himself was a victim of the repressive morality that hung
over Philadelphia like a blanket. The Pennsylvania Academy of the
Fine Arts dismissed him from his teaching post for removing the
loincloth of a male model in front of a class of female pupils, and
the nude photographs of his family and students which he used
in his work also contributed to his isolation within the straitlaced
community. Eakins died in 1916. His American reputation is entirely
posthumous; very few of the paintings on view in this exhibition were
sold during his lifetime.

Walking through this show, we begin to realise that Eakins was
assembling a sort of sociological scrapbook in which he chronicled
the psychological reality of ordinary American lives. Like a series
of mugshots for police records, just beginning to come into use in

the 1890s, a series of relatively small head-and-shoulders portraits amount to a roll-call of the disappointed, the broken-hearted, the lost and the troubled. The excellent catalogue confirms what our eyes tell us, detailing the incidents of suicide, syphilis, madness and early death among his sitters.

Sadly, a number of Eakins's finest works could not be loaned to this show. The selection of about fifty paintings is adequate but not outstanding and, among the many gems, I spotted half a dozen or so duds. But please, don't let that deter you from going. If you don't know his work already, this exhibition will come as a revelation – and encourage you to visit the extensive collection of his work which is housed, naturally enough, in the Philadelphia Museum of Art.

Gustave Caillebotte

Like most myths, the one about the Impressionists starving in their garrets while waiting for recognition is at best only partially true. Manet and Morisot, Degas and Mary Cassatt all came from prosperous upper-middle-class families, while Toulouse-Lautrec was an aristocrat and Cézanne's father a *nouveau riche*. They could all afford to experiment with new ways of painting for the simple reason that they didn't have to sell their pictures to earn a living.

Gustave Caillebotte, whom the Royal Academy's Spring exhibition dubs the 'The Unknown Impressionist', is another case in point. The large private income that enabled him to bequeath his incredible collection of Impressionist pictures to the Louvre also allowed him to treat painting as another gentlemanly pursuit, along with stamp-collecting, gardening, architecture and rowing – in each of which he effortlessly excelled. And yet at his best Caillebotte is a more original artist than the label of gentleman-amateur implies. The years when he was actively exhibiting before his early death (in 1894, aged forty-five) coincide with the age we feel we know through Impressionist depictions of ballet and boulevard, racecourse and seaside.

What is odd about Caillebotte is that his pictures often show an edgy, out-of-joint world, a world in which the sweetness of life is curiously absent, and where material comfort seems only to increase social and psychological tension. Here's an example. In the 1870s, progressive artists had no difficulty in showing the city of Paris as a place of parks and flowers, chestnut trees and beautiful buildings. But in 1876 Caillebotte sent to the second Impressionist exhibition his picture *Le Pont de l'Europe*. It shows a newly constructed bridge over a railway in a treeless part of the city near the Gare St Lazare, its deep and startling perspective serving to emphasise the rigid geometry of Baron Haussmann's city plan. The long straight lines and iron barrier seem to channel the men and women crossing the bridge into a pre-

3 April 1996

Caillebotte: The Unknown Impressionist

Royal Academy, London

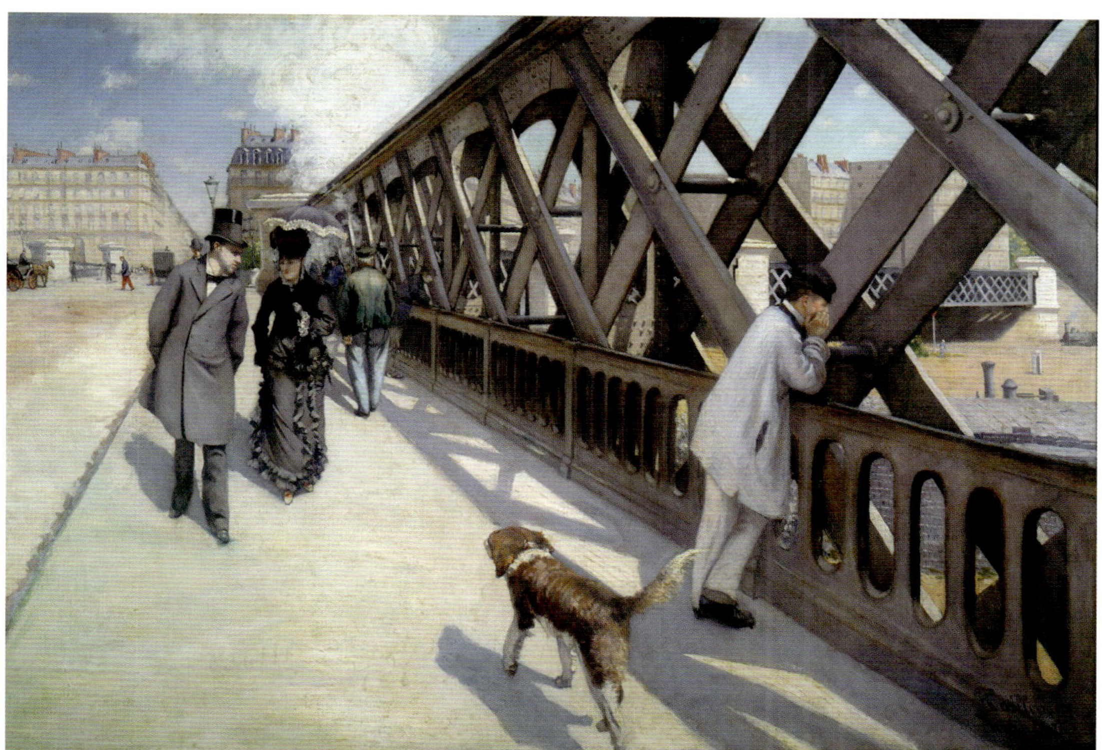

ordained groove. In the work of Degas or Manet, we could identify the bearded man in top hat and frock-coat walking towards us as a *flâneur*, or man of leisure. But the whole point of Caillebotte's picture is that the man is nothing of the sort. This is a businessman hurrying from the station to his morning's work, perhaps on the Bourse, so intent on getting there in time that he overtakes an elegantly dressed widow without pausing to remove his hat.

The man represents a new breed of bourgeoisie, one as single-minded in its pursuit of money as the mongrel is in dutifully trotting at a distance behind his master from the other direction. His opposite number the labourer, leaning on the parapet, idly watches the trains shunting into the station below. The long blue shadows that tell us it is early morning also suggest that this fellow has nothing to do, is unemployed. The man's smock identifies him as a member of the working classes whom Haussmann's urban development drove out of central Paris. Caillebotte depicts a city that would have interested the Futurists, a place of dynamic intersections and personal anonymity, where human relationships count for nothing.

In *A Traffic Island, Boulevard Haussmann* of 1880 we look at a bird's-eye view of a perfect circle, just after noon on a hot summer's day, when few people have ventured on to the streets. The traffic island is empty apart from two men dressed in black frock-coats, tiny specks poised on opposite sides of its perimeter, like two hands on a giant clock. Caillebotte shows a city where isolation and alienation is the norm, and where a sense of community hardly exists.

And what is true of his cityscapes is true of his genre and portraiture. In *The Luncheon* Caillebotte shows his mother and younger brother in the heavily curtained dining-room of the family's *haute bourgeois* Paris flat. It takes a moment in front of the picture to figure out why it is so depressing. Caillebotte has tilted the dark table upwards, pushing his widowed mother towards the top of the picture to emphasise the emotional as well as the physical distance that separates her from the empty place-setting at the bottom of the table – presumably the artist's own. Meanwhile, his brother rudely begins to wolf down his lunch before his mother has been served. That the house is beautifully run we know from the rigid arrangements of cut-glass decanters and goblets in the centre of the polished table. But we can be sure that mother and son will not speak to each other during the meal.

I don't mean to imply that Caillebotte is painting's answer to Ibsen, for there are plenty of pleasant pictures of gardens and flowers in the Royal Academy show. Over and over again he surprises us with the novelty of a subject (a male nude towelling himself after a bath: as far as I know a theme unique in art before the twentieth century) or his viewpoint (two rowers seen from the front and from below as they bend over their oars). But why, if Caillebotte's is such an original voice, is he not better known?

The answer is that he painted only about a dozen pictures that remotely come up to scratch. At his best, he was dazzling. But most of the time he was nothing more than a superior illustrator. Pictures that look wonderful in reproduction are consistently disappointing on the gallery wall. While he had an eye for unusual shapes, and a sensibility attuned to psychologically fraught situations, he didn't have the ability to make ordinary things beautiful simply by the way he painted them. Looking at his still lifes showing a side of beef or dead rabbit, we instinctively compare them to works by Rembrandt and

Chardin – and instantly see how turgidly painted their surfaces are. Whereas Manet could turn a few stalks of asparagus into a work of transcendent beauty, Caillebotte's real talent was for observation and narration, not painting.

But Caillebotte possesses one quality that confers on him near-mystical status in the 1990s: he was an Impressionist. No reservations about his artistic competence, nor even the absence of some of his most famous pictures from this show, is going to prevent a public stampede.

Vincent Van Gogh

The title of the Royal Academy's groundbreaking new show, *The Real Van Gogh: The Artist and His Letters*, signals the intention of the curators to dispense with the myth of the madman touched with genius, to present instead the art of a consummate professional. From the first gallery, we realise that Van Gogh's primary purpose in writing (about art or anything else) is to communicate his thoughts and needs as clearly as possible. The artist whose voice we hear in this show speaks not about suffering, but about the practical business of how to draw and paint, whether telling a friend about a new type of pencil he's discovered or drawing pictures of the kind of brushes he wants his brother Theo to send him from Paris.

If that makes the show sound a trifle dull, trust me, it is anything but. With sixty-five paintings and thirty drawings, including major loans from abroad, dramatically displayed and beautifully lit in the great galleries, it's that rare thing, a blockbuster on a manageable scale. Just don't expect to breeze through it. With the written word given equal importance to the painted image, you have to concentrate from the first picture to the last.

Sometimes, the letter itself is of such intrinsic interest it stands on its own. In the summer of 1882, for example, he describes learning to master the science of perspective by using a perspective frame – a wooden frame with wires stretched across it, through which the artist views his subject 'as if through a window'. Then, a few days later, he sends Theo a sketch that shows him at work on a beach, a tiny figure looking out to sea through a perspective frame, palette in hand, painting directly from nature.

More often, though, Vincent's letters are shown next to the pictures they describe or illustrate, so that by turning from one to the other we can see the paintings through his eyes. Only after reading his description of an early watercolour showing a bird's-eye view from

19 January 2010

The Real Van Gogh: The Artist and His Letters

Royal Academy, London

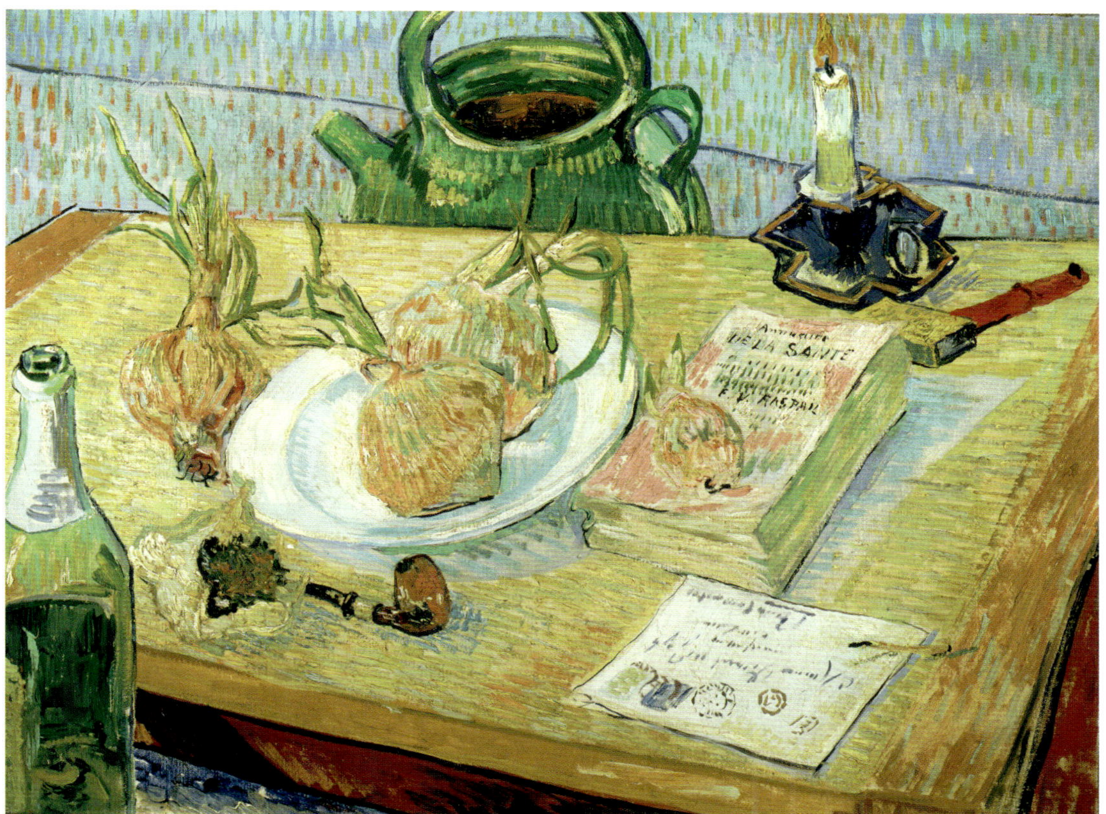

Vincent Van Gogh
**Still Life: Drawing
Board, Pipe, Onions
and Sealing-Wax**,
1889
*Kröller-Müller
Museum, Otterlo*

his attic studio in The Hague do you notice among the myriad details
the 'bird on the wing, the chimney smoking, the figure far below
ambling along'. Other letters discuss the artists he reveres
(Rembrandt, Delacroix and Millet), the books he is reading in the
original English, French and Dutch, or his developing sense of how
colour can be intensified by placing complementaries side by side
('No Blue without Yellow and without Orange').

You can see him experimenting with colour combinations in a
wall hung with flower paintings and still lifes. It begins with the
relatively crude *Vase of Cornflowers, Daisies, Poppies and Carnations*
(1886) and culminates four years later in one of the last pictures he
painted in the asylum at Saint Rémy, the monumental *Roses*, cascading
over a background of light green irradiated by waves of creamy white
paint.

And when there are no letters to help us chart his development –
as in the transitional years 1886–88 when Vincent was living with

Theo in Paris and in contact with Gauguin, Signac and Seurat – the pictures themselves show how he incorporated into his art the non-Western perspective, asymmetry, flat tones and strong colour of Japanese woodblock prints. In these years, colour is at last separated from its descriptive function in pictures that fuse Japanese decorative patterning with realism based on direct observation.

Van Gogh frequently mentions that he has taken only an hour or so to paint a picture – but what he doesn't always say is that before he started, these pictures were carefully planned. One of the masterpieces of the Arles period, *Tarascon Diligence,* is so freely painted that it looks and feels as though improvised on the spot. But the more we look the more we see how artfully Vincent has structured his composition. Our eye enters the picture through the upward diagonal of the ladder at the left, which is immediately countered by two downward diagonals – the driver's whip at front of the diligence and the whip protruding from the carriage behind it. Together, these diagonals turn the vehicle, which otherwise would float unanchored in space, into a stable triangle locked in place by an astonishing smear of violet shadow linking it both to the ground and to the yellow wall behind it.

When we turn to the letter to Theo in which Vincent talks about the picture, we see that, far from being accidental, the diagonal line formed by the coachman's whip was important enough to his composition to include it in the little sketch at the bottom of the page.

Composition is one thing, painting technique another. To paint the two coaches, Van Gogh 'draws' their intricate outlines in black paint. His brush hardly loses contact with the canvas, as he then neatly fills the interstices between the black lines with thick green, red and white paint. But to paint the yellow wall and the medley of white, yellow and blue in the foreground, he uses a different technique, letting his hand move quickly over the canvas with a loaded brush in what looks like a loose, slapping motion.

What this means is that before his brush touched the canvas he had mixed or chosen the precise colour and tone he wanted to use, and calculated how much turpentine and linseed oil to mix it with. When he began to paint, he knew exactly how much paint he needed to have on his brush and how much pressure each of the hundreds of brushstrokes in a picture required. Though he worked quickly, there are few corrections and revisions in his pictures, indicating that he

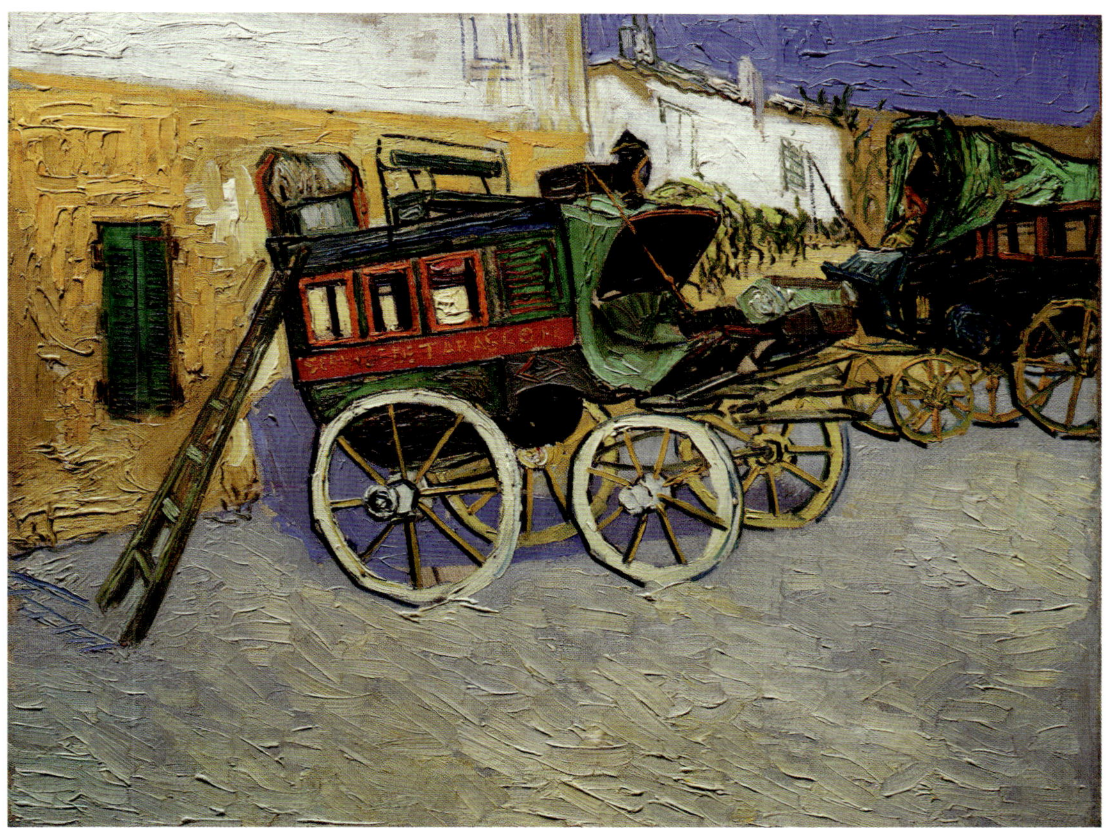

Vincent Van Gogh
Tarascon Diligence,
1888
Princeton University
Art Museum

must have known exactly how he wanted each one to look before he began it. All this took as much forethought and sustained concentration as you find in the paintings of Cézanne. And here is the point: it is simply not possible to paint like this in a mad frenzy.

If you didn't know who was writing these letters, it would be hard to guess the long, hard struggle Vincent endured to become an artist, or the terrible illness that stopped him from working for long periods in the last years of his life. We do not know the precise nature of that illness, but what we can say is that unlike the schizophrenic Richard Dadd, whose pictures are symptomatic of his madness, Van Gogh's mental state hardly finds its way into his art at all. And so, Vincent painted his *Still Life with a Plate of Onions* soon after his first breakdown in Arles.

There is nothing about the way the picture is painted that suggests the recent turmoil in his life, though some of the objects in it – a handbook on homoeopathy, a coffee pot and an empty bottle of absinthe – are reminders of his illness, and the letter on the table is the very one in which Theo told Vincent of his engagement, a psychological blow that is sometimes cited as a factor contributing to his breakdown.

In the last letter posted to Theo, written on 23 July 1890, only two days before he shot himself in the chest, Vincent writes not of depression or anxiety but that he is applying himself to his canvas 'with all my attention'. He encloses a sketch of *Wheat Fields After the Rain*, which hangs nearby and is one of the most radiantly serene pictures in the show.

In it, Van Gogh is working at the height of his powers, so completely in control of his medium that he uses two different viewpoints – the foreground seen from close to (painted with short flicking brushstrokes) and the patchwork of fields in the distance, painted with parallel ribbons of light yellow, apple and forest green edged with dark blue. The newly washed fields stretch on forever under an aquamarine sky filled with blowsy whorls of woolly white clouds, an image of pure bliss.

It is easy to let what we know about Van Gogh's life to colour the way we look at his art. The genius of this show is that the artist himself tells us in his own words to look again and see what is really there, not what our imaginations have added to it.

John Singer Sargent

In a crucial scene in Henry James's novel *The Portrait of a Lady* the heroine Isabel Archer is speaking to her nemesis Madame Merle about what makes each of us uniquely ourselves. Young and naive, Isabel maintains that she is whole and complete in herself. She knows who she is. Her identity will not change irrespective of the clothes she wears or where she lives. Older and far more worldly in her outlook, Madame Merle gently rebukes her. 'What do you call one's self? Where does it begin? Where does it end? It overflows into everything that belongs to us . . . I know that a large part of myself is in the dresses I choose to wear . . . one's house, one clothes, the book one reads, the company one keeps – these things are all expressive.'

As a portrait painter and an expatriated American, James's friend John Singer Sargent must have thought every day of his life about the question of identity and how it is expressed – and in precisely the terms framed by Madame Merle. His successful portrait practice depended, of course, on his ability to capture a likeness. But in commissioned portraits he was frequently called upon to indicate status through clothing, furniture, jewels and setting. In many of his most admired portraits, sheer visual panache takes precedence over the revelation of character. As a result he emerges as a far more complex and multi-faceted artist than the mere society portraitist he has sometimes been derided as.

What makes the National Portrait Gallery's exhibition of Sargent's portraits of artists and friends so rewarding is a sense that we are seeing Sargent when he is most true to himself, responding in paint not to patrons who paid him to make them look glamorous but to people he liked or admired or simply thought interesting. When painting family and intimate friends Sargent was free to probe character without flagging up their position in the world. And so his vivacious sketch of his close friend Violet Paget (who wrote under the

10 February 2015

Sargent: Portraits of Artists and Friends

National Portrait Gallery, London

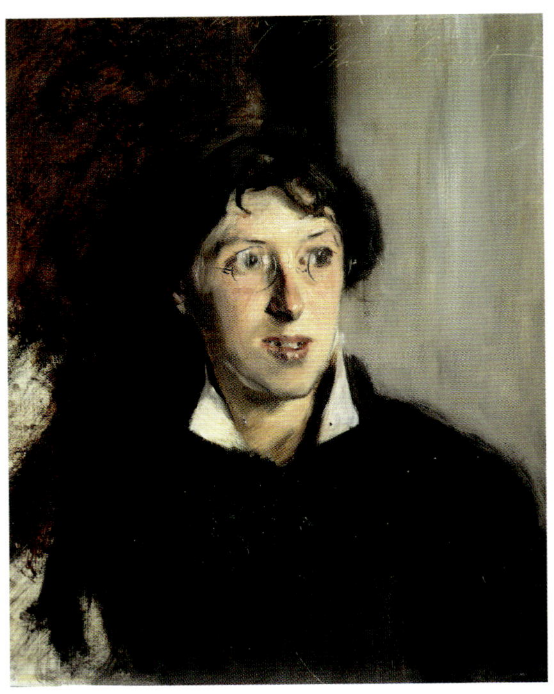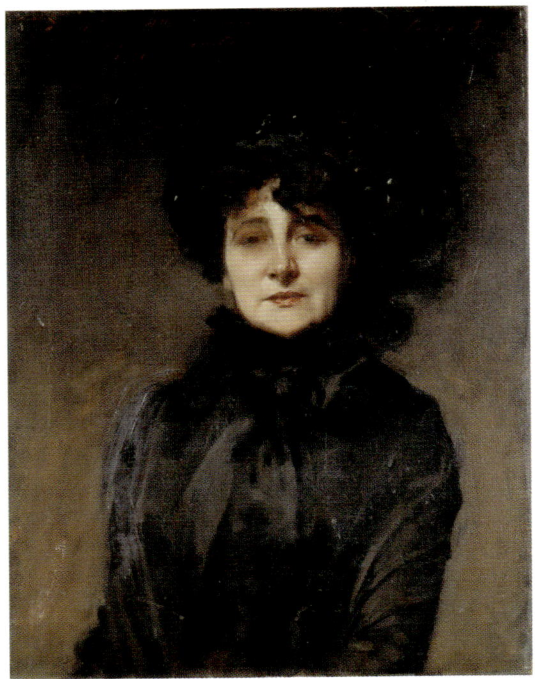

name of Vernon Lee) shows a boyish, plain, and highly intelligent young woman speaking with such animation that her features are slightly blurred, as though the artist's brush couldn't keep pace with the whirl of her conversation. The picture looks like a snapshot because Lee appears to be unaware that the artist is sketching her. Not only can she not keep still, but she hasn't bothered to remove her spectacles, close her mouth, or tidy her hair.

Hanging next to this masterly character study is Sargent's sublime half-length portrait of the French writer Mme Allouard-Jouan, a distinguished beauty even in middle age, fine-boned, composed, and commanding in her presence. In complete contrast to Lee, she has prepared for her encounter with the young painter. Elegantly dressed in black and shown full face, she fixes her hooded eyes straight ahead, the flicker of a wintery smile suggesting curiosity, amusement, or perhaps appraisal. Simply by being so completely themselves both women in different ways gave Sargent the raw material he needed to bring their personalities to life – and to do so without recourse to props or accessories.

In that sense, all of Sargent's most successful portraits are collaborations between the artist and sitter. In his show-stopping full-

Above left:
John Singer Sargent
Violet Paget
(Vernon Lee), *1881*
Tate Gallery, London

Above:
John Singer Sargent
Mme Emma-Marie
Allouard-Jouan,
1882
Musée du Louvre,
Paris

length 1881 portrait *Dr Samuel Jean Pozzi at Home,* the spectacularly good-looking surgeon surely risked public ridicule by posing against a crimson swag of drapery and with one hand on his breast like a matinée idol taking a curtain call. His floor-length scarlet dressing gown serves to accentuate his jet-black hair and beard, while drawing attention to the delicacy of his impossibly long fingers. This was to court controversy: everyone in Parisian society knew that Dr Pozzi was – wait for it – a famous gynaecologist notorious for his numerous love affairs including a long liaison with Sarah Bernhardt.

But what if a sitter wouldn't cooperate? This is what I think is happening in the double portrait of sixteen-year-old Edouard Pailleron and his six-year-old sister, Marie-Louise. At first sight, the picture seems simply to represent two beautifully dressed and impeccably behaved children. But the longer you look, the more uneasy you feel. Neither child smiles nor looks comfortable in the poses they've been instructed to take. Then it dawns on you. These offspring of the *haute bourgeoisie* understand all too well that their lives are constricted on every side by the expectations of their parents. They are being put on display– beautiful, defenceless and sullen as animals in a zoo. Rather than try to make them likable, Sargent respects their passive aggression by letting us see it. Nothing specific such as a frown or a tear accounts for the picture's strange atmosphere, but that 'nothing' is like the silence that is more eloquent than speech in James's novels.

Things become even more ambiguous when Sargent conflates portraiture and narration in that hybrid genre, the conversation piece. In his *A Dinner Table at Night,* the portrait's subject, the wife of an industrialist, sits at the head of a candlelit table in a dining room suffused with the warmth of crimson walls and lampshades. Dinner is over, port and cigars have been passed around. Much has been drunk; the atmosphere is mellow. By extending the tablecloth into the foreground plane, Sargent creates the illusion that we are seated opposite our hostess and so deep in conversation that it takes a moment before we notice her husband. Seated at the table in profile on the far right, he is an afterthought, cut out of the conversation (and almost out of the painting) by the brutal truncation of his head and body. Far from suggesting any estrangement between the couple (as Degas might do), the picture subtly describes an easy relationship

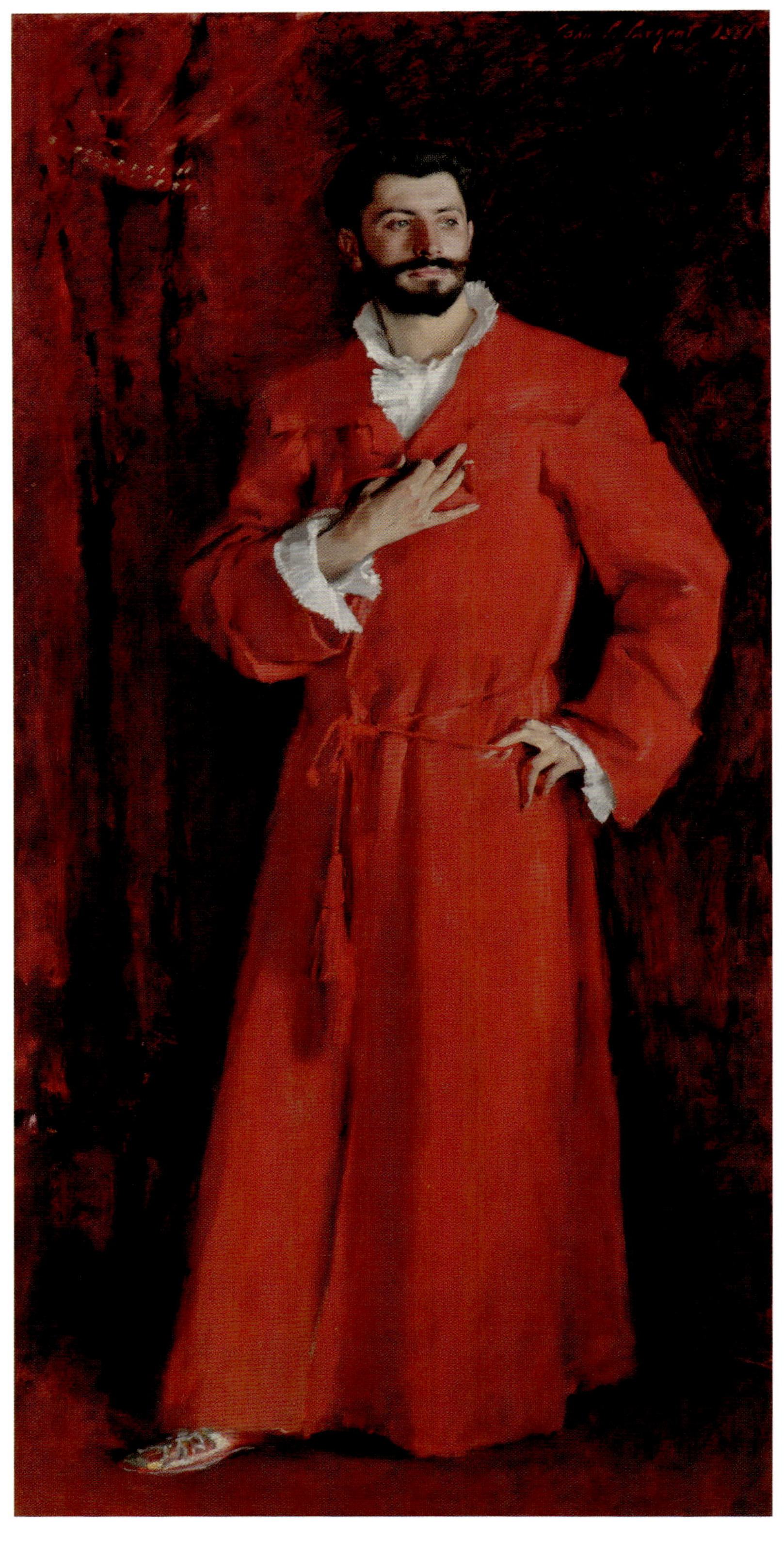

John Singer Sargent
Dr Samuel Jean
Pozzi at Home, *1881*
Armand Hammer
Collection of Art,
Los Angeles

between two people completely relaxed in the painter's presence. Look again and you realise that the husband must have moved from the other end of the table where he started the meal to sit closer to his wife, happy to listen and smoke his cigar while she leads the conversation. In many society portraits, sitters flaunt their wealth and privilege. With these close friends, that's irrelevant.

Perhaps because he was a bachelor, Sargent is particularly acute in portraits of married friends. The consumptive novelist Robert Louis Stevenson is shown stalking on long thin legs across the picture, leaving his wife as though stranded on the opposite side of the room. Very different is his sunlit portrait of painter Paul Helleu, painting from nature in his straw boater with his beautiful wife leaning comfortably at his side. Compare her body language with that of Mme Monet, who sits with her legs inelegantly stretched straight out as Claude gets on with his work.

When Sargent fails, it is because the sitter doesn't give him enough to work with – either because they are reticent, or because their own sense of themselves is not firmly established. Confronted with the pale worried face of his rival portraitist Jacque-Emile Blanche, his inspiration failed.

And the best example of all is Sargent himself. Of the several self-portraits in this show, in not one do you feel any sense of his personality. Since he was an accomplished pianist, spoke four languages, and was a passionate lover of music, literature and art, this withholding of information must be deliberate, or perhaps a better word is instinctive. These self-portraits are, after all, profoundly revealing. They are of a piece with the single most important fact about his private life – that, as far as we know, he had no sustained physical relationship with either a man or a woman. I'm guessing here, but could it be that in painting those people who attracted him – whether because of their talent or personalities or beauty – he found the intimacy that eluded him in his own life?

Many curators and writers contributed to the making of an outstanding exhibition, one of the best I've ever seen at the National Portrait Gallery. But the final bow has to be taken by Richard Ormond, whose life-long study of Sargent's once-disparaged work has restored him to his rightful place in the pantheon of great European artists.

Georges Seurat

Until last week I had always thought of Georges Seurat's *Bathers at Asnières* as a serene picture, as uncomplicated in its way as the boating and seaside scenes of Renoir or Manet. Now I'm not so sure. The National Gallery's new exhibition *Seurat and the Bathers* made me think again about the picture and ask a question it had never occurred to me to ask before: what, exactly, is going on?

Ostensibly, the answer is simple. Five swimmers and idlers are shown basking on the banks of the Seine on a hot summer's afternoon. In the distance three more men sit or stretch out on the grass, while on the river itself there is a sailing boat, a man rowing a scull, and a ferry transporting two middle-class passengers with a furled tricolour to the opposite bank. The railway bridge and smoking factory chimneys in the background confirm what the picture's title tells us: that the setting is a nondescript, semi-industrial suburb of Paris.

The twenty-five-year-old Seurat painted the *Bathers* in his Paris studio during the winter of 1883–84. When it was rejected at the Salon of 1884, he showed it instead at the Groupe des Artistes Indépendants. Unsold, it remained in Seurat's studio until his death in 1891. Nine years later the critic Félix Fénéon bought it from the artist's heirs. Unlike many of the other great milestones of Impressionism and Post-Impressionism, France showed no interest in purchasing it for the Musée du Luxembourg. Instead, as late as 1924, Fénéon sold the painting to Samuel Courtauld, who presented it to Britain. What is it about this apparently innocuous image that made it so unloved for so long?

The problem could not have been Seurat's working method or painting technique, both of which were straightforward. Working directly from nature on small wooden panels, he first made more than a dozen freely painted landscape, figural and compositional studies in

2 July 1997
Seurat and the *Bathers*
National Gallery,
London

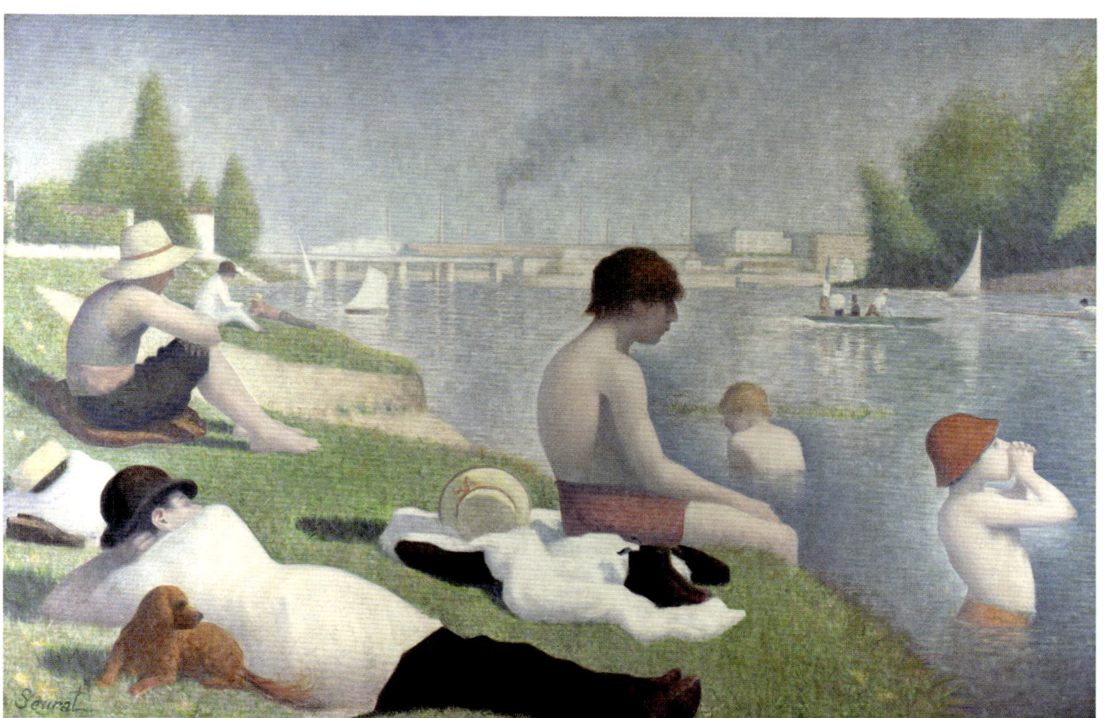

Georges Seurat
Bathers at Asnières,
1884
National Gallery,
London

oil. Once he had found his composition he returned to the studio
to make highly finished tonal drawings from the nude model using
black conté crayons. Finally he began to paint directly on to the
primed canvas. Using a palette of pale creams, blues, pinks and
reddish browns, he laid on coat after coat of luminous colour
with criss-cross brushstrokes in a technique closer to Monet's
Impressionism than to the pointillism that Seurat would develop
in *Sunday Afternoon on the Island of La Grande Jatte* a year later.

As for the subject of the *Bathers*, that wasn't controversial either.
Scenes from modern life were commonplace in the Salons of the
1880s, and there is nothing to suggest that the ambitious young artist
intended his *Bathers* to shock. Indeed, he was careful not to show one
of the more disagreeable activities that actually took place along this
stretch of the river. As we can see in the preparatory studies, this spot
was dedicated not only to bathing, but to washing the ugly dray
horses which were used for transporting goods to and from Paris.

Nor is the setting problematic. The suburb of Asnières is a two-
hour walk north-west of Paris. Unlike in Clichy on the opposite

bank, with its gas and chemical works, the factories at Asnières were devoted to light industry. This is where Louis Vuitton had been manufacturing luggage since 1860, and where the Goupil company printed its famous reproductions of works of art. Beyond the railway bridge that connects pristine Asnières to grimy Clichy in the distance of Seurat's scene, the river became badly polluted. Seurat could easily have walked a few hundred yards downstream to show men and cranes unloading coal from trains and barges. Instead, he chose a stretch of river where there was little evidence of industrial activity and where the water was fairly clean.

And cleanliness is what the picture is all about. The boys shown here are not the rough youths who scrubbed down mud-caked horses for a few centimes. The neat straw hat, clean boots and spotless white linen of the large seated bather suggest that he is a respectable member of the lower middle class, perhaps a clerk in one of the factories. We can even guess the reason he and his fellow bathers are off work for the day: the tricolour in the distance suggests that it is Bastille Day, proclaimed a national holiday only four years earlier, in 1880. The boy in the straw hat on the left, sitting on his smock, could be a carpenter or boat-builder. The one incongruous figure is the older man in derby hat and white frock-coat who reclines in the foreground. He is not a bather, but a middle-class interloper. Out for a walk with his dog, he has stretched out on the grass to watch the swimmers.

You come closer to answering the question of why the picture is so difficult to like when you examine its curious atmosphere. Why is everything so still? Why is there no splashing, no movement of any kind? Why do the figures seem so isolated, with four of them shown in strict profile, arranged in a frieze across the picture? One explanation is that they are concentrating on something that is happening outside the picture. The dog has just turned to look, while the boy in the water whistles or calls out to someone or something out of our sight.

But there is another explanation. Three of the preparatory oil sketches reveal that in reality the boys sometimes swam naked – as men are shown doing in other paintings included in this show, such as Léon-Augustin Lhermitte's *Bathers at Mont-Saint-Père*. What's more, when preparing his figure studies, Seurat worked from the nude model. But, just as he edited the work-horses out of the final composition, the artist chose at a relatively late stage in the picture's evolution to give the two boys on the right of the picture bathing trunks.

A clue as to why Seurat may have done so is provided by the lovingly painted still-life in the exact centre of the picture. It consists of a white linen shirt, boots and a round straw hat with a delicate pink bow. To Seurat and his contemporaries, discarded clothes seen in conjunction with a nude figure by the bank of a river would have recalled the scandal created by Manet's *Déjeuner sur l'herbe* twenty years earlier. That picture was rejected from the Salon on moral as well as aesthetic grounds, for it showed not a nude goddess in a sylvan glade but a contemporary woman, stark naked, having a picnic with two clothed men.

By placing unclothed youths in proximity to a fully clothed man, Seurat ran the risk that the boys would be seen not as classically nude, but as naked, thereby introducing an element of sexual tension into the *Bathers* which he evidently didn't want. Just imagine the bathers without their trunks. Suddenly the reclining man looks all too much like the male equivalent of one of Ingres's odalisques, or, even more dangerously, of Delacroix's Sardanapalus presiding over his harem. Far-fetched? Not a bit. A subterranean world in which older men preyed on younger ones in *fin-de-siècle* Paris was described in obsessive detail by Marcel Proust in *A la Recherche du temps perdu*. How could Seurat not have known of its existence?

By comparison with Manet's *Déjeuner sur l'herbe* Seurat's *Bathers* feels not so much innocent as repressed. In cleansing the image of dirt – moral as well as material – Seurat created a picture which is cold and still, frozen at its core. I hasten to add that this interpretation is mine, not the National Gallery's.

Impressionism: Painting Quickly in France

Edouard Manet must have painted *The Races at Longchamps* at top speed, for the excellent reason that he would have been killed if he hadn't. That, at least, is our first thought in front of the canvas, which shows six horses thundering down the race track and past the finishing line from head-on. Since it looks as though Manet was standing directly in their path, he has another ten seconds or so to get out of the way before he is trampled to death. Swiftly co-ordinating hand and eye, his brush was engaged in its own race, against time. And the question of speed – of how long it took artists to paint works which they then exhibited as finished paintings, not sketches – is central to the National Gallery's thrilling new exhibition, *Impressionism: Painting Quickly in France 1860–1890.*

Did Manet really paint *The Races at Longchamps* quickly, or, for that matter, on the spot? Well, he could have. We know that he moved around Paris with a satchel containing his brushes, tubes of oil paint and canvases strapped to his back, searching for suitable motifs to capture in paint. Having found this one at Longchamps, the relatively small size of the canvas meant that he could almost have covered it in the time it took for the horses to run a race, or perhaps several. You can imagine his loosely held brush moving swiftly over the background to lay in broad areas of sky, cloud and landscape. Then, he switched to a smaller brush to dash off the dark blur of oncoming horses with tight, staccato flicks of paint. And it must have taken only a few moments to scumble in the monochrome mass of spectators at left and right.

But then we begin to have our doubts. Look at the carefully delineated lady with the parasol at the lower left, and the man with the binoculars up in the grandstands. Surely both figures must have been added back in the studio. Come to that, aren't the jockeys riding steeds that look more like rocking horses than real ones? The

1 November 2000

Impressionism: Painting Quickly in France 1860–1890

National Gallery, London

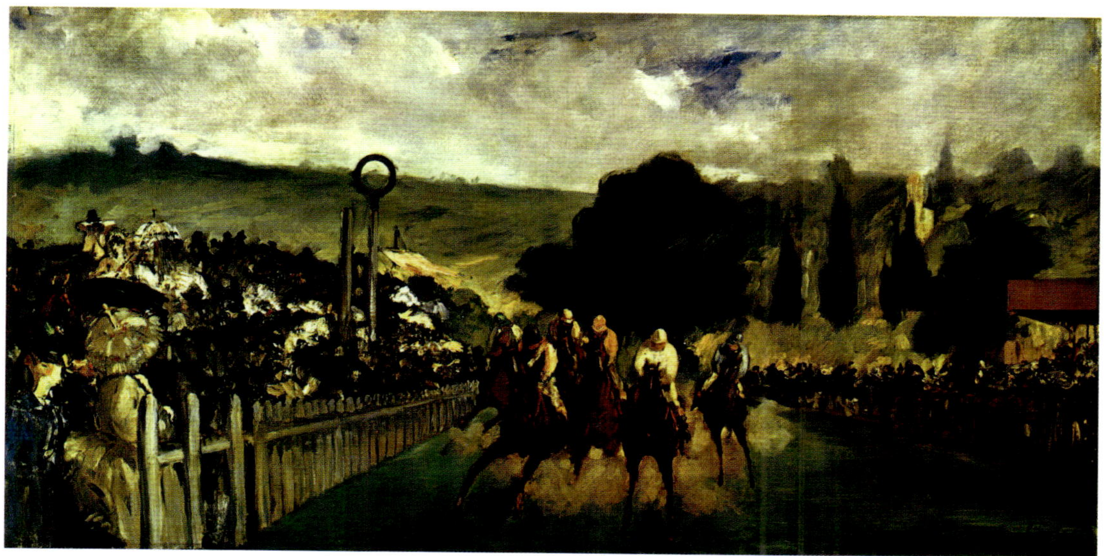

important thing about the picture is not that Manet painted it at speed, and during the race itself, but that he wanted us to think he did. It's the impression of haste, of ephemerality, of reportage that makes the picture look so modern.

In another canvas, *The Funeral*, Manet uses speed for another purpose: to express emotion. The painting is not sketched from life, but from Manet's memory of an actual event, his friend Baudelaire's funeral three years earlier. On that hot September day in 1867, as a procession of mourners in black straggled behind a hearse through Père Lachaise cemetery, a thunderstorm broke over Paris, and the city itself seemed to partake in the calamity. Here, the frantic, turbulent brushwork in the sky and skyline – the way that streaks of dark grey and black-green slash and stab the canvas, obliterating all traces of light – stands for the anguish felt by the painter himself. As Richard Brettell says in his superb catalogue, 'if ever a painting wept, this one does.'

Because each stroke of the brush is so apparent in works by Manet, Monet, Pissarro and Sisley, it is often possible for Brettell to estimate how many sessions a painter took to complete a canvas. In Monet's *Towing a Boat, Honfleur* of 1864, for example, you can see from the two different paint layers that the artist first laid in the sky and sea, then waited for these areas to dry (or at least become tacky) before adding the lighthouse, boat and fishermen. Once again, a sense of the passing moment is central to the picture's meaning, for Monet intended us to imagine him working flat out to capture the few moments of light left before night rolls over the lurid yellow and purple sunset, the shimmering sea and darkening coastline.

But how was it possible for Monet to work so quickly? One answer is that before beginning a work, he had already prepared his canvas and planned the composition. Take his *The Seine at Petit-Gennevilliers* of 1872, which shows a grubby dockyard on a bleak winter's day from the water. Clearly Monet worked from nature. But this doesn't mean the composition is artless, for the horizon line bisects the canvas horizontally exactly at its centre, while the tallest mast performs the same function vertically and other verticals further divide the canvas into quarters. Monet's composition provides clarity and structure and above all stability. Having established that, it would not have taken more than a few hours to paint in the boat-houses and boats. Then, possibly even towards the very end of the painting process, Monet adds the free brushstrokes to suggest the scudding clouds, icy water and rising smoke – the elements that give the scene its freshness and immediacy.

Don't forget that these artists were like concert pianists or Chinese calligraphers – years and years of practice enabled them to set down each swift touch of the brush with unerring precision. So great is their control that no matter how free the painter's arm or wrist movements may be, we viewers read the marks they make as evocations of wind, of smoke, of snow or of water. In short, we trust the Impressionist to give us accurate information about what he saw in that place, at that time, on that day. To represent the still life of bottles and glasses in the left foreground of his *Sketch for 'The Bar at the Folies-Bergère'*, Manet employs a visual shorthand so economical that it verges on the incomprehensible, trusting that the sympathetic viewer will instinctively read the shapes.

Then, too, it is of the essence of the Impressionist technique that the artists opened up their brushstroke to let the priming colour show through. Before beginning to paint, an artist would prime the canvas with light grey, white or violet, then use the colour of the underpaint to 'induce' colours that aren't in reality there at all. The best example in the show is in Manet's *Girl Reading*, where from a distance we read the half-shadows of the girl's face as green. But step closer and you

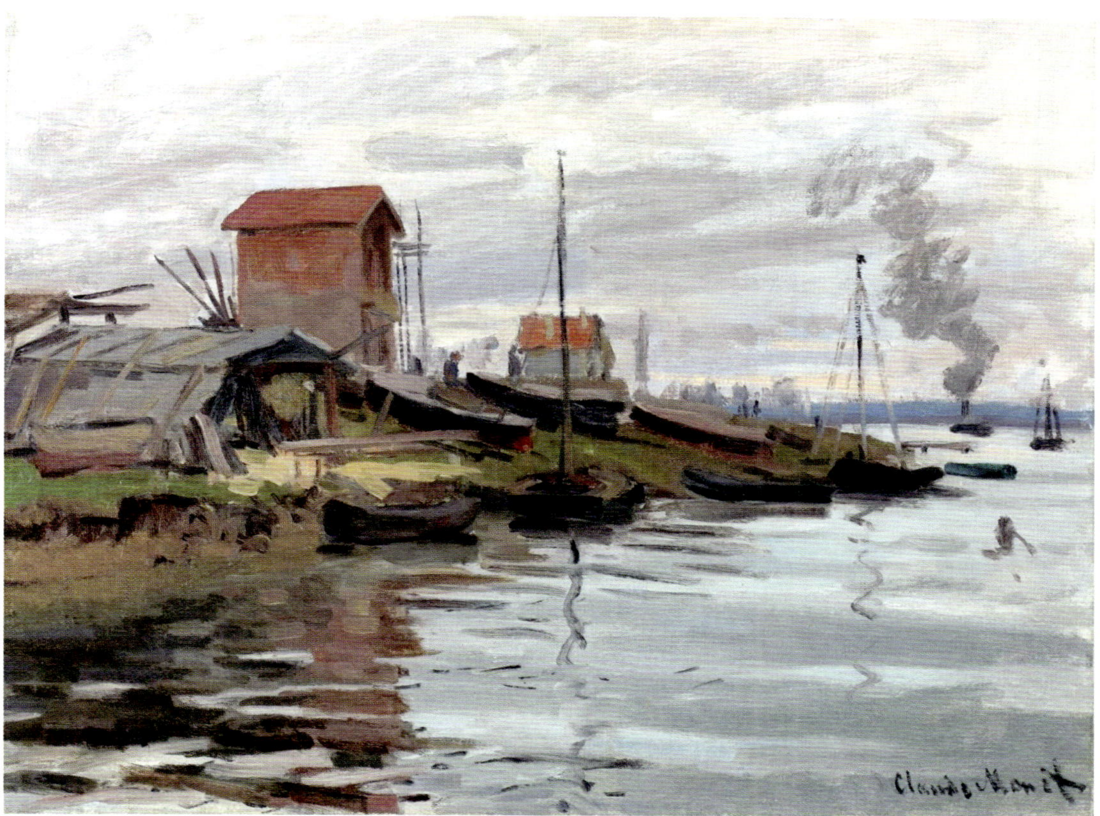

Claude Monet
The Seine at Petit-Gennevilliers, *1872*
Private collection

see that those shadows are in fact the grey ground which Manet has left bare. As the National Gallery's conservator David Bomford points out, the illusion of green has been induced by the proximity of the grey ground to areas of pink and orange in the rest of the face.

When you go to this show, stop and ask yourself how and why and under what circumstances each picture was painted. When Manet paints a glimpse of a besieged Paris under snow during the Franco-Prussian war, dates it to the day like a diary entry, and inscribes it to a friend, it is impossible to believe that he didn't paint it on the spot and then spontaneously present it to a fellow soldier. But when Renoir paints what I believe to be an imaginary view of a fashionable Parisian boulevard, he must have worked in the studio with the sole purpose of making a few bob from the tourists.

One artist actually painted quickly, the other wanted us to think he did. Neither of those works could be called an aesthetic jewel, but even if there is a sprinkling of really bad pictures in the show they hang near some of the greatest works in the history of art, such as Monet's *Bathers at La Grenouillère* and Manet's portrait of Georges Clemenceau – a picture which demonstrates that speed can be suggested by the removal of brushstrokes as well as by their application.

Henri de Toulouse-Lautrec

In Toulouse-Lautrec's famous poster, *Moulin Rouge, La Goulue*, the dancer Louise Weber, who was known as La Goulue, kicks up her heels for a circle of silhouetted spectators. It is easy to become caught up in the abandoned high spirits of the wonderfully drawn central figure, a creature of polka dots, flying legs and fancy underwear. But if we allow our attention to stray from her, we understand why, of all Lautrec's posters, this one packs such a particularly strong punch.

Imagine the audience stretched beyond the edges of the poster, then follow the deep perspective of the floorboards, and it becomes clear that the artist intends us to see the space of his poster extending into the real space of pavement or gallery. He places us among the faceless audience, voyeurs in spite of ourselves. Dancing just in front of us is La Goulue's double-jointed partner, Valentin le Désossé ('the boneless'), lightly shaded in grey, the profile of his body wobbling like a pall of cigarette smoke settled over the dance hall. Lautrec's colours imitate the sickly, yellow-green glare of early electric lighting, but in the upper-left-hand corner the words 'MOULIN ROUGE' are repeated three times in a garish shade of red, like a neon sign flashing on and off, luring us into the noise and naughtiness of Montmartre's demi-monde.

Then comes Lautrec's masterstroke. As we pause in front of the poster we notice a star-shaped patch on La Goulue's knickers. There is writing on it. Of course we are curious. With our noses all but pressed up against the poster we make out the letters: 'M-O-U-L-I-N R-O-U-G-E'. We can almost hear Lautrec laughing. He has successfully tempted us respectable bourgeoisie to inspect La Goulue's posterior.

Tricking us into taking a second, and then a third look is what Lautrec's art is all about. We might think we can take in his prints and posters at a glance, but we soon find ourselves staring at a face that has not proved so easy to pass by. Lautrec is our friend, introducing us

22 October 1988

Toulouse-Lautrec:
The Graphic Works

Royal Academy,
London

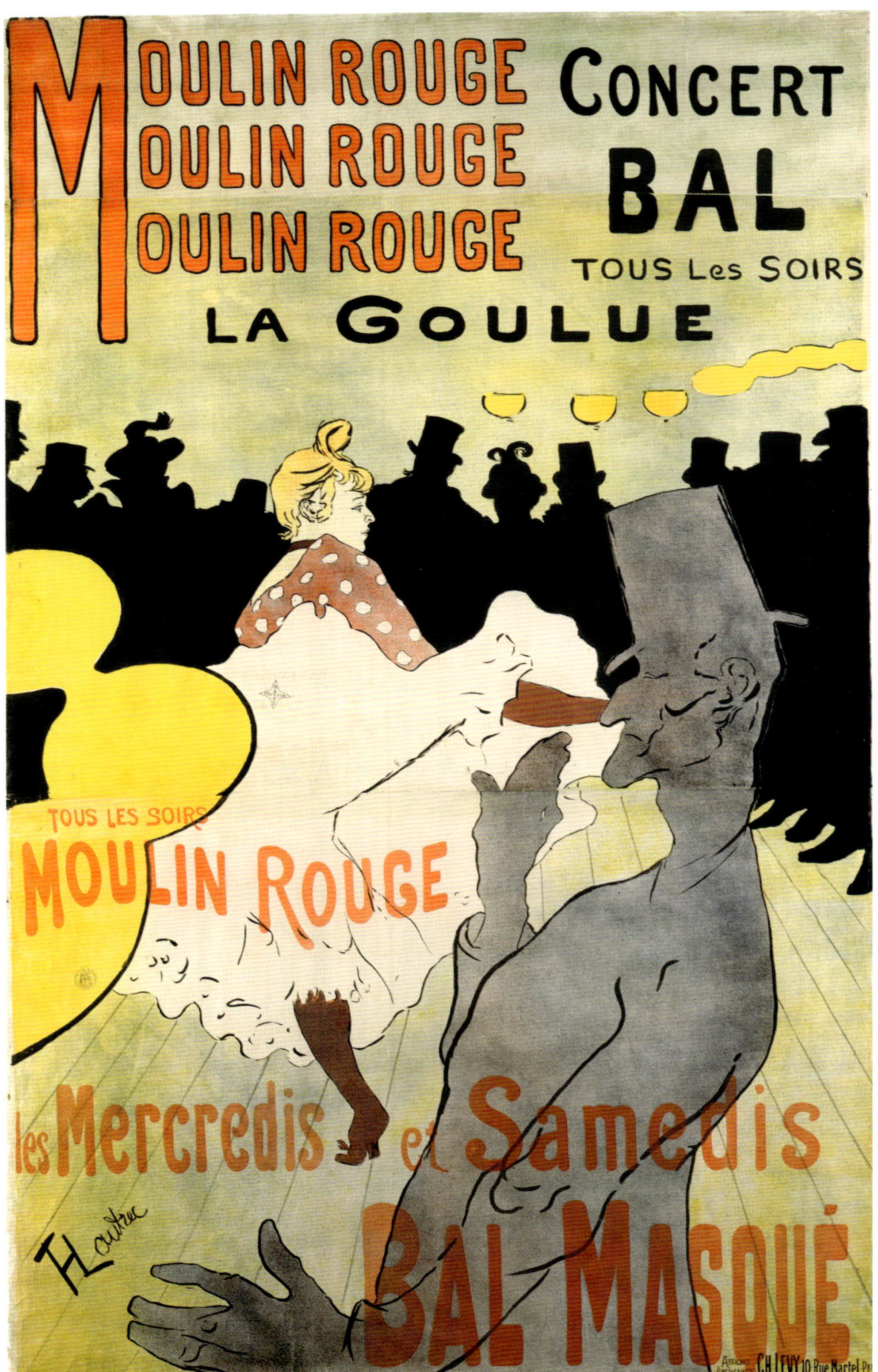

MOULIN ROUGE
MOULIN ROUGE
MOULIN ROUGE
LA GOULUE
CONCERT
BAL
TOUS LES SOIRS
TOUS LES SOIRS
MOULIN ROUGE
les Mercredis et Samedis
BAL MASQUÉ
HTLautrec
CH LEVY 10 Rue Martel Pa

to the hard-drinking, high-living denizens of the Boulevard Montmartre and the rue de Clichy. He is the great celebrator of Paris, as Dickens was of London or Damon Runyon of Broadway. We soon become familiar with his night-time world of dance-hall performers, prostitutes, clowns, perverts and *boulevardiers*, all dressed up to the nines, men and women alike heavily made up, exhibitionists every one. In a picture by Degas we peep through the keyhole at dancers and models who do not know they are being observed. The opposite is true of Lautrec, who reserves a ringside seat for us to ogle performers who would be devastated if we were to turn away.

A grotesque like May Belfort, a hideous Irish woman who lisped ribald nursery rhymes dressed in a little girl's pinafore and Kate Greenaway bonnet, must have attracted Lautrec with her outrageous appearance. But in his many lithographs of her we sometimes catch a glimpse under her coarse features of something like girlish beauty, humorous self-mockery, even grace.

And then there is the ageing singer Yvette Guilbert, obviously revelling in her tenth curtain call, swooping down to the footlights and hanging on to the stage curtain with her long black-gloved hands, delighted to have pleased yet another audience, and desperately needing even more applause.

Though related to Daumier's comic savagery, Lautrec's art transcends caricature simply because he is so fond of the people he draws, many of whom were his close friends. One cannot exactly speak of compassion or understanding in his work because these words imply condescension, and Lautrec certainly did not pity his subjects. Indeed, he admires their talent, humour and, above all, the moral courage and honesty with which they live their lives. If at first the prints he made while living in brothels seem cruel, we soon come to feel that he was paying the women who worked in them the ultimate respect of showing them just as they were.

Only rarely does he make a moral judgement, as in his terrifying lithograph *Idylle Princière* of 1897, which shows the American-born Princess de Caraman-Chimay and her lover, the pockmarked gipsy Rigo, whom she was to marry in 1904, sitting together in her box at the opera. Lautrec lingers on the dead pallor of the princess's skin, her bleached hair and vacant expression. For all her sophistication, she is presented as a bird-like creature, preyed upon by her lover, a grinning cat whose hair and moustache are slick with brilliantine. He is the incarnation of pure evil, and he is about to pounce.

The huge show at the Royal Academy of Toulouse-Lautrec's complete graphic works is pure pleasure. Very few of the prints on view – there are more than three hundred of them – could be removed without diminishing our experience of some further aspect of Lautrec's nearly inexhaustible talent. Considering that he died at the age of thirty-six, his dwarfish body destroyed by alcohol and syphilis, and that the exhibition includes nothing of his 5,084 drawings, 275 watercolours or 737 paintings, we get some idea of his staggering energy.

Vilhelm Hammershøi

It is a winter afternoon, around three o'clock. The house is silent, the rooms empty. Where you are sitting, weak sunlight irradiates the wall and furniture near the window, but leaves everything else in a grey half-light. With the world drained of colour but not of natural light, forms become clearer and more defined, emerging from their surroundings, distinct and whole. Such moments of clarity and composure don't happen often and don't last long, vanishing with the ring of the doorbell, the key in the lock, the lighting of the lamp.

The artist who captured them in paint is Vilhelm Hammershøi, who died in 1916 at the age of only fifty-two. Hammershøi spent most of his life in Copenhagen. Though he is regarded as one of Denmark's greatest artists, his name is hardly known in the rest of Europe. Yet the exhibition of his work at the Musée d'Orsay is the talk of Paris. Tucked into a few galleries on the main floor, this understated show of sixty interiors, portraits, nudes, landscapes and architectural studies has had an impact out of all proportion to its size.

To describe a typical work by Hammershøi is to describe nothing special. *Motes Dancing in the Sunlight* shows something we see all the time in real life but rarely in art: millions of particles of dust suddenly made visible by a shaft of sunlight. Where the slanting rays of the sun stream through a window into an empty room, they form parallel bands of transparent grey light, interspersed with darker bands where the light doesn't fall and the dust motes can't be seen.

It is the sort of subject the American Andrew Wyeth would vulgarise later in the century. But in Hammershøi's painting you find nothing illustrative or anecdotal. As you look, you become mesmerised by the geometry of the square window panes set within the larger rectangular frame, the relationship between these shapes and those of the door and the panelled walls, and the contrast between the white winter light and the infinitely subtle modulations

3 December 1997

The Poetical Universe
of Vilhelm Hammershøi

Musée d'Orsay, Paris

of grey interior light that it penetrates. For all the formal perfection of the compositions, there is nothing cold or cerebral about Hammershøi's art. He lays on his monochrome pigments with tenderness and deliberation. You feel his touch in every inch of a painting. Architectural forms are rendered by the deft co-ordination of eye and hand, not by a measuring instrument. Hammershøi didn't have a studio, but worked at home, in the very rooms depicted in these interiors. Knowing this, it is easy to visualise the neat palette, the clean brushes, the immaculate craftsmanship he brought to his art.

In other paintings a solitary woman is shown with her face turned away from us. Sometimes she is reading a letter facing a blank wall, at other times she is seated in the middle of the room, her back to us. Often the door on the far wall is open, affording us a view of the space beyond, where yet another open door leads our eye to a glimpse of window in the far distance. In such works voids are given the same value as solid forms, and space is as important as the figures and things it surrounds.

But how are we to understand these pictures? We know very little about Hammershøi, who left no letters or diaries, and who, apart from two early trips to Paris and several low-key visits to London, had few friendships outside a small circle of Danish artists and critics – some of whom appear, seated around a dining-room table illuminated by candlelight, in the famous but not typical group portrait now in Stockholm. Because he doesn't fit into any of the international art movements of his time, it is almost easier to say what his art is not than what it is.

First, it is not Romantic. In the Northern Romantic tradition exemplified by Caspar David Friedrich, a figure looking out of an open window suggests a longing for spiritual freedom, a dissatisfaction with the confined interior in which they find themselves. But in Hammershøi, the light always penetrates into the enclosed spaces, suffusing his figures with a silvery radiance, integrating them into their surroundings, creating an effect of wholeness.

Second, his art has nothing to do with Expressionism. In Expressionist pictures, such as those of Hammershøi's Norwegian contemporary Edvard Munch, domestic interiors are settings for playing out tragic family dramas. But in Hammershøi's work the

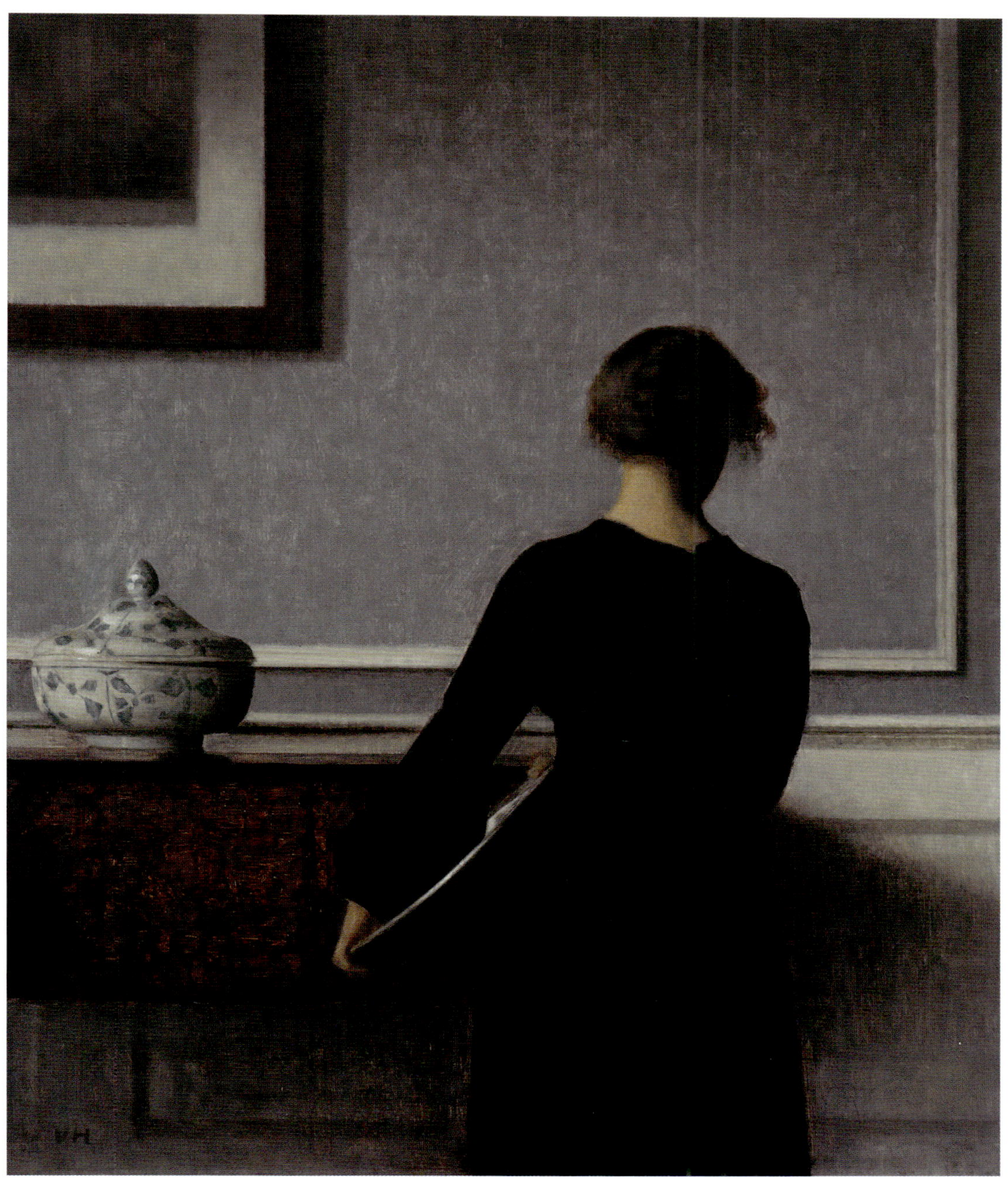

Vilhelm Hammershøi
Interior with Young Woman from Behind, *1904*
Randers Art Museum

mood is of utter peace. In every picture a window is shown or implied to alleviate any potential sense of claustrophobia.

Third, there is no temptation to read these pictures as symbolic. These are not paintings about loss or absence. They tell no story. No, they are what they appear to be: meditations on the complexity and beauty of form and space. Though the Parisian press has compared Hammershøi to Vermeer and Piero della Francesca, I think there is a closer precedent for what he does in the art of the eighteenth-century still-life painter Chardin.

For me, these interiors are in a sense still lifes – arrangements of doors, tables, windows and furniture in space. Seen in this way, we understand why the figures turn away from us, or sit in places where no one would dream of putting a chair. Figures function as formal elements in the composition, deliberately placed where they are needed, as abstract and yet as tangible as the bottles and jars painted by Giorgio Morandi.

There is something else about Hammershøi that is hard to put into words. Though there is nothing remotely mystical about his art, he is the painter of still interior moments, when thoughts are subdued and the mind is at rest. His art is about the clarity and order we experience when we accept the world as it is, when the imagination is quiet.

Symbolist Landscape

In 1886 the French poet Jean Moréas defined Symbolism in art as the attempt to 'clothe the idea in sensuous form'. The important word to pick out in that sentence is 'idea'. In the last decades of the nineteenth century, Symbolism emerged as a reaction to the naturalistic styles of realism and Impressionism. It evolved in parallel with similar developments in music (Debussy), theatre (Maeterlinck) and poetry (Mallarmé).

Ravishing though an Impressionist picture might be, it can only present the viewer with facts, not ideas. Impressionism celebrates the visible world, the here-and-now, the passing moment. Take a view by Monet of a railway bridge over the Seine. You can, if you wish, learn a lot from it about the effects of the railroads and the subsequent industrialisation on the suburbs north of Paris in the 1870s – but nothing at all about less tangible areas of human experience such as love, grief, imagination or forgiveness.

Likewise, Degas and Manet paint prostitutes but not erotic experience. Whistler paints the Thames at night but has little to say about melancholy. Symbolist painters of mythological and allegorical subjects like Gustave Moreau, Jan Toorop and G. F. Watts addressed a new subject in art – the inner world of feeling, yearning and aspiration.

Did I say new? Actually, a century earlier William Blake, Caspar David Friedrich and J. M. W. Turner used symbols and allegory to convey ideas that are otherwise barely expressible in words, while the cult of the picturesque revelled in the melancholy sense of time passing, conveyed by the sight of bare ruined monasteries. So it is more accurate to say that Symbolism is a resurgence of the idealism last seen in Northern European painting during the Romantic period. This summer a sensationally good show at the Scottish National Gallery looks at an aspect of the movement that has not yet received

7 August 2012

Van Gogh to Kandinsky: Symbolist Landscape in Europe 1880–1910

Scottish National Gallery, Edinburgh

much attention – the Symbolist landscape in Europe from 1880 to 1910. As well as bringing together scores of first-rate paintings by artists whose names are scarcely known even to art historians, it refuses to oversimplify the surprisingly difficult question of what exactly a Symbolist landscape is.

Why, for example, is the barren landscape peopled by classically draped women in Puvis de Chavannes's 1885 canvas *Vision of Antiquity* Symbolist, when a classical landscape containing the same elements by the seventeenth-century painter Claude Lorrain is not? The answer is that Puvis makes no attempt to replicate in paint the tangible reality or the appearance of the natural world, however idealised. His fantasy of an Arcadian idyll has nothing to do with illusionistic or atmospheric truth. It was painted in reaction to the visual and moral squalor caused by the rapid industrialisation and rampant materialism that was transforming the social fabric in France. His rhythmic disposition of figures swathed in soft blue, pink and green against a colourless landscape implies some underlying moral order, the sense of calm that characterises a society at peace with itself and with the outside world. Because the women are not differentiated as individuals, Puvis implies that they live as equals in a democratic society. The picture's absence of colouristic intensity, tonal contrast or dramatic action is part of its point — for in a socialist utopia, life is pleasantly dull.

Although Symbolism is not a style of painting, the technique used to paint a Symbolist picture often conveys a deeper meaning than the banal subject matter may seem to warrant. The myriad dots of paint in pointillist seascapes by Paul Signac and Henri-Edmond Cross, for instance, create uninflected screens of colour in which no area of the canvas has more dramatic or chromatic interest than any other. Embedded into the very fabric of pictures showing sailing boats and cultivated fields, therefore, are utopian notions of harmony between man and nature.

But beware of generalisations. In the hands of the little-known Alphonse Osbert, the pointillist technique beautifully evokes a mood of soft, dreamy reverie. In his *Evening Poem* of 1897 three white-robed women are shown against an imaginary landscape created by horizontal bands of black and blue dots. A strip of water irradiated by a few thin strokes of orange paint runs from left to right across the centre of the composition. The picture is a melancholy reverie on the closing of the day and the transience of life. The artist depicts not something he saw, but the feelings the landscape evoked in him.

Some Symbolists chose subjects quintessentially associated with Impressionism, like beaches and urban vistas. But look what they did to them. The Belgian Léon Spilliaert paints the beach at Ostend in 1908 but shows the colonnaded galleries of the royal pavilion receding in vertiginous perspective into the distance in the dying light of a cold winter's afternoon. The Dane Vilhelm Hammershøi paints the square in front of the Amalienborg Palace in Copenhagen, but at a time of day when it is deserted, making it look frozen in time, like something dreamed up by de Chirico.

All but one of the Nordic painters in this show studied at some point in their careers in Paris, and then went home to paint the muted colours and fading light of Northern forests, lakes and coastlines. But even when such landscapes appear to be naturalistic they can be loaded with symbolic meaning. Sweden's Prince Eugen paints a dense screen of tree trunks running from bottom to top of the canvas. The repeated verticals block out the light except for the distant shimmer of the setting sun. In this way the artist conveys the idea that through life's dark maze of obstacles and complexities lies something more. What that 'more' is – death, eternal reward, hope – is unstated, for in Symbolism to name an object, an idea or a feeling is to diminish its potency. The painter only suggests, and by suggestion reveals not what he saw but what he thought or felt.

If those feelings or thoughts were easily expressed, Symbolism would have little value. Where it is unrivalled is in conveying complex or even contradictory ideas using the formal means available to all painters – the choice of subject, the painting technique, and the composition. In his 1908 *Woods Near Oele* Mondrian uses ribbons of dark red, streaks of undulating pink and smears of black and indigo paint to convey a sense of nature in constant flux, but then uses a geometric grid formed by vertical trees and the horizontal mountain range to stabilise his composition – and by implication to suggest that some invisible force holds the universe together. This is religious painting for an age of unbelief.

This distinguished show genuinely adds something to our knowledge about late nineteenth- and early twentieth-century

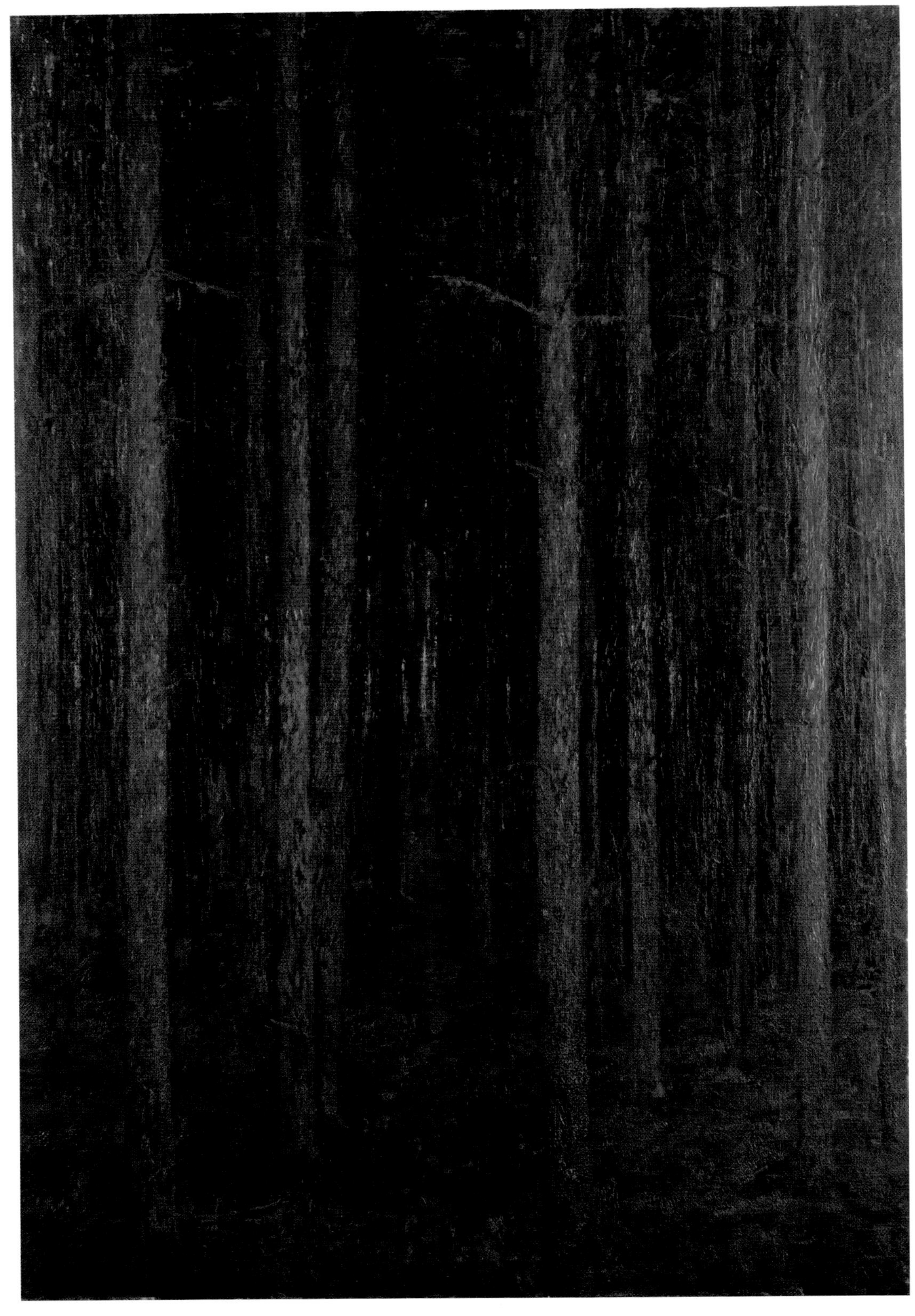

painting. That I profoundly disagree with the inclusion of a substantial number of artists in it under the Symbolist umbrella only goes to show how serious a show it is. Whistler, for example, was a student of the realist painter Courbet. He remained a *plein air* realist throughout his career. Though he wrote poetically about his views of the Thames at night his intention in them was purely descriptive. His urban views have no hidden or secondary meanings. I would argue that the same is true for Monet and I have reservations about the inclusion of Leighton, Gauguin and Van Gogh.

These distinctions are important. The realist tradition extends from Impressionism and Post-Impressionism in the nineteenth century to Cubism and Abstraction in the twentieth. Symbolism appeared to die out by about 1910, but in fact lived on in the art of Marcel Duchamp, whose ready-mades are the continuation of the Symbolist idea that what is important about a work of art is not only (or even primarily) what you see but what it makes you think or feel. But that is the kind of controversy that makes this such a terrific show.

Prince Eugen
The Forest, *1892*
Gothenburg Art
Museum

1900: Art at the Crossroads

The concept behind the Royal Academy's *1900: Art at the Crossroads* is as simple as it is audacious: to look at the condition of painting and sculpture at the turn of the century by cutting across national boundaries and different schools of artistic practice. The idea is to show what was happening in Tokyo and Melbourne, Helsinki and New York at the very moment when Monet was painting *Charing Cross Bridge* and Picasso was exploring the dives and dance halls of Montmartre. But what aesthetic criteria do you use to select pictures for such a show?

The answer has been to build 1900 around the Exposition Universelle, the most glamorous of all world fairs, which opened in Paris in April 1900. Among its many attractions, it featured a vast show of international contemporary painting and sculpture which was held in the newly built Grand Palais. Twenty-nine countries were represented, each sending a group of artists selected by a committee of their own countrymen. Each nation was given a separate space in which to show and, as at the Venice Biennale, competition between countries was fierce. France took the lion's share of space to show the overwhelming majority of artists (2,612 works by 1,066 artists). By general consensus, however, the country that sent the best art was Belgium, and everyone expressed amazement at the beauty and originality of the work sent by the Scandinavian countries. But naturally the quality of what was on view varied wildly.

Recognising this, the curators of the Royal Academy's exhibition have not tied themselves down by limiting the selection to works actually sent to Paris in 1900 (though one section of the exhibition does so). Instead, from the long list of artists who exhibited at the Exposition Universelle, they have chosen works of art painted, carved or modelled between 1898 to 1903. Almost three hundred works jostle for space in the beautiful galleries at Burlington House. They range

12 January 2000

1900: Art at the Crossroads

Royal Academy, London

from a spectacular mural-sized altarpiece by the arch-academician William-Adolphe Bouguereau to an Expressionistic landscape by a part-time artist, the playwright August Strindberg; and from the calm monumentality of Aristide Maillol's life-sized reclining nude to the neurotic intensity of British sculptor Alfred Gilbert's Virgin Mary in polychromed bronze.

London has not seen anything like it since the RA's sprawling Post-Impressionist exhibition in 1979. The difference is that that show had a theme, a thread to guide the visitor through uncharted waters; *1900* is like a gigantic fishing net dipped into the ocean of art history to come up with a pictorial catch of every possible type and variety, scale, quality and importance, from the sublime to the risible. I must admit that I haven't yet come to grips with it all. I'll have to go back again and again.

The show is not hung by school but by theme – the Bather, the Interior, Religion, the City, Portraits, Landscape and so forth, so that within each section the works on the wall might be Impressionist, Post-Impressionist, Academic, Symbolist or Realist. Visually, the whole thing is a mess, but what a glorious mess! With the benefit of hindsight, art historians invariably shape and prune and tie up loose ends: *1900* tries to show what actually happened at the turn of the century, not what the history books tell us happened.

In doing this the curators Robert Rosenblum, Mary Anne Stevens and Ann Dumas took an enormous risk. As we know from the RA's summer exhibition, when you hang bad art next to good it drags the good down to its level. But it was a risk worth taking. In the gallery devoted to Bathers and Nudes, for example, a shimmering little Cézanne *Grandes Baigneuses* rubs shoulders with the French academic painter Paul Chabas's nearly life-sized *Joyous Frolics*. We find ourselves looking at both pictures harder than ever before, trying to analyse what it is that makes the Cézanne look forward to the twentieth century, while the Chabas belonged, even in the year it was painted, to the past.

The answer has something to do with the degree to which the artist seeks or rejects naturalistic illusion. Chabas's circlet of scantily clad young women frolic in a pool of shallow water which floods over the picture plane in such a way that nothing comes between the figures in the picture and the viewer standing in front of it. The dark-eyed minx

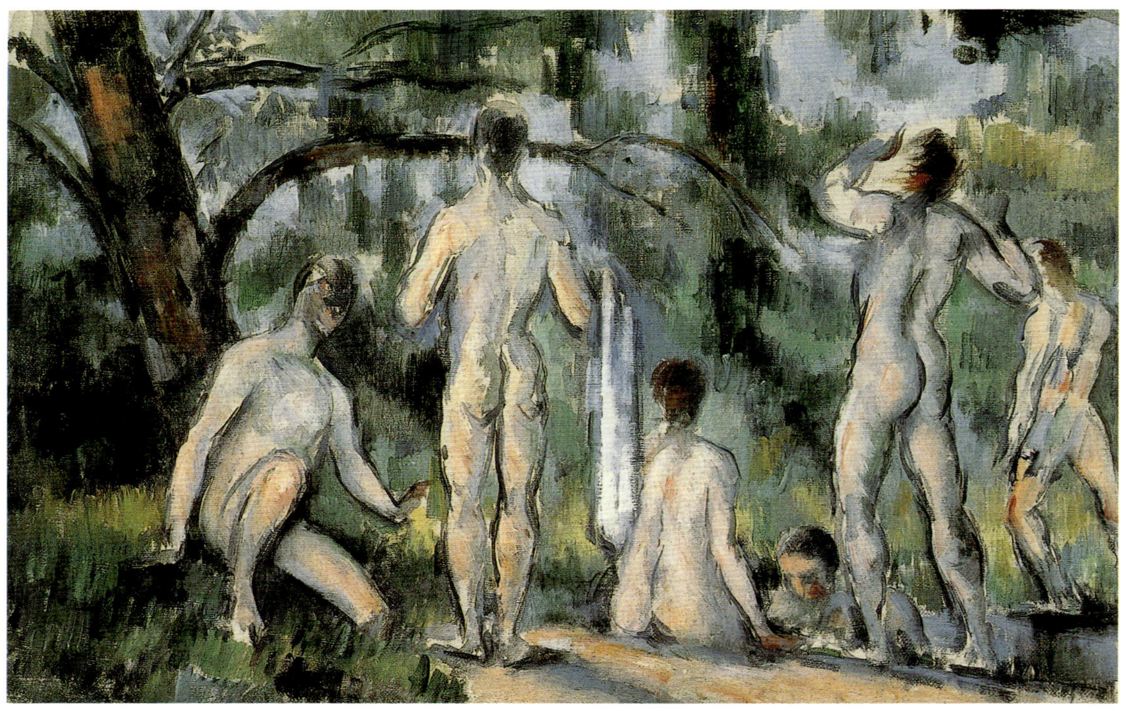

nearest to us looks boldly out of the painting, as though she could
stretch out her hand and drag us through the invisible picture plane
into her pictorial space.

The Cézanne too shows a group of nude bathers, but has almost
nothing else in common with the Chabas. Cézanne allows us to see
how each brushstroke is laid on to the flat canvas, an intricate medley
of tiny patches of pure colour used to create mass and volume as well
as flickering movement. History has of course decided that Cézanne
was a genius, Chabas second-rate. I don't think the curators are asking
us to re-evaluate their respective reputations, but to understand the
historical context in which they were made.

For in 1900 artists such as Chabas, Jean-Léon Gérôme and John
Singer Sargent were bringing to a close the nineteenth century's
dialogue between painting and photography. Their successors would
be found in the directors of the early cinema (indeed, I'm not sure that
Hedy Lamarr's famous nude scene in *Ecstasy* doesn't owe something
to a painting in this show by the Swedish artist Anders Zorn). But
at this very moment progressive artists such as Cézanne, Gauguin,
Munch and Klimt were attempting to analyse the nature of visual,

Paul Cézanne
Study of Bathers,
1895–98
Pushkin Museum of
Fine Arts, Moscow

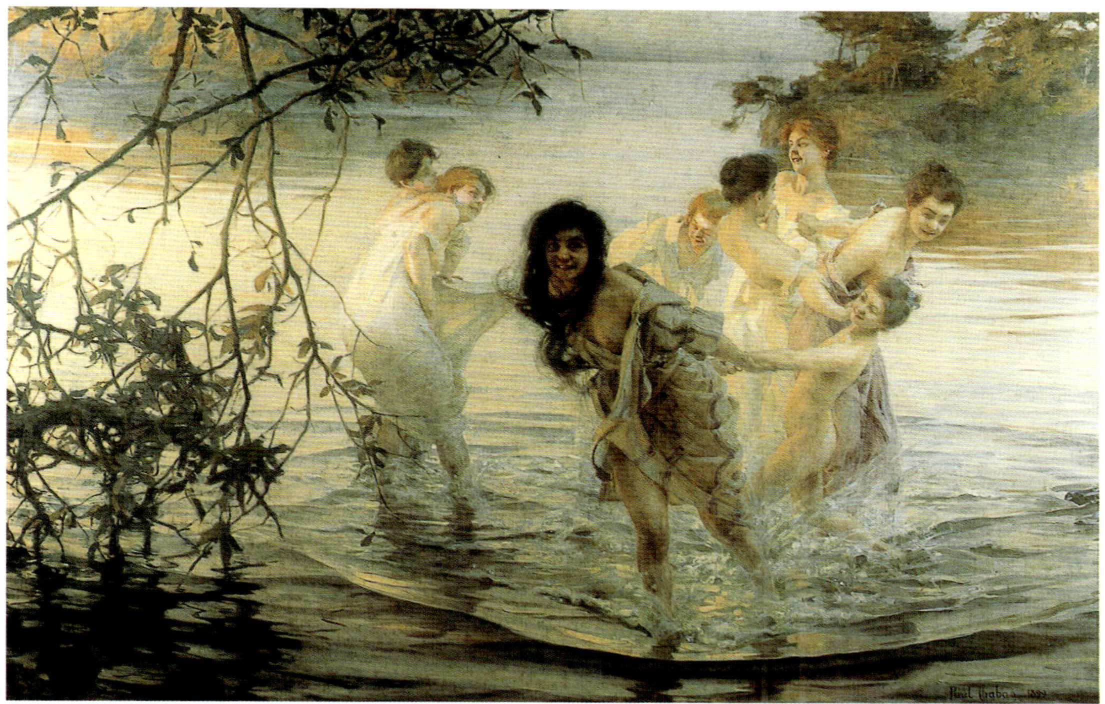

Paul Chabas
Joyous Frolics, *1899*
Musée des Beaux-Arts,
Nantes

spiritual and psychological experience. The question the exhibition asks us to consider is whether one set of artists is better than the other – or just different. How we answer this will depend on what value we place on originality.

Take the example of Childe Hassam, an American follower of Monet. His *Late Afternoon, New York: Winter* is a masterpiece of American Impressionism painted long after Impressionism had become a spent force in France. Seeing it next to Monet's *Charing Cross Bridge* in this show, I actually preferred Hassam's magical evocation of a winter's evening, though Monet is unquestionably the greater artist. I suppose the lesson is that we must judge works of art by our response to them, not by the date they were painted or the order they were painted in. But do we gain anything by such comparisons?

When the young Mondrian paints wind-tossed willows reflected in the River Gein by evening light, his mood is echoed across Europe in Klimt's brooding poplars silhouetted against the cloudy night sky. But this kind of juxtaposition makes you think you're learning something when really you aren't because both pictures were inspired by a series painted by Monet in the early 1890s, *Poplars on the Epte.*

Maybe I'm asking too much of *1900*. Who can complain about an exhibition that brings to London Valentin Serov's penetrating *Portrait of Maria Morozova*, Sir John Lavery's terrifying *Father and Daughter*, Ludvig Find's endlessly touching *Portrait of the Norwegian Painter Thorvald Erichsen*? And I was stopped in my tracks by the thousands of naked children who tumble like so many gurgling sperm down a hideous but unforgettable masterpiece by the Belgian Symbolist Léon Fréderic. I'm still trying to imagine what the young Picasso made of the naked women who stare out at us from Emile Bernard's *The Three Races* when he came to paint the *Demoiselles d'Avignon*. This is a show in which we finally get to see the works of artists who are always mentioned, but rarely illustrated in biographies of Picasso and Matisse – the Spaniard Ramón Pichot Gironés's interior of a church in Barcelona, and the Belgian Henri Evenepoel's *The Spaniard in Paris*.

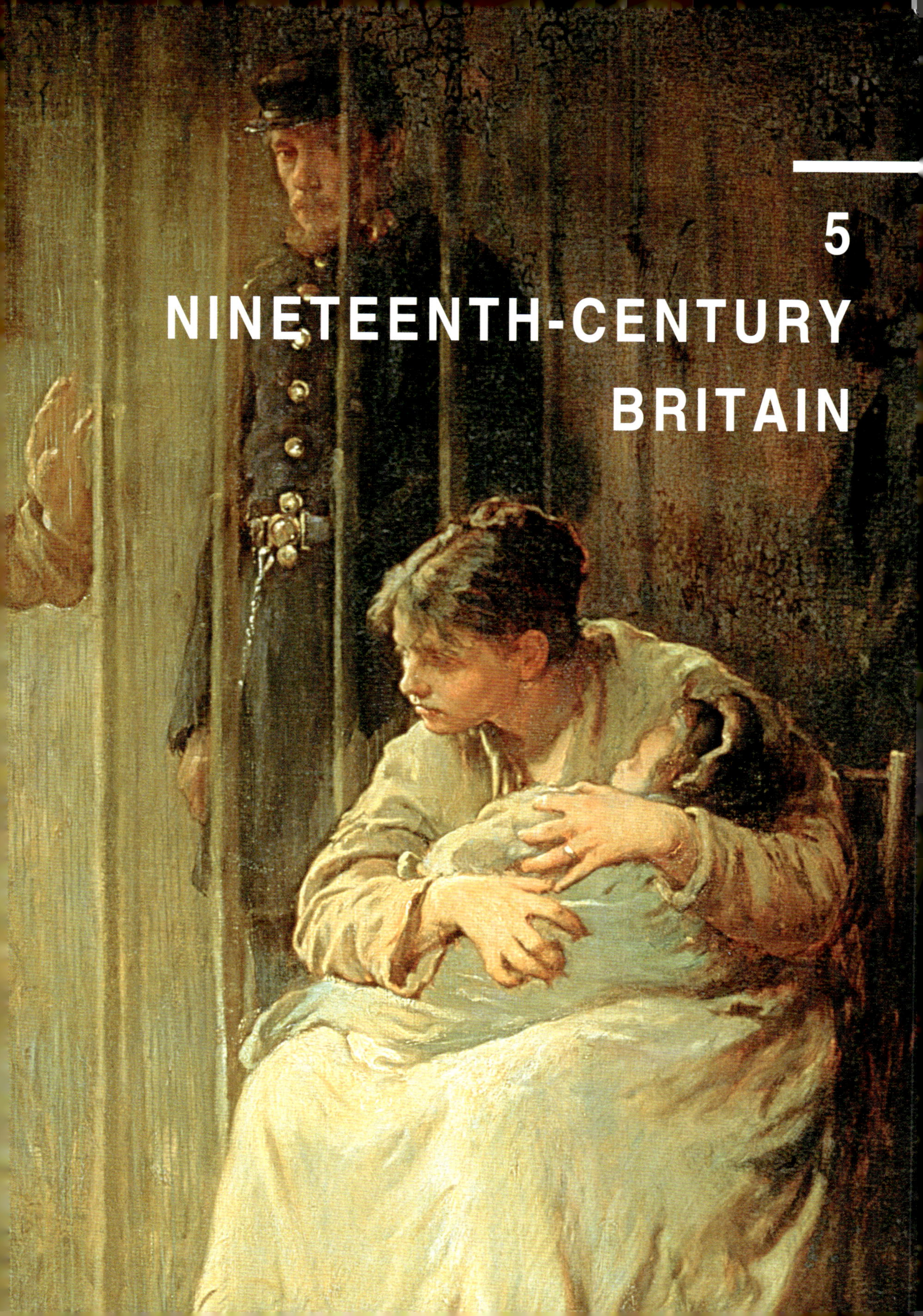

5
NINETEENTH-CENTURY
BRITAIN

Thomas Lawrence
**Portrait of Elizabeth
Farren**, *1790*
*Metropolitan Museum
of Art, New York*

Thomas Lawrence

One of the pictures that launched the twenty-one-year-old Thomas Lawrence's career when it was shown at the Royal Academy in 1790 was his full-length portrait of the celebrated actress Elizabeth Farren, engaged at the time to marry the Earl of Derby. Miss Farren is shown against a landscape of rolling hills on a clear spring morning, with sheep grazing peacefully in the distance. But instead of a simple frock suitable for such a time and place, she's heavily made up and dressed to the teeth, as though out for a night on the town. She is also wearing clothes more suitable for winter than spring. Swathed in silk and clutching her fur-trimmed evening cloak to her throat with one hand, she carries a huge fur muff and an elbow-length kid glove in her other. Moving from right to left across the canvas, she appears to stop, turn her head in our direction, smile and throw us a mischievous glance. It's as though we'd spotted her hurrying home in the morning after a late-night assignation. Elizabeth Farren specialised in comic roles: if she were on stage, she'd be giving her audience a wink.

And that word 'wink' exactly captures Lawrence's ability to let his viewers in on the joke, to turn us into his accomplices. In his lifetime, a contemporary accused him of being a 'male coquet' and the National Portrait Gallery's glorious exhibition *Thomas Lawrence: Regency Power and Brilliance* allows us to see his seductive technique in action – especially when he's painting a beautiful young person of either sex.

Take his three-quarter length 1792 portrait of Arthur Atherley, a banker's son just down from Eton, who was only two years younger than the painter. A decade before Byron's debut, Lawrence transforms this ordinary young man into a Regency buck by showing him standing against black storm clouds with Eton College in the far distance. Looking straight at the viewer, Arthur politely doffs his top hat with one hand, as though meeting us for the first time. Then look

19 October 2010

Thomas Lawrence:
Regency Power and
Brilliance

National Portrait
Gallery, London

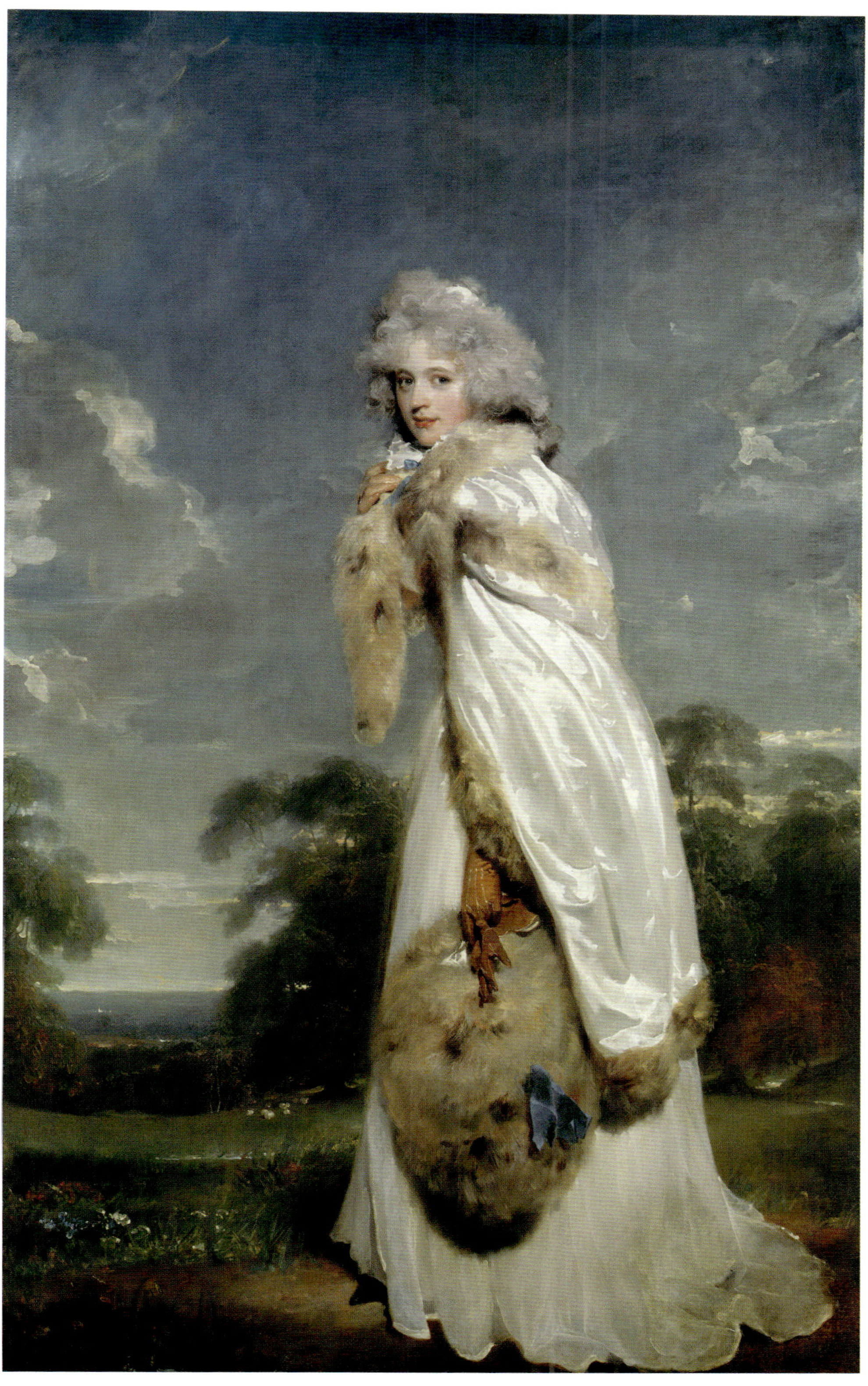

what happens. Casually flipping back his scarlet coat to show off
a slim waist, he rests one gloved hand on his hip. He then lowers
his head slightly to allow his long hair to tumble down over his
shoulders, and with the hint of a smile passing over his lips, locks
his eyes with ours. Georgette Heyer, eat your heart out.

With older men, Lawrence is usually less successful, unless they
are in uniform. Art historians love his triple portrait of the bankers Sir
Francis Baring, John Baring and Charles Wall because it so cleverly
incorporates references to group portraits by Titian and Reynolds. For
all the liveliness of the picture's conception, however, I find the poses
and gestures stilted and unconvincing. I suppose that since time
immemorial bankers and businessmen have been no fun to paint, but
then neither were young noblemen who didn't look particularly
noble. Faced with painting a lump like John, Lord Mountstuart,
Lawrence's solution is to wrap him in a cloak to disguise his girth. In
what had by now become a well-worn trick of the trade, frumpy Lord
John is seen from below, romantically silhouetted against storm-tossed
skies – and fooling nobody.

But if a male sitter could pose in a costume that presented
Lawrence with a challenge, he didn't have to resort to such gimmicks.
He loved a man in uniform, particularly hussars in gold braid and
field marshals enveloped in greatcoats. But there was nothing he liked
better than a king or a duke in full regalia. As a general rule, a sitter's
merits or accomplishments were usually less important to him than
the appearance he presented to the world.

So imagine how thrilled he must have been when George IV
commissioned him to paint Pope Pius VII, the finest of the 24 portraits
that now hang in the Waterloo Chamber at Windsor Castle. The Pope
sits enthroned in the new Vatican galleries with the antique statue of
the Laocoon behind him, simply dressed in a white silk cassock and
red velvet jacket trimmed with ermine. Even here, Lawrence's wit is
irrepressible. No British monarch had commissioned a portrait of a
pope, and certainly not one intended to hang in a royal residence. For
this reason, no overt symbols of papal authority such as the triple tiara
are visible. But Lawrence shows the Pope resting one embroidered
slipper on a plump velvet cushion jutting out over the step to the dais
into the viewer's space. Right up until the twentieth century, etiquette
during a private audience at the Vatican required the visitor to kiss the

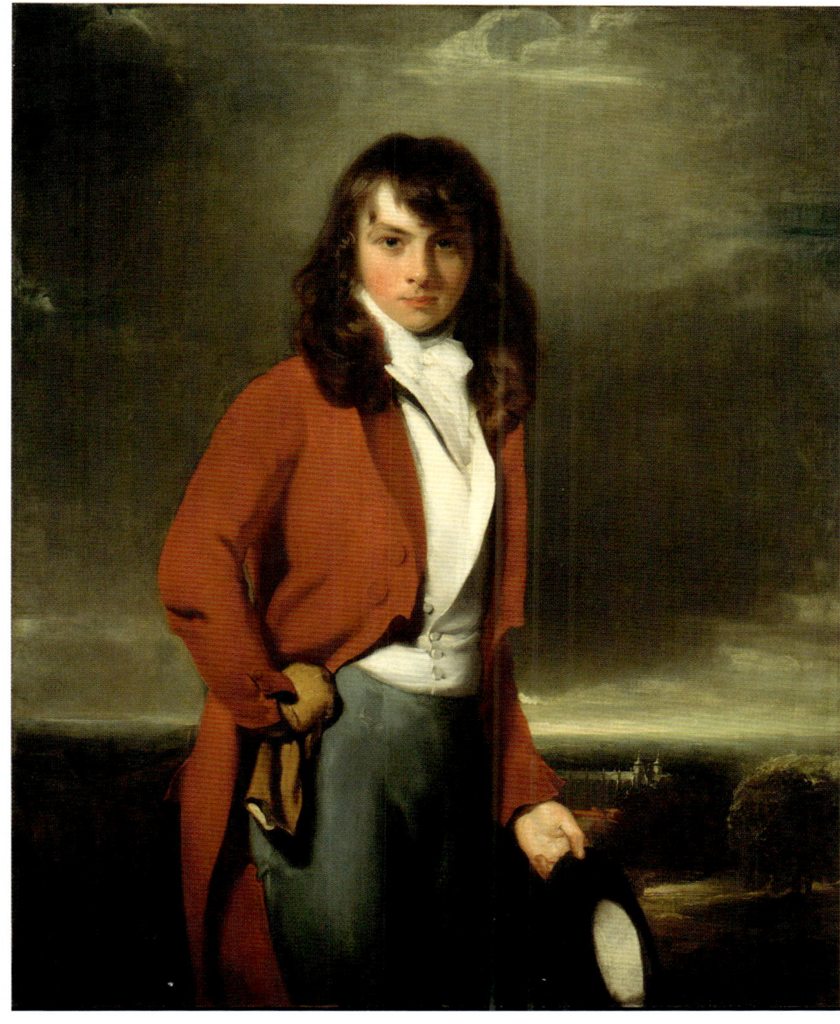

pope's foot. Since the portrait would hang just above eye level, that red velvet slipper becomes its dramatic focus, a (possibly facetious) invitation to the British monarch to submit to the Roman obedience. Only George IV would have let Lawrence get away with it.

Lawrence's portraits of women follow a similar pattern. Unless they are as old and as fierce as the wonderful Lady Robert Manners, the exploration of character is rarely the point, particularly if a woman didn't dress to impress. For example, the Duchess de Berry was such an important player in French politics after the Restoration that she could choose to be painted wearing a simple sleeveless gown, with only a rose and single pearl pendant at her breast. Since she was not a pretty woman, Lawrence doesn't know what to do with her, and so concentrates all the picture's visual excitement in the tartan bonnet she wears in tribute to the historical figure she most admired, Mary Queen of Scots.

As well as being a sublime portraitist, Lawrence was also a ravishing still life painter: in this show you can feast your eyes on a diamond-encircled portrait of the King on Queen Charlotte's wrist, or the giant amethysts worn by Frances Anne, Marchioness of Londonderry. Such jewels were, of course, important symbols of the sitter's status – the Queen's as consort of the incapacitated George III, Lady Londonderry's as tokens of esteem presented to her by no less a figure than the Russian tsar.

One of Lawrence's best-known female portraits is also one of the strangest: his double portrait of the voluptuous Frances Hawkins and her son, John James Hamilton. Frances was the mistress of the handsome, vain and much-married Duke of Abercorn, who was also the father of the boy in the picture. She looks straight out at us with her fresh and open face, but instead of showing us her body, Lawrence places a slobbering Newfoundland dog between her and the viewer, one that turns towards the irritating little boy as though unsure whether to lick his face or bite his head off.

And speaking of irritation, Lawrence must be the worst painter of children in the history of art. Lawrence gets it wrong every time by making them too coy, too knowing and too much like adults. In his celebrated portrait of seven-year-old Charles William Lambton in his red velvet playsuit and frilly open-necked shirt, for example, the child places one hand behind his head, like a Mack Sennett bathing beauty. And what on earth is he doing, sitting alone on a rocky outcrop at night, looking out over a moonlit sea?

Though nothing can be done about the sadly inadequate temporary exhibition spaces at the National Portrait Gallery, the selection and the installation do full justice to the visceral intensity of Lawrence's best work. And I loved the catalogue's old-fashioned, deeply satisfying entries that answer all the questions you have about each picture.

Turner and the Sea

One of the first pictures in the National Maritime Museum's *Turner and the Sea* is the early nineteenth-century equivalent of a disaster movie – the kind filmed in 3D that you have to see in an Imax cinema. Painted in 1810, *Wreck of a Transport Ship* makes your stomach lurch by plunging you headlong into chaos. The scene is a storm at sea. With no land in sight and no barrier between us and the mountainous swells that rise up on either side of the picture, we look down into dark roiling waters, our equilibrium destabilised by the up-and-down, back-and-forth rocking movement in a composition that has no centre on which the eye can focus.

Transfixed by the furious brushwork and naturalistic detail with which Turner depicts the frenzied waves lifting the lifeboat in the foreground into its vertiginous diagonal, it takes a moment for the viewer to understand that while the boat's passengers and crew desperately struggle to haul a drowning soldier on board, their fate is already sealed. For the fishing boat attempting to rescue them has been tossed back with such violence that it too looks likely to break up.

Having witnessed the impending doom of perhaps two dozen souls in the foreground, our eye moves at last to an even more horrific tragedy unfolding in the upper left-hand corner where, in the distance, scores of terrified passengers still cling to the deck of the listing ship. By painting them as an indistinct mass of humanity Turner emphasises nature's indifference to their imminent annihilation. Though muffled by wailing winds and deafening waves, you can almost hear their final cries of terror as the ship turns over.

For all its immediacy, *Wreck of a Transport Ship* is an imaginary scene that may have been inspired by newspaper accounts of the loss of a real ship, the *Minotaur*. By the time he painted it, Turner had been depicting the sea in all its moods for ten years. In the decades to come he would become so well known for his engagement with maritime

26 November 2013

Turner and the Sea

National Maritime
Museum, London

subjects that the Victorian artist Robert Leslie recalled his father describing the great man to him as 'Mr Turner the famous *sea* painter'.

The show at Greenwich doesn't go quite that far, but it does place Turner firmly within a long and distinguished tradition of maritime painting that includes Willem van de Velde the Younger and Jan van Ruisdael in Holland, Claude-Joseph Vernet in France and both Philip James de Loutherbourg and Thomas Gainsborough in Britain.

However talented his predecessors or contemporaries, Turner transcends them all. As a student at the Royal Academy Schools he was taught by the president Joshua Reynolds to idealise nature in the manner of the Old Masters. But can the sea be idealised in the way a landscape can? I don't think so. That is why it was just as important for the formation of the painter Turner would become that as well as studying the paintings of Poussin and Claude he loved to visit the panoramas and dioramas that were such a feature of late eighteenth-century popular entertainment. There he would have seen spectacular images of shipwrecks and other natural disasters, many of them based on events that had recently been in the news. For accounts of shipwrecks haunted the imagination of the British, who depended on the sea and its vagaries for the country's naval supremacy and economic prosperity.

Throughout his career, Turner was always drawn to current events, sketching the ruins of a theatre on the day after a fire, or the burning of the Houses of Parliament as it was happening. As we see in this show his method was to fill notebooks with quick sketches that became the raw data he used for finished landscapes and seascapes in watercolours or oils. It's what he did with that data that is the key to understanding Turner's art. For his landscapes and seascapes divide into different categories: sensational crowd-pleasers; accurate topographical views primarily intended to convey information; and scenes in which he omitted, distorted or added details to express his thoughts on history, nature, politics or society.

I would argue – perhaps counter-intuitively – that *Wreck of a Transport Ship* belongs in the first category, as does his monumental *Battle of Trafalgar* of 1823. Commissioned by George IV in 1822, it is easy to imagine this scene of awesome destruction, violence and chaos as an exhibit in a popular diorama. Turner's intention is to thrill and inform by presenting his audience with a realistic (though by no

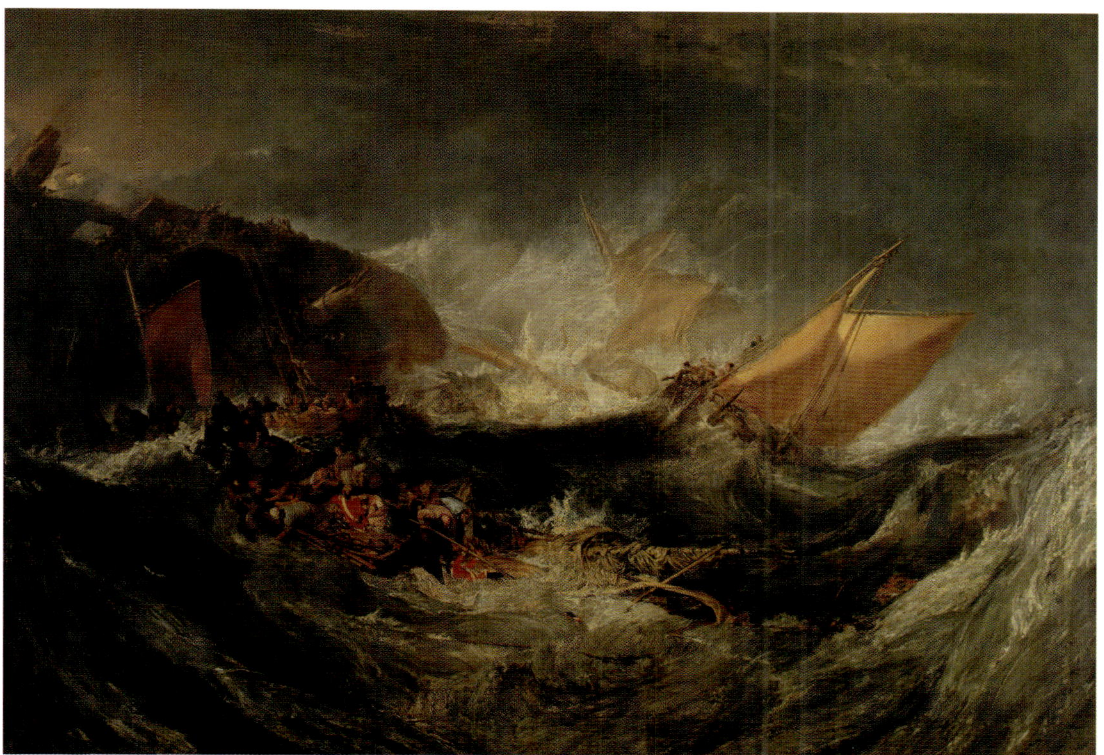

means historically accurate) evocation of a naval battle seen from close to.

Realising that most representations of naval battles are unintelligible to anyone who wasn't present, he chooses to show a static moment at the end of the fighting when the French ship *Redoubtable* surrenders to the English. Through the smoke of battle the hull, sails, cannon and rigging of Nelson's great flagship *Victory* loom up in front of us, its sheer scale dwarfing everything below it. In the foreground, English sailors, rowing around the periphery of the battle to rescue survivors, cheer Nelson's victory.

Battle of Trafalgar is a technical *tour de force*. Had any other artist painted such a picture, you'd say it was a masterpiece. But whether because it was a royal commission or because Turner dared not project his own thoughts and feelings on to so iconic a subject, what's missing for me is the ineffable dimension that makes Turner so much greater than contemporaries like Clarkson Stanfield or Francis Danby. For in his most profound works, Turner had the ability to weave into his imagery a sense of the past impinging on the present. This is particularly true in many of the oils he painted at the height of the Napoleonic wars, such as *Hannibal Crossing the Alps,* but it is there, too, in *The Fighting Temeraire Tugged to her Last Berth to be Broken Up, 1838* (1839).

Then, too, Turner had so much to say about so many subjects that he often expressed his ideas about history and destiny indirectly – for example, by pairing two pictures in such a way that meaning is conveyed not in one or the other painting but in the difference between them. In this show, we can see this happening in the pairing of *Venice* (1834) and *Keelmen Heaving in Coals by Night* from the following year. The first is a view of the church of San Giorgio under blue skies on a summer's day, when the Grand Canal is crowded with pleasure-seekers and no one is doing a hand's turn of work. The second is a night scene set on the Tyne, with watery moonlight irradiating the sky with silver as workmen load coal on to barges for shipment to London.

Far from despising the industrial north, Turner pays tribute to the hard-working men who laboured through the night to create the wealth that made Britain the nation it was. He even dares to suggest that beauty can be found even in an industrial environment at the mouth of the River Tyne. By contrasting this with the idleness and luxury depicted in the Venetian scene, Turner turns the table on us. Against strength, independence and energy he juxtaposes lassitude, subjugation and corruption.

What a show this is. The organisers have snagged all the great maritime paintings and chosen works on paper that reveal so much, not only about how Turner worked, but how he thought.

Turner's *Fighting Temeraire*

Yet another illusion shattered! Like most visitors to the National Gallery I had always assumed that one of J. M. W. Turner's most popular paintings, *The Fighting Temeraire Tugged to her Last Berth to be Broken Up, 1838*, is an accurate visual record of an event the painter actually witnessed: the last journey up the Thames of the ship whose crew had fought so heroically at the Battle of Trafalgar. The latest exhibition in the National Gallery's excellent *Making and Meaning* series shows that it is nothing of the sort. When in August 1838 the Admiralty sold the 98-gun fighting ship *Temeraire* at auction in Sheerness, it first stripped her of her masts and rigging. What was towed 55 miles upriver to a wharf in Rotherhithe was a bare, distinctly unheroic hulk. What's more, the journey took place on 5 and 6 September – when Turner is thought to have been abroad. The closest he came to witnessing the *Temeraire*'s last hours was to have read an account of them in *The Times*.

What, then, makes *The Fighting Temeraire* one of the most compelling images Turner ever painted? When John Ruskin came to examine Turner's works in *Modern Painters*, he interpreted them as symbolic warnings against the moral and physical decline of Great Britain. Certainly Turner, like Blake, was a visionary, a man out of his own time rather than, like Constable, a seeker after objective visual truth. Turner saw the *Temeraire* as the embodiment of England's naval glory, a symbol for the passing of a whole age. That the ship, which had seen no action for thirty-three years, was towed not at sunset but during daylight hours, and that the two steamers which towed her looked nothing like the one in Turner's painting, was immaterial to his purpose. Turner needed the setting sun to suggest the end of an era, just as he needed the prosaic tug as a pictorial foil to the romantic, high-masted ship.

12 July 1995

Making and Meaning.
Turner: *The Fighting Temeraire*

National Gallery,
London

The more I learn about Turner, the more I admire him not for the accuracy of his observation but for the fecundity of his invention. By placing the tug's smokestack just where he did (and not towards the stern, where it belongs) he ensured that a stream of smoke would obscure the jackstaff – where the Union Jack once had flown.

It is often said that in contrasting the stately ship to the squat steamer Turner expressed his dismay at the passing of an heroic age for a utilitarian one. Yet in other pictures Turner betrays no particular antipathy towards the effects of the Industrial Revolution. In his thrilling evocation of the railway age, *Rain, Steam and Speed*, for example, he stresses not the destructive aspects of change, but its inevitability.

Then, too, there is nothing crabbed or petty about Turner. Particularly in late paintings such as *The Slave Ship* and *Peace – Burial at Sea*, he strikes at the deepest chords of human experience, for they are about, respectively, the nature of evil and of grief. *The Fighting Temeraire* moves us so because it is about history – or, perhaps more accurately, about how the love of one's country is inseparable from a reverence for its history. When Turner painted *The Burning of the Houses of Parliament* in 1834, he had shown crowds of onlookers cheering as flames leaped and timbers crashed, destroying St Stephen's Chapel, the architectural symbol of England's medieval past. In that picture, as in *The Fighting Temeraire*, he criticises what he sees as Britain's lack of a proper regard for its own history.

Still, what I have said so far is not quite enough to explain the depth of emotion that resonates through the picture. For one thing, the *Temeraire* is a ghost ship. Its white, vaporous immateriality reminds me of the ghostly white forms swirling through Turner's *Interior at Petworth* – a picture which expresses the artist's personal desolation at the loss of his great patron Lord Egremont. And the silence that permeates *The Fighting Temeraire* is present, too, in one of the most beautiful of all Turner's paintings, *Peace – Burial at Sea*, his private tribute to his friend, the painter David Wilkie.

Perhaps what moves us so about *The Fighting Temeraire* is hidden, and has to do with Turner himself. We usually think of Turner as a nineteenth-century painter, but in fact he was born in 1775 and so reached maturity in the eighteenth century. The *Temeraire* had been built in 1798, the year after Turner exhibited his first oil at the Royal

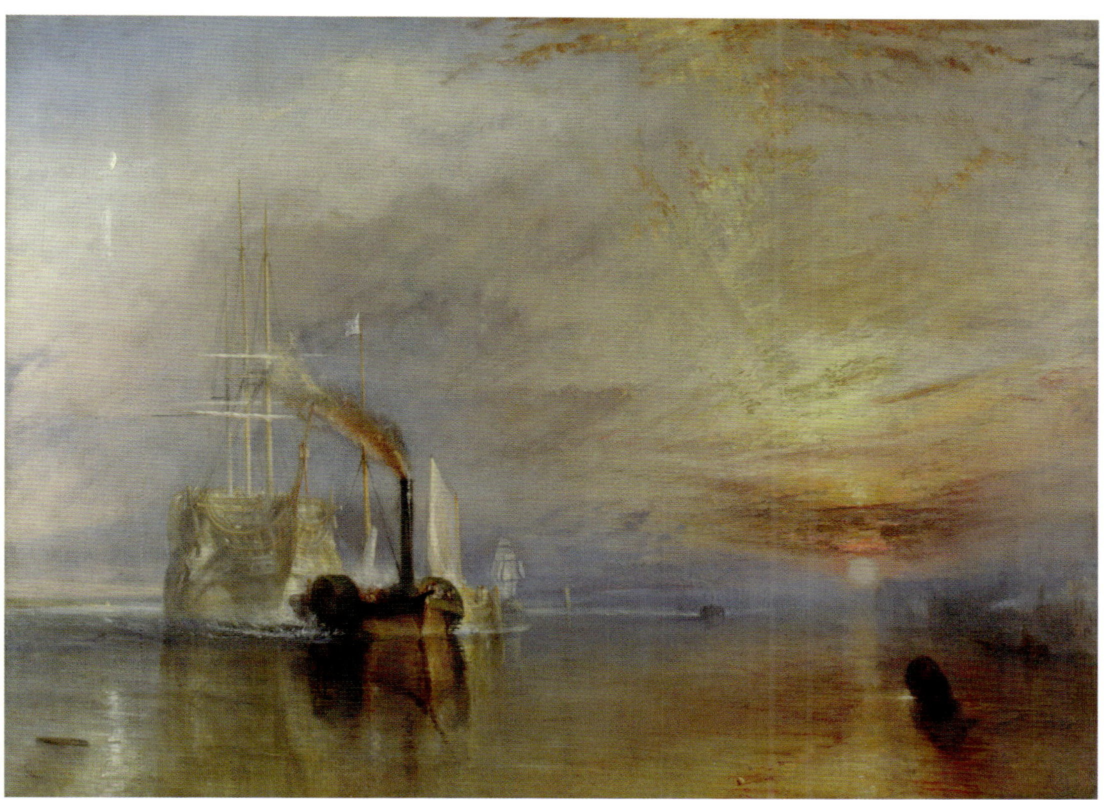

J. M. W. Turner
The Fighting Temeraire Tugged to her Last Berth to be Broken Up, 1838, *1839*
National Gallery, London

Academy. As a fiercely patriotic young man he certainly had followed her exploits at Trafalgar and subsequent roles as a prison and victualling ship. Could it be that the sixty-three-year-old Turner saw in the warship nearing the end of its useful life something of his own situation? As a lover of the sea and of ships, and as a man of the eighteenth as much as of the nineteenth century, he could have hit upon no more fitting a symbol of the passing of time, of the inevitable approach of his own death. Thinking of this, I looked again at the picture, and saw something I had not seen before: that there is a mythic quality about *The Fighting Temeraire*, with the black tug acting the role of the boatman Charon ferrying his ghostly galleon across the River Styx. So you give up one illusion – that the picture is a simple document – and you gain something infinitely more interesting: that its references range from the historical to the political to the deeply private.

Late Turner

Every generation makes J. M. W. Turner over in its own image. The phenomenon started in 1840 when John Ruskin, who was raised in the evangelical church, told readers of *Modern Painters* that Turner's pictures should be read as moral allegories – to which Turner replied that the critic 'sees more in my pictures than I ever painted'. More than a century later another critic and painter, Lawrence Gowing, staged an exhibition at New York's Museum of Modern Art in which he presented the great man essentially as an abstract artist, thereby turning him into a precursor of Pollock and Rothko.

Then came Turner and the written word. Beginning in the 1980s scholars began to study the many allusions to history, science, philosophy and myth embedded in his landscapes. They showed that what distinguished Turner from eighteenth-century predecessors such as Richard Wilson is that he used the medium of paint to express his thoughts on subjects ranging from morality and religion to current events. Next it was travel. We had exhibitions about Turner in central Italy, Turner in Venice, Turner in France and Switzerland, and Turner and the sea. Interesting though all this has been, in recent years I'd begun to ask myself where Turner studies would take us to next.

The answer is to Tate Britain's *Late Turner – Painting Set Free*, which in large measure is about Turner's body – or rather, it's about how infirmity and ageing impinged on his work in the sixteen years before his death in 1851. Such an approach takes us right back to the pictures and how they are painted.

It is well documented that in later life Turner used drink as a form of self-medication to control a tremor in his hands associated with Parkinson's disease. His alcohol consumption inevitably contributed to weight gain and that led to diabetes, which in turn affected the eyesight of a man already afflicted with cataracts. These ailments, as well as chronic fatigue and the loss of his teeth, imposed limitations

9 September 2014

Late Turner –
Painting Set Free

Tate Britain

on his physical and possibly mental capacities that could not but have impacted on his art.

The show, which is largely drawn from paintings and watercolours Turner bequeathed to the nation, starts in 1835. By then he was sixty and had long been one of the most famous artists in England. In late middle age he still undertook arduous painting tours at home and abroad, exhibited regularly at the Royal Academy and relished business dealings with patrons and engravers. The catalogue essay makes much of how spiteful critical writing about his pictures could be – but these were attacks on a financially successful artist, secure in his place at the heart of the establishment.

The question to ask as you walk through this show is not whether the onset of old age affected Turner's later paintings (of course it did) but at what point that physical deterioration can be detected and how that affects our understanding of his work. It's a very tricky subject. I'd be very careful about suggesting old age as the cause of a picture's success or failure because Turner had hits and misses at every period in his career. Even so, it is inarguable that the simple passage of time in a painter of Turner's age makes a huge difference to what a painter can and cannot do. Here is an example.

On his last trip to Venice in 1840 he created a series of watercolours as fresh and as seductive as anything he'd ever painted. In *Fishermen on the Lagoon, Moonlight*, for example, his ability to suggest delicate blues, greens and greys in the water melding imperceptibly into a midnight-blue sky irradiated by moonlight sends a shiver down the spine. But several views resulting from that same trip are unpleasantly harsh in colour and overworked in texture. For instance, both his habitual lightness of touch and descriptive precision are lost in the clogged and finicky paint surface of *Going to the Ball (San Martino)* while his overuse of chrome yellow quite simply ruins the picture. I was puzzled as to how Turner could have painted both the watercolour and the oil at the same date, until I read the label, which tells us that the oil was exhibited in 1846. I'd suggest that in the six years between the two works he experienced some impairment of his motor control, while that excess of yellow may be explained by the fact that oranges and yellows are the last colours a person with cataracts sees before he goes blind.

As in that lovely Venetian watercolour, many of the most beautiful pictures in this show are set either at night like *The Parting of Hero and Leander* or in violent storms like *Snow Storm Steam-Boat off a Harbour's Mouth*. Perhaps Turner in old age found it easier to control his blues, silvers and blacks than he did the spectrum of yellow, red and orange. Compare his moonlit elegy to the painter David Wilkie, *Peace – Burial at Sea*, with the lurid sunset in *War. The Exile and the Rock Limpet* which shows Napoleon surveying a world that looks drenched in blood. He exhibited both in 1842, but the miraculous tonal control in the nocturnal scene makes the heavy-handed application of oranges and reds in the sunset look all the cruder. Most of his best-loved late pictures are low in tone.

In these late works is paint really 'set free' as the title of the show proclaims? Turner experimented with octagonal and round formats and explored ever wilder colour combinations. And yes, scumbled and glazed picture surfaces reveal a more complex painting technique than he used in the 1820s. But then Turner had always flung, spattered and slapped paint on to canvas and he had always used brushes, a palette knife, rags and fingers to rub, smear and scrape his paint surfaces. In terms of pictorial innovation, the astonishing *Rain, Steam and Speed – the Great Western Railway* (1844) challenges the idea of what a finished picture could be at this period – but then so did *Hannibal Crossing the Alps* and that was painted in 1815.

My point is that you can't quite say what quality there is in 'late Turner' that makes his last pictures so very different from everything that went before. Towards the end of this exhibition we see luminous canvases such as *Northam Castle, Sunrise* in which Turner seems to be discarding extraneous detail, to reduce painting itself to colour and light. Some of these sublimely empty pictures consist only of bands of soft yellow and blue, while in others he seems to be reprising motifs from pictures painted decades earlier as though painting his own memories, confronting his own mortality.

Had the show ended here, I'd have wiped away a tear and gone home happy. But there is still one more gallery yet to see and in it are highly finished exhibition pictures on the theme of Dido and Aeneas. They are dreadfully overworked, and overcrowded to the point of incoherence. Yet Turner exhibited them at the Royal Academy in 1850, implying that these were the kinds of pictures by which he wished to

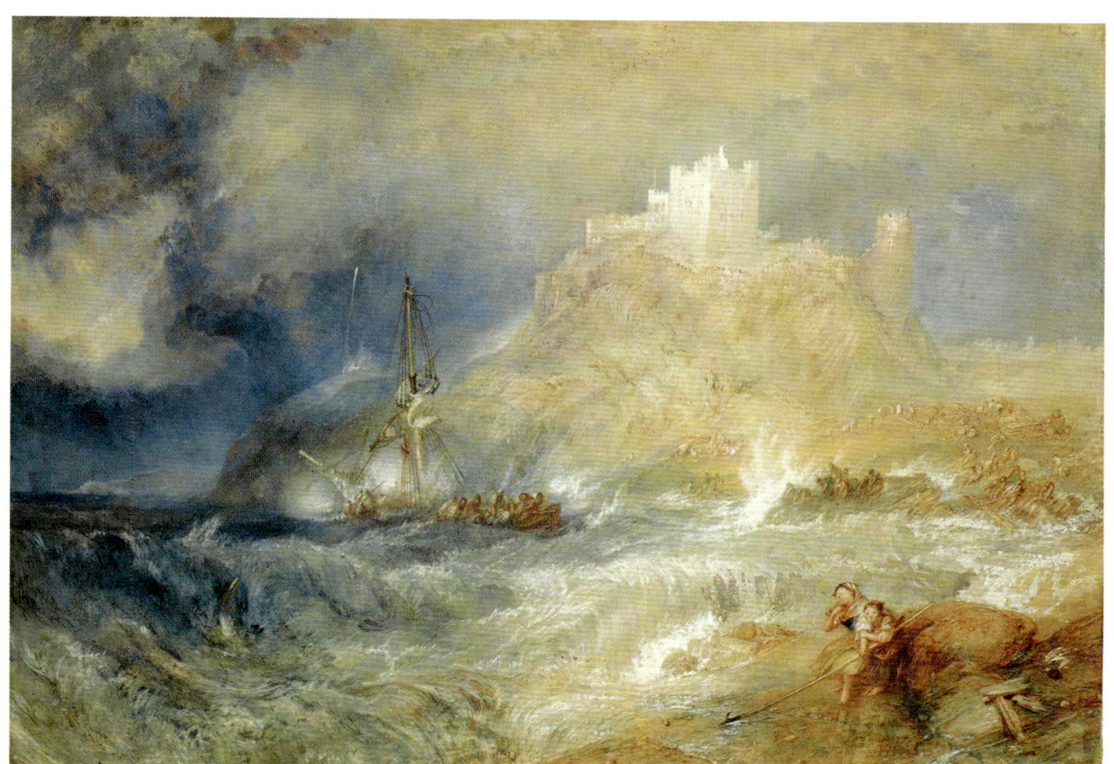

be judged, not those light-filled washes of colour we all love, which may, after all, simply be unfinished.

So let's not get all sentimental about Turner in old age. This is an ambitious show that asks important questions but if you go, remember what Turner told Ruskin and do not read more into the late work than the artist put in.

John Constable

Over the years I've seen many exhibitions of the work of John Constable, but the one organised by the British Council and opening tomorrow at the Grand Palais in Paris is by far the best. Selected by Lucian Freud, it does not try to be comprehensive or balanced; nor does it offer much in the way of historical context. Instead, it represents something increasingly rare in art exhibitions – a display of pictures chosen for no other reason than for their aesthetic quality.

Whatever a picture's scale, medium or subject, if it gives off that pleasurable shiver we feel in the presence of luscious pigment slapped on a flat surface, Freud has put it in the show. On and on they come, one gem after another, revealing Constable not just as a great British artist but as a great artist, full stop. By mounting the exhibition in Paris, the British Council reminds us that the French recognised Constable's genius long before we did. In 1824, at the age of forty-eight, Constable had still not been elected to full membership at the Royal Academy. But in that year his *Hay Wain* won the gold medal at the Paris Salon, and the French government attempted to buy the picture for the nation. Both Géricault and Delacroix enthusiastically admired his work. In the 1820s, the dealers most anxious to handle his paintings were French. In England, Constable was still an outsider, cut off from patronage and denied the approval of his colleagues. In France, he was seen to be painting landscapes as revolutionary as anything exhibited in Europe in their time.

But what was it, exactly, that so impressed the French? To answer the question, you really have to go back to the beginning of Constable's career. Although he was born in 1776 on the Essex–Suffolk border, and although he was to paint the scenery along the River Stour all his life, Constable was not some untrained local artist. After studying at the RA Schools in London, for most of the first decade of the nineteenth century he groped from style to style, imitating now

9 October 2002

Constable: Le Choix de Lucian Freud

Grand Palais, Paris

Claude, now Gainsborough, now Girtin. Early in this show we come across a pastiche of Gainsborough called *The Reader in the Woods* which he probably exhibited at the RA in 1802. This sensuously painted depiction of a clearing in a forest reveals a technical proficiency in the handling of pigment that Constable isn't usually credited with at this early date. But, for all the richness of the paint surface, in terms of the picture's composition, the young artist is still in thrall to the eighteenth-century tradition of the picturesque. It is precisely such conventional ideas about landscape composition that Constable would learn to discard.

In 1809, he made the decision to paint directly from nature and as though he had never before seen a picture by another artist. Narrowing his subject matter to encompass only places and scenes he had known since his youth, in a series of oil sketches and drawings, often inscribed with the location and date when he made them, he sought to record what he saw in front of him as it was at the moment he saw it, not with the objectivity of a topographer but with his own feelings and sensations as he stood before the scene recorded intact.

Rising at dawn, he looks out from his bedroom window over to the village rectory, where the girl he loved (and would eventually marry)

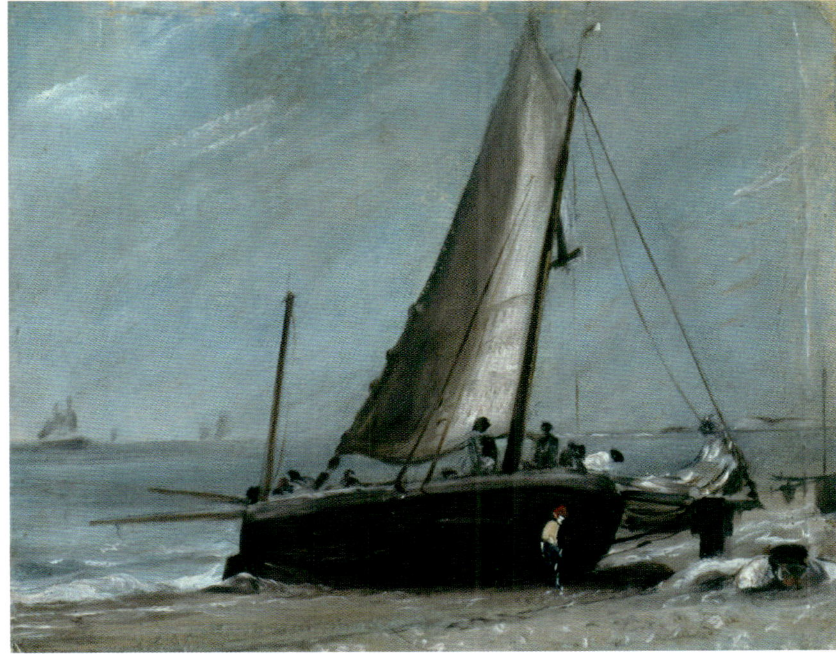

John Constable
Brighton Beach with a Fishing Boat and Crew, *1824*
Victorian & Albert Museum, London

lay sleeping. With the sun rising behind the house and distant birds wheeling across the orange- and rose-streaked clouds, the little oil sketch exudes the longing of a love letter and the urgency of a poem by Keats.

In another oil sketch, a traveller sleeps by the side of a field on a nondescript dirt track. There is nothing intrinsically memorable about the landscape, but Constable's bleached colours convey the stillness of early afternoon, the deadening stupor that descends on the countryside on a stiflingly hot summer's day. In another little sketch, barges float down the River Stour under a darkening sky, the silvery light behind the clouds of the coming storm reflected in the rushing waters below.

In such works Constable evolved an expressive and precise sketching style with which to catch brilliantly transient effects of light, motion and time. There is no sense that such pictures are deliberately composed at all. Note, too, how commonplace the subjects are. Of these scenes, Constable wrote: 'It is the business of the painter to make something out of nothing, in attempting which he must almost of necessity become poetical.' The sentence may sound innocuous but, in fact, it is making a claim that no English artist had ever made before: that beauty is independent of subject matter.

However, what is permissible in a sketch was not, until Constable's own breakthrough, permissible in a work of art of the sort then considered acceptable for exhibition at the Royal Academy. And, for a successful career in England, the academy was the arena in which all artists had to compete. In terms of subject matter, Constable continued for the most part to paint scenes of ordinary life and landscape in rural Suffolk and Salisbury (and increasingly, after 1821, Hampstead Heath). But, in other ways, he conformed to prevailing academic practice.

In *Boat Building at Flatford Mill* (1814–15), for example, the theme is still mundane. But now Constable gives a sharper focus to his forms and strengthens his outlines and colours. The result is ever so slightly slick. It conforms to conventional notions of academic 'finish', but in doing so loses some of the spontaneity and urgency that make the sketches so thrilling. Here we come to the crux of Constable's dilemma. He needed to find a way to translate the spontaneous brushstrokes of his spirited little sketches into full-size canvases without losing the freshness of the original moment of inspiration. The means he found to do this was the full-size sketch, which he used in preparation for a great series of six-foot-high pictures exhibited at the Royal Academy in the early 1820s, including *The Hay Wain* and *The Leaping Horse.*

These sketches are painted with an unselfconscious freedom that corresponds to everyone's idea of a sketch of 8 × 12 inches, but which in the early nineteenth century was unacceptable in a large-scale exhibition picture. In them, he could block out the masses and work out the composition while minimising differences in tone and texture, in background and foreground, and even in colour. These famous sketches are truly, radically modern. They are exercises in self-referential painting, painting as painting – rather than as a view into the real world.

But, of course, it was not the sketch for *The Hay Wain* that the French saw in 1824. In the finished picture, Constable reintroduces focus, clarity and notes of strong colour but without wholly discarding the painterly vivacity of the sketch. Even more important for artists such as Delacroix and Géricault was the way Constable alters and shifts elements in the composition to make the subject more monumental, more intense and more teeming than it would have been in real life. For those who first saw these pictures, it must have been like seeing the first films in CinemaScope with stereophonic sound. In *The Hay Wain*, a perfectly humdrum view of a cottage and field has been given a dignity and grandeur we associate with the compositions of Claude or Rubens.

This sort of critical analysis of Constable's career is all very well, but the best way to approach this particular exhibition is simply to revel in the pleasures of each picture at random, without worrying too much about how it fits into Constable's artistic development. Freud has done us all a remarkable service in reaffirming Constable's reputation as a painter of landscapes, but also in calling our attention to his abilities as a black-and-white draughtsman and above all as a portraitist.

Edwin Landseer

No novelist has ever based a fictional character on the Victorian painter Edwin Landseer, and yet the story of his life would make a plot worthy of Trollope at his darkest, involving as it does spectacular worldly success, a passionate love affair with a married woman, public scandal, mental instability, alcoholism and madness – all set against the glamorous background of royal, aristocratic, artistic and literary Britain in the mid-nineteenth century.

Born in 1802 into a family of London artists, Landseer, like Turner, was a child prodigy. After his election to the Royal Academy as an associate member at twenty-four (the youngest permissible age), he became a full RA in 1831. By the time Queen Victoria knighted him in 1850, he was one of the age's most popular and highly paid artists.

From the beginning of his career, his dazzling talents were appreciated by aristocratic patrons, in particular by the Duke of Bedford and a network of Bedford family connections that included the Dukes of Gordon, Athol and Abercorn. Soon, the handsome young artist won the heart of the Duchess of Bedford, becoming so close to her that her youngest daughter was rumoured to be the painter's child. Their friendship scandalised London. A rival artist, Benjamin Robert Haydon, wrote bitterly that he, Haydon, had never 'seduced the Wife of my Patron and accepted money from the Husband while I was corrupting his Wife & disgracing his family'. And yet the Duke and Duchess stayed together, Landseer continued to be received everywhere, Queen Victoria called him her favourite painter, and Prince Albert took drawing lessons from him. But worldly success brought no inner peace. In 1840, he experienced his first mental breakdown, and thereafter the shadows of depression, drink and an unstable temper dogged him. He died in 1873, certified as a lunatic.

Landseer is one of the giants of nineteenth-century British painting, a major artist who has been unfairly relegated to the ranks

27 April 2005

Monarch of the Glen: Landseer in the Highlands

Royal Scottish Academy, Edinburgh

of mere animal painters. In fact, as a hugely enjoyable exhibition in Edinburgh shows, Landseer was also a portrait, figure, genre and landscape painter of breathtaking talent. *Landseer in the Highlands* looks at only one aspect of his art, the work he did on his annual summer visits to Scotland, but this includes such iconic British paintings as *The Monarch of the Glen* and *Flood in the Highlands*. A gallery hung with landscape sketches, each one painted swiftly from nature for his own pleasure, is as bracing as a blast of Highland air.

As we shall see, whole sections of the population, from Sir Sean Connery to members of the League Against Cruel Sports, should probably avoid this show, but for everyone else, I say Landseer is a major Romantic painter who, at his best, bears comparison with Géricault and Delacroix. That 'at his best' is an important qualification. Landseer also painted utterly charming but silly pictures in which comical dogs wear bonnets and smoke pipes. Though I confess to a more than sneaking affection for pictures like these, though they are just as beautifully executed as the large hunting scenes they are not the works by which he should be judged. For me, his highest achievements include the extraordinary series of large-scale paintings of stags in the wilderness hung to stunning effect in the great gallery of the Royal Scottish Academy.

The Sanctuary, for example, shows a stag that has escaped from its pursuers by swimming a loch and now, at sunset, staggers on to dry land. What a masterpiece of narrative description it is, from the animal's dripping fur and lolling tongue to the way ripples on the still surface of the loch reflect the dying light, while the sky fades from a faint yellow glow to the most delicate shades of mauve, blue and grey. Or look at *The Challenge*, in which a rutting stag confronts an approaching rival in the moonlight. How perfectly the artist captures the cold, silence, desolation and piercing beauty of the wilderness on a starry night. In pictures like these, Landseer is not simply an illustrator. His theme is that, in the animal world, violence is mindless, death arbitrary. The stags will fight to the death in this lonely place, and we can never know why or for what purpose.

If you are ever tempted to dismiss Landseer as a sentimentalist, look at pictures such as *The Random Shot*, showing a hind mortally wounded by an irresponsible hunter. After staggering through the snow leaving a trail of blood, it has now collapsed, its carcass lying

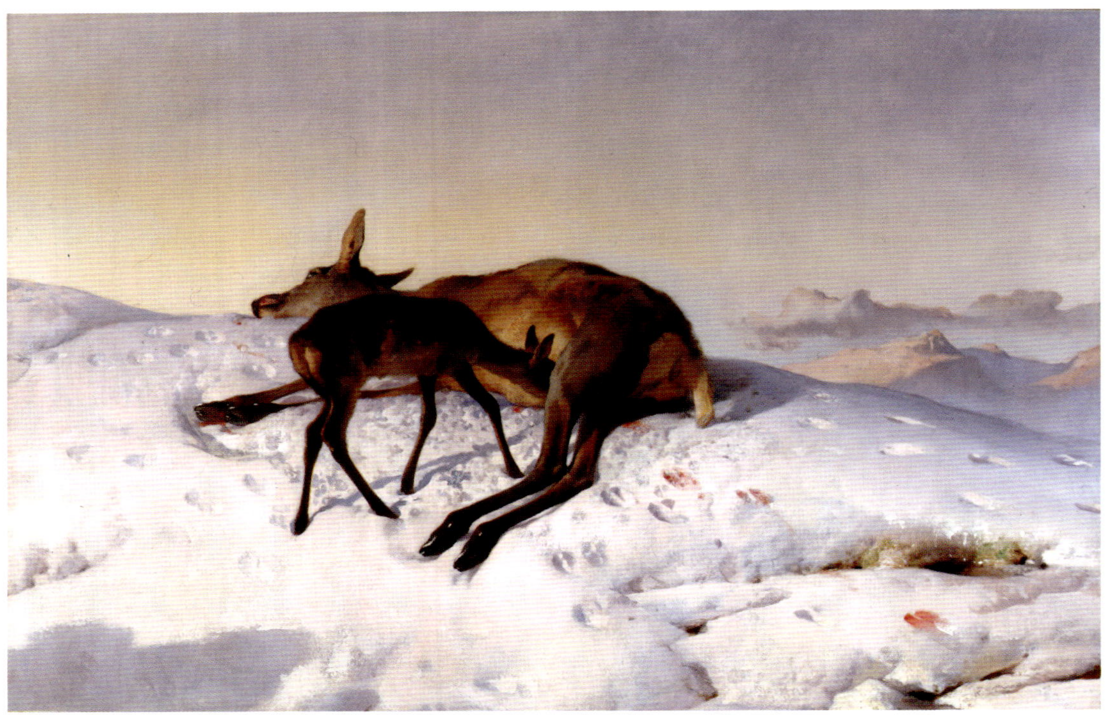

in a landscape of unearthly beauty. Adding to the horror and the
pity of the scene, a fawn, attempting to suckle at its mother's corpse,
will now die of starvation. In such pictures Landseer expresses
complicated emotions (including his own anger) simply and directly,
without descending into melodrama or sentimentality.

I can't help but feel that some of the mental anguish that poisoned
Landseer's life found its way into pictures such as *None but the Brave
Deserve the Fair* in which rutting stags lock horns on a mountain pass,
watched impassively by the herd as though at a performance in the
theatre. And call me a softie, but when I look at the dog that paws
the coffin in *The Old Shepherd's Chief Mourner*, I find the emotion
expressed in it true, deep and without a false note.

And now for a word of caution. Landseer's art gets up a lot of
people's noses. Whether you are a Scottish Nationalist, an animal
rights activist, or even simply an animal lover, from the political point
of view these pictures are hopelessly, gloriously, deliciously incorrect.
The fact that he offends pretty much everybody is part of what I like
about him.

Edwin Henry Landseer
The Random Shot,
1848
Bury Art Museum

And so Scottish critics object to the way in which Landseer, like Walter Scott, colluded in the tartanisation of Scotland. From his first visit in 1824, his pictures helped to create the image of a country that never existed, one with the phoney 'traditions' of pipers and kilts, and an ersatz history featuring chivalrous nobles and a poor but happy peasantry. To other critics, what is truly unforgivable is that Landseer ignored the poverty, dispossession and social collapse that were taking place in the Highlands during the very years when he was moving from one ducal summer residence to another.

Certainly it is true that the crofters and shepherds in his canvases always have a roof over their heads and a pot on the fire. A number of his paintings show strong, manly gillies kneeling at the slippered feet of effete English noblemen without a hint of irony or criticism. When you turn to the hunting pictures, he is just as controversial. Even if you are neither anti-hunting nor an animal rights activist, it can be hard to take the cruelty, suffering and downright sadism he depicts with such apparent relish in *The Stag at Bay* or *The Otter Hunt*, two of the most violent pictures ever painted by a British artist.

Now for the defence. Landseer was an artist, not a social critic. His idealised depictions of a medieval Scotland are but another aspect of the Gothic revival that elsewhere in Britain saw the building of Pugin's Palace of Westminster. As for his failure to confront the clearances, in the present catalogue it is argued that Landseer may not have seen the worst of them, nor realised the extent of the suffering they caused. And we can no more denigrate him for portraying the savagery of the stag hunt in *The Hunting of Chevy Chase* than we can take Rubens or Franz Snyders to task for their equally violent depictions of dogs sinking their fangs into the flesh of lions and boars.

Judge Landseer simply as an artist and you quickly conclude that no nineteenth-century painter apart from Delacroix painted animals in conflict with the same brio and fluency, none applied paint so lusciously, and none created compositions so rich in drama, movement and colour.

William Bell Scott

'A lying, backbiting, drivelling, imbecile, doting, malignant, mangy old son of a bitch . . .' From Swinburne's verdict on the character of the painter William Bell Scott it would still be difficult to dissent. By all accounts one of the least attractive figures in the Pre-Raphaelite circle, Scott's dour manner set him apart from a group of artists renowned for their high spirits and bohemian mode of life.

Scott's total lack of a sense of humour was not mitigated by a flat Scottish accent and dry delivery, both of which were complemented by his curious appearance: in 1863 he lost all his hair (including his eyebrows and beard) from a disease contracted in Italy, and was therefore obliged to wear a wig, kept in place by a bowler hat which he seems never to have removed in public.

After Scott's death in 1890 his *Autobiographical Notes* appeared posthumously, revealing long-nurtured resentments against the more successful Pre-Raphaelites. The publication caused a furore. When Swinburne reviewed the book he declared that Scott's 'name would never have been heard . . . but for his casual and parasitical association with . . . the Rossettis and myself.' This is unfair. Scott was a considerable artist and poet in his own right, and in recent years we have come to see that he played a crucial role in the dissemination of British avant-garde painting from its centre in London to the great industrialist collectors in the north-east.

The son of a Scottish landscape artist and engraver (and brother of one of the most interesting visionary artists of the Romantic period, David Scott), William was born in Edinburgh in 1811. In 1843 he submitted a cartoon for the competition to paint the murals in the newly built Houses of Parliament. Though his entry was not chosen, it resulted in Scott being offered the job of supervisor of the Government School of Design in Newcastle upon Tyne, where he would live and teach for the next twenty-one years.

21 October 1989

Pre-Raphaelites: Painters and Patrons in the North East

Laing Art Gallery, Newcastle upon Tyne

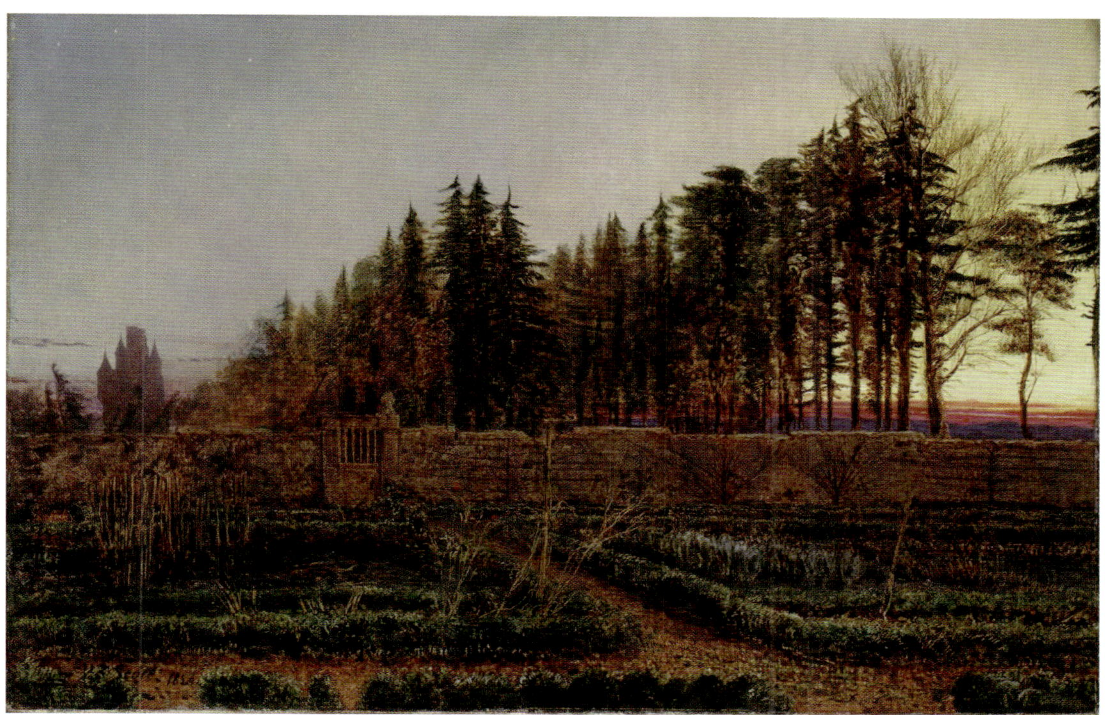

Scott's official position at Newcastle changed the pattern of
patronage in the area. Because he travelled south to London every
summer to renew his association with the Pre-Raphaelites, he formed
a one-man conduit between the great collectors in the north and the
work of avant-garde painters in the capital. Although Scott never
became a Pre-Raphaelite Brother, he was in close contact with the
Brotherhood from the late 1840s to the 1860s. His best paintings
date from the later part of his career, when he began to work in their
characteristic glowing colours and fine detail, choosing subjects
inspired by the romantic landscape so near to him in Scotland and
the Borders.

William Bell Scott is a central figure in the exhibition *Pre-
Raphaelites: Painters and Patrons in the North East* at the Laing
Art Gallery, Newcastle upon Tyne. Perhaps his most important
contribution to the arts in the north were his mural paintings at
Wallington Hall, the Northumberland home of Ruskin's friends, Sir
Walter and Lady Trevelyan. These illustrate scenes from the history of
Northumberland and the Borders, and, with the fading of the frescoes
in the Houses of Parliament and those in the Oxford Union, they

represent the most successful fully extant mural scheme of the first half of Victoria's reign.

His role as teacher to local painters such as Henry Hetherington Emmerson turns out to be far less interesting than his position as trusted adviser to the great Newcastle collector James Leathart. Leathart's magnificent collection of the works of Rossetti, Burne-Jones and Ford Madox Brown was among the best in the Victorian age.

The exhibition also includes works from the collections of other patrons, such as the engineer and armaments manufacturer Sir William Armstrong, who built a castle, Cragside, which would have impressed King Ludwig of Bavaria. He filled it with paintings by his Pre-Raphaelite and Aesthetic contemporaries. Here, too, is Thomas Eustace Smith, a rope manufacturer whose rise (and eventual fall) in London society was accompanied by his patronage of the most fashionable painters and architects. The aristocracy is represented by examples from the collections of George Howard, himself a landscape painter of considerable talent, who decorated the chapel at Castle Howard with stained-glass windows by Burne-Jones.

The only name missing in this survey of collectors is that of Frederick Leyland, owner of Whistler's Peacock Room and in my view the greatest patron of them all, but he belongs to the history of Liverpool, not Newcastle.

The organisers have done an excellent job in re-assembling collections that have been dispersed for almost a hundred years, thereby giving us some idea of the richness that so astonished the art critic (and founder member of the Pre-Raphaelite Brotherhood) F. G. Stephens when he first realised the scope of depth of the collections of the north and began to write about them for *The Athenaeum* in the 1870s. Stephens was amazed that 'pictures which may be called poetical . . . [are] encountered in unexpected numbers near Newcastle', and more surprised to discover Leathart's collection in 'the unlovely town of Gateshead', so near 'noise, smells, and unmitigated squalor'.

Edward Burne-Jones

When Edward Burne-Jones's late masterpiece, the *Briar Rose* series, was first shown at Thomas Agnew's in the spring of 1890, the occasion attracted so many members of the public that queues snaked from the venerable firm of art dealers all the way down Bond Street. The carriages of the curious clogged Piccadilly. For the fame of the artist was then at its height, and it had been widely reported that the financier Alexander Henderson, later Lord Faringdon, had just paid the colossal sum of £15,000 for the four large canvases that made up the series. This was at a time when a skilled labourer earned about £10 a month. At today's prices, the figure would be somewhere around £750,000.

Based on Charles Perrault's fairy-tale *The Sleeping Beauty*, as a narrative cycle the *Briar Rose* series represented the culmination of a literary tradition in painting that stretched back to the Renaissance, but which was even then being eroded by the naturalism of French Impressionism. As Burne-Jones himself defiantly retorted when told that French painting was not based on literature, 'What do they mean by that? Landscape and whores? That's what they want – nothing but landscape or if any figure pictures, more or less languid whores. But what do they mean by literary painting? All the Greek art was about their heroes and gods, and all the medieval art was concerned with the religion of the time.' His own pictures, he added, were 'so different to landscape painting. I don't want to copy objects, I want to tell people something.'

But he protested in vain. By the end of the decade, Burne-Jones's reputation had begun its long descent into twentieth-century oblivion, as taste turned against Victorian art in general and the romantic medievalism of his own painting in particular. For most of this century, the *Briar Rose* series existed in a twilight world, frozen in the past, unappreciated in the present. But as in all good fairy-tales, the

24 November 1999
The *Briar Rose* Series
Agnew's, London

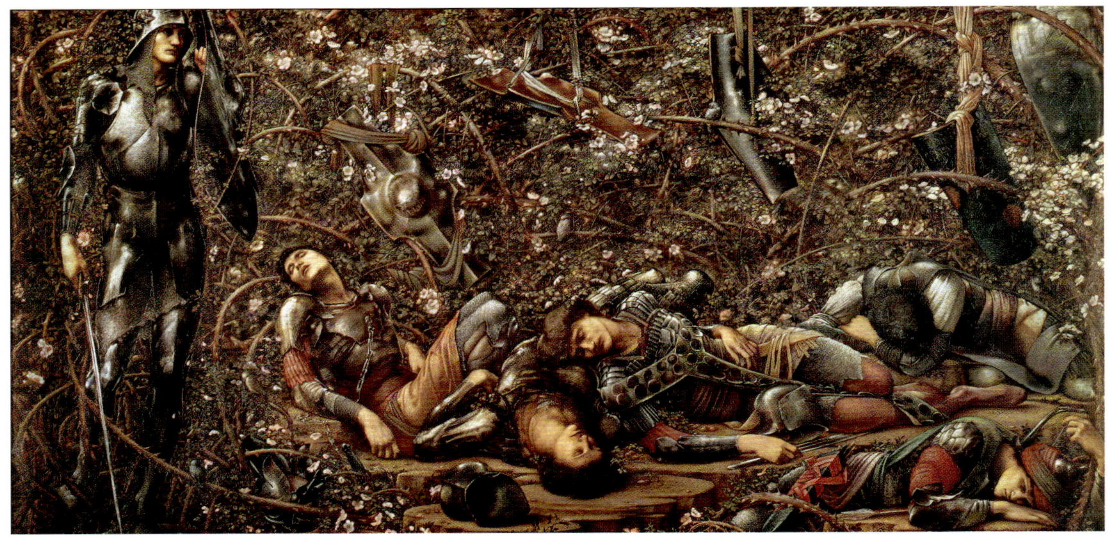

spell was at last broken – this time by the art historian John Christian, whose pioneering exhibition at the Hayward Gallery in 1975 woke us all up to the long-neglected beauties of this most enchanting of all English painters.

Now, to complete the awakening, the *Briar Rose* series has for the first time been temporarily removed from Lord Faringdon's beautiful Oxfordshire house, Buscot Park, and is again being shown at Agnew's in memory of the great connoisseur and collector Sir Brinsley Ford, who died earlier this year. At Buscot, which now belongs to the National Trust, the pictures hang in the music room, in frames designed especially for them by Burne-Jones and inscribed with verses by William Morris.

To the original four paintings, Burne-Jones added ten smaller connecting scenes so that the pictures form a continuous frieze around the walls. The artist intended us to feel on entering the room that we had actually stepped into the Briar Wood, to find ourselves surrounded by the spellbound sleepers of his imagination. Seeing the pictures at Agnew's, hung lower on the walls, unframed, and in a room much smaller than the one at Buscot, it is easier to grasp that the series forms a single unified composition in four main parts, beginning with the standing figure of Prince Charming, who opens the story at the far left, and ending with the sleeping Princess Aurora, who closes it at the far right.

Edward Burne-Jones
**The Briar Rose
Series, 1: The Prince
Enters the Briar
Wood**, *1870–90*
Faringdon Collection

Between these two figures, Burne-Jones takes us on a room-by-room tour of the enchanted castle, moving as in a cinematic tracking shot from the enchanted wood littered with the entwined bodies of sleeping knights, into the Council Chamber where the wise men slumber, past the handmaidens dreaming by loom and fountain in the Garden Court, until we arrive at last on the balustraded terrace where the Princess lies on her embroidered palanquin. Everywhere you look you see images and objects reflected in the mirror-like surface of polished stone floors, as Burne-Jones makes his surrealistic inventory of the make-believe contents of a non-existent building.

Looking back over the whole history of art, can anyone think of a composition containing so many figures in which absolutely nothing happens? The whole point of the *Briar Rose* series is that the action has either taken place in the past or will take place in the future. For the present, nobody moves, silence reigns, time stands still. Even the handsome Prince shows no sign of wishing to proceed through the Briar Wood. Frozen with indecision, he appears to have neither the will nor the desire to bestow the kiss that will awaken the Princess.

The *Briar Rose* initiates the decadent tendency in the art of the 1890s not because of the way it is painted (Burne-Jones's academic draughtsmanship and solid painting technique strike me as the opposite of decadent), but because it leaves open the question as to whether a state of eternal, careless dreaming is not preferable to the messy reality of waking life. For by kissing the Princess, the Prince not only awakens sexual desire, he revives the forces of belligerence, the life of the mind, and the necessity of toil, each of which is specifically referred to in one of the four canvases. Beautiful as the series is, its subtle undercurrent of *fin-de-siècle* languor feels like a celebration of inertia, a turning away from reality – a fear of life itself.

Then, too, the picture had a highly personal meaning for the artist. Princess Aurora is a portrait of Burne-Jones's much-loved daughter, Margaret. It doesn't take Sigmund Freud to figure out that when time stands still, children don't grow up, and marauding princes don't carry away cherished daughters. And only in a place where sleep is eternal can young bodies lie touching and intertwined, as they do in the *Briar Rose* series, without the arousal of dangerous desires which, as we saw, Burne-Jones associated with the moral depravity of modern French painting.

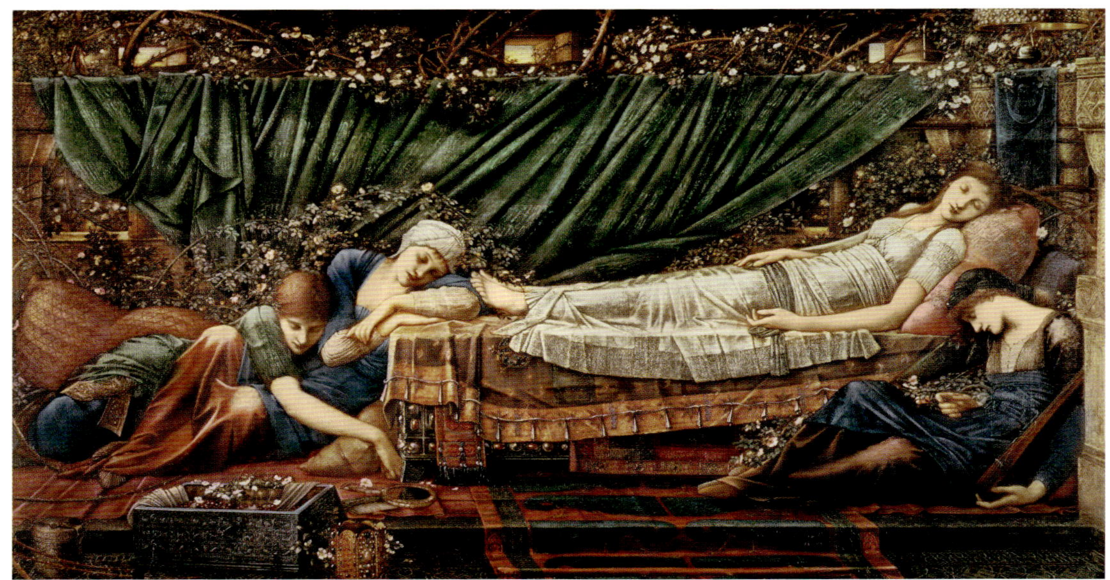

Here is a test. Try to name the century or country in which the *Briar Rose* series is set, and then try to identify the primary visual sources on which Burne-Jones drew for inspiration. See? It can't be done. The *Briar Rose* series is timeless in every sense of the word. The Prince wears a set of fanciful armour vaguely Renaissance in design, while the architectural details, clothing, ornaments and caskets belonging to the court are an eclectic mix of Romanesque, Byzantine, Gothic and Islamic design.

Notice too how aware Burne-Jones is of how his viewers will read the pictures. He keeps all his figures well within the shallow space of the foreground plane to ensure that there are no abrupt changes in scale, and that our eye moves easily from figure to figure, as in a relief sculpture. Using a dry brush, he then weaves his soft palette of mauves, dusty roses, bronzes, sea-greens and blue-greys into the texture of the canvas, as though it were a tapestry. But then, in a sense, these pictures are a tapestry – or, rather, a fusion of Eastern and Western, classical Renaissance and medieval art into one seamless and near-perfect whole.

Edward Burne-Jones
The Briar Rose Series, 4: The Sleeping Beauty*,
1870–90*
Faringdon Collection

Frank Holl

Born in 1845, the Victorian social realist painter Frank Holl's early career coincided with a late glorious flowering of the Victorian subject picture, a phenomenon paralleled (and to an extent created) by the popularity of the novels of Charles Dickens and Charlotte M. Yonge. No less a figure than Vincent Van Gogh admired the wood engravings in which Holl portrayed the poor and dispossessed not as generic types, but as real people, while his narrative paintings were sensationally popular at the Royal Academy in the 1870s. But towards the end of that decade, as advanced taste and critical opinion shifted towards an 'art for art's sake' aesthetic, it became more difficult to sell harrowing scenes of death and destitution. Once Oscar Wilde had quipped that 'one must have a heart of stone to read the death of Little Nell without laughing', life became very hard for Royal Academicians who specialised in pictures of dead babies.

This is why as early as 1880 Holl abandoned painting what had come to be seen as his 'morbid sentimental pictures' to become a hugely successful portrait painter. He died at the age of forty-three in 1888, and within a few decades had been forgotten, along with almost everything else Victorian.

That may now change, thanks to an ambitious loan exhibition at the Watts Gallery in Compton, near Guildford. Aptly entitled *Emerging from the Shadows,* it is the first retrospective of Holl's work in 125 years – and what a knockout of a show it is. Congratulations to the organiser Mark Bills for putting Holl back where he belongs, centre stage. For at his best Holl emerges as a painter of modern life who handled paint with the confidence of a Manet or Courbet, but who also had a flair for dramatic narrative that sits firmly within a specifically English tradition stretching back from William Powell Frith to William Hogarth.

16 July 2013

Frank Holl: Emerging from the Shadows

Watts Gallery, near Guildford

Rigorously trained as a draughtsman and painter at the Royal Academy Schools, Holl found both his subject and his voice in 1870 when he spent four months living in the fishing village of Cullercoats on the coast of Northumberland. There he grew close enough to the fishing community to be able to sketch and even to paint women and children inside their cottages. So accurate was his attention to detail that today these pictures are considered unique records of the clothes and living conditions in nineteenth-century Britain.

Holl is sometimes accused of sentimentality, but what you notice about his work is its restraint. In *No Tidings from the Sea*, for example, the anxiety and grief of a fisherman's wife are expressed not with histrionic gestures but in the way she buries her face in a hand she's clenched into a fist. While other artists of the time chose to depict heroic scenes of men in action, Holl invariably focused on women and their reactions to catastrophe and loss.

The veracity of Holl's paintings is linked to the origin of many of them in the wood engravings he created for that extraordinary publication *The Graphic*. Founded in 1869 as a rival to *The Illustrated London News*, the weekly periodical employed fine artists like Holl, Hubert Herkomer and Luke Fildes to represent the destitute denizens of London's streets and slums. Like Dickens on his 'night walks', Holl tramped through highly dangerous areas of London including the East End, the Docks, and the notorious slum of St Giles to show readers scenes they may have read about in the books of Henry Mayhew and Dickens, but had never seen.

And so *Gone* simply shows a cluster of poor women and children standing together on a dark, smoke-filled platform at Euston Station. They have gathered to wave goodbye to husbands and fathers who have just boarded the night train to Liverpool where they will make the crossing to America. The scene is completely static and almost devoid of drama. What makes it poignant is the realisation that these women may never see their men again. As a viewer, you sense that Holl may have come across his subject by accident, grasped its implications at once, and drew it on the spot.

Often, the scenes he sketched or painted of his 'tramps' provided him with the raw material out of which he constructed complex works of art that portray individuals in desperate and sometimes heart-breaking situations. In order to paint *Newgate: Committed for Trial*,

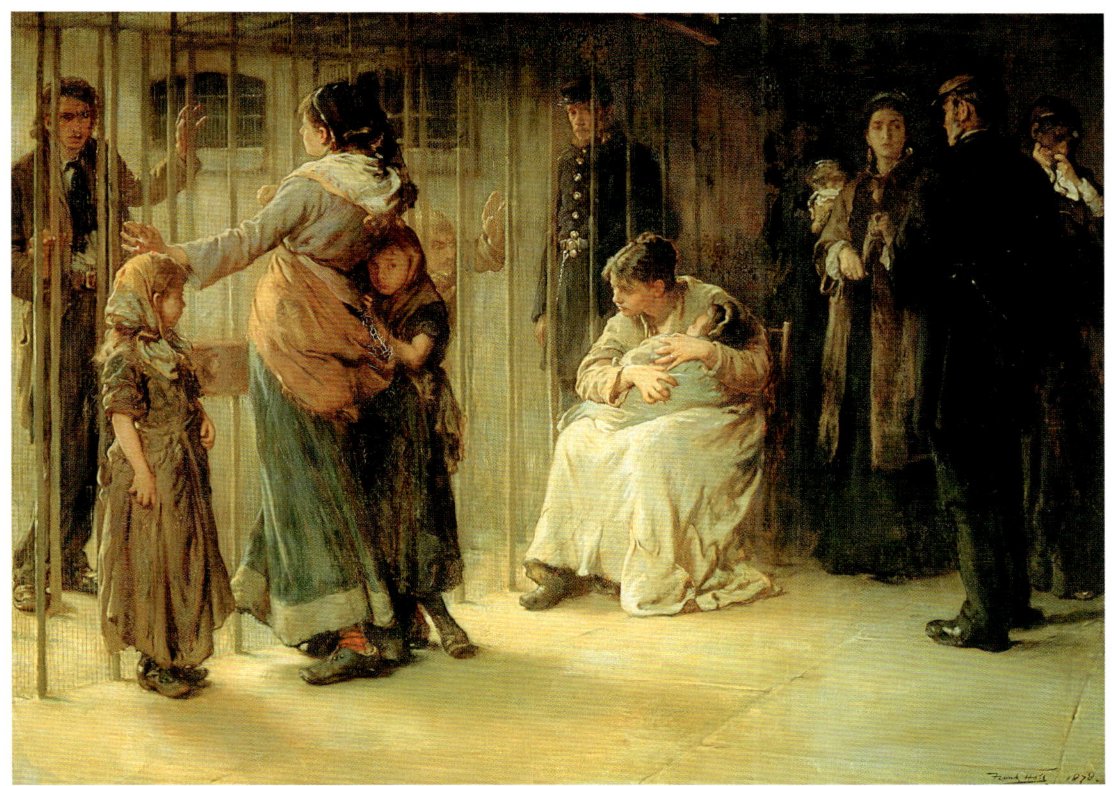

Frank Holl
Newgate:
Committed for Trial,
1878
Royal Holloway,
University of London

for example, Holl made several visits to the infamous prison where he was allowed to paint in the barred area known as 'the cage' where inmates could meet their families after sentencing. Out of the real-life dramas he witnessed there, he created a composite composition in which at least three separate narratives unfold simultaneously. At the left a shabbily dressed young woman with two little girls stands face to face with her husband, a bank clerk who has just been sentenced to five years' penal servitude for embezzlement. Holl characterises the husband as a weak man from a genteel background, while the wife is working-class.

By contrast, the other prisoner is like a caged animal who lunges against the bars that prevent him from ripping the throat out of the woman who has turned him in. As long as he is in prison, she and the baby in her arms are safe, but as soon as he is released, she will once again become the victim of his alcoholic abuse.

But who is the grand lady, swathed in fur and dripping with jewels, who has just entered at the far right? Her presence is inexplicable unless, as I believe, she is the young bank clerk's mother. If so, then Holl adds what we would now call a back story to his tragedy. For the state of near-destitution of the wife and children suggests that the bank clerk had been cut off from his family for marrying beneath him. The motive for his crime was therefore to raise his wife to a station in life acceptable to his proud mother, who makes her appearance too late to be of use to him, but perhaps in time to make some amends by looking after her grandchildren and daughter-in-law.

I don't have space to discuss Holl's portraits of men such as Gladstone and Sir William Gilbert (of Gilbert and Sullivan) but then I don't need to. You'll see for yourself that they are every bit as powerful as his subject pictures and their impact just as visceral. Still. Though I don't regret for a moment Holl's decision to concentrate on portraiture, when he abandoned narrative painting, this country lost an irreplaceable storyteller in paint.

Fairy Paintings

Though many important nineteenth-century British artists worked in the curious genre of fairy painting, it is surprising how few first-rate paintings you find in the Royal Academy's exhibition *Victorian Fairy Painting*. Even Ruskin admitted that Turner's magical landscape *Queen Mab's Cave* didn't quite come off. In depicting his sprites wafted along by the wind like a swarm of insects, Turner hints at a rational explanation for a supernatural phenomenon. He is vague when he should be specific, whimsical when the subject calls for absolute conviction. Like science fiction, the genre of fairy painting requires not only imagination but belief that such things are possible. To paint fairies you have to enter fairyland.

And so the greatest fairy painter of all, Richard Dadd, was schizophrenic, confined to Bedlam for murdering his father. His *Fairy Feller's Master-Stroke* mesmerises us because at some profound level Dadd 'saw' the beings he was painting. The clarity and detail with which the tiny, unexpectedly scary figures are realised in paint underlines their existence for the artist. We viewers approach their hidden world at ground level, parting the tall grass in the foreground to peep at creatures who would vanish if they became aware of our presence. In front of Dadd's picture, we stand in spellbound silence – 'fairy struck', like all mortals who stumble upon the elfin folk.

For Victorian fairies are by no means harmless, benign creatures. The frightening intensity of David Scott's *Ariel and Caliban* of 1838, for example, suggests a preoccupation with the morbid, bizarre and menacing. For a long time I couldn't put my finger on the visual source for this imagery. Then I realised how much Scott and several other artists in this show owe to Goya's suite of visionary etchings *Los Caprichos*. John Anster Fitzgerald's *The Artist's Dream*, for example, could be seen as a drug-induced reworking of Goya's *The Sleep of Reason Produces Monsters*.

19 November 1997

Victorian Fairy Painting

Royal Academy,
London

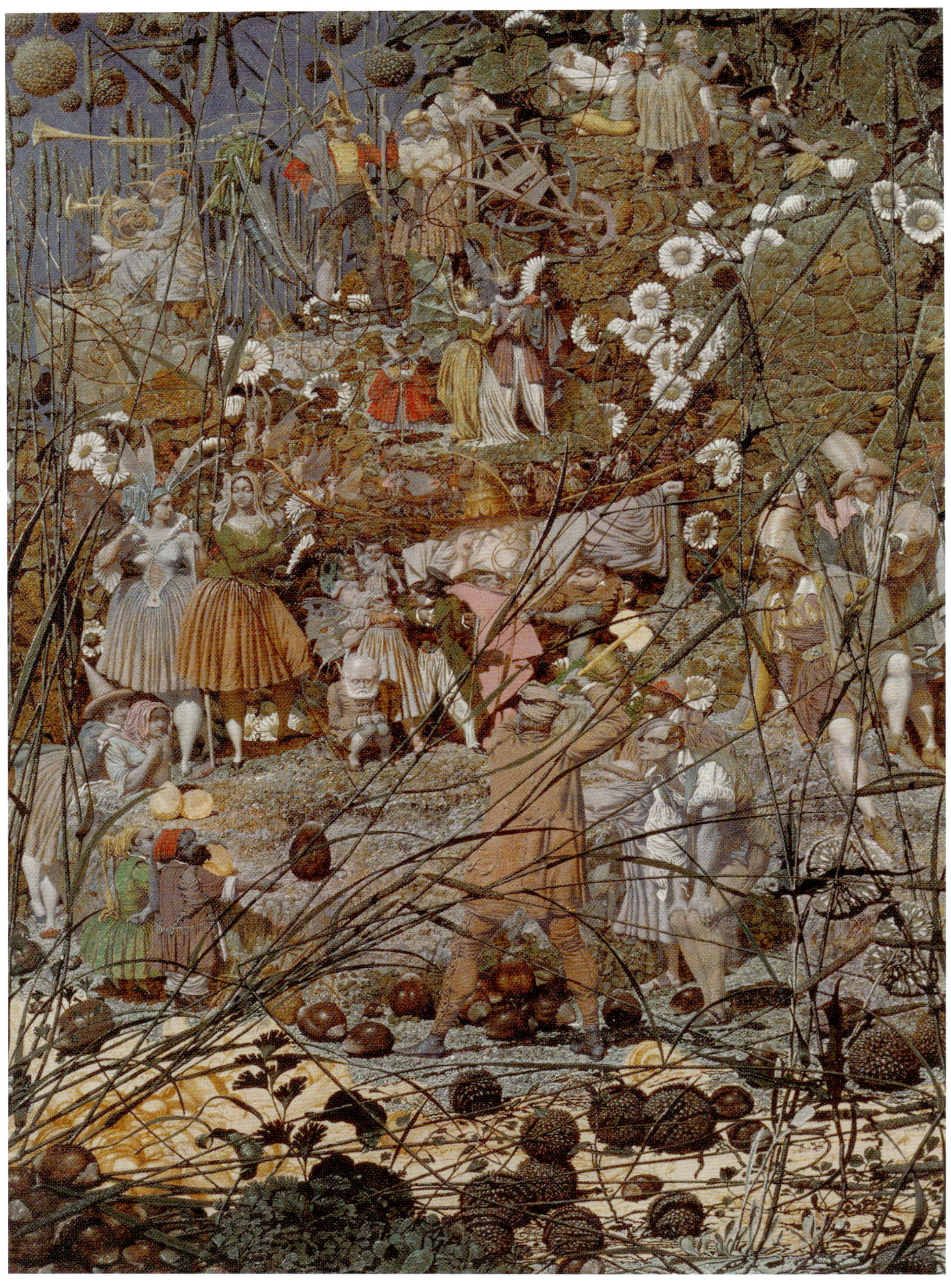

Not that this art has the grandeur or psychological complexity of Goya. Sometimes fairy painting was simply a way of smuggling into Victorian England a kind of Continental naughtiness. Look at Thomas Heatherley's charming if inconsequential *Fairy Seated on a Mushroom*. Isn't the nude fairy with her back to us one of the odalisques from Ingres's *The Turkish Bath*? And would this Second Empire nudity have been exhibitable had it not been distanced by being assigned to tiny, mythical beings whom everyone knows don't really exist?

Fairy painting is usually said to be an excuse for the Victorians to unleash a pornographic flood of unbridled eroticism. I don't see it. True, the usually innocuous Scottish painter Sir Joseph Noël Paton felt free in *The Reconciliation of Oberon and Titania* explicitly to depict shameless shenanigans among the wee folk, but the painting has a kind of prepubescent innocence that could never have caused serious offence.

If you want to see the modern equivalent to fairy painting, go to the *Sensation* exhibition downstairs at Burlington House, where you'll find the Chapman brothers' tableau of naked, little-girl manikins scampering through an artificial woodland setting, at once openly sexual and totally bland. If you think there is something limited – not to say pointless – about what the Chapmans do, that could equally be said about their Victorian predecessors.

Having said this, the freshness of Fitzgerald's morbid imaginative vision is compelling still. Peer closely at what is going on in his *Fairies in a Bird's Nest*, where the fairy babies hatching from fairy eggs and witches staring with eyes in their nipples can be traced back to Hieronymus Bosch. Fitzgerald, who was untrained, is technically a terrible painter, but arguably the most original artist in the exhibition after Dadd. For, unlike the others, he makes it clear that the fairies and demons who writhe around sleeping artists and nightmare-racked ladies are hallucinations emanating from the opium bottle.

Don't go to this show if you aren't willing to look at the pictures with close attention, and without condescension. This means that you have to learn a little about the characters you encounter in fairyland before you can understand what is going on. From the excellent catalogue, by Charlotte Gere, Jeremy Maas, Pamela White Trimpe and others, we learn the sinister fact that robins are the enemies of fairies because they were thought to bury human dead in the woods, polluting the fairy domain. Did you know that fairies hide in hawthorn trees because the hawthorn was thought to grow from the thorn of Glastonbury? Or that Red Cap is a fairy of malign aspect, whose headgear is dyed in human blood?

At every turn you encounter the most fascinating links with science, religion and the theatre. The great ballerina Marie Taglioni has an honoured place in this exhibition because when she first danced on point dressed as a fairy in *La Sylphide* in 1832, fairies in art immediately rose up on tiptoe.

Among the many explanations for the existence of fairies was the theory that they were spirits of the dead, who could be contacted through mediums. Knowing this, you look at John Simmons's *Titania* and realise that what you took to be diaphanous drapery surrounding the Queen of the Fairies may well be intended to suggest ectoplasm. In pictures by Charles Doyle and John Atkinson Grimshaw, we run across crackpot pseudo-scientific ideas, including levitation, spiritualism and belief in the 'aura'. When George Cruikshank depicts *The Fairy Ring*, he is like a magazine illustrator trying to depict a UFO sighting based on the description of eye witnesses.

Fairy painting had a kind of afterlife in Edwardian illustration, with such masters as Edmund Dulac and Arthur Rackham working at the height of their powers. But even in Rackham's poetic nocturne *The Serpentine is a Lovely Lake and there is a Drowned Forest at the Bottom of It*, painted to illustrate a J. M. Barrie book, I detect a condescension that isn't there in Victorian fairy painting. Like the creator of Peter Pan, Rackham can conjure up a world that adults no longer believe in for an audience of children who do. The beauty is still there, but the innocence is gone.

And finally a quibble. Was it the First World War that killed off the belief in fairies, as the show's organisers believe, or the publication in 1900 of Freud's *The Interpretation of Dreams*? I'd say that once you find a rational explanation for the visions that disturb our sleep, you've dealt the fairies a blow from which they can't recover.

Walter Sickert

Developed in the 1820s, the London suburb of Camden Town never quite succeeded in attracting the middle classes. Already by the 1840s the tall houses in its handsome crescents were being subdivided into multi-occupancy dwellings, rooming houses for Irish immigrants working as cheap labour on the stations at Euston, St Pancras and King's Cross. In *Dombey and Son* Dickens memorably describes the urban desolation wreaked on Camden Town by the arrival of the railways. In their wake, a transient population flooded in, so that to this day the area attracts prostitutes and their clients, down-and-outs and persons of no fixed address.

A Victorian temperance hospital still stands just off the Euston Road; side streets near the stations are full of cheap hotels, newsreel cinemas, porn shops. And the laureate of this anonymous, constantly changing part of the city was Walter Richard Sickert, an exhibition of whose work, *Sickert: Paintings*, is currently at the Royal Academy of Arts.

Perhaps because he was born in Munich of a Danish father and English mother, Sickert brought to his work a detachment not typical of native-born artists. His was a London few Englishman saw or wished to see, a London of mean streets and marginal people. Sickert hated gentility. He was not interested in London's picturesque Georgian squares, the fog-bound Thames or chintz-covered drawing-rooms. He lingers instead in shabby rented rooms with their unwashed windows and the lavatories down the hall. Nobody starves in Sickert's London, but his is a hand-to-mouth world, half-lit, without expectations.

And yet Sickert is an English artist. How many Continental painters would have treated the working-class audience in the galleries of the Old Bedford Music Hall as Sickert did, without a trace either of condescension or of glamour? The harmless working men in

25 November 1992

Sickert: Paintings

Royal Academy, London

several of these pictures seem to be caged like animals behind the safety railings – a surging, faceless mass illuminated by the stage lights reflected from below. In other pictures in the series, the powerful baroque sweeps and swirls of the theatre's architecture stabilise the composition. But perhaps more importantly, the architecture acts as a metaphor for the rigid social structure keeping this audience in its place: the cheapest seats in the highest balconies.

Technically, the music-hall pictures are among Sickert's most complex compositions. Often the performers or audience are shown reflected in gigantic mirrors which apparently hung to the right and left of the stage, so that the picture's central motif may be 'behind' the spectator as it was behind the artist when he drew it. Understanding this, we then begin to read what appear to be incoherent compositions as straightforward records of what Sickert saw in front of him: the lights and fug and smoke of the Victorian theatre darkly reflected in smeared glass.

Pretty though Sickert's many studies made in Venice and Dieppe are, in most of them he remains just another Post-Impressionist. He is truly original only when he takes England itself as his subject. We see this clearly in a masterpiece of Sickert's mid-career, the *Brighton Pierrots* of 1915. The picture shows a troop of vaudeville comics performing on a rickety open-air stage on the beach. It is dusk, around 9.30 on a summer's night. The pink sunset on the horizon merges into a haze of yellow-brown pollution hanging just below the darkening blue sky, while the performers in their straw hats and electric-pink blazers seem to hover around the illuminated stage-lights like moths round flames. There is no audience – most of the deckchairs are empty. In the surrounding silence we can almost hear the furious tinkling of the old upright piano. Gradually it dawns on us that the empty seats and desperate gaiety reflect the news that summer that British losses at the front had reached 230,000. Sickert finds beauty as well as sadness in the transitory theatrical performance, the ephemeral burst of laughter, the moment caught on the wing. But the nuance he captures most tellingly is specifically English: a certain gallantry. The Pierrots might represent England itself, desperately trying to hold back the night. This is Sickert's version of Dover beach.

The Camden Town Murder is based on newspaper reports of an actual murder. The series of pictures always includes a fat, naked

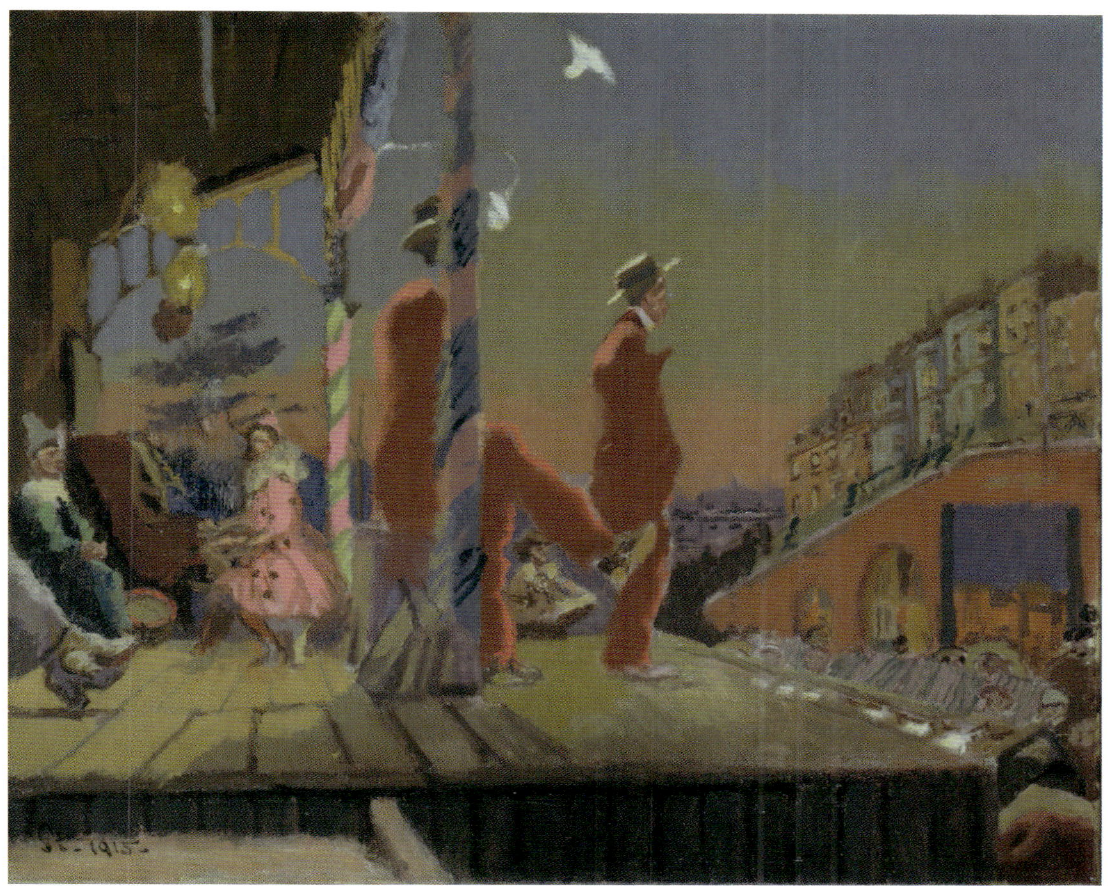

Walter Sickert
Brighton Pierrots,
1915
Tate Gallery, London

woman lying on the sagging mattress of a cheap iron bedstead.
Next to her stands or sits a clothed man, her client. Thickly painted
in dark colours, all the paintings have that grainy, blurred quality
of newspaper photography. It is as though Sickert wanted to create
an art with the very texture and feel of life in the streets. The use of
glancing Impressionist brushstrokes, alternating with thick gobs of
stabbed-in pigment, at once suggests the prostitute's features while
at the same time denying her the dignity of an individual portrait. In
this way the painting technique itself becomes a metaphor for faceless
anonymity.

What one might call the artistic provenance of Sickert's aesthetic
vision stretches deep into the nineteenth century. His first and most
important teacher, James McNeill Whistler, was himself the disciple of
the realist painter Gustave Courbet. When Sickert in his turn came to
repudiate Whistler's radical version of art for art's sake (conveniently

forgetting how important Whistler's early etchings had been for his own development) it was to re-introduce something like Courbet's gritty actuality into British art.

As early as 1906 Sickert was working directly from photographs, not drawings, which gave certain pictures such as *Lady in Red: Mrs Swinton* a flat, muzzy, unreal quality which I find disagreeable. Later, however, he showed the way to a whole new conception of portraiture by emphasising the ephemeral nature of these photographically based images. He found his subjects in looming close-ups of film stars on illuminated screens in darkened cinemas, or else in tabloid snaps of famous figures like Edward VIII or Amelia Earhart stepping into history for their allotted five minutes of fame.

To those used to the shrieking, wham-bam colour of the French Impressionists and Fauves, Sickert's tonal Impressionism will at first seem muted, his subject matter sadly restricted. But if we open ourselves up to the quiet intelligence of these pictures, we find in them a formal complexity and thematic richness which sometimes eluded even his two mentors Whistler and Degas. It is not that every picture in the very well-chosen exhibition succeeds – Sickert is far too experimental and ambitious an artist for that – but that he brought his own quirky intellect, humour and feel for the craft of painting to everything on view.

Aubrey Beardsley

Aubrey Beardsley's black-and-white illustrations are said to capture the spirit of his age so perfectly that Max Beerbohm dubbed the 1890s 'The Beardsley Period'. And yet the fashion for Beardsley's work lasted for only about a year – from April 1894, when the first number of *The Yellow Book* brought him notoriety – to the spring of 1895, when Oscar Wilde's trial for indecency created a public backlash leading to Beardsley's dismissal from the magazine. Referring to Beardsley's drawings in *The Yellow Book*, one reviewer called for 'an act of Parliament to make this kind of thing illegal'. These may seem like strong words to use about mere illustrations. But unless we recognise that to his contemporaries those illustrations posed a danger to the very fabric of society, we can't understand his role in creating the myth of the Naughty Nineties.

What exactly was the nature of that danger? Wilde had never been invited to contribute to *The Yellow Book*, and Beardsley neither liked nor admired the writer, whom he considered to be a plagiarist and fraud. But there was a connection between the two men, for Beardsley had illustrated Wilde's play *Salome*, and these illustrations are among the most subversive and endlessly fascinating images in British art. Like much of Beardsley's work, the *Salome* illustrations have become so familiar through frequent reproduction that it can be difficult to understand why they were once so threatening. The Victoria & Albert Museum's exhibition marking the hundredth anniversary of Beardsley's death gives us a chance to look at them as though we had never seen them before.

In one of the most famous images from the series, *Enter Herodias*, the magnificently bare-breasted queen is led on stage attended by a grotesque dwarf and an effeminate, heavily made-up page. Though the setting of Wilde's play is vaguely Byzantine, Beardsley here works in the fashionable Japonisme of the period, drawing on the

7 October 1998

Aubrey Beardsley

Victoria & Albert
Museum, London

asymmetry, economy of line, and decorative flatness of the Japanese woodblock print. Of course, many artists before Beardsley had studied the prints of Hokusai and Hiroshige. But he alone looked attentively at the Shunga genre of printmaking, which is so pornographic that such prints were sold under the counter in bookshops specialising in erotica or 'curiosa'. In his published work (as opposed to the obscene drawings he produced for private collectors) there was no question of directly quoting from such a visual source. But then sex, like wit, can be even more effective in art when it is used discreetly, and Beardsley became adept at slyly inserting schoolboy smut in otherwise blameless illustrations.

When his publisher, John Lane, first saw *Enter Herodias* he instructed the artist to add a fig leaf to cover the loins of the girlish page. Beardsley meekly complied. But Lane did not notice the real indecency in the drawing – and I'll wager that most of you haven't spotted it either: the tent-like swelling on the front of the dwarf's costume. Clearly, this grotesque fellow is as aroused by the Queen's nudity as her fig-leafed page is indifferent to it.

Because of shenanigans like these, Beardsley is usually bracketed with the 'decadent' school of British art. But you have to be careful how you use the term, because in his case 'decadence' refers to his subject matter, not his style. The use of black and white; the way the figures appear to be arbitrarily cropped; the exquisite calibration between the flowing lines and the flat areas of black and white: all these make Beardsley's style feel closer to that of Toulouse-Lautrec or even to Egon Schiele than to the hesitancies, evasions and misty outlines of the British decadents. As for Beardsley's treatment of his subjects, there too he was subtly different from his British contemporaries.

When Whistler or Charles Condor (1868–1909) showed prostitutes parading London streets at night, for example, the women are as vague and poetic as figures in a painting by Watteau. Beardsley's retinue of leering streetwalkers and vicious catamites could hardly be mistaken for anything other than what they are. For all the extravagance of Beardsley's imagination, at one level his art is highly realistic. This is what made it so threatening.

There is another aspect to his work that is often lost on modern audiences: he was a master caricaturist. In *Enter Herodias* the

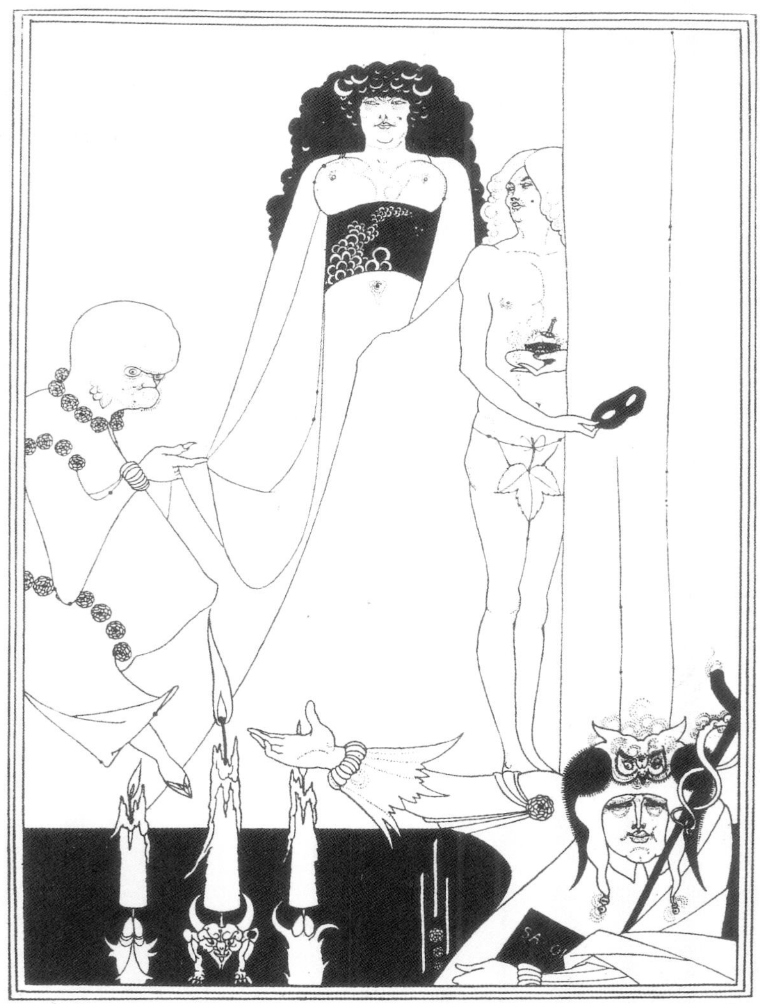

fairground barker in the foreground who introduces Herodias is none other than Wilde himself, so bloated and pasty-faced that the critic for the *Saturday Review* concluded: 'Mr Beardsley laughs at Mr Wilde.'

Beardsley was also a natural parodist. Even in his first major project, the illustrations to a popularly priced edition of Malory's *Le Morte D'Arthur*, he couldn't resist sending up the mannered intensity of Burne-Jones and Rossetti by filling his pages with androgynous knights and droopy nymphs. Though he brilliantly adapted their slightly old-fashioned Pre-Raphaelitism to the more refined taste of the 1890s, he correctly described the art of Morris and Burne-Jones as 'old stuff'.

With equal correctness, he added that his own art was 'fresh and
original'. That is in part because Beardsley was capable of working in
several different styles at once. His later infatuation with the French
rococo informs the suitably frothy illustrations to *The Rape of the
Lock*, the silhouetted outlines of the figures on Greek red-figured
vases served him for Aristophanes' satire *Lysistrata*, while for the
illustrations to Ben Jonson's *Volpone* he used a heavy cross-hatch
to create a richly baroque effect.

Remember, Beardsley was dead at the age of twenty-five from
consumption. We are dealing with a talent as prodigious in its way
as Picasso's – but one cut short at the height of his powers.

The last show of Beardsley's work at the Victoria & Albert Museum
in 1966 contained more than seven hundred works, and created
a national craze for his art. This time round, the V&A's Beardsley
exhibition is a low-key affair. The curator, Stephen Calloway,
has limited the exhibits to prints, drawings and posters from the
museum's own holdings, supplemented by a few strategic loans
from British collections. This means that what is on view are mostly
line-block prints. To compare these to the relatively few original pen-
and-ink drawings – for *Lysistrata* and for Gautier's *Mademoiselle de
Maupin* – is to become aware that when you look at a print, you lose
much of the freshness and subtlety of Beardsley's work.

Nothing is harder to recapture than the sense of danger in a work
of art once that danger has passed. When you leave this show, try
to exit through the nearby Canon photography galleries. Not only
will you find that Beardsley's greatest influence was on fashion
photographers such as Irving Penn, but in the photographs of Robert
Mapplethorpe you may feel a bit of the frisson that Beardsley's work
once gave the Victorians.

The Aesthetic Movement

In English art of the mid-1860s, the curtain was coming down on Pre-Raphaelitism and a full-scale neo-classical revival was in full swing. Stimulated by the rearrangement of the Elgin Marbles in the British Museum, a new generation of artists was ready to take centre stage with work that sought to reject Ruskinian realism and yet to avoid the superficialities of academic neo-classicism.

Whether you think of Albert Moore's rhythmic friezes of toga-clad Greeks, the languorous reveries of Edward Burne-Jones or the little-known Thomas Armstrong's enigmatic women in a hayfield by moonlight, these artists turned their backs on the natural world. Even more controversially, what mattered in their pictures was not the subject but the emotions stirred in the viewer by the delicately restrained colours, exquisite compositional balance, and sultry, dream-like atmosphere.

The work of these progressive young painters struck a chord with the French-trained American James McNeill Whistler. In what they were doing he found something he felt had been missing from the art of the realist painters Courbet and Manet, whom he had known in Paris: an emphasis on the purely formal or abstract qualities of painting at the expense of conventional subject matter. Whistler in turn introduced his British colleagues to the relentless simplification of form he had discovered in the art of Japan. Discarding narrative, minimising perspective, and eliminating detail, British art in the decades to come would draw closer than it had ever come to architecture, design and the decorative arts. This is what the Aesthetic Movement is all about.

Aestheticism can be defined as a philosophical position in which aesthetic values are placed in the foreground of human experience. The Aesthete saw art as a supreme good in itself, not (as John Ruskin or William Morris believed) as a means to make us all better people.

12 April 2011

The Cult of Beauty:
The Aesthetic
Movement 1860–1900

Victoria & Albert
Museum, London

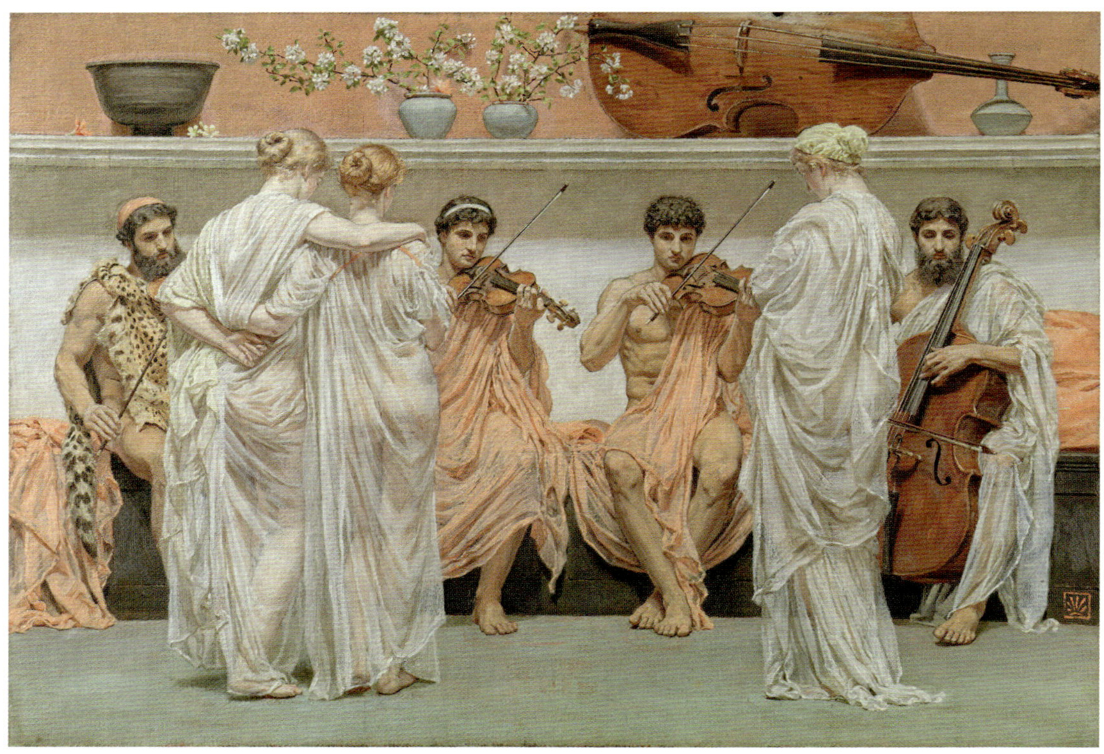

Whistler declared that 'art should stand alone and appeal to the artistic sense of eye or ear, without confounding this with emotions entirely foreign to it, as devotion, pity, love, patriotism'. The French critic Théophile Gautier succinctly referred to 'art for art's sake'.

The title of the Victoria & Albert Museum's masterly survey of the Aesthetic Movement, *The Cult of Beauty*, is apt. For a 'cult' is exactly what it was. Exponents said openly that art was for the chosen few whose temperament enabled them to see it where it had not been seen before. At the height of the Industrial Revolution, that meant finding beauty in the flow of a great river at night or in a London fog that the man on the street saw as mere pollution.

For the Aesthete, art had nothing at all to say about morality. That was what critics on both the right and the left hated about it. When the socialist designer William Morris moved to a house beside the Thames at Hammersmith, he was appalled by the nightly spectacle of drowned bodies dragged from the river's depths. Responding with outrage to Whistler's exquisite studies of the Thames at night, Morris declared that 'we cannot look upon the world merely as if it were an

Albert Moore
A Quartet: A Painter's Tribute to the Art of Music, *1868*
Pérez Simón Collection, Mexico

Impressionist picture', and yet that was exactly what Whistler urged his followers to do with his poetic evocations of the river at twilight shrouded in mist.

For others, however, what was truly suspect about Aestheticism was all its carry-on about beauty with nary a word about God or nature. Where would it end? In this show, exquisitely bound volumes of Swinburne's and Rossetti's poems, displayed near works by Simeon Solomon, Aubrey Beardsley and Alfred Gilbert, exude a worrying whiff of forbidden sensuality. Next stop: Reading Gaol. Aestheticism represented not so much a taste in art as a style of life – one that didn't come cheap. For artists such as Whistler, for collectors like Frederick Leyland, or for a gallery owner like Sir Coutts Lindsay, how pictures and *objets d'art* were displayed was a matter of overwhelming importance. To decorate the house Edward William Godwin designed for him in Chelsea, Whistler chose restrained colours against which to display his collection of blue-and-white Chinese porcelain, simple floor coverings and plain eighteenth-century English furniture.

His *Harmony in Blue and Gold: The Peacock Room* is both a work of art and an architectural interior. Though Leyland only commissioned him to finish the decoration of a cheerful morning room in his London townhouse, Whistler created what looks like the inside of a Japanese lacquer box, a room that only comes to life at night, under artificial light, as golden peacock feathers appear to spill out from its closed shutters on to the turquoise-blue walls and ceiling.

As you can see, Aestheticism was also a way to justify materialism and consumer consumption of luxury goods. From 1873 to 1881 in his *Punch* cartoons, the great George du Maurier both fuelled the public's curiosity about the Aesthetic Movement and ridiculed its pretensions in cartoons that hit on truths the Aesthetes themselves would never have admitted. In his drawings, characters such as the poet Jellaby Postlewaite, the painter Maudle and the 'intense' hostess Mrs Cimabue Brown gush about art when what they are really doing is fetishising their own possessions. In one of the most famous, the Aesthetic bridegroom says of his blue-and-white teapot, 'It is quite consummate, is it not?' to which his intense bride replies, 'It is indeed! Oh, Algernon, let us live up to it!'

Though we see du Maurier's satires as good fun, Whistler bitterly resented them, correctly understanding that they played to the pervasive British mistrust of the visual arts. But the person to bring Aestheticism into most disrepute was not du Maurier but Oscar Wilde, a lousy art critic who appointed himself its spokesman without knowing the first thing about either art or design.

The Age of Enchantment

27 November 2007

The Age of
Enchantment

Dulwich Picture Gallery,
London

Dulwich Picture Gallery's *The Age of Enchantment* looks at the art of Aubrey Beardsley, Edmund Dulac and other artists who worked during one of the golden ages of British book illustration, from the 1890s until the 1920s. It is also the first exhibition I can remember to deal directly with the phenomenon of decadence in art.

Every artistic style, like every historical cycle, has its decadent stage – a perceived decline from its initial vigour and strength, as, for example, when the self-conscious artificiality and elegance of the Mannerist period superseded the classical art of the High Renaissance. But you have to be careful when using such a loaded word: what for one person constitutes a lowering in standards to another is freedom from unnecessary rules and restraints. Decadence isn't necessarily the opposite of progressive art. It can just as easily represent a rearguard action fought by the avant-garde against both the accepted art of the time and conventional cultural values.

Beardsley is the epitome of *fin-de-siècle* decadence. With almost no formal training in art, he learnt to draw by imitating engravings by Mantegna, Japanese erotica, and Walter Crane's picture books for children. A technical genius with no allegiance to one school or style, he also possessed an imaginative vision as far-reaching as any in British art. But his is an art of surface, not depth. It appeals to the eye and to the mind, but rarely touches the emotions.

'Decadent', too, is his ability to change his style of drawing with each new subject. In this show we move from his stiff, medievalising illustrations for Malory's *Le Morte D'Arthur* to one of his most famous drawings for Oscar Wilde's *Salome*, in which he imitates Japanese art, treating pictorial space as a flat field on which to dispose figures and near-abstract forms. And, in his frothy illustrations for Pope's *The Rape of the Lock*, he turns for inspiration to the French Rococo at its most frivolous. But what is truly decadent – and absolutely inimitable –

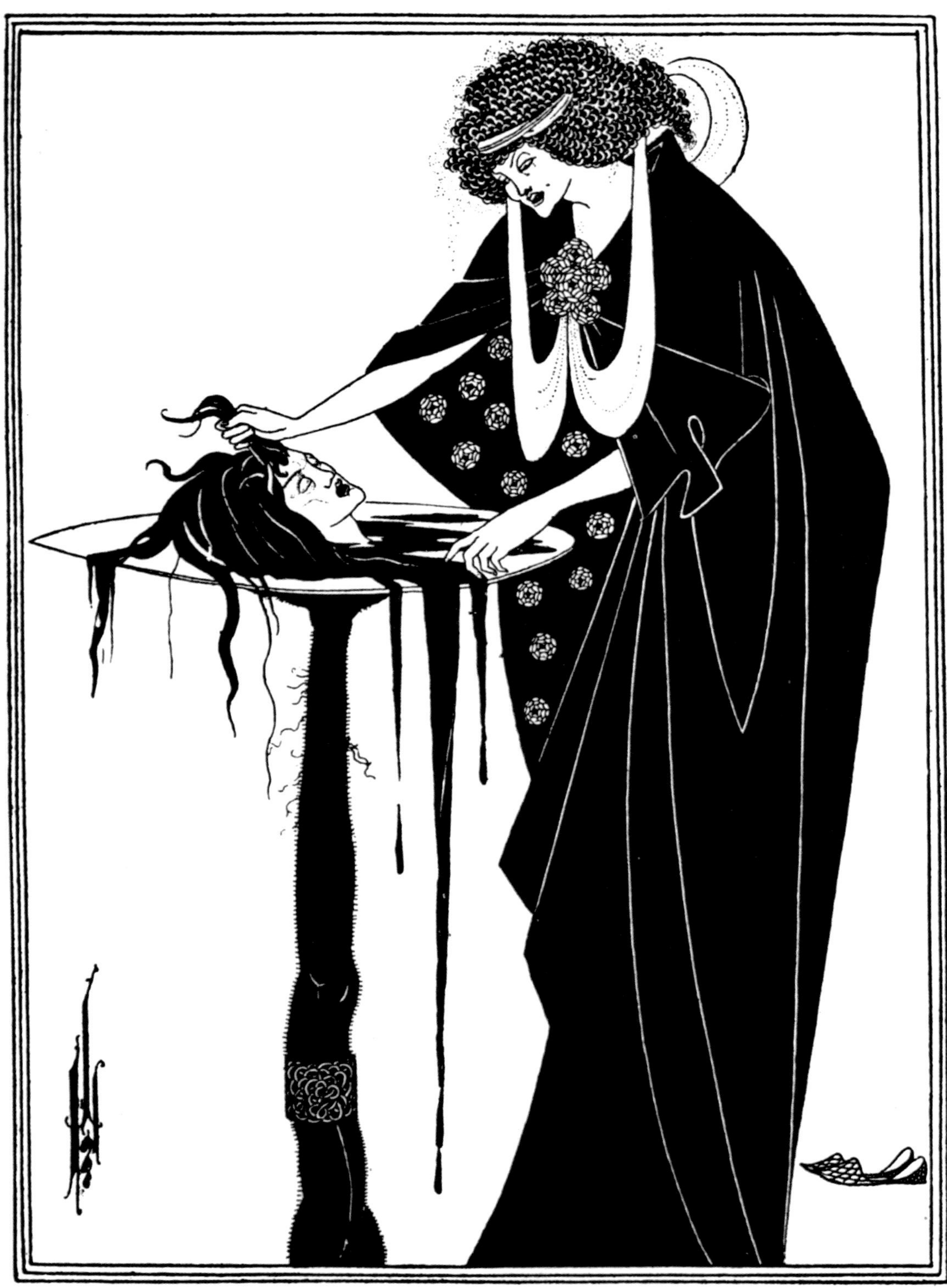

about Beardsley has nothing to do with his eclectic visual sources, his exquisite draughtsmanship or his boldly original compositions. It is that his drawings exude a sense of evil so pure and palpable that it can almost make you reel. Look at the face of Salome as she prepares to kiss the severed head of John the Baptist: no other artist conveys malevolence the way Beardsley does, and none is as frank in his depiction of sadism, lust and moral degradation.

When his contemporary James McNeill Whistler painted prostitutes cruising for custom in Cremorne Gardens, he veiled the sordid scene in mist and darkness, turning it into a *fête galante* worthy of Watteau. But you could never mistake Beardsley's leering, predatory street walkers for anything other than what they are. Whatever subject he is treating, he uses wit and sex as subversive weapons, trusting that his audience will spot the sexual puns discreetly inserted into apparently harmless illustrations and, in doing so, become complicit in the act of schoolboy transgression each represents.

This sense of danger died in British art with the trial of Oscar Wilde for indecency in 1895. Wilde's conviction had catastrophic consequences for any artist associated with symbolism or decadence. In particular, those identified with *The Yellow Book* had to be careful. When one review of the notorious periodical called for an Act of Parliament 'to make this kind of thing illegal', he was referring primarily to Beardsley's illustrations – but 'this kind of thing' could easily be construed to refer to the crime for which Wilde was sent to prison.

At a stroke, a deeply ingrained visionary tradition in British art – extending from Burne-Jones and Rossetti to John Martin, Fuseli and Blake – was wiped out as a whole generation of artists either left the country or toned their work down. By 1900, British art had been reduced to the Frenchified banalities of the Newlyn School and the third-rate 'Impressionism' of the New English Art Club. Art in this country has never, before or since, sunk so low.

Except, that is, for illustration. Taking their cue from Beardsley, black-and-white illustrators such as Laurence Housman, Sydney Sime and Charles Ricketts all turned their backs on nature. It is as though they pulled down the blinds of their studios, the better to cultivate their beautiful – and often violent and erotic – fantasies. Now, too,

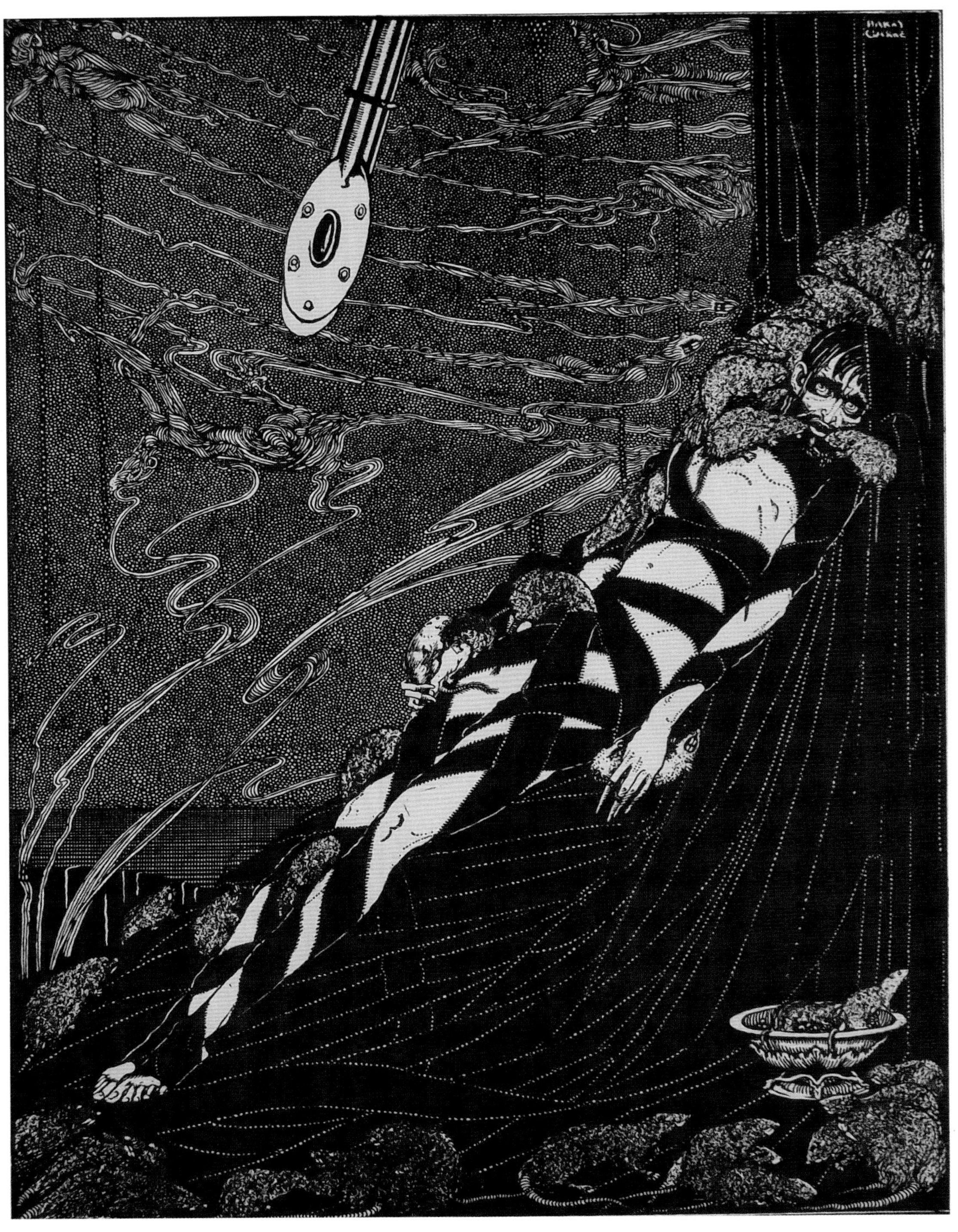

they begin to send themselves up. For the first time ever in British art, we can detect a distinct note of high camp.

The one who came closest to catching the transgressive quality of Beardsley's art was the Irishman Harry Clarke, whose illustrations to Edgar Allan Poe's *Tales of Mystery and Imagination* were directly responsible for the night terrors that helped to ruin my childhood. In this show, we see Clarke's visualisation of the horrifying scene from *The Pit and the Pendulum* in which the narrator, bound to a plank with criss-crossed strips of thick black cloth, stares out at us with fear-crazed eyes as rats swarm over his naked body, including his mouth and groin. Clarke's genius resembled Beardsley's because he did not just illustrate Poe's stories – he brought out their sadomasochistic subtext. The work of Beardsley and Clark was intended for grown-ups, not children.

But the extraordinary illustrations of the amazing Sidney Sime aren't so easy to categorise. They can be frightening and funny at the same time. His illustration of a fairy tale in which a malignant elf who keeps a boiling pot filled with the limbs of little children is a throwback to the fairy painting of the 1860s, but his invented creature, the Zagabog, looks forward to Maurice Sendak's illustrations for *Where the Wild Things Are*.

Of the two great rival illustrators of the Edwardian era, I'm impervious to the charm of Arthur Rackham, whose work I find so sanitised that it loses all its edge. The French-born Edmund Dulac is altogether different, the last truly Romantic artist, whose gorgeously decorative style encompassed both orientalism and the Rococo revival. For sheer invention, he is second to none. It was he who produced the haunting image of *The Ice Maiden*, a fairytale vision of an albino woman flanked by two polar bears tiptoeing through the snow under a star-studded sky – and holding in her open palms a human heart dripping with blood.

Such vivid, visceral imagery became ever more diluted in British illustration. Though I love the work of Charles Robertson in small doses, the cute moppets he never stopped drawing can fairly be described as saccharine. And for all their flowery delicacy, Jessie M. King's illustrations preserve the romance of Pre-Raphaelite painting, without its solid grounding in draughtsmanship or its close observation of the natural world.

What is hard for us to recapture today is how much more
important illustration was at this period. As late as the Sherlock
Holmes stories, books for adults were routinely illustrated, and de
luxe colour annuals sold in their tens of thousands right through the
First World War.

The show ends with wonderful costume designs by Leon Bakst for
the Ballets Russes, and by an artist who is completely new to me, the
incredible German illustrator Alastair (Hans Henning von Voight),
whose perversely stylish Art Deco fantasies somehow feel closer to
the world of fashion design than to literary illustration.

I could easily have done without the hideous 'Fairyland Lustre'
of the ceramicist Daisy Makeig-Jones, and a print cabinet designed by
Frank Brangwyn so ugly it has to be seen to be believed. But these are
quibbles. This is the perfect show for the holiday season, enjoyable for
anyone old enough to see the pictures without standing on a chair.

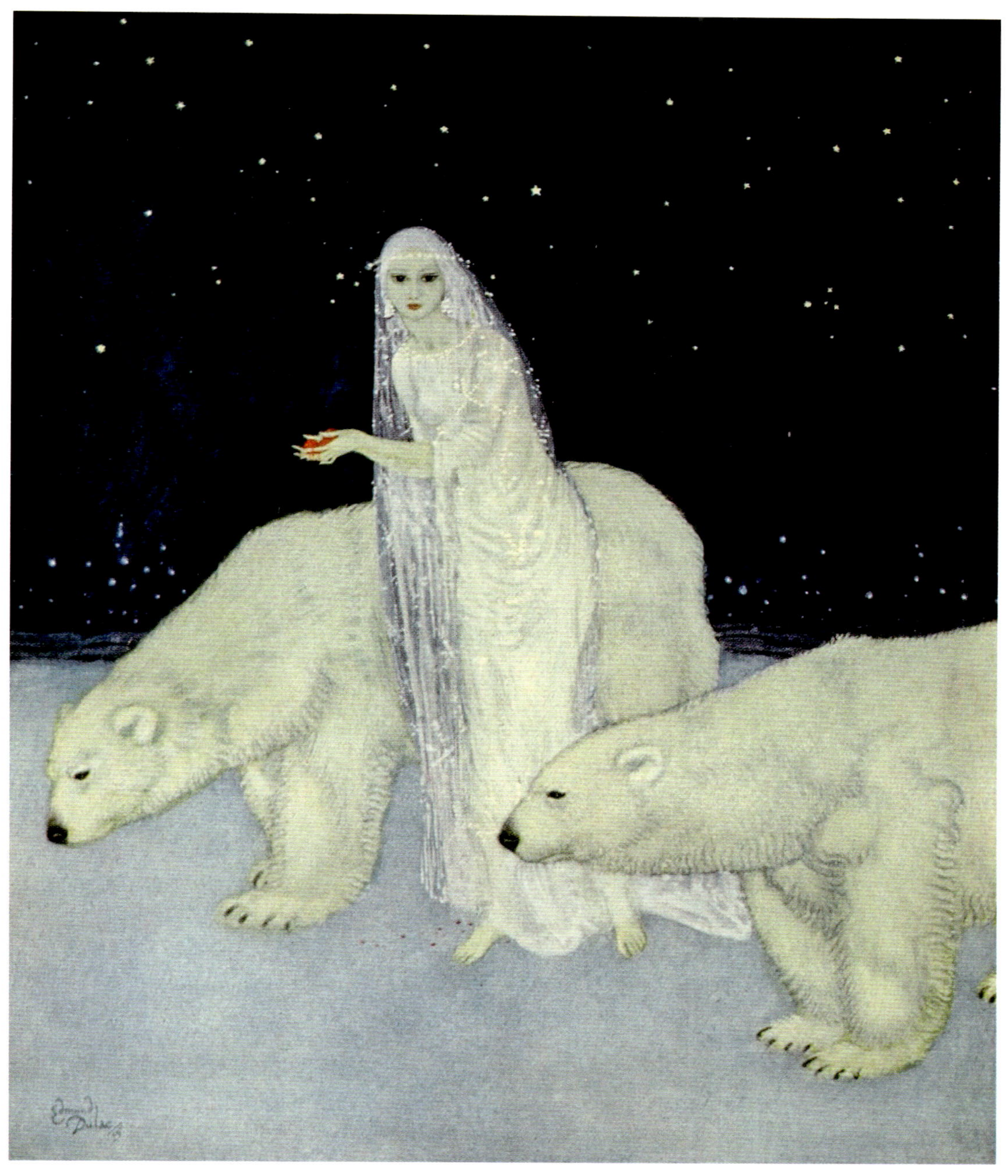

Edmund Dulac
The Ice Maiden, 1912
Illustration to Marie
of Romania's 'The
Dreamer of Dreams'

PHOTOGRAPHY

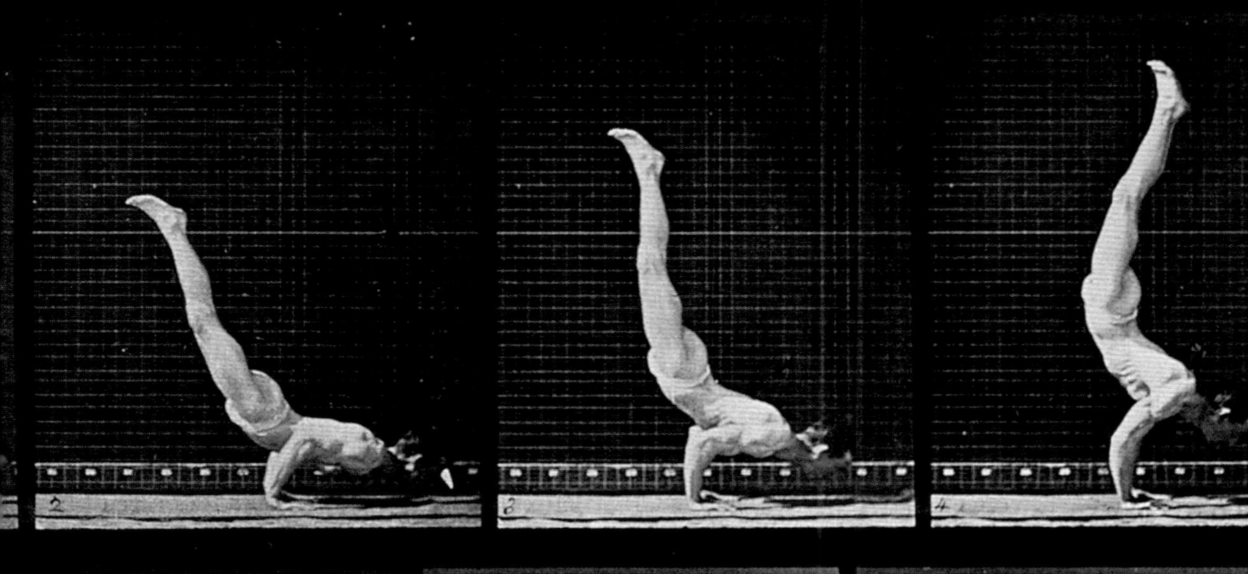

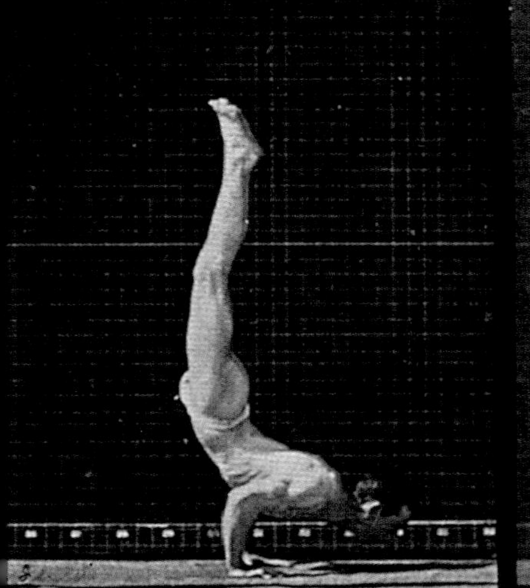

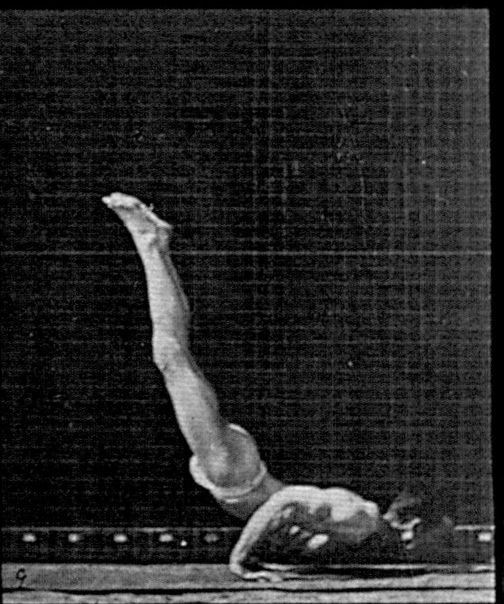

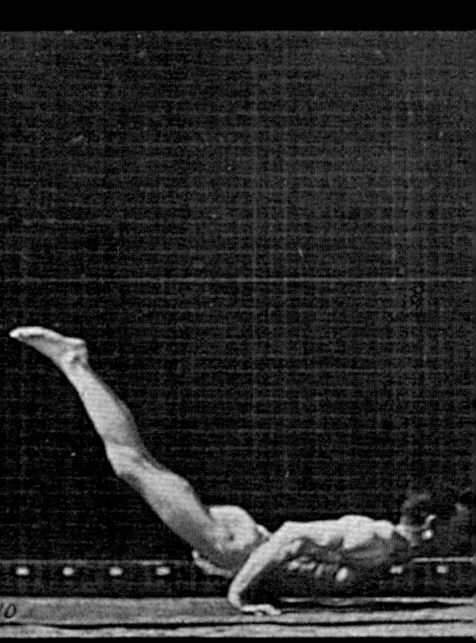

La Divine Comtesse

The exhibition everyone was talking about in New York last week was neither the Museum of Modern Art's continuing thematic rehang of its permanent collection, nor Damien Hirst's hugely successful show of recent works at the Gagosian Gallery, but a modest display of nineteenth-century French photographs at the Metropolitan Museum of Art. *La Divine Comtesse* is a selection from the more than four hundred photographs that Pierre Louis Pierson took of one woman, Virginia Oldoini, Countess de Castiglione. From a technical point of view, they are nothing very special. But as a private archive of photos spanning a period of more than forty years (1856–98) they at once testify to the narcissism of a legendary Second Empire beauty, and document her decline into solitude and madness.

Her story is the stuff of a romantic novel. The Italian-born Virginia married the Count di Castiglione, a rich widower ten years her senior, in 1854, when she was sixteen. Two years later she arrived in Paris on a mission from Count Cavour, prime minister to King Vittorio Emanuele II, to help advance the cause of Italian independence from Austria. Taking Parisian society by storm, the raven-haired *femme fatale* soon became the mistress of Napoleon III.

Like other ladies of high fashion but limited means, she also found her way to the studio of a firm of commercial photographers, Mayer and Pierson. Early photographs show a plump and extremely pretty young woman, as round and ripe as a freshly picked peach. Though she isn't shy, initially she appears to be intimidated by the camera. Her repertoire of poses is conventional, borrowed from portraits by Ingres and Winterhalter. Clearly she is assuming poses suggested by the experienced photographer, Pierson.

But before long, the balance of power begins to shift, as the Countess discovers the true love of her life, the camera, and finds that her infatuation is reciprocated. Rather in the way that photography

11 October 2000

La Divine Comtesse

Metropolitan Museum of Art, New York

transformed the late Diana, Princess of Wales from a pretty young thing into one of the most glamorous women in the world, the camera's lens turned the teenage Castiglione into La Divine Comtesse, a dark-eyed seductress whose aristocratic profile, high cheekbones and bitter, downturned mouth lent her an air of frigid allure.

Like the late Princess of Wales, she appears to have become addicted to the contemplation of her own beauty. She fed this habit by commissioning more and more photographs of herself, apparently oblivious to the fact that the more glamorous the image the less relationship it bore to an increasingly pathetic life. For after an attempt was made on the Emperor's life as he left her house late one night in 1857, the Countess, though innocent of any involvement in the plot, was banished from court. Having made a powerful enemy in the Empress Eugénie, Castiglione never regained her place in French society. At first she lived in seclusion with her son near Turin. On her return to Paris in 1861 she became a figure of scandal and then of ridicule. Her heyday had been short-lived.

Yet all the while she continued to work with Pierson, dressing up in costumes so extravagant that the bills for her wardrobe and jewels finally bankrupted her long-suffering husband. Like a living statue in one of the *tableaux vivants* popular at the time, she faced the camera in the roles of characters from history and fiction, from Marie Antoinette to Lady Macbeth. In this she could be compared to a notorious beauty from another age: Emma Hart, Lady Hamilton, whose one-woman mime shows, the Attitudes, electrified visitors to the British Embassy in Naples at the end of the eighteenth century.

But, for the Countess de Castiglione, posing was no frivolous pastime. It wasn't fame that the camera gave her (most of these photographs she neither sold nor circulated), but something far more precious – it stopped time. With her identity inextricably bound up with her beauty, photography validated her existence by fixing her image for eternity. When one thinks of all those 'celebrities' who turn up in the pages of *Hello! Magazine*, her situation begins to seem curiously modern.

It was Madame la Comtesse, not Pierson, who was in charge of each photo shoot. She not only dictated the subject, costume, pose, gestures, coiffeur and props, but also chose the camera angles and marked up the proofs to indicate where she wished the final print to

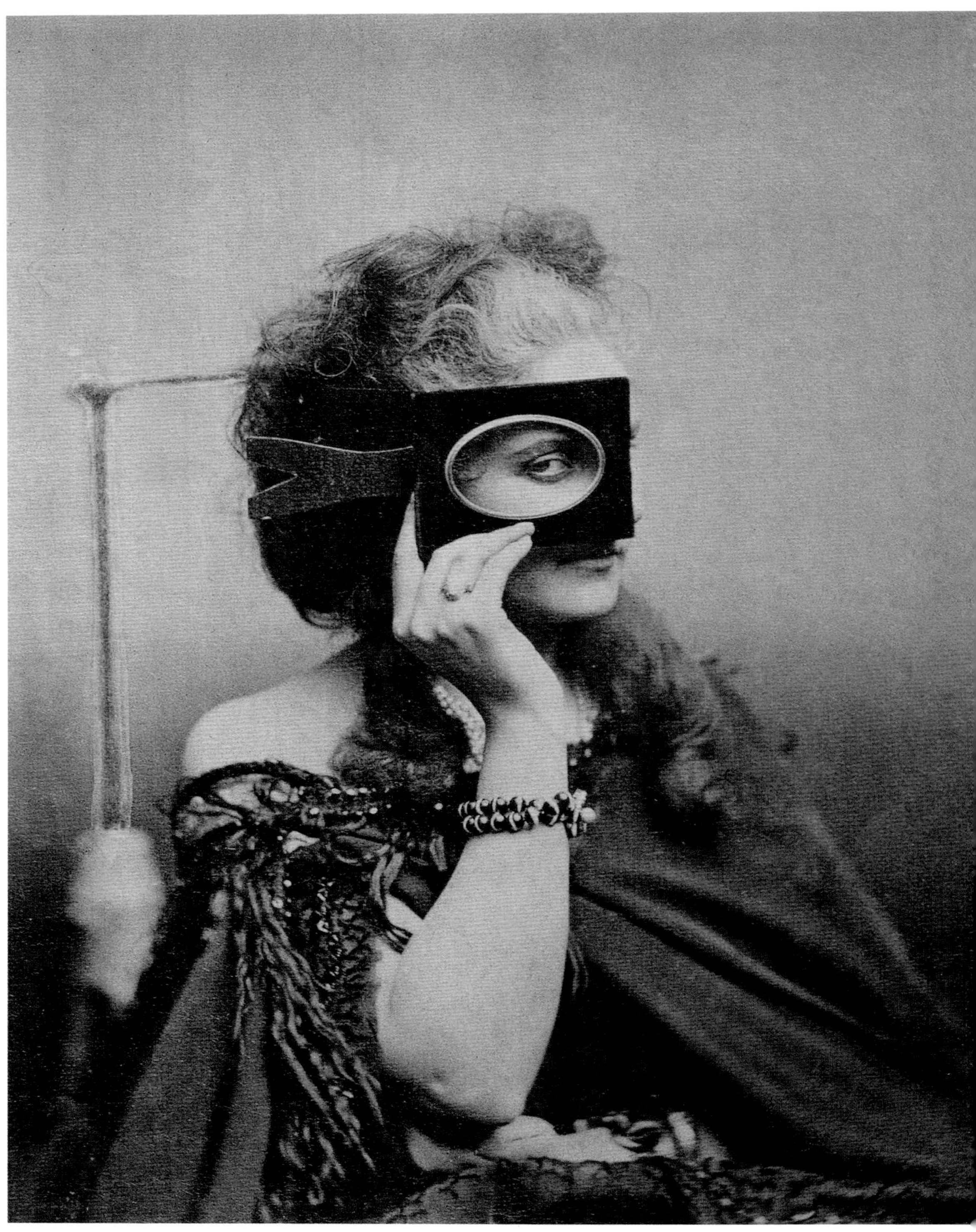

be cropped, enhanced, airbrushed or accented with colour. Any physical shortcomings she detected in herself she corrected, as when she elongated her dumpy figure by standing on a footstool. (Weirdly, she doesn't conceal such stratagems, for in some shots we can see the stool partially concealed under her billowing crinolines.) In the most famous image of her, endlessly shown in surveys of the history of photography, she picks up a black picture frame, holds it to her eye and looks out from the oval window, reducing herself to a lens: I am a camera.

The title of this work, *Game of Madness,* was apt. For, although by this time ill, she was having her boudoir re-created in Pierson's studio in order to have herself photographed in bed. Clearly the distinction between artifice and reality had begun to crumble in her mind. The photographer's studio became for her a private stage on which she was the only actress. She took the leading role in the drama of her own life – a life produced and directed by her own imagination.

It is always fascinating when the work of a contemporary artist makes us see the art of an Old Master in a new light. Twenty years ago the body of work produced by Pierson and the Countess was no more than an eccentric footnote to the history of photography. But since the American artist Cindy Sherman began using costumes, make-up and accessories to transform herself into a series of characters from the cinema, which she photographs and exhibits as works of art, it has become possible to recategorise the Countess not as an eccentric society woman who dabbled in photography, but as almost an artist in her own right. The man behind the camera, Pierson, was simply her collaborator, the tool she used to investigate a subject of endless interest to her, her own identity.

In 1878, her beauty fading, she moved to an apartment in a corner of Place Vendôme above the jewellers Boucheron. Painting the walls black and banishing mirrors, she emerged only at night and heavily veiled to wander the streets of Paris. As her fragile mental stability finally gave way in the 1890s, this relic of the long-vanished Second Empire had a series of final sessions with Pierson, and these are the most disturbing photographs in the show. Now she is Norma Desmond, toothless and bewigged, her eyes frighteningly outlined in mascara, ready for her close-up. Dressing up in her tawdry finery, what was left of her mind fed on memories of her former beauty.

With Pierson – who must have found these last photographs
unbearably poignant – she outlined her plans to mount a retrospective
of their work together at the Exposition Universelle of 1900. She
intended to call the show *The Most Beautiful Woman of the Century*.
She died, in 1899, before this could happen.

La Divine Comtesse will not be coming to London. But the
catalogue, written by Pierre Apraxine and Xavier Demange and
published here by Yale University Press, is endlessly fascinating.
I can honestly tell you that I read it straight through without stopping.
And don't, whatever you do, skip the footnotes.

Eadweard Muybridge

When a magisterial survey of the photographs of Eadweard Muybridge opens in London on Wednesday, the venue – Tate Britain – signals a subtle change in the way we look at his work. Muybridge's stop-action photographs and moving images are, of course, precursors of the early cinema and not so long ago this show would probably have been staged at the Science Museum or the National Media Museum. By showing these photographs at Tate Britain the organisers encourage us to look at them as art – and not just as art, but as British art. The new context adds yet another dimension to our understanding of this extraordinary man's achievement. After visiting the show last week, I realised for the first time that Muybridge was probably the most important artist/scientist since George Stubbs.

Not Stubbs the painter, but Stubbs the anatomist, draughtsman and engraver whose *The Anatomy of the Horse* (1766) and *Comparative Anatomical Exposition of the Structure of the Human Body with that of a Tiger and a Common Fowl* were direct precedents for Muybridge's *Animal Locomotion* (1887). Just as Stubbs's painstakingly detailed drawings of dissected cadavers synthesise scientific accuracy and aesthetic perfection, so Muybridge's 20,000 stop-action photographs of animals and humans make visible something the human eye had never before seen: the beauty of movement itself.

Born in 1830 plain Edward Muggeridge in Kingston upon Thames, at the age of twenty-two this strange man emigrated to the United States, initially to work for a publisher and then as a seller of books, prints and sheet music. After his return to England in 1860 he must have taken up photography – because when he turns up again seven years later in San Francisco, having changed both his first and last names, he set up a photographic studio that operated under yet another pseudonym, 'Helios'.

There is little in the first few years of Muybridge's career to suggest

7 September 2010

Muybridge

Tate Britain, London

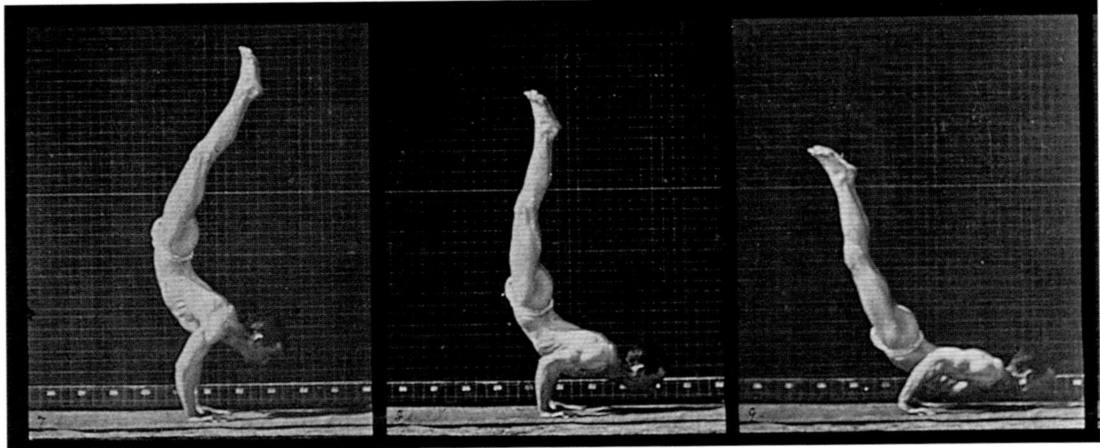

his future reputation as one of the supreme innovators in the history
of photography. Many of the early photos look like the work of
a talented jack-of-all trades, happy to photograph the mansions
of railroad magnates or document a day in the life of workers
on a Guatemalan coffee plantation. More interesting is his photo-
journalism. A series of photographs commissioned by the American
government shows the terrain, ports, frontiersmen and Indians in
the newly acquired Alaskan territory. When he accompanied the US
Cavalry to north-east California to record their suppression of an
uprising by the Madoc Indians, the series movingly conveys the harsh
reality of conflict in the Wild West.

By this time Muybridge had already been acquitted of the murder
of his wife's lover, Harry Larkins, 'a roguish theatre critic'. At the trial,
a self-portrait in which Muybridge perches at the edge of a precipice
was produced as evidence of a deranged mind. I don't know about
deranged, but to me the image speaks of profound loneliness and
emotional isolation.

When Muybridge photographed the Yosemite Valley he used large
glass negatives to achieve images of startling clarity, distinguished by
his determination to show the natural world as he found it. In these
photographs Muybridge first confronted one of the limitations of
early photography: exposure times were too long and shutter speeds
too slow to capture rapid movement. Whenever he photographed a
waterfall, the result looks unnatural, since the camera shows running
water as static, like a long white ribbon. In this very year, 1872, he first

Eadweard Muybridge
*Detail from **A man**
standing on his
hands from a lying
down position, 1887*
Wellcome Library,
London

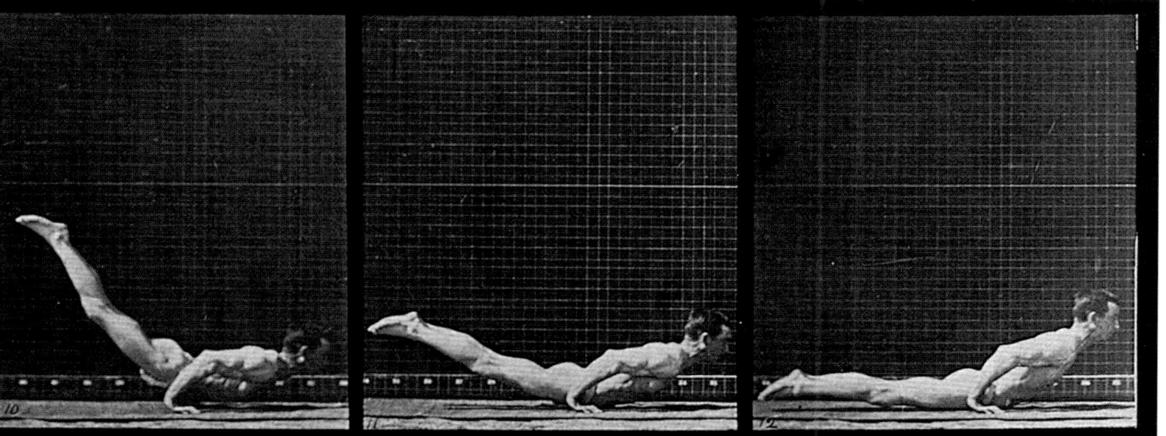

began to experiment with multiple cameras in an attempt to capture on film the precise movement a racehorse breaks into a trot.

Muybridge developed a shutter that worked at the speed of one-thousandth of a second and used plates which he treated with chemicals to reduce their exposure time. Then he set up batteries of cameras connected to trip wires that triggered the shutters as the subject moved. This enabled him to create stop-motion images showing movements the human eye had never seen. Not only did he prove that for a split second a trotting horse lifts all four hooves from the ground, but he invented a device he called a zoopraxiscope, in which drawings derived from his photographs could be projected in sequences so rapid they appeared to move.

In the mid-1880s he moved to America's east coast, where, with financial support from the University of Pennsylvania, he began to photograph people. Installing 36 lenses in three groups of twelve, he photographed naked or semi-naked male athletes fencing, wrestling, running, walking or performing somersaults and back flips against a background grid. The presence of the grid indicates that Muybridge's purpose was not purely scientific – for, like a squared drawing, the grid made it possible for an artist looking at the photograph to measure the height of a foot or arm in any given position, and therefore to draw them correctly. He also photographed naked women performing less strenuous activities, famously inspiring Marcel Duchamp to paint his *Nude Descending a Staircase*.

From the beginning, Muybridge was obsessed with optical

phenomena, fascinated by how the eye works. By taking two photographs of the same scene from slightly different perspectives and viewing them through a hand-held device called a stereoscope he created the illusion of depth and was able to show the world in 3D. To create his 360-degree panoramic view of San Francisco he exposed thirteen large plates, then put the photographs together to make a single image that can only be seen by moving from left to right, as in a Chinese scroll painting. Years later, in his Philadelphia studio, Muybridge developed this idea by photographing the same subject from several different camera positions, opening up a whole new world of visual experience, later to be explored by the Cubists. He also prepared the way for motion pictures.

Otherwise, I can't see that his motion studies had any serious scientific use. He invalidated any pretence the photos might have had to scientific accuracy by sometimes re-shooting a photo within a sequence, or leaving a movement out of the sequence when one of his cameras failed. In some photographs of female models a whiff of voyeurism creeps in – at least it is hard to see what scientific purpose was served by showing a naked woman smoking a cigarette or getting into bed. But that, I think, is part of the point. While his technical innovations belong to the realms of science, Muybridge's photographs are also objects of elusive beauty, mysteriously imbued with the powerful personality of a man you feel by the end of this show you have come to know.

Julia Margaret Cameron

Julia Margaret Cameron's daughter presented her mother with her first camera with the words: 'It may amuse you, Mother, to try to photograph during your solitude at Freshwater . . .' The year was 1864, and Mrs Cameron was in her late forties, her children grown, her nest (on the Isle of Wight) empty. Although she had known about the new invention of photography since 1839, and had certainly done some photographic work herself, it seems from the tone of her daughter's letter as though Mrs Cameron might just as easily have taken up painting in watercolours to fill the empty years that stretched ahead of her.

But Julia Margaret Cameron was far from a conventional Victorian matron. Photography was a distinctly unladylike pastime. It required a camera and tripod so heavy that two men were needed to move them. The wet collodion process for taking and developing photographs in the 1860s was complicated, messy and extremely dangerous – especially when it came to using potassium cyanide to remove excess developer from the plate. On the other hand, one of the advantages photography possessed for a person in her position was that it is a mechanical process. It didn't require years in an art school to learn how to do it, and even in late middle age you could start.

Photography is also a medium in which the amateur has certain advantages over the professional. One was time. Mrs Cameron had the leisure to arrange her models in any way she chose, and, if a photograph failed, she could retake it as many as a dozen times, experimenting with lighting effects and correcting technical and compositional flaws as she went along.

Another was her sex. Living as she did in a domestic circle of friends and family, she could command an endless supply of children, neighbours and servants to endure the tedium of sitting absolutely still during the long exposures photography then required.

29 January 2003

Julia Margaret
Cameron:
19th-Century
Photographer of Genius

National Portrait Gallery

Finally, she approached photography as an art, not a craft. Dressing many of her sitters in exotic costumes, she did not intend her photographs to be seen as pure portraiture, but as the equivalents of genre, myth, religious or history paintings.

She chose her sitters well: Alfred Tennyson, John Herschel, Thomas Carlyle and G. F. Watts all have strong, worn, craggy faces, lined with years, and full of character. Dressing them neutrally or even wrapping them in cloaks, she placed them against dark backgrounds. Before taking the photograph, she first mussed their hair to give them the farouche appearance of inspired prophets.

It must have taken great courage for Mrs Cameron to dispense with the conventional props that tell us who these sitters are – the telescope for the astronomer, the easel for the painter, the pile of books for the poet. It was her genius to use light and shade alone to convey their moral and intellectual weight. In each, a looming face fills the frame, floating against the darkness like the ectoplasmic spectres you see in 'spirit' photos. These great men stare off into the distance, thinking their great thoughts. To me, they foretell the Symbolist art of Redon, Carriere or Rodin.

All of Mrs Cameron's photographs are just slightly out of focus. In part the reason was technical, because the type of lens she used made it impossible to photograph a subject from close to and still retain focus. But it was also a deliberate attempt to imitate in photography the effect that in painting is called *sfumato* – a vaporousness created by making the transitions from light to dark so gradual that they are imperceptible. In doing this, Mrs Cameron dragged the twenty-five-year-old medium of photography into a debate that had raged among artists and connoisseurs since the Renaissance.

Which was superior – line or colour? Michelangelo or Titian, Poussin or Rubens, Ingres or Delacroix? Mrs Cameron was in the camp of the colourists. The most Venetian of Victorian artists, G. F. Watts, her lifelong friend, helped to form her aesthetic sensibility. But her rivals instantly pounced on her penchant for soft focus. Henry Peach Robinson, for example, wrote of Mrs Cameron's photos as 'failures from every point of view. It is not the mission of photography to produce smudges.'

Precisely what we admire today about these photos is the depth and richness of their tone, the velvety shadows and romantic play of

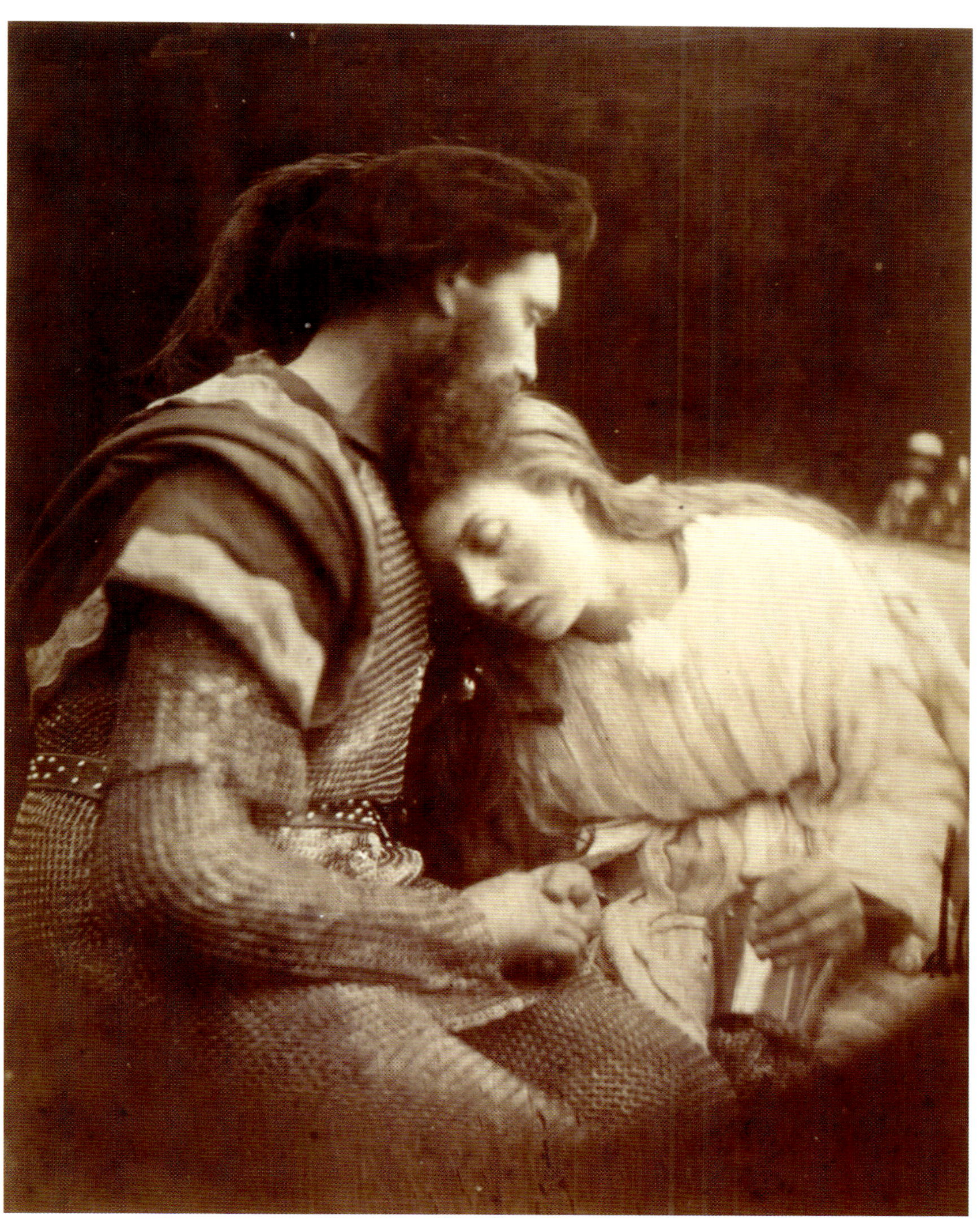

light and shade that reveals softly modelled forms. What is more, they are in some ways deeply private, very revealing portraits. You have only to look at the downcast eyes and full lips of the Italian Angelo Colarossi or at the many portraits of beautiful teenage girls, who, in an age of tight stays and crinolines pose in loose flowing gowns, to trace a seam of open sensuality and the frank appreciation of animal beauty in her work.

For twenty-first-century sensibilities, the modernism of Cameron's approach to portraiture can be obscured both by her predilection for fancy dress and for a tendency to exaggerated expressiveness. But this is unfair. Mrs Cameron was a highly educated woman whose photographs openly acknowledge her debt to Old Masters such as Perugino, Raphael or Sassoferrato. As for the white draperies, lilies, children dressed up with fake angel wings: some critics have been put off by the air of the dressing-up cupboard or amateur theatrical in certain photos, but I see an extraordinary artist trying to wring from the camera the same depth of feeling that Old Masters achieved with their brush.

Even more interesting to me is the knowledge she shows of the art of her own time. The long-necked beauties photographed with frizzy hair tumbling around their shoulders come straight from Pre-Raphaelite painting; Mrs Cameron's chubby-cheeked children could have stepped out of the canvases of Sophie Anderson, her lovers from Arthur Hughes.

It is true that Mrs Cameron did not always succeed in her aims, but even in failing, she told us a great deal about herself, her family, her circle of friends and the world she moved in. The show of her work at the National Portrait Gallery is as perfect as an exhibition can be: the right size, the right choice of photographs, the right lighting and labels, and a superbly produced catalogue by Colin Ford that tells you everything you need to know about the subject – and not a syllable more.

TWENTIETH-CENTURY EUROPE

7

Matisse

In *Henri Matisse: A Retrospective*, which opened at New York's Museum of Modern Art last week, we come upon *Harmony in Red*, the artist's first indisputable masterpiece, only after tracing Matisse's slow metamorphosis from a painter of dark, voluptuously modelled nudes in the 1890s into the controversial Fauve innovator, his landscapes vibrating with broken touches of crudely applied pigment. Born in 1869, Matisse was already thirty-nine when he painted *Harmony in Red* in 1908, and yet nothing in this utterly straightforward picture of a woman in a richly decorated bourgeois dining-room looks backward. In it, he gives us a near-inventory of the themes that will preoccupy him throughout his later career.

In place of the fragmented brushstrokes of the Fauve years, we find broad, flat areas of pigment; instead of depth and volume, space is compressed and form is flattened. The twisting arabesque pattern of the bright red tablecloth seems to flood over the frontal plane of the canvas, its tendrils appearing to climb the wall and to submerge individual details in a riot of pattern and colour.

This is an art of purification and simplification, but also an art in which perceptions and emotions are intensified and enhanced. By setting the yellow lemons within a surrounding field of scarlet, Matisse creates an aching, almost blinding yellow, a yellow of an intensity one has never seen before. By showing the white trees outside the window apparently covered in snow, the artist makes us feel the heat and light of the crimson interior.

The modernity of *Harmony in Red* lies in its artifice, its frank admission that it is not a view into a fictive world but a flat canvas covered with pigment. Fundamentally abstract, it is concerned with flatness, pattern, surface and colour. Matisse dreamt of an art which was essentially decorative in conception, instinctive rather than

23 September 1992

Henri Matisse:
A Retrospective

Museum of Modern Art,
New York

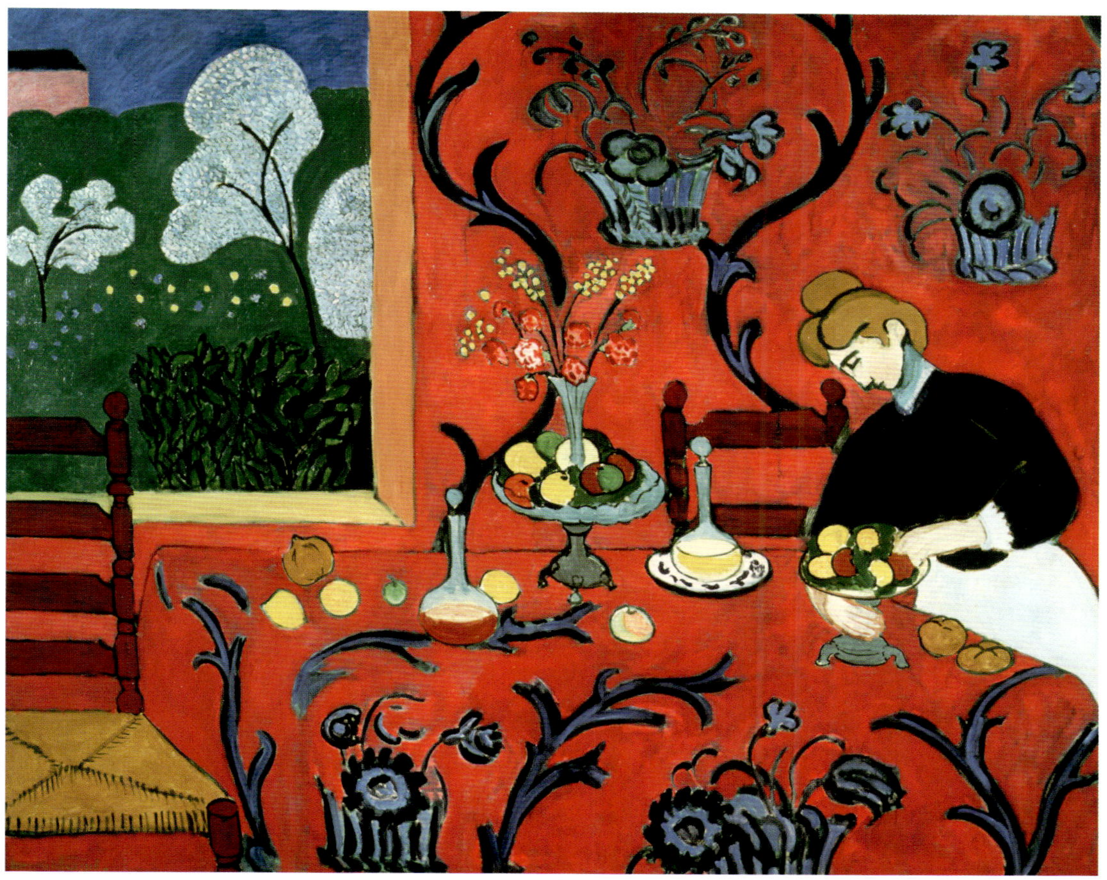

cerebral, and wholly dependent on the feelings of the painter for his subject.

Those who see Matisse entirely as a formalist overlook the powerful subjective content of his paintings: *Harmony in Red* functions as a metaphor for emotional warmth, security, and for the sensuous enjoyment of good food and wine. It represents an artificial garden in a remembered paradise – not, perhaps, as it really was, but as the artist would like it to have been. The picture is one of thirty early masterpieces lent to the exhibition by the Hermitage Museum in St Petersburg and the Pushkin in Moscow, originally purchased by Matisse's great Russian patrons Sergei Shchukin and Ivan Morosov. In gallery after gallery these pictures come at us, pounding our senses with waves of light and rhythm and almost impossibly beautiful colour. One room is hung entirely with pictures from his two Moroccan journeys of 1912–13, some smouldering with deep pinky reds, others awash with aqueous blues and submarine greens. If one has not seen these sublime canvases at first hand, one simply does not know the art of Matisse.

The show helps us to understand the way in which Matisse works – indeed thinks – in terms of pairs of pictures. For the first time since they were painted in 1909, the two versions of the monumental *Dance* are hanging side by side in a gallery of their own, the figures in one painted in a shade one might describe as dionysian red, those in the other a cool light pink. The former appear to perform some slow, savage, prehistoric rite of spring, like dancing Bacchae in the circular frieze around an Attic vase; the latter, by contrast, seem to join hands for a graceful Arcadian reel.

During the second Moroccan sojourn, Matisse became aware of the geometric shapes made by slanting shadows and shafts of light as they fall through doorways on to figures and faces. Building on these discoveries in the years 1914 to 1917, the artist painted a series of ambitious architectonic masterpieces in which he came to terms both with Cubist severity and with the sombre mood of a world at war. Though many experimental pictures from this period are flawed or unfinished, seeing them in sequence like this demonstrates that Matisse was a great artist precisely because he was constantly breaking new ground, losing his way, and sometimes running up against a blank wall.

A much more serious problem arises with the long Nice period, from about 1917 to 1943, when the artist simply ceased to be an avant-garde painter, churning out what sometimes seem like the same colourful but empty pictures over and over again. This show deals with the 'soft' Matisse by arguing that the best of these images are among Matisse's most memorable productions.

In many of the 'odalisque' pictures the model is treated as a single, uninflected element within an intricate latticework of colour created by juxtaposing oriental carpets, patterned fabrics, striped silks and brilliant flowers. Within this Aladdin's cave, our eye is never allowed to come to rest on one part of the canvas rather than another. Matisse's models seem to play at harem life for the delectation of the detached, impassive artist. These paintings are not, therefore, about reality, or even about the present, but about erotic memory.

To achieve all this, Matisse banishes ugliness, pain and anxiety from his Nice period pictures. Some would say he banishes life itself. A criticism often made of his art is that, compared to Picasso's austere confrontation with the darkest aspects of human nature, Matisse is far from profound. But such misgivings – even in this selection not entirely unfounded – vanish when one comes to the sublime late period, the ecstatic, visionary final years, when Matisse began to work with paper cut-outs.

Always aware of 'the eternal conflict of drawing and colour', the tendency for artists to divide into draughtsmen (Michelangelo, Ingres) or colourists (Titian, Delacroix), late in his life Matisse discovered that he was able to conflate the two elements by cutting out shapes of pre-painted paper, which he then pasted on to a neutral background. 'Instead of drawing an outline and filling it with colour,' he said, by this method he could 'draw directly in colour'. The contour of a shape and its colour were formed simultaneously.

Among the many masterpieces of the years before his death in 1954, my own favourite is the decorative frieze entitled *The Swimming Pool* of 1951. Here, blue cut-out shapes mounted on a background of white paper seem to register first as positive then as negative, first as totally abstract then as seagulls and swimmers splashing in the surf. Look again and one can make out a swan dive, cannon ball, the backstroke and a joyful, exuberant belly-flop.

Henri Matisse: A Retrospective is the artist's first full-scale exhibition since 1970, and the first show ever to give a comprehensive overview of his art, to reveal the seamlessness of his achievement. Of the four hundred works on display in the Museum of Modern Art, three hundred are paintings and the rest are sculptures, drawings, paper cut-outs and prints (but not ceramics or stained glass).

Matisse Picasso

Matisse Picasso at Tate Modern explores the life-long artistic dialogue between the two men who dominated twentieth-century art – a dialogue all the more remarkable because, until now, even art historians and biographers hardly realised its importance or how it enriched every phase of their long careers. To tell this remarkable story, the show's organiser, John Golding, devotes each of the fourteen galleries to a different theme and hangs the works of art in pairs and clusters, so that we never see a painting or sculpture in isolation but always in relation to the works around it. Aesthetic concerns explored early in the century are echoed in work made decades later, for the show isn't only about the relationship between the two artists, but about how each kept returning to earlier themes in his own work, inspired not only by what each had learned from his rival, but by war, illness and by the changing circumstances of their own lives. I can't remember an exhibition in which I become so engaged with the artists' creative process, or one in which I learned so much about how to look at a work of art.

The first phase of the dialogue began in 1906, when the two first met, and lasted until 1917, when Matisse left Paris for the South of France. When the exhibition starts, Matisse is the more progressive and experimental figure. At first, Picasso has to catch up with his fierce Expressionism, which the Spaniard always filters through his great intellect, even as both artists respond to the common stimulus of Cézanne and African art. But, with Picasso, to borrow from another artist's work is also to criticise and to improve upon it. In his *Bather* of 1908, for example, he simply rotates by 90 degrees the odalisque in Matisse's *Blue Nude (Memory of Biskra)* of 1907, turning a horizontal figure into an upright one. But, at the same time, he shows us what Matisse only implies – the back as well as the front of the figure simultaneously.

8 May 2002

Matisse Picasso

Tate Modern, London

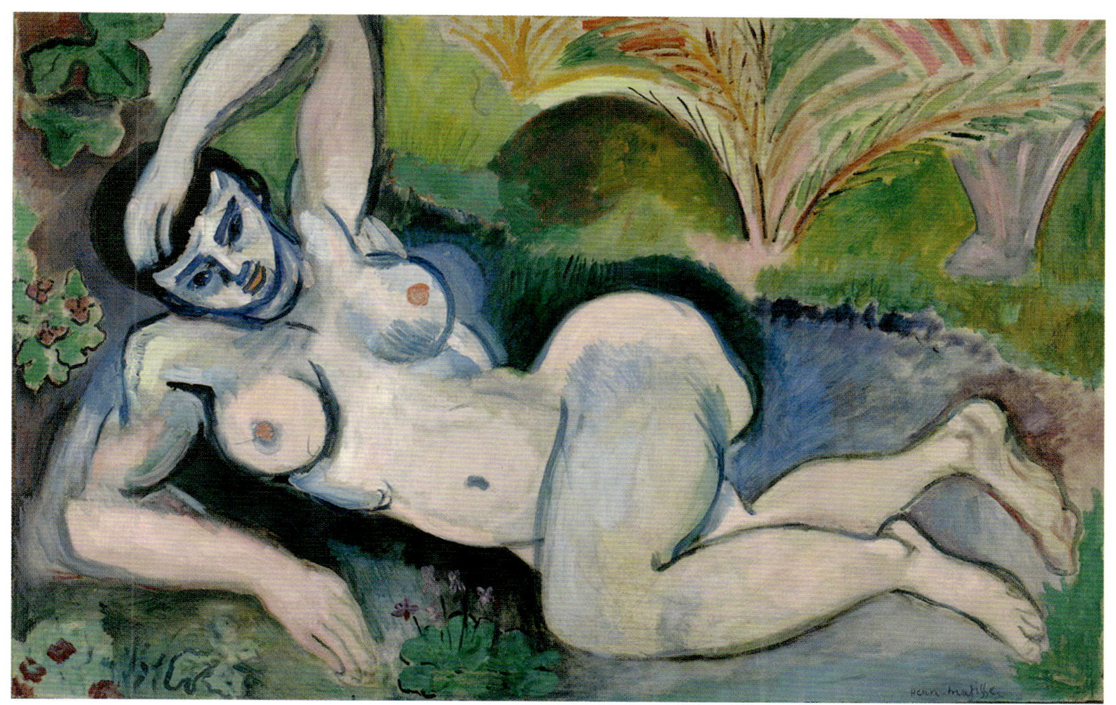

Above:
Henri Matisse
**Blue Nude (Memory
of Biskra)**, 1907
Baltimore Museum
of Art

Right:
Pablo Picasso
Bather, 1908–9
Museum of Modern
Art, New York

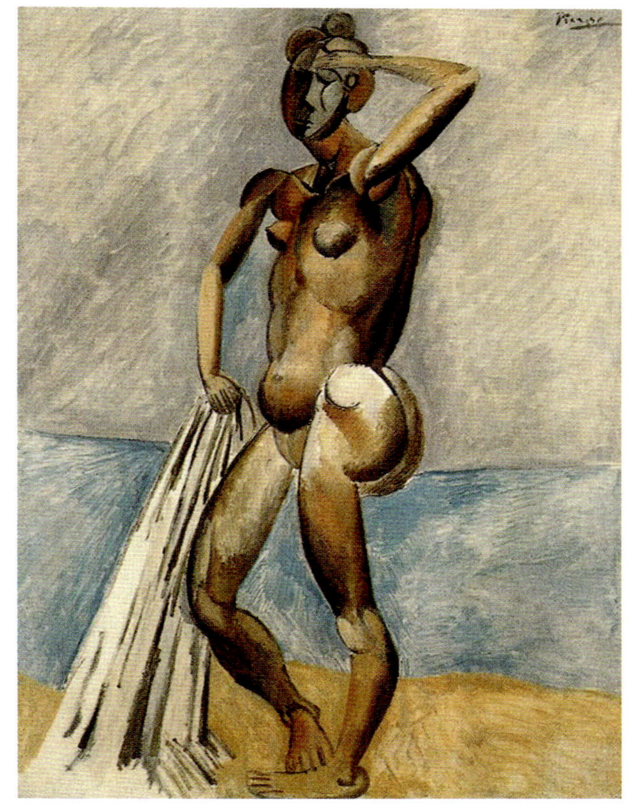

On the other hand, inspired by Picasso's muscular *Two Nudes* of 1906, Matisse painted a small *Standing Nude* the following year, which is even uglier than Picasso's squat monsters and which he shows lumbering across the canvas, too powerful to be contained within its top and bottom edges. Then, in 1909, Matisse began work on the first version of his monumental relief sculptures on the theme of the nude, *Back 0*. As is clear from the bronze versions in the show, even in 1930 the memory of Picasso's *Two Nudes* was present in Matisse's mind, for *Back IV* could be the nude in Picasso's pictures, just swivelled to face away from us.

To round out this extraordinary artistic dialogue between Matisse and Picasso (which is also a dialogue between painting and sculpture), and to remind us that both Picasso and Matisse were painters who thought in three-dimensional terms, remember that the work that started it all, Matisse's *Blue Nude (Memory of Biskra)*, was itself inspired by one of Matisse's own early sculptures, the *Reclining Nude (Aurora)* of 1907.

Cubism did not come naturally to Matisse – or, rather, his exploration of Cubist space initially feels tentative, as though the style in its first, formative phase was too austere and too cerebral for an artist of Matisse's sensual temperament. But, by 1914, with *Goldfish and Palette*, he has absorbed Cubism in its second, synthetic phase, which is characterised by the use of colour, decorative shapes and the incorporation of lettering, stencilling and pieces of newspaper into the composition.

Matisse does not at this stage work with *papier collé*, or collage, but the large, flat geometric shapes that appear in Matisse's art have their origin in Picasso's use of similar shapes of pasted paper in works such as the small *Guitar* of 1913. Here, tight rectangles of newspaper and wallpaper are pasted over each other in such a way that each seems to occupy a separate plane, and each functions as a semi-abstract and semi-independent element within the composition as a whole.

You can see Matisse demonstrate that similar effects can be achieved through colour and shape alone in the way triangles and rectangles of grey and green pigment are used to represent landscape or shadow in his famous *Piano Lesson* of 1916. And the influence ran the other way, too, for the much larger scale of Picasso's later Cubist paintings, such as the wonderful *Three Musicians*, and his use of notes of strong colour in the great *Harlequin* surely reflect an awareness of Matisse's practice.

But then, when one of these artists takes something from the other, he will make it his own, show his rival how it should be done. An example is Matisse's joyful *Still Life* after Jan Davidsz de Heem's *La Desserte* of 1915, his homage to a specific seventeenth-century Dutch still life, and his critique of the Cubist still life in general. Matisse breaks the green tablecloth into Cubist facets, so that the plates, goblets and fruits seem to hang in space, as though in front of a curtain, while, in true Cubist fashion, he shows us both the front and side of the mandolin in the corner. And yet, at almost 6ft high and 7ft long, the canvas has a scale and an exuberant colourfulness that is like a rebuke to the small size and near monochrome palette of Picasso's early Cubist still lifes.

But only when you see Picasso's 'reply' to Matisse's work, the 1924 *Mandolin and Guitar* hanging nearby, do you see something else about the Matisse: that Picasso's palette of sky blue, rust and ochre is very close to the warm Mediterranean colour and light with which Matisse has flooded his cold northern landscape.

One quality Picasso has that Matisse doesn't is a sense of humour. In his painted sheet metal sculpture of 1924, *Guitar*, Picasso peels back the body of the guitar to reveal its hollow interior. The complex arrangements of metal flaps painted with horizontal stripes parodies the open and half-open shutters and windows in Matisse's wonderful painting of 1917–18, *Interior with Violin*. And, if Matisse shows you the violin in its open case (the intense blue of its cover, by the way, one of the exhibition's many ecstatic moments of pure visual pleasure), Picasso goes one better by wittily showing the guitar and its case as one and the same thing.

The humour in Picasso's *Painter and Model*, hanging near Matisse's *The Studio, quai Saint Michel*, is not so obvious. Visually, it's hard to see what the two works have in common, but Picasso's joke is to identify the painter who sits so close to his model as Matisse himself by the patterned yellow fabric on the chair he sits in. Picasso didn't use models; Matisse did. And, as we can see from the ravishing drawings in this show, Matisse always sat very close to his models as he drew them. Adding to the dry wit of *Painter and Model*, I think, is that its squares and rectangles of pure red, yellow, blue and black parody the work of Mondrian, an artist who had less need of the living model even than Picasso.

Throughout the show, we watch each artist explore in three dimensions the implications of the other's work in two. The similarities are astonishing when you place Matisse's small bronze sculptures of women with boneless, snake-like limbs in front of Picasso's *The Painter*, in which the woman's torso almost disappears altogether, as her arms and legs are transformed into the writhing tendrils of a plant. And when, in the Sixties, Picasso responded to Matisse's late cut-out acrobats and nudes by realising them in three dimensions, he balances solids and voids as interestingly as Matisse did when he played with the relationship between figure and ground in his cut-outs – which are themselves, you could argue, a late variation on the technique of *papier collé* Picasso developed in his Cubist years.

Time and again this exhibition astonishes us by adding whole new dimensions to pictures we thought we knew well. Picasso's famous *Girl Before a Mirror* of 1932, for example, is as familiar to me as the *Mona Lisa*. How could I not have seen that by piling on strong colours and frantic patterns and stripes, Picasso identifies her as one of the orientalised women in luxurious interiors that Matisse was painting in the Twenties and Thirties? In an installation filled with felicitous juxtapositions, it was thrilling, too, to look past *Girl Before a Mirror* into another gallery and see Picasso's *Two Nudes* of 1906, and to realise how inevitably the later painting develops from the earlier one.

I walked through this show before there were any labels, so I can truthfully say that the exhibition is so limpidly and clearly installed that you don't need any. John Golding tells a story he justly calls 'one of the most compelling and rewarding in the entire history of art' through the works of art themselves. What I've left out of this review is perhaps the most important thing of all: that, in gallery after gallery, we come across some of the most beautiful and complex works of art ever made. But you don't need me to tell you that.

Matisse: the Cut-Outs

Tate Modern must know that with *Matisse: the Cut-Outs* they have a winner. I guarantee that this exhibition of the colour-saturated works Henri Matisse made by cutting out shapes from pre-painted sheets of paper during the last seventeen years of his life will be among the most popular ever staged in this country. And why not? With their lively rhythms and lusciously inventive colour combinations of yellow, pink, cerise, blue, violet, magenta and apple green, the aesthetic qualities of this body of late work are self-evident.

But what makes the exhibition outstanding for me is that the curators have imbued the cut-outs with a quality that at first glance they appear to lack: complexity. They do this by placing Matisse's creative process at the heart of the exhibition. Starting with the works of art as they exist today, they spool back in time to look at the methods and materials he used at each stage in their transformation from the raw materials of paint, paper and scissors to the transcendent works of art we see before us.

But is that really necessary? The joy of the cut-outs is their simplicity. They are made out of modest materials using basic techniques, and in them Matisse reduces art to the essentials of colour, shape and pattern. Yet precisely because they offer us instant visual gratification, it is easy to forget how innovative they actually are. We need to be reminded that they grew out of a lifetime of hard work, painful searching, and persistent questioning.

For there was nothing safe or pre-ordained about the cut-outs. Matisse developed them late in life not as an end in itself but as a working method for trying out different compositional and colour arrangements in the models or maquettes he made for the illustrations to his book *Jazz* (1943–46). As he grasped the implications of what he had done, the cut-outs evolved into a new art form in which drawing,

15 April 2014

Matisse: the Cut-Outs

Tate Modern, London

painting and sculpture were fused into a whole so perfect that it is impossible to separate one medium from another.

The process starts by cutting out shapes from sheets of paper that have already been painted in gouache with the colours chosen by the artist. The act of cutting into pure colour became for Matisse the equivalent both of drawing (outline) and sculpture (revealing form by cutting into his material). These cut-out shapes are then pinned (but not glued) to a support, which might be a sheet of paper, a wall, or a canvas. The use of pins meant that the bits of paper could be moved or rotated at the artist's will. In one of the larger cut-outs, for example, conservation scientists have counted as many as a thousand pin pricks, indicating that Matisse must have drastically altered the composition as he worked.

Then, too, because the shapes of palm fronds, mermaids, parrots and coral reefs were not fixed permanently to a flat surface, they have a degree of physicality which mediums like painting and collage do not. It changes your understanding of the cut-outs to learn that in their original form they might flutter slightly in a breeze, so that their sense of dynamic movement was at once visual and actual – a little like Calder's mobiles.

Today we look at *Oceania, the Sea* (1946), his monumental evocation of a silent, silvery underwater world teeming with stylised sharks and jelly fish, coral and starfish, and marvel at the elegance of white shapes pasted against a soft beige-coloured canvas edged with lapping waves. But can you imagine if those swirls and tendrils moved ever so slightly as we passed in front of them?

After the war, the bedridden artist used assistants to climb ladders with hammers in hand and pin cushions strapped to their wrists in order to pin cut-outs to the walls of his studio in Nice. In effect the studio wall replaced the canvas as the physical ground over which he could deploy shapes both abstract and figurative. As before, Matisse had assistants move, rotate or invert the shapes, but now the waving leaves, swirls, eddies, amoebas, faces and nude figures seem to float over door frames and around the corner of one wall to another. Because nothing was fixed, this was a world in constant flux, like life itself.

It was at a moment when the cut-outs were still pinned to the walls that Matisse turned down a rich man's offer to buy his entire studio

Henri Matisse
Icarus, *plate VIII of 'Jazz', 1946*

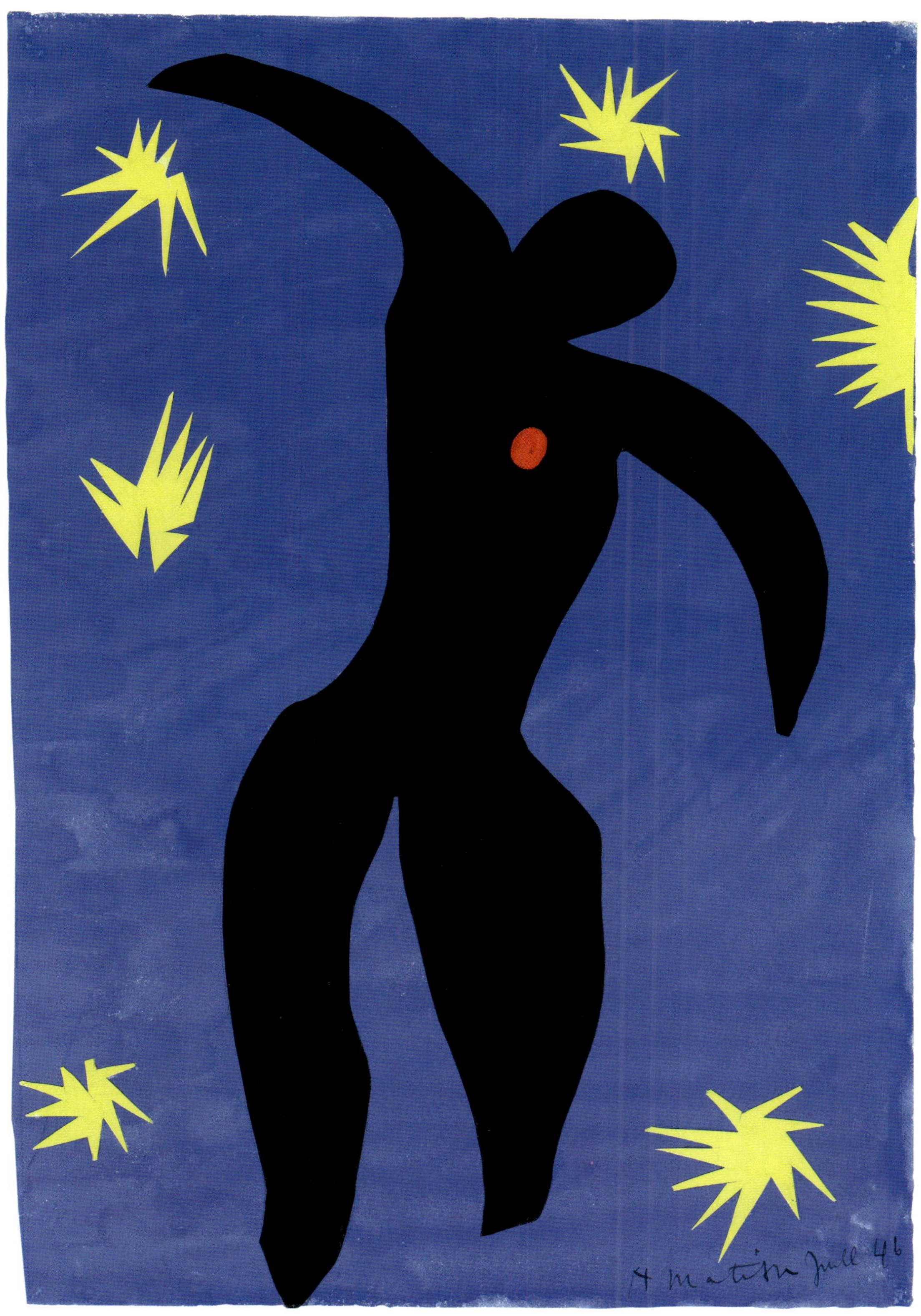

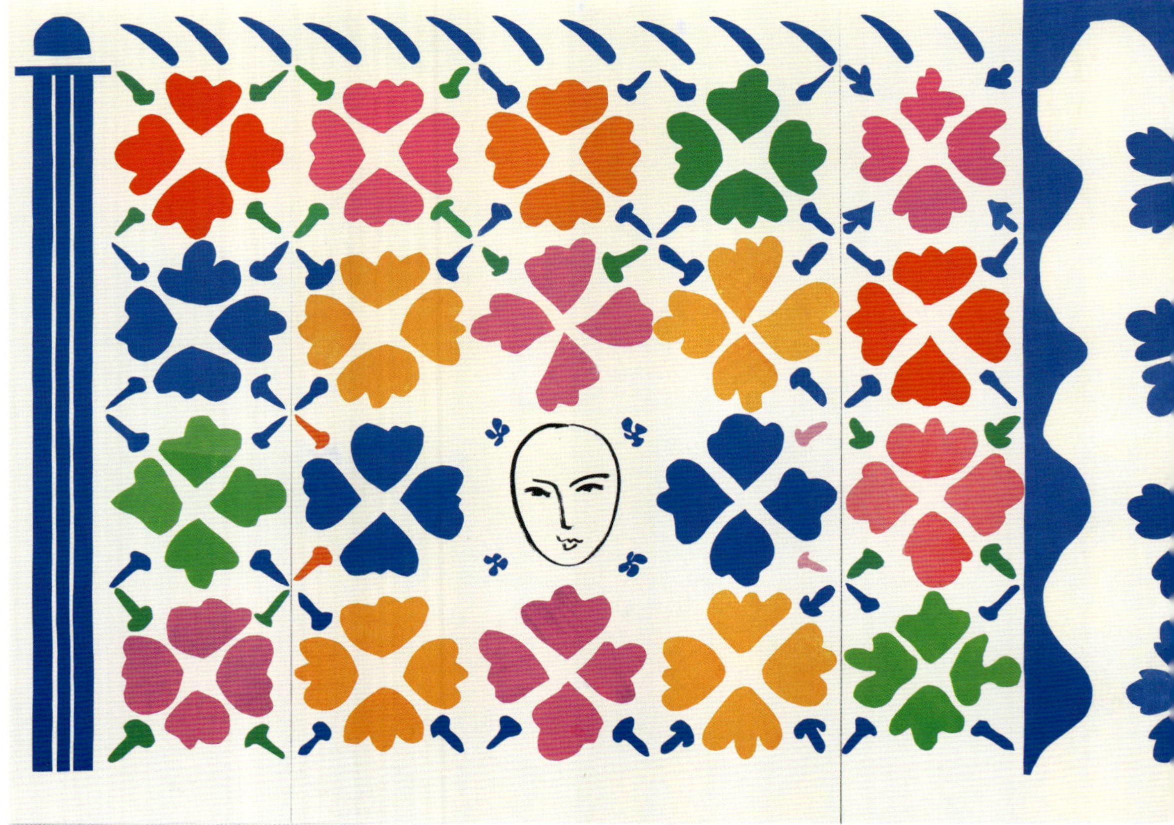

and put it under glass. Had he accepted, he'd be considered the father of installation art. But he didn't accept, so let's not turn him into a more influential figure than he really was.

Matisse could only use pins during initial phases of his work. Of necessity, the next step had to be to glue the paper shapes to the support, thereby destroying (or at least diminishing) the work's ephemerality in order to preserve it. For purely practical reasons, then, Matisse had the cut-out shapes taken off the wall, traced, and glued on to canvas. In the process, new compositions were created. For example, several images that are today framed separately were once part of much larger compositions originally on the walls of his studio. It's the artistic equivalent of taxidermy. The works that now give us so much pleasure are a step removed from the ones that Matisse made.

Even so, what we see in this show is a body of late work so exceptional that it can feel as though it came out of the blue, a glorious coda to the career of a very great artist who had been running out

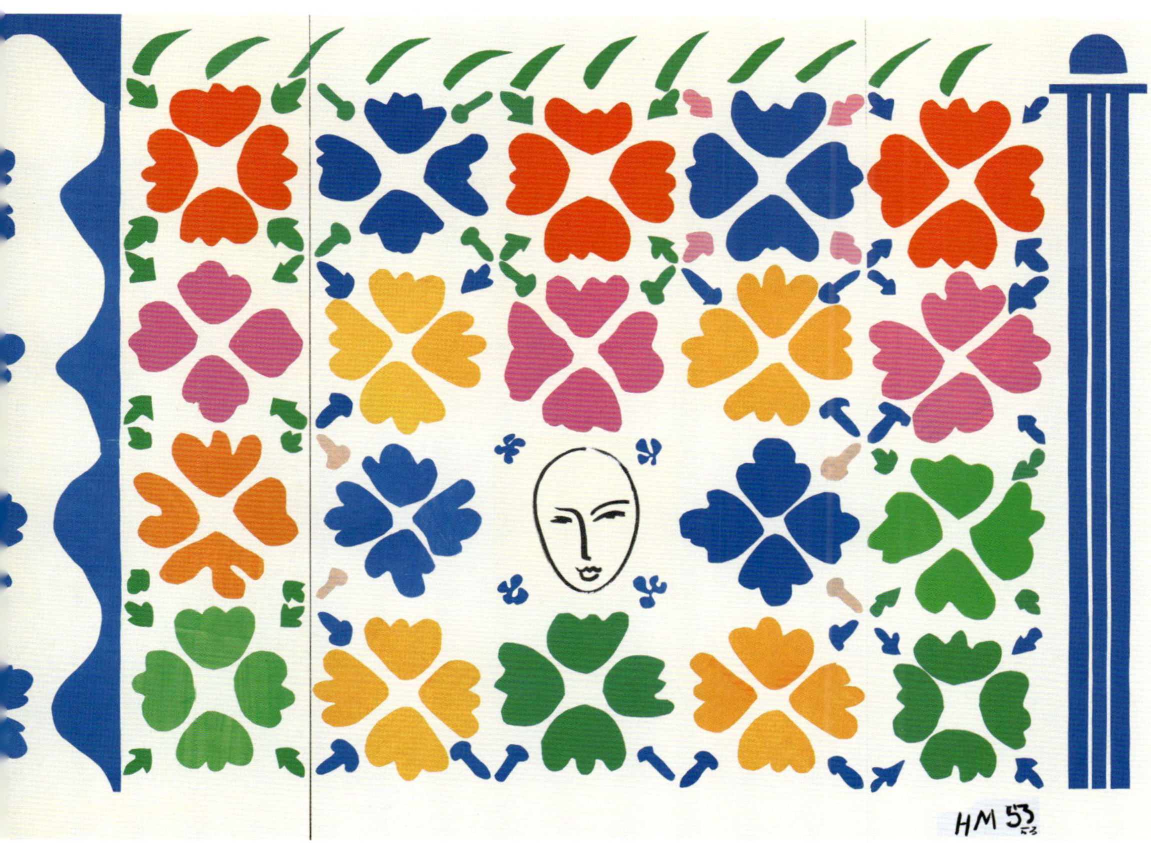

Henri Matisse
**Large Composition
with Masks,** *1953
National Gallery of
Art, Washington DC*

of steam for decades. But of course that isn't the case. The cut-outs
evolved logically out of formal and thematic ideas the artist had
first explored as early as the first decade of the twentieth century.
Matisse had long been interested in the theme of the artist's studio
and the decorative interior. But an even more direct precursor to the
astonishing rooms we see in photographs of his studio in Nice in
the early 1950s is *Harmony in Red*, a painting of 1908 now in the
Hermitage.

This shows a bourgeois dining room in which the arabesques and
tendrils of a *toile de jouey* tablecloth seem to flood over the frontal
plane of the canvas, then rise up to cover the walls in a riot of pattern
and colour. An ordinary interior is therefore re-cast as a fantasy of all-
encompassing abundance and delight, a crimson dreamscape. This is
largely true, too, of the enveloping cut-outs covering the walls of his
studio in Nice.

His fantasy of creating a unified decorative ensemble became a reality in the stained glass, painting, fabrics and metalwork he designed for the Chapel of the Rosary at Vence. Here Matisse could realise many of the artistic aspirations that at some level had been compromised in the cut-outs. For the chapel, too, is a kind of dream. Sometimes misinterpreted as an expression of faith, it is Matisse's attempt to replace the grim Catholicism of his youth in a bleak industrial town in north-eastern France with an architectural interior that surrounds both believers and non-believers with colour and light.

A round of applause, therefore, for curators Karl Buchberg, Nicholas Cullinan, Jodi Hauptman and Nicolas Serota. Their beautifully realised exhibition changes our understanding of what Matisse achieved in the cut-outs. From now on we'll see them not simply as delightful arrangements of shapes and colours but as works of art that touch the spirit through the imagination.

Mondrian: Nature to Abstraction

Which is the real Piet Mondrian, the passionate young painter of vibrantly coloured Expressionist landscapes, or the ice-cold intellectual who painted nothing but grids of vertical and horizontal lines enclosing flat planes of primary colour? So deep does the fissure dividing early from later Mondrian run that we might be dealing with two artists, the first loved by the public, the second the darling of museum curators and art historians.

The question arose two years ago when the Gemeentemuseum in The Hague mounted its massive Mondrian retrospective. Confident that Mondrian's significance as an artist lay in the mature work of the 1920s and '30s, the organisers excluded virtually all the early naturalistic and Symbolist pictures. Even the Fauve period was represented sparingly: the earliest painting in the show dated from 1911, when the artist was thirty-nine. Mondrian came across as the austere, exalted, fanatically pure modernist. The public stayed away in droves.

The Tate Gallery's *Mondrian: Nature to Abstraction* might have been conceived as a corrective to this view. The show looks at the period from 1900 to 1914 in depth and sums up the last twenty years of his career with a dozen or so fully abstract pictures. In fact, Bridget Riley, who with Sean Rainbird selected the show for the Tate, had limited control over its balance. During the closure of the Gemeentemuseum for renovation, the Tate was invited to choose sixty Mondrians from its extensive holdings. In the Netherlands, Mondrian's abstracts have never been popular with collectors, so the collection is weighted towards the early work.

But who's complaining? By topping up the selection of later paintings with loans from British institutions and private collections, the Tate has put together a ravishing little show which is expected to be so popular that it has instituted timed admissions.

2 August 1997

Mondrian: Nature
to Abstraction

Tate Gallery, London

The exhibition gives us a chance to correct some misconceptions about Mondrian's art, beginning with the supposed dichotomy between early and later styles. Seeing the two together it is no longer possible to look at the early representational work without seeing it in terms of the abstraction that was to come. It is easy, for example, to respond to the Expressionistic *Trees on the Gein, Moonrise* of 1907–8 in terms of pure emotion. You don't need formal analysis to see that its frieze of tormented trees the colour of coagulated blood writhing against a rust-red sky could be a backdrop for Strauss's *Elektra*.

But this doesn't mean that the same painting can't be seen in purely formal terms. Step back a bit and it becomes a series of vertical lines evenly spaced across the picture plane, with the middle vertical in the exact centre dividing the canvas in half. In this analysis, you don't see a shadowy riverbank and livid moon, but a line bisecting the composition horizontally and a yellow circle placed just off centre to create depth and add a degree of asymmetry to a rigidly geometric design. So the subject of the picture is indeed trees by a river – but it is also the tension between depth and surface, symmetry and asymmetry, frontality and dynamic distortion.

If the living forms in Mondrian's early pictures can be reduced to abstract lines and planes, the converse is also true: we must look for the humanity in Mondrian's abstract works. Take the lovely *Composition in Oval with Colour Planes* of 1914. Painted in Paris, the picture is made up of a maze of overlapping vertical and horizontal lines, interspersed with the occasional diagonal and curve. But no one would describe its medley of smudged blacks, powder blues, dusty pinks and semi-transparent greys as cold or mechanical. Its numinous, silvery tonality is the colour of Paris in winter, its linear rhythms a cityscape of rooftops, windows and billboards.

In the purely abstract work of the 1920s, the smallest formal details – a line stopping just short of the canvas edge, an area of impastoed paint – create areas of tension or voluptuous sensuality or limpid calm. In *Composition with Red, Blue, Black, Yellow and Grey* of 1921, each patch of pure colour has a specific physical and emotional weight. A rectangular lozenge beautifully painted in red seems to float above the picture plane, while a yellow rectangle feels anchored in the fabric of the canvas. Only when you take time in front of a picture like this, pressing your nose right up against the canvas, do you begin to

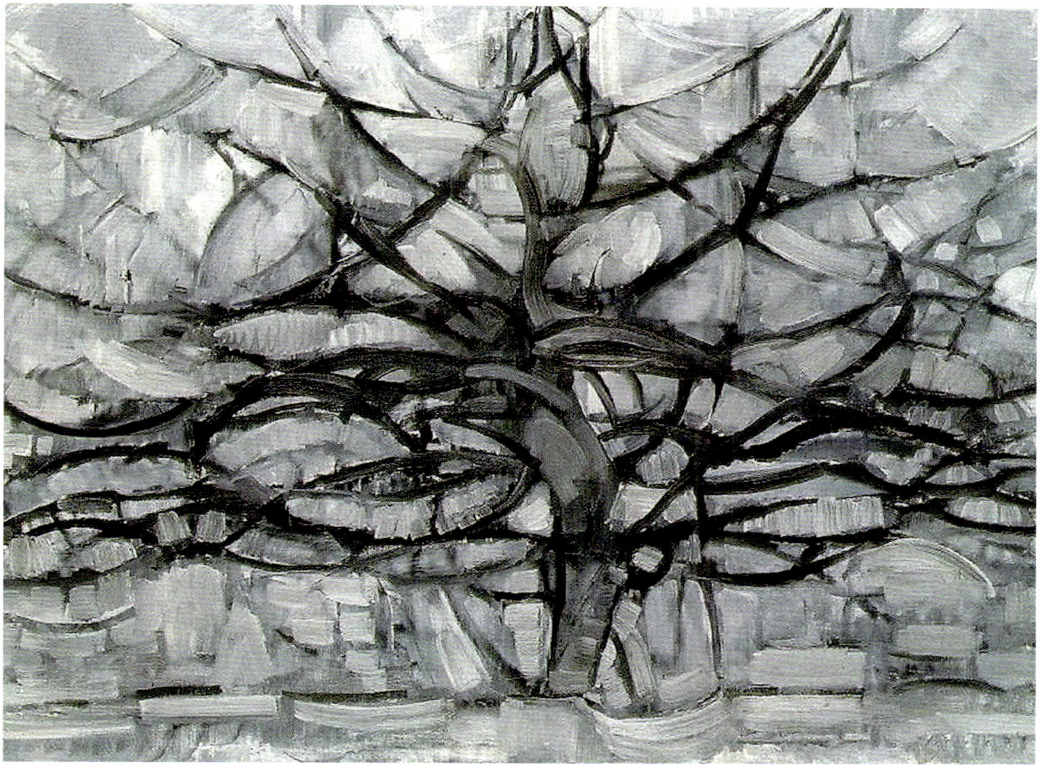

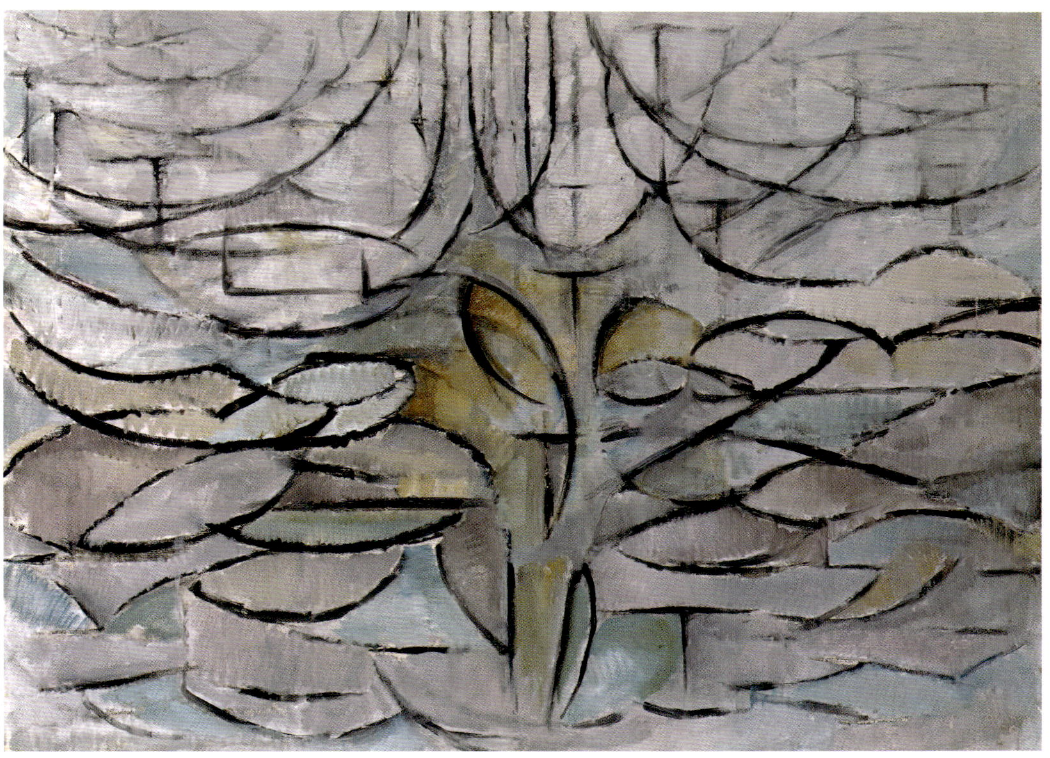

feel the trembling sensitivity and ardent emotion with which Mondrian infused every brushstroke.

This is because Mondrian came to abstraction through the exploration of the underlying structure of the natural world. His passionate emotional response to that world never changed – it only deepened. You can see this happening along one amazing wall in the second gallery, where four studies of a single tree, two from 1908 and two from 1912, are hung in the sequence in which they were painted.

In the first two, Mondrian stands far enough away to show the whole tree surrounded by earth and sky. The arched trunk, top-heavy with its mass of bare branches, provides his motif, while emotion is created by the use of intense colours – a livid red contrasted against nocturnal blue in one painting, dense indigo against fierce stabs of lighter blue in the other. Then, in the monochromatic *Grey Tree* of 1912, he moves closer to his motif. Now the branches stretch from one edge of the canvas to the other, creating a semi-abstract pattern of intersecting curves. The tree is still recognisable, but it is the rhythmic criss-cross of crescent-shaped lines radiating from a central vertical that constitutes the picture's true subject. Now the interstices between the branches are as carefully painted as the branches themselves. Mondrian was no longer trying to capture in paint the illusion of reality, but thinking of the canvas as having an autonomous reality of its own.

Soon after this, in *Flowering Apple Tree* – a magical image in aquamarine, charcoal grey, silver and ochre – he has moved so close to the tree that the curved branches extending out from the central vertical fill the canvas. Mondrian doesn't show how the branches are attached to the trunk: it simply isn't important. The sequence shows how he stripped form down to its bare essentials, then reconstructed it as a semi-abstract study in line and colour. Yet even when the motif finally disappeared, the emotional response to nature remained. *Flowering Apple Tree*, the last in the series, has a visionary intensity that put me in mind of Samuel Palmer.

And so the answer to my question is that there is only one Mondrian. The external appearance of the paintings changed, certainly, but not the passionate response to the visual world that inspired them.

The Stein Family

When Gertrude Stein published *The Autobiography of Alice B. Toklas* in 1933, all hell broke loose. Her hugely entertaining memoir tells the story of her early years in Paris, when her apartment in the rue de Fleurus became the most celebrated literary and artistic salon of the twentieth century. Readers were gripped by accounts of Gertrude's Saturdays when visitors mingled with avant-garde artists, writers and collectors in rooms hung from floor to ceiling with the paintings by the artists she collected and promoted – including Renoir, Gauguin, Cézanne, Toulouse-Lautrec, Matisse, Picasso and Juan Gris.

Her account of those years became an instant bestseller, but within the Stein family circle its publication caused consternation. For in it, Gertrude implied that she alone discovered Matisse and Picasso, downplaying the contribution of her two brothers Leo and Michael, and of Michael's wife Sara. In truth, the four siblings acquired no fewer than 180 works by Matisse and Picasso alone, and all four were equally generous in providing financial and moral support to unknown artists. Leo was particularly scathing about the way his self-promoting sister wrote him out of the story. 'Practically everything that she says of our activities before 1911 is false both in fact and implication . . . God what a liar she is!'

The massive exhibition devoted to the Stein family that opens tomorrow at the Grand Palais sets the record straight. As the show documents in works of art, written and spoken words and scores of photographs, the Steins may not have been midwives at the birth of modern art, but they were certainly in the delivery room. What's more, by admitting into their Saturday soirées anyone, whether they were interested in progressive painting or not, the Steins did as much as anyone to promote the culture of modernism. In the years when Picasso did not exhibit publicly, the only way to see his work was to show up at an evening either with Gertrude and Leo in the rue de

4 October 2011
L'Aventure des Stein
Grand Palais, Paris

Fleurus or with Michael and Sara around the corner in the rue
Madame. Matisse's colour-saturated portraits and landscapes
looked much less alarming when seen in a domestic setting, hanging
alongside Renoirs or Gauguins, than they did in the scrum of the
Salon d'Automne.

An educated, upper-middle-class family originally from
Pennsylvania, the Steins had money, but not a great deal of it, and
were Jewish, but not religious. It was Leo who set the ball rolling
when in 1902 he settled in Paris after two years studying art history in
Florence. Shy and introspective, he was the driving force behind the
collection and was able to recognise the ways in which young artists
built on the achievements of the giants of French art in the 1870s such
as Degas, Renoir, Cézanne and Manet.

Leo could see that Picasso's *Boy Leading a Horse* looked back to
Cézanne's *Bathers*, and Matisse's *Blue Nude (Memory of Biskra)* (1907)
to the reclining nudes of Giorgione and Titian by way of Manet's
Olympia. It was Leo who (with Gertrude) bought Cézanne's *Woman
with a Fan* and he who acquired masterpieces from Picasso's blue and
rose periods. Leo defied conventional taste to purchase Matisse's *Lady
in a Hat* from the Salon d'Autumne of 1906 – not to mention owning
the same artist's *Joy of Life*, now in the Barnes Collection. Little wonder
that Alfred Baar, the first director of the Museum of Modern Art, said
of Leo that 'for the two brief years between 1905 and 1907 he was
possibly the most discerning art collector in the world'.

Why such a short period? Leo looked at the art of his time through
the lens of art history, and was unable to comprehend the work of an
artist who stepped outside that history. Although he was the first of
the siblings to acquire a Picasso, and though he continued to support
the artist as late as the pre-Cubist *art nègre* period, Cubism offended
his sensibilities because it broke so completely with the past. In 1914,
he quarrelled with Gertrude and returned to America – taking with
him all of the Renoirs, but leaving the Cézannes, Picassos and
Matisses to his sister.

One reason that this show is so fascinating is that by looking
at some of the most famous works of art of the twentieth century
through the eyes of each sibling in turn, we come to know a great
deal about their personalities. Leo and Gertrude, for example, bought
Matisse from 1904 to 1907, but lost interest when they felt that his

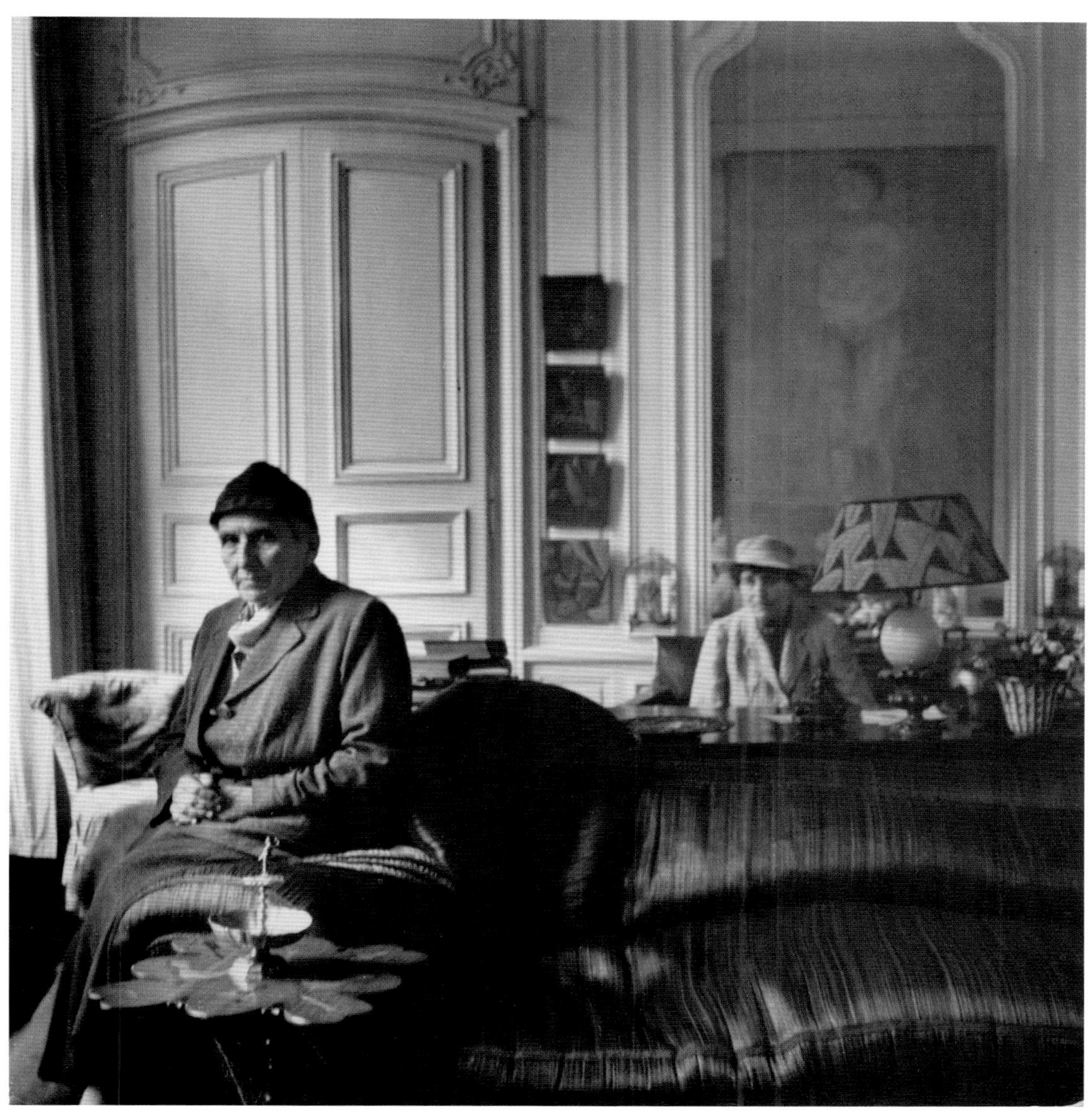

work had become too decorative. But Michael and Sara focused on Matisse to the exclusion of most other artists, supported the academy where Matisse taught painting between 1908 and 1910, and remained the artist's lifelong friends and supporters.

Yet I respect them more for their generosity as patrons than for their judgement. Although they formed an exceptional collection of Matisse's early bronzes, all but a few of the best paintings by Matisse in their collection were bought from Leo and Gertrude. Michael and Sara acquired too many inconsequential studies, academic nudes and pre-Fauve still lifes. In 1914, they sent nineteen paintings by Matisse to an exhibition in Berlin, and then lost them forever when America entered the war. Perhaps their greatest act of patronage was to commission Le Corbusier to design their palatial villa west of Paris, where they lived from 1928 until they returned to live permanently in the US in 1935.

Despite what I said at the start, Gertrude is the heroine of the show. Her debt to Leo was incalculable, but in the long run she had the best taste and surest judgement. Soon after meeting her in 1905, Picasso asked to paint her portrait, that masterly psychological study that owes so much to Ingres and Cézanne and yet was transformed by Picasso's inspired decision to repaint the head after seeing a display of African masks. Seeing the picture next to Cézanne's *Woman with a Fan* (1878–88), what is so striking is how Picasso is able to convey both the sense that Gertrude is thinking, and also that her thoughts are impenetrable. Elsewhere, it is not so much Gertrude's mind as her solid bulk that inspired the lumbering nudes that precede *Les Demoiselles d'Avignon*. During the sittings for the portrait, Gertrude and Picasso became lifelong friends. She continued to buy his work until Sergei Shchukin and Ivan Morosov, the Russian collectors with bottomless pockets, pushed his prices out of her range.

Although the exhibition tells us what the Steins thought about these artists, we learn little about what the artists thought of them. Picasso adored Gertrude but was baffled by her writings. Not speaking English well, he could never be sure that her books were as incomprehensible as he found them. 'With lines and colours one can make patterns, but if one doesn't use words according to their meaning, they aren't words at all,' he said. When Gertrude's description of Picasso's creative process as 'he empties himself and the moment he has completed emptying himself he must recommence emptying himself' was explained to him, he commented, 'She's confusing two functions.'

From 1914 through the Twenties, Gertrude bought the art of Juan Gris in depth but, as happens to many collectors, her eye failed her when it came to the next generation, when she briefly bought artists associated with the Ballets Russes, including Pavel Tchelitchew and Eugene Berman – two mistakes that only add to the interest and complexity.

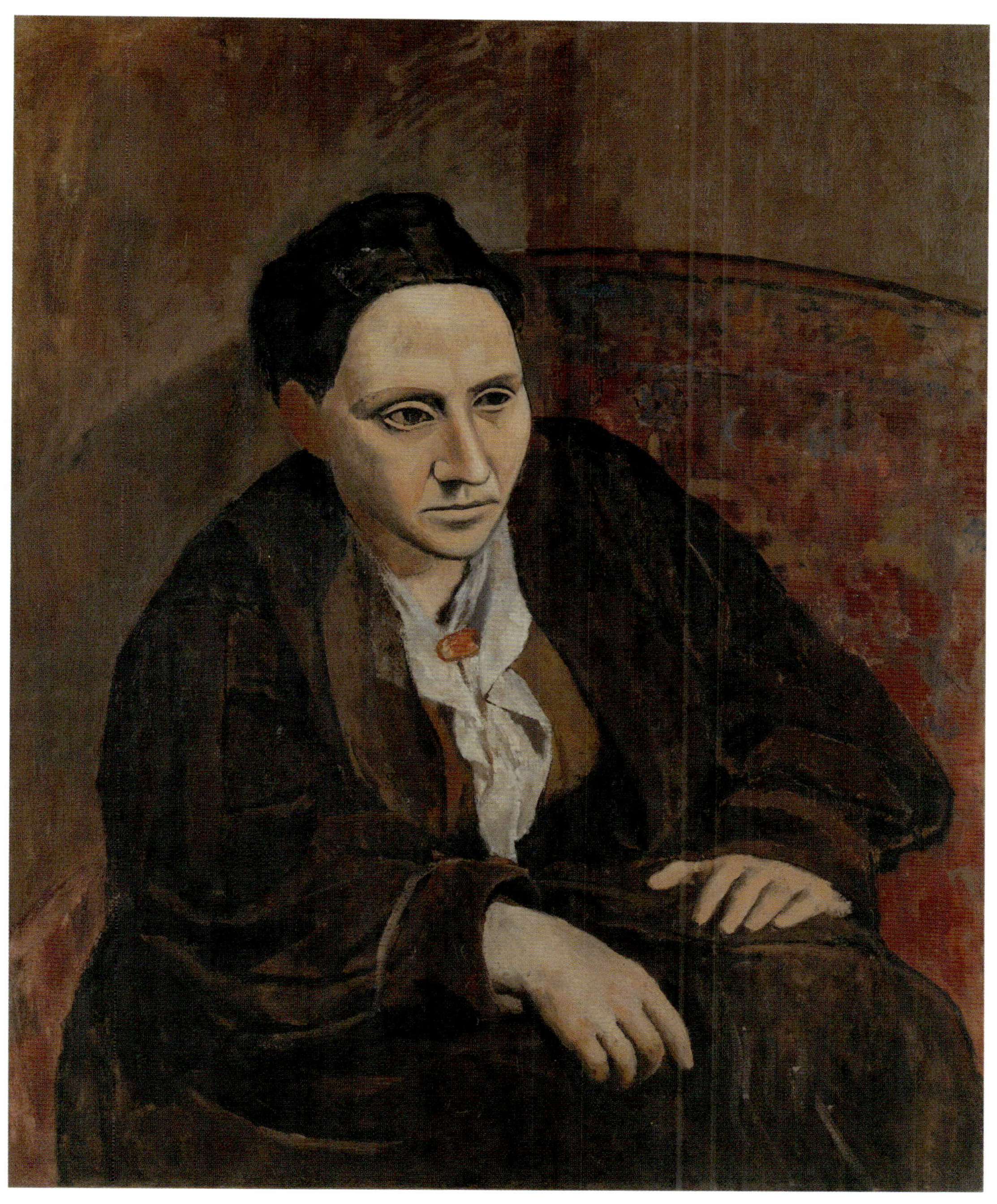

Pablo Picasso
*Portrait of Gertrude
Stein*, 1905–6
Metropolitan Museum
of Art, New York

Picasso: The Early Years

Walking through *Picasso: the Early Years* at the National Gallery in Washington DC last week I played a little game with myself. The show covers the period 1892–1906, that is, from an eleven-year-old living in provincial obscurity to a twenty-five-year-old on the brink of international celebrity. My game was this: had Picasso died young, at what stage in this exhibition would he have left a significant mark on the history of art? *Fin-de-siècle* Barcelona? The first years in Paris? The Blue Period? The Rose Period? The answer isn't clear until the end of the exhibition, most of which chronicles the cul-de-sacs down which he stumbled before reaching his first stage of artistic maturity with the *Demoiselles d'Avignon* of 1907.

The show begins with precocious studies by a young boy trained in traditional academic methods. Although Picasso quickly came to reject those methods, he never despised the discipline they required, nor the results they produced. Years spent drawing from plaster casts and from live models in art schools turned him into one of the most accomplished draughtsmen of all time. But turgid oil studies such as *Girl with Bare Feet* of 1895 show how hard he had to work, demonstrating once and for all that the fourteen-year-old Picasso was neither the prodigy nor the natural-born painter he later claimed to have been.

The first intimations of what was to come can be seen in poster designs and caricatures executed in the years Picasso spent hanging around the Els Quatre Gats café in Barcelona. Heavily dependent on the modern art he knew only at second hand through art magazines, these works mingle the linear Art Nouveau of Aubrey Beardsley with the social realism of Theophile Steinlen and the Symbolism of Edvard Munch. Had the train from Barcelona crashed *en route* to Paris in 1900, the nineteen-year-old would be remembered as a gifted but minor figure in the orbit of the Catalan avant-garde.

2 April 1997

Picasso: The
Early Years

National Gallery,
Washington

It would be charitable to describe the first years in Paris as a period of confusion and self-discovery. Gauguin and Cézanne were alive and working in 1900–1. Precisely because he found it so easy to assimilate other artists' styles, Picasso at first ignored their work, instinctively imitating painters who posed little threat to his emerging identity. In the gallery devoted to his first two trips to Paris, we find skilful pastiches of the Impressionism of Camille Pissarro and the sulphurous Rococo of Charles Conder. His imitations of Toulouse-Lautrec, distinguishable as Picassos largely by the heavy-handed use of black to create an aura of decadence, extended to the very titles of the paintings.

But during these years Picasso was also forming friendships in Paris's literary bohemia, particularly with the poet Max Jacob, who introduced him to the poetry of Verlaine and Baudelaire. Literature, not painting, transformed Picasso into an artist of intellectual substance, by teaching him that 'art emanates from Sadness and Pain', as he later said. The suicide in 1901 of his friend the Spanish painter Carles Casagemas, a charming manic depressive who blew his brains out in a Montmartre restaurant, triggered the sad imagery and saturated palette of the Blue Period.

The paintings immediately inspired by Casagemas's death begin with a portrait of the artist on his bier. Typically, Picasso used the flickering brushwork and high-keyed palette of another painter who committed suicide, Vincent Van Gogh. There follows the blasphemous *Burial of Casagemas*, a parody of an El Greco altarpiece in which stocking-clad whores escort the painter to heaven on a white charger. It is dismissed by Picasso's biographer John Richardson as 'art-school facetiousness', but I think this picture is more touching than that. It represents a boy's attempt to keep at bay the reality of death by turning it into a joke.

But the pictures that followed – of emaciated paupers and syphilitic prostitutes shuffling across empty landscapes, or of blind men and beggars huddling in the cold moonlight – are no joke. By choosing such subjects Picasso was trying to discard the second-hand sentiment of *fin-de-siècle* art and to replace it with something more shocking and more direct. Unfortunately, the figures he used to do so were borrowed from the Symbolist painter Puvis de Chavannes. They are too classical, too decorative, too lyrical for his purpose. As a result, when Picasso aimed at tragic emotion he ended up with self-pity. The best Blue Period pictures deal with the one emotion Picasso couldn't simulate: fear. His portrait of Celestina, a one-eyed procuress, depicts a powerful personality who clearly frightened the young painter as much as she fascinated him.

In the Rose Period, which began in the middle of 1904 and lingered until 1906, the artist allowed his draughtsmanship to come to the fore, relegating his palette of soft rose and light blue to a secondary role. The new colouristic delicacy and linear precision perfectly suited the gentler imagery of circus performers and harlequins. Now the poet Apollinaire introduced Picasso to the poetry of Mallarmé and Rimbaud, the first infusing into his friend's art a sense of the ephemeral, the second a new sensuality.

Drugs, too, played their part. It was Jacob who supplied Picasso with the opium and hashish that contributed to the lack of tension, dulled eyes, emotional isolation and dreamy moods of pictures such as the large *Family of Saltimbanques* of 1905 or, from the same year, the stoned young man holding his opium pipe with practised hands in the marvellously druggy *Boy with a Pipe*. To get their full flavour, you have to imagine these pictures as they must have looked in Picasso's Paris studio in the Bâteau Lavoir, at night, by gaslight, through clouds of opium.

But, for all their exquisite prettiness and comforting evasions, the pictures of the Rose Period still belong to the nineteenth century. Picasso didn't really find the key to a truer and more direct approach to experience until the summer of 1906, spent in the mountain village of Horta in the Spanish Pyrenees. Perhaps in these months he realised at last that he had been in error about the nature of his talent. He discovered that his art's closest affinities were with sculpture. In the monochromatic *Two Nudes* it is as though Picasso had walked around the massive torso of a single woman to show it from two different points of view. The monumental solidity of the *Seated Nude* from Prague or Picasso's own sculpture of the *Head of Fernande* shows how closely he had looked at medieval Iberian stone carvings, while both the sculpture and the painting of the *Woman Combing her Hair* are directly inspired by the sculpture of Gauguin.

And so to answer my question: it is not until the portrait of Gertrude Stein, finished in the autumn of 1906, where the bulky figure

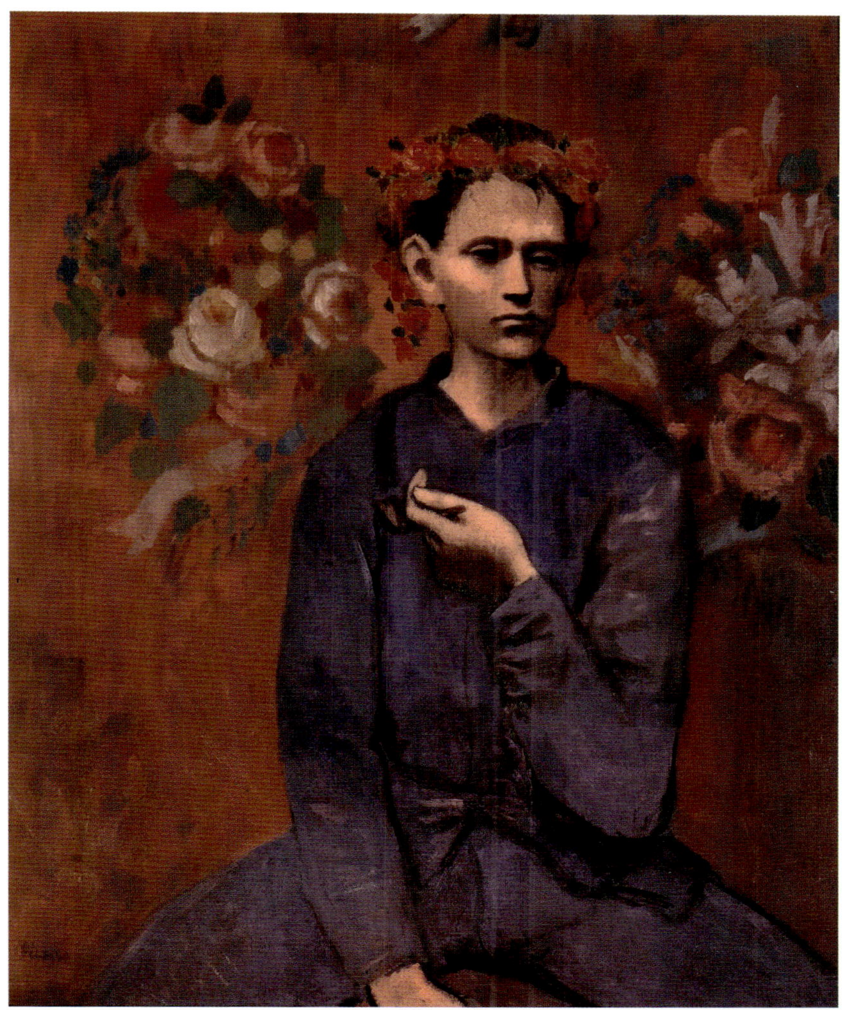

occupies pictorial space like a stone displacing water, and the face has
the impassivity of a carved mask, that Picasso became the twentieth-
century master we know. It comes as something of a shock to realise
that this exhibition of 152 paintings, drawings, prints and sculpture
is but a prelude to the great career that still lies ahead, with the
discovery of Cézanne and tribal art.

Georges Braque

As well as being the man who painted the first Cubist work, Georges Braque also painted the last. Unlike Picasso, his partner in the Cubist adventure from 1909 to 1914, he continued to explore ways of creating non-perspectival space until the end of his life. The protean Picasso would exploit the formal possibilities of each breakthrough in Cubism, then move on. Braque, by contrast, never discarded anything he had learned. The pictures painted in his later life deepen and expand the pictorial discoveries of his youth. New materials and new techniques interested him not for their own sake but because they helped to make the picture in hand more tactile or palpable or poetic. Caring much more than Picasso did about how he applied pigment to canvas, Braque was a slow and fastidious craftsman.

Or he usually was. By no means all of the forty-five pictures in the Royal Academy's exhibition of Braque's late works are successful. His tributes to Van Gogh's sunflowers and landscapes look back to his own early Fauve period – and fail because hot colours and bravura brushwork are alien to his methodical temperament. Braque is an artist of elegance and restraint. His best pictures have a chic worthy of one of the great couturiers of the period.

He's also such a gentle artist. Though there is no denying the structural complexity of individual paintings in the series devoted to the artist's studio, we sense that the objects depicted are there for specific reasons, having to do with memory or affection. And, as we shall see, at least two kinds of Cubist space can be found in these pictures, as though Braque were making an inventory of the discoveries of a lifetime. This lends to the late works a personal dimension which I find immensely moving.

The earlier pictures are easier to read and – initially at least – easier to like. In his 1942 *Large Interior with Palette* the space is so shallow that the potted plant seems to sit on the surface of the picture, while the

29 January 1997

Braque – The
Late Works

Royal Academy,
London

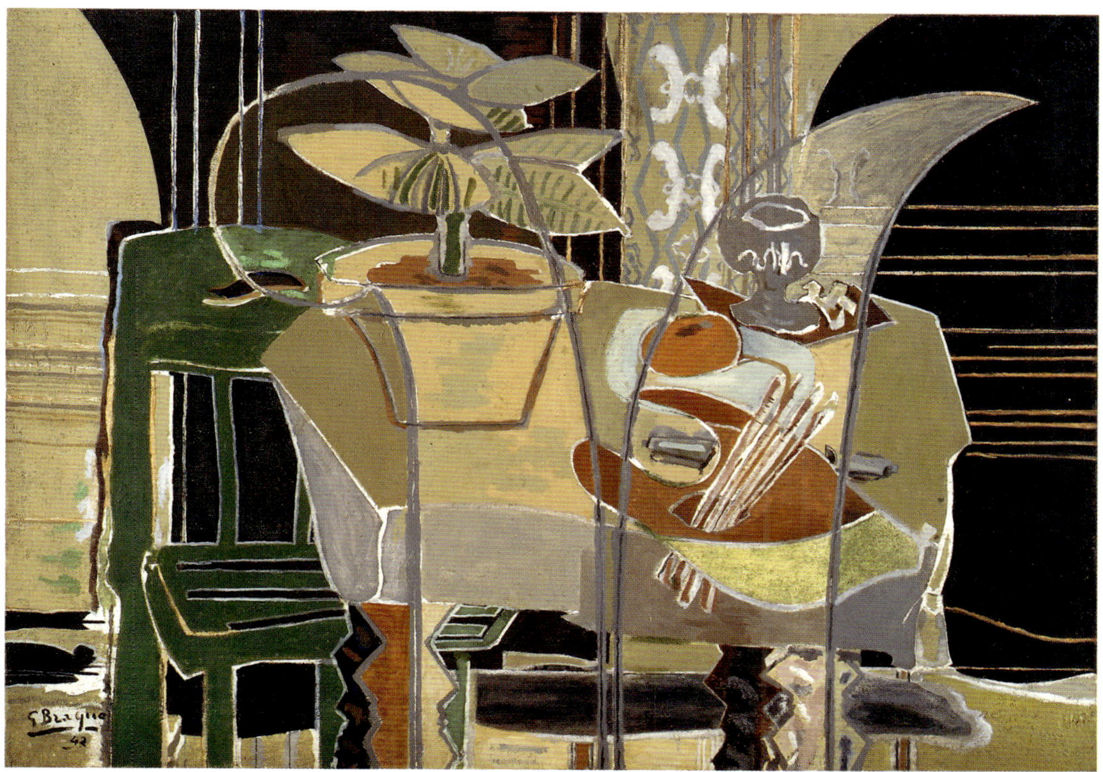

table top is tilted forward in such a way that the palette and brushes appear to be slipping out of the canvas. Braque holds the disparate elements in the composition together by 'rhyming' the shapes of the leaves and the palette with the decorative squiggle on the back of the chair. You have to step close to savour the texture of the paint surface, created by adding sand to the pigment. And look at the colours in the tablecloth, with its undulating edge of stone grey, and its centre of warm ochre scumbled with touches of palest green.

Standing in front of the picture, it is as though we viewers were seated at a piano, looking through the transparent, lyre-shaped music desk to a score suggested by the parallel lines of the wainscotting on the far wall. Not only do the curving lines help establish our distance from the objects in the picture; through them Braque (who was very musical) suggests an analogy between the act of painting and musical composition. But what sort of music? Though comparisons with composers are rarely useful in art criticism, the interiors of the early 1940s have something of Schubert's rippling clarity, whereas many of the pictures of artist's studios from the 1950s are as dense and sombre as late Beethoven string quartets.

The transition between the two styles can be seen in *The Terrace*, begun in 1948. Whereas the objects depicted in his earlier pictures are fairly easy to make out because Braque surrounds them with naturalistic space, here the forms have become so impacted that the eye has difficulty separating the jug and glass on the table from the wood-grained background. Braque is reverting to a method of working that has much in common with *papier collé*, the collage technique which initiated the second, 'synthetic' phase of Cubism in 1912. Although now all the elements in the picture are painted and not pasted on, the effect is much the same: by layering one flat shape on another, he all but banishes two-dimensional space.

By contrast, pictorial space is practically excavated in the first two canvases in the series of billiard tables. By tilting the massive rectangular table on its side and positioning it so close to us that we cannot see its bottom edge, Braque puts us in the position of looking down on its green baize surface. It is as though he were inviting us to pick up one of the cues that lie so near the surface of the canvas, and join him in a game. But to do this, we must imagine entering the picture's warped space and moving around the table, just as we would in a real billiard match.

In the artist's studios Braque uses the techniques of both analytical and synthetic Cubism in the same canvas. To take the clearest example, the large jug and goblet at the centre of *Studio VIII* are surrounded by the shallow space that characterises the first, analytical phase of Cubism. But at the bottom and side of the picture the flattened shapes of a bottle, palette, newspaper and bunch of grapes are 'collaged' one on top of another, as in synthetic Cubism. The picture becomes an inventory of Cubist clichés, a kind of symbolic diary of Braque's entire artistic career.

But unlike classic Cubist still-lifes, the studios are full of movement, and there is constant tension between surface and depth, top and bottom, forward and backward, and left and right. In *Studio VIII* the bird, which for Braque embodies the creative spirit, seems to soar free of its red background and float above the picture. In other pictures in the same series Braque corrugates these birds with vertical pleats or folds, like folding screens or things seen through a prism. In

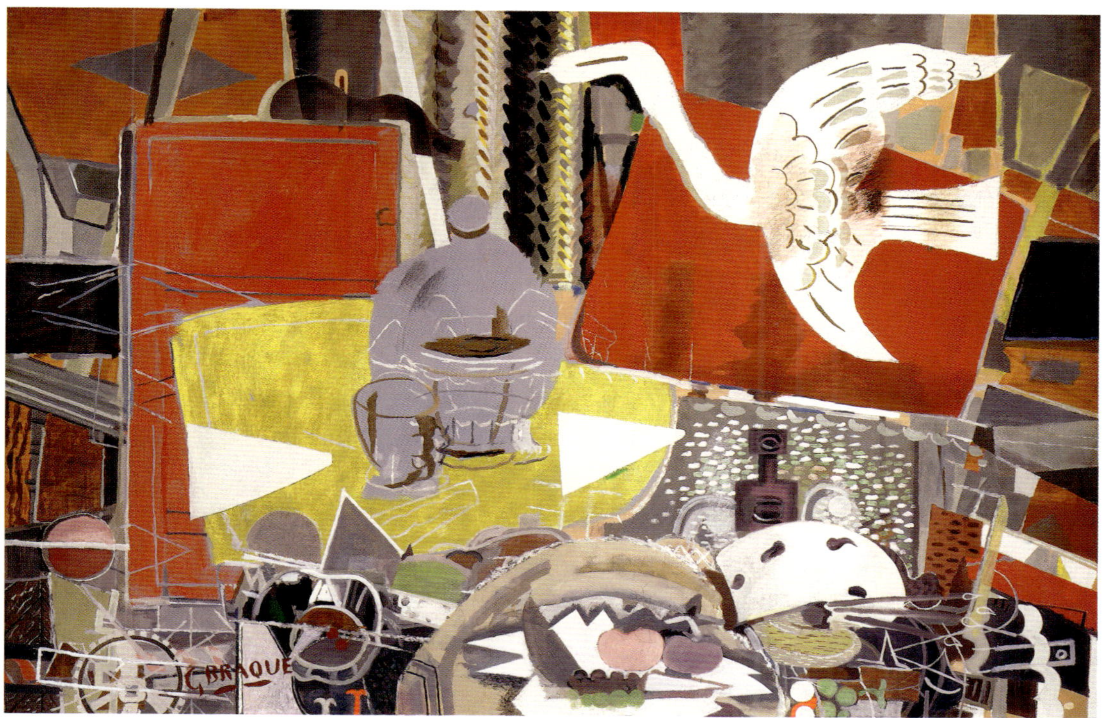

Georges Braque
Studio VIII, *1942*
Colección Masaveu,
Madrid

the most poetic picture in the show, *Composition with Stars*, forms seem to implode and explode at the same time, and the original image dissolves into a shiver of stars and feathers.

The exhibition has a coda. In the late 1950s Braque abandoned Cubist space. In the series devoted to birds, he builds up the light-blue ground with layer upon layer of impastoed pigment until the surface is almost like a low relief into which he incises the simple black, bird-like shapes. In these late and still highly experimental canvases, Braque achieved the illusion of infinite depth through colour, shape and texture. Almost at the last (he died in 1963), he again found a way of depicting space that had not been seen before.

Joan Miro

Snails, dragonflies, stars, birds, flowers, and a little dog barking at the moon: just listing the subjects for which Miró is famous makes him sound childlike and charming – twentieth-century art's own Dr Seuss. Now, an exhibition of Miró's early work at the Centre Pompidou in Paris gives us a very different view of his work. *Joan Miró 1917–1934: The Birth of the World* traces the years of turmoil and experiment that began in earnest in 1922, and found some degree of resolution only in the so-called 'savage pictures' of 1933–34.

Displaying Miró's paintings and drawings in the order he painted them, the organisers show that the dark and destructive side of his art is just as important as its humour and high spirits. We watch him as he first shatters the formal geometry of Cubism, then attacks its dry subject matter, and finally moves on to the destruction of painting itself. 'Painting disgusts me profoundly,' he once said. 'The only thing that interests me is pure spirit.' In the first half of his career, at any rate, Miró's art is as searching as that of any artist in the twentieth century.

Born in Barcelona in 1893, as early as 1916 the teenage prodigy was combining Fauve colour with Cubist abstraction. An incongruously faceted nude standing against a riot of patterned wallpaper is the work of a young man who has learned to imitate the appearance of avant-garde painting without understanding the logic behind it. This was to change when Miró moved to Paris in 1919 and established himself as an accomplished follower of his fellow Catalan, Picasso.

Every summer, Miró returned to the family's property at Montroig near Barcelona. In the low-toned landscapes started in Spain and finished in Paris, we first glimpse an artistic sensibility more engaged with the messy vitality of the real world than the French Cubists ever were. *The Farm* of 1921–22 is his precise, beautifully wrought inventory of all the things you might find on a working farm. As

5 May 2004

Joan Miró 1917–1934:
The Birth of the World

Centre Pompidou, Paris

though instructing a child in its ABC, Miró keeps things simple: A is for ass, B is for bird, C is for cock, and so on, all placed in a landscape which, in true Cubist fashion, gently tilts upward so that we look down on the objects in it.

Only a few months after finishing *The Farm*, Miró began *Interior (The Farmer's Wife)*. Now, suddenly, objects float free in space, while geometric forms are simplified so that they can be read in more than one way. And so a white triangle becomes a dishcloth hanging from a nail by the stove, but it can also be seen as a handkerchief held by a weeping lady in a wide skirt. Grotesquely enlarging the feet of the farmer's wife to express her connection to the soil, Miró abandons naturalistic representation in favour of emotional or psychological truth.

In *Catalan Landscape*, painted in 1923–24, the floodgates of Miró's invention, wit and fantasy have opened wide. Gone now is the Cubist grid, gone its solemnity, and gone its tendency to make the motif inseparable from the ground. The monstrous peasant who pees and squats and smokes his pipe has a triangle for a head, a few lines for a body, and another (elongated) triangle for a gun. While the first words

Joan Miró
The Hunter (Catalan Landscape), *1923–24*
Museum of Modern Art, New York

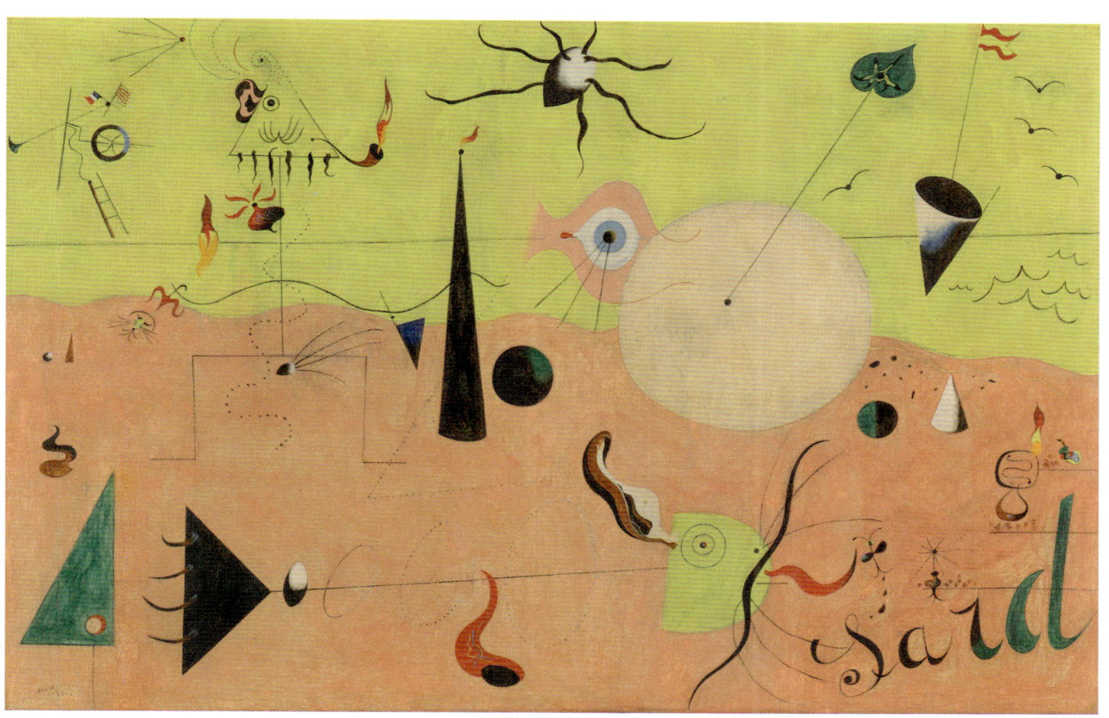

of a Catalan folk song float across the canvas, a giant hare bounds
after a darting insect. Meanwhile, all nature is in a comical frenzy.
Sunlight pours down on countryside in which worms, insects, snails,
leaves, spiders and birds are all happily eating each other in a
deliriously good-natured food chain.

Within a year or so, Miró has reduced painting to a matter of
graffitied words and simple shapes, often drawn on landscapes
rendered as diagrams. In these 'dream' paintings, Miró is trying
to create a painterly language that is less tied to the real world, one
so light and fine that the work of art will cease to have material
importance, and only the poetry will remain. He is on a quest to
restore painting to its essence. And so, in *Maternity* of 1924, human life
is reduced to a triangle, a hole, curved lines, and squiggles of paint
floating on a blue ground. Instead of painting a mother and child,
Miró breaks the subject down to the components of womb, sperm,
embryo and breast.

The show also reveals that Miró constantly zig-zagged between
bringing his art to the brink of annihilation and then pulling back.
In the great canvas *The Birth of the World* of 1925, Miró places totally
abstract geometric forms on a picture surface that has been stained
and scarred as though attacked by vandals. Miró's real struggle in
these years was to detach his subject from the ground it is painted on,
to allow these abstract forms to float free of the canvas's gravitational
pull.

But only a year later, with *Dog Barking at the Moon*, Miró returned
to the delightful imagery of 1920–24. Now using areas of flat saturated
colour, he depicts the earth and sky united by an endless ladder with
which the artist hopes one day to reach the stars. Meanwhile, the
foolish pup (surely Miró's alter ego) yelps in vain at the red-nosed
moon. What an eloquent symbol for the futility of Miró's search for a
new artistic language. No wonder he kept giving up in despair, and
then deciding to try again.

Around 1931–32 he abandoned paint and canvas in favour of
making collages and constructions with new materials such as sand,
tar and Masonite. These are violent, nasty and unremittingly ugly. It
is with a sense of relief and calm that we come to the 1933 paintings
where organic forms outlined in black are superimposed on blurred

backgrounds painted in deep, rich, iridescent purples, blues and greens.

Now the ground seems to penetrate and surround the abstract shapes that swirl over it, as though swimming slowly through viscous liquid. The gaiety and sunshine that had for the most part characterised Miró's earlier work is entirely absent, leading many critics to see this series as his premonition of the Spanish Civil War. But seeing them in the last gallery of this show, they feel instead like the resolution of a problem Miró had struggled with for a decade – the tension between the ground and the motif – here seamlessly harmonised in the lowest registers of his palette. They bring an unforgettable show to a close on a note of resignation and serenity.

René Magritte

Try to set aside, for a moment, your image of the Surrealist painter René Magritte as a man in an overcoat and a bowler hat. The selection of his paintings on view at the Hayward Gallery emphasises a much darker, more dangerous artist than the one whose sly visual jokes have held so much appeal for advertisers and cartoonists. This Magritte explored the corroding anxiety at the heart of human experience.

He has been given an appropriately sombre, moody exhibition, beautifully selected by David Sylvester and Sarah Whitfield. In the early rooms blues, blacks and greys establish an atmosphere of nameless foreboding. Like the nineteenth-century Belgian Symbolists, Magritte used bizarre imagery not simply to disconcert his audience, but to give visual form to psychological truth.

An early work, *Nocturne*, shows an empty stage on which there lies a framed picture of an isolated house, at night, ablaze. A bird seems to flutter out of the fictive canvas towards a strange object that is in fact a banister rail imprinted with musical notes. *Nocturne* is about the fear of calamity. It implies that for Magritte night was a time of dread, a time when physical security and emotional stability could vanish before morning.

Again and again in his early pictures Magritte returns to his childhood traumas, recovering (or uncovering) a strange and strangulated world of buried emotion. An untitled work in *papier collé* shows the torso of a bourgeois woman whose head has been replaced by a swirling, shapeless pall. This disturbing image surely echoes the circumstances surrounding the death of the painter's mother, who drowned herself when he was thirteen. Remembering the night when his younger brother awoke in her room to find his mother's bed empty, then roused the family, who followed her footsteps to a nearby bridge, the painter later added this unforgettable detail: '. . . when

27 May 1992
Magritte
Hayward Gallery,
London

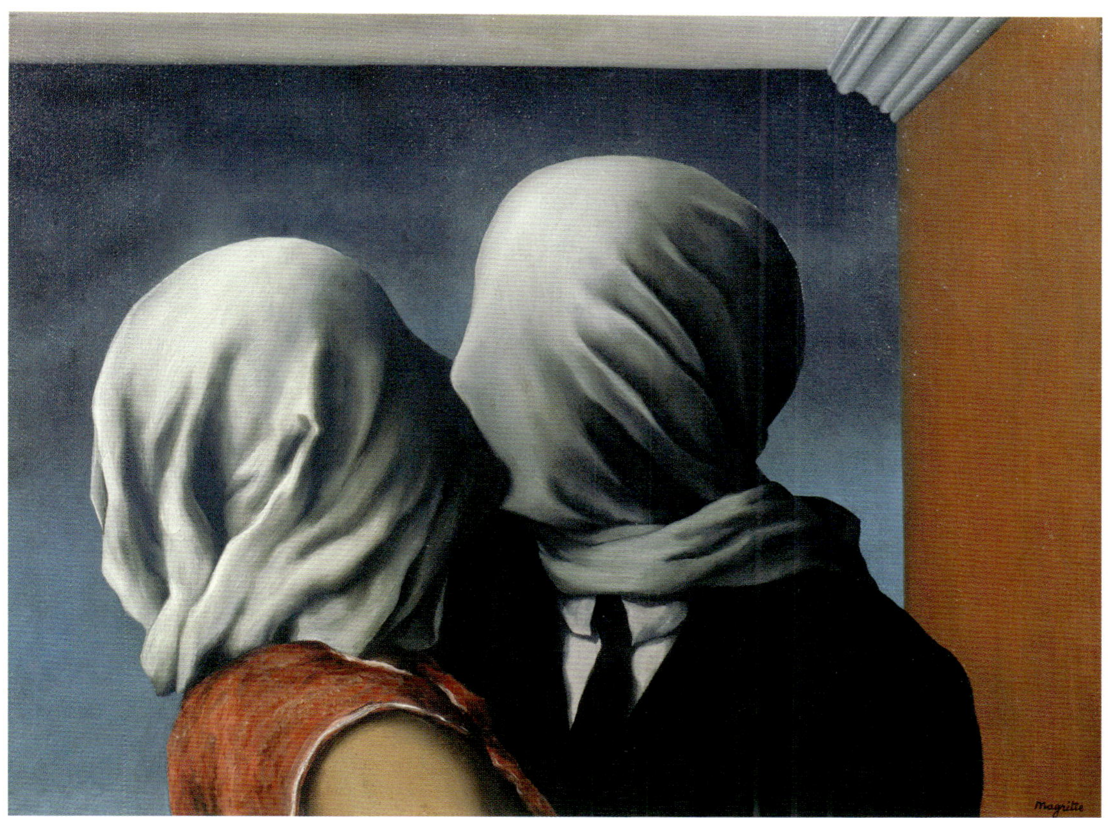

René Magritte
The Lovers, *1928*
Museum of Modern
Art, New York

they recovered the body, they found her nightgown wrapped around her face. It was never known whether she had covered her eyes with it so as not to see the death she had chosen, or whether she had been veiled in that way by the swirling currents.'

A number of early paintings show the fictional criminal Fantomas, a sort of arch-fiend capable of any crime, whose novelistic adventures were wildly popular when Magritte was a child and who was taken up as a subversive hero by other members of the Surrealist movement. But for Magritte Fantomas is no joke. In his work, the monster emerges headless from a mist-laden sea, a terrifying creature who walks by night, able to unlatch any window and creep into any drawing-room. He is the very incarnation of all childhood fears, inexplicable anxieties, dreadful mental oppressions.

Magritte is the painter of neurotic suffering. Of all artists I can think of he is the one who makes us feel what it is like for a dark curtain to descend over the mind, for every door to open on to a black chasm, for each enclosed space to become a place of sepulchre. In *The Central Story* of 1928, a figure whose head is muffled in a cloth demonstrates, as in an advertisement, the suffocating effect of depression, the inability of the sufferer to do anything about his or her distress. And it is this passivity that seems to me the most menacing thing about Magritte's world. By and large his figures remain silent and motionless, as in a dream: there never seems to be a solution to the state of psychic immobility in which they are stranded. It is not the anonymous man in the bowler hat that interests Magritte, it is his desperation.

Magritte's famous retreat into a life of solid bourgeois respectability amounted to a strategy in the game of trying to outwit first society, then life itself. Like a Belgian version of Burgess or Maclean, while appearing to conform to the social order, Magritte was in fact engaged in the serious game of trying to undermine it. In his art he fought a subtle rearguard action designed to point up the futility of trusting to appearances. One by one Magritte examined the bland certainties of our everyday lives, calling into question the two pillars of our sanity, language and perception. Nature he turned upside down and inside out, showing the sky as the lining of a curtain that is drawn back to reveal an empty stage; day descends over night; time turns to stone.

Magritte went through a phase of painting linguistic conundrums, naming the thing represented in the picture rather than painting its image, as when a shapeless object is designated *Femme Triste*. The famous picture *This Is Not a Pipe* simply makes us aware of the arbitrary way in which we use language. The sentence makes no sense without the picture of the pipe, but even with the picture the statement as written is meaningless, whether stated positively or negatively. (Were the inscription to read 'This is a pipe' it would still not be true.)

Was Magritte a painter of landscape? portrait? still life? genre? The answer, of course, is that he was a painter of ideas. He was a great figure not because he used his meticulous technique to fool the eye, but because, having accomplished that, he went on to fool the mind. And yet for me Magritte is at his best when he mingles private memory with surrealist absurdity. *The Future of Statues*, a work of 1937, consists of a plaster cast of Napoleon's death-mask, the surface

of which is painted with passing clouds against a blue sky, pitiless
and indifferent to any death, whether of the illustrious or the
unknown. But this strange object stirs memories of another famous
death-mask, *L'Inconnue du Seine*, a beautiful young woman, a suicide
like Magritte's mother, whose body was fished out of the Seine at the
turn of the century.

This show is so big that there is room to show Magritte's
weaknesses as well as strengths, from the thrilling early years to
the flabby Impressionist period in the mid-1940s to the splendid
but undeniably slick and often jokey late works, including old
favourites like *Golconde*, in which it is raining men, or the haunting
daytime/night-time landscape, *The Dominion of Light*. The show
closes with a selection of Magritte's dreadful bronzes.

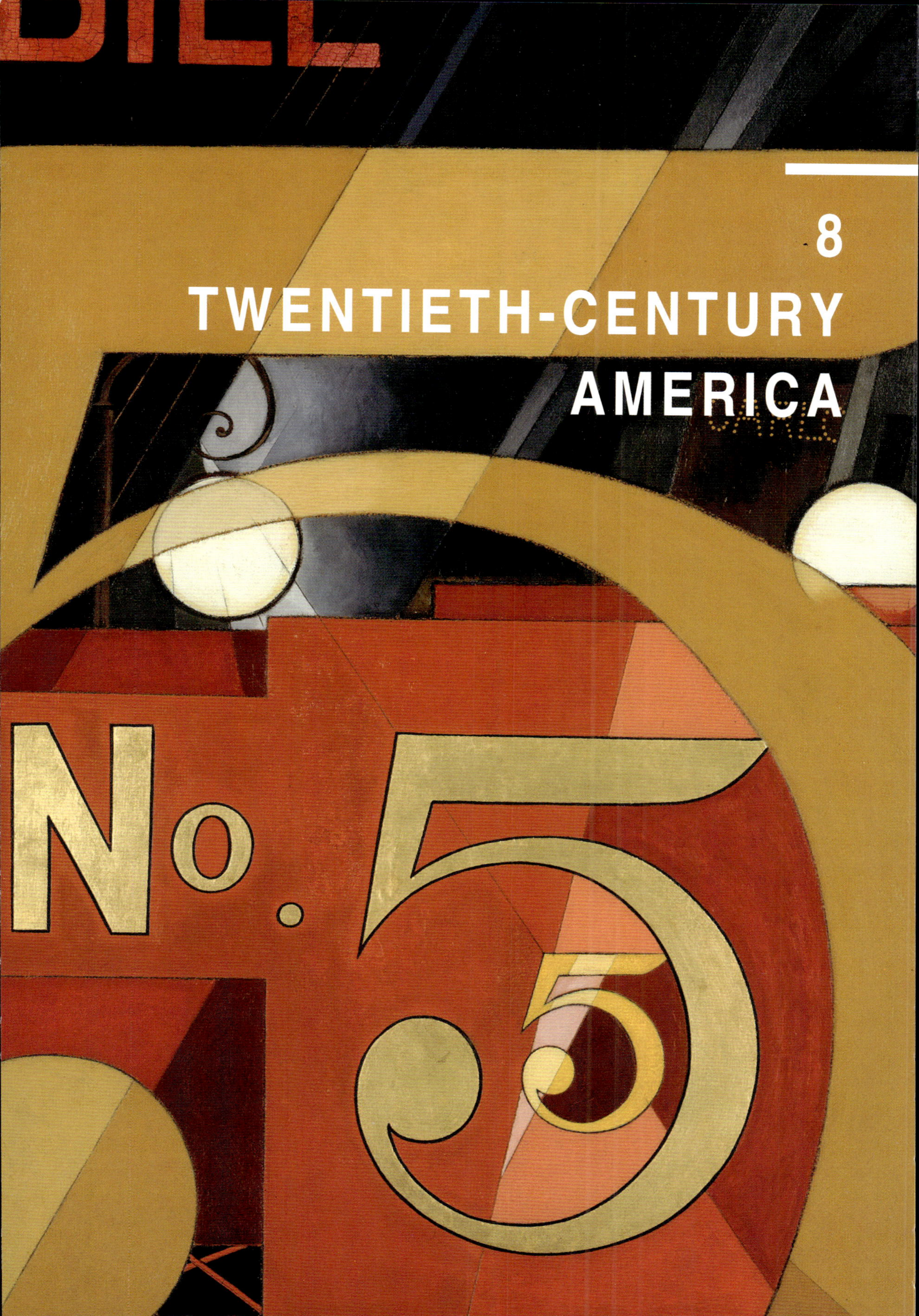
BILL
8
TWENTIETH-CENTURY
AMERICA
No. 5

American Art in the Twentieth Century

Early in the Royal Academy's *American Art in the Twentieth Century*, we come across Charles Demuth's *Buildings, Lancaster*, a view of nondescript offices and warehouses on the edge of a small Pennsylvania industrial town, painted in 1930. It is not the dreary Victorian facades that interest the artist, but a giant blue-and-yellow billboard, which cheerfully tells the world that Lancaster has been the home of Eshelman's Feed Company since 1881.

The America we see in paintings by avant-garde American artists in the first half of this century is very different from the optimistic land of opportunity of European cliché. A forlorn, empty and soulless place, it is a country where what is made and sold is far more interesting than the lives wasted in making and selling it. Advertising animates this landscape, a substitute for life itself. No matter how banal, the billboard is a barrier between individual Americans and their terror of being left alone with drab buildings and impersonal machines. The common language of commercial hype symbolises the American experience.

From the French Symbolist poets and Cubist still-life painters, American artists learned to approach their subjects obliquely, through allusion and suggestion rather than by naming or depiction. From Marsden Hartley in 1914 to Jasper Johns in the 1960s, remarkably few artists in this show deal directly with the human figure. Even when painting what are essentially portraits, Americans sought to express their feelings by following Stephane Mallarmé's advice to painters: 'Paint not the subject, but the effect it produces.'

Take Demuth's evocation of William Carlos Williams's poem, 'The Great Figure', *I Saw the Figure 5 in Gold*. Poem and painting simply describe a number five fire truck clanging down a canyoned city street at night. The repeated number five emerges from the tunnelled space, growing bigger and bigger, closer and closer: a hallucination with

14 September 1993

American Art in the Twentieth Century

Royal Academy, London

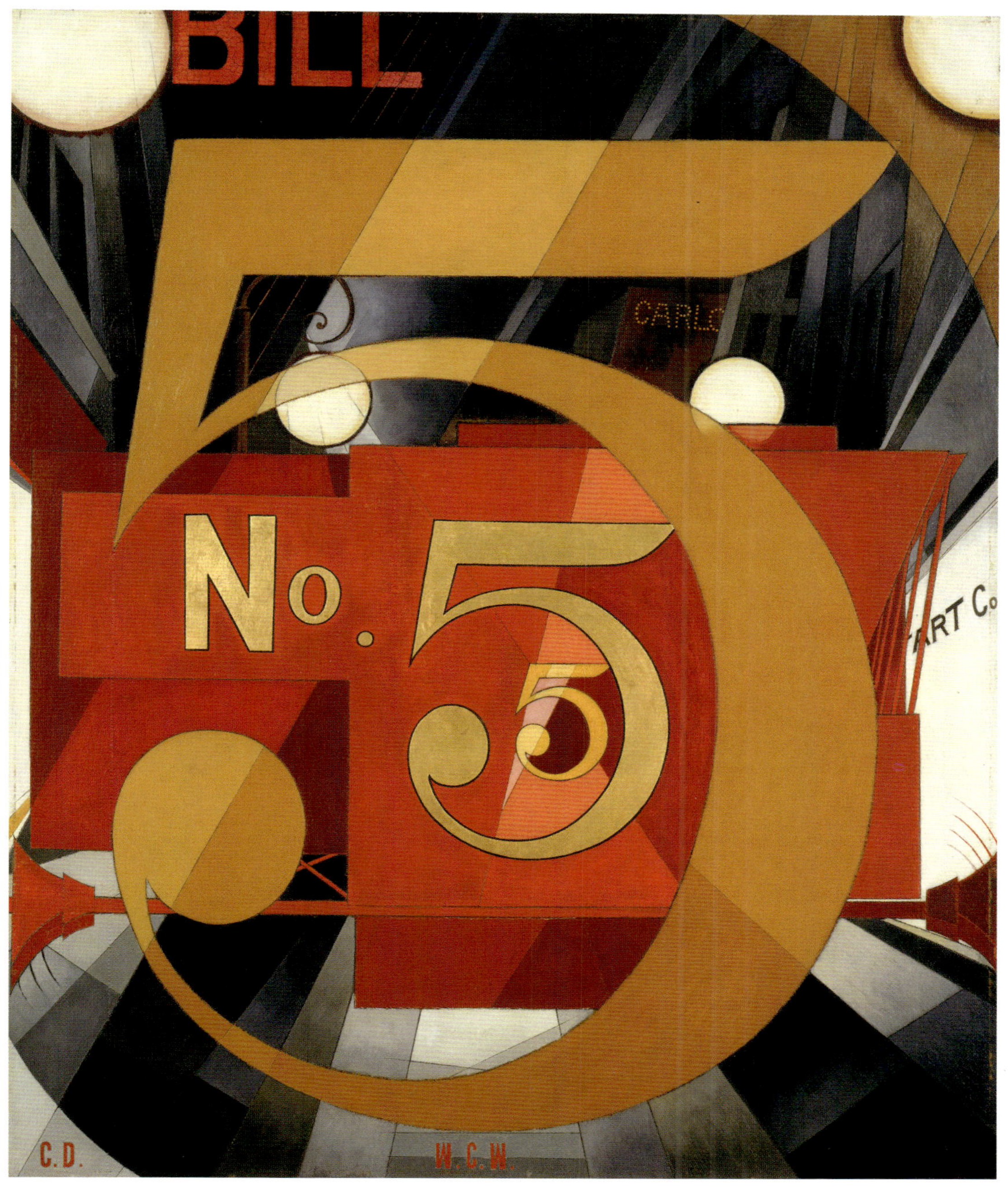

BILL
NO. 5
CARLO
ART Co
C.D.
W.C.W.

Charles Demuth
**I Saw the Figure 5
in Gold**, 1928
Metropolitan Museum
of Art, New York

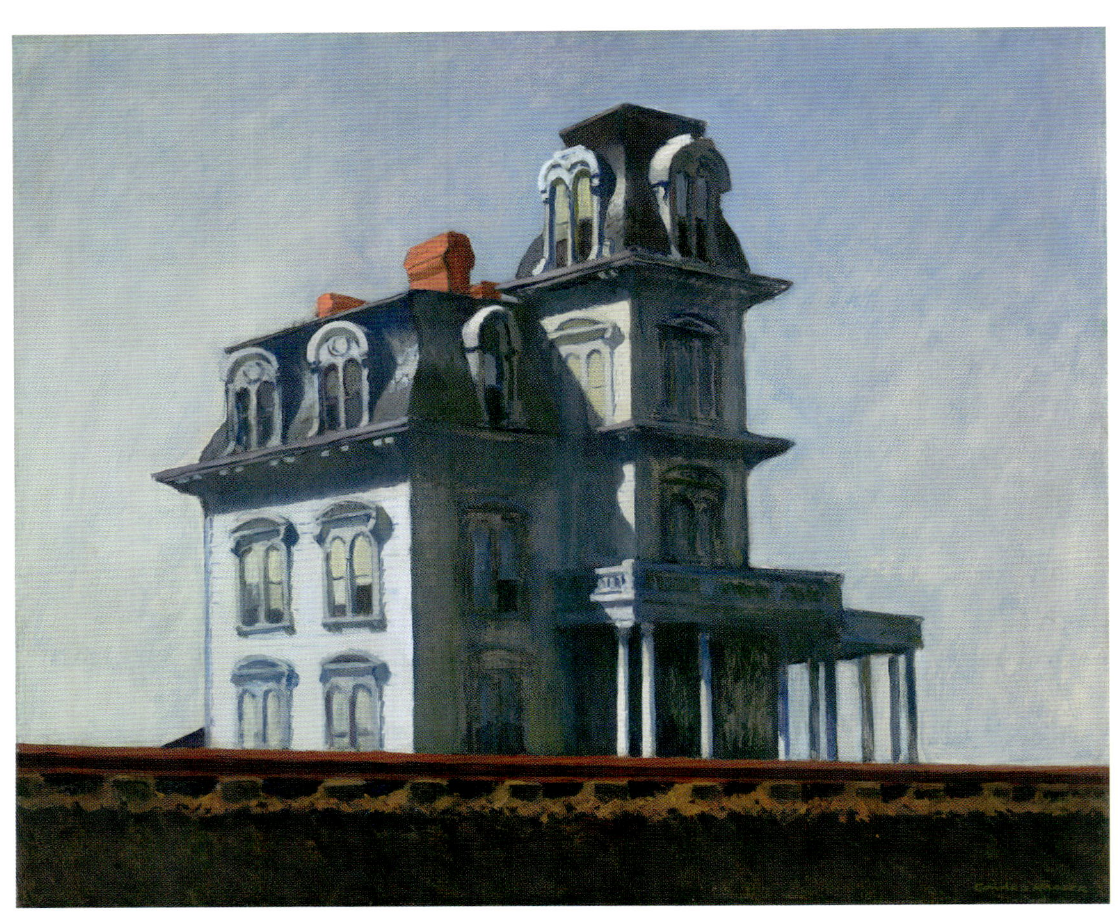

Edward Hopper
**The House by the
Railroad**, 1925
Museum of Modern
Art, New York

headlights, careering straight at us. The poet's name in electric lights
against the surrounding darkness co-signs the picture, a shared
valentine to New York in which a number is the only text.

Europe-trained and steeped in French painting and poetry,
American artists of the 1920s treated art as a sophisticated game.
Their work virtually excludes overt emotion. When Gerald Murphy,
Stuart Davis and Charles Sheeler responded to Cubism, they did so
as though translating French poetry into American slang, trading
the wine bottle and pipe of the Cubist still life for machinery, flags,
detergent bottles and cigarette packets.

It is only when we see the paintings of Edward Hopper in the
context of a survey like this that we realise how utterly original his
genius was. With his training as a commercial illustrator, his odd little
genre scenes might almost belong to the vigorous (but provincial)
regionalist school of the 1930s, were it not for the *fin-de-siècle* tone of
longing and absence that characterised everything he painted. Like
many of the other artists in this show, Hopper painted the marginal
areas of American life – the edge of town, the railway siding, the other
side of the tracks. But he alone explores relationships between people.

Like his contemporary, Alfred Hitchcock, Hopper is a voyeur
whose dramatic vignettes examine played-out marriages and dead-
end lives. And yet the heavy sense of *ennui* brings us back to the
world of the Symbolists: Hopper paints not just the humdrum
commonplaces of everyday life, but the inarticulate yearning for
something beyond them.

It is a tone he shares with the surrealist Joseph Cornell, whose
three-dimensional collages, assembled in cunningly crafted boxes,
are among the most likeable works of art in the show. Cornell, a near-
recluse who lived in the New York borough of Queens, loved the
poetry of Mallarmé and Charles Baudelaire, the collages of Max Ernst
and the paintings of René Magritte. The faded photographs of movie
stars and Old Master paintings in his work speak of a life not quite
lived – or rather, lived vicariously through art, literature and the
cinema. Behind Cornell's art lies the fantasy that the artist–collector
can capture and imprison youth, innocence, beauty, history and
romance.

Like Arshile Gorky's painted abstractions, the sculptor Alexander
Calder's hanging cascades of brightly coloured metal evolved out of

memories of landscape, insects and animals. But Calder's eternally
circling mobiles also suggest nature's eternal flux, the impossibility
of stopping the world in its tracks even for a split second. Unusually
for an American artist before Jackson Pollock, Gorky's thinly painted
canvases are drenched in emotion, their drips and stains somehow
suggesting tear-drops on an intimate letter. Lovely though they are,
the Symbolist reveries of Gorky, Calder and Cornell exude a sense of
exhaustion. Looking over their shoulders at European artists, they are
more self-conscious than their predecessors, with the result that their
art teeters on the edge of whimsy. By the 1940s, American art had
reached what one might almost describe as a premature decadence.

Suddenly, like a meteor out of nowhere, the genius of Pollock
hurtles into the New York art world. American art roars back to life,
born again. I can't remember another exhibition in which a single
work of art holds a place comparable to that occupied by Pollock's
Mural in this exhibition. Painted in 1943, it is like a great hinge
opening a door to the golden age of American art. Pollock grew up
in the American West, studied under the figurative painter Thomas
Hart Benton, and lived and worked in New York. Instead of going
to Europe, Europe came to him in the forms of war-time Surrealist
refugees and of the art-crazed heiress Peggy Guggenheim. For her
he painted *Mural*, the 20-foot long abstract panorama in which he
enacted before our eyes his struggle between representation and
abstraction, consciousness and the unconscious, his will to create and
his need to destroy. The picture changed the course of American art.

Overnight, the tendency in American art to filter experience
through literature and poetry disappeared. In its place Pollock put
something else, something much less comforting but much more
powerful: the artist's ego.

Alexander Calder

Born in 1898 into a dynasty of distinguished American sculptors, Alexander Calder set out to dematerialise the sculptor's traditional materials, to open up the medium and to set it free. Both his grandfather and father had specialised in ponderous bronze statues of colonial patriots at a time in American history when such civic monuments served to create a common history binding together a heterogeneous population.

Alexander Calder saw sculpture's function differently. Whereas the materials with which his forebears had worked were colourless and dense, his would be bright and transparent, limpid and light, as pure as air itself. What had been inert would be filled with movement. With his lifelong dread of the pompous and boring, Calder intended to make an art whose purpose was to 'do' nothing. Nothing, that is, except to delight. Calder took a degree in mechanical engineering before entering art school and finally moving to Paris in 1926. By the time he made his first 'mobile' in the early 1930s, he was in a unique position to apply scientific laws of balance and stress to create free-hanging constructions in wire and metal. In doing so, he made the severe geometric abstractions of Mondrian, his idol, come to life. With their graceful shadows cascading down the gallery wall like feathers, the mobiles change configuration with every passing air current. Watching *Roxbury Flurry*, moving soft and silent in its unpredictable orbit, the wire armature seems to disappear and the circular metal discs to fall freely in space, a snowfall at night.

As in Eric Satie's music or in the poems of e e cummings, Calder's early sculptures have an understated, playful quality, as though each mobile was cobbled together out of old studio scraps and leavings, magically manipulated by a doting grandfather to amuse a grandchild. And yet what looks improvised is as precisely crafted as a Swiss watch, the larger mobiles carefully worked out in maquette

25 March 1992
Alexander Calder
Royal Academy,
London

before being sent to the founders to be enlarged. Calder, who died in 1976, is often spoken of as an abstract sculptor, but in fact the imagery in many of his works is perfectly recognisable. References to fish, birds, leaves, wind and sun can all be present in a single mobile.

While it is true that Calder was one of the relatively few American artists to spend time in Paris between the wars, he also belonged to that generation of American poets and painters who sought to exploit a colloquial idiom in their work. Using the vernacular, they would cut American art and literature free from the deadweight of European tradition. As soon as we become conscious of the essentially American character of Calder's art, we realise what a vital source of inspiration he found in the simplicity and humour of New England folk art. The influence of Mondrian and Arp, Miró and Duchamp, though important, begins to look distinctly secondary when compared to that of the brightly coloured wooden toys and painted weather vanes once ubiquitous throughout the rural North-East.

Entering the Royal Academy's exhibition of Calder's art, which has been sent over by the Whitney Museum of American Art in New York, the visitor might, for an instant, think that the beautiful Sackler Galleries were deserted. It is only the sound of laughter from a far gallery that makes one realise that virtually every visitor is clustered not around a work of art but around a film of one: the fifteen-minute documentary made in 1961 showing Calder manipulating his sculptural assemblage, *The Circus*.

Calder created *The Circus* in Paris in the 1920s. He and his wife frequently 'performed' the piece (as though it were a concerto and not a work of visual art) before the cream of Parisian artistic society. I like to picture Picasso and his first wife Olga Koklova, Hemingway, Fitzgerald and the Murphys, Gertrude Stein, Cocteau and Miró all crowding into the Calders' tiny apartment at the same time: for all I know, maybe they did. Though tiny in scale and made of bits of painted metal, fabric and cork, *The Circus* has all the self-parody and predictable pomposity of the real thing. Mrs Calder operates a tinny Victrola playing a scratchy 78 rpm record of *Ramona* over and over, while Calder himself manipulates the sword swallower, the trapeze artists and the stretcher bearers – as well as firing the toy cannon and making the clockwork kangaroos and horses move. Though I generally find all manifestations of whimsy very resistible, I was won

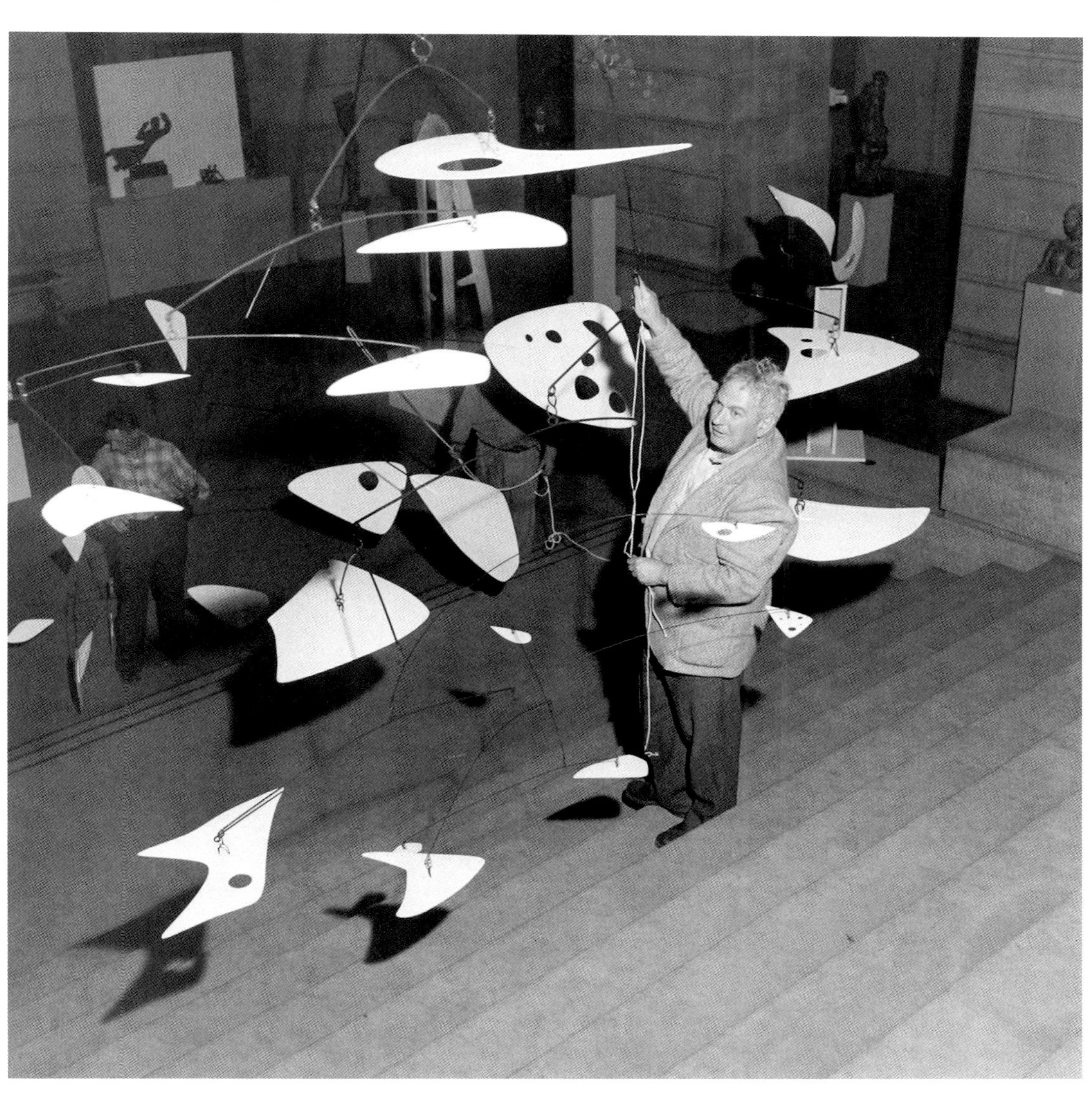

*Alexander Calder
installing his*
International Mobile
*at the Philadelphia
Museum of Art, 1949*

over by the personality of the unsmiling, bear-like Calder, who is shown supplying the sound-effects, including a bloodcurdling lion's roar and the ringmaster's introduction of each act in French pronounced with a broad Yankee twang. Unfortunately, *The Circus* itself, which is now in the National Gallery of Art in Washington DC, is not in the exhibition. This is a serious loss: without its physical presence Calder's status as a major artist hangs too much on the mobiles. For as a draughtsman and as a more conventional sculptor Calder is not quite first-rate.

The stabiles, abstract constructions standing on the gallery floor, consist of cut-out sheets of metal ingeniously fitted together into a series of intricately interlocking arches. These depend for their effect on the constantly changing point of view of the circling spectator. But when placed beside the fascinating mobiles they are always doomed to look pedestrian, like attractive modernist knick-knacks.

As a graphic artist, Calder likes to play the game of 'taking his line for a walk' without lifting the pencil from the page. But whereas Picasso's or Klee's lines tremble with life and nuance, Calder's are as inanimate as the thin wire he was so used to manipulating into images of clowns and strongmen.

Calder is that rarity in the history of twentieth-century art, a major artist whose work as a decorative artist is just as important as his work as a sculptor. Indeed, as a designer of jewellery, textiles and (particularly) children's toys, he himself would perhaps have drawn no distinction between the fine art and decorative sides of his work. Instead of trying to classify him, perhaps we should try to take Calder on his own terms. The critic who provides the most penetrating insight into an artist like Calder is Baudelaire, who defined genius as 'childhood recovered at will'. For such a man, he says, no aspect of life is stale.

George Bellows

There are many reasons to visit the Royal Academy's exhibition
of the work of George Bellows, but you only need one – to see that
quintessential depiction of boxers in the ring, *Stag at Sharkey's*. Painted
in 1909, only five years after the twenty-two-year-old Midwestern
artist came to New York, it is one of the most startlingly original
pictures in American art. Two sinewy boxers hurl themselves at each
other with such force that, like stags locked in mortal combat, neither
is able to displace the other. This is the climactic moment just before
the boxer on the right delivers a powerful right hook to his opponent's
rib area. The referee crouches down and moves in close. If there's
been no foul and the punch lands where intended, the match will
be over.

The ferocious dynamism of the action is held in check by a tightly
structured composition in the form of a massive triangle that fills the
canvas from edge to edge, starting with the long diagonal that begins
with the boxer's leg at the left, and closing by the extended arm of the
referee at the right. As viewers, we look up at the picture's powerful
vectors as though seated in the darkness a few rows back from
ringside. Even from this vantage point, the pain the boxers inflict on
each other is palpable. But then, like other members of the audience
revelling in the cruel spectacle, that is what we've paid to see.

Stag at Sharkey's has been reproduced so often that it comes
as a shock to see how beautifully painted the original is. In certain
passages, the young artist seems to be applying paint with a few
sweeps of a loaded brush that looks as though it never lost contact
with the canvas. Though the inspiration of Goya and Daumier is
clear in his treatment of the grotesque faces of some of the onlookers,
the urgency and expressiveness of the brushwork he uses to describe
the arms, legs and torsos of the fighters has no real precedent in
American art.

12 March 2013

George Bellows:
Modern American Life

Royal Academy,
London

Bellows does not approve or disapprove of boxing. He once said that he knew nothing about the sport, joking that in *Stag at Sharkey's* he was 'just painting two men trying to kill each other'. But he was doing much more than that. Until 1911 boxing was illegal in New York. In order to circumvent the ban, spectators and fighters were made members of private clubs like Sharkey's for one night only. Matches were therefore held behind closed doors with a largely male audience. *Stag at Sharkey's* was the only one of the three boxing pictures Bellows painted in 1909 that was sold during his lifetime. Americans were shocked both by the near-nudity of the boxers and by the brutality of the subject.

Even more controversial was the depiction in one of the pictures of an interracial fight that, in a segregated society, could only have taken place in a private club. Ultimately, I think, these pictures hit a nerve because they look at the violence and racism at the heart of American society. This is what makes Bellows a more important artist than his master, Robert Henri, or his contemporaries John Soane and the Ash Can school of painters. He harnesses a bravura painting technique to an intelligence that continually probed beneath the mere surface of things. In his best paintings he does for New York what Walter Sickert did for London – captured the roiling energy of poor or marginal areas like the Docklands tenement buildings.

In his early *Forty-two Kids*, a posse of street urchins cool off in the filthy waters of New York's East River. By tilting the rickety pier from which they swim upwards and eliminating the horizon line, Bellows creates a false picture plane over which he arranges dozens of small figures to create a lively, apparently random pattern. But there is nothing abstract about the boys. They are cocky creatures with simian faces who fight, pee, puff on fags and inspect each other's willies in a parody of decorous male nudes by Thomas Eakins and Henry Scott Tuke.

When he paints a conventional subject, Bellows often hints that there is more to his subject than he is prepared to tell. The smart, suspicious face of the little laundry girl in an early portrait hardly conforms to the sugar'n'spice idea of childhood expected by the American public, while to show an adult female model in the act of undressing is more unsettling than to show her in a pose, especially when her body is imperfect and she is wearing make-up. When he

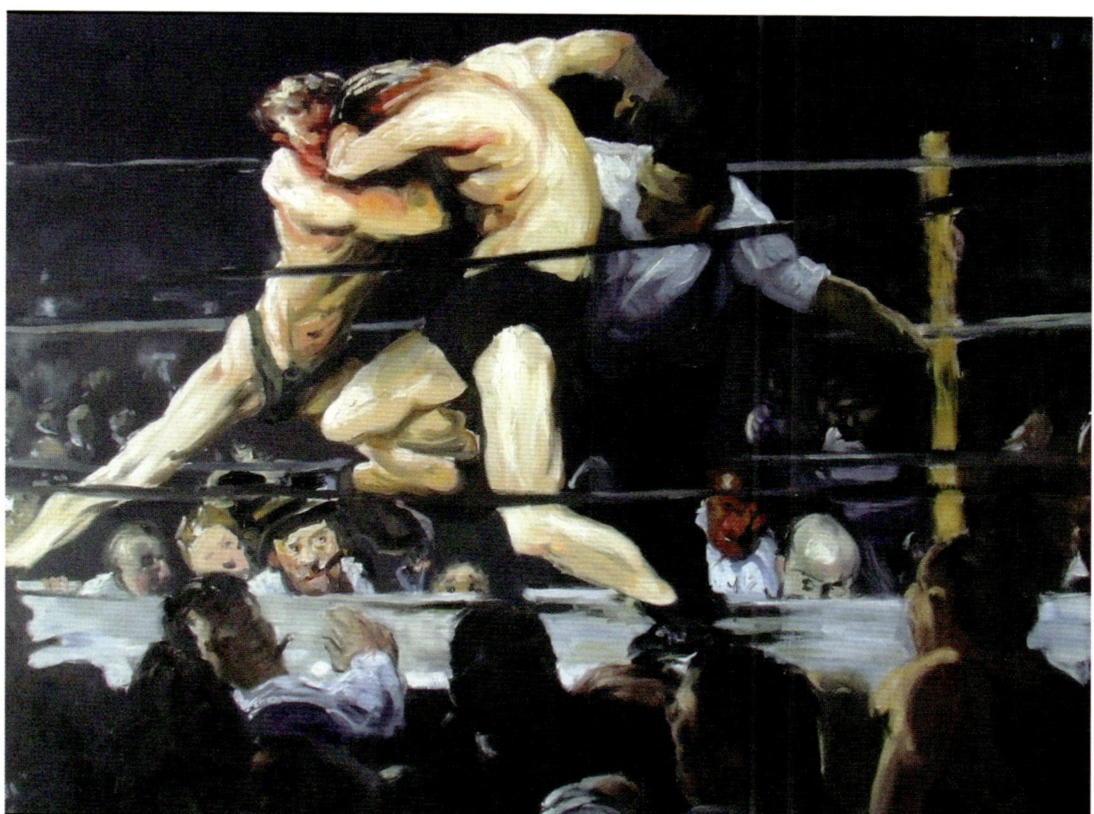

paints the crowded beach at Coney Island or rush hour in midtown Manhattan, he makes them look like hell on earth.

Where Whistler and Sickert painted London's fogs, Bellows found beauty in tugboats butting through the icy waters of the rain-sodden East River. He also paints Manhattan under snow and the lovely sight of the Palisades rising up on the Jersey side of the Hudson and some pretty views of summer fêtes in Central Park, but for all their craftsmanship, these subjects don't have quite the edge of the superb studies of working-class and poor New Yorkers.

American landscape painters in the nineteenth century focused on awe-inspiring natural phenomena like the Grand Canyon or Niagara Falls. Bellows paints the man-made equivalent, the excavations for the foundations of Pennsylvania Station – effectively a giant hole in the ground conceived on a scale that turns the workmen we see in its depths into insect-sized flecks of paint. Nowhere in this show is the balance between representation and abstraction more evenly balanced and not until Frank Auerbach's paintings of London building sites do we see anything like this in art again.

Bellows died young, in 1925, at the age of forty-three. The work he did in the last few years of his life has never been critically acclaimed – and indeed there is something lubricious about his wartime propaganda paintings showing German atrocities against Belgian civilians. In *The Barricade*, for example, it feels as though a hint of voyeurism and sadism have crept into a picture that shows naked and defenceless villagers walking with upraised arms to form a human shield in front of German troops.

But the show's organiser, Charles Brock, convincingly argues in his catalogue essay that we should all look again at the family portraits of Bellows's last years. These ravishingly painted pictures look strangely out of place in the oeuvre of an artist so closely associated with masculine subjects like boxing matches, field sports and locker rooms. Painted in the early 1920s, they show well-dressed, middle-class women and girls in claustrophobically enclosed spaces. In one, his wife and daughters sit awkwardly in a darkened room filled with heavy furniture. Emma Bellows wears a floor-length dress that looks about thirty years behind the times and no one looks remotely at ease. Once again, it is not really American art I think of when I look at these pictures, but of the unsettling portraits of the German realist Otto Dix.

Arshile Gorky

The real name of the painter known to the world as Arshile Gorky was Manoug Adoian. He was born in the western part of Armenia to a family of prosperous Christian traders. One morning, when he was about five years old, his father took his son and daughter to a field by a lake. There they sat on the ground, sharing a last meal before his father emigrated to America, where, he promised, they would join him soon. Before kissing his children goodbye, he presented his son with a pair of pointed wooden shoes, traditional footwear for Armenian men.

But the years went by and his father didn't send for them and didn't return, in effect abandoning his wife and children not just to hardship, but to mortal danger. In 1915 the Turks began their campaign of extermination against Christian Armenians, and more than 1.5 million people were either massacred or died during deportation. Amid horrific violence, the young family fled for their lives, making their way on foot to Russian Armenia 150 miles away. In the winter of 1918–19, temperatures sometimes dropped to -30°C. Manoug's mother lay down on the floor of a derelict house and died in the arms of her fifteen-year-old son. She had starved to death.

In 1920, through the generosity of a relative, the children reached America, where in due course the exiled painter would draw on imagery culled from memories of his boyhood to forge a new language of lyrical abstraction. It was a long time before he could confront his past, but when he did he lit the way for two generations of American artists.

To make sense of the magnificent retrospective of his work at Tate Modern, go straight to gallery seven, where you will find both versions of *The Artist and his Mother*, an image that distils the experience of the millions of immigrants who made their way from the old world to the new in the early years of the past century. Based

9 February 2010

Arshile Gorky:
A Retrospective

Tate Modern, London

on a black-and-white studio photograph taken in Armenia in 1912,
it shows Manoug and his mother posing stiffly in front of the camera
like figures in a Byzantine icon. The little boy stands like a bridegroom
at his mother's side, wearing a coat with a velvet collar and shyly
holding a bouquet of flowers. Seated next to him, monumental as
a Madonna by Giotto, his mother wears the traditional Armenian
headscarf and long apron. His round eyes look out pleadingly,
hers are full of accusation.

Manoug's mother had gone to the expense of having the
photograph taken to send to her husband in America, a reminder
of his family's existence. The person to whom Manoug offers the
bouquet is his absent father. Both versions are unfinished. Was it that
Gorky could not bear to let his mother go a second time? Or did the
picture bring back too many painful memories and too much anger
to work on for long periods? His pseudonym, after all, is the Russian
word for 'bitter'.

At the beginning of his career, Gorky painted dead pastiches of
Cézanne, Picasso, Léger and Miró, remarkable mainly because he
knew the European modernists he was imitating only through the few
examples of their work he could see in New York, or from black-and-
white reproductions in art magazines. For me, the most interesting
thing about these pictures – far too many of which are included in
the exhibition – is what they tell us about the mind of the artist, who
applied paint to his canvases so thickly that their surfaces feel airtight,
closed shut, lifeless.

In an important series of black-and-white drawings in pencil
and pen-and-ink from the early 1930s called *Nighttime, Enigma and
Nostalgia*, Gorky combines the biomorphic shapes of Miró and Picasso
with the Surrealist imagery of de Chirico. But Gorky was always a
superb draughtsman, and the most beautiful works in the series are
drawn with dense hatching to create an overall black tonality, from
which amoeba-like organisms that suggest nascent eyes, mouths, lips
and breasts struggle to emerge. For the first time we sense that the
difficult-to-decipher imagery has some deeply personal meaning for
the artist – that it comes from some dead zone of memory and feeling
in his unconscious.

His meeting with the European Surrealist artists in New York in
the early 1940s was the catalyst that enabled him to break free from

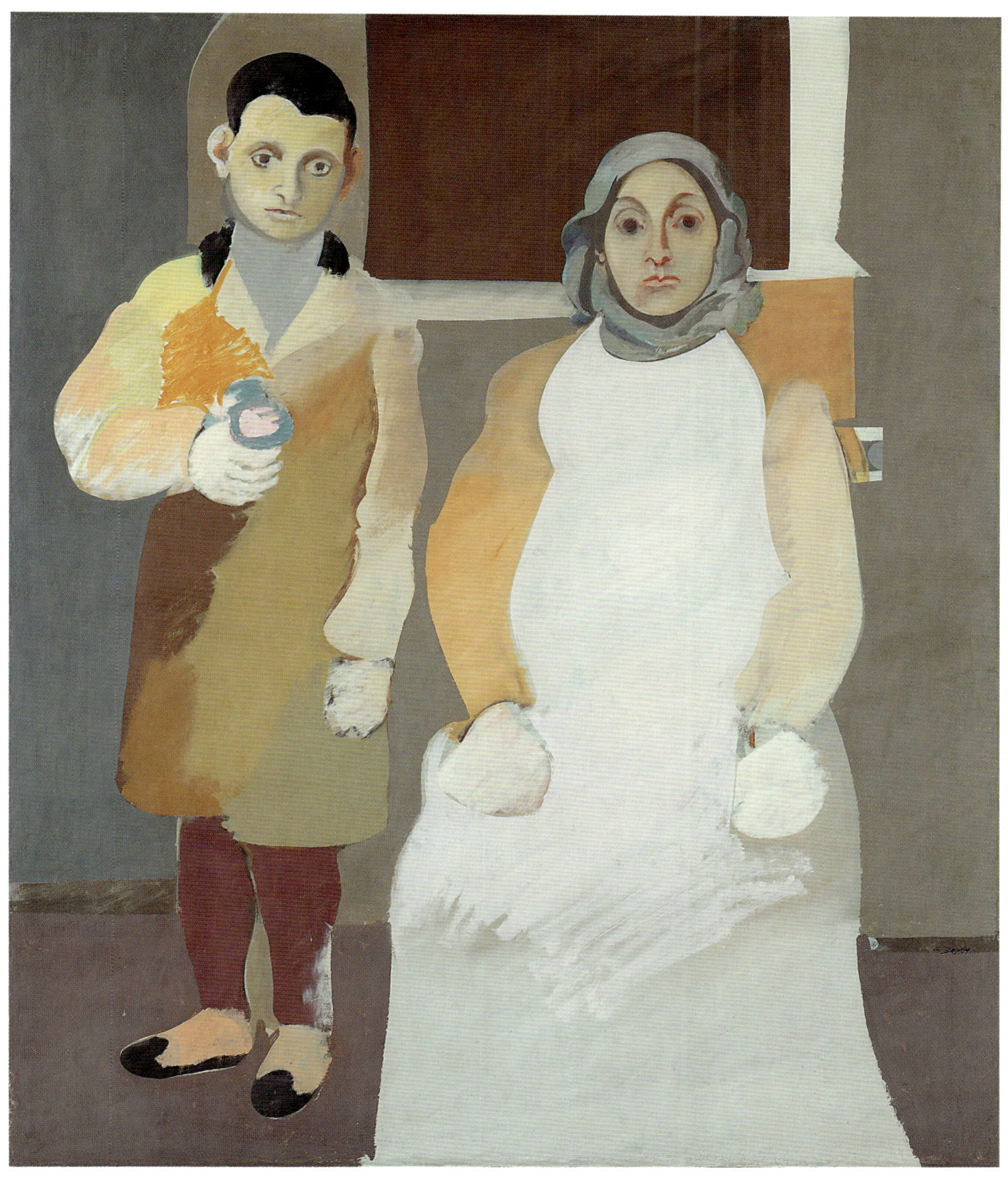

Arshile Gorky
The Artist and his Mother, c. 1926
National Gallery of
Art, Washington DC

the stifling influence of Picasso and Miró. From the moment he found
the courage to look inside himself for his subject matter, he also found
a new painterly freedom. The series *Garden in Sochi* (1940–41) is still
stylistically dependent on Miró, but its imagery is drawn from
childhood memories – the family's sunny garden, the butter churn
and plough, a rug, a butterfly, a tree's branches hung with strips of
fluttering cloth, and the Armenian slipper his father had given him
that long-ago morning.

By unlocking memories of his childhood, Gorky opened himself
up to the world around him. His colour-filled semi-abstract
landscapes from the 1940s are filled with animal, bird and insect
life. Their joy and sensuality reflect the personal happiness he found
in marriage and a new life outside New York. They can combine
eroticism and playfulness with a sometimes sinister undertow that
you don't find elsewhere in American art from this time.

In *Love of the New Gun*, for example, he uses swift sweeps of a
brush dipped in grey and black paint with the assurance of a master
calligrapher to summon up a landscape that you just know is alive
with birds and insects. But since their presence is indicated by a
snatch of green plume, a glimpse of yellow breast, a black beak, or an
open wing, it is very hard to say exactly why these incomplete shapes
represent birds. Then you spot the smears and drips of red paint
and the title tells you the rest: this is what remains of the beautiful
creatures the hunter has just shot with his brand new weapon.

In other works, spidery calligraphic lines create biomorphic shapes
that feel as though they are in perpetual movement, while washes,
drips and smears of colour suggest second thoughts and erasures. The
canvas has become a palimpsest in which feelings and memories stir
only to be buried again in an endless cycle of consciousness and
repression.

Gorky's life started and ended in tragedy. Just as he began to
receive critical recognition, a series of personal disasters took away
everything he valued in his life – his work, his health and his family.
First, a fire in his Connecticut studio destroyed a lifetime's drawings
and paintings. Then an operation for cancer that required a proud,
handsome and fastidious man to wear a colostomy bag broke his
spirit. A late picture entitled *Charred Beloved* evokes the fire's
aftermath in black paint over raw canvas. But it is also one of

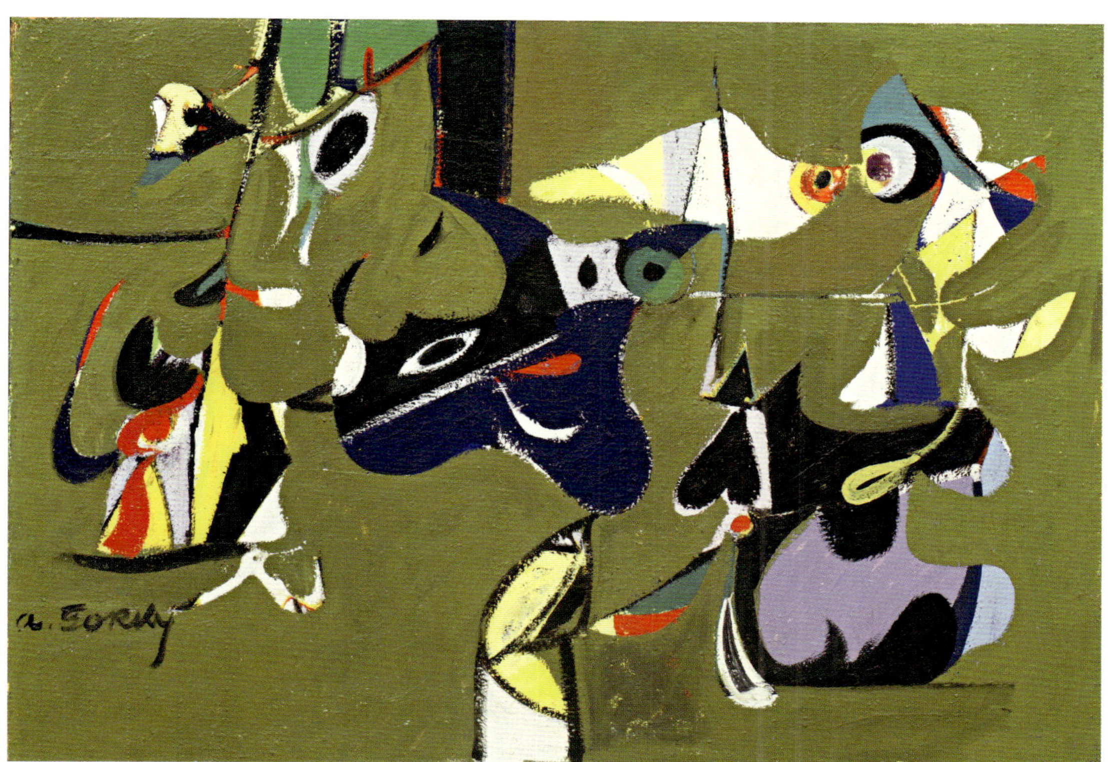

Arshile Gorky
Garden at Sochi,
1941
Museum of Modern
Art, New York

the most shockingly intimate self-portraits ever painted, for the rivulet of scarlet paint inside an intestine-shaped blob must refer both to rectal bleeding and post-operative pain, while black smudges evoke both human waste and the cancer that had invaded his body and made him feel unclean. After the collapse of his marriage and a car crash that left him in agony, he could take no more. On 20 July 1948, Gorky hanged himself.

What a loss. Gorky was the link between European Surrealism and American Abstract Expressionism. The passion, enigma and autobiographical dimension of his work would find their way into the art of Jackson Pollock, Willem de Kooning and, above all, Cy Twombly.

Jackson Pollock

It's the roiling, brooding human drama of the New York Museum of Modern Art's magnificent Jackson Pollock retrospective that captures the imagination. The largest show of his work in thirty years – which opened this month – unfolds like a novel of epic scope, telling the story of a depressive and a violent alcoholic born with no discernible artistic gifts, who by sheer force of will transformed himself into the greatest of all American artists. Pollock's personality and troubled emotional life come across in these paintings more intensely than in any retrospective I've ever seen.

Jackson Pollock was born in 1912 in Cody, Wyoming, the youngest of five sons. Less than a year later, the family moved to California, where his father more or less abandoned them, leaving Jackson to be raised by his weak but possessive mother and by his four older brothers. He first began to study art at his Los Angeles high school, making his way to New York in 1930 to study under the American regionalist painter, Thomas Hart Benton.

The paintings he produced under Benton, and for a brief period working alongside the Mexican muralist David Alfaro Siqueiros, aren't particularly impressive. The young Pollock had little facility as a draughtsman and no feel at all for the handling of paint. Had he died in his thirties, he'd have been no more than a footnote in the history of American art. But, in the light of what was to come, we look at the paintings of the Thirties and see in Pollock's imagery an authenticity and force of feeling which render the crudity of the execution irrelevant.

An untitled oil from about 1938–41 shows the body of a naked man surmounted by a head which takes the form of an abstract circle of swirling paint. Some have seen the figure as a mythological creature, the Minotaur. I regard it as a self-portrait, Pollock's highly original way of representing a person whose corporeal existence feels real

14 November 1998

Jackson Pollock

Museum of Modern Art, New York

enough, but whose identity, the internal 'I' most of us take for granted, is obliterated in a maelstrom of violent and angry fantasy. For, by the time he painted it, Pollock had endured long years of loneliness, poverty and failure, gradually sinking into the alcoholism that would ultimately lead to his death.

Throughout this period, he was learning to paint. In his awkward use of fragmentation, meandering lines and the surrealist merging of one form into another, Pollock's early paintings chronicle his successive absorption with the art of Siqueiros, Picasso, Miró and André Masson. But whoever he imitated, the images of devouring, biting, stabbing and strangulation in paintings such as *Birth* or *The Moon Woman Cuts the Circle* are so urgent and intimate that it is hard not to see in them expressions of some catastrophic, aboriginal hurt deep within Pollock's psyche.

Though we can never know what went wrong in Pollock's life, his preoccupation with wombs, pregnancy and parturition may have less to do with unconscious memories of physical birth than with his longing for the emergence of a separate and secure self, an identity strong enough to struggle against the chaotic emotions which threatened to engulf him. This he began to find in the late Thirties under the guidance of a Jungian analyst who encouraged Pollock to explore his unconscious fears and desires through his art. The danger of this approach to painting is that it can so easily become self-conscious. I find the portentousness of one of the best-known canvases from the early Forties, *Guardians of the Secret*, somewhat contrived. With its imagery of a recumbent she-wolf and two sentinel-like forms keeping watch over a sealed sarcophagus covered in hieroglyphics, it is as though Pollock were glancing over his shoulder, aware of exactly the sort of picture his analyst would expect a man tormented by his inability to contact the deepest wells of his own being to paint.

The picture that actually marks Pollock's artistic birth is the great *Mural* painted for the heiress Peggy Guggenheim in 1943–44. For five months, Pollock is said to have sat and stared at the blank canvas, 19 feet long and almost 10 feet high. With the work due to be delivered the following day, he locked himself in his studio and worked all night, painting the picture using the Surrealist technique of automatic drawing. From his deepest unconscious a great panorama began to emerge, wild horses, bulls, antelopes and human figures. Gradually, as the great curves and swirls of brushed and splattered paint obliterated the original shapes, all that remained of his terrifying plunge into the unconscious was a phalanx of giant black brushstrokes marching like primitive stick figures across a jungle of olive greens, raspberry reds and sickly yellows.

When *Mural* is hanging on a wall, a six-foot-tall man standing close up to it feels like a child overwhelmed and confused by a world of frightening adult figures. Since Pollock never allows our eye to rest, and charges every inch of the canvas with violence, the effect is to plummet the viewer into a new and intimidating world, one in which we feel utterly and unexpectedly helpless. This is something new in American art. No longer does Pollock filter experience through literary or poetic imagery. In its place, he gives us experience itself, forcing us to share with him the awe of an infant confronting a world of elemental chaos. In *Mural*, we come face-to-face with a reality which our minds are incapable of either encompassing or controlling.

Brutally aggressive, *Mural* offers the viewer neither comfort nor beauty. It did not lead immediately to the drip paintings of 1947–50 on which Pollock's reputation ultimately rests. In the years following its creation, Pollock married the painter Lee Krasner, who got him off the bottle by moving with him to East Hampton on Long Island in November, 1945. Almost overnight, Pollock's art changes. Tense and violent abstractions painted in New York give way to radiant, colour-drenched landscapes reminiscent of Matisse. This period in his life coincided with the beginning of Pollock's first critical and financial successes. With the support of a sympathetic wife, reassurance from the critic Clement Greenberg, and a small income from the gallery owners Peggy Guggenheim and Betty Parsons, he achieved enough inner security to leap into the unknown world of Abstract Expressionism.

In describing the sober Pollock, eye witnesses use words such as 'cold', 'dead' and 'monosyllabic'. Depressed, or else so intensely preoccupied with his inner world that the real one had little relevance for him, his face is said to have looked like a mask, registering neither pleasure nor pain. But this is not how most of us imagine Pollock. That is because the photographer Hans Namuth's famous films of the artist at work in 1950 show quite a different person. With his canvas

laid flat on the studio floor and the cans of paint, dry brushes
and sticks at the ready, he stands up tall, smoking a cigarette and
contemplating the white rectangle at his feet. Then, suddenly, he
picks up a dripping brush and begins to move back and forth over the
canvas with the grace of a dancer and the concentration of a lover. At
times, he is so close to the canvas that he seems to become part of it.

Far from relying on chance or accident, we can see the enormous
control with which he 'draws' with the dribbles and splashes of paint,
using the flick of his wrist or the sweep of his arm to place the
pigment on the canvas exactly where he wants it to go. So complex is
the technique he used to create these winding skeins and interlacing
webs of squeezed pigment that our eye soon gives up trying to
disentangle line and colour. It is easy to see why so many critics
have likened the drip technique to bodily functions, including the
ejaculation of semen, the spilling of blood, and the boyhood game
of 'drawing' in the sand with a stream of urine.

The drip paintings have also been compared to things in the
natural world, from galaxies and fireworks to sea foam and the
tangled undergrowth. But, then, their rich allusiveness is part of their
greatness. While painting them, you sense that Pollock was in touch
with that part of himself which was most alive. That is why they
speak of an infinite variety of experience, from the light-filled
Cathedral and the aerated *Galaxy*, to the coagulated depths of
Full Fathom Five and the intimidating grandeur of *Autumn Rhythm
(Number 30) (1950)*. But how are we to interpret such works? At one
level, the answer is straightforward. With its palette of black, white
and light brown set on a beige ground, *Autumn Rhythm* is just what
the title says it is, a November landscape of gusting winds and
whirling leaves set against the stormy skies Pollock could see every
time he looked out of his window.

But new research suggests that it is more. By analysing Namuth's
contact sheets, studying his films frame by frame, and then using the
latest computer technology to assemble composite images of Pollock's
pictures at earlier stages in their development, the scholar Pepe
Karmel has shown that he never wholly abandoned the human figure.
Whether dripping or pouring paint, his first 'hit' at the blank canvas
often resulted in recognisably human forms, not unlike those that had
appeared in his work in the Thirties and early Forties. As he worked,

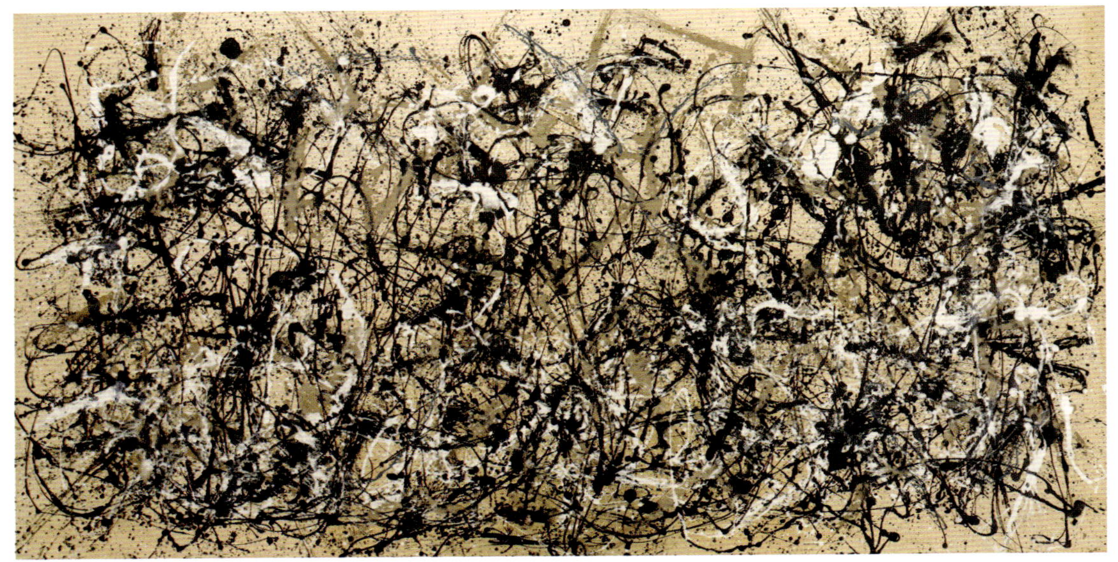

these figures were overlaid by paint, sometimes re-emerging at a later stage in the picture's evolution, but ultimately disappearing again under multicoloured skeins of pigment. Whereas in the past it was necessary to distinguish between Pollock's early figurative and symbolic work on the one hand and the Abstract Expressionist drip paintings on the other, now the gulf between the two has narrowed.

Since the late Thirties, Pollock's great subject had been his own unconscious, the tension between his will to create, love and imagine, and the murderously self-destructive forces which threatened to overwhelm his fragile ego. But we now see that the drip paintings are themselves an extension of Pollock's inner world, depictions of his unconscious at a moment of relative equilibrium.

As he worked, he was re-enacting the central drama of his life, his struggle to allow a recognisable identity (the figure) to emerge from within him, and the equally powerful compulsion to destroy or bury it again. Even as he was destroying the figure, the 'allover' painting technique meant that he was creating connections between areas of the canvas which would otherwise have been isolated and separate. If we accept that the paint somehow felt to Pollock like a part of himself, then the act of painting these pictures enabled him to draw together into a coherent whole those parts of himself to which he had no conscious access. That is why they are so beautiful.

But that beauty, like those feelings, was unsustainable. By the time

Jackson Pollock
Autumn Rhythm
(Number 30), *1950*
Metropolitan Museum
of Art, New York

of *Lavender Mist (Number 1) (1950)*, something is wrong. With its spider-web surface and luminous pastel palette, the picture is too beautiful to have been painted by a man so filled with anger and self-hatred. Having been sober for two years, after Namuth's last photo-shoot in November 1950 Pollock downed the tumbler of whisky that would initiate the six-year period of drunkenness and increasingly erratic work, which would end in his death in 1956.

As he got drunker and drunker on that November afternoon, he obsessively repeated to himself the phrase, 'I'm not a phoney.' I find this profoundly moving. Here was a man whom *Life* magazine had described as the most famous painter in America, and whom many saw as the first American artist to attain truly international stature. But, while the world exclaimed at the ethereal beauty of his paintings, Pollock had come to feel increasingly out of touch with that part of himself which also felt real, the dark, destructive forces that he now used alcohol to unleash. In the 'black' paintings which emerged in 1951, figurative imagery returns. Though the oppressively heavy forms and crushing sense of doom in these works speak of his depression, they are also ferocious depictions of the cruelty and aggression which he had somehow been able to contain and control in the drip paintings of 1947–50.

Pollock's tragedy is that he found it impossible to integrate both sides of his nature – the lyrical and creative with the destructive and violent. This may be the meaning of the painting that closes this unforgettable show, *Portrait and a Dream* of 1953. On the right-hand side of the large canvas he paints a multicoloured human head, almost certainly a self-portrait. Opposite on the left, drawn in black paint on the raw canvas, is a violently agitated, near-abstract tangle of stars, knives, female shapes and spatters that look like blood. What is important is the empty space which separates the portrait from the dream. In the drip paintings, there are no such empty spaces, and, therefore, no sense of fragmentation and desolation. The picture eloquently describes Pollock's predicament: his inability to find a bearable psychological identity which could incorporate both the creativity and the violence which were equally part of his nature. Pollock died in 1956 by crashing his car when drunk at the wheel. In the end, he succeeded in murdering not only himself but an innocent young woman as well.

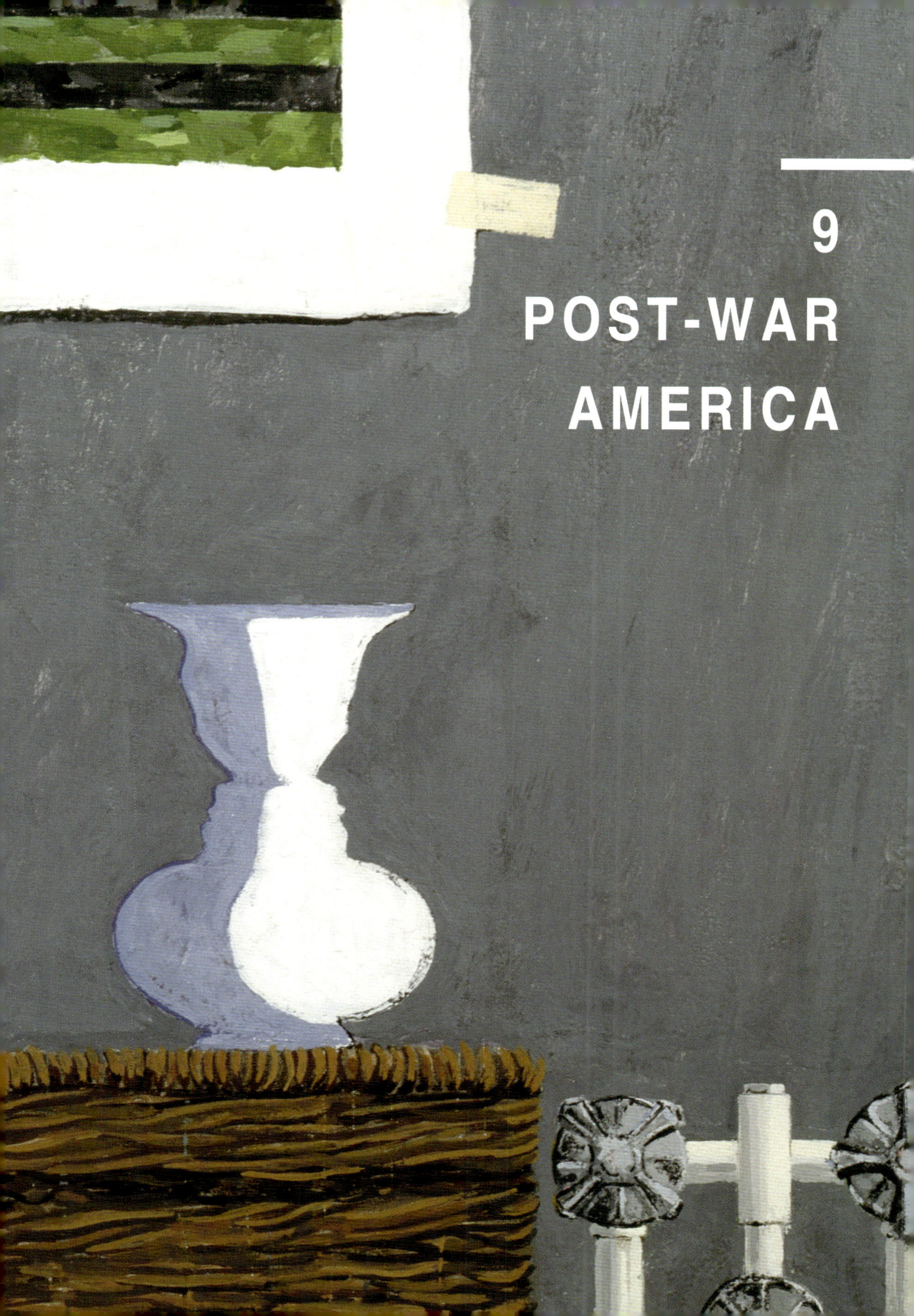

9
POST-WAR
AMERICA

Roy Lichtenstein

Tate Modern's magnificent Roy Lichtenstein retrospective arrives in London hot on the heels of both the Royal Academy's exhibition of Edouard Manet's portraits and the Barbican's of Marcel Duchamp. After seeing the three shows in quick succession, I was surprised to realise that Lichtenstein's work felt far closer in spirit and intention to the nineteenth-century French master than to that of his contemporaries. Both Manet and Lichtenstein were innovators, yet both worked within the framework of existing artistic traditions. Neither artist sought to break with the past: Lichtenstein's entire career can be seen as an extended dialogue with the Old Masters.

One of the earliest paintings in this show is a spoof Lichtenstein painted in 1951 of Emanuel Leutze's *Washington Crossing the Delaware*, an academic history painting reproduced in every school textbook of the time. What is striking is not that Lichtenstein's picture looks as if it was painted by a four-year-old, but that a young artist at that date would have bothered to parody an academic history painting. Why mock a work that was universally despised in progressive artistic circles?

But did he despise it? Or by re-doing it in the style of the then-fashionable Dubuffet, was he slyly conveying his admiration for the time, talent and skill that went into the making of a large-scale exhibition picture? At the very least, the jokey little picture reveals that he was thinking about art in terms of the hierarchies formulated in the French Academy in the seventeenth century – with prestigious history painting at the top, followed by portraiture, landscape and the lowly still life. Lichtenstein would spend the next forty years exploring the challenges presented by each genre and in every case finding ways to make it look new.

His breakthrough came in the early 1960s, when he began painting images he found in comic books, anonymous mail-order catalogues

19 February 2013

Lichtenstein:
A Retrospective

Tate Modern, London

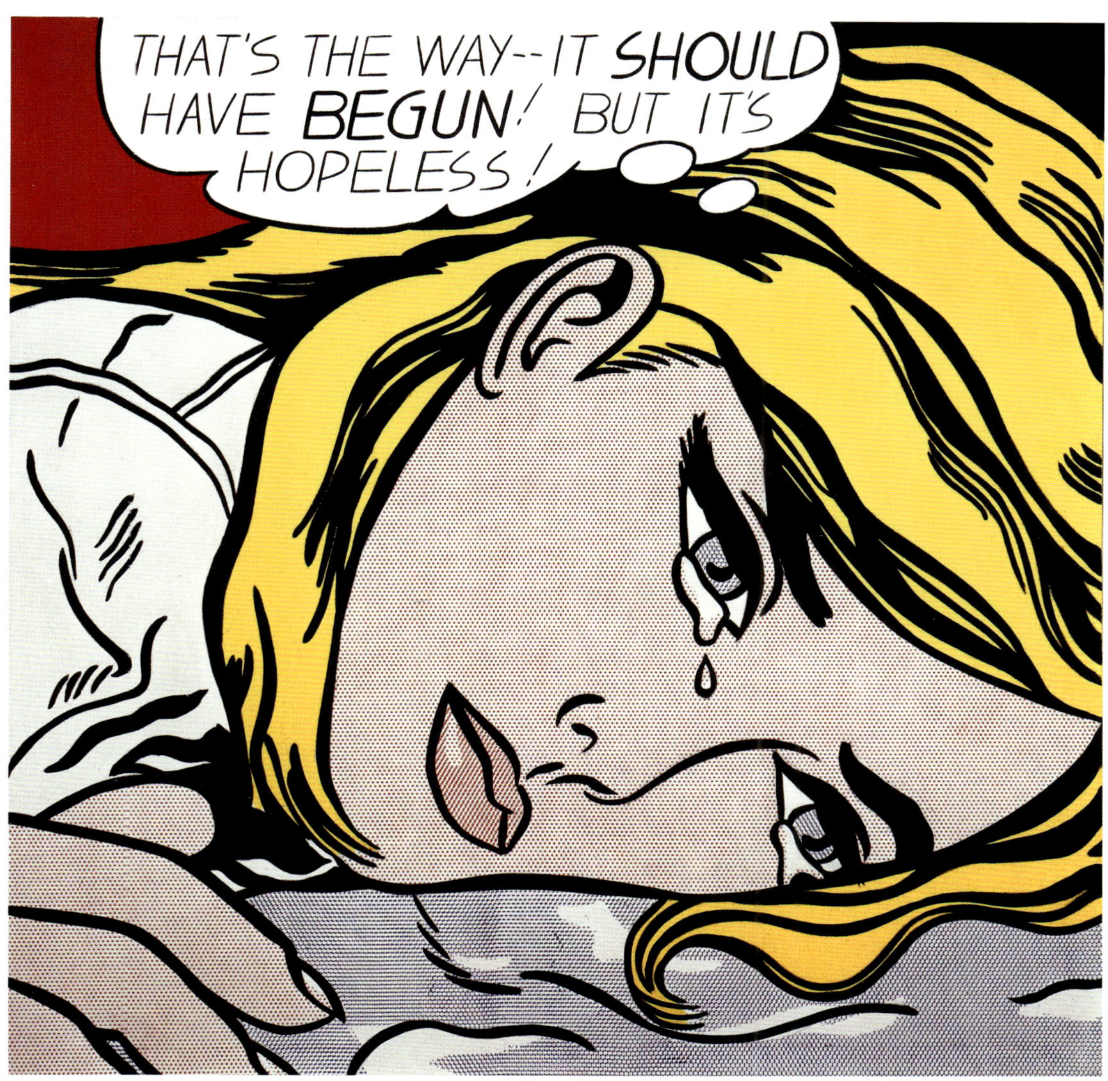

Roy Lichtenstein
Hopeless, *1963*
Kunstmuseum Basel

and *True Romance* magazines. They depict all-American types in close-up, so that the giant heads of handsome Brad and his generic blonde girlfriend fill our field of vision just as they do on movie and TV screens. Speech and thought bubbles above lovers' heads tell us that they are talking about profoundly serious things – love, death, abandonment, suicide, ambition – and yet every thought is banal, every word a cliché, and every breathless sentence ends in an exclamation mark!

But then Lichtenstein wasn't painting actual feelings, but mass-produced representations of feelings in pictures that are as carefully constructed and carefully executed as any nineteenth-century salon picture. Take a moment to look at the actual comic-book illustration that Lichtenstein used to paint *Whaam!* and you'll see that he altered the original by removing a second explosion between the hot-shot fighter pilot and the bad guy he blows to smithereens. What had been an aerial battle involving several planes becomes a one-to-one struggle between good and evil. The change emphasises the actuality of the foreign pilot's violent death, which becomes at once both intimate and depersonalised. I see these pictures of love and war as Lichtenstein's version of history and genre painting conceived on the grand scale of Salon or exhibition pictures. Like Manet, he's a controlled and cerebral artist, a detached observer who rarely strays into the realms of feeling. Both artists make art about art.

The original cartoons he used as visual sources for these early pictures belong to a particular moment in America's history, the innocent post-war decades before the Vietnam War. Lichtenstein's paintings of the same cartoons address the superficiality of a culture that was turning real people into automatons, whether in a cashier's soon-to-be-ubiquitous 'have a nice day,' the pressure to conform to Madison Avenue's idea of beauty, or even the soul-destroying banality of daytime TV. It is hard to look at the war pictures today without thinking of the American belief that acts of unimaginable violence have no consequences as long as they are directed at foreigners.

Crucial to what Lichtenstein was doing was his use of Ben-Day dots, a printing process in which small, closely spaced dots in different colours were used to create half-tones in cheap newsprint. Though not a new invention, Ben-Day dots are specifically associated with comic books and illustrations in pulp magazines from the 1950s and 1960s. By using them, Lichtenstein signalled the modernity of his visual sources. But they also force the eye to slow down, so that the viewer has to work his way across an image that otherwise he'd be tempted to take in at a glance. Look for example at Lichtenstein's brushstroke paintings at the beginning of the show. They show you something that in real life you can't really see – the speed with which a brush loaded with paint can create the illusion of depth on a flat canvas. We 'see' that speed because the undulating ribbon of pure red or yellow sweeps across a field of laboriously painted Ben-Day dots.

One of the revelations of the show for me was the gallery of black-and-white still lifes showing a single golf ball, a ball of twine, a composition notebook or Alka-Seltzer tablet dissolving in a glass of water. Each object is shown in close-up, and all are painted in a dreary monotone palette of black and grey. Tired and worn out, these pictures look like the endlessly reproduced advertisements you'd find in the small ads in tabloids. But look for a few minutes at each and you see that the linear patterns made by the loops of twine or the bubbling water are described with an economy of line that Hokusai would have admired. These are at once graphic images and representations of graphic images – pictures of pictures that, for all their low-key perfection, give nothing away.

By isolating each object and then zooming in to enlarge it, Lichtenstein does the most old-fashioned thing a twentieth-century artist could do – he makes you see an everyday object not as a symbol of something else but as a thing of beauty and complexity. And if Lichtenstein finds visual inspiration in low art, he frequently gives us a little wink to remind us of Japanese printmakers or Art Nouveau painters – and sometimes the wink becomes a nudge when he takes a motif from Klimt, Picasso or Rauschenberg.

This is a big show, and these are only brief observations about the early work. I came away with a new respect for the way Lichtenstein used the work of other artists as a means to analyse, explore and sometimes subvert the building blocks of art – illusion, perspective, line and colour.

Once you see him 'doing' a Mondrian or Picasso, you look at their art with a new sense of awareness. But I also have to say that work he did in the two decades before his death in 1997 looks to me like a revisiting of the Pop years. There are successes even towards the end but the extraordinary energy, curiosity and sense of discovery you find in the 1960s and 1970s have gone.

Cy Twombly

Cy Twombly is the odd man out in the great generation of American artists that also includes Jasper Johns and Robert Rauschenberg. Born in Lexington, Virginia in 1928 and educated in the South, he went north to study art before attending Black Mountain College in North Carolina. Coming of age during the high noon of Abstract Expressionism, his early black-and-white paintings are indebted to the art of Franz Kline and Willem De Kooning, but his sculptures look like nothing else in American art at the time.

After a trip to Morocco in 1952 he began to work with found materials, making crude pan pipes by bandaging together pieces of wood with fabric, or an altar decorated with palm leaves mounted on wooden sticks. All his sculptures are painted white so that, for all their simplicity and lightness of touch, they look as though they had been excavated from an Etruscan grave site, or like fragile offerings found in the tomb of an Egyptian pharaoh. It is one of the many strengths of Tate Modern's survey, *Cy Twombly: Cycles and Seasons*, that the curator Nicholas Serota has given so much space to the relatively little-known sculptures, for in them Twombly finds a depth of poetic feeling that exists nowhere else in twentieth-century art.

Seeing the early sculptures near the beginning of this show, you understand at once why Twombly could not have stayed in the US. In 1957, at the very moment when Pop Art and Minimalism would usher in a golden age of American art, Twombly moved to Rome, where he has remained ever since. With hindsight, it is obvious that it was the only city in the world where an artist so temperamentally attuned to the art and poetry of the ancient world could possibly have lived. Like an earlier American expatriate, Ezra Pound, Twombly needed to feed at the source of classical and Renaissance culture – to immerse himself in European art, yet to stand apart in order to make it modern, make it new. What enabled him to do this, I think, was his American identity –

24 June 2008

Cy Twombly:
Cycles and Seasons

Tate Modern, London

the essence of which is detachment from the past.

In *The Italians* of 1959 he uses oil paint, pencil and crayon to capture the chaos, gaiety and unfocused energy of Italian life. As you look at the airy, free-floating composition, your eye moves restlessly from one cluster of visual activity to another, much of it in the form of cartoon-like scrawls of buttocks, breasts and male and female genitals, many of them half-erased or painted over, a palimpsest in which the past, though hidden, is only just beneath the surface. The picture is like a diary in which Twombly evokes his experience of living in the hedonistic city Fellini had just celebrated in *La Dolce Vita*. Whenever I look at it I see Vespas roaring past the Pyramid of Cestius, and rude graffiti chalked on the ruins in the Largo Argentina.

There is no illusion in these early paintings – you can see for yourself exactly how the artist made every mark in them, using a brush, a pencil or paint squeezed straight from the tube. In his homage to Raphael's *School of Athens* he uses pencil to draw the highly structured composition, which is loosely inspired by the architecture in the Renaissance picture. Then he applies squiggles and smears of white, yellow and pink paint like blasts of helium gas to fill the picture with light and make it airborne. In this way, the usually spontaneous act of drawing in pencil becomes the delicate armature that holds the picture together, while the more ponderous medium of oil-based paint is made to look light and impulsive.

Though his calligraphic and episodic style of painting doesn't fundamentally change in these early paintings, the mood of the pictures varies dramatically. Six paintings executed over the stifling hot summer of 1961 make up the series called the *Ferragosto* paintings. In them, fluid smears of purple, pink and magenta gradually turn into impastoed blobs of faecal brown and sanguinary red, which are sometimes slapped on to the canvas with an open palm. These impacted, violent compositions exude heat, frustration and low-down sex. Beauty and filth exist side by side in pictures painted by a man fully in touch with own polymorphous perversity. In them, paint becomes a metaphor for sexual experience, at once violent and tender, exciting, degrading and shameful.

In a New York art world that was attuned to Pop and Minimalism in the Sixties, this kind of thing looked too much like a revival of the emotional excess the now passé Abstract Expressionists had wallowed

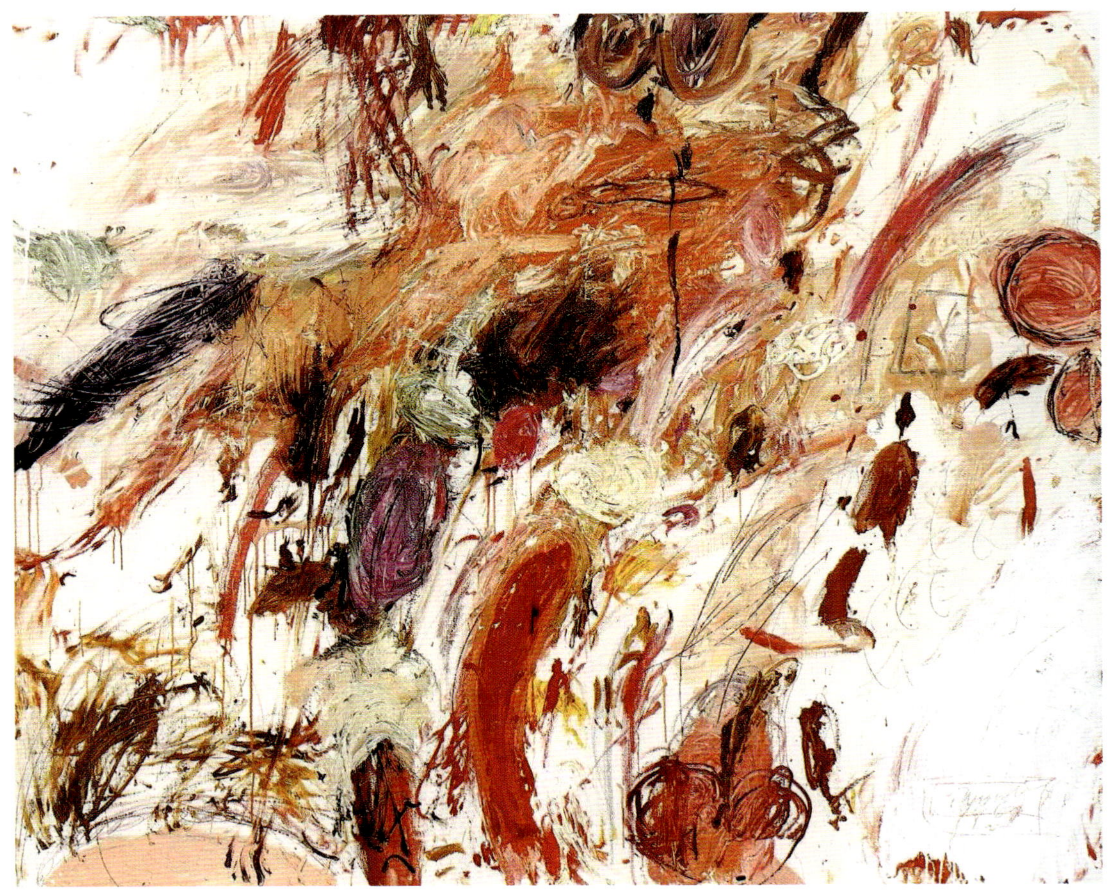

Cy Twombly
***Ferragosto V**, 1961*
Private collection

in. Reacting to this criticism, Twombly reined in his sensuality to create works in which he reduced his paintings to white marks on a grey-black ground, painted with a dragged brush or drawn in white chalk. One of the greatest of these 'blackboard' paintings is the vast *Treatise on the Veil* which was apparently inspired by a photograph by Eadweard Muybridge showing the progress of a veiled bride passing in front of a train. More than anything he had done so far, these works spoke not just of movement but of the evanescence of human experience – what remains when time erases words and images, like film exposed to sunlight.

Close in spirit to the blackboard paintings are Twombly's sublime later sculptures, including a ravishing piece from 1979 made out of the simplest materials to evoke a ghostly barque, which you could imagine carrying Orpheus to the underworld.

Critics have been getting Twombly wrong for sixty years, and I count myself among them. In 1987 he showed a series of dark-green paintings that simply depicted flowing water, like Monet's late waterscapes. When I saw these at the Venice Biennale I found them corny and disliked their lush romanticism and hated their shaped frames, which resembled painted ceilings in Italian baroque palaces. Seeing them again at the Tate in the context of Twombly's entire career, it is clear that they are the culmination of a lifetime's interest in depicting water that began with his series of 24 works on paper, *Poems to the Sea*, in 1959. What's more, the emotion he'd held in check in the blackboard paintings and sculptures suddenly pours out in floods of intense magentas, forest-greens and silvers.

From this point on we can speak of Twombly's late style, which includes the well known *Four Seasons* at Tate Modern, and culminates in his most recent series, a cycle of eight monumentally scaled paintings collectively entitled *Bacchus*. Now great loops of bright crimson paint cover an orange ground in a sort of orgy of visual pleasure and sensual release. Throughout his career there has always been a dialogue in Twombly's art between the Apollonian restraint of the sculptures and blackboard pictures and the Dionysian excess you see in the *Ferragosto* series. These paintings are at once exalted and barbaric, elegant and crude – the summation of a life lived through the senses.

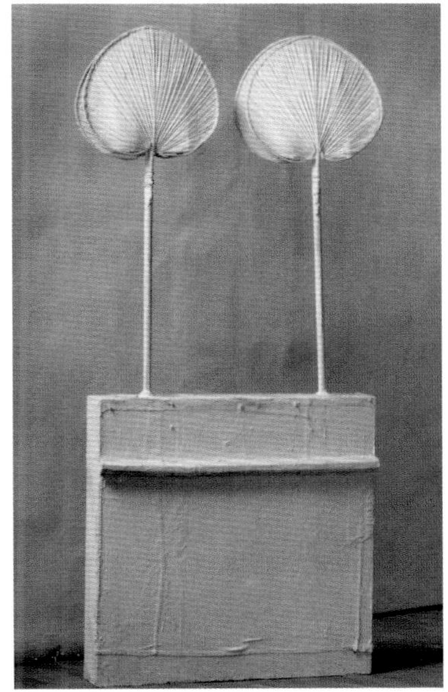

Cy Twombly
Untitled (Funerary Box for a Lime-Green Python), *1954*
Private collection

The Warhol Look: Glamour, Style, Fashion

On the night that Damien Hirst won the Turner Prize in 1995, his companion chose to wear to the Tate a frock printed with a pattern of multicoloured spots inspired by one of the artist's paintings. Only a year or so ago Tracey Emin was an *enfant terrible* of the art world, nowadays she appears in advertisements for a brand of vodka.

Trivial though these details are, they perfectly demonstrate the way the avant-garde has been co-opted by the worlds of fashion and advertising. How can artists be subversive, radical or challenging when the moment they are successful their art is absorbed into mainstream popular culture? For although Marcel Duchamp showed that things taken from the real world have the potential to be turned into art, he didn't foresee that they would not be allowed to remain art for very long.

And for that state of affairs, we have to thank one artist: Andy Warhol. Before Warhol, modern art was unashamedly elitist – it was made to hang in the homes of sophisticated collectors or else on the walls of museums. But the exalted status accorded to art ended in the 1960s, around the time when the all-black paintings of Ad Reinhardt finally brought the modernist tradition to an end on a note of emptiness and despair. More than any other artist of his time, Warhol put life back into art; and by life I mean content, colour, meaning and interest, the things you see not when you look at a black rectangle, but when you look into a mirror.

Everything that passed before Warhol's basilisk gaze – people, pop music, film and fashion – he imprinted with his deadpan mixture of glamour and humour, then cast them back into the world as narcissistic reflections of his own personality. To take just one example, when socialites, drag queens and street hustlers came to call on the artist, they emerged from his aptly named Factory as superstars, parodies of the stars created by the Hollywood studio

10 June 1998

The Warhol Look: Glamour, Style, Fashion

Barbican Art Gallery, London

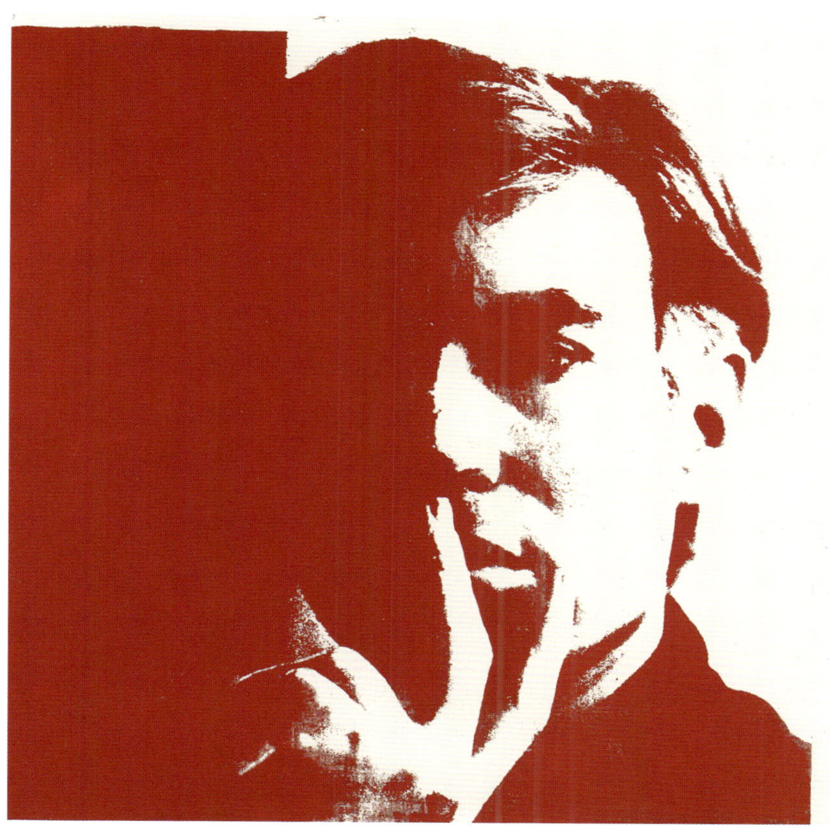

system. Films such as *The Chelsea Girls* (1967) conferred on these sad, beautiful, talentless people artistic immortality.

Fame and fashion are by definition fleeting. One of Warhol's great discoveries was that they are no less worthy of the artist's attention for being ephemeral – indeed, their transience is an intrinsic part of their fascination. In closing the gap between art and fashion, Warhol opened a Pandora's box which has sometimes threatened to bring about the end of art itself. Even while he was transforming Brillo boxes and Campbell's soup cans into high art, he was silkscreening popular logos and trademarks on to fabrics, moving away from the art gallery back into the world of fashion and commerical design. Because of him, we no longer require a work of art to last for ever. While a lot of art (including Warhol's) still ends up in museums, much of it now has a limited lifespan, and is no less entertaining or valuable for that.

Like all great historical changes, it was hard to see what was happening while it was going on. More than a decade after Warhol's death in 1987, the Barbican Art Gallery's exhibition *The Warhol Look: Glamour, Style, Fashion* puts into historical perspective his extraordinary role in the transformation of Western culture. From the beginning, Warhol's was a highly public art, one that criss-crossed between high art, popular culture, commerce and daily life.

Early in his career he created window displays for Bonwit Teller department store using his own paintings, props, lights and objects. Framed as they were behind glass on Fifth Avenue, these can be seen as precursors of installation art. Although their primary purpose was to sell clothes, they gave Warhol far more public exposure than an exhibition at the Museum of Modern Art could ever have done.

Unlike the art then being shown in museums, however, the window displays were temporary. Not even a catalogue recorded their transitory existence. Because he was willing to accept that impermanence, Warhol could bypass critics and curators and appeal directly to a mass audience. This is exactly what fashion designers or film-makers had always done, if only because for them to ignore public taste was to go broke.

And so, in addition to his Brillo boxes and Campbell's soup cans, Warhol began to experiment with forms of communication that had not until then been categorised as art. Warhol himself didn't write the songs or play an instrument in his rock band Velvet Underground, but everything about their act reeked both of elegance and of the twilight world of drugs and sex that surrounded him. The 'look' of Velvet Underground, from the helium-filled silver pillows that floated above the stage to the catatonic stage presence of the singer Nico, was imprinted with Warhol's personality.

It doesn't really matter that all that's left of Velvet Underground are their records. Anyone who saw them play will attest to the powerful visual dimension that their performances had – and that the Rolling Stones, for example, didn't.

It is sometimes held against Warhol that he fed off the creativity of other artists or the beauty of other people. Well, of course he did. Warhol's genius was to bring America's deepest secrets to the surface by putting them under the spotlight of art. In the 1960s he took the American obsession with glamour and celebrity and forced his countrymen to see that these values lay at the very heart of their culture.

Once again, not all of this was obvious at the time. Take the film *Poor Little Rich Girl*, a 40-minute interview with a beautiful but disturbed member of Warhol's factory named Edie Sedgwick. At the time it was made, the film's lack of plot, dialogue and structure looked inept. But, as details of Edie Sedgwick's extraordinary life have since emerged, it has become clear that, like any traditional artist, Warhol was simply making a portrait, rather than telling a story, of a beautiful and tragic young woman. And if you want to gauge the sheer extent of his influence on portraiture, go to the National Portrait Gallery where the portrait of Evelyn Waugh – by far the most compelling portrait of a twentieth-century writer – takes the Warholian form of the constantly replayed tape of his television interview with John Freeman.

The most disturbing section of this show, 'Drag and Transformation', looks at Warhol's obsession with the relationship between identity and appearance. He had himself undergone plastic surgery, always wore a wig to disguise his premature baldness, and held his stomach in with a surgical corset after being shot by Valerie Solanas in 1968. Long before the current generation of artists began to explore how liposuction, plastic surgery and Prozac allow us to alter the bodies and minds we are born with, Warhol saw that this was a great subject for late twentieth-century art, whether in his early painting, *Nose Job*, or in the late videos of himself in drag.

It is a weakness of this endlessly fascinating show that it all but ignores the role of drugs in Warhol's life, but I suppose that with so much art and social history to cover the organisers couldn't explore every aspect of this extraordinary man.

Andy Warhol: *Outer and Inner Space*

Any attempt to list the most important artists of the first half of the twentieth century would start with the names of Picasso, Duchamp and Pollock. But, when you try the same exercise for the second half of the century, the picture isn't nearly as clear. I suppose Joseph Beuys, Jasper Johns and Richard Serra are all possibilities, but, in terms of the range, depth and variety of his work, one artist emerges head and shoulders above all his contemporaries – Andy Warhol.

For some reason, this surprises people. Perhaps it was the silver wig, or the deadpan humour or the obsession with celebrity, but the idea persists that Warhol was somehow a lightweight. In fact, everything he touched – from portraiture and printmaking to magazine publishing, filmmaking and set design – bore the stamp of his genius. Fourteen years after his death, we are only just beginning to grasp the full range of his activities. Like Picasso, he seemed to have an intuitive command of whatever medium he chose to work with and a compulsion to explore that medium until he had exhausted it.

Outer and Inner Space, a 16mm black-and-white film made in the summer of 1965, demonstrates my point. Virtually forgotten until recent years, this milestone in twentieth-century art is being shown at the ICA this summer. It consists of a monologue by the most charismatic of Warhol's superstars, the twenty-two-year-old Edie Sedgwick, who appears 'live' twice – once on either side of a dual screen. With her short, blonde hair and huge dangling earrings, she is the epitome of Sixties glamour. The film opens with Edie in mid-sentence. Her face turned to the camera, she is talking non-stop to someone off screen, presumably Warhol himself.

But there is another Edie in the film, a ghostly *doppelgänger*, whom we can see on a TV monitor behind her. This Edie appears on pre-recorded videotape, her head shown in profile and looking slightly

8 August 2001

Outer and Inner Space

ICA, London

upwards. Once more, she is talking to someone out of our range of vision. The quality of the film is grainy, the lighting harsh, and the soundtrack so dodgy that we pick up only bits and pieces of what Edie is saying ('Oh, what a waste!' 'I can't remember.' 'That's absurd! Do people really do things like that?'). And yet Edie's incandescent beauty and enchanting personality hold us mesmerised for the 33 minutes of the film. When Warhol dubbed her a superstar, he knew what he was doing. Her gaiety and charm, her dumb-blonde chatter, infectious laugh and self-deprecating clowning combine sensuality with a quality very close to innocence. She was Warhol's answer to Marilyn Monroe.

And like Monroe, Edie was frighteningly vulnerable, a borderline psychotic whom the film shows near the end of her short life. As she smokes cigarette after cigarette, sometimes chewing gum at the same time, you begin to realise that Warhol is using the camera to probe the manic, desperate quality underneath her apparent vivaciousness.

At one moment, for example, the camera zooms in for a close-up of the face on the TV monitor, so that Edie's alter ego becomes as big as her 'real' face in the foreground. At the same time, Warhol turns up the volume of the soundtrack on the TV monitor so that the voice on the videotape drowns out Edie's own voice. This flusters Edie, who turns to look over her shoulder, momentarily distracted by her own image. Then she continues her chatter, as though determined to ignore her other 'self'. But the real woman has been reduced to silence; the false one on the TV screen takes over. This must be what happens to certain celebrities when the glamorous images they see of themselves on screen or in photographs begin to feel more authentic than the self they know in their everyday lives.

What Warhol is doing here is remarkably similar to what Picasso did in those images of women in which the subject's face is shown twice within the same head, once in profile and again full face. Both artists are suggesting that the sitter's personality is split between an outer (social) self and hidden, inner (private) self. Since Warhol shows Edie's face four times in one work, you could justifiably describe the film as 'Cubist'. Remember, too, that in addition to being a film star Edie was Warhol's model and muse.

I've often imagined that the atmosphere in Warhol's New York studio, the Factory, must have been a bit like that in Picasso's studio

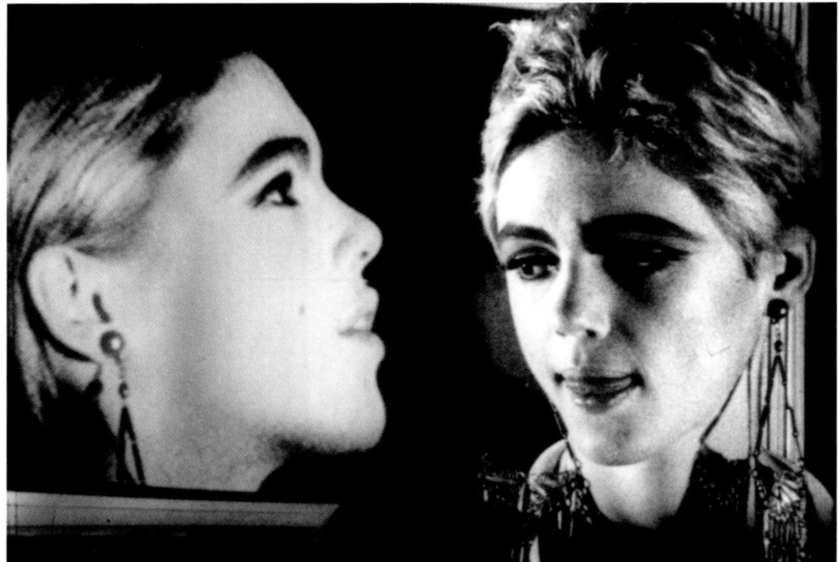

complex, the Bateau Lavoir in turn-of-the-century Paris. For Warhol drew on his entourage of beauties and eccentrics, art dealers, drug dealers and conmen for inspiration in much the same way that Picasso did. In his reliance on the living model, Warhol was unlike any other artist of his generation.

With hindsight, *Outer and Inner Space* is even more powerful today than it was to those who first saw it. We now know that Sedgwick was soon to go into a mental hospital and would eventually take her own life. Warhol certainly realised how disturbed this young woman was, and throughout the film one of his assistants fiddles with the knobs on the TV monitor to create visual effects that would mimic the mental turmoil underneath her chitter-chatter.

When, late in the film, the profile on the TV monitor begins to 'roll' alarmingly, and then fades to a ghost before blinking out altogether, this is Warhol's way of indicating the disintegration of a personality before our very eyes. Only at the end of the film did it finally dawn on me that Sedgwick's gaiety was in all probability drug-induced. When the film ran out, the lights went down and the amphetamines wore off, she would crash into an abyss of black depression.

With *Outer and Inner Space*, the ICA is showing Warhol's 'Screen Tests', a series of eighteen very short films, in which Warhol asked friends and hangers-on to sit in front of a camera for a few minutes. As the camera rolls and the minutes tick away, each subject gradually

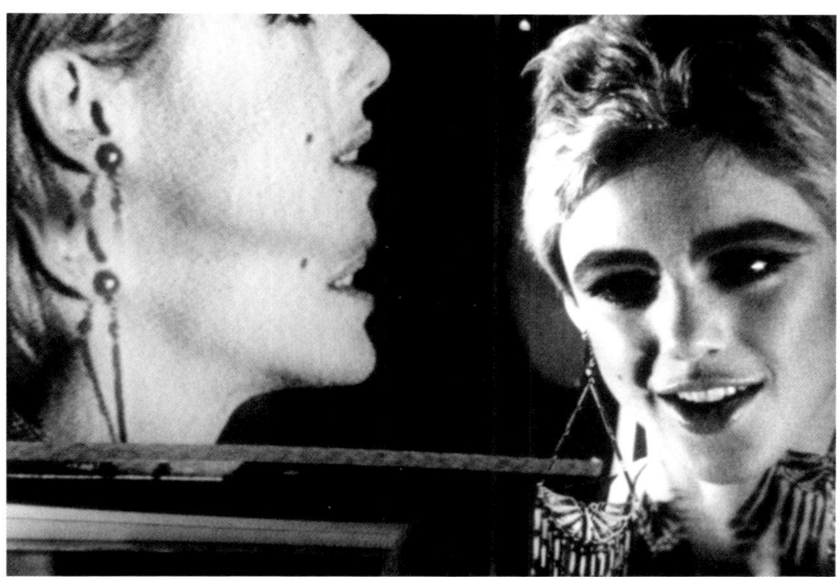

reveals his or her personality to the artist. One young man – furtive, bored, insolent – simply can't look at the camera straight on. Others preen, flaunt or sit there without moving a muscle.

After 'Screen Tests', traditional portraiture would always look limited, because it has the ability to capture only one mood, one expression and one aspect of the sitter's character. Because Warhol uses the camera as a neutral recording instrument and not for editing or creating a composition, he does not impose his own feelings or thoughts on his subjects.

Both works deserve to be seen by as many people as possible. But what do the idiots who install the shows at the ICA think they are doing here? Not only is 'Screen Tests' a silent movie, it is one in which silence is integral to what is happening on screen. For it is that uncomfortable empty space created by the combination of silence and the recording eye of the camera that the subjects are trying to fill in any way they know how. The film is utterly spoiled by being shown next door to the distracting soundtrack of *Outer and Inner Space*.

One last thing. Some of Warhol's early films (*Sleep, Empire*) are both interminable and unwatchable. Because they are shot in a loop anyway, you can look at them for a few minutes, get the idea and then leave. But you can't do that with these films. You simply have to sit down and watch them straight through from beginning to end, or you miss their point.

Jasper Johns

'Impersonal', 'detached', 'neutral' – when we use these words to describe the art of Jasper Johns, we are thinking of the early pictures of maps, targets, flags and numbers. *Past Things and Present: Jasper Johns since 1983* at the Scottish National Museum of Modern Art in Edinburgh undermines the usual minimalist reading of the American's work, forcing us to re-evaluate our received ideas about the nature of his art.

If the paintings, drawings and prints of the past two decades are often baffling, that is because their imagery is highly personal. These pictures need to be interpreted because they describe the way Johns's mind works, the thought process itself. You come away from the show realising that no artist of the last century has more poignantly or more consistently tried to tell us who he is than Jasper Johns.

Here is an example of what I mean. In about 1995, Johns based a series of pictures on a twelve-year-old schizophrenic's drawing of her mother, who had died when the child was two. This extraordinary image shows the mother though the eyes of the disturbed child, who drew eyes and breasts in each of the four corners of the blank page, with a mouth and nose in the centre.

As discussed by psychoanalyst Bruno Bettelheim in the essay in which Johns found this image, the drawing shows how, when sucking at the breast, the infant apprehends the mother not as a whole person but as two breasts and two eyes split off from the rest of the body. As though in sympathy with the child's skewed interpretation of reality, in Johns's paintings and prints based on the image by the disturbed girl, he places two enormous eyes and a pursed mouth at the edge of our field of vision, where they surround his copy of the drawing.

The question we ask ourselves is why Johns was particularly attracted to this strange, unsettling image. When we do, we discover something surprising: that within the context of Johns's work, the

4 August 2004

Past Things and Present: Jasper Johns since 1983

Scottish National Museum of Modern Art, Edinburgh

image isn't so unusual at all; he has been using drawings and casts of detached body parts right from the beginning of his career.

In the famous *Target with Plaster Casts* (1958), for example, he arranged three-dimensional casts of different parts of the male anatomy in a row of boxes above a painted target. Just as in the schizophrenic's drawing, Johns's fragmented image of an adult man omits the body that would connect the different sensory and sexual organs and so render the person whole. I suggest that in both works – from the '50s and the '90s – Johns obliquely alludes to his deepest and most protected feelings, a sense that people are real and lovable only in parts.

The human body has been a consistent theme throughout Johns's career, both through its presence and in its absence. *Ventriloquist* (1983) is set in the bathroom of the artist's house, as we can see from the painted bath taps in the lower right-hand corner. At first, we see no human figure in the picture. Then we realise that the artist himself is present by implication, lying naked in his bath, thinking about the things he can see in his field of vision: a framed print by his friend Barnett Newman, one of his own prints (a double American flag in orange and black), pots by the visionary American ceramicist George Orr, and an illustration from *Moby-Dick* showing the great whale. A *trompe l'oeil* nail appears in homage to the nineteenth-century American still life painters John F. Peto and William Michael Harnett.

The title *Ventriloquist* suggests that the artist is like a man who can throw his voice, make it appear to come from inanimate things. Each of the separate elements in the still life on the wall 'speaks' for the artist in the sense that each has personal meaning for him. And, as so often in his work, what is not there is as important as what is. Were any of us to give visual form to our thoughts as Johns does here, we'd probably include photos or memorabilia connected with parents, children and partners. There is something faintly melancholy about their total absence here.

Two details help us to understand how Johns's mind works. The first is the white vase above the wicker hamper at the lower right. This is one of those visual jokes that Johns loves because it demonstrates the unreliability both of the mind and of the eye in determining reality. When our eyes focus on the outline of the vase, the silhouetted portraits of the Queen and Prince Philip become visible. For Johns,

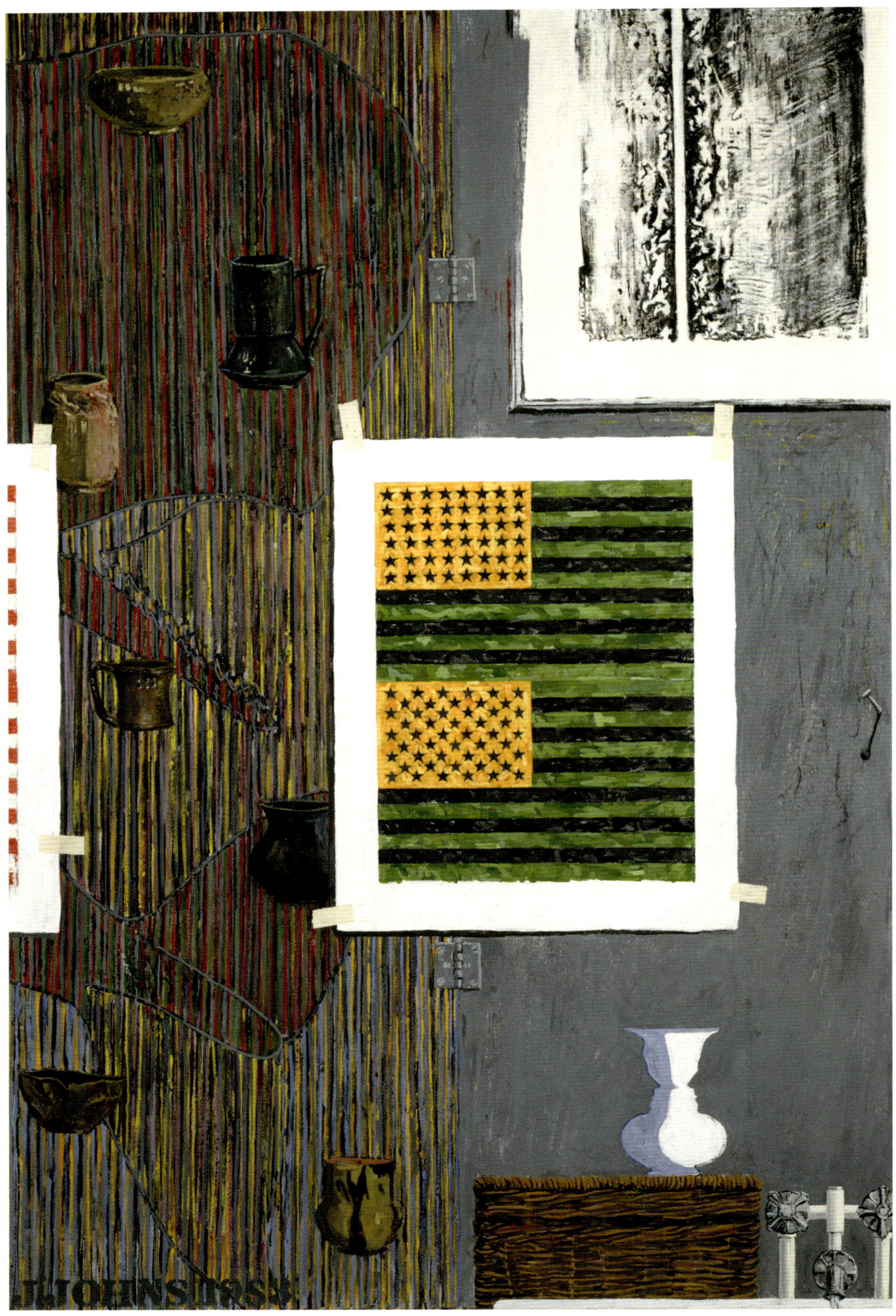

day-dreaming in his bath, the now-you-see-it-now-you-don't illusion replicates the way we see and think, for a thought or an image can be held in the mind for only an instant before disappearing, and what is not there (the portraits) is as real as what is (the vase).

Now look at the two *trompe l'oeil* hinges that 'join' the two sides of a canvas divided vertically in half. They turn the painting into a notional diptych, reiterating the theme of splitting or division (between body and mind, sight and thought, the real and the imaginary) that runs consistently through Johns's work.

The beautiful *Winter* from the series of *The Four Seasons*, for example, is also a diptych. In it, Johns paints two self-portraits, both oblique. In one, the artist's shadow falling over the right side of the canvas stands in for his body, while on the left side he symbolises the things of the mind by painting an inventory of objects and artworks piled up in his studio. But the two sides remain separate. 'Only connect,' said E. M. Forster. To connect is precisely what Johns in these paintings can't seem to do.

Before you accuse me of gratuitous psychobabble, look at the new and surprising imagery that has entered Johns's paintings, drawings and prints in recent years. In a group of works from 1997 called the *Catenary* series, he shows a flexible cord hung loosely from two fixed points to make a curve. Engineers use catenary curves when designing suspension bridges, but for Johns the curve becomes a symbol for joining things that time and memory have separated. In the Catenary pictures, the imagery becomes surprisingly, embarrassingly intimate. In some, he paints the pattern of a clown costume he wore as a little boy, a photograph showing his grandparents with their young family in 1904, a fragment of the American flag, and a representation of the universe – all 'connected' by a catenary curve.

I've only skimmed the surface of this dense, slow-moving show. From what I've written, you'd never guess at the grave, melancholy beauty of so many of the works on view, or at the exuberant calypso colours of cockatoo green, red and yellow in pictures painted on the Caribbean island of St Martin. Believe me, you can go to this show without attempting to interpret the pictures and you will still come away besotted with the textures, images and colours of Johns's wonderful paintings.

Brice Marden

I well remember how shocked I was when I first saw the American artist Brice Marden's *Cold Mountain* series in, I suppose, the early Nineties. In the Sixties and Seventies, Marden had become known for painting severe monochromatic rectangles in a medium composed of oil and wax. Human in scale, and irradiated by Marden's ultra-refined colour combinations, his mute, beautiful canvases made other art of the period look loquacious, vulgar. Then, in the *Cold Mountain* paintings, he introduced all the things that the minimalist work had rejected: line, brushwork, atmosphere, space and depth. It was as though he had taken a can-opener to the closed, impenetrable surface of the earlier works to allow deep draughts of air, movement and light to blow through his art.

What it took some time for me to realise was that the discipline and restraint on which Marden's whole aesthetic project had been based had not disappeared, just taken a new direction. Take, for example, *Cold Mountain 2*, on view in the Serpentine Gallery's new exhibition of Marden's recent work. It is inspired by Japanese and Chinese calligraphy, and elegant skeins of dark-grey paint have been laid over a network of opaque green and light-blue lines to form vertical 'columns'. The eye instinctively moves down and across the picture surface, trying to 'read' the abstract brushstrokes as though they were written characters. Only then do we discover the painting's unexpected depth, for the lighter and thinner lines register as being further away than those that are darker and thicker.

And, as though all this weren't complex enough, you can sense Marden's own presence in the canvas in the way that pigment is applied with loose arm and wrist movements, the brush travelling lightly and rhythmically over a grey ground filled with erasures and pentimenti (evidence of an artist's change of mind in a painting). Nothing feels fixed, nothing static. Shapes constantly dissolve and

15 November 2000

Brice Marden

Serpentine Gallery, London

merge into new forms, even as our eye tries to pin them down, creating a palimpsest.

Cold Mountain 2 was painted more than ten years ago, so now is an excellent moment for the Serpentine to mount a show of twenty-eight paintings and drawings, executed over the past decade. Broadly, the main thing that has happened in Marden's work in this time is the ever-more apparent presence of the figure. Whereas the pictures in the *Cold Mountain* series were fundamentally landscapes, in paintings such as 1990's *Kalo Keri* (meaning good season, or summer, in Greek), ordered rows of calligraphic shapes have given way to more loosely structured, looping lines of blue, orange, yellow and white.

Though we first see the canvas as wholly abstract, when we step back from the painting and our eye picks out and begins to follow the blue lines, we soon sense the presence of two vertical figures, one on each side of the canvas, connected by areas of yellow and orange between them. Then, looking again, we find that we may be mistaken: in fact, it is the yellow/orange lines that form the figure – a vaguely female shape, like Venus emerging from the sea, perhaps attended by two flanking figures. But when we try to hold on to any of these figures, they disappear, lost again in the tangled web in which they are embedded. Eternally frustrated, we find ourselves again moving close to the picture surface. And when we do, we discover how rich and complicated the painting technique is, with one colour scumbled into another, as in an Old Master painting.

The effect is similar in a slightly later canvas called *The Sisters*, in which the two large figural shapes – one in plum, the other in deep blue – are entwined against a brilliant yellow background. In all these pictures Marden allows us to participate in his creative process by leaving evidence in the brushstrokes themselves of his struggle to balance line and colour, spontaneity and control. Look for a few minutes, and you feel you could look for ever.

The masterpiece of this period is *The Muses* (1991–93), for me one of the most beautiful pictures in post-war American art. In a 15-foot-long horizontal frieze, tendril-like coils of dark green, chartreuse and light violet appear to move across a background of the lightest possible green to evoke the procession of the nine daughters of Zeus, as they might be carved on the pediment of a Greek temple. At once landscape and figure subject, in *The Muses* the goddesses are not

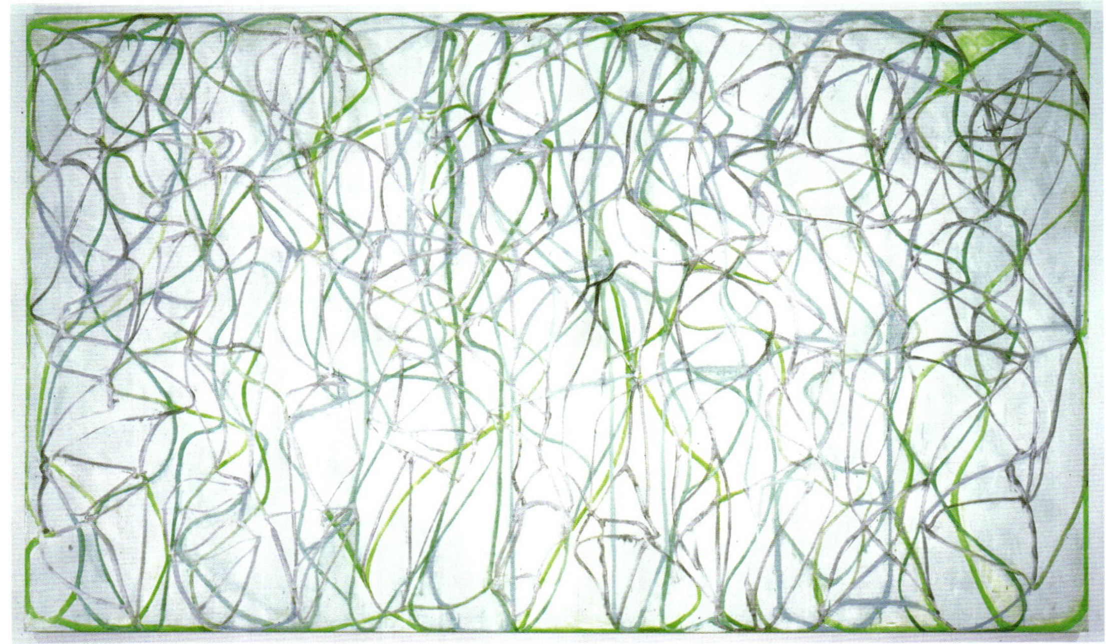

visible exactly, but miraculously present, immanent, all-pervading.
When you realise that the figures are the landscape you understand
why, almost as soon as you sense their presence, they disappear. This,
surely, is the way the gods would have materialised to the Ancient
Greeks. And this too is the way that artistic inspiration, which is the
gift of the Muses, can arise and evaporate in a twinkling, like the
deities themselves beyond mortal control.

Formally, the obvious comparison is to Jackson Pollock's 19-foot-
long canvas of 1943–44, *Mural*. Neither artist ever allows our eye to
rest, with every centimetre of the canvas charged with energy. But the
differences are telling as well. Pollock used pain aggressively, flinging
it at the canvas until he had almost obliterated the underlying
figurative imagery. Marden too is able to contact something elemental
and dangerous within himself, but then contains it and uses it to
create patterns of lyrical beauty.

In his most recent body of work, six paintings called *Attendants*
(exhibited for the first time in this show), it is as though the figures
latent in earlier works have at last fully materialised. Now Marden,
just into his sixties, not only leaves us with fully recognisable forms,
but, by using lines of equal thickness, minimises depth and allows us

Brice Marden
The Muses, *1991–93*
Museum of Modern
Art, New York

to follow the order in which he laid each layer of paint on the canvas. Inspired by tomb figures of the Han Dynasty (206 BC–220 AD), each painting shows a servant to the emperor crouching, sitting or kneeling. The snaking lines of deep, throbbing red, hot orange, green and turquoise fill each canvas, as though the figures were hemmed in, entombed within the dark-grey ground.

These are slow pictures, easy to follow, leaving you plenty of time to discover the inexhaustible richness of Marden's painting technique. At the same time, it is as though the artist has begun a return journey to a simpler, more minimal aesthetic, one that may end up closer to the art of the Sixties than to the mid-Nineties. But, whatever happens next, his work offers a quality that has become very rare in modern art: in the words of one recent commentator, 'a truly profound aesthetic experience'.

Richard Serra
*Detail of **Weight and Measure** at the Tate Gallery, London, 1992*

Richard Serra

The San Francisco-born sculptor Richard Serra once recounted a childhood memory that explains a lot about the work he does now. On his fourth birthday he was taken by his father, a pipe fitter in a shipyard, to watch the launching of a ship. Crossing the Golden Gate Bridge, they reached the dockyards, where the awesome sight of the new tanker's hull loomed up in front of the little boy – a gigantic steel-plated arc as tall as a skyscraper, obliterating everything else. Then suddenly, while the crowds cheered, whistles shrieked and horns tooted, the cables holding the ship on its track were released, ripping the scaffolding apart. Slowly the ship slipped down its chute to the sea, sliding off its cradle, picking up momentum until – terrifyingly – it 'swayed, tipped, bounced into the sea, half submerged, to then raise and lift itself and find its balance'. As a sculptor, Serra could be said to re-live that memory over and over in his work. 'My awe and wonder of that moment remained. All the raw material that I needed is contained in the reserve of this memory which has become a recurring dream.' Like his father, Serra welds, rivets and casts enormously heavy slices of steel which cut through and disrupt tranquil space.

He recreates – in galleries and public spaces – the abstract equivalent of his four-year-old's eye-view of that vast, unexpected ship's hull. His is a belligerent, confrontational art – an art you can't ignore, that won't fade politely into the background. Serra's work is very beautiful, but its beauty is of the sort eighteenth-century theorists categorised as the 'sublime'. Even as we react to its scale and proportions, our response is edged with fear. We step back from the towering steel girders of his *Fulcrum*, erected in London's Broadgate development in 1987, just as we instinctively back away from a derrick or a crane on a building site. The viewer hesitates to approach too close to the four heavy steel plates that make up *One Ton Prop (House of Cards)* because they look as though they might collapse in on themselves and seriously hurt somebody.

21 October 1992

Richard Serra:
Weight and Measure

Tate Gallery, London

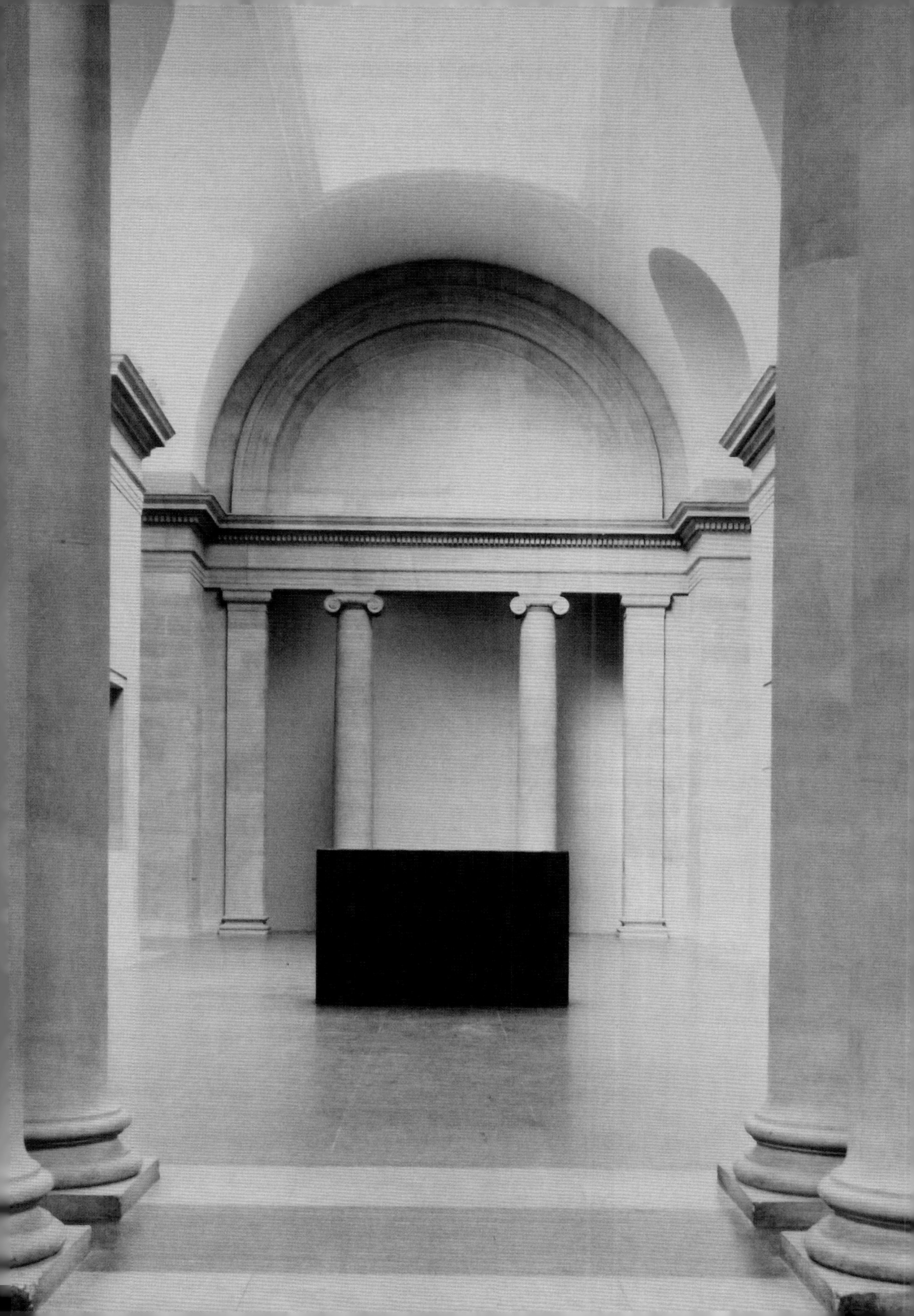

In one of the most memorable of his works the artist violently flings hot molten lead against the gallery wall and floor. The splatter at the moment of impact cools and then solidifies into permanent form. In the poster showing Serra actually hurling the poisonous hot lead against the gallery floor, he wears a heavy protective industrial mask, emphasising the danger in which the artist places himself.

For many people Serra is the foremost living sculptor. The decision of the Tate Gallery to invite him to use the central spine of the Duveen Galleries to create a work of art was therefore not in itself particularly adventurous. But it took courage perhaps to accept and install the work he actually made, *Weight and Measure*. This consists of nothing more elaborate than two forged steel rectangles, each carefully placed at intervals on the gallery floor, leaving the central octagon empty. As the title tells us, the work is as much about weight as it is about measurement. Each rectangle weighs between 35 and 40 tons, so that its density becomes an element in the sculpture as real and measurable as colour or scale or texture would be in another work of art. Had Serra miscalculated and made the two rectangles too small, the piece would not stand up to the surrounding space; had he made them too big he would relegate them to the category of *objet d'art*. But *Weight and Measure* works. Its drama is contained not so much in the massive rectangles as in the surrounding space they displace – just as the launched ship displaces water when it slips into the sea. *Weight and Measure* could also be likened to a black hole in outer space. Vampire-like, it seems to suck all the surrounding space into itself, apparently drawing its immense weight and density from the vacuum around it, and incidentally making the pompous surrounding architecture seem lighter and purer than we've ever seen it.

So powerful is the result that it has had a negative effect on the rest of the Tate's collection, making it all seem fussy, over-elaborate, concerned with the emotional and ephemeral instead of the pure and eternal. In saying this I am pin-pointing the underlying aggression in Serra's aesthetic. Abhorring anything picturesque or decorative, his art demands a lot of his audience. Human beings seem only to get in the way of this sculpture, which almost ceases to exist if there are too many spectators milling around the Duveen Galleries, rather in the way that the Parthenon is ruined when seen at high noon crawling with tourists. Ideally one should arrive at the Tate at the time of opening to see the work in pristine viewing conditions.

Susan Hiller

12 May 2004

Susan Hiller:
Selected Works
1969–2004

Baltic, Gateshead

9 February 2011

Susan Hiller

Tate Britain, London

Susan Hiller does it big or she doesn't do it at all. Her retrospective at Tate Britain charts a career that burned for two decades on a long slow fuse without going anywhere in particular. Then, in the series of ambitious multimedia installations for which she is now famous, she began to look at areas of human experience that had rarely been explored in art before. Now over seventy and one of our most influential artists, she could easily take on the commission for Tate Modern's Turbine Hall, but I still can't imagine her having a show in Cork Street.

Hiller came to London from the US in the early 1970s. I don't want to dismiss the work she did during her first decade here, but neither do I want to linger on it. The text- and photo-based pieces you encounter at the beginning of the show are much more interesting after you've seen the installations she was to make thirty years later. That is because in early pieces exploring dream-states, unconscious thoughts and automatic writing, Hiller wasn't so much looking for her voice as finding her wavelength. That's the right word to describe her developing interest in unseen realms of human experience – things you can't see, touch or measure and yet know to be real.

The breakthrough came with *Monument* in 1980, her meditation on the meaning of the commemorative plaques in Postman's Park in London. Created by the visionary Victorian artist G. F. Watts to call attention to acts of 'heroic self-sacrifice' in everyday life, each memorial briefly recounts the story of a man, woman or child who gave their life attempting to save another person from drowning, a fire, a runaway horse or an oncoming train.

In a tape recording we listen to while seated in front of enlarged photographs of forty-one memorial plaques, Hiller speaks movingly of how these terse inscriptions can be experienced as channels through which the dead live on in our imaginations.

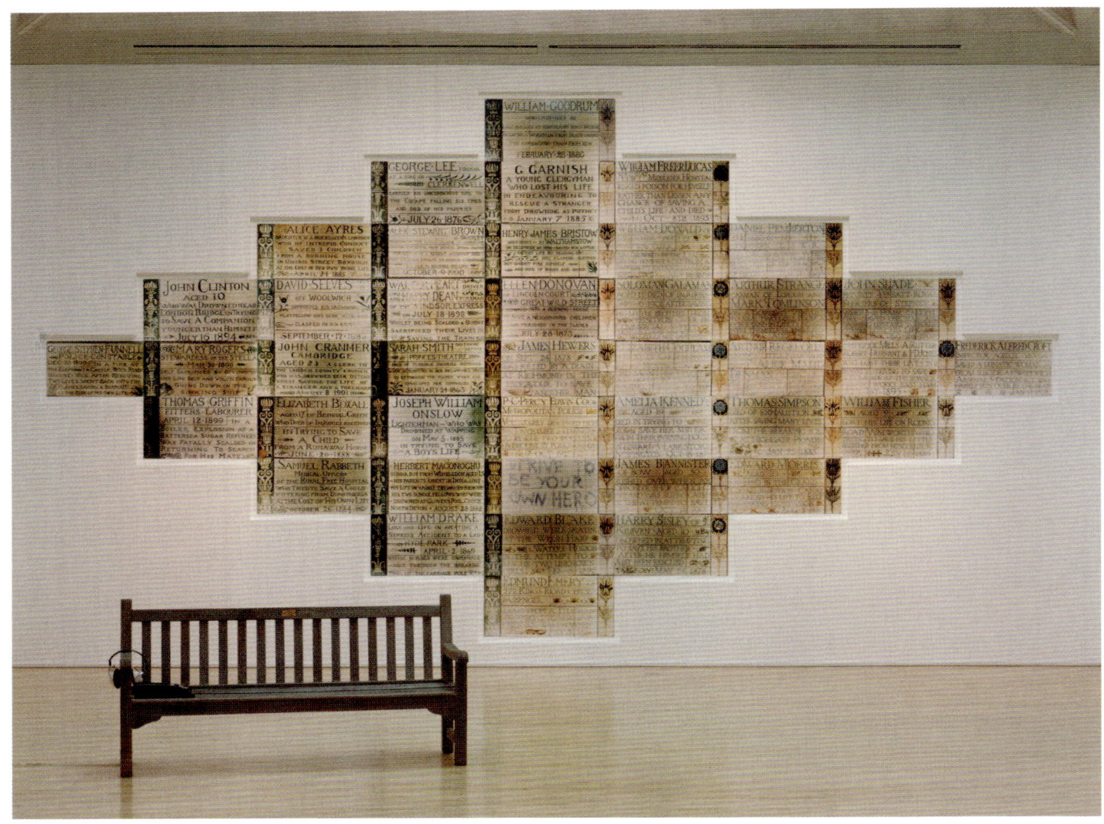

Here, for the first time, Hiller states the great theme that underlies all her mature work: the deep human need to be held in the memories of others. If, ultimately, *Monument* fails, it is because in taking on the role of commentator, Hiller interprets the meaning of the memorial for us. What she needed to do was to find a way to step back from her own work, to place nothing between her audiences and the 'voices' she wants us to hear. Only then can we confront the universal fear of our own extinction. But to achieve this, she first has to locate that fear in our collective unconscious – and then make it audible as well as visible.

It took another ten years, but when it happened it was in one of the most upsetting works of art I've ever seen. I still remember the moment in 1990 when, completely unprepared for what I was about to see, I stepped into the exhibition space where Susan Hiller's nineteen-minute DVD installation *An Entertainment* was being shown. Within a few seconds, it felt as though I'd been pinned to the wall, unsure

Susan Hiller
Monument, *1980*
Tate Gallery, London

of how to respond to a work of art this harsh, this brutal and this
unrelenting.

To make *An Entertainment* the artist travelled to seaside towns
throughout the British Isles, filming and recording Punch and Judy
shows. Back in her studio, she deftly edited out the narrative
elements, and then spliced together the fights, murders and
executions to make a filmic collage of the most gruesome scenes from
the different productions she'd seen. From the moment the curtain
rises on *An Entertainment* a screeching Mr Punch pummels Judy,
beats her with his club, tosses Baby into the air, and goes to the
gallows for his crimes. The giant puppets are projected on to the
full height of two walls on opposite sides of the gallery. Because the
projections are slightly out of synch, everything that happens on
one wall happens a few seconds later across the gallery, doubling the
impact of word and image. We viewers become like small children
watching non-stop altercations between angry adults. Caught in the
middle, we turn our heads from left to right as though watching Mum
and Dad trade blows and insults.

Almost as soon as the well-loved cast of characters make their first
appearance, the screams are so loud we want to stop our ears. Because
the sound quality is not good and it is important to Hiller that we hear
every word of the dialogue, we also hear Hiller's calm voice repeating
the words after each verbal exchange, like a police officer reading
the transcript of the interrogation of a witness at a murder trial. Words
are repeated not once or twice but many times, so that, after Punch
throws sleeping Baby against a wall, Judy's high-pitched hand-
wringing begins to sound like a mantra. 'Oh, What a Pity, What
a Pity, What a Pity!' or 'Wicked! Wicked! Wicked!'

After each act of violence, the soundtrack picks up the squeals and
laughter of the children in the audience, who are of course delighted
by the cruelties of psychotic Mr Punch. And had we been present at
just one of these performances, we too would have been amused. It is
the cumulative effect Hiller achieves by excerpting the most extreme
moments from many separate performances that is so distressing.
For it doesn't take long to realise that a Punch and Judy show is a kind
of public enactment of things that go on behind closed doors every
day, in towns throughout the country – wife beating, child abuse
and infanticide. By removing the humour from Punch and Judy and

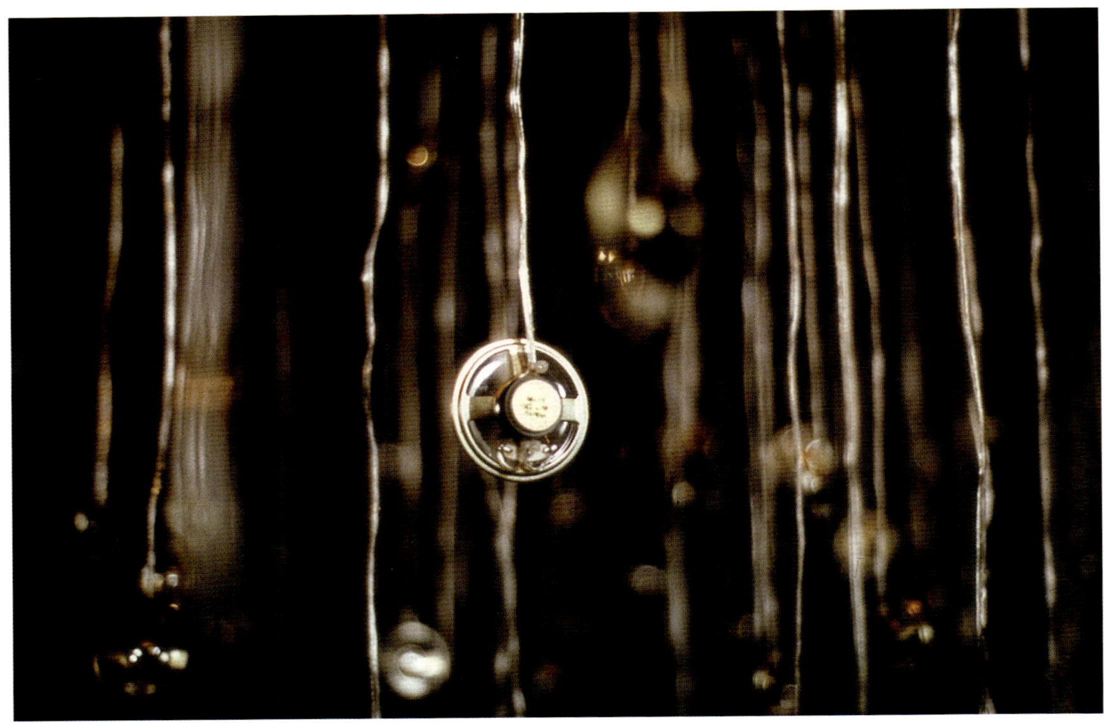

concentrating on the violence, Hiller shows us that what happens in the play is not so very far from things that we read about in the papers every day – things we know happen but pretend we don't until we read about cases like Victoria Climbié or Baby Peter.

Children love these entertainments because they can watch from a safe distance as the puppets act out the deepest fear of all – that Dad will kill Mum and then come after me. I suppose a psychoanalyst would say that such entertainments are projections of thoughts and feelings that we don't know what to do with and have to put somewhere safe like a book or a play.

To see Hiller's breathtakingly beautiful 2000 installation *Witness* the viewer enters a darkened gallery in which six hundred circular microphones dangle from wires attached to the ceiling. Place a microphone to your ear and you'll hear a muffled voice speaking in English, French, Russian, German, Japanese or Swedish, each telling his or her story of an encounter with an alien being or UFO. All speak in matter-of-fact, earnest voices that blend into a soft babble rippling through the galley. Then, suddenly, all quieten down as one voice rises above the din to tell us what must have been the single most

Susan Hiller
Witness, *2000*
Tate Gallery, London

memorable experience of their life. The speakers appear sane and we listeners have no reason to suppose they are lying. And yet what they are saying cannot possibly be true.

So what are these stories? Fact? Fantasy? Psychiatric disorder? When I reviewed *Witness* eleven years ago, I concluded that the answer is 'art'. Hiller's true subject was the human need to tell stories, to hold a listener spellbound and in doing so to join hands with Homer or the Brothers Grimm. This time I saw something else – that the work is also about listening. Whether or not the storyteller is telling you a verifiable fact, he or she is always telling you something about himself – that he or she is unable to bear the thought that when they die, there will be no memory of them. So powerful is the need to live on that the unconscious takes over and convinces the storyteller that what he saw in his imagination is actually true. Hiller asks us to pay attention to stories that are usually consigned to mouldering police reports or the pages of the tabloids and to respect them for what they are: a means to eternal life.

A darkened gallery; a black screen; the voice of an unseen man or woman speaking in an unintelligible language: *The Last Silent Movie* (2007) takes the theme of extinction and memory and what remains of us when we die to its logical conclusion. For what we are listening to are the last speakers of extinct or endangered languages. Hiller found their voices in archives and libraries and had their words translated into English. As they speak their words appear on screen. A few seconds later, we hear an English speaker repeating their words. It takes a moment to grasp the strangeness of the experience. For as we stare into the darkness, we listen to the voices of the dead speaking languages that are also dead. What must these people have felt as they spoke these words for the last time, knowing their language would die with them? The moral beauty I find in these works sends a shiver down my spine. How appropriate that through them she will live forever.

Bruce Nauman

Although Bruce Nauman has been the presiding genius of American art for almost two decades, a show of his neon and video work isn't something you'd want people to stumble upon unprepared. Perhaps that is why Nauman's 1985 audio-visual installation *Good Boy, Bad Boy* is being shown in the entrance foyer of the Hayward Gallery, to accompany his latest exhibition. It is as though the organisers had decided to give visitors a taste of the complexity and ferocity of Nauman's art – and a chance to turn back while they still can.

It consists of two separate TV monitors placed side by side. On the first a young black man appears, on the second a middle-aged white woman. Both are well dressed and agreeable-looking. Looking us directly in the eye, they start to recite a series of simple declarative sentences: 'I was a good boy. You were a good boy. We were good boys. He was good. / I was a bad boy. You were a bad boy. We were bad boys. He was bad.' When they have said a hundred simple phrases using verbs such as 'to be' or 'to like' followed by a simple adjective or verb such as 'good', 'alive', 'work' or 'play', they start again, until they have recited the whole sequence five times. Though they begin together, they soon fall slightly out of synch, so that they never quite speak in unison.

In the first recital, their voices are studiously neutral. The second time through, though, they emphasise and draw out certain words, 'I like to sleep' or 'You are alive'. This makes the sentences sound syrupy, as though the man and woman are desperate to persuade us that they sincerely mean what they say. But getting no reaction either from us or from each other, with each repetition of the sequence, frustration and anger creep into their voices.

As we watch, kindness turns imperceptibly into irritation, and then into pathological hatred. By the end, they are shrieking at the monitor: 'I am alive! You are alive! This is life!' / 'I play. You play. This is play!'

22 July 1998

Bruce Nauman

Hayward Gallery, London

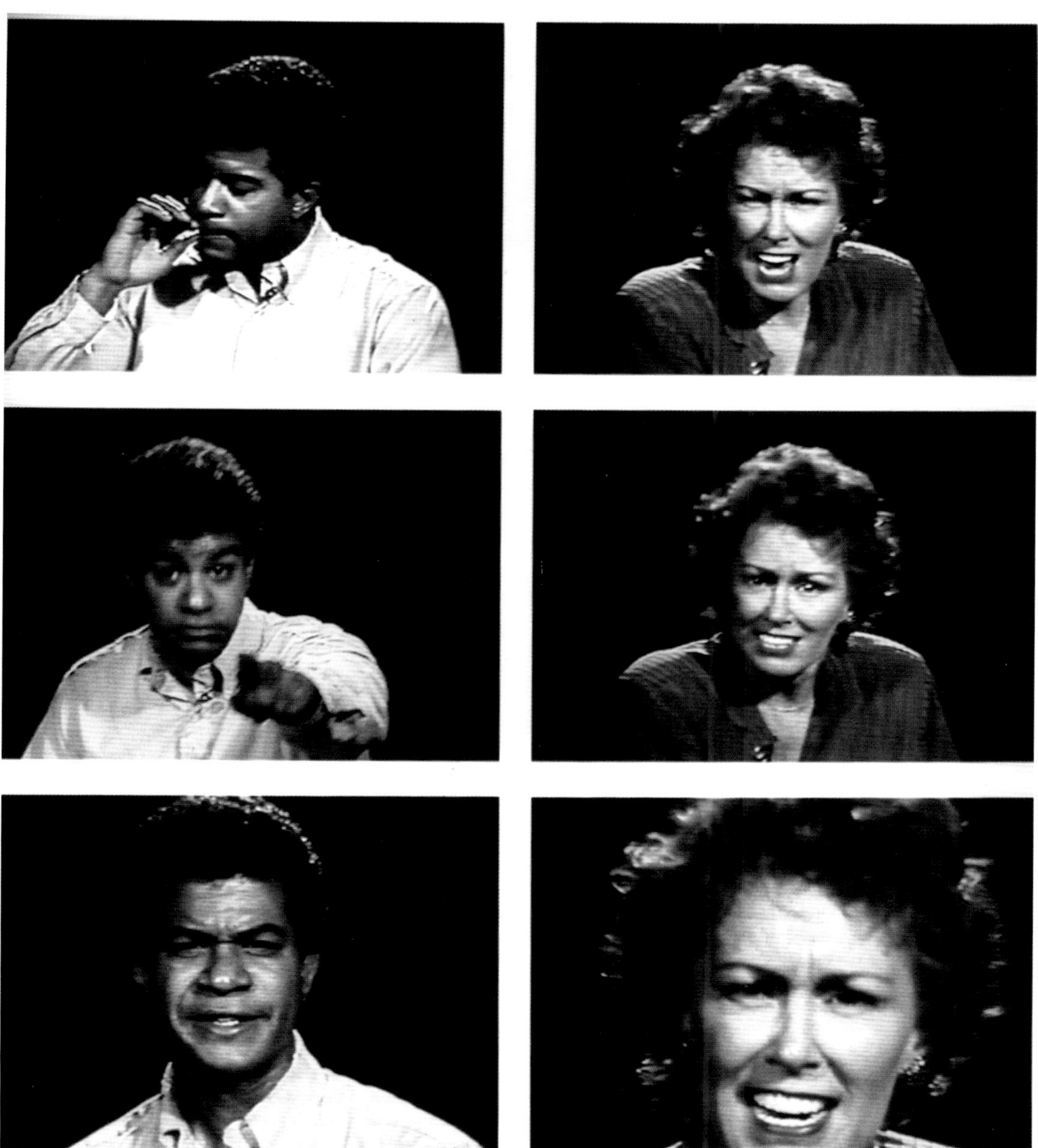

*Bruce Nauman
Detail from **Good Boy, Bad Boy**, 1985
Tate Gallery, London*

What went wrong? How did something so innocent turn so nasty? Only after we've seen all five sequences do we realise how important the sex and race of the actors are to the work's meaning. For although the words they recite are exactly the same, the meaning of those words changes subtly depending on the inflection in each actor's voice, and on whether they are spoken by a black man or a white woman. When she screams 'This is work!', for example, she sounds like an angry right-wing zealot accusing black men of not working. When he spits out the words 'You have work!' he could be a black activist replying to her slur.

Good Boy, Bad Boy is in part about sexual and racial divisions within American society. The actors are not necessarily addressing us, the viewers, as we first assume, but could be engaging in a debate which can never be resolved. This is because at a deeper level it is language itself that is under Nauman's scrutiny. Communication depends on words, he suggests, but words are useless when even the simplest ones mean different things to different people.

And yet words are all we have. One of the most depressing works in this show is a recent audio-visual installation entitled *World Peace (Projected)*, in which five videos project the images of five actors on to the gallery walls, while ten loudspeakers amplify their voices. Once again, the people who perform in the video are fairly ordinary – a young woman who signs in deaf and dumb language, a middle-aged man who could be a TV presenter or a politician, an elderly woman you might take for an official at the UN, and so forth.

All the actors say (or sign) the same two phrases, over and over again: 'I'll talk. You'll listen.' / 'You'll talk. I'll listen.' These are the words a patient might say to a psychotherapist (or vice versa). They are the words with which a diplomat might open peace negotiations, or the way a politician might address his constituents. At first they sound so reasonable. Surely it is obvious that world peace, sanity or political stability can be achieved if only we talk to and listen to one another.

But gradually the phrases come to sound either meaningless or sinister. What some of the actors are really saying is 'I'll talk.' (I will impose my will.) 'You'll listen.' (You will do as I say.) And even when the question of intonation doesn't arise – as in the case of the actress who signs the words – the phrases are meaningless unless they are intoned as a command. This is because no amount of talking or listening brings about change unless will and action are involved. The piece ends up as a plea for the imposition of change by force, a hymn to fascism.

But with Nauman, there's no way out of the human predicament. In other works in the show he demonstrates what happens when reason sleeps and people are told what to do. You enter a completely

empty room where Nauman's growling, snarling voice orders you to
'Get out of this room. / Get out of my head.' Even if we obey the first
command (and sever our connection with the work of art) we can't
do anything about the second (because it's Nauman's voice that has
got into our heads, not the other way around). In Nauman's world
there's always a catch – no matter what you do, you become either the
aggressor or the victim, the stalker or the stalked, the passive voyeur
or the object of the artist's belligerence.

For the duration of this show the Hayward Gallery is like the
seventh circle of Dante's *Inferno*. All around you voices shriek,
demand, accuse, wheedle and snarl. In a spectacular video installation
that gives new meaning to the expression 'in your face', a gigantic
male head cries out over and over again, 'Feed me. Eat me. Hurt me,'
like an enraged, demanding infant. Yet I don't want to imply that all
this aural and visual sadism is mindless. If you spend time with this
work, you discover the deep, irremediable melancholy beneath its
superficial aggression.

Fluxus

The Tate Gallery's *Flux-britannica: Aspects of the Fluxus Movement 1962–73* is not so much an exhibition as a haphazard collection of posters, artworks, letters, photographs and newspaper clippings documenting a phenomenon unique in my experience: art that has stopped being art. The vitality of Fluxus, a radical collective of international artists that flourished in the Sixties and Seventies, depended on experiencing it at first hand, at the time it was made, like the 'happenings' that were so much a part of the same period. What is on view at the Tate has the sad, distant, fitfully moving quality of memorabilia.

Founded by a left-wing, Lithuanian-born American named George Maciunas, and heavily influenced by the Zen-inspired composer John Cage, Fluxus had only one member anybody has ever heard of: Yoko Ono. And there is a reason for this. Fluxus was an underground anti-art movement, a rearguard action fought against the museum and gallery system, the art object and the cult of the personality of the artist. You might call Fluxus the flip side of Pop. It valued poor materials, ephemerality, mass production and anonymity. Maciunas called it 'art amusement . . . a game or a gag'. According to another member, 'Fluxus is inside you, is part of how you are. It is part of how you live.' That traces of it survive at all seems to me a miracle, but more miraculous still is its continuing influence. In advertising, rock 'n' roll, video and visual art, Fluxus is enjoying a comeback in the 1990s. This is because its aestheticising attitude towards life, its idealistic belief that young artists can change society by turning people's attention to the quality of everyday living, is compelling still.

The several hundred artists who made up Fluxus wanted to transform society through social change. If that sounds pretentious, in reality Fluxus was light and witty, more Monty Python than Bertolt Brecht. It drew heavily on non-Western visual traditions, refusing to

20 April 1994

Flux-britannica:
Aspects of the Fluxus
Movement 1962–73

Tate Gallery, London

distinguish between high and popular art, designating as 'art' formal gestures, ritualised actions and the conscious aesthetic appreciation of the mundane.

Members of Fluxus were musicians, artists, designers, dancers and poets – but what each individual did or played or made or wrote was of relatively little consequence, since all were working together. It was fun to know someone associated with Fluxus, since communications with them, often by post, were apt to contain bits of collage, poetry or instructions to perform a series of absurd ritualistic acts. Here is a particularly silly one called *Subway Event*:

> *Have a quarter and a token and enter a station*
> *Use token for turnstile*
> *Leave by nearest exit*
> *Buy one token at booth*
> *Say yam instead of thank you*

Fluxus performance with prepared piano.

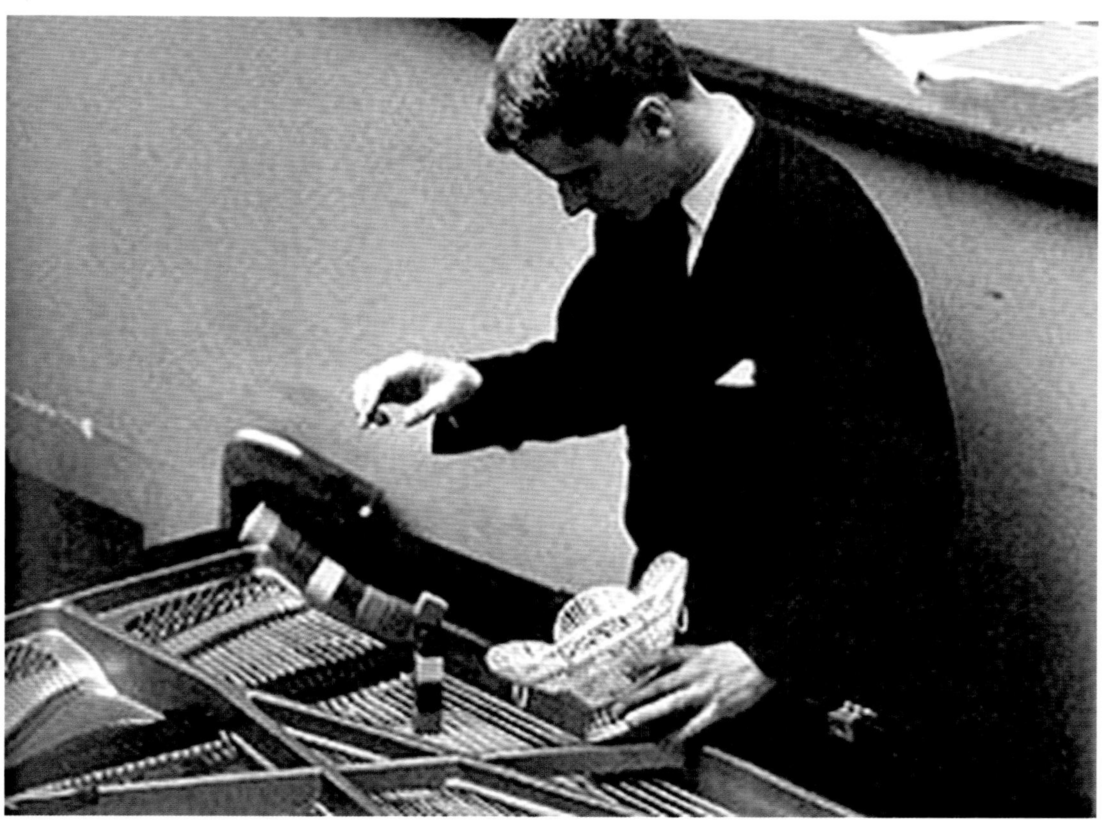

But if I've made Fluxus sound dumb and pointless, it wasn't. Fluxus was also highly political. William Morris was an important figure for British Fluxus because he argued for the role of art as a weapon for social change. Morris spoke with contempt of the middle classes who used art to camouflage what he saw as the visual and moral wasteland created by the Industrial Revolution.

Like Dada, Fluxus flourished in part as a protest against an art world that could go on buying and selling aesthetic objects at a time when there was a war in progress. Among the few memorable surviving artefacts in this show are Fluxus posters (now almost as quaint as First World War recruiting posters) protesting against the war in Vietnam ('US surpasses all Genocide Records!'). Remember when John and Yoko took to their bed to demonstrate against the war? Fluxus. Or when Yoko made a film descriptively entitled *Bottoms*? Some of Fluxus's events were genuinely subversive, others amounted to little more than art-school facetiousness. As a teenager I first became aware of the avant-garde when I saw a picture of the cellist Charlotte Mormon playing bare-breasted on the same stage as the Fluxus artist Nam June Paik. But what had once seemed so outrageous to a boy from the suburbs soon began turning up everywhere. When The Who began smashing guitars on stage, or the former art student Brian Ferry formed his own rock 'n' roll band, they were acting out ideas that had first surfaced in Fluxus.

And the influence of Fluxus on the mainstream of the visual arts has been enormous. In this show I was intrigued to see photos of the work of the French artist Ben Vautier. For an exhibition at Mayfair's Gallery One in 1962, he lived in the gallery window for two weeks, labelling everyone who walked through the door a work of art, and offering himself for sale as a 'living sculpture' for £250. Like so much else in this exhibition, all that is left of Vautier's action is a dim photo redolent of youthful high spirits. But it must have touched two young art students named Gilbert and George, who would soon designate their entire lives 'living sculpture' and who, though not (as far as I know) a part of Fluxus, brought many of its ideas to a much wider British public.

The show will appeal to people who were there at the time and who want to remember, and to young artists who are curious to know what happened. But visual interest has almost nothing to do with it.

Objects made by Fluxus should have been stamped with a 'sell by' date: the most radical thing about the movement was its proposal to replace museum art with ephemeral experience. Part of the bargain these artists struck with life is that what they did in their youth would not survive. Me, I'm too old, too mortgaged and too jaded really to respond as I'd like to this art. But it is reassuring to realise that another generation is touched by some of its energy and idealism.

I must add a coda to this. After a decade when Fluxus's emphasis on immateriality made the movement seem totally irrelevant, it is appealing again to a new generation of young people repelled by the commercial excesses of the 1980s. I found my daughter's seventeenth birthday present at a Fluxus-inspired art gallery in Limehouse devoted to artists' books. Almost everything there was cheap and fun and light in spirit.

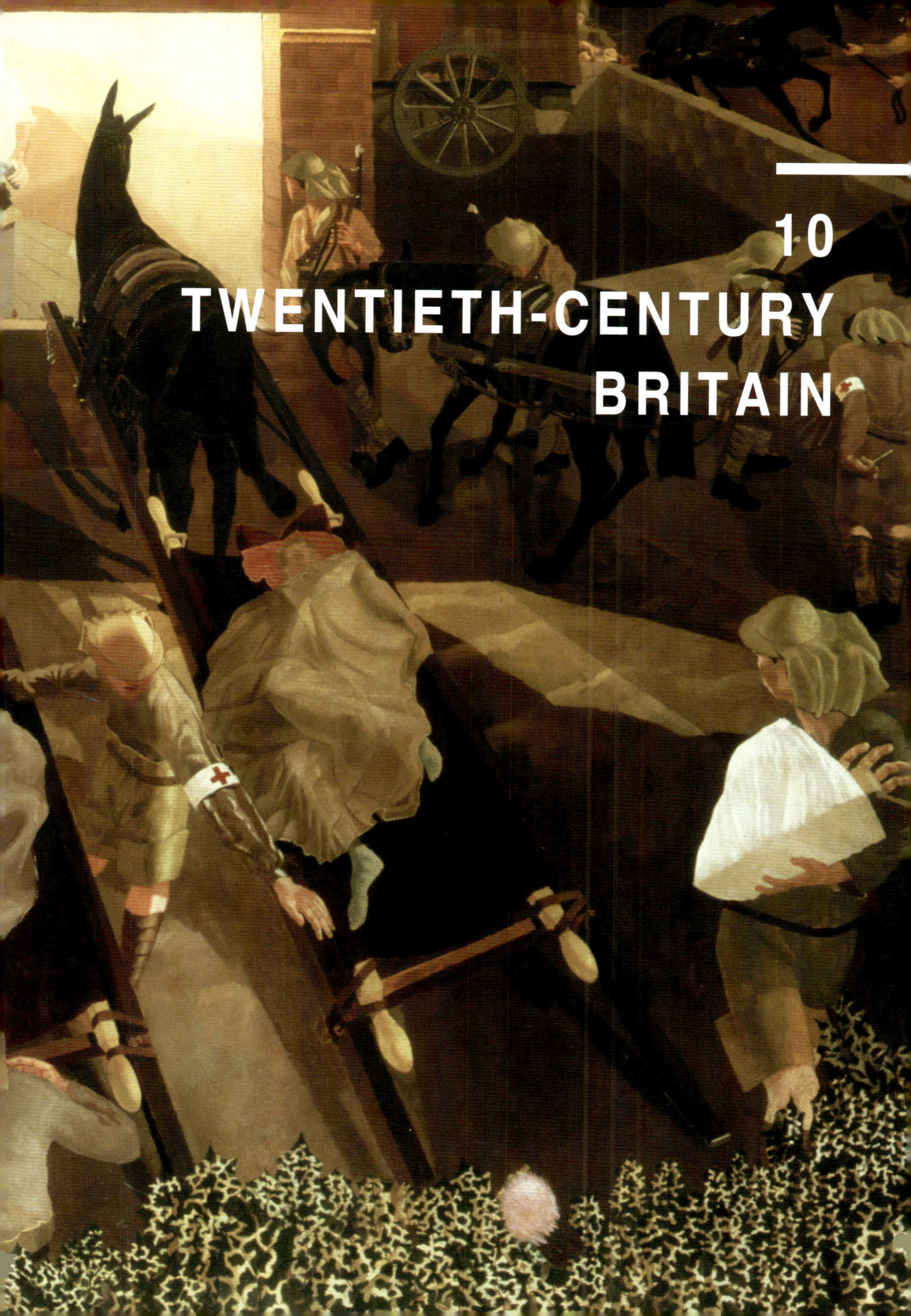
10
TWENTIETH-CENTURY
BRITAIN

Algernon Newton

Notwithstanding the myth of the undiscovered genius, it's actually pretty rare for an exceptional painter to go unrecognised during his lifetime – and rarer still that the neglect should persist almost fifty years after his death. But Algernon Newton is just such an artist.

Born in 1880 into the family that made Winsor & Newton paints, he left Cambridge without a degree to study art in London. Having married young, he then lost decades of his youth moving around England, trying to eke out a living as a painter. Invalided out of the Army in 1916, divorced and living apart from his children, at a low moment he was reduced to selling his paintings on street corners, so ashamed of his failure that he pretended to be disabled, and wore a mask to disguise his identity. By the time he was forty, he had long been familiar with what the nineteenth-century critics Jules and Edmond de Goncourt described as 'the bohemia that embitters'.

Like Constable, Newton's early life was one of deep frustration, of gratification delayed nearly beyond endurance. His first mature works date from the 1920s, but thereafter his pictures seem to have sold well, and he received public recognition in the form of election to the Royal Academy of Arts. But after his death in 1968 there was no retrospective, no biography, and not even an entry in *The Macmillan Encyclopaedia of Art*.

All that is going to change because a small loan exhibition of Newton's work is about to open in the Bond Street gallery of art dealer Daniel Katz. Newton emerges from the show as a strikingly original eccentric whose closest affinities are with neo-Romantic twentieth-century British painters. As far as I am aware, this is the first time enough of his work has been brought together to give us some sense of his artistic personality and stylistic development.

The show starts with his 1929 view of warehouses along the Regent's Canal north of Paddington, west London – vast featureless

27 November 2012

The Peculiarity of Algernon Newton

Daniel Katz Gallery, London

brick blocks built during the industrial revolution that had by then fallen into a state of dereliction. We know that Newton had an obsession with the work of Antonio Canaletto in the National Gallery, but as the presence of a smokestack, wooden shacks, washing on the line, and industrial rubble in the foreground of this picture tells us, the focus of his attention was not only on Canaletto's light-filled views of the Grand Canal but the Italian's early *Stonemason's Yard*, with its crumbling stone tenements in a backwater inhabited by poor and working-class Venetians.

Unlike Canaletto, Newton never moved on to paint the kind of subjects that would have made him popular with the public. At every stage in his career, he chose motifs that were the antithesis of the picturesque – the parts of London tourists never see, where, he said, we glimpse the city as if 'from the wings in a theatre'.

That's because he was essentially not a topographical painter. Whatever the motif, Newton was always ready to alter reality to create an underlying abstraction based on formal arrangements of geometric shapes. Look, for example, at the way the diagonal shadow falling over the building in the left-hand foreground rhymes with the slanting roof of the warehouse at the right. In *Spring Morning Camden Hill*, he paints nothing more exciting than an empty London street. With no people or cars in sight, only a 'To Let' sign suggests human habitation, while the rigour of the one-point perspective makes the street look like a stage set before the first actor makes an entrance.

In a thoughtful catalogue introduction, Andrew Graham-Dixon reasonably proposes that the deserted street and inexplicable sense of menace here reflect the artist's early experience of domestic unhappiness and (possibly) post-war trauma. Certainly, this is the kind of picture that you'd expect a man suffering from shell shock or chronic depression to paint.

Except that *Spring Morning Camden Hill* was painted in 1940, which is decades after you'd expect some of those traumas to have been laid to rest. Forget for a moment the painter's life story, and look instead at how Newton plays light against dark and solid against void to draw attention to the picture's essential abstraction, and how the low monochromatic tonality unifies the composition. Notice that the empty spaces of sky and street are accorded the same visual importance as solid form.

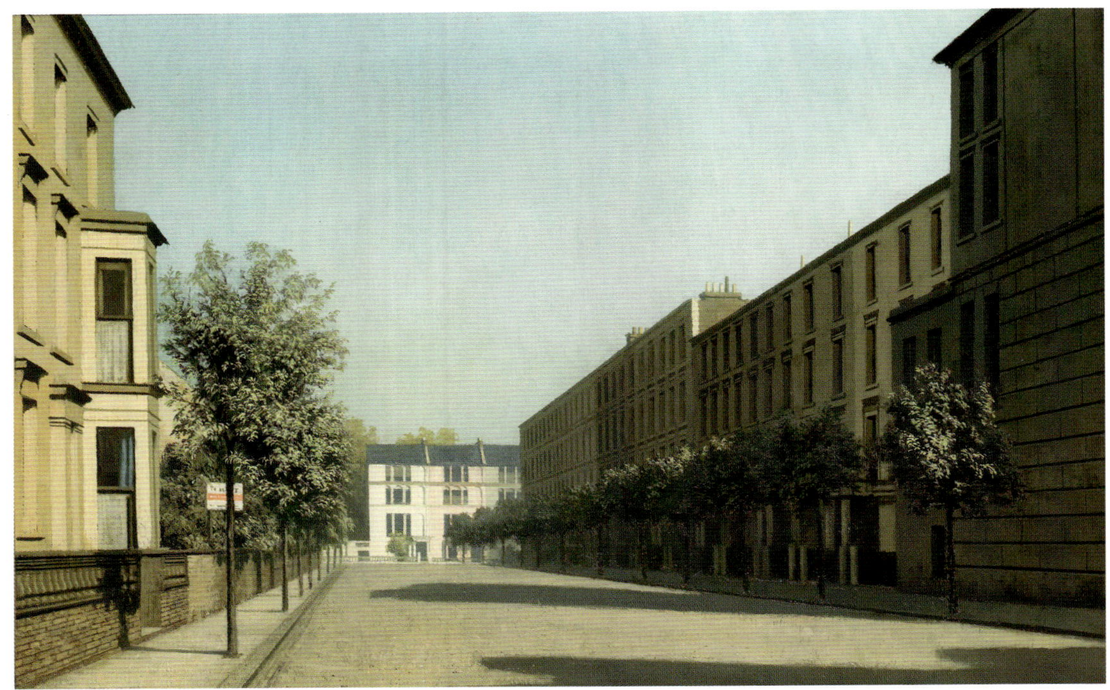

I do not deny that the atmosphere in the picture is unsettling, but what I can't quite put my finger on is why. Perhaps it is because Newton achieved his effects by painting with transparent glazes, a technique that leaves virtually no evidence of the painter's touch in the form of brushstrokes or impasto. But if Newton is consciously or unconsciously revealing something about himself here, then his is a rare example of Expressionism without distortion.

By the late 1930s, he consistently uses thundery clouds and the silvery light of an impending storm to ratchet up the atmosphere of dread both in his views of vacant London streets and in his no less disturbing landscapes. In pictures from this period, black, implacable storm clouds rolling in from the sea or casting grim shadows over the English countryside can only refer to the expected German invasion. But in this, Newton was hardly unique, since many Neo-Romantics including John Piper, John Nash, Graham Sutherland and Cecil Beaton were doing the same thing.

And looking back to the earlier views of London, my guess is that these have less to do with Newton's personal psychodrama than with the views of empty fog-bound streets around the British Museum that the Dane Vilhelm Hammershøi painted on his visit to London in the winter of 1905–6. So close are these Whistlerian cityscapes to Newton's work that it is hard to believe that he did not see them at the very moment when he was starting out as a painter.

And the more you look at Newton's pictures, the more you see quotations from artists as different as Thomas Jones and George Stubbs – suggesting to me that what lies at the root of his creative genius is not so much his personal history (significant though that may be) but his early and profound immersion in art and its history.

The Sitwells

The Sitwells and the Arts of the 1920s and '30s starts with a great big thumping lie. John Singer Sargent's conversation piece shows that famously dysfunctional family as the epitome of aristocratic style. The scene is Renishaw, the family pile in Derbyshire. The dashing young paterfamilias has just strolled into the drawing-room after riding in the park. Naturally, he finds his beautiful wife idly arranging flowers while their infant sons play on the floor. That Sir George rarely rode, and that Lady Ida wouldn't have dreamt of fiddling with the flowers are merely the conventional lies of the British portrait tradition.

But to one person who posed for it, the picture reeked of a more corroding hypocrisy. The fact that Sir George places one protective arm around the shoulder of his thirteen-year-old daughter Edith made her 'white with fury and contempt, and indignant that my father held me in what he thought was a tender paternal embrace'. The portrait enraged Edith because it used art to disguise the lack of parental love that had poisoned her childhood.

Yet one lesson their father taught his children all too well was the superiority of style over substance. When Edith and her brothers Osbert and Sacheverell set out to scale the peaks of culture and fashion in the 1920s, they might have been drawn to that aspect of Modernism which tore away polite falsehoods in pursuit of deeper and more primitive truths. But that would have struck them as such a frightful bore. Instead, they used art as their father had, to present themselves to the world in the guise they wished it to see. Not wounded, insecure and relatively uneducated, but sophisticated, disdainful of the philistine horde. Through sheer force of personality this is the vision they imposed on the world. Wyndham Lewis caught their tone best in his great portrait of Edith in the Tate, where the artificialities of twentieth-century Futurism somehow merge with those of sixteenth-century Mannerism.

19 October 1994

The Sitwells and
the Arts of the 1920s
and '30s

National Portrait
Gallery, London

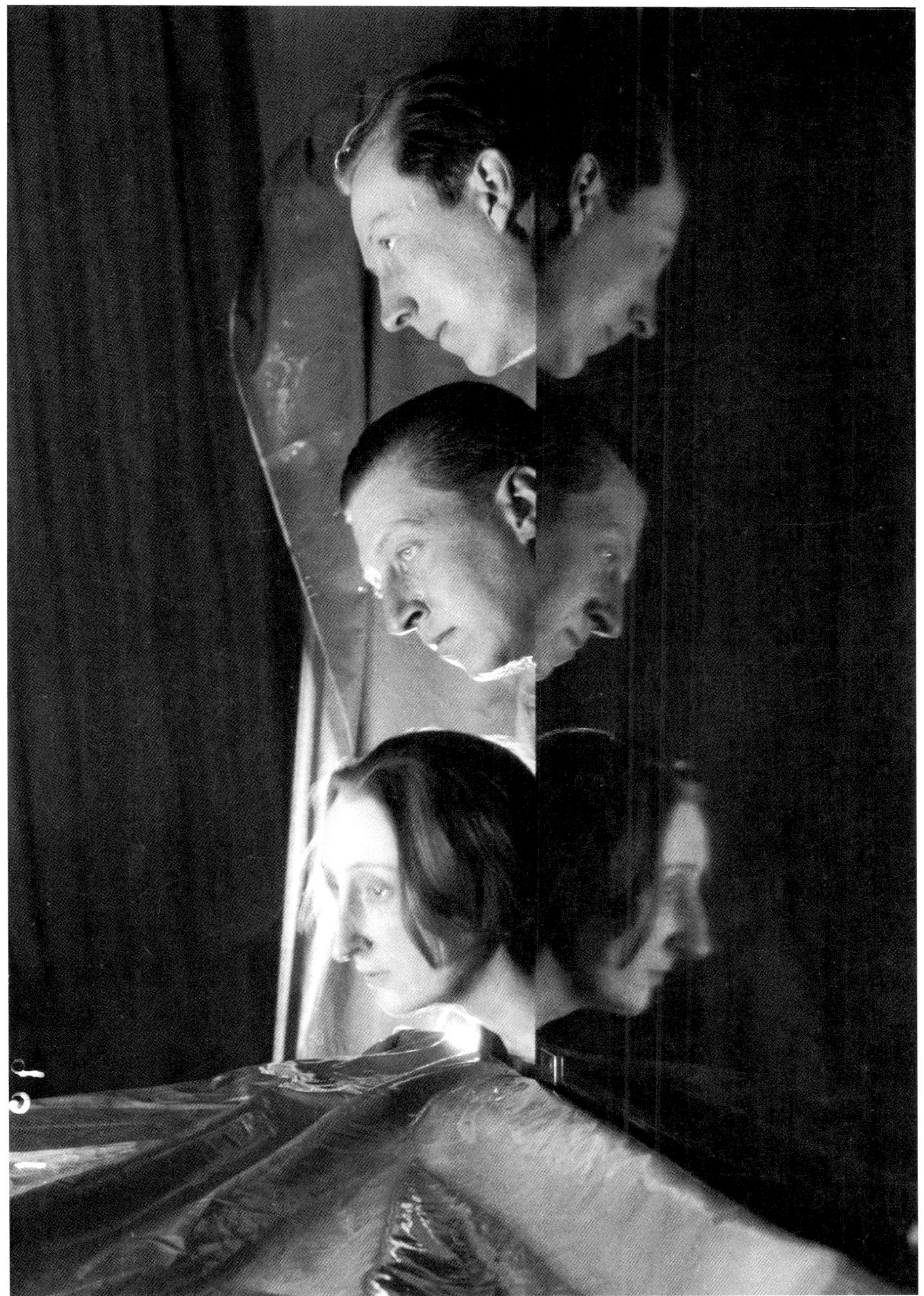

As patrons of the visual arts, you can't begin to compare the Sitwells to their counterparts in Paris – Gertrude, Michael and Leo Stein. But this is one exhibition in which the quality of the art is irrelevant. The Sitwells wouldn't be the Sitwells if they had collected art that disrupted the status quo too seriously. So it's Modigliani not Matisse, Tchelitchew not Dalí, Frank Dobson not Brancusí.

But to grasp what the Sitwells' patronage meant to the history of taste in this country, look not at the dispiriting works of art around you, but at the photographs and paintings of Osbert's drawing-room in Carlyle Square, Chelsea. With its regency stripes and gilded flowers, Osbert's aristocratic flair gave even second-rate art a decorative grace that eludes them in the NPG.

Patronage is only part of the story of the Sitwells and the visual arts. When you enter their world, art and fashion, reality and illusion, become inextricably intertwined. Cecil Beaton's photograph of Edith, turbaned and impassive as a pasha in one of Renishaw's stately, high-canopied beds, is so convincing an image of aristocratic hauteur that it takes an effort of will to remember that Edith lived through the 1920s in a dingy flat in Bayswater, often with just enough to eat.

When F. R. Leavis described the Sitwells as belonging to the history of publicity, not poetry, he could not have known how prophetic of much late twentieth-century art his remark would be. With her barren childhood, grotesque appearance and deeply shy nature, life had dealt Edith one losing hand after another. It is her response that seems so modern. By emphasising her physical defects, she turned the tables on those of a conventional cast of mind. In an age of sleek yachts, she transformed herself into a Spanish galleon under full sail in heavy brocaded cloaks, huge aquamarine rings and golden pectoral crosses: a living work of art. Let me assure you that when Dame Edith made her famous appearance on *This Is Your Life* on American television in 1962, among those watching and taking notes were young Andy Warhol and little Cindy Sherman.

The Sitwells are of enduring interest because they formed a crucial link between the polite distortions and evasions of the past and the wholesale unrealities of the present. But if all the Sitwells did was relentlessly to promote themselves, I don't think we'd be bothering much with them today. The fascination the Sitwells still exert can be explained by the myth of the transforming power of art. Art saved

them from their loveless childhood and half-mad parents. Take away
their profound and sincere love for poetry, music and painting, and
what do you have? Three sad, aimless members of their class.

For dedicated Sitwellians I recommend a visit to the delightful new
museum devoted to the family, designed by Alex Cobb at Renishaw.
For others, the classic biographies by John Pearson and Victoria
Glendinning are two of the most compelling I have ever read. And to
these pleasures we can now add the NPG's first-class exhibition and
perhaps even more enjoyable catalogue, which I devoured in one
long, mesmerised sitting. My only serious criticism of an otherwise
triumphant show is the inexplicable decision not to run John
Freeman's televised interview with Edith continuously, just as the
National Portrait Gallery does Freeman's interview with Evelyn
Waugh. Not only is it the greatest single portrait of Edith, but the
abysmal quality of the portraits in the new twentieth-century galleries
leads me to conclude that photography and video are the only lasting
answers for late twentieth-century portraiture.

Stanley Spencer

In the British wartime film *Went the Day Well?*, a nest of German spies has cunningly taken up residence in a typical English village. In every outward aspect, these blond fiends look and speak like their neighbours. Only a simple grammatical error – a slip of the tongue that no native would ever make – arouses the suspicion of the alert villagers, who raise the alarm, unmask the interlopers, and, in due course, save Blighty from the depredations of the Hun.

And so it is with culture: there are places in the nation's psyche that those of us who come from abroad can never hope to fathom. As an American who has lived in this country for thirty years, I feel so much at home that I sometimes forget I was not born here. But occasionally, when the conversation comes round to art, music and books, I am reminded of just how much of an outsider I still am. For there exists in Britain a passion for a certain kind of art that, to put it tactfully, finds no echoing sympathy in the foreign breast.

When a true Briton holds forth on the power of Elgar, the hilarity of Betjeman, or the rib-tickling fun of P. G. Wodehouse, the foreigner either falls strangely silent, or changes the subject to the excellence of Purcell, Auden or Waugh. Oh, we aliens pretend to find Gilbert and Sullivan great fun, but we are only trying to ingratiate ourselves with the natives. While they tap their feet and guffaw, we secretly cringe. Here is an easy test. If you harbour any suspicions as to your best friend's true origin of birth, the next time you meet, sidle up to him and casually bring up the subject of Stanley Spencer's *New Testament* paintings. If he begins to rave about Spencer's originality and sense of humour, and especially if he uses the word 'visionary', you may be sure that pure English blood flows through his veins. But, if he sputters in embarrassed confusion, anxious not to cause offence but clearly at a loss as to what to say, you've got him – Johnny Foreigner!

26 March 2001
Stanley Spencer
Tate Britain, London

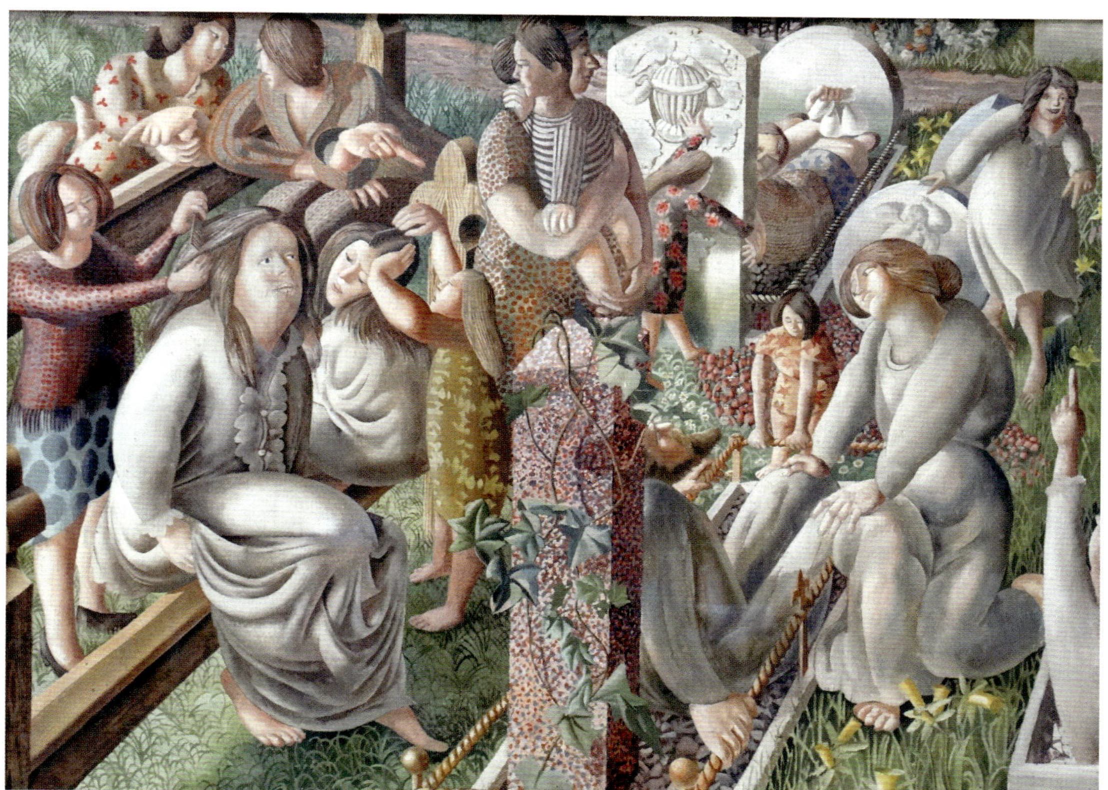

I am not saying that the British are wrong, exactly. If we benighted souls miss the point of Spencer's religious images, it may be because we simply don't have the cultural references to appreciate them. I wonder, for example, whether Spencer is popular in this country because he devoted his entire career to painting a distinct social class (lower middle) that does not feature much in the art of other countries, where artists are happier painting pictures of peasants on the one hand, or of the well-heeled middle classes on the other. Or could it be that in Britain to discuss religion publicly is perfectly acceptable, whereas in other countries it constitutes an egregious breach of good manners?

Still, there it is. Stand me in front of Spencer's mural-sized *The Resurrection, Cookham* of 1924–27 – the one with all the comical villagers rising out of their graves – and you set my teeth on edge. It's no use pretending that I find the picture of the dustman kissing the housewife, or the one of the old men falling down in adoration before ladies of the Women's Institute, either funny or moving. To me, they

are whimsical, horribly self-conscious and
not terribly well-painted – a hair's breadth
away from that bottomless pit of bad art,
Beryl Cook.

But, as the Stanley Spencer show at Tate
Britain makes clear, the fantastical paintings
aren't the whole – and certainly not the
best – of Spencer's work. The exhibition
starts with a room full of paintings executed
before Spencer was twenty-three, and
these show us exactly why contemporaries
regarded him as the most talented young
artist of his generation. Even here, I'm not
100 per cent 'on message' about Mr Spencer.
Even if the early *Zacharias and Elizabeth* could
be said to have something of Samuel
Palmer's intensity and naivety, it is a little
too cartoonish, a little too knowing and

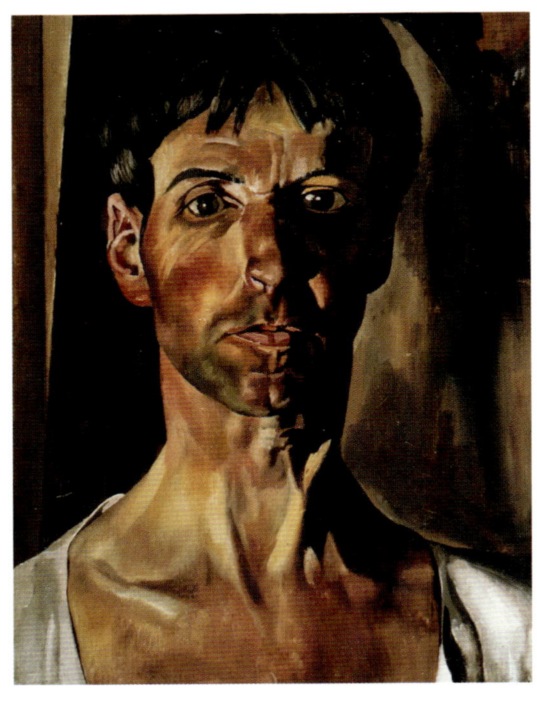

Stanley Spencer
Self-Portrait, *1936*
Stedelijk Museum,
Amsterdam

superficial for my taste, and doesn't show off Spencer's superb gifts as
a draughtsman. But *The Centurion's Servant*, that extraordinary image
of the physical and psychological torments of adolescence, is not only
the most powerful of all Spencer's early inventions, but contains, in
the rendering of the striped yellow blanket or the rose dust-skirt
under the mattress, some of the most beautiful passages of pure
painting that he ever did.

Here, or in *Mending Cowls, Cookham*, or in the over-life-size *Self
Portrait* of 1914, Spencer worked directly from nature. The Great War
was, on the whole, a good thing for Spencer's art because it forced
him to engage with the real world, even if he then simplified and
stylised that world in his painted images. In *Travoys Arriving with
Wounded at a Dressing-Station at Smol, Macedonia, September 1916* he
gives us a bird's-eye view of horse-drawn stretchers bearing wounded
soldiers to the medical station shown at the top of the picture. The
power of the image lies in the tension between the writhing men
under their blankets and the rigid order of the lined-up stretchers;
between the urgency of the soldiers' need and the absolute immobility
imposed on the travoys by the order and discipline necessary to run
an army. Spencer understood that, in war, soldiers, orderlies and

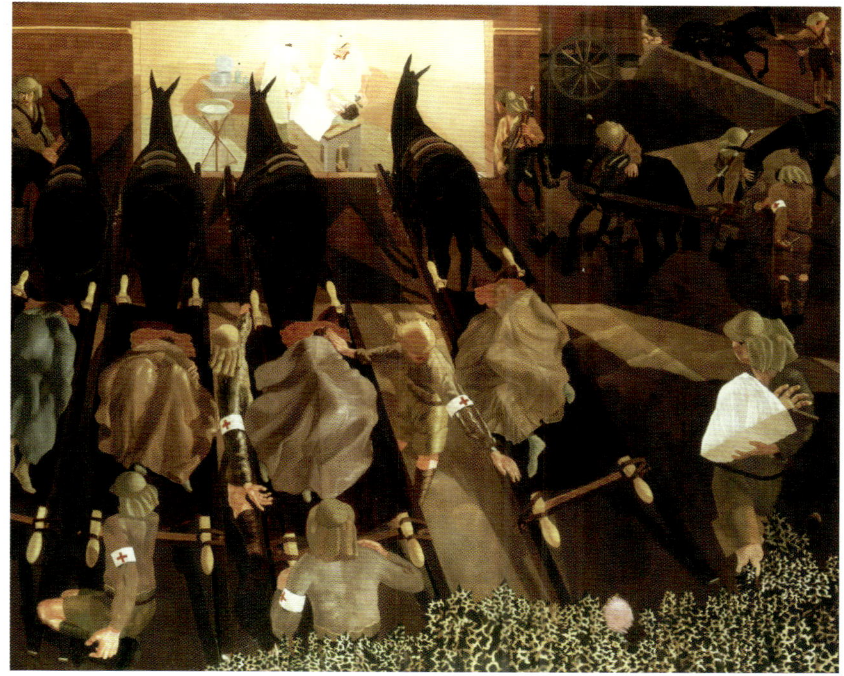

doctors are all faceless and mute; no one is more important than anyone else; each man must wait his turn. Other artists showed the horror of the battlefield. This is a rare picture about goodness in a time of war, for it is about patience, generosity, kindness and healing.

Spencer's discovery of evil, like his discovery of sex, came relatively late in his life. Whatever anguish both areas of human experience caused him, they served only to deepen and enrich his art. The great artistic period celebrated in this show is the Thirties, when he underwent the famous marital crisis, leaving his wife and young children for the lesbian Patricia Preece, with whose scarred and flabby body he had become obsessed. The nude portraits of Preece are harsh, cruel and loveless. The cold light that mercilessly reveals her tight lips and mean eyes suggests that Spencer had no illusions about her feelings for him, even as he handed over to her his house and money. And, though she certainly played the role of the villain in Spencer's life, if you look hard at these pictures, you see a look of infinite sadness in her eyes, a sense that Spencer's naked body intruded upon and stifled her. It is her own absence of desire – an absence provoked by Spencer's attentions – that renders her isolated and alone, like a character in Sartre's play *Huis clos*.

What makes the naked portraits of Patricia even more compelling
is that they are hung in such close proximity to Spencer's magnificent
drawings of his wife, Hilda, the most tender, sexy and deeply
felt works in the show. And nearby hangs his unflinching
acknowledgment of the mess that he has made of his life, the portrait
of his uncomprehending daughter, Unity, standing with an armful of
grimacing dolls in front of the weary, wary Hilda. The picture is all the
more chilling because it lacks even the possibility of atonement. What
a sad man Spencer was. And what a creep. It is part of the power of
these images that few personalities in the whole history of art repel
me as Spencer's does. But though the man may have been awful
and his work uneven, the exhibition itself is very good. Rigorously
selected by Timothy Hyman and Patrick Wright, the show stops
just when you think that, if you see one more picture of whimsical
villagers doing wacky things in Cookham High Street, you'll vomit.
Unlike the massive Royal Academy show of twenty or so years ago,
this exhibition compresses the last twenty years of Spencer's working
life into a single gallery, thereby minimising his later penchant for
banality, sloppy draughtsmanship and dry paint.

The selection of landscapes, which emphasises his love for
suburban gardens, scrap heaps and scruffy back yards at the expense
of the more conventionally beautiful motifs that he also painted, is
particularly good. It is also the first show I remember at Tate Britain
to use video to represent the unexhibitable aspects of an artist's
work – the decoration of the Sandham Memorial Chapel, Burghclere,
and Spencer's unrealised project to create a church dedicated to telling
the story of his own life through his pictures.

The uncompromisingly modernist exhibition design by the
architect Claudio Silvestrini is intended to banish the received image
of Spencer as a cosy British eccentric, but the long perspectives and
lime-green walls serve to make an edgy, uncomfortable artist even
harder for me to take than usual.

Ah well, I guess I'll never make it as an Englishman.

Herbert Read

There are only three words on the tombstone of Sir Herbert Read in the tiny churchyard at Kirkdale, Yorkshire. Those who think of him as the most influential British writer on art of this century may be surprised to find that 'critic' is not among them. Engraved on Read's tombstone is: 'Knight / Poet / Anarchist'. To understand this inscription, we might start by asking why he is called a poet. The reason is that Read can't really be compared to a controversialist such as Ruskin, Clement Greenberg or John Berger. Much closer to his gentle spirit are the poet–critics Baudelaire or Apollinaire. A literary man, Read happened to be present at the birth of the British Modernist movement and wrote about it – brilliantly – from the point of view of an insider.

Just as Baudelaire had once known Manet and Apollinaire had known Picasso, Read was himself a creative artist who maintained intimate friendships with the young Henry Moore, Barbara Hepworth and Ben Nicholson. And, like his French predecessors, his genius was to translate into words the ideas the artists had expressed in purely visual terms. In doing so, he enabled a bewildered British public to enjoy the art of its own time much earlier than it might otherwise have done.

An exhibition at the Leeds City Art Gallery, celebrating the centenary of his birth in 1893, reminds us that Read came late to art criticism. His earliest publications included a collection of his own First World War poems, followed by a study of Wordsworth's poetry. Just as important, his first job was at the Victoria & Albert Museum, where he spent ten years as curator of ceramics and where he published then-definitive studies on medieval stained glass and Staffordshire pottery. Later, he edited the *Burlington Magazine*. When he began to write about modern art in the *Listener* in 1929, therefore, his audience responded to the words of a poet, literary critic and art

15 December 1993

Herbert Read: A British Vision of World Art

Leeds City Art Gallery

historian. He gained the respect of his readers because he was able to bring to his subject both poetic intuition and a profound consciousness of the visual and literary traditions within which the artists he wrote about were working.

From the Thirties to the Sixties, Read's genius was to explain to the intelligent and receptive layman the nature of Henry Moore's semi-abstract sculptures. He was able to do this effectively because he could relate Moore's art to Greek, late Gothic and Renaissance sculptural traditions, and also because he realised that Moore's attitude towards man and landscape had its roots in British Romantic poetry and painting.

As this exhibition makes clear, Read also introduced the British public to Barlach, Munch, Klee, Kokoschka and Nolde – all northerners whose work looked barbaric to sensibilities predisposed to admire the Mediterranean classical tradition. This openness to competing visual experiences was not wishy-washy, as later detractors claimed, but broad-minded. Read was striving not to impose his own theories on what he saw but to judge art unblinkered by nationalistic or aesthetic preconceptions.

Even his willingness to trust the judgements of critics he respected seems to me a strength. Read was a journalist, after all, with an obligation to report fairly on what was happening in the visual arts. For his book, *Art Now* (1933), he allowed Douglas Cooper – a much more original critic whose eye for quality was unquestionably more acute than Read's – to influence his selection of illustrations, and so became the first major critic to publish one of Francis Bacon's earliest paintings, *Study for a Crucifixion*, which is in this exhibition.

The more successful an art critic is at his job, the harder it is for subsequent generations to understand why what he did was in any way remarkable. It is easy to forget the derision with which this country greeted the work of Moore and Picasso in the Thirties. Read courageously praised these artists when the public considered them simple charlatans, and regarded the critics who wrote about them as frauds. I am not, of course, suggesting that he accepted and praised new art because it was new. Far from it. Sir Herbert (as he became in 1953) deeply disliked Pop Art, as, with perfect consistency, he had once had reservations about the Euston Road School. For Read, the function of art was to create a better society, not to reflect a sick one.

By the Sixties, his interest in the writings of Carl Jung had led him to the view that the disintegration of visual form would lead to society's disorientation.

If that's what Read thought, no wonder Pop Art revolted him. In the Sixties he continued to defend the abstract painters Terry Frost and Patrick Heron, and the sculptors Reg Butler, Lynn Chadwick and Kenneth Armitage, all of whom represented to him the continuation of the humanist tradition on which he had based his life's work. Whether or not one agrees with it, how can one feel anything but respect for such a position?

And this brings us to the last word on Read's tombstone, 'Anarchist'. As one realises from reading his 1935 novel, *The Green Child*, Read's anarchism was philosophical, not political. He believed, simply, in personal freedom and uninhibited self-expression. Utopian tosh? Absolutely. Read's books were read by every art student in England and America. They not only prepared the way for the great upsurge in interest in the visual arts that took place in the Fifties and Sixties, but also led to the unheard-of liberation of form that occurred in the following decades. The belief that art leads to a better society may have been a chimera, but it was based on the optimism and idealism that characterised everything this remarkable man thought or wrote or did.

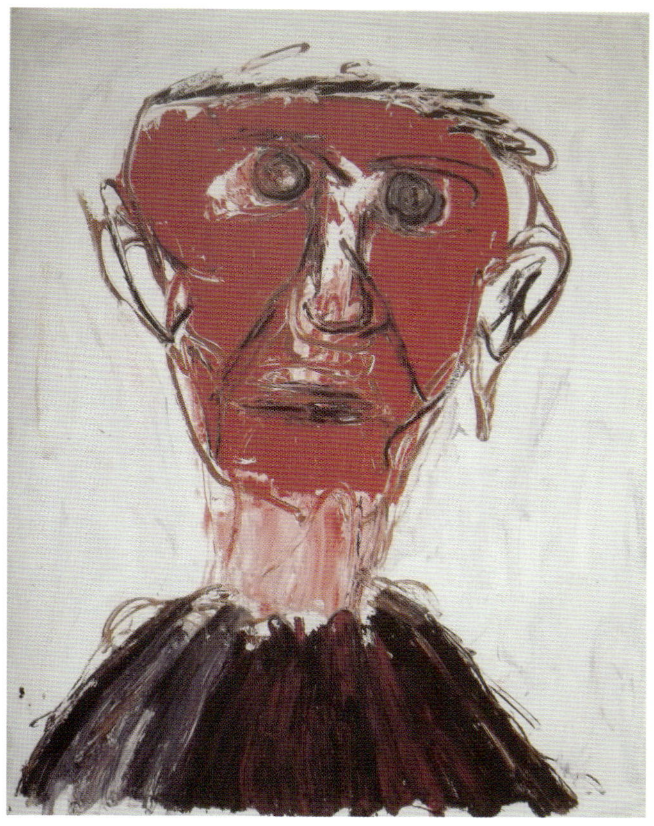

Karel Appel
Portrait of Herbert Read, *1962*
Montreal Museum of Fine Arts

Douglas Cooper

A famous passage in Sir John Rothenstein's autobiography recounts the former director of the Tate Gallery's last nightmarish run-in with the art historian and collector Douglas Cooper.

'Immediately on arrival [at the Diaghilev exhibition on the night of 2 November 1954], I encountered Douglas Cooper, who promptly began to shout at me in a French accent. I hurried into the next room. Cooper followed me from room to room, shouting taunts from a distance.

'I tried to get further away. Several of those present remonstrated with him, but he persisted, and presently caught up with me in a room from which there was no escape. I turned and faced him. As the big face loomed close, anger welled up in me and I punched it hard. In a moment he was crawling on hands and knees, searching for his spectacles among the feet of the guests crowding around.' Rothenstein concludes: 'Congratulations from all sides.'

Rothenstein's well-publicised blow formed the climax of the notorious 'Tate Affair', a vicious two-year campaign by Cooper and his allies to hound Rothenstein, whom they considered a reactionary, from the Tate. Almost four years after Cooper's death, and in a final ironic postscript to the affair, a selection of works on paper from Cooper's incomparable collection of Braque, Gris, Léger and Picasso goes on view at the Tate.

By the time of his death, Cooper had quarrelled with just about everybody in the art world, from his own protégé Graham Sutherland to his old friend Pablo Picasso. His legacy, apart from his great collection and an arm's-length bibliography of books and articles on nineteenth- and twentieth-century French art, is his independence, intelligence and generosity – as well as his paranoia, bitchiness and wit. After the publication of Rothenstein's autobiography, for

Douglas Cooper with Pablo Picasso and his sculpture **Femme au chapeau** *at La Californie, Cannes, 1961*
Photograph by Edward Quinn

30 January 1988

Picasso, Braque, Léger, Gris: Drawings from the Douglas Cooper Collection

Tate Gallery, London

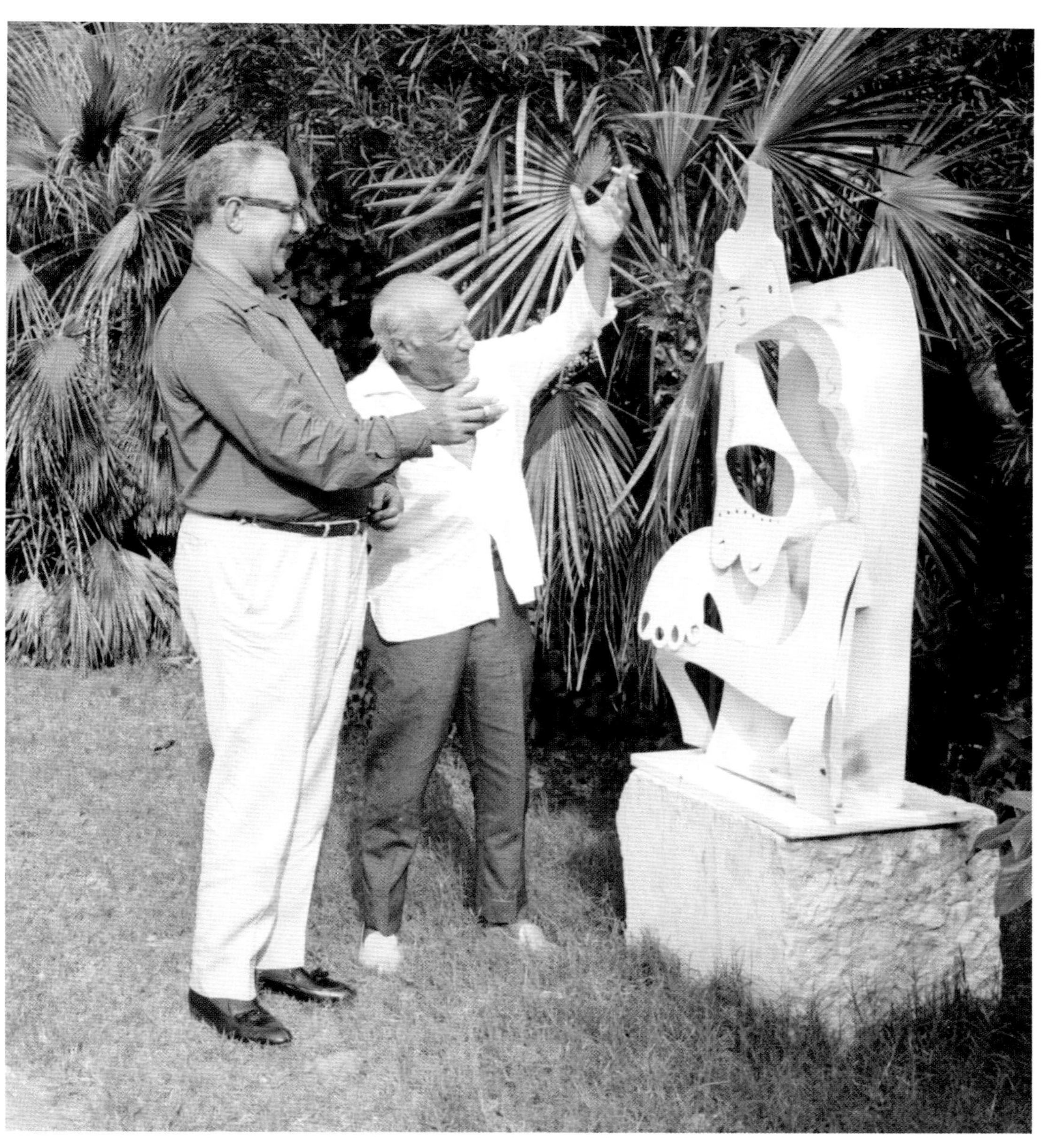

example, Cooper remarked that the last word in the title, *Brave Day, Hideous Night*, should have been spelled with a 'K'.

Even visually he cut an unforgettable figure. A big, powerfully built man with a piercing voice, he normally dressed with a flair for colour and pattern to rival the Brighton Pavilion, mixing in one outfit herringbone trousers with a bright striped shirt, fantastic polka dot tie, screaming plaid jacket and, latterly, one of his many pairs of multi-coloured running shoes. Physically he was strong enough to recover from being stabbed three times in the stomach by a North African soldier in 1961.

Born in 1911, Cooper came from a middle-class English family whose fortune had been made in Australia in the nineteenth century. Educated at Cambridge, Freiburg and the Sorbonne, he spoke French and German perfectly though, curiously, in later life he sometimes affected to speak English with a heavy foreign accent. In 1932, influenced by his uncle, the musicologist and collector of musical manuscripts Gerald Cooper, he set aside a quarter of his inheritance, £25,000, to form a collection of Cubist art.

The sales in the 1920s of several important early private collections, followed by a slump in prices for Cubist pictures in the 1930s, meant that many great pictures were on the market, and for Cooper the pursuit of Cubist paintings 'became [for me] the adventure of a lifetime'. In less than a decade he had put together one of the finest collections in Europe, a collection, moreover, which methodically charted the stylistic development of each of the four artists whom Cooper considered 'true' Cubists – Braque, Picasso, Gris and Léger.

Cooper's great contribution to art history was to approach the study of these artists with the same rigorous historical method hitherto reserved for Old Masters. He was an absolute authority on Cubist painting, and besides his many books and articles on the subject, he organised classic exhibitions in Edinburgh, Chicago, Los Angeles, New York and London. The last of these, *Essential Cubism*, was seen at the Tate in 1983.

The Tate Affair of 1954 shows Cooper at his best and worst – though any number of anecdotes could do that, for, in the words of his obituarist John Richardson, it was as though an angel and a demon child were perpetually fighting for control of his personality. Cooper was not wrong to call attention to the backwardness of the Tate's acquisitions policy. At a time when the Museum of Modern Art in New York under Alfred Baar was putting together its extraordinary collection of twentieth-century art, the Tate either did nothing or bought the wrong paintings. For a man of Cooper's energy and intelligence, the Tate's apathy and failure to cultivate private donors (including, one suspects, Cooper himself) was frustrating. Had Cooper been another man, able to use his considerable influence in a civilised way to put right a sad state of affairs, he might have played an extraordinary educative role in this country, like that, for instance, of Sir Roland Penrose, founder of the Contemporary Art Society.

Indeed, given the force of Cooper's personality and the violence of his opinions, he might, with a soupçon of diplomacy, have changed the way the English looked at art. Instead, the breathtaking venom of his attacks actually lost him support, and finally confirmed Rothenstein as director of the Tate for a further ten years. By the 1950s Cooper was no longer in the vanguard of thinking about twentieth-century art. What he didn't like he rejected out of hand, and although his eye was extraordinary his taste was extremely narrow. The exhibition of selections from his collection at the Tate is a fitting tribute to a brilliant monster.

Robin Ironside and Keith Vaughan

Two shows running in parallel at the Pallant House Gallery raise an issue I can't remember writing about before – the relevance or not of an artist's sexual orientation in assessing his work. Robin Ironside and Keith Vaughan were both born in 1912 and were both self-taught. They are usually grouped with Neo-Romantic artists such as David Jones, Denton Welch, John Minton, Francis Bacon and Graham Sutherland. But in almost every other respect they are as different as chalk and cheese – the one a romantic expressionist, the other a neoclassical modernist. By scheduling their exhibitions concurrently, Pallant House draws attention to one thing they did have in common: both were gay artists working at a time when the open expression of homosexuality in art was not possible. Though the imagery of neither artist is overtly homoerotic, the way each man dealt with his sexuality is a crucial component in how we look at and interpret their art.

Robin Ironside, rake-thin and dirt-poor but always exquisitely dressed, looked as if he'd stepped out of the pages of some nineteenth-century novel. Edgar Allan Poe, Charles Baudelaire or Joris-Karl Huysmans would all have recognised him as a spiritual kinsman. A glittering-eyed dope fiend addicted to both Benzedrine and opium, Ironside was a chain-smoker who also experimented with mescaline and LSD. I picture him with tiny brushes and magnifying glass in hand, obsessively painting, correcting, erasing and repainting through the night to create the phantasmagorical images of sensuality, excess and decay we see in this show.

In the 1940s, Cyril Connolly published Ironside's stunningly original articles on art in the magazine *Horizon*; in 1949 his paintings were shown alongside Francis Bacon's at the Hanover Gallery; and he was responsible (sometimes with his brother Christopher) for the designs of operas and ballets at Covent Garden and Sadler's Wells. But for all his gifts and many admirers, he never became a major

20 March 2012

Robin Ironside: Neo-Romantic Visionary

Keith Vaughan: Romanticism to Abstraction

Pallant House Chichester

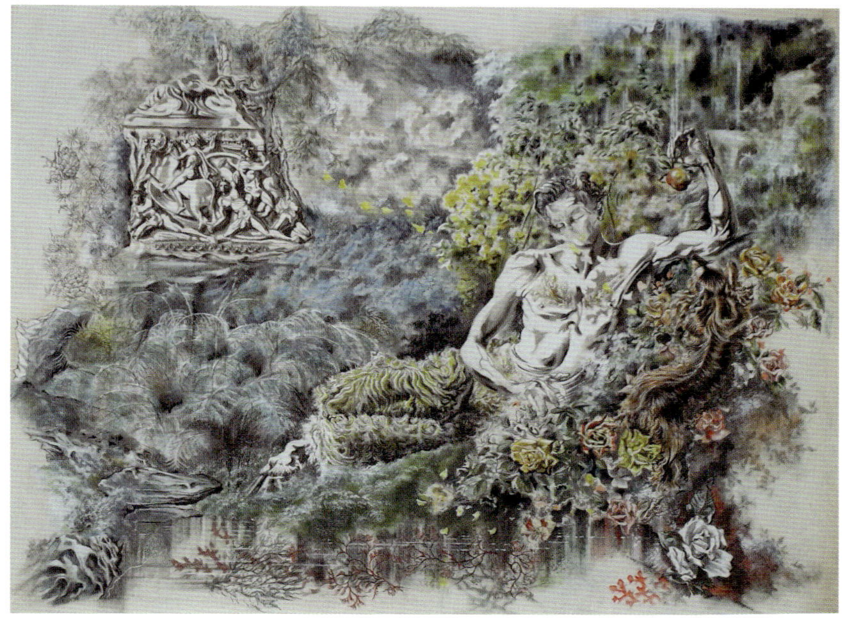

figure in British art, and since his death aged fifty-three in 1965 he has been all but forgotten. This first-rate show of his watercolours will help to introduce his work to new audiences.

I must acknowledge my own debt to Ironside, whose superbly crafted essays on nineteenth-century British art opened my eyes to the possibility that the disciplines of art history and art criticism are not necessarily mutually exclusive. Though not a prolific critic, he was a spellbinding, mind-expanding one. Trained at the Courtauld and a keeper at the Tate Gallery from 1937 to 1946, in writing about the art of the past Ironside questioned the critical orthodoxies of the present. At a time when Clive Bell's one big idea – that what was important in a work of art was 'significant form' – Ironside observed that 'the interpretation of the subject matter, the beauty of the conception, must be the basis for appreciation or criticism of a work of art'.

Ironside only wrote about the art he loved or felt was insufficiently appreciated. Because he was a painter and draughtsman himself, what he had to say was direct, deeply felt and extravagantly personal. Though I revere Ironside as a critic, his work as a watercolourist comes as a revelation. He is a painter of baroque palaces fallen into ruin and the corpses of beautiful youths decomposing in overgrown gardens, of dying poets, escaped madmen and clandestine burials.

Much of this imagery is tongue-in-cheek, but for all their camp
theatricality, the atmosphere of melancholia even in these small-scale
watercolours is palpable. The symbolic content of many pictures is
obscure, all are at some level autobiographical, or at least reflect the
emotional desolation of a gay man whom the catalogue essay tells us
was ill at ease with his sexuality. When he contrasts the horror of a
boy with half his face blown off with the beauty of an English manor
set in a peaceful valley, he speaks of longing, isolation and exclusion.

Just as in his critical writings the reader scarcely notices a phrase
from Tennyson or Rossetti inserted into a sentence, in the paintings
he slips in figures borrowed without change from visual sources
ranging from Harry Clark's illustrations to Poe's *Tales of Mystery and
Imagination* and Henry Wallis's *Death of Chatterton* to Delacroix's *Raft
of the Medusa*. With his delicate rococo sensibility and almost
imperceptible black humour, Ironside is a lightweight – but then the
roll call of lightweights we cherish in this country includes Saki and
Firbank, the Sitwells and Rex Whistler. Though I regret the curators'
decision to omit his oil paintings, the show is superb and the
catalogue includes an essay on Ironside by his niece Virginia that
is a joy to read – a rarity in my experience.

Ironside turned his back on modernism to claim a place in a
specifically English line of visionary poets and painters. After his
initial Neo-Romantic phase, Keith Vaughan chose to follow in the
footsteps of the modernist giants Cézanne, Picasso and, to a lesser
extent, Matisse. As we've just seen in Tate Britain's show about
Picasso and British art, he was lucky to get out alive. Picture after
picture is weighed down by his struggle to hew the human figure
from canvas using faceted planes and a limited range of colours.
Ultimately his confrontations with Cézanne's series of bathers and
Picasso's pre-Cubist and neo-classical figures were battles to assert
an artistic identity in constant danger of being subsumed by theirs.

This is why he clings so tenaciously to a subject that he could
identify as his own: the male nude shown either alone or in groups.
Apart from his competent but not particularly individualistic
landscapes, the male nude was the only motif he ever painted.
Though at times the figures verge on abstraction, these pictures are
not simply formal exercises in the arrangement of shapes like, say, the
still lifes of Giorgio Morandi. Somewhere between figurative and

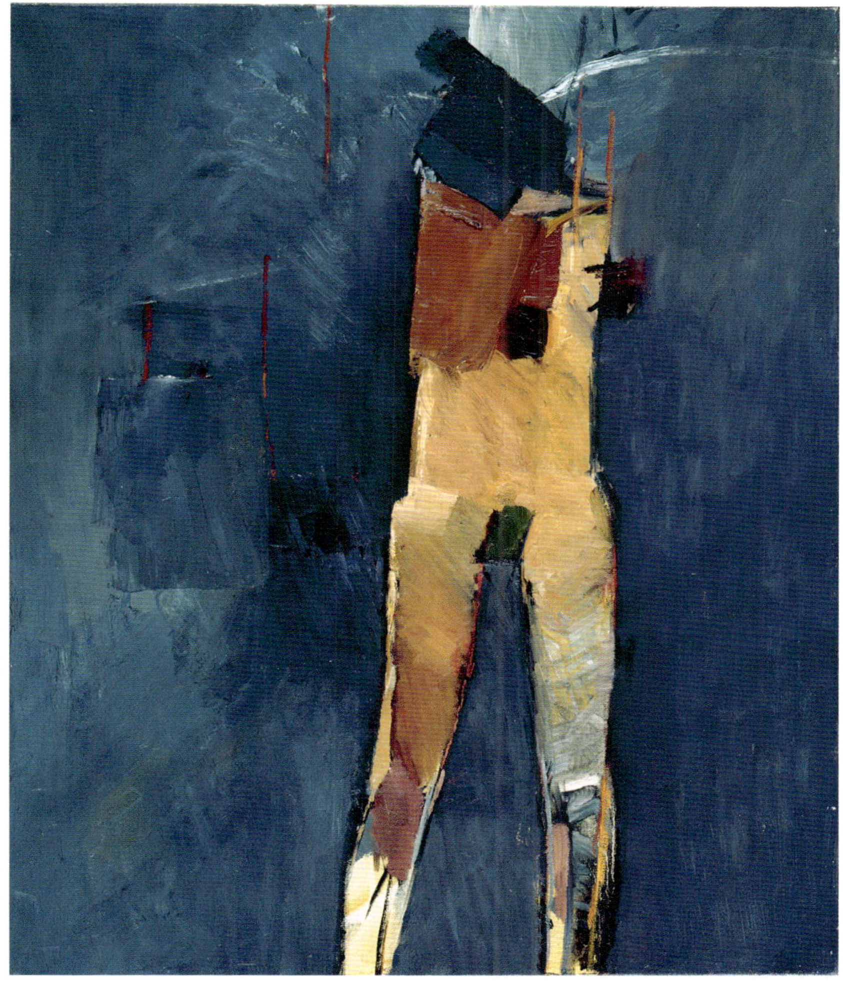

abstract, in a remarkable number of pictures the sex of the figures is either omitted or obscured. In those showing groups of men, the figures interact in some way but it is difficult to say what they are doing. Only once you've seen Vaughan's erotic drawings (which are not in this show) do we grasp what that might be.

The conclusion I draw from all this is that to exhibit and sell these pictures, Vaughan had to disguise their origins in living experience. Any erotic charge they may have had for him could not be openly expressed; but even so, his best pictures pack a visual punch that took me by surprise. We need to look at Vaughan again, but to see his work as a whole by showing the paintings alongside the drawings and written works.

Picasso and Modern British Art

When Tate Britain announced plans for an exhibition about Picasso's influence on British artists such as Duncan Grant and Graham Sutherland, my snorts of disbelief could be heard in Sidcup. Recent exhibitions have pitted him against Titian, Rembrandt, Velázquez, Goya, Delacroix and Matisse. To hang important works by him in a show full of his British imitators would be an act of cruelty.

I wasn't wrong, but neither is the show the disaster I imagined. The perverse brilliance of *Picasso and Modern British Art* is to take a non-subject (Picasso's impact here was limited to a handful of artists) and turn it into a gripping indictment of British culture in the first half of the twentieth century.

First, a brief look at the context in which the exhibition is set. In the last decades of the nineteenth century the British public tended to confuse innovation in the visual arts with political anarchy. As late as 1905, when the French dealer Paul Durand-Ruel held an exhibition in London of works by Monet, Degas, Manet and Renoir, he sold fewer than ten pictures. Roger Fry's Post-Impressionist shows at the Grafton Gallery in 1910 and 1912 suffered a similar fate, and an indication of a deeper malaise in British culture is that, at no stage in Picasso's career, did Britain's most progressive art critics, Roger Fry or Clive Bell, fully understand what he was doing.

Without critical guidance and with few opportunities to see his work, collectors of progressive painting in this country could be counted on the fingers of one hand – Samuel Courtauld, Sir Michael Sadler and a few figures connected with the Bloomsbury Group. Compared with what was happening in the US, Germany and France, it makes you want to sit down and weep. Not until the Thirties did collectors like Hugh Willoughby and Douglas Cooper acquire major Picassos. They had no competition from the Tate, which only made its first Picasso purchase in 1933, when it acquired a banal 1901 still life

13 February 2012

Picasso and Modern British Art

Tate Britain, London

entitled *Flowers*. In the words of John Golding, Cubism was 'the greatest artistic revolution since the Italian Renaissance'. How heartbreaking to learn that the Tate purchased its first Cubist Picasso only in 1949, the same year the BBC broadcast stupid opinions about Picasso's work expressed by an inebriated president of the Royal Academy. In this climate, no wonder British visual culture stagnated. The public could not appreciate new art if public galleries did not show it. Ironically, when the Tate finally did mount its legendary Picasso retrospective in 1960, it attracted more than 460,000 visitors across two months.

It is in this context that *Picasso and Modern British Art* looks at how his art was understood and absorbed by British artists who saw it either on visits to Paris or in shows at the Grafton, Mayor and Leicester galleries in London. What they took from him inevitably depended on the style Picasso was working in when they discovered him, so that Duncan Grant's Picasso is a Cubist while Francis Bacon's was a Surrealist. Of the six artists the show looks at in depth, only Ben Nicholson and Henry Moore emerge from their encounters with Picasso as greater artists than they were before. The others divide into those who retained their artistic identity (Wyndham Lewis, Bacon) and those who didn't (Grant, Sutherland). As always, David Hockney fits into neither category.

I won't waste space ridiculing Grant's brainless imitations of Picasso, except to say that, like all the Bloomsbury painters, he was a glorified decorator. Sutherland is the hollow man of British art whose artistic integrity was subsumed in Picasso's powerful personality. In this show, his 1946 *Deposition* is a pastiche Picasso manufactured out of passages from *The Three Dancers* and *Guernica*, but altogether missing the frenzied anguish of the originals. Wyndham Lewis is an artist of much greater stature, but his work has little to do with Picasso except by way of Italian Futurism.

For me Francis Bacon is the artist who suffers most in the show from comparison with Picasso, but also the one I learned the most about. The grossly distorted limbless torsos and gaping mouths are close to the similarly distorted figures in *Guernica*. The difference is that Bacon moves into the realms of abstraction to express horror and disgust, whereas Picasso never strays from the here, the now, and the specific.

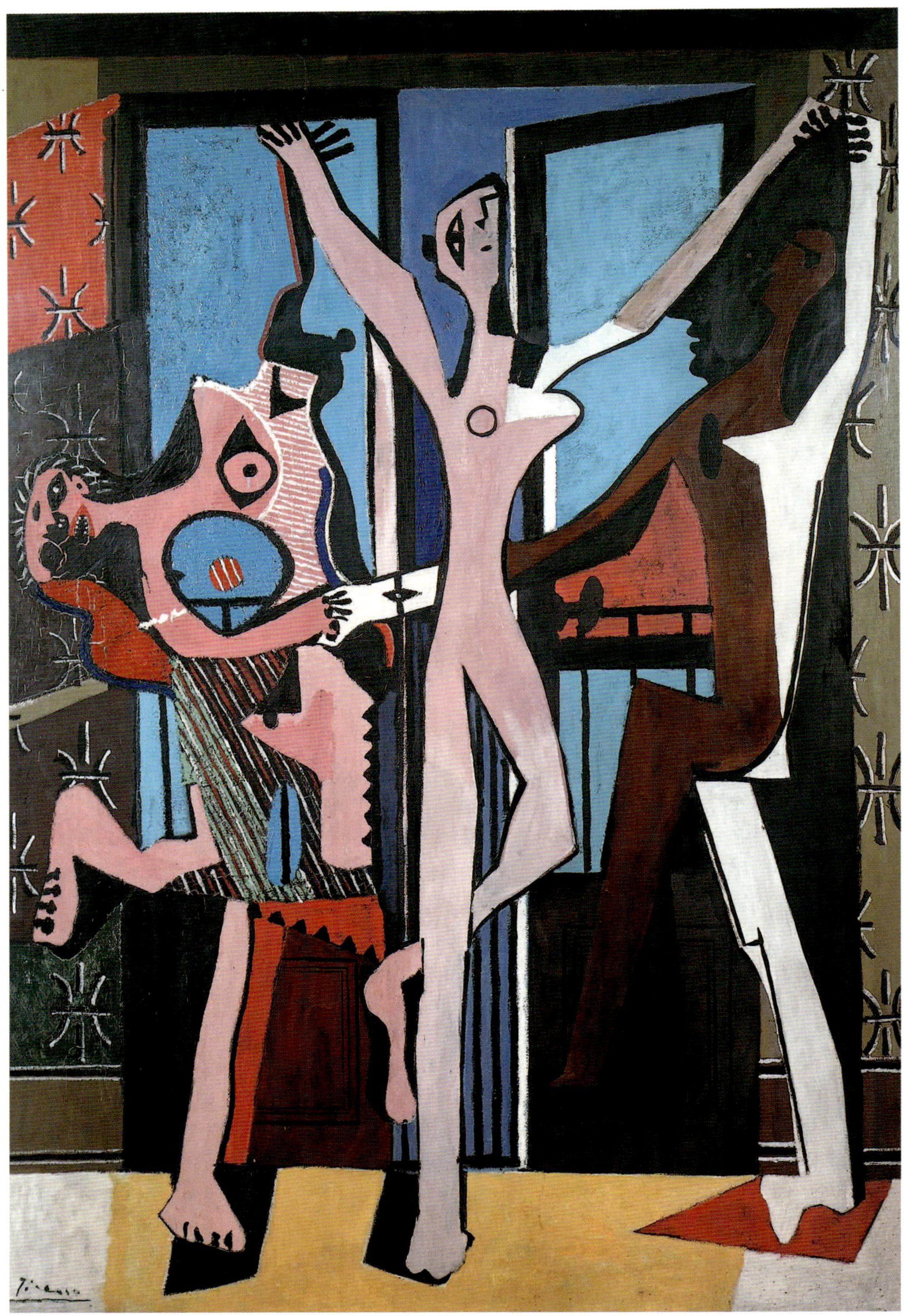

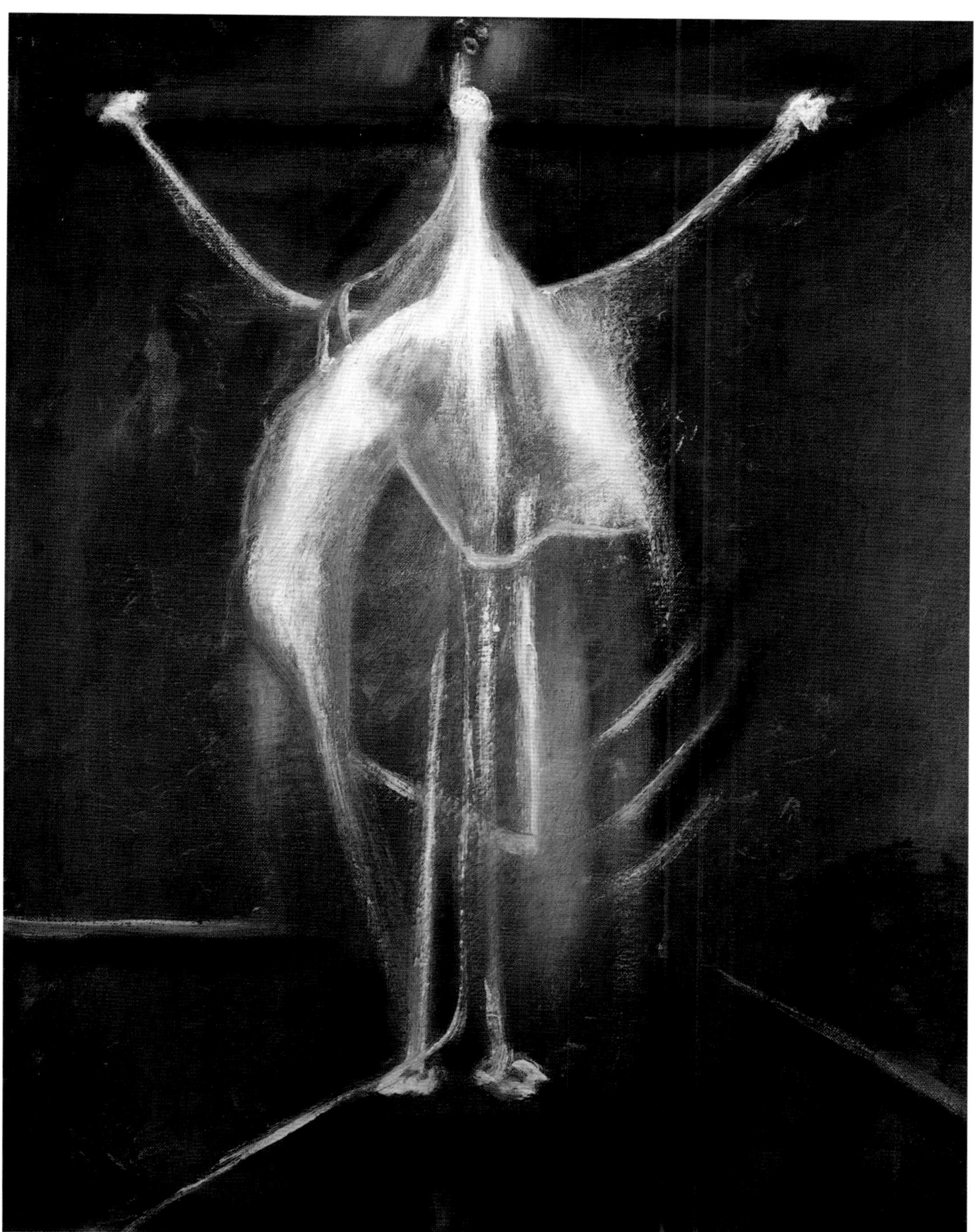

Opposite:
Pablo Picasso
The Three Dancers, 1925
Tate Gallery, London

Above:
Francis Bacon
Crucifixion, 1933
Private collection

Picasso's importance for Ben Nicholson lasted only a few years, but such was the British painter's intelligence that he was able to take what he needed and turn what he learned into something uniquely his own. For example, look at Picasso's 1921 still life, *Guitar, Compote Dish and Grapes* for a few minutes and you will see the picture miraculously change before your eyes. The guitar's sound hole becomes an eye, its neck a tail, a crisscross pattern on the body of the instrument fish scales – and you are looking at a fish on a platter with a figure sitting down to dine at one end of the table. It is this playful, chimeric aspect of Picasso's art that Nicholson explores in *Au Chat Botté*, where a view through a glass shop-front blurs distinctions between what is real and what is reflected.

What Henry Moore learnt from Picasso was monumentality. The great neoclassical female nudes Picasso painted in the Twenties inspired Moore's reclining figures in the following decade, while the purity of Picasso's line reappears in some of Moore's most beautiful drawings. Perhaps because Moore was a stone and wood carver, his contacts with Picasso are the most straightforward in the show, amounting to a rare case of influence without anxiety.

David Hockney's self-confidence is so absolute that he can admire and imitate Picasso to the point of idolatry and yet surrender not one iota of his artistic identity. I love the costume and stage designs, but wish he had not spent so much time attempting to replicate with photographs the unfathomable space in Picasso's Cubist works. He's the odd man out in this show – the one who cheerfully strolled into the dragon's open mouth, was happy to be swallowed whole, and carried on painting pictures that somehow manage to owe everything to Picasso and yet look nothing like him.

Neo-Romantics

English art took fifty years to recover from the trial of Oscar Wilde in 1895. In the wake of his conviction and imprisonment, a whole generation of Romantic artists – artists who worked in a uniquely English tradition – sought the more tolerant atmospheres of Dieppe, Mentone, Paris and Venice. In this country Aestheticism became unfashionable and art intensely serious.

The departure of the Symbolists and Decadents left a vacuum to be filled by members of the New English Art Club, the Camden Town Group, Bloomsbury or the Euston Road School, who all looked not to their native country but to France for stylistic inspiration. Post-Impressionism and Significant Form triumphed. The long line of Symbolist artists descending from Blake and Rossetti to Burne-Jones and Beardsley was snuffed out, and the English tradition of the poet–painter ceased for a time to exist.

So complete was French (and later American) hegemony that the recent British *20th-Century Painting* exhibition at the Royal Academy actually defined the mainstream of British art in this century as consisting of only those artists who worked in the International Modernist style. How such a development in the history of English art would have astonished Blake, Turner and Constable! In telling the story of English painting from the viewpoint of Paris and New York, the Royal Academy necessarily ignored precisely those qualities that make English art English in the first place: a proud insularity; an ecstatic, visionary love for Engand's history and landscape; the intermingling of art and literature, and – pervading all this – a profound Symbolist orientation.

The Barbican Art Gallery has tried to rectify the omissions of the Royal Academy in a huge, amazing, over-the-top survey, *A Paradise Lost: The Neo-Romantic Imagination in Britain 1935–1955*. Neo-Romanticism might be defined as the attempt on the part of certain

25 May 1987

A Paradise Lost:
The Neo-Romantic
Imagination in Britain
1935–1955

Barbican Art Gallery,
London

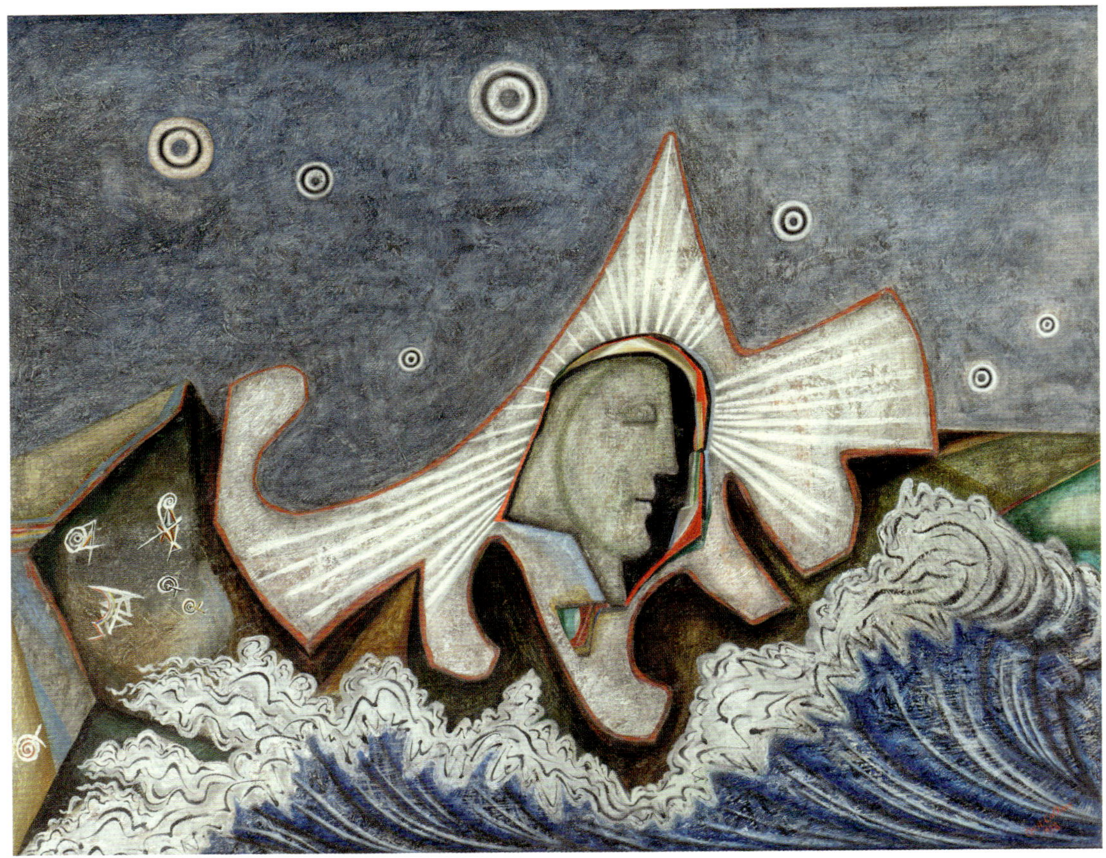

Cecil Collins
The Voice, *1938*
Offer Waterman
Gallery, London

English artists to recover the intensely subjective vision of Blake, of Samuel Palmer and the Ancients, of certain Pre-Raphaelites, and of the black-and-white artists of the 1890s. More a shared sensibility than a movement or style, at its heart were the large number of artists such as Cecil King, John Craxton, Mervyn Peake and Denton Welch who were also poets and book illustrators.

Like their predecessors in the Nineties, John Minton, Keith Vaughan and David Jones introduced into their art a flamboyant sexual – and more specifically homosexual – subject matter. Theirs too was a decadent art. As in the days of the first generation of Romantic landscape painters, John Piper painted the English landscape with an intensity fuelled by the threat of foreign invasion. Many Neo-Romantics looked beneath the surface of their cherished countryside to paint the geology of the land, its bones, or looked to the origins of English history for themes taken from Celtic or Arthurian legend.

From the Neo-Romantic point of view the 1939–45 war was

on the whole a good thing, cutting artists from the Continent and strengthening their English identities. Not until after the war did they see real suffering in photographs that came out of Belsen and in descriptions of Hiroshima. Only then, it seems, did a sort of frenzied despair set in, best seen in the work of Francis Bacon and Gerald Wilde. Ironically, as soon as many of these artists were free to travel after the war, they could hardly wait to leave the island that had so inspired them for the light and warmth of the Mediterranean. Who can blame them? Yet the pictures that Michael Ayrton and others produced in the south could not shake off the cynicism and cruelty of the war years.

One criticism I have of the current exhibition is its sheer size, which tends to throw so many artists and photographers into the Neo-Romantic pot that it is hard to separate the core from the rather blowsy periphery. Then, too, whereas a lot of Neo-Romantic painting is beautiful, some is almost unbelievably ugly. It was left to the abstract artists like Gabo, Nicholson and Hepworth to pursue beauty for its own sake. In their lack of interest in pure painting and in their idealisation of art as a metaphysical experience, the Neo-Romantics were apt to produce *objets d'art* that seem wilfully crude. Sometimes an artist such as Leslie Hurry produced pictures I felt compelled physically to turn away from. Hurry did design posters for horror movies, so I suppose this is a measure of his power as an artist.

The catalogue, really a series of essays on Neo-Romanticism edited by David Mellor, is a delight. Once one gets the hang of the thing, one begins to identify what is Neo-Romantic and what is not. Apparently there is such a thing as a Neo-Romantic novel (Daphne du Maurier's *Rebecca*, John Wyndham's *Day of the Triffids*, T. H. White's *The Sword and the Stone*); there are Neo-Romantic films (Michael Powell's *The Red Shoes* and David Lean's *Great Expectations*), aristocrats (the Sitwells) and even a Neo-Romantic television programme (*Quartermass II*). One thing the catalogue does not say: Neo-Romanticism is also Neo-Conservatism. Its revival in the 1980s was almost as inevitable as the popularity of *Brideshead Revisited* and the current obsession with Evelyn Waugh, whom incidentally, both as artist and writer, the exhibition curiously ignores.

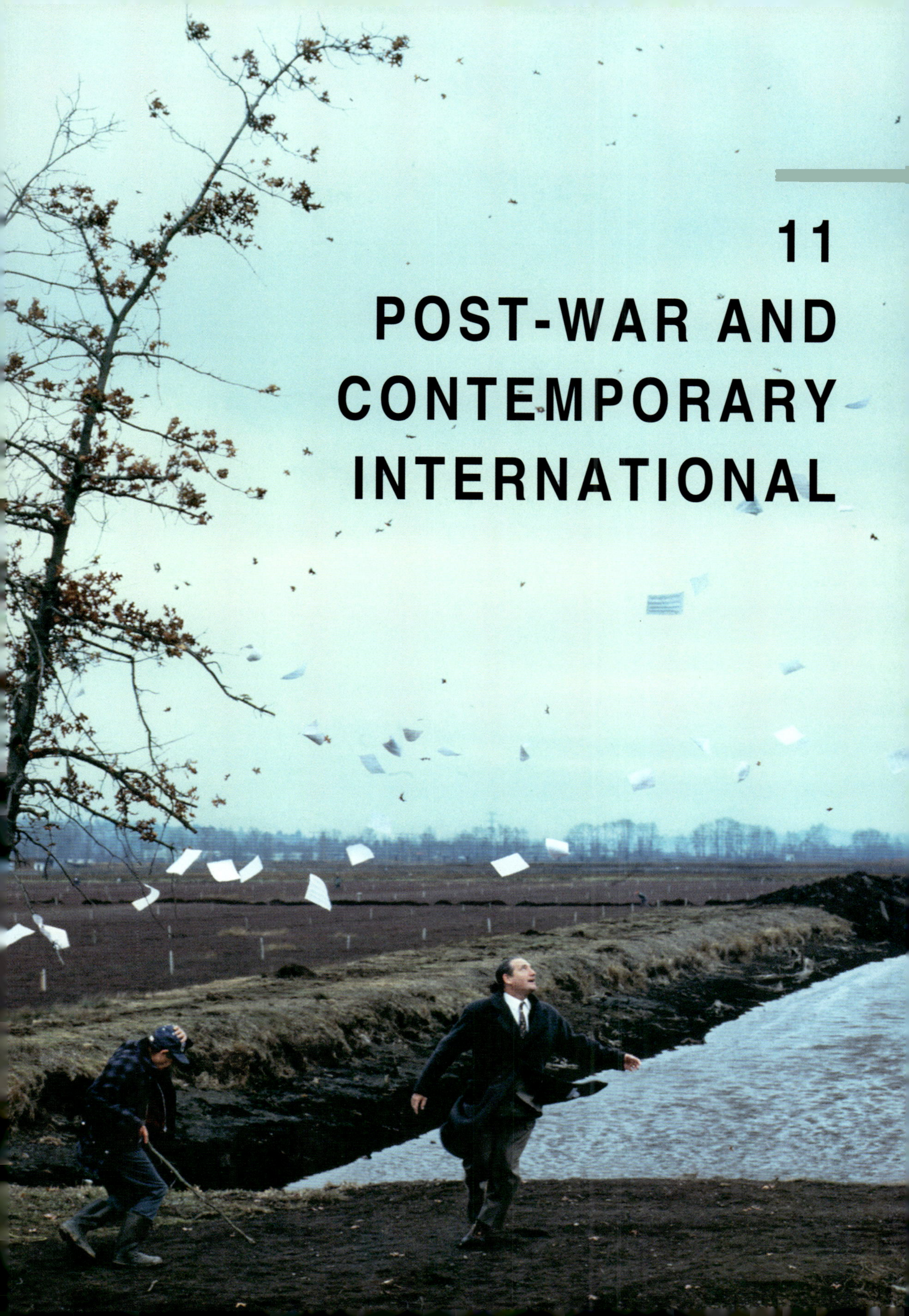# 11
POST-WAR AND CONTEMPORARY INTERNATIONAL

Modern Art

This year marks my tenth anniversary as art critic for *The Daily Telegraph*. Vermeer, Poussin, Fragonard, Degas, Gauguin, Cézanne, Matisse, Picasso, African Art: it has been a golden age for art exhibitions and I was lucky enough to see them all. Yet for all the pleasure these shows have given me, the part of my job I've most enjoyed has been writing about contemporary art. I wish I could do it more often. Critics hostile to modern art describe it as banal, incomprehensible and visually boring. All I can say is that that hasn't been my experience. So indulge me while I recall my first encounters with the work of five modern artists.

These are not the only ones I could have written about – Richard Serra's *Weight and Measure* at the Tate, for example, was hard to leave off the list – but I've chosen these particular artists because I hadn't seen their work before, and because I wanted a list that reflected the internationalism of the art I've seen over the past decade.

Much of this art is ephemeral. If my words can't persuade readers to go to see a show during the few weeks it is on, then there isn't going to be a second chance. And you do have to go to see it, because most of it is unphotographable. Next week, for example, the Japanese artist Tatsuo Miyajima will plunge the Hayward Gallery into darkness for a series of installations made out of coloured LEDs (light-emitting diodes). When I last reviewed a show by Miyajima, the article couldn't be illustrated because no photograph captured the hypnotic beauty of formless, constantly moving impulses of light flickering in the dark like thousands of fireflies.

That is why, when writing about modern art, the critic has to seduce and cajole readers into making the effort to see new work. But before this can happen, the critic himself must be persuaded of its beauty and importance. Take that first encounter with Miyajima. It started inauspiciously. Late on a freezing afternoon in February 1995,

14 June 1997

I'd driven through appalling traffic to see an installation called *Running Time* at the Queen's House in Greenwich.

After climbing a winding staircase to a gallery overlooking the Great Hall, I saw a spectacle that made me forget the slog I had to get there. Below, in the pitch darkness, a mass of blinking, restlessly moving electronic counters glided silently through the darkened space. Made of red LEDs and mounted on tiny wheels, the endlessly changing numbers careered aimlessly around the floor, like millions of atoms under a microscope. But just as one counter was about to collide with another, a light sensor made it bounce off in a new direction, like a bumper car in a fairground.

Each counter counted from one to nine, then repeated itself, just as the minutes repeat themselves every hour, and the hours every day. Miyajima described the work as 'a poem about time' but it was also about space, chaos and infinity. Because the surrounding darkness gave the viewer no sense of scale, the whole scene seemed to be happening in a void. As if viewing the lights of downtown Tokyo from the air at night, you sensed that there might be some underlying structure to the whole system, but that it was beyond our grasp or understanding. Much later, a friend who was present on the last day of the exhibition told me that, in the final moments, the running numbers blinked off, one by one, until the room was left in total darkness. Time had come to an end.

Another day, in 1993, I drove down to Oxford to see a show by a young Californian named Gary Hill who worked in video. I went without enthusiasm or expectations and came home unable to stop talking about what I'd seen. The work that moved me so much, *Tall Ships*, consisted of small photographs of ordinary people – a student, a housewife, a child, a businessman, a schoolteacher and elderly grandparents – each picture only a few inches high.

But the act of stopping in front of each image triggered a hidden electronic mechanism which made the person depicted appear to stir to life. One by one they seemed to notice my presence and to step forward to take a good look at me. As each moved towards me, he or she became bigger until I was standing face to face with a whole gallery of life-sized phantoms, separated only by the invisible barrier that divided my world from theirs. As we looked at each other, the figures began to react to me, some with joy, others with dismay or fury. A few walked away in apparent disgust, one child ran towards me with open arms, some tried to greet me, then gave up. *Tall Ships* was like a house of spirits, a gallery of the dead, a work about dreams or memory. I may well not see it again, but it is now a part of me.

Zurich, summer, 1995. I am in the art museum, standing in front of a mural-sized work by the American artist Bruce Nauman entitled *One Hundred Live and Die,* and I am mightily bored. It is composed of a hundred short, deadpan phrases made of neon tubing in all the colours of the rainbow. Half of these phrases are made up of a simple verb followed by the word 'live', the other half of the same verb, followed by the word 'die', as in 'Eat and Live' / 'Eat and Die', 'Sleep and Live' / 'Sleep and Die', 'Love and Live' / 'Love and Die'. Only one phrase lights up at a time, vanishing at the instant another is illuminated.

This is philosophy stripped to its bare essentials: Nauman lists all of the basic, ordinary things we do and feel every day of our lives: love, hate, eat, sleep, sit, walk, etc. Either we do these things and continue to live, or we do these things and then die. For the nihilist, that is all there is to be said about life.

Standing there, watching the phrases blink on and off was a deadening, melancholy, apparently pointless experience, and more than once I thought I had seen enough and would move on. But for some reason I stayed for the full twenty minutes or so it took to watch all hundred phrases light up and blink off. And I'm glad I did, because only at the very end of that time did I understand what the work was about. In the final moments of the cycle, the viewer is rewarded with a frisson of pure visual bliss as all hundred phrases light up simultaneously, and more than two hundred brilliant colours and combinations of colours come on at once – a glorious finale, like the catherine wheel closing a firework display.

At that moment I realised that *One Hundred Live and Die* was about life itself. Of no particular interest in themselves, individual actions feel mechanical and meaningless as we do them, and yet the sum total of those actions makes up a person's life, the most joyous and exhilarating thing there is. As usual with Nauman, there was a sting in the tail. Because the work was fully illuminated only for a minute or two at the very end of the cycle, the implication was that we can't see how beautiful life is until we are near the end of it.

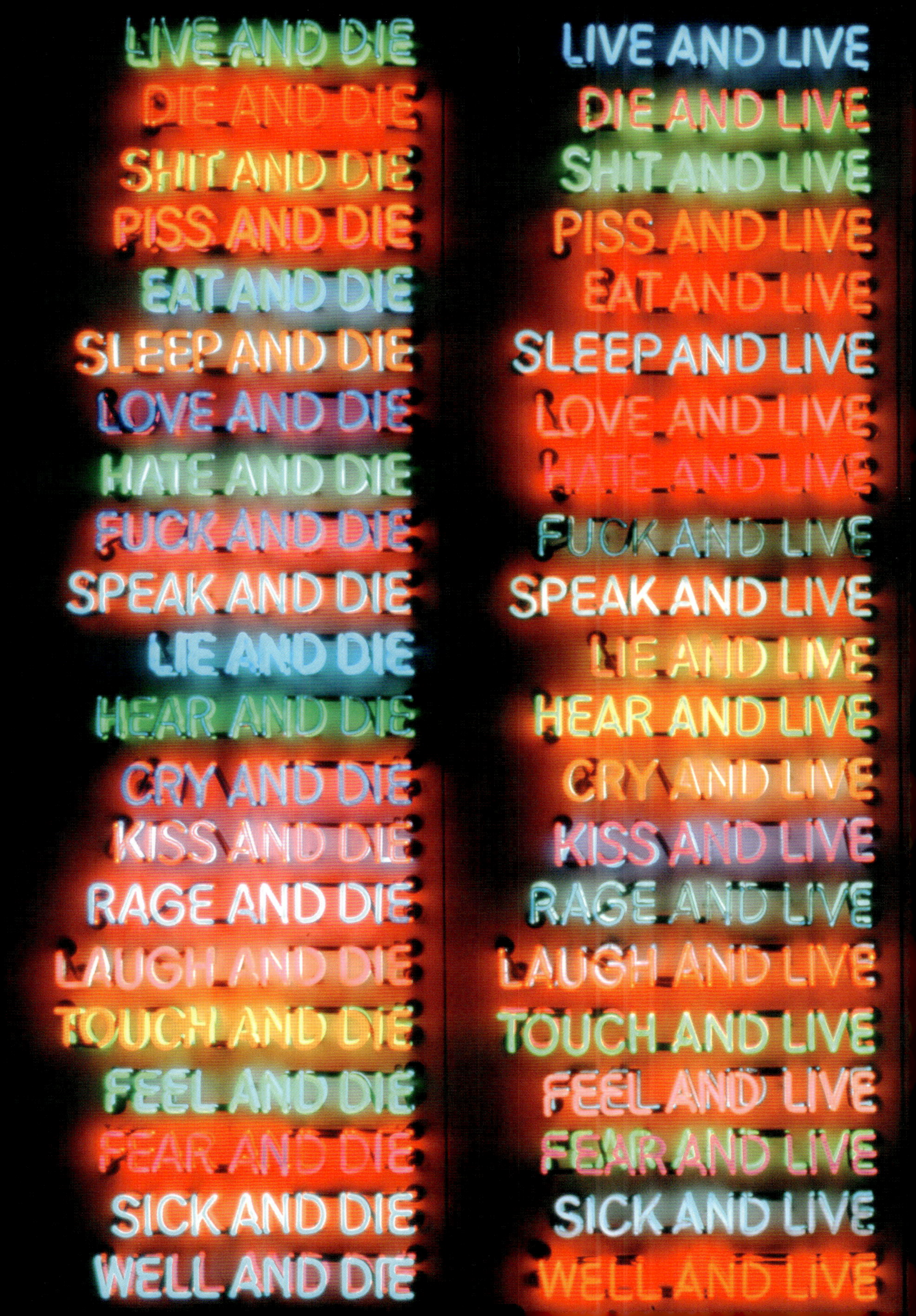

LIVE AND DIE
DIE AND DIE
SHIT AND DIE
PISS AND DIE
EAT AND DIE
SLEEP AND DIE
LOVE AND DIE
HATE AND DIE
FUCK AND DIE
SPEAK AND DIE
LIE AND DIE
HEAR AND DIE
CRY AND DIE
KISS AND DIE
RAGE AND DIE
LAUGH AND DIE
TOUCH AND DIE
FEEL AND DIE
FEAR AND DIE
SICK AND DIE
WELL AND DIE

LIVE AND LIVE
DIE AND LIVE
SHIT AND LIVE
PISS AND LIVE
EAT AND LIVE
SLEEP AND LIVE
LOVE AND LIVE
HATE AND LIVE
FUCK AND LIVE
SPEAK AND LIVE
LIE AND LIVE
HEAR AND LIVE
CRY AND LIVE
KISS AND LIVE
RAGE AND LIVE
LAUGH AND LIVE
TOUCH AND LIVE
FEEL AND LIVE
FEAR AND LIVE
SICK AND LIVE
WELL AND LIVE

Then there is the surprise of seeing a familiar building utterly transformed through the intervention of an artist whose work you hadn't known before. That happened in April 1990 when I walked into the Whitechapel Art Gallery and discovered that the French artist Christian Boltanski had used lamps, candles and paper cut-outs to throw weirdly distorted shadows, mysterious and insubstantial as supernatural apparitions. Cut-out devils danced on walls illuminated by stubby candles while ghostly shadow puppets stirred in unseen breezes. Never has the Whitechapel looked so beautiful.

But there was a serious point to Boltanksi's work. He was trying to make us aware that our lives are as ephemeral as those shadows. In one piece, he arranged on the gallery walls framed photographs taken in the early 1930s of children who attended a Jewish high school in Vienna. Then he built what could only be described as altars to their lives, lighting each photo with a dim electric light bulb, like so many votive candles flickering in front of holy pictures in a Catholic church. As we gazed at the innocent faces of the anonymous children, we became aware that most of them were dead.

Finally, I have a memory connected with one visit to see Rachel Whiteread's *House*, which has little to do with the work's intrinsic artistic quality. On this occasion I arrived around four o'clock on a November afternoon in the street in the East End of London where *House* stood. With the darkness closing in and a light rain falling, spotlights had been turned on to the hauntingly beautiful white plaster cast of the interior of what had once been a nondescript, late Victorian terraced house. From a distance, you could see dozens of other visitors standing under umbrellas or silently circling the house like pilgrims around the Kaaba in Mecca.

England was going through one of its periodic outpourings of almost hysterical hostility to contemporary art – this always happens when art is on the move. Graffiti had been scrawled over *House*, and after Whiteread had won the Turner prize, a bunch of failed artists attempted to humiliate her with a cheque for the 'worst artist of the year' which she promptly donated to charity (this week she refused the Royal Academy's invitation to become the youngest Academician this century).

Thinking about all this, I felt what I can only call *House*'s moral beauty. There was something touching about this monument to a building in which generations of ordinary, anonymous Londoners had lived and died. As I stood in the darkness watching the scene from across the road, I sensed that *House* was an important moment in twentieth-century British art. Its mixture of visual beauty, poetic allusion and ephemerality are precisely the qualities that have characterised the best British art that has emerged in its wake. Looking back now, I see that *House* opened up a path to the twenty-first century.

Admittedly this list is highly selective – unlike our film and theatre critics, I get to choose what I review, and I'd rather write about something that interests me. When I review Vermeer or Degas I am writing about artists I know in advance will interest readers. When I write about modern art, I take risks. But the rewards are enormous, too, for it gives me great pleasure to receive letters thanking me for recommending shows readers would not otherwise have considered going to see. Now that, I think, is a job worth doing.

On Kawara

Since 1966, the Japanese artist On Kawara has made more than 2,000 'date paintings', monochromatic rectangular canvases on which the only image is the date on which the work was made. At this point, I can almost hear the soft swish of thousands of pages of this newspaper being turned. But, if you will bear with me, I shall do my best to explain why Kawara is one of the most unsettling artists working anywhere in the world today, one whose art I often feel unable to think about for more than a few seconds at a time without anxiety. A small show entitled *Consciousness. Meditation. Watcher on the Hills* at Birmingham's Ikon Gallery demonstrates that it is not so much the individual works of art that can chill you to the bone, but the breadth and scope of Kawara's 36-year project.

To make the date paintings, Kawara works by a rigid set of self-imposed rules. The letters and numbers are always centralised on the rectangle, hand-painted in a basic sans serif font. The depth of each canvas is the same and each is painted on the sides where the canvas wraps round the edge of the stretcher. They are flawlessly finished, with no trace of the artist's touch visible. This gives them a cold, funereal look, like memorial tablets hanging on the gallery wall. And yet the effect is not entirely uniform, since, within his own strict boundaries, Kawara permits a surprising number of variations. The size of each canvas varies significantly, and the background colours range from black to grey, navy, slate blue and even red. The format of the composition can change, too, depending on whether the work was painted in Europe (day, month, year) or America (month, day, year). Kawara spells the abbreviated word for the month in the language of the country in which he painted the work, so you know that '11.Fev,1973' was painted in France, and 'Aug.27,1972' in the USA.

To make each work is a laborious process involving the application of four or five coats of paint and outlining the date by hand. But how

11 December 2002

Consciousness.
Meditation. Watcher
on the Hills

Ikon Gallery,
Birmingham

these works were created seems to me beside the point. What is
significant is that, if Kawara does not finish a canvas by midnight,
he destroys it. Once finished, the canvas is catalogued and then placed
in a cardboard box especially made for its size. Though he no longer
does so, Kawara used to include a copy of the day's newspaper in
the box, creating a sort of time capsule or memorial to the passage
of that particular day. It is a serious flaw in this exhibition that no
newspapers are included with the paintings.

From what I have said so far, you can see that Kawara deals with
the most fundamental reality of all, the passing of time. I will return
to the date paintings in a minute, but it will be easier for me to explain
his purpose in making them if we first look at other works in the
show. In *One Million Years – Past* (a companion work to *One Million
Years – Future*), Kawara counted backwards from the year 1970 (1969,
1968, 1967 . . . and so on) until he had compiled a list of one million
dates. These he divided into ten separate bound volumes of 100,000
dates each. Open any volume and all you see are rows of numbers,
each row consisting of ten dates. The rows in turn are divided into
units of ten lines each. A single unit, therefore, records the passage

On Kawara
*From **Today**,*
1966–2013
Private collection

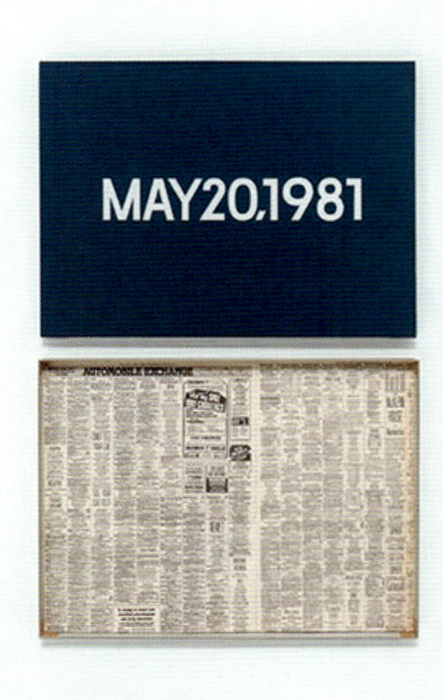

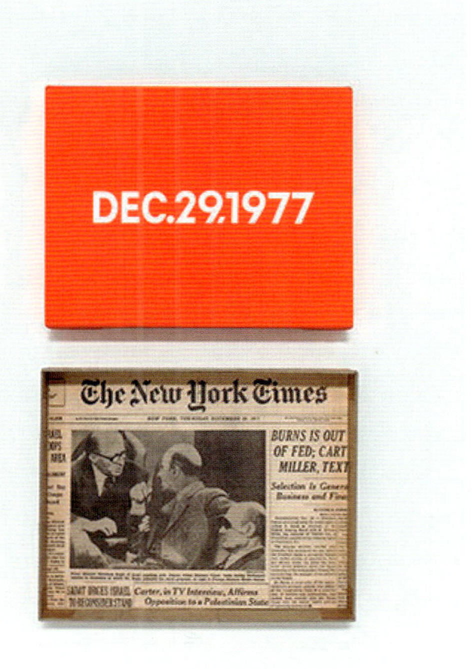

of a hundred years. If you open to page 94 in one of the later volumes, for example, you start in the upper left-hand corner with the date 952000 BC. Reading from left to right to the end of the line, you come to 951991 BC, and end the page in the lower right-hand corner with 951001 BC.

I have described this work in detail because, until you know exactly what you are looking at, it is virtually impossible to respond to it with anything but bafflement. And the response, when and if it comes, must come through the imagination, not the eyes. For, as you contemplate the seemingly endless columns of dates, it begins to dawn on you that a human life consists of only about seven or eight rows of numbers, that whole dynasties rose and fell in the space of two pages, that the Ice Age hardly registers against the immensity of time recorded in a single volume.

Suddenly, you have a tiny glimpse of the awesome expanse of time, a sense of your own brief flicker of life across a medium in which 20,000 years is but one chapter. This consciousness of time reminded me of the feeling of personal annihilation I used to have as a student studying geochronology, where an epoch is measured in millions of years, and an era in tens of millions.

Once Kawara gets under your skin, you start to think as he does. As you leave this show down a back staircase, you hear the sound of two people intoning another list of dates, counting backwards. Each performer takes exactly one second to say a number – 415 BC, 414 BC, 413 BC – relentless, implacable, like a ticking clock that can't be turned off. It takes the visitor about thirty 'years' to reach the bottom of the staircase, and each second it takes the performers to say a year is about how long that year lasted in the perspective of eternity. What's more, each second represents a second of your own life gone for ever. Not only do you want to scream, 'Stop it!' but you leave the show with a profound sense of melancholy, conscious of the brevity of your existence in the infinite, invisible and inexorable ocean of time.

Now go back to the date paintings and you see that they have the exact opposite purpose. For, when the passing years coincide with our own lives, time slows down. Having looked at time through the wrong end of a telescope in *One Million Years – Past* and *One Million Years – Future*, we now see it close up, a slow, heavy trickle of passing days. The changes in the size, background colour and format of each canvas simply register the idea that, although each 24-hour cycle of time is in all fundamental ways exactly like the one before it, in fact, each of our days is different. Particularly when you see the date paintings displayed with the relevant newspaper of the day, they speak of time as a medium full of life, events, things and people.

It is this meditation on the ambiguous nature of time that lies, I think, at the heart of On Kawara's work. And it is a meditation that you simply can't 'get' unless you stop in your tracks, draw in your breath and concentrate on the terrifying implications of the dimension he has made you concious of. For there comes a moment in all our lives when we start counting the years and days left to us, becoming aware that the amount of time allotted to each of us is not infinite. Kawara is about seventy. His death may be two years away or twenty, but it is within sight. Whether he has a lot of time or very little depends on the perspective from which you see it, up close or from a great distance.

Spare and elegant as the show at the Ikon is, with only 36 date paintings (one for every year since 1966) it is much too small. I once saw a huge On Kawara retrospective, where scores of the date paintings were shown alongside the relevant newspapers, and the cumulative impact was overwhelming.

The Ikon should be congratulated for doing in a small way what the Hayward or Tate Modern should do on a proper scale, but I have to warn you that, if you don't know Kawara's work, seeing it here you have to make a great leap of the imagination to submerge yourself in the terrifying medium that he has somehow made visible.

Eva Hesse

If ever an artist deserved cult status, it is the American sculptor Eva Hesse. Had she not died so young – in 1970, at the age of thirty-four – she would today have attained a stature in American art comparable to that of Richard Serra or Brice Marden. In the five years of her maturity, 1965–70, her achievement was to take the severe minimalist aesthetic then prevalent in progressive American sculpture and infuse it with an emotional resonance associated with European artists such as Joseph Beuys, whose work was then all but unknown in New York. At the time of her death, her sculptures were only just becoming widely known, but since then they have inspired a generation of younger artists. Judging by the crowds now packing into her retrospective at Tate Modern, her work is about to be discovered by a second wave of young admirers.

Hesse's art combined natural and industrial materials, from paper, wood, cotton, rope and string to wire, rubber tubing, plastic, galvanised steel, latex and fibreglass. She wasn't afraid to make pieces that were ugly, but, more often than not, her sculptures have an ethereal, melancholy radiance. The formal rigour of her work stands on its own merits irrespective of the circumstances under which it was made. But, at a time when minimalist sculptors such as Donald Judd and Carl Andre were denying that a work of art could have any subject (except for its own texture, proportions and the material from which it was made), it took enormous courage for Hesse to put her life – her family's flight from Nazi Germany in 1938, her mother's suicide, her emotional vulnerability and mortal illness – into her art.

The show starts slowly. In the first gallery, a number of pen-and-ink studies of dark, dramatically charged landscapes made in 1961 foretell the themes of grief and loss you find in the mature work. But the titles of some of these works (*Erasing a Girl*, *Finding a Girl*) are ominous, and, over the next four years, it is as though Hesse tried

21 November 2002

Eva Hesse

Tate Modern, London

to become the artist her mentor at art school Josef Albers wanted her to be, not the one she was. The result isn't a disaster, but neither is it memorable.

After four galleries of student work – brightly coloured paintings by an artist who would soon reject both colour and painting – the visitor who doesn't know what is about to happen may begin to wonder what all the fuss was about. Then we enter the gallery containing the work created after Hesse had spent a year in Germany, and it is as though some barrier to creativity had crumbled, enabling her to speak at last with her own voice.

In *Hang Up* (1966), Hesse confronts the problem all young artists of the period faced. What kind of artwork can you make when the boundaries between the formerly separate mediums of drawing, sculpture and painting no longer seem relevant – and when everything about the work of art is being questioned – including its materials, its subject matter and the role the viewer might play in completing it?

What we see is a large rectangular frame surrounding nothing. It has been meticulously bandaged and then covered with subtle

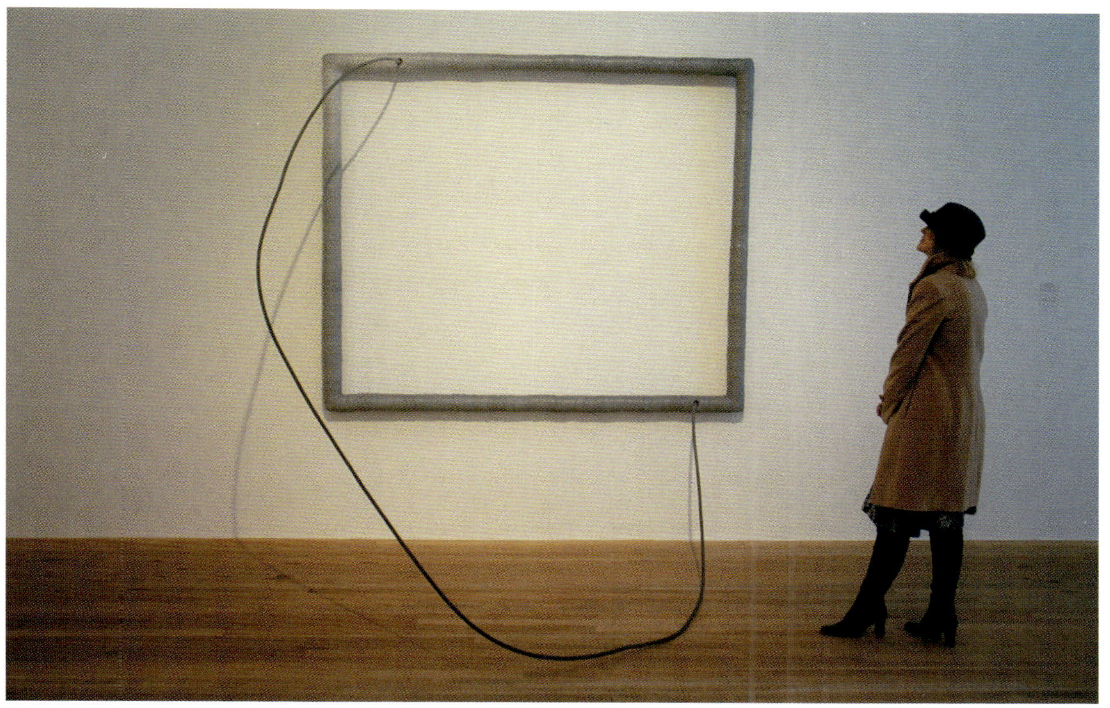

Eva Hesse
Hang Up, *1966*
Art Institute of Chicago

gradations of industrial grey paint. Abruptly, out of the upper left-hand corner of the frame, a thick metal wire leaps out and into the gallery space, then swoops down to touch the floor before looping back again into the frame. So a frame surrounds a 'painting' that doesn't exist, and a wire loop defines a volume of empty space, as though lassoing a sculpture that isn't there.

Because *Hang Up* hangs on the wall, its strongest affinities are with relief sculpture. But it is also a drawing of sorts, for, just as Paul Klee drew a work called *Taking a Line for a Walk*, so Hesse's 'line' seems to have a life of its own. What Hesse is doing, I think, is taking an inventory of all the traditional means of making art (painting, drawing, free-standing and relief sculpture) and then mocking each one. What is more, this impudent young woman, tipping her hat to Marcel Duchamp, tells the viewer who stands in front of *Hang Up* that if he or she wants a traditional painting or sculpture they have to imagine it for themselves.

Hang Up is cheeky and beautifully made, but it has a darker side, too. For the bandages also suggest something damaged about art itself, something in need of nursing or nurturing. The theme is emphasised by the way the wire, doubling back on itself, is like an umbilical cord that hasn't been cut. I interpret this as Hesse's comment on minimalist art. In *Hang Up*, she sends up the idea that art begets art, that a work of art is a closed circle that can't be broken in to. The work is a sort of artistic manifesto in which Hesse accepts the myriad freedoms and possibilities of the new art, while rejecting its sterility. From this point on, her work would make explicit references to the human body and to emotions.

There is something defiant as well as vulnerable, for example, in the wonderful *Not Yet*, in which she crumples clear polyethylene and paper into nine fishnet bags, and then hides a metal weight in each bag. Nailed to the gallery wall, the soft, heavy sacks hang down, pendulous, like testicles or breasts, at once male and female, castrated but curiously sensual, too. In *Metronomic Irregularity I*, she connects two painted wooden rectangles with a delicate skein of criss-crossed wires like a switchboard – or a nervous system sending signals from one part of the body to another. In *Accession II*, she parodies Judd's minimalist boxes by making one with an interior bristling with 'nails' made of plastic tubing. At once elegant and threatening, it is as overtly

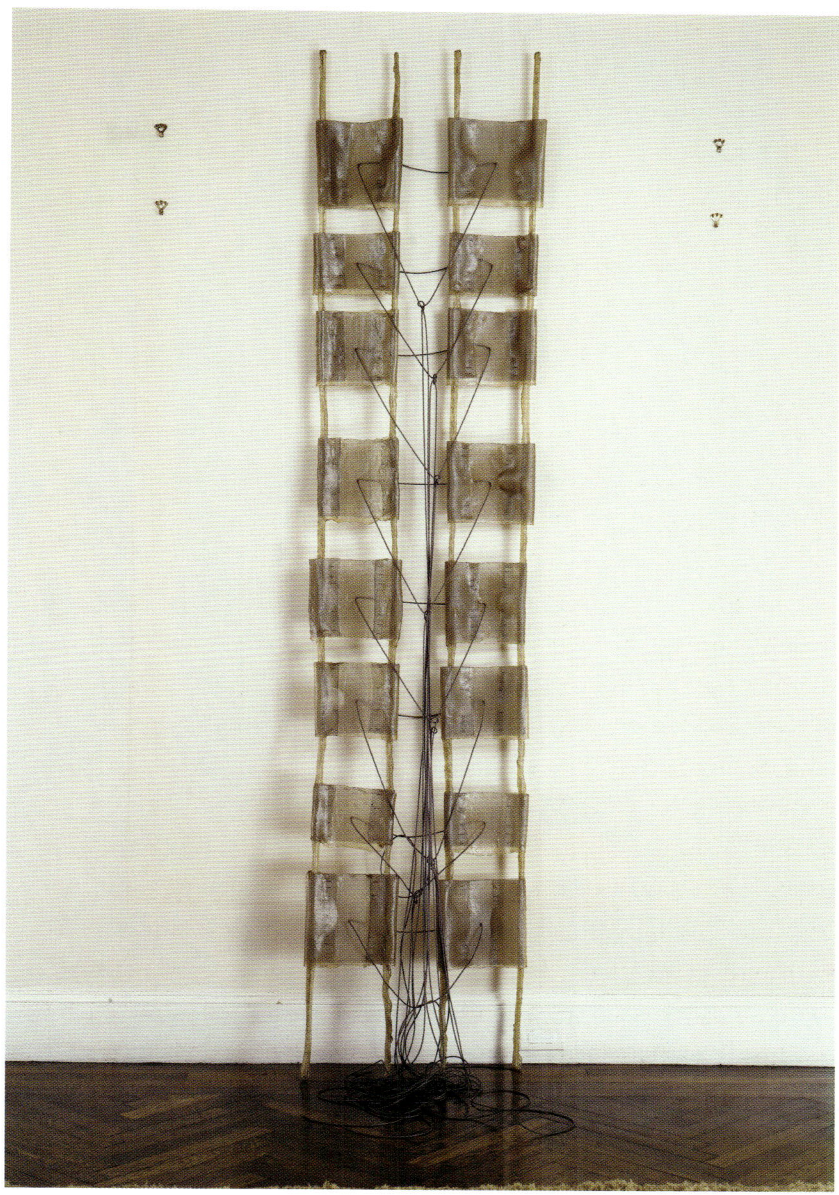

sexual as Meret Oppenheim's Surrealist icon the fur-lined teacup, but updated to an age of female empowerment.

Most beautiful of all is *Vinculum*, in which she uses fibreglass, polyester resin, metal screening and tubing to create a delicate, fragile sculpture that looks like a stretcher or palette leaning against the gallery wall. But, as you begin to analyse the way the piece is assembled, you see that it breaks down into two parallel sides, apparently stitched together like a human spine that has been opened up and then surgically closed again. Here, the non-colours of grey and discoloured white add to the sense of melancholy, as though *Vinculum*, like so many of Hesse's works, was damaged, split and only imperfectly repaired.

In *Sans*, she creates a minimalist progression of almost identical fibreglass boxes, then hangs the long line of rectangular voids on the gallery wall at breast height. Something about the deadening repetition of the translucent, parchment-like boxes feels funereal, like empty niches for ashes in a crematorium. But then, the theme of death becomes ever more palpable in the sublime late fibreglass pieces, where a rich layer of medical imagery emphasises the frailty of the human body and the transience of our lives.

Tori is a multi-part sculpture consisting of fibreglass sleeves or envelopes of dark silvery-grey fibreglass, each one ripped open like a pod. These lie on the gallery floor next to the remarkable untitled work in which Hesse strung from the gallery walls an elegant tangle of ropes dipped in latex, like great festoons of Spanish moss. But, seen together as they are at Tate, the two works suggest the opening of human torsos and revelation of the intestines within.

The show closes with the most ravishing corridor hung with late gouache studies based on repeated rectangles, like the window motifs that recur throughout her art, all associated with the window out of which her mother had fallen to her death. Trembling with veils and washes of soft grey and blue colour, these exude a sense of bafflement as to what might lie beyond or behind the blank window, but also a sense of acceptance and finality.

Bas Jan Ader

In Search of the Miraculous, the last and most poignant work by the Dutch-born artist Bas Jan Ader, was intended to be a performance in three parts. On the afternoon of 9 July 1975, the thirty-three-year-old artist said goodbye to his American wife and set sail from Cape Cod on a solo voyage across the Atlantic. His boat, the *Ocean Wave*, was only a little over 12 feet in length, the smallest craft in which such a feat had ever been attempted.

On the night before his departure, he arranged for a student choir to sing sea shanties around a piano in the gallery of his Los Angeles dealer. The voyage was to be the central element in the performance. To end it, Ader planned a second sing-song when he reached Falmouth eight to ten weeks later. But, after three weeks, radio contact with his boat was lost. Although it was spotted sixty miles out to sea and again near the Azores, he was never seen again. To this day, no one knows whether Ader was swept to his death by a freak wave, became disorientated and jumped overboard, or whether, from the first, his intention in staging his last work had been to commit suicide.

The body of work Ader left behind is extraordinary, but it isn't extensive – only a few short films (most of which were made in a single weekend), plus some photographs and several performance pieces. In short, he is a classic cult figure, an artist's artist. His work was enormously influential, but of limited popular appeal. At least, that's what I thought until I saw *All is Falling*, the heartbreaking retrospective of his work at the Camden Arts Centre.

I can't remember another exhibition that so completely transformed my understanding of an artist's work. Before I went to this show, I thought of Ader as a conceptual artist in the mode of Chris Burden and Bruce Nauman, unusual only in that he was such a romantic figure – young, handsome and melancholic. Now I realise

9 May 2006
All is Falling
Camden Arts Centre,
London

his life and work were tragically intertwined in ways that remind me
of Egon Schiele or Vincent Van Gogh.

In his few silent black-and-white films, he performs a series of
actions that are both dangerous and clown-like in their absurdity. In
one, he sits on a chair balanced on the pitched roof of his house and
allows himself to fall off. In another, he hangs from the branch of a
tree until his strength fails and he drops into a muddy stream. And in
a third, he steers his wobbly bicycle into an Amsterdam canal. In these
falling pieces, Ader's medium is the force of gravity, which launches
him into the unknown – much as Yves Klein had done in his famous
photograph of 1960, *Leap into the Void*. Thematically, Ader sets himself
up for failure in these works, presenting himself as hopelessly
incompetent, unable to hold on, to keep his balance, or to stand
upright – the artistic heir to Buster Keaton. All this is charming
enough, but, taken at face value, it's a little too whimsical to be the
stuff of great art.

At first sight, Ader's photographs and installations feel similarly
slight. In one of his best-known works, he photographed all of his
clothes chaotically spread out on the roof of his house. Another piece
consists of two photographs shown side by side. In the first, he stands
in a forest clearing looking directly out at us; in the second, he lies
prone on the forest floor.

His films and photos combine an element of slapstick with an
undertow of melancholy. Only a few express grief outright. In *I'm too
sad to tell you*, we see him in close-up weeping uncontrollably for a full
ten minutes, a Man of Sorrows. In one of his installations, he scrawls
the words 'Please don't leave me' on to the gallery wall.

What the Camden show reveals is that the terrible events of Ader's
early life inform the art he was to make as an adult. Ader was born in
1942, the son of a Calvinist minister living in northern Holland. His
idealistic parents had turned their home into a refuge for Jews, hiding
them from the Nazis and so saving their lives. When Ader was a few
months old, his father was arrested, imprisoned, taken into the woods
and shot. Suddenly, the photos in which Ader stands in the forest and
then falls down look like a re-enactment of his father's execution.

Ader's mother wrote a book about her experiences during the war,
in which she recalled that when her young son realised his father
would never return, he said, 'Mama, please don't leave me' – the title

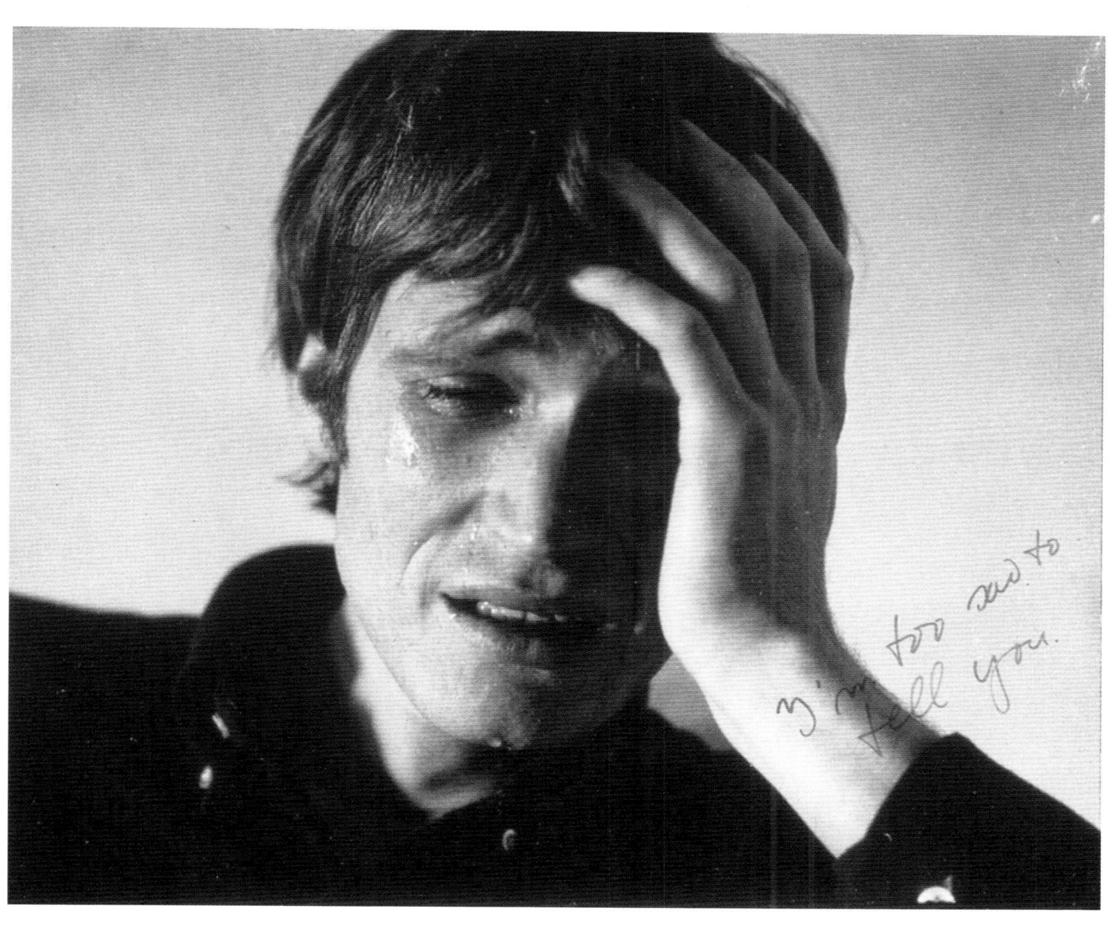

Bas Jan Ader
*Still from **I'm too sad to tell you**, 1971*

of a later artwork. When the Germans gave her fifteen minutes to
gather her belongings and leave the family home, she rushed through
the house, flinging the family's clothes out of the windows into the
garden, intending to come back later to retrieve them. Knowing this,
the photo of Ader's clothes thrown on to the roof of his house no
longer looks like a piece of whimsy, but an act of homage to his
mother.

And the film of Ader weeping uncontrollably is surely about
a sense of mourning and loss so great that it cannot be articulated.
Death haunts this work. In his film *Nightfall*, he lifts a concrete paving
slab and allows it to fall on to the only light source in a dark interior,
a cluster of light bulbs – an act symbolic of sudden and violent death.
A psychoanalyst might say Ader's work documents his attempt to
find his irretrievably lost father within himself. I'd go further. In some
works, it feels as though Ader is trying to become his father, and that
for this reason his early death was entirely predictable.

Whatever else is true about Ader, I think it is safe to say he was
a profoundly depressed man. It is in this light that we should see the
films in which he falls from a roof, a tree or into a canal. In order to
fall, you have to let go, to lose control – just as you must if you allow
yourself to feel the full force of overwhelming grief. In a superb
documentary film Rene Daalder has made about Ader's life and work,
it is suggested that the act of crossing the Atlantic in such a small boat
was another way to lose control, to place himself at the mercy of a
force greater than himself. Perhaps he let go of the steering wheel,
surrendering himself to the ocean as he had surrendered to the force
of gravity. We will never know.

For some, I realise, such a biographical interpretation diminishes
Ader's art, which should be allowed to stand on its own. But I think it
makes it richer by adding another layer of meaning and resonance to
work that was already original, touching and meticulously executed.

Jeff Wall

At one level the forty-nine-year-old Canadian artist Jeff Wall is simply an accomplished photographer whose still-life and landscape studies can be enjoyed for the perfection of their lighting, colour and composition. But Wall also uses the medium of photography to create large-scale narrative pictures, and these belong to a tradition of history painting which stretches back to the seventeenth century. Wall's art has a panache and theatricality nowadays more in evidence on the stage or in the cinema than in the visual arts.

All the pictures in the Whitechapel Art Gallery's exhibition of Wall's recent work are mounted on aluminium light boxes. Although the luminous effect is familiar to us from modern advertising techniques, back-lighting was first used in this country in the late eighteenth century by the painter and stage designer Philippe de Louterbourg. His celebrated exhibition of illuminated scenes painted on transparent material – his Eidophusikon – was imitated by no less an artist than Thomas Gainsborough. Spectacle is very important to Wall's aesthetic, for his larger works feel like panoramas, those all-enveloping paintings mounted on slowly revolving drums which attracted huge audiences in the nineteenth century. In the mural-sized *Restoration*, he actually shows conservators at work on a late nineteenth-century panorama depicting Napoleon's retreat from Moscow.

But a technology that was once capable of mesmerising spectators has now become a relic of a bygone age. The conservators' attempt to restore life to a moribund art form can at best only partially succeed. In Wall's art it is the camera, assisted by the computer, that creates the illusions which were once the sole province of painting. And illusion is what Wall's work is all about. The Tate Gallery's *A Sudden Gust of Wind (after Hokusai)* looks like a spontaneous photograph showing four men walking in a landscape at the very moment when a whoosh

13 March 1996

Jeff Wall

Whitechapel Art
Gallery, London

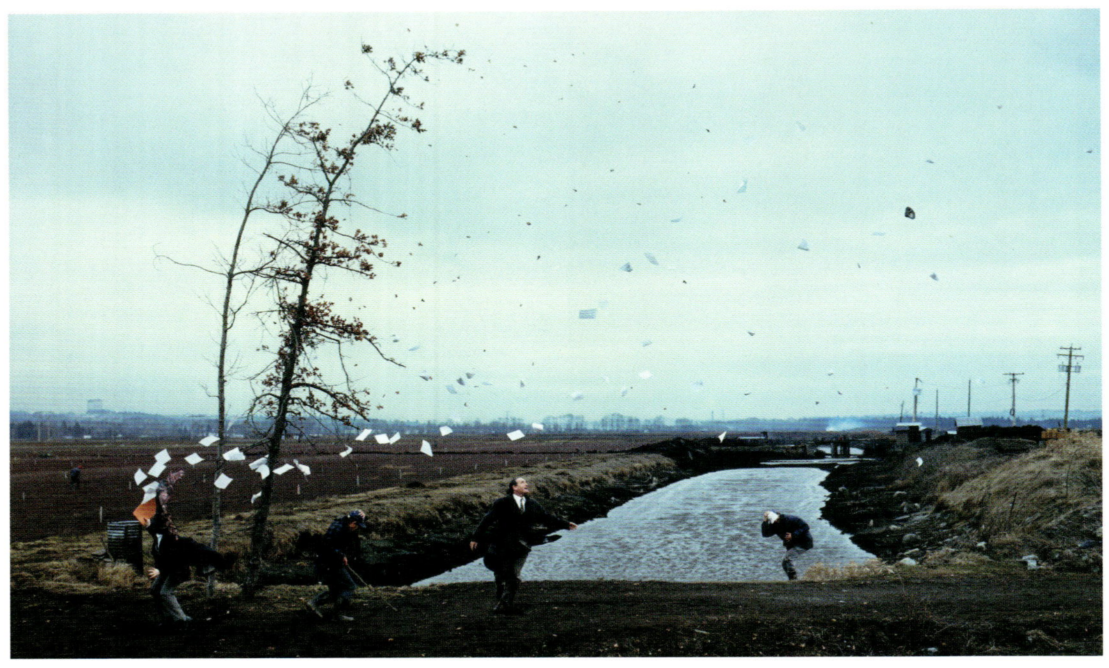

of wind blows papers, hats and leaves sky
high. But the title tells us that it is in fact a
meticulously staged tableau in which Wall
wittily updates the famous print from
Hokusai's *Thirty-six Views of Mount Fuji*. Like a
film director, Wall set up his shot using actors
posed individually against the same landscape
background. With advanced computer
technology he then spliced the separate

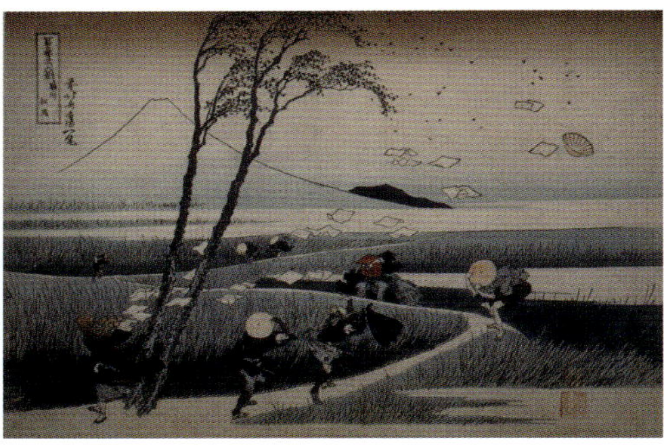

photographs together to create the illusion of instantaneous action. As
a former graduate student at the Courtauld Institute, he is well aware
that this technique resembles that of an academic artist preparing
a vast canvas in his studio. First he makes studies of the individual
figures, then he seamlessly joins them all together in the finished
composition. 'The fascination of this technology', he says, 'is that
it alone permits me to make pictures in the traditional way.'

But if Wall were using photography merely to make pastiches of
the Old Masters, he would be a far less interesting artist than he is.
Look closely at *A Sudden Gust of Wind* and it soon becomes evident
that Hokusai's image is the starting-point for a complex narrative

which is very much Wall's own. The setting is a scruffy wasteland
on the edge of a city, an area still under cultivation by local farmers,
but which a high-rise building in the distance suggests could be ripe
for development. Two of the men wear baseball caps and country
clothes – implying that they are local farmers, and therefore the
owners of the land. But the central figure with the ponytail comes
from another world. His overcoat and tie suggest that he is a
businessman of some kind, perhaps a property developer. At the left,
the fellow whose scarf has so comically blown up into his face looks
like another spiv, logically an accountant or lawyer. From his bright
orange folder (the only strong colour accent in the picture) the wind
has sent flying a flurry of business letters and contracts.

So, just as the river divides the composition into two halves, the
picture is about the meeting of two different cultures. It is a scene
that could be full of dramatic tension, but instead has been turned
into a gentle allegory. The sudden change in the direction of the wind
turns potential confrontation into communal fellowship by making
everyone ridiculous for a few moments. It is awfully difficult to look
at this picture without sharing the expression of amused surprise that
registers on the face of the central figure. *A Sudden Gust of Wind* is one
of the most infectiously joyous images I know.

What Wall does so brilliantly is to make the pomposities of
academic painting palatable to a modern audience by infusing them
with a wickedly black sense of humour. In both *The Vampire's Picnic*
and *Dead Troops Talk* he gives us modern versions of Géricault's *The
Raft of the Medusa*, but so thoroughly disguised under buckets of fake
blood and dime-store wigs that there is no temptation to respond to
them with undue solemnity. In these pictures Wall reintroduces into
modern art costumes, props, gestures and lighting in a way that
would have been familiar to artists ranging from Caravaggio to
Delacroix. But in his beautifully spare still-lifes he demonstrates a
concern for abstract formal values which would be recognisable to
Vermeer or Mondrian. The show at the Whitechapel includes both
aspects of Wall's art, and makes an excellent introduction to the work
of this unique voice in contemporary art.

Gary Hill

The best way to introduce the Californian video artist Gary Hill is to describe one of his works in detail. The trouble is, I am not entirely sure I have the words to do so. *Tall Ships* is a highly theatrical video installation, which can be seen in Hill's current exhibition, *Gary Hill: In the Light of the Other*, at the Museum of Modern Art in Oxford. To see it, the visitor walks down a darkened corridor in which the walls are illuminated by sixteen dim pools of light.

As our eyes grow accustomed to the gloom, we realise that these lights are actually indistinct black-and-white photographic images of the kind of people one passes in the street every day of one's life without noticing. But we are, after all, in an art gallery, so we pause to examine these figures more closely. Each image is only a few inches high, and each shows a person standing or seated at some distance from the spectator, at eye level. But wait. The very act of stopping in front of each image activates an electronic switch.

One at a time, the figures seem to notice our presence. As they come towards us, they grow larger, until each is the size of life. And because these ghostly presences are projected directly on to the wall, and are not 'framed' by a border of light around them, the effect is disturbingly realistic. As we approach these figures, some are already facing us. Others have their backs turned and therefore have to swivel around when they hear us coming. Still others are seated and rise politely to greet us as soon as they become aware that we are watching them. (This is the first art exhibition in my experience in which the art looks at you, as well as the other way around.)

But, as soon as they come close to the wall – the invisible barrier that separates our world from theirs – their reactions vary greatly. One woman appears to be overjoyed to catch sight of us. Incredulous, she strains to make us out, as though she can't quite see us through a fog, or as though trapped behind a sheet of plate glass. A burly gent

8 December 1993

Gary Hill: In the Light of the Other

Museum of Modern Art, Oxford

scowls as he takes out his pocket handkerchief to mop his brow. Only gradually do we realise that he may be wiping away tears, and that his face registers not anger but anguish. Some try to contact us, others look at us with eyes full of reproach or despair, then turn away. In the one that upset me most, a little girl ran towards me in slow motion, as though about to jump into my arms.

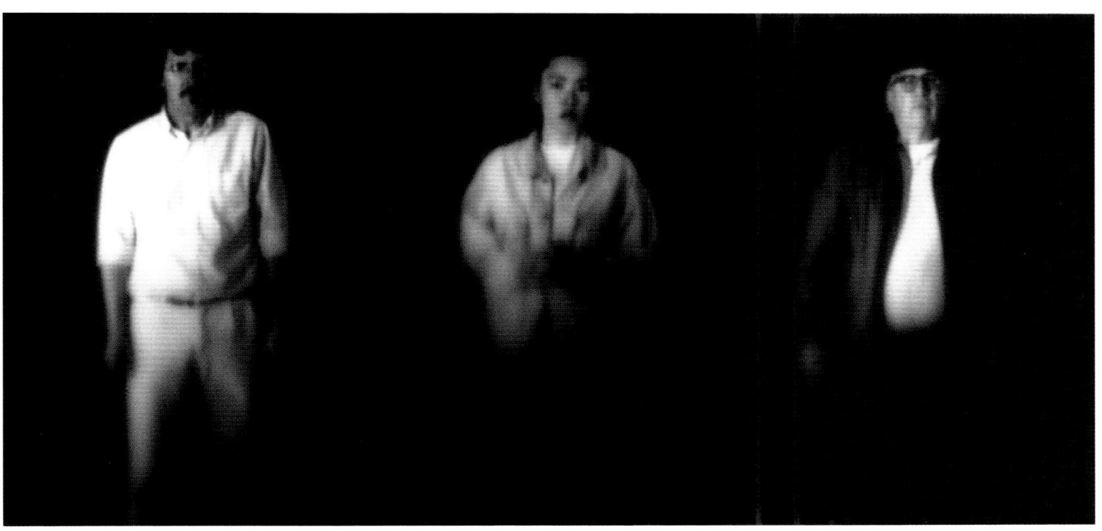

Gary Hill
*From **Tall Ships**, 1992*
Private collection

There will be many different interpretations of *Tall Ships*. For me, Gary Hill evokes a spirit world, a house of the dead. I was haunted by a sense that I had seen all this before, but couldn't quite put my finger on where. Then it came to me. *Tall Ships* reminded me of Virgil's description of Aeneas's visit to the Underworld in Book VI of the *Aeneid*, and particularly of the Trojan hero's encounter with the ghost of his beloved father Anchises. At the thought that the people in *Tall Ships* could be those we have known and loved, tears pricked in my eyes. But, of course, this interpretation is highly personal: each visitor projects his or her own feelings, fears, fantasies on these images. I can well imagine others being comforted by *Tall Ships*, or feeling that the work is not about death but about life, about how one can never truly make contact with another human being, about the mystery we all finally are to each other.

Francesco Clemente

I learned a new word – 'ideogram' – at the Royal Academy's new exhibition, *Francesco Clemente: Three Worlds*. It means a picture or symbolic image which stands for an idea or an emotion, and it accurately describes what Clemente does in his ravishingly beautiful pastels and watercolours. Ideograms work rather like dreams. For ideas that may otherwise be too subtle or difficult to express, Clemente will substitute one or two simple images in bizarre and allusive juxtapositions, thereby creating a third image containing a new meaning. In this way he can communicate sensations we all share but which lie outside our powers of speech.

The subjects of these radiantly colourful works include the physical senses of taste, smell and touch – as well as more incommunicable sensations like boredom or hunger. Then there are the visual equivalents for experiences we normally keep hidden like ejaculation and evacuation: Clemente sometimes seems like some modern Linnaeus classifying every aspect of our common humanity. At the same time, in his seemingly primitive ideogrammatic images Clemente resembles the ancient storytellers who accounted for human feelings by inventing myths in which the aboriginal gods partook of experiences which even the naive listener could share. In Hindu mythology an inexhaustible number of fantastic stories chronicle the adventures of thousands of major and minor deities. Such fables serve to explain every aspect of existence, from the creation of the Ganges to the infertility of a new bride.

At the RA exhibition, a six-foot-high banner made of sheets of handmade Indian paper sewn together with strips of cotton muslin is entitled *Hunger*. Designed by Clemente but painted in brilliant gouache by commercial sign-painters from Madras, it shows a little man biting into a huge snake, which in turn bites its own tail. Crude but unforgettable, the image suggests the idea of man cruelly

30 September 1991

Francesco Clemente:
Three Worlds

Royal Academy,
London

condemned to eternal insatiability. Another gouache, *The Four Corners*, depicts a gigantic hand rising up from the sea against a starry blue sky. On its palm we can read mankind's destiny in a map of the world so drawn that the future belongs to Africa, India and South America.

Clemente's preoccupation with his own face, body and sexuality is often described as narcissistic. It might be more true to say that his body is the vehicle he uses to explore universal states of being. In addition to his remarkable technical command over his various mediums, part of the discipline of what he does lies in his ability to reach deep within himself to recover and bring to the surface visual equivalents for his own most private experiences and emotions.

Francesco Clemente was born in Naples in 1952. In 1970 he moved to Rome where, it would seem, Cy Twombly's ethereal evocations of the classical myths were more important to him even than the ubiquitous Arte Povera of his own era. In 1973 Clemente first went to India. Just as late nineteenth-century avant-garde artists turned to Japan in order to shed the burden of their classical academic training, in the East Clemente found a way to slough off the stale onus of Modernism. Yet the fascination with India was less of a break than it might at first seem. 'The gods who left us thousands of years ago in Naples are still in India,' he has said, 'so it's like going home for me. In India I can feel what it was like [in Italy] many years ago.'

Over the years, Clemente has lived and worked for long periods in the South Indian city of Madras. As admirers of Clemente's art, several years ago my wife and I made our own pilgrimage to the ashram outside Madras where Clemente then had a studio. On the road out to the ashram, which is run by the Theosophical Society of Madras, we became aware of the characteristic reddish-brown earth around the city, and of the presence of the sea (the Bay of Bengal) and of the fishermen, even when both were out of sight. This is a strange, haunted – and, for India, relatively empty – coast. The huge scale of the skies and beaches gave us a feeling of being on the edge of the world. We passed gigantic modern billboards advertising new Indian movies (Madras is an important film-making centre), with huge close-up faces of kissing film stars, often heavily made-up and in exotic costume.

Close to Madras are some of the most exotic temples in India. Here the younger Clemente must have spent his days observing the

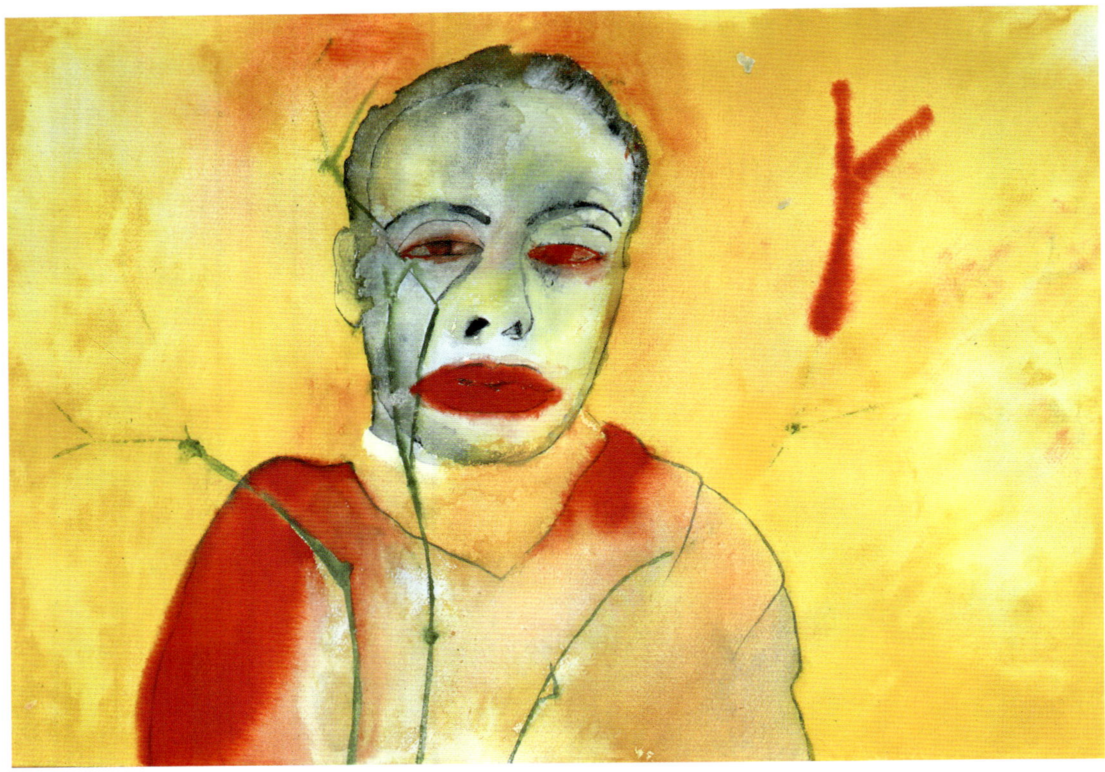

teeming spectacle of South Indian temple life, including the gorgeous crimson and saffron-coloured fabrics worn by the women, the dyes used for cosmetics, and the garish flower and souvenir stalls. All this inevitably finds its way into Clemente's art. The materials with which he works are very pure and wonderfully tactile – from the dry, powdery red and orange pastels on thick rag paper to the liquid watercolour washes that seem mysteriously to flow into one another without becoming muddy.

At these temple sites Clemente (like the young Picasso) learned the palmistry, prediction and numerology to which he refers so often in this show. And not far from Madras he could see the erotic temple sculpture, the struggling with powerful demons, or the marvellous bestiaries of carved animals – all of which seem to reappear in one form or another in almost every work on view. In short, the melange of new and old, which at the Royal Academy looks so strange and so surreal, in India seems utterly natural and ordinary.

In 1982 Clemente moved to New York. Though the exhibition attempts to divide his life and work into three separate sections

Francesco Clemente
The Four Elements:
Fire, *1982*
Private collection

corresponding to his life in Rome, Madras and New York, what quickly emerges is that there is really very little difference for him between the three worlds. In New York the inspiration he had once found in Indian high and low culture is replaced by daily contact with poets, critics, painters and filmmakers. Above all, there is the idol of Clemente's early youth, Allen Ginsberg. Working closely with Ginsberg to illustrate – or, better, illuminate – the great American poet's work, Clemente has discovered the perfect collaborator.

Felix Gonzalez-Torres

The mature work of the Cuban-American artist Felix Gonzalez-Torres coincided with the nightmare years of the Aids epidemic in New York. The themes of sexuality, death and fear are therefore central to his art, though it must be said too that it is also about life, hope and personal responsibility for our actions. Though he himself died of the illness in 1996, aged thirty-nine, the superb exhibition of his work at the Serpentine Gallery is anything but gloomy, and has none of the explicit sexual imagery of his contemporaries Robert Mapplethorpe or Keith Haring. The gravity of his subject matter and the poignancy of the circumstances under which he worked are leavened by his delicate wit and a deep undercurrent of emotion that never descends into self-pity.

Gonzalez-Torres emerged in the 1980s, at a moment when minimalist sculptors such as Carl Andre and Donald Judd were denying that a work of art could have any content at all. Appropriating minimalist forms such as grids, stacks and rectangles, it was Gonzalez-Torres's achievement to invest them with meaning, and to show that the materials an artist uses can in themselves set in motion poetic, personal and political associations of quite extraordinary resonance.

In *Untitled (Placebo)* from 1991, for example, he took thousands of sweets, each one wrapped in silver foil, and spread them out on the gallery floor to form a perfect rectangle, so that the shiny paper spotlit from above looks like the rippling surface of a silvery lake. At first glance, you could easily mistake the work for a floor piece by Andre. But unlike Andre, with Gonzalez-Torres what you see is only part of what you get. Equally important is what you do. For it is at the moment when a viewer picks up one of the sweets, unwraps it and puts it into his or her mouth that the work's many meanings begin to unfold.

7 June 2000
Felix Gonzalez-Torres
Serpentine Gallery,
London

By yielding to our hunger, we become participants in the making, or rather unmaking, of the work of art. Our desire for sensual gratification eventually alters the shape of *Placebo*. Soon it has diminished in size, and ultimately it will disappear, only to be renewed again by the gallery staff overnight. This is one work of art that exists in a constant state of flux, for after several thousand visitors have taken what they want from it, we all pay the price: the beautiful rectangle which in the morning offered the promise of endless pleasure has by evening been ravaged, the few remaining sweets scattered over the bare floor amid the detritus of cast-off wrappers.

Since most of us will not be content with one sweet, it isn't hard to see how our behaviour mimics the causes and effects of the Aids epidemic. Because the very act of unwrapping and consuming the sweet is fraught with sexual innuendo, *Placebo* might be interpreted as a warning that promiscuous consumption of sexual partners (or any other natural resource) destroys the source of our gratification, and may in the end destroy our world as well.

But with Gonzalez-Torres, nothing is ever simple. Are we really meant to stand there, confronted with this carpet of delicious M&S chocolate caramels and not participate, not take pleasure when it is offered to us? The work's final meaning has to do with personal freedom, with the moral and ethical choices that we make. It is essential to Gonzalez-Torres's purpose in making *Placebo* that we be allowed to destroy or preserve it, as we wish.

He comes back again and again to this theme. Right at the beginning of the show, a more or less empty gallery is casually strung with a swag of light bulbs, as though for a party. On one wall we find two Walkman headsets. Visitors are encouraged to switch on a Walkman, grab a partner, and waltz under the lights. It goes without saying that few of us would dream of doing any such thing. But the very austerity of Gonzalez-Torres's work has a way of needling you, of getting under your skin. Entering into the artist's way of seeing things, we ask ourselves why in the world we aren't dancing. We preserve our dignity, certainly, but at the cost of not participating in life. By taking the risk of inviting a stranger to have a twirl, we engage not only with the work of art, but with life itself. It is by surrendering our pride, chancing humiliation, that we become fully human.

But here's the sting in the tail. Even if we do participate, we

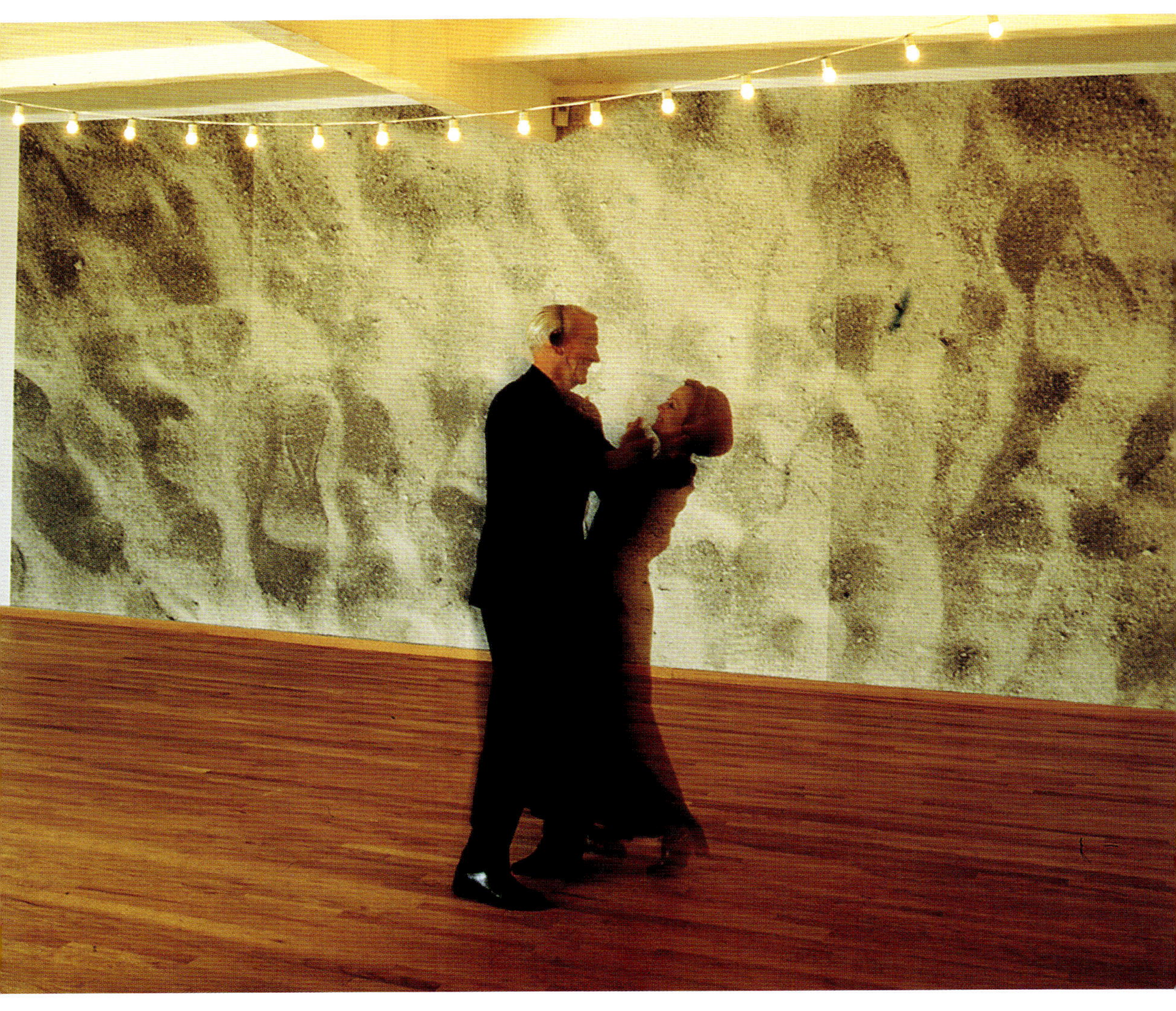

discover that we are dancing to the music in our own Walkman, music that no one else, including our partner, can hear. Even a long-married couple may find themselves out of synch, dancing to a beat utterly different from that of the person in their arms. Life is never perfect, human relationships are never without pain, but they are better than the alternatives of loneliness and death.

Gonzalez-Torres was also a highly political artist. A piece on one of the most hardline American lobby groups, the National Rifle Association, is particularly effective: visitors are invited to take a paper doormat from an 8-inch-high stack on the gallery floor. Each one has a green border and blood-red centre. The idea is that members

Felix Gonzalez-Torres
***Untitled (Arena)**,*
1993
*View of the installation
at the Serpentine
Gallery, 2000*

of the NRA can put one on their front doorsteps to symbolise their complicity in leaving a trail of blood through America.

But the works I find most moving are those that reflect the artist's constant awareness of his own mortality. He was attracted to cheap, gaudy materials, materials that in any setting but the art gallery you would describe as camp. In one piece, a rather pretty curtain of silver and blue glass beads is simply hung between the passage from one gallery to another. Because we know something about the circumstances under which Gonzalez-Torres made the piece, it suggests that the passing from life may not be so terrible after all, that it may simply be a transition from the place in which we are now standing to one in which we can dimly make out the shapes of people moving on the other side.

And when we walk through the curtain, we find one of Gonzalez-Torres's late black-and-white photographs of birds wheeling high up in the sky, remote, untouchable and free. The last thing that happens before we leave the gallery is that we see two stacks of paper, each ideally 26 inches high. The first reads 'Somewhere better than this place'; the second 'Nowhere better than this place'. Obviously one sentence is for optimists, the other for pessimists. But which is which? Are those who believe in an afterlife condemned to be unhappy in this one? Or are those who are greedy for life in the here and now doomed to live without the promise of some future joy? Gonzalez-Torres provides a partial answer, leaving instructions for visitors to take one piece of paper from each stack. For him, both statements were true.

Despite Gonzalez-Torres's intensely personal involvement with his subject matter, he never actually appears in his work. Far from sharing the romantic anguish of contemporaries such as Mapplethorpe or Robert Gober, Gonzalez-Torres strikes me as a profoundly classical artist, one for whom emotion is all the more heightened for being contained, kept at bay. Death-haunted though it is, this show never at any point feels lachrymose. At the end it is the beauty, joy and generosity of his art that makes it so memorable. This is one of the few exhibitions that I can honestly say brought a lump to my throat.

Matthew Barney
(*Il Tempo del Postino*)

'In consideration of the bull's well-being, please refrain from making
any startling noise whilst he is in the theatre.' When I read this
programme note while waiting for the curtain to go up at the Opera
House in Manchester, something told me this wasn't going to be
a run-of-the-mill theatrical experience. In fact, *Il Tempo del Postino*
('Postman's time') was an art exhibition, an international group
show of fourteen artists selected by celebrity curators Hans Ulrich
Obrist and Philippe Parreno. They commissioned works of art to be
presented sequentially on stage, accompanied (where appropriate)
by music, just as in a play or opera.

The element of time, intrinsic to the theatre but surprisingly
irrelevant to the way we usually look at visual art, was to play a major
role in the proceedings. Each artist was allotted no more than fifteen
minutes to present an artwork, film or performance before the
interval. The entire second part of the evening was given over to the
night's star attraction, the staging of a new work by one of the most
influential artists in the world today, Matthew Barney. Anyone who
has the slightest acquaintance with his art will have guessed that it
was he who required the live bull.

Things got under way with a delightful 'overture' by performance
artist Tino Sehgal, who made the Opera House's heavy, red velvet
curtains dance, swing, shimmy and shake in time to music provided
by the orchestra. Then the lights went down and Los Angeles-based
installation artist Doug Aitken wowed us with a performance by
two auctioneers from the American South patrolling the aisles with
torches, taking bids so fast that we were all hypnotised by that
singsong unearthly sound, hardly noticing that what they were
auctioning off wasn't tobacco or cattle, but members of the audience.

Albanian-born Anri Sala made me melt by staging an aria from
Madam Butterfly in the darkened theatre using four sopranos in full

17 July 2007

Il Tempo del Postino

Opera House,
Manchester

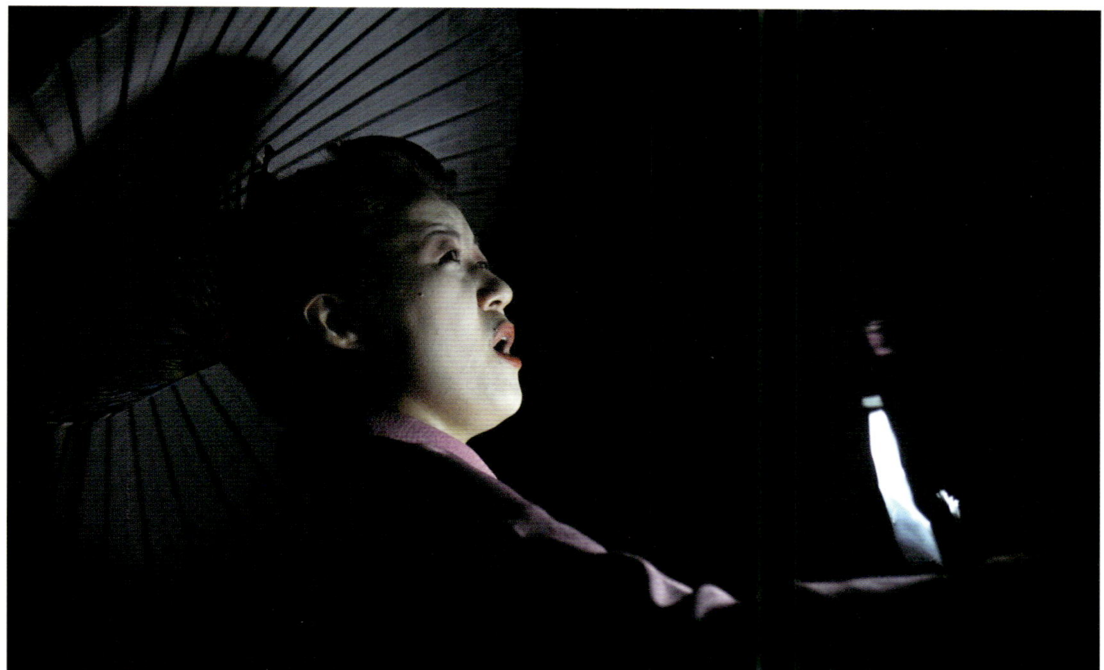

Japanese costume who stood both on stage and in the amphitheatre illuminated only by lights concealed behind their fluttering fans. They sang their hearts out, but only one at a time, tossing the aria back and forth to each other across the theatre while the villain Pinkerton ratcheted up the emotion by singing while walking slowly backwards down the central aisle. This was spine-tingling stuff, and also a deeply felt homage to all those lushly romantic moments the opera house had seen over the years.

All these works used the architecture of the Victorian building where the event took place to explore themes of theatricality and that was true too of Olafur Eliasson's *Echo House*. The curtain rose on a mirror in which the audience saw its own reflection. Then a conductor silently mounted a podium to face the (real) audience and proceeded to have the orchestra imitate every cough, sniffle, catcall, joke or whistle we made – in fact, to 'play' the audience back to its own reflection.

The great Douglas Gordon had a torch singer in a black dress come on stage, then turned the lights off while she broke our hearts with the ballad *Love Will Tear Us Apart*, sung without accompaniment. It's been a long time since I've lain in bed at 3 a.m., listening to the wireless after a lovers' quarrel, but Gordon made me remember what it was like.

Best of all, Dominique Gonzalez-Foerster created the most moving work of the evening out of a piece of music. First, she asked fifty or so players from the Orchestra of the Royal Northern College of Music to play a Beethoven symphony. Gradually, one by one, each player picked up his or her instrument and slowly left the pit, walked up on to the stage, and then disappeared into the darkness of the wings. As this happened, the orchestral sound became thinner and thinner until at last, with violins, horns and flutes gone, the melody was lost. Then the conductor exited, leaving a lone cello, and the orchestra fell silent.

Gonzalez-Foerster had created a simple metaphor for what happens in life, as each generation starts with hope and talent and promise, and then slowly breaks up as each of us dies and at last the generation passes away. Liam Gillick, Pierre Huyghe, Koo Jeong-A and Rirkrit Tiravanija: all staged work that was just as inventive and entertaining. But the best was yet to come. After the interval, Matthew Barney came on – and made everything we had just seen look like child's play. Barney is the real thing. When he brings his boundless imagination to a subject he goes down to its depths to create images and implant ideas that stay in your mind for ever.

Guardian of the Veil seems to be about nothing less than the psycho-sexual origins of Islamic fundamentalism. As the curtain rises, four pall-bearers dressed in paramilitary fatigues place the corpse of a woman wearing a sequinned, Western-style cocktail dress on the roof of a crashed car. Barney then enters wearing a Masonic leather apron and a headdress containing a live dog to represent the Egyptian god of the dead, Anubis. He then symbolically 'embalms' the woman and the values she represents, by opening the car bonnet, and removing parts of the motor which he deposits in Egyptian funerary urns at the front of the stage.

As balaclava-wearing terrorists roam the stage playing a haunting score composed by Barney's collaborator Jonathan Bepler, a series of symbolic actions take place: a naked woman who stands motionless throughout the performance and whom we see only from the rear is ritually 'veiled' in black plastic of the sort used to make bin bags; a female contortionist, naked apart from a veil over her face, stiletto

heels and claw-like nail extensions bends over backwards in such
a way that all we see of her are her legs and vagina, then urinates
spectacularly and copiously over the stage; a ritually garlanded bull
is escorted on stage in too-close-for-comfort proximity to the still-
exposed vagina, then urged to mount the crashed car, which, as we
saw, Barney uses as a symbol of the female body. At the stomach-
turning finale, the naked woman we see from behind defecates on
stage.

Shocking as some of this is, nothing that goes on in Barney's
dream-like, surrealistic performance is gratuitous. He is meditating
on the psychic catastrophe that is Islamism, whereby men who
possess power over women express their fear and disgust at the sight
of the female body by forcing their daughters and wives to cover
themselves completely. Drawing on Freud's writings, he shows that
women who are made powerless express their rage in the only way
they can – by using their own bodies to urinate and defecate.

The corpse we saw at the beginning is that of a Westernised
Muslim woman, embalmed and replaced by women made faceless
by men who deny their existence as real people. This breakdown of
human interaction is completed when the men then cover their own
faces in balaclavas, losing any sense of themselves as individuals and
allowing them to be subsumed in their sick ideology. Barney seems to
be saying that the horrors we see nightly on news bulletins from the
Middle East have their origins in sexual dysfunction.

The cause of Islamists' hatred of the West has nothing to do with
Israel or Iraq but with fear of the other. They hate everyone who isn't
like them, beginning with their own mothers, sisters and wives. And
orchestrating this perversion of human nature is the god of death.
At the end of *Il Tempo del Postino*, I felt I'd been present at a historic
occasion when the ambitions of the curators were perfectly matched
by the quality of the art, and when we saw the premiere of one of
Barney's most profound and powerful works.

Olafur Eliasson
The Weather Project,
2003
Tate Modern, London

Olafur Eliasson

I promise to resist the temptation to unleash a torrent of purple prose
about Olafur Eliasson's *The Weather Project* at Tate Modern. It is more
in keeping with the spirit of the piece to describe it with clinical
detachment, and to trust that my words can convey something of its
beauty and power. The fourth in the series of artworks commissioned
by Unilever to fill the vast space of the Turbine Hall, *The Weather
Project* is, essentially, a vast optical illusion. As the visitor enters the
building, he is confronted by what looks like a gigantic illuminated
orange disc suspended from the ceiling at the far end of the hall.
Discreetly placed humidifiers pump a mixture of sugar and water
into the air to create a fine mist.

Seen through this soft haze, the light of the great disc is filtered and
diffused so that it looks like the flaming ball of the setting sun. Then,
as we start to walk down the long entrance ramp, we realise that the
entire ceiling is covered in what appears to be a single huge mirror.
The tiny specks of humanity we see far, far, above us are our own
reflections.

That is the illusion. The reality is that Eliasson has hung a semi-
circle of light from the mirrored ceiling in such a way that its reflection
creates the appearance of a full circle. There is not just one mirror on
the ceiling but hundreds, fractionally offset where they are joined.
This makes the edges at the upper (illusory) half of the great disc
appear slightly jagged or uneven, which is what makes the ball of
light look so uncannily like the sun. Had the mirrors on the ceiling
been level or flat, we would see a perfect circle and the whole thing
would have looked unreal.

What the artist began, the audience completes. It is the visitors
that make *The Weather Project* unforgettable. From any distance at all,
people in the Turbine Hall are seen as tiny black silhouettes against
a field of orange light. Minuscule in scale and robbed by the orange

12 November 2003
The Weather Project
Tate Modern, London

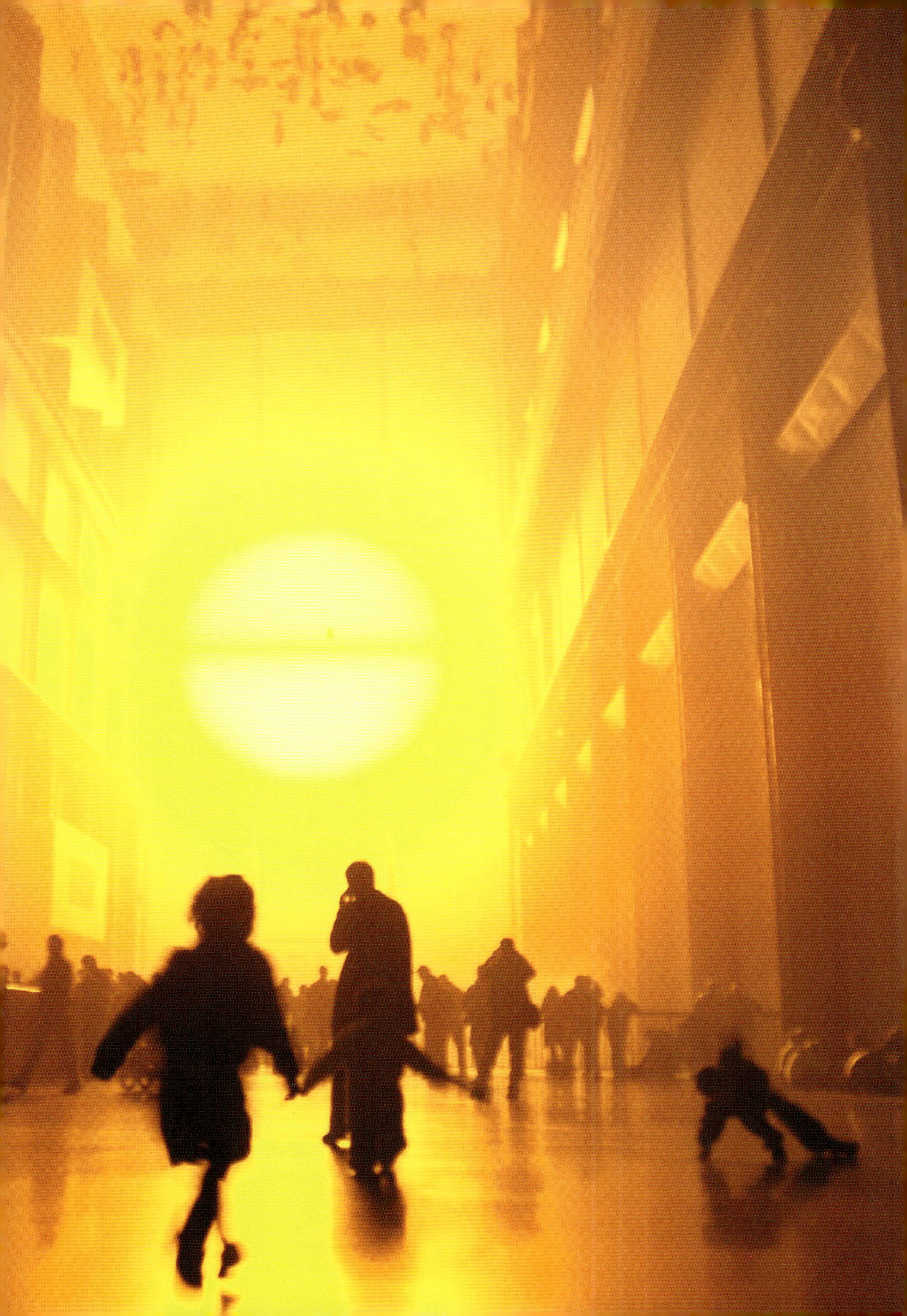

glow of their individuality, they are diminished by the spectacle they have come to the Tate to see. Paradoxically, the less we look like individuals, the more aware we become that we share a common humanity, that we are all members of the same species. Against the cataclysmic beauty of the evening sun, we sense our insignificant place within the infinity of our solar system.

When I first saw *The Weather Project*, I thought of the sun rising through vapour in one of J. M. W. Turner's landscapes. But, late on a Saturday or Sunday afternoon, when hundreds of people stand mesmerised in the face of the glowing disc, the work becomes truly frightening, a modern interpretation of one of John Martin's or Francis Danby's apocalyptic visions of the end of the world. A close encounter of the third kind.

Not only does the audience help to create Eliasson's work of art, but, in the weeks since the exhibition opened, the behaviour of that audience has added another layer of meaning to it. Visitors respond not only to the circle of light, but also to the mirror above their heads. Adults and children lie on their backs staring up at the ceiling, often moving their arms and legs in a sweet, sad effort to find their own reflections in the swarming mass of undifferentiated shapes in the distance. It is as though some deep primeval instinct compels us to do something – waving our hands, scissoring our legs, huddling in groups, forming shapes with our partners – to reassure ourselves of our individual existence in the universe. What this great artist has done, literally, is to hold up a mirror and show us who we are.

Francis Alÿs

Tate Modern's impeccably curated retrospective of the work of Belgian artist Francis Alÿs starts in silence, with a 16mm film of a mirage shimmering on a horizon, forever out of reach. It's an apt introduction to an elusive artist who uses gentle wit and inexhaustible invention to make work that is at once sad, serious and almost impossible to pin down.

Take *Rehearsal*, a 30-minute performance on video that Alÿs, who lives in Mexico, staged on the outskirts of Tijuana. To the joyful sound of one of the town's famous brass bands, the driver of a battered red Volkswagen Beetle repeatedly tries and fails to reach the top of a steep dirt track. As in slapstick comedy, there is something both comical and touching about the plucky little car's eternal optimism and unending failure.

As we watch the apparently random stopping and starting, the structure of the film gradually becomes clear. The constantly interrupted music is the sound of a brass band in rehearsal. The driver of the VW steps on the gas pedal whenever the band starts to play, but brakes, and then allows the car to roll back down the slope the moment the musicians stop – either because they've gone wrong or to take a coffee break. Because the rehearsal is interrupted so often, the car never goes anywhere.

For all the lightness of his touch, Alÿs is incapable of making art that isn't imbued with gravity. The location, in the violent border town of Tijuana, suggests that the piece is a bittersweet metaphor for Mexico's chronic inability to solve its economic, social and political problems. The band that can't seem to finish the song and the car that can't reach the summit symbolise the paralysis that poisons a country where change is always promised, but never happens.

For Alÿs, who trained as an architect, the act of making a work of art requires careful preparation, compositional rigour, deep thought

22 June 2010

Francis Alÿs:
A Story of Deception
Tate Modern, London

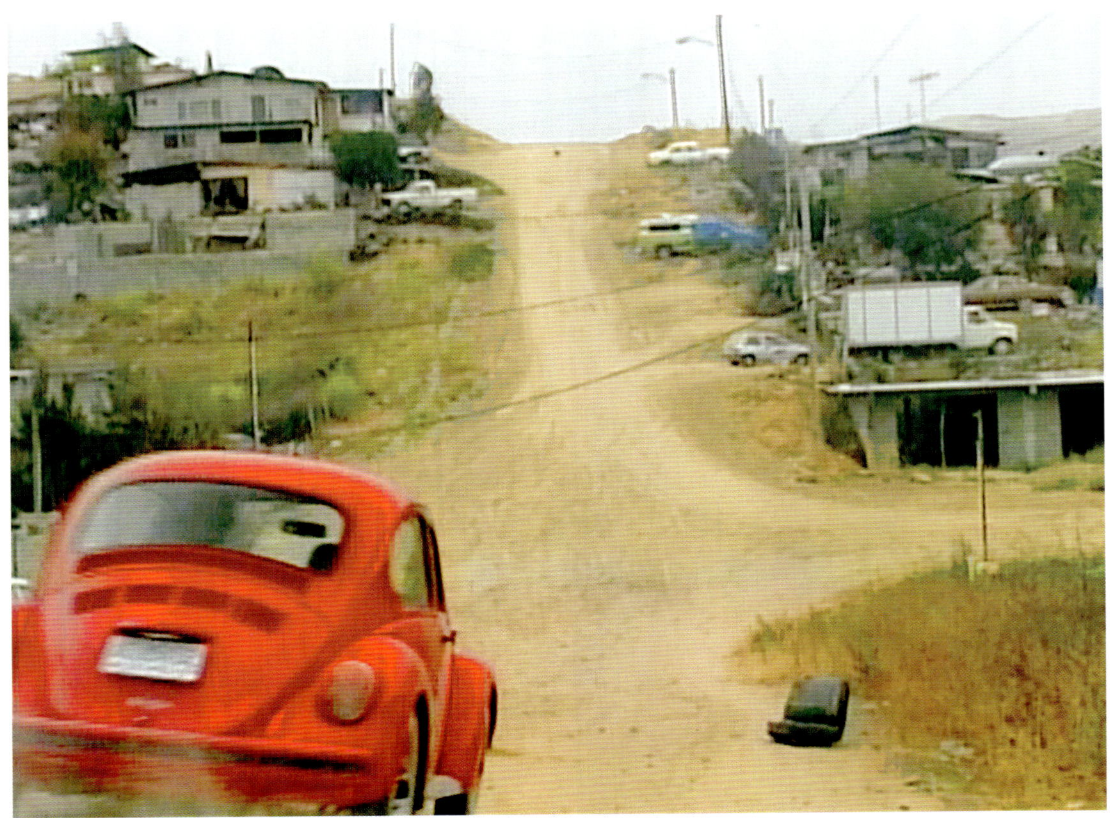

and continuous revision. After watching the film for a few minutes, you notice that the camera is positioned so that the dirt track bisects the screen, with the bright red Beetle the only note of strong colour running up and down the lateral stripe in the centre of the dun-coloured landscape. In case we miss this, the curators show a scale model of the VW and the terrain in which it will be driven made by the artist before the filming of *Rehearsal* began.

Alÿs seems to have taken to heart Samuel Beckett's injunction to the artist to 'Fail, fail again, fail better.' Following an early work in which he photographed small tradesmen and street vendors pushing, hauling and carrying a surreal variety of objects through the streets of Mexico City, he staged a physically gruelling performance in which he is filmed pushing a large block of ice through the same streets on a hot day. After nine hours, he is left with a puddle of water at his feet – to the joy of the street children on hand to witness to the gringo's stupidity. As always, the pointlessness has a point – or rather, poses a question.

Francis Alÿs in collaboration with Rafael Ortega **Rehearsal I (El Ensayo), Tijuana,** *1999–2001 Private collection*

Is the result of pushing a giant ice cube around town ultimately so very different from hauling mattresses or kitchen equipment? For the poorest-paid workers in Mexico, isn't all effort finally met with failure? Might it not be wiser to do nothing at all rather than use up all your energy and still end up with nothing? That, in a nutshell, is Mexico's problem. Then, too, the very absurdity of Alÿs's action imbues it with the universality of a myth: for in re-enacting the story of Sisyphus, he touches a nerve with anyone who has spent their life working hard to no obvious purpose or tangible reward.

Even when filming or documenting ephemeral actions or chance encounters, Alÿs shapes his material, with the result that apparently trivial incidents are made to take on new meanings. Whether leading a flock of sheep in a circular walk around the flagpole in the middle of Mexico City's main square, or marshalling five hundred volunteers with shovels to displace 10 cm of sand from a giant dune on the outskirts of Lima, an action that might begin as a comment on a local political issue is filmed in such a way that it resembles a sacred ritual. This, in turn, invites the viewer to interpret it as a parable about how we might live our lives.

Even at his most playful, Alÿs is thinking hard about meaning. Early one morning in July 2004, he asked an entire regiment of Coldstream Guards to dress in their red tunics, bearskin caps and highly polished boots, as though on duty at Buckingham Palace. He then took the 64 men to the City of London and handed them their instructions. They were to disperse, and each was to walk alone through the almost deserted City's narrow streets, Edwardian thoroughfares and modern piazzas. When one soldier met another, they were to fall in together and march until they came upon another soldier or group of soldiers. Finally, when they had re-formed into a complete regiment, they were to march to the nearest bridge and disperse.

As the long day wears on, Alÿs lovingly films the soldiers as their shadows fall on empty courtyards and desolate streets, emphasising the loneliness of the ones who take the longest time to find their comrades. Though the heat is fierce, their self-discipline is incredible. Without breaking rank, they swerve around parked cars and march up steps as if it were the most natural thing in the world: a gorgeously costumed army of robots. And at the glorious finale, when the regiment has been reunited and it reaches the bridge, the men break step, laugh, talk and tear off their furry hats to mop foreheads pouring with sweat.

Instantly, what had been a robotic military machine becomes human again. Hot, exhausted and delighted, they have overcome their ordeal, their individual identity is no longer subsumed into the regiment. And that's the point. Armies can only function when individuals merge into a group identity. Their uniforms are certainly picturesque, but don't underestimate their power to turn men into soldiers.

At one level, all Alÿs did in *Guards* was to devise an elaborate game of 'sardines' – but one that is unexpectedly mesmerising to watch, and even more amazing to hear. In fact, children's games are an important source of inspiration for Alÿs, who has a child's ability to take such activities as building sandcastles or skipping stones as seriously as children themselves do. But don't be alarmed; far from there being anything fey or whimsical about this show – the best by a contemporary artist I've seen at Tate Modern – after seeing it you will understand what Baudelaire meant when he said that genius was 'childhood recaptured at will'.

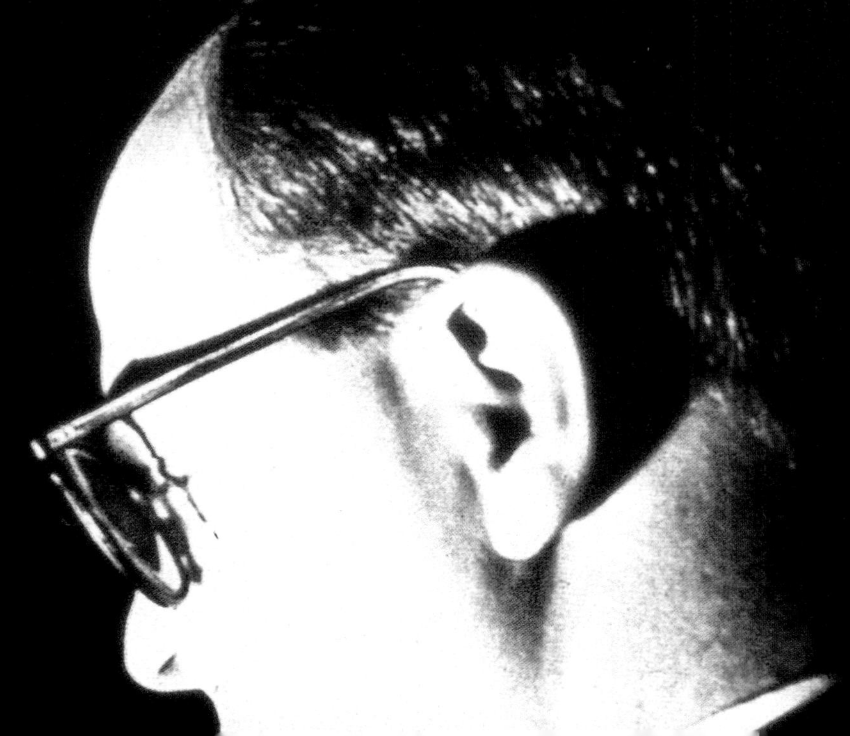

12

POST-WAR AND CONTEMPORARY BRITAIN

David Hockney

What a bright idea it was to mount a show about David Hockney's work in the Sixties for the inaugural exhibition at Nottingham Contemporary, the new arts centre for yet another British city that crass urban development robbed of its soul. Though I was underwhelmed by the serviceable shed Caruso St John has designed for the awkward site in that blighted city centre, it was a stroke of genius to bring these glorious pictures and prints from Hockney's finest period together for the first time.

Only twenty-two when he arrived at the Royal College of Art, it wasn't so much that the boy from Bradford set out to break the rules – he didn't know there were any rules to break. In the faux-naïf, graffiti-inspired work of the early Sixties, he revelled in his freedom to paint the figure unfettered by the disciplines of drawing, proportion, composition or perspective. The camp humour and high spirits of the earliest works go hand-in-hand with the erasures, pentimenti, secret codes and in-house jokes that are delivered with offhand defiance, as if to say to his elders, 'So what are you going to do about it?'

To paint (as opposed to draw) two young men in an amorous clinch wasn't done in 1962, but Hockney got away with it in *We Two Boys Clinging* because the 'boys' look like crudely painted strawberry and chocolate ice-lollies and it is 'love' in the form of Valentine hearts that the picture celebrates, not illegal sex. But sex is what interested Hockney, and the rest of the show tells the story of how he came to discard these early evasions and circumlocutions to put it at the heart of his work.

He followed up his initial success with the series of etchings updating Hogarth's *A Rake's Progress*. Setting his story in a specific time and place (New York, early Sixties) with extraordinary graphic fluency, Hockney tells the familiar tale of drink, drugs, sex and death in a jokey visual language that anyone could understand.

24 November 2009

David Hockney:
1960–68

Nottingham
Contemporary

But here, and in many other pictures painted right after he left the Royal College, it feels to me that Hockney introduces passages of surrealistic whimsy as a tactic to avoid having to deal with naturalistic description. I find paintings like *Great Pyramid of Giza with Broken Head of Thebes* (1963) repellently slick and superficial. With their echoes of the cartoons of Saul Steinberg, they are the reason the painter William Scott dismissed Hockney at this period as a 'colour supplement artist'.

And then it happened. The day he stepped off the plane at Los Angeles, everything changed. In a moment that I would seriously compare to Vincent Van Gogh's arrival at Arles, it is as though the heat, light and colour of southern California entered Hockney's bloodstream. Overnight, a talented British artist became a major international star. Seeing it happen in this show is like watching a plane taxiing down a runway – on and on it trundles, gathering speed and power and then, suddenly, when you come to the first LA pictures, whoosh – the wheels lift and one of the great artistic careers of the twentieth century takes off.

From the first picture, the mannerisms and the obscurities of the London years begin to fall away. In the flourishing gay subculture in California, the young artist could assert his sexual identity in a way that was not possible under the watchful eyes of the British police and the Lord Chamberlain's office. Now he could paint the subjects that interested him, sun-struck male bodies lying under blue skies beside rippling water. What's more, he could paint them in focus, using academic draughtsmanship and Renaissance perspective without having to blur, erase, or otherwise disguise his imagery.

And so the nude in *Man Taking Shower in Beverly Hills* (1964) is painted from a black-and-white photo Hockney found in a beefcake magazine. But now Hockney's brush describes the slow-moving jets of water hitting the man's arched back and the light tan line on his buttocks so caressingly that the three palm fronds in the foreground look carnivorous, like a Venus flytrap about to eat him alive.

The Californian equivalent to *A Rake's Progress* are his wonderful illustrations to fourteen poems by C. P. Cavafy. What before had only been implied, he now spells out in elegant line drawings showing young men nude, or in their underwear, or lying in bed together. The catalogue essay rightly discusses all this within the historical context of the sexual revolution that was taking place in these years. But though that is certainly true, what struck me so forcibly in this show is not so much the explicit subject matter of these pictures and prints as their formal perfection.

One small canvas shows the black-and-white street sign for Wilshire Boulevard against a sky of light blue, with a few green palm fronds. Its not what Hockney paints that's interesting but how he paints it. Remembering the insouciant way Hockney used to paint in his earlier work, what is so striking here is that each brushstroke is laid on the canvas with a slow deliberation that's as ravishing as any patch of colour painted by Vermeer or Mondrian. This quality is very hard to put into words, but it is covered by the term 'facture' which refers to the artist's touch, or feel for the paint – which in Hockney's case is almost palpable. Forget spontaneity – that's a distant memory, the indulgence of his youth. As Hockney matures, the pictures become quiet, measured, almost solemn – as if he realises that what he is doing in them is too important to make light of.

Take the most famous of all, *A Bigger Splash*. For years, I looked at that picture and all I saw was the meticulous way Hockney paints the two sprays of water arrested in mid-air forever, dutifully noting the picture's gentle send-ups of Abstract Expressionism, geometric abstraction and post-painterly abstraction. But now that I am more familiar with Ed Ruscha's paintings and photographs of LA, it's clear that Hockney's picture also captures the emptiness, sterility and an element of the sinister in Los Angeles. Notice, for example, the dark grey buildings and palm trees reflected in the sliding doors in the middle distance. We often think of Hockney's Californian pictures as hymns to flesh and sexuality but this picture has none of that. Instead, what it gives us is an element of film noir, a side of LA that all this prosperity serves to keep at bay.

The culmination of the swimming-pool pictures came in 1966 with *Peter Getting Out of Nick's Pool*, that hypnotic masterpiece in which Hockney paints water as a series of intertwined lines of white and mauve paint, rippling over bands of light blue, dark blue and aquamarine. At first, it's hard to take your eyes off the figure at the centre, the linchpin that holds the composition together. But after a while, your eye starts to move over the picture surface to discover the patch of radiant green Hockney uses for the back of the deck chair, or the horizontal bands of yellow, white and moss green interrupted by

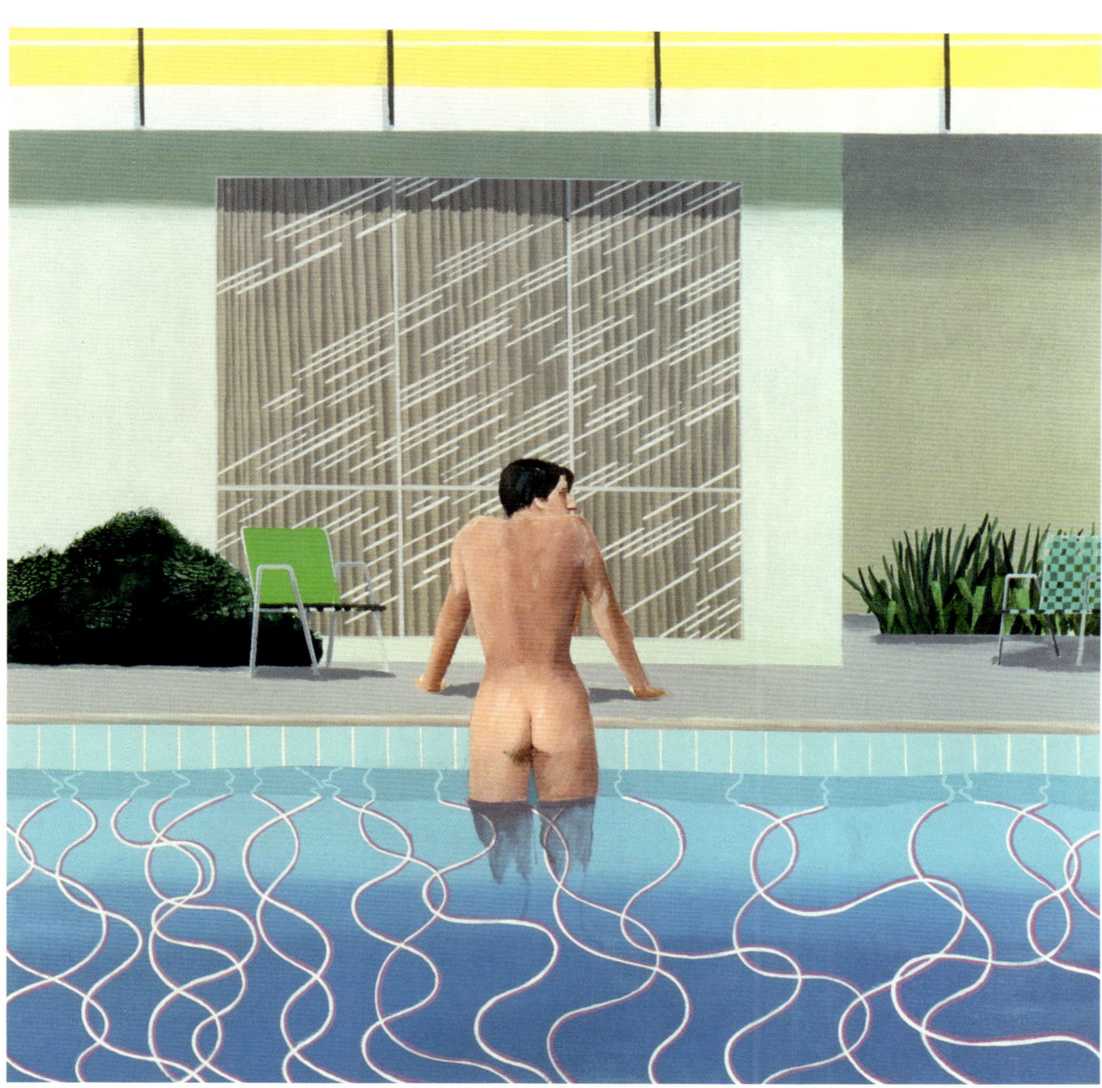

evenly spaced black verticals at the top of the picture, surely his homage to Mondrian.

With time, you notice that, as in a work by Josef Albers, the composition here consists of a series of progressively smaller squares, beginning with the 'frame' of the bare canvas, and ending with the glass picture window streaked with white diagonal lines that for some mysterious reason we read as reflections. Hockney has found a visual language that combines geometric abstraction with minimalism and naturalism. He plays off the straight lines of the architecture with the curving ripples and round flesh, all in colours as pure and as vibrant as a Matisse.

Gilbert and George

After Gilbert and George's 26 *Dirty Words Pictures* were first shown (in Amsterdam, Brussels and New York) in 1977–78, all but two were sold to foreign individuals or museums. Apparently, in the year of the Queen's Silver Jubilee, British institutions and collectors did not want to hear what the pictures had to say about this country.

On view 25 years later in the first complete exhibition of the series at the Serpentine Gallery, they look every bit as threatening as they did then – but now they also look frighteningly familiar. For the violence, racial tension, class war and psychological dislocation that Gilbert and George saw embedded in the fabric of British society then are now openly acknowledged as facts of urban life. Time has proved the artists to be prophets, unsung in their own country.

To make *The Dirty Words Pictures*, Gilbert and George photographed graffiti they found scrawled on walls within a ten-minute walk of their home in London's East End. They then enlarged these swear words, insults and political slogans and integrated them into a photographic grid, the panels of which show the artists themselves surrounded by the streets, the vistas and the populace of London.

The enlarged scale of the individual letters ('Angry', 'Fuck', 'Bugger') puts the written words on an equal footing with the cityscapes and portraits. The camera lens pulls back for panoramic shots of London landmarks, or zooms in for close-ups of individual faces or groups of people. There is no visual or moral hierarchy in the sense that everything shown in each picture is given equal emphasis, and all the pictures are unified by an overall grainy black-and-white tonality, sometimes tinted with areas of deep, saturated red.

Each picture has a different theme. In *Piss*, for example, the graffitied word takes up four panels at the top of the picture. At the bottom of the grid are photos of the then-new National Theatre, while

26 June 2002

Gilbert and George:
The Dirty Words
Pictures

Serpentine Gallery,
London

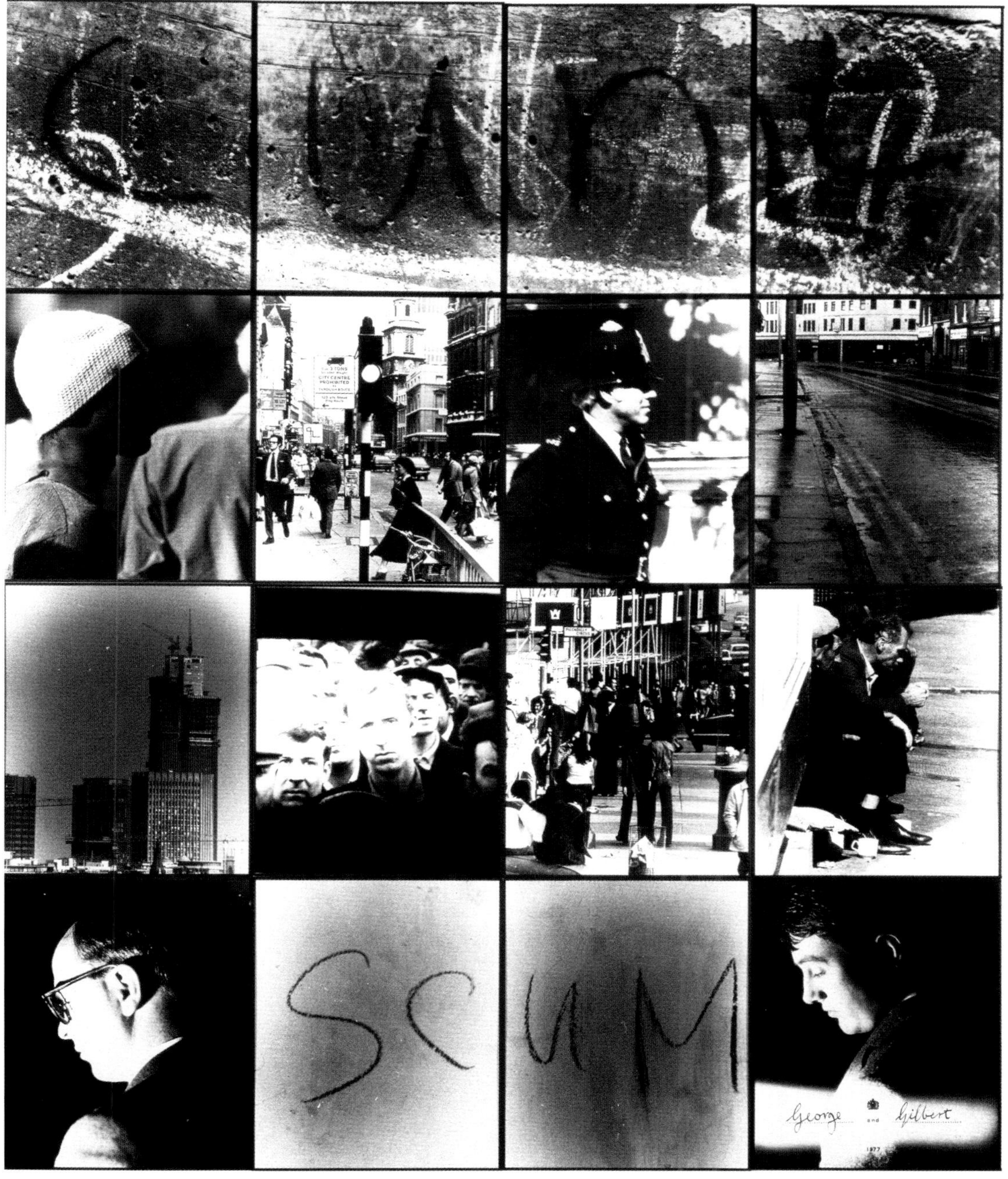

Gilbert and George
Cunt Scum, *1977*
Tate Gallery, London

in the middle Gilbert and George appear, flanked by images of down-and-out men drinking in the doorway of what looks like an eighteenth-century building. The artists contrast Denys Lasdun's brutalist fortress of high culture with the underclass excluded from it. They point to what they see as the inhumanity of contemporary architecture compared to that of the past.

But the work isn't the boring, left-wing agitprop it might have been in the hands of other artists of the period. Having shown us how modern architecture helps to create or reinforce polar extremes in British society, Gilbert and George neither comment nor condemn. In picture after picture they play the role of Everyman, the detached but thoughtful observers who look out on the spectacle of modern life and simply ask us not to turn our eyes away from it. As you walk through this show, just try to imagine what the pictures would look like without the melancholy figures of Gilbert and George in them. Most of the humanity and the intimacy would vanish; the pictures would look like grim posters for the Socialist Workers' Party.

In other pictures, they contrast the tourist sites of Westminster Abbey, the Houses of Parliament and St Paul's with the reality of life in the streets of London. Gilbert and George are here working on a scale no other artists I know have attempted. All of London is here – its parks, monuments, office blocks, council housing, circuses, traffic. Homeless men sleeping rough, City traders, pedestrians at Piccadilly Circus, Rastafarians, Muslims – all are covered in a pall of rain and soot that makes the city look timeless. Gilbert and George join a list of artists including Hogarth, Dickens, Sickert and Orwell who have created supreme works of art out of the sheer spectacle of London life.

But even this doesn't begin to convey the richness of these works. The dirty words themselves are like cries from the ciy's collective unconscious. Like bursts of gunfire, they contain all the buried violence, desperation and loneliness of anonymous voices in a vast metropolis. Whoever felt compelled to take his magic marker and write 'smash', 'shag' or 'queer' on a public wall was in some weird way telling the world that he exists, but also revealing his own sense of powerlessness.

Never confuse what Gilbert and George do here with the aestheticising of graffiti by artists such as Jean Dubuffet or Jean-Michel Basquiat. The London artists do not treat ugly, violent, sexual and angry words as artistic statements, but as urgent communications from the mad, the horny and the dispossessed.

The device of the grid – which isolates each separate view or figure and cuts it off from the other images – implies a fracturing of society. The pictures look like banks of television monitors or even surveillance cameras, enabling us to see different parts of the city and different sections of society at the same time, and to see that each sector – office workers, the Bangladeshi community – ignores the others. The grid format has become something of a cliché, but when these pictures were first shown, they looked like nothing else in art.

This is a picture of British society at boiling point. 'ARE YOU ANGRY OR ARE YOU BORING?' are the words scrawled on a wall at the tail end of James Callaghan's Labour government, a time of strikes, uncollected rubbish, unburied bodies, riot police. Anyone who lived through this period will remember how troubled the times were, and how accurately Gilbert and George capture the mood of those years.

Some of it I had forgotten. In many of these pictures, you are surprised to see how omnipresent the police and army seem to be, how London looks like a place of riot and roiling insurrection. From a distance of 25 years later, we know what form the boiling-over took: the government of Mrs Thatcher, who came to power two years later. What we can't see in this exhibition is how accurately Gilbert and George went on to show what happened next, in pictures inspired by the Wapping riots, which are heroic, gigantic in scale, ignited with colour, like posters from the Russian Revolution. But politically, it is hard to say that the artists are either left- or right-wing: clearly horrified by the state of Britain under the last socialist government, they are equally appalled by the social conditions that cause such poverty, alcoholism and depression. Probably the best description of them is liberal humanists.

For years now I've been saying that Gilbert and George are the most important artists to emerge in Britain since the war. Having now seen *The Dirty Words Pictures* together for the first time, I don't hesitate to say that these are among the most powerful works of art made in this country in the twentieth century.

Andy Goldsworthy

To create *Moonlit Path*, the British artist Andy Goldsworthy first pulverised white chalk from the Sussex Downs and then used it to lay out a winding trail through an ancient wood in Petworth Park on the Leconfield Estate in West Sussex. Even on the darkest night, the dazzling white path is luminescent enough to guide the visitor on a gentle, hour-long ramble through the woods. But, since the path will be open to the public only on the three nights of the month around the full moon, Goldsworthy intends it to be seen when its pale radiance is augmented by unearthly light from above.

You reach the entrance to the path long after dark, of course, and admittances to the wood are timed so that the already apprehensive visitor sets off alone and in silence. This is an important part of the experience. As you walk through the woods guided by the shining path in front of you, the softest sounds become intensified. By this hour, even the hum of distant traffic has died down. The crack of a twig, fronds or branches brushing against your side, invisible footfalls in front or behind you: each is heard with a clarity that would be lost in the daytime.

On a clear night, milky light flooding a forest clearing becomes confused in your mind with the artificial 'moonlight' at your feet. At the same time, the world has become infinitely strange, a place drained of colour, reduced to tones of light and dark. Like animals, the longer we stay in the wood, the more acute our sense of sight becomes.

To see a landscape by moonlight is rare in an age of sodium street lamps and brightly lit houses. At its simplest level, Goldsworthy's project connects us with something elemental in ourselves, some instinctive fear of the night and awe of the moon, worshipped by the ancients in the form of Hecuba or Diana. But, if *Moonlit Path* is a landscape, it is also a metaphor. For Goldsworthy lays out his path

10 July 2002

Moonlit Path

National Trust at Petworth House and the Sussex Downs Conservation Board

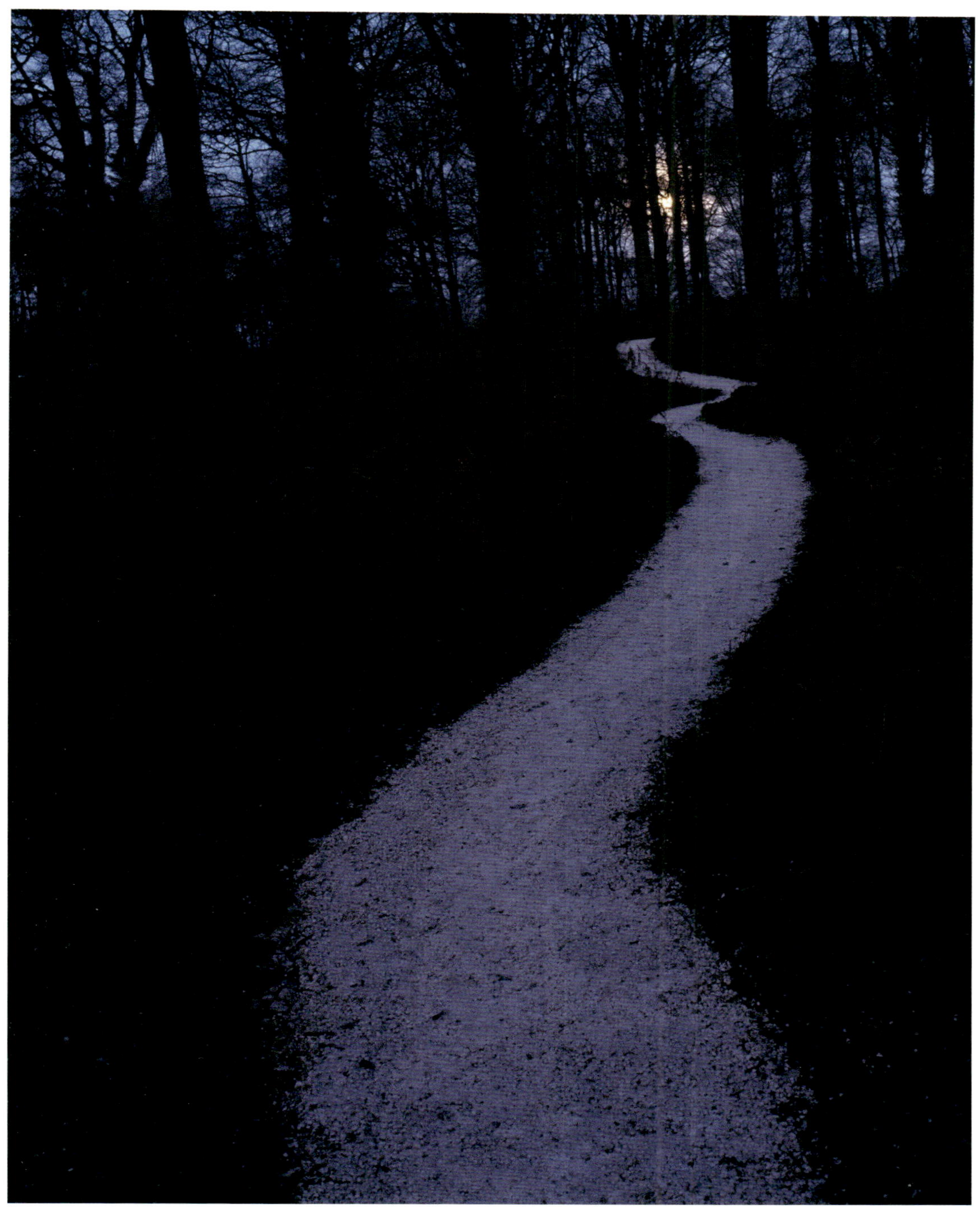

Andy Goldsworthy
Moonlit Path, 2002–3
Petworth Park,
West Sussex

in such a way that it constantly twists and turns, taking you up hillocks and down hollows, never for an instant allowing you to rest. At times, your path looks clear and straight and easy, with the real moon at your back, shedding light on the way ahead. At other moments, the trees close over your head, and the path you are following becomes almost invisible. Now you have to trust your instinct and find courage to continue on in the darkness until you find your way – and the comforting light – again. In short, the path is like life itself. Inseparable from its beauty is its ephemeral nature: since it won't last for ever, and most people will walk it only once, its value to us is connected with a sense of loss.

Moonlit Path is one of the most original and poetic works Goldsworthy has ever made, and yet it is very much connected to the art of the past. Artists as different as Chopin, J. M. Whistler and Debussy would have recognised at once that it is, in essence, a nocturne. Even stronger are its links with Eastern art. Many times during the walk, I was reminded of the Japanese artist Yoshitoshi's series of woodblock prints, *One Hundred Aspects of the Moon*. And, in both Japanese and Chinese culture, to witness the ephemeral manifestation of the full moon is considered a refined aesthetic pleasure, celebrated with parties and festivities.

What's more, *Moonlit Path* is constantly changing. No two people will experience it in the same way. I saw it at the end of June, when the woods looked as lush and romantic as a set for *A Midsummer Night's Dream*. But I can imagine that in the autumn, as the leaves turn colour and cover the ground underfoot, the atmosphere will be one of contemplation and nostalgia. In the depths of winter, the ghostly path snaking through leafless trees will feel have a fairytale feel, like a scene from *Hansel and Gretel*.

Mark Wallinger

Among London's many eyesores, one of the most familiar is the massive granite plinth in the upper left-hand corner of Trafalgar Square, originally intended as the base for a bronze equestrian statue of William IV that was never made. It has stood vacant for the past 150 years – not so much because we can find no British heroes to commemorate, but because to place any statue in Trafalgar Square is to consign it to oblivion. One of the most desolate public spaces in London, the 'square' is really a sunken horseshoe-shaped bowl, closed off by high walls at its northern end, open at its southern. Only under Nelson's Column and around Landseer's lions does it come to life, a mecca for pigeons and the tourists who feed them. No Londoner deliberately sets foot in the place.

Landed with the thankless task of finding a suitable statue to place there permanently, the Royal Society of Arts decided first to give three young artists a free hand to do whatever they fancied atop the vertiginous granite monolith, with the stipulation that each project would remain in place for only six months. The two 'safe' choices were Rachel Whiteread and Bill Woodrow, both sculptors whom we know to be capable of working on a monumental scale. But to commission the first work in the series from one of the quirkiest figures in British art, Mark Wallinger, took courage and imagination.

Wallinger is a conceptual artist who works with materials ranging from paint on canvas to photography and video. In the past he has made art about the British obsession with class and breeding, as manifested in the national mania for horse racing. In one project, he bought a thoroughbred racehorse, dubbed her *A Real Work of Art*, trained her at Newmarket, and created what was, for me, one of the few conceptual works made by a British artist in the Nineties that may find a place in the history books. The interesting and dangerous thing about Wallinger is that you can't tell what he is going to do next.

25 August 1999

Mark Wallinger:
Ecce Homo

Trafalgar Square,
London

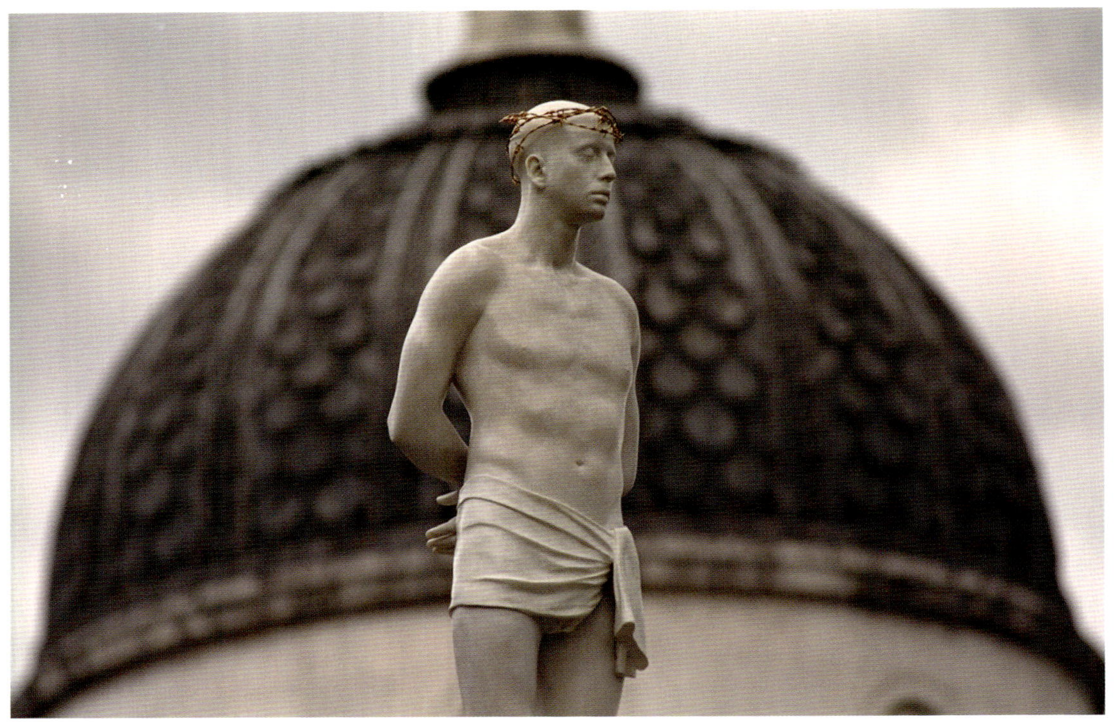

In recent years he has turned his attention to religion, making videos in which he played the part of a blind deity descending an escalator in the London Underground, or a crazed prophet raving from a soapbox in a public park. But nothing in his previous career prepared us for the work that was unveiled last month, a 6-foot statue of Jesus Christ entitled *Ecce Homo*.

Made of sanded polyester resin (a hard material resembling white marble), and wearing only a loincloth and a crown of gilded barbed wire, the figure stands precariously on the edge of the plinth with his hands bound behind his back. The milky-white colour and the bland, over-smooth surface create a spectral, washed-out effect, like a bar of soap left out in the rain. The impassivity and vulnerability of the pose is emphasised by the scale of the plinth, which is 24 feet high, or quadruple the size of the figure. When seen from the ground, the human scale of the statue makes Christ look insignificant.

This disparity in scale between plinth and figure is, like the setting of Trafalgar Square, as important to the meaning of the work as the figure itself. To take the statue away from this particular site would be to vitiate its impact. For it is not simply a statue of Christ, but a narrative work which illustrates a specific scene in the story of his Passion. This is the moment when Pilate displays to the crowd a man he has already scourged and crowned with thorns, with the words '*Ecce homo*' ('Behold the man'), before ordering his execution.

By placing the statue high up on this enormous plinth, Wallinger implicates us as spectators in the drama. As in a traditional passion-play, we become participants in the unfolding narrative, taking the part of the mob, baying for blood. In the visual arts, I would compare Wallinger's work to the Belgian symbolist James Ensor's famous painting of 1899 *The Entry of Christ into Brussels*, which shows Christ jeered by contemporary Belgians as he carries his cross thorough the streets of the modern city.

Up close, what is most striking about the figure of Christ is that he has been given the face and body of a modern man. (Wallinger cast the figure from life, using a friend who is also an artist.) Though the marble resin is as prosaic as it is possible for a substance to be, the contemporaneity of the face is startling. Like Caravaggio's smooth-shaven Christ in the *Supper at Emmaus* in the National Gallery, this isn't the traditional image of the deity. Like the naturalistic depiction of the Holy Family in John Everett Millais's *Christ in the Carpenter's Shop* (Tate Gallery), which was considered (by Dickens, among others) to be blasphemous, Wallinger's Christ looks too much like someone we know for comfort.

But then, this isn't a statue many people are likely to want to pray in front of. Wallinger describes himself as an agnostic, and the feeling of the work isn't so much religious as it is moral. In its exaltation of humility, of suffering and of acceptance, it questions the values by which we live our lives. Instinctively we contrast this human-scaled Christ with the giant figures of Sir Charles Napier and General Havelock nearby. Admiral Nelson has been raised on his column so high above mortal men that he is almost invisible. What Wallinger has really done is to turn Trafalgar Square into something akin to a *vanitas*, a meditation on the transience of earthly things. However brave, well-born or distinguished these worldly heroes may have been, compared to a spiritual leader such as Jesus, they are nonentities. Wallinger's Christ seems to rebuke a city that exalts their lives.

One effect the RSA didn't have in mind when they gave Wallinger the commission is that it would make all other statues in the square look hopelessly pompous, and ultimately unnecessary. In fact, he has presented us all with the obvious solution to the problem of the empty 'fourth plinth': not to fill it with yet another bronze statue of someone whom our descendants are likely to forget, but to banish all the sculpture from the square, leaving only the lions, the column and the fountains, to create a gigantic open space, like the square in front of St Peter's in Rome.

Tracey Emin

With almost daily bulletins in the press recording her every passing thought, Tracey Emin is so overexposed that when I heard she was having a full-scale retrospective at the Hayward Gallery, I couldn't imagine what she could possibly show or write or say in it that I hadn't already seen or read or heard. She's told the whole world the story of her progress from small-town slag to notoriety on television, media celebrity, a Turner Prize nomination, financial success and critical acclaim.

Along the way she's shared with us graphic details of her abortion, her alcoholism and her inability to find love or have a child. Her solipsistic obsession with her own trials and tribulations has always struck me as a major weakness in her art, one that explains why the commentators who have served her best have not been art critics, but personal friends who write about the woman and not her work. The Hayward show – the best I've seen by some distance – turns this weakness into a strength. Carefully selected and beautifully installed, the exhibition looks at Emin's whole life as a performance, a soap opera in real time, like *The Truman Show*.

The exhibition starts with a selection of embroidered wall-hangings into which she stitches drawings, words and text. The stop-and-start, patchwork nature of these remarkably ugly textiles is a metaphor for the chaotic way Emin lives her life. In them her mood veers between pathetic (*I Didn't Know I had to Share Your Life*), to enraged (*You Cruel Heartless Bitch Rot in Hell*) and the triumphantly vengeful (*Harder and Better Than All of You F – ing B – – s*). Had Emin attempted to present herself as nicer than she is, these works would fail completely. It's because she is by turn loving, needy, vicious and smug that they feel authentic.

The quilts introduce us to the paradox at the heart of her work: you can't judge it using formal criteria such as design or composition, and

17 May 2011

Tracey Emin: Love Is What You Want

Hayward Gallery, London

you can't speak of her stylistic development, because there isn't any.
All you can do is see each individual painting, film or object as a
fragment of a multimedia biography-in-progress.

Here's an example. At the show she staged in the British Pavilion
at the Venice Biennale in 2007 she exhibited a series of feeble
watercolours made at the start of her career and in the aftermath of
a traumatic abortion. Viewed on their own, they felt like a gratuitous
exploitation of a personal tragedy. But in a film at the Hayward called
How it Feels, Emin talks about the abortion, the depth of her physical
suffering, her emotional distress and heartfelt consciousness of
irreparable loss. That film relates to a series called *Feeling Pregnant*
in which the psychological cost of her termination is again expressed,
in vitrines filled with clothes and tiny shoes created for the baby she
didn't have. The thread that began with the abortion isn't complete
until you see a later film in which she is seen talking to her mother,
who tells her, with casual brutality, that she's glad Emin didn't have
a child because she was unfit for parenthood.

Each work in this show seems to dovetail into the others. In an
early film, *Why I Never Became a Dancer*, Emin describes how teenage
sexual abuse left her with a sense of worthlessness mitigated only by
her power to attract men. After seeing it again in this show, I began
to look at Emin's paintings with the kind of attention a psychoanalyst
brings to the words of a patient. What I saw was that in picture after
picture she portrays herself as a pair of spread legs – often without
a head and sometimes without a torso. These images are visual
expressions of the damage inflicted by sexual abuse.

The show isn't nearly as grim as I'm making it sound. Two talents
have been key to Emin's success: the first is that she can draw like an
angel, albeit one with a bad hangover, and the second is that she is
smart enough to know how to parody herself. It's hard not to warm
to someone who can photograph herself in the nude joyfully scooping
gold coins into her crotch, like a modern Danae who's just been
visited by some art-world Jupiter like Charles Saatchi and can't
believe her luck.

So am I born again? Has this long-time sceptic now become an
ecstatic fan? Not quite. The triumph of this Hayward exhibition is to
show that with Emin's work the whole is much greater than the sum
of the parts. But the reverse is also true – without the autobiographical

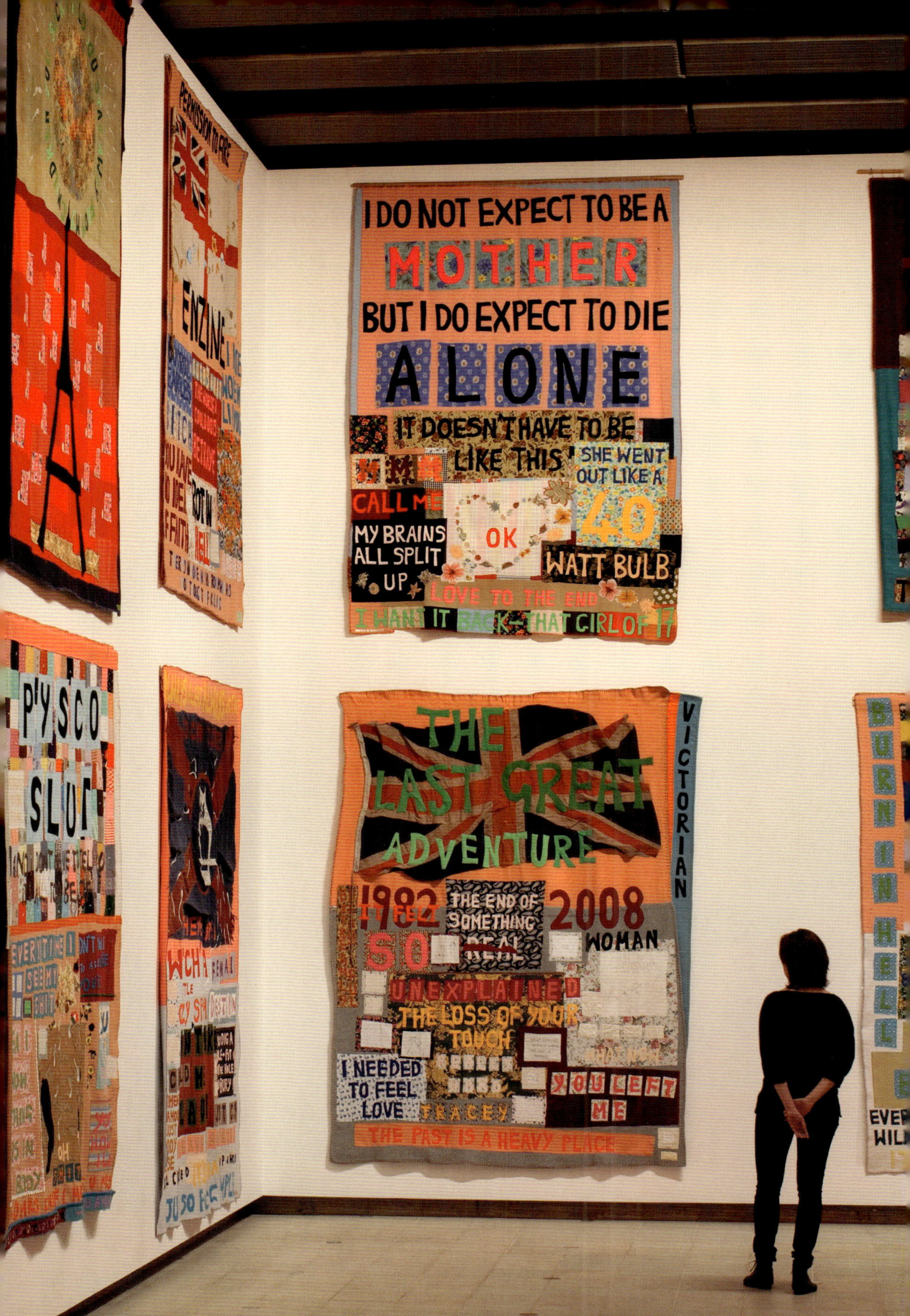
PERMISSION TO FLY
ENZINE
I DO NOT EXPECT TO BE A
MOTHER
BUT I DO EXPECT TO DIE
ALONE
IT DOESN'T HAVE TO BE
LIKE THIS
SHE WENT OUT LIKE A
CALL ME
OK
40
MY BRAINS ALL SPLIT UP
WATT BULB
LOVE TO THE END
I WANT IT BACK - THAT GIRL OF 17
PYSCO SLUT
THE LAST GREAT ADVENTURE
VICTORIAN
1982
THE END OF SOMETHING REAL
2008
WOMAN
UNEXPLAINED
THE LOSS OF YOUR TOUCH
I NEEDED TO FEEL LOVE
YOU LEFT ME
TRACEY
THE PAST IS A HEAVY PLACE
BURN IN HELL
EVER
WIL

context in which the exhibition places them, many of the works here aren't strong enough visually or conceptually to stand on their own.

For example, the curators have grouped most of Emin's neon signs together on the long wall of a darkened gallery, their garish lettering made to look like shop signs on the sleazy side of town. The installation is so effective that it is easy to forget that, seen on its own, a pink neon heart surrounding Emin's handwritten message in blue neon saying 'Love Is What You Want' has no artistic merit at all.

Then, too, her artistic heroine is Louise Bourgeois, a bad choice for a role model. Just as Bourgeois spent her career tediously recounting the story of her father's betrayal of her mother, so Emin is still banging on about traumas and tragedies that feel worried to death. Feelings of anger and resentment are the wellspring of her art and arrested emotional development is what you'd expect of someone with her history. What's hard to reconcile is her presentation of herself as utterly abject, when her worldly success must provide a measure of the self-esteem that was lacking at the beginning of her career.

Marcus Coates

Try to imagine a digital art video set in a block of high-rise council flats on a run-down estate on the outskirts of Liverpool: if there is a more dispiriting description of a work of art in the English language I have yet to hear it. But I've now seen Marcus Coates's *Journey to the Lower World* several times, and each time it is just as funny, just as tense, and just as strange as I remembered it.

Coates, who is having his first retrospective in this country at the Milton Keynes Gallery, is the kind of British eccentric I thought they didn't make any more, a man so attuned to the bird and animal world that he believes he can communicate freely with starlings and crows in their own language, speaks fluent rabbit, pretty good badger and passable deer, but has never managed to master the difficult dialect of the plover. Certainly, the animal noises that come out of his mouth are eerily life-like, and if the film in which he transforms himself into a seal is anything to go by, his knowledge would interest David Attenborough.

I know what you are thinking – I did, too – but bear with me. On the day of the filming, eight mostly elderly residents of the ageing tower block have gathered together in a small flat on the twentieth floor. They are worried about their future, for the bleak monstrosity they call home appears to be under some kind of threat. They have a question for Coates to ask his friends in the animal kingdom: 'Do we have a protector?' At this point I should mention that Coates is clean-cut, well mannered, and a total geek.

What he is going to do, he politely explains, is to perform a shamanistic ritual during which he will fall into a trance and then descend to the netherworld to converse with the spirits of small dead animals. With luck, he will bring back their wisdom to help these feisty Liverpudlians. Since he is standing only a few feet away from his audience, this takes a straight face and a lot of nerve. After

2 February 2010

Marcus Coates:
Psychopomp

Milton Keynes Gallery

drawing the curtains and pressing 'play' on a portable CD player, the
sound of hypnotic drumming fills the room. First he ties two anklets
of keys to his feet, and then emerges from the kitchen in a reindeer
headdress and pelt. Coates appears to fall asleep. When he awakes,
he is a different person, more animal in his movements than human.
The audience watches with a mixture of stifled amusement, fear
and intense concentration as he walks around swaying, spinning
in a circle, all the while making realistic animal grunts, barks, howls
and hisses. When the performance ends, he is covered in perspiration.
Speaking in a normal voice, he describes a journey of the imagination
in which he wandered through dark caves and dense forests before
encountering the sparrowhawk who gave him the answer he was
seeking.

What that folksy answer is doesn't particularly matter – because
the artwork isn't about Coates, it's about his audience. His camera
returns constantly to faces that unselfconsciously register their
responses to what they are seeing. Just like us, these good people
don't know whether to laugh out loud or sit in solemn silence
watching this complete stranger behave like a lunatic. Like us, most
of them think it's all a lot of hokum but, like us, they can't be 100
per cent sure. Not only is this ambiguity created deliberately, I'd
say it is the whole point of his work. He could be the real thing,
or a screwball, or a good actor – and
how we choose to see him holds a
mirror up to who we are.

For Coates, the world is divided
into two kinds of people – the ones
who are able to entertain the possibility
of the paranormal, and those unwilling
to suspend belief even for an instant.
All these residents live on the same
grim housing estate. For those who are
able to enter into an artist's imaginative
world, their surroundings are
immaterial. Those who can't will
never transcend them.

At forty-two, Coates has clearly
learned a lot from the performance art

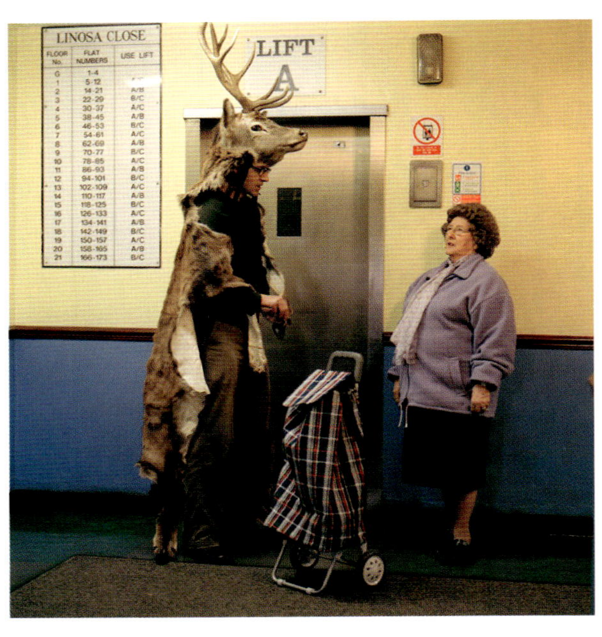

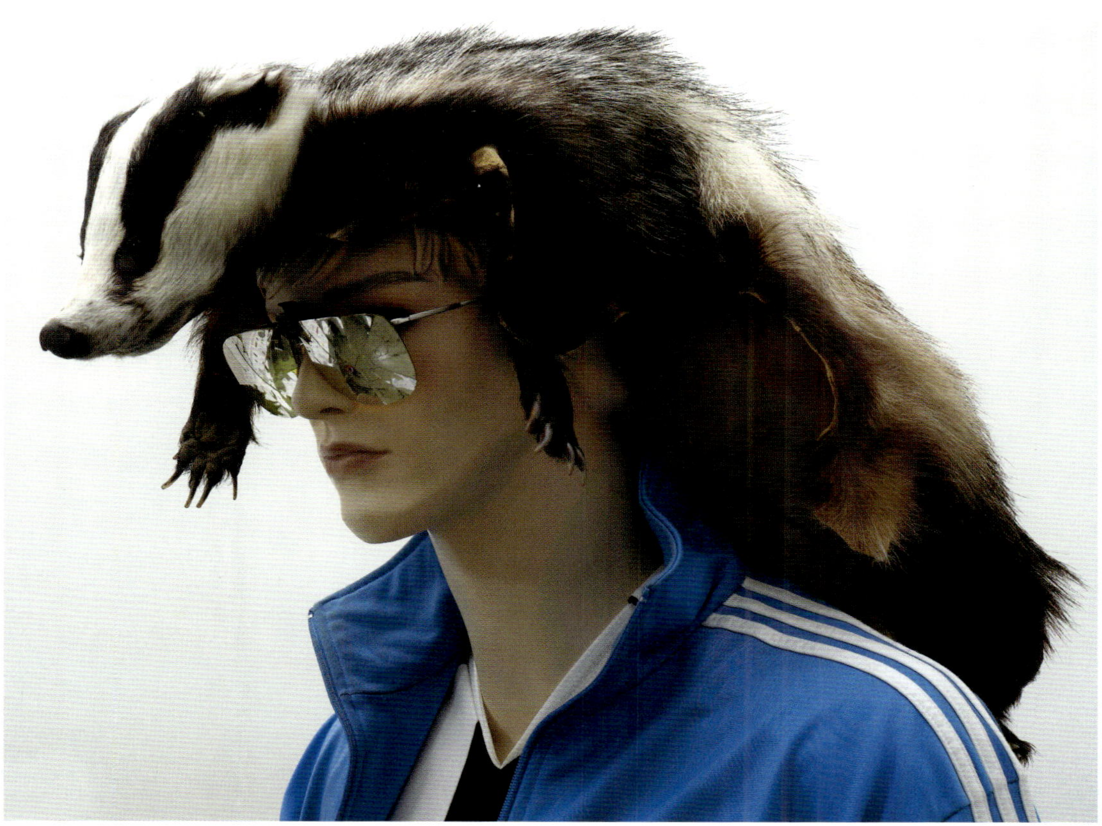

of Joseph Beuys. But for me he is one of the most intelligent and original artists in this country today. Deliriously odd, he dresses up in animal skins and travels the world performing magical rituals for the unimpressed mayor of a town in Israel, or at an open-air festival in Japan. Each time, his camera searches the audience for the exquisite moment when, if only for a split second, a face registers the possibility of belief.

Just as inspired is *Dawn Chorus*, a multi-screen film and audio installation in which the human voice is made to replicate the sound of birdsong. Early one morning in May 2005, Coates had a wildlife sound recordist capture on tape the cacophony of a dozen varieties of birds chirping, chattering, squawking and twittering simultaneously. Coates slowed the recording down to human pitch, and then taught human volunteers to mimic the song of each bird. Finally, when each volunteer had learned the song of the bird assigned to him or her,

Coates accelerated the recording so that the result sounds like the real thing.

But that's not all. Treating each participant like an instrument in an orchestra, he filmed these men, women and children at home or work. On one screen, a young woman lies in her bath, chattering like a starling, on another an old man reads the paper, tweet-tweeting like a chaffinch. Here's the amazing thing: as far as I could tell, they aren't making these sounds at random. They are following the 'score' of the original dawn chorus on that May morning.

One of the things good art can do is change the way we look at the world. By assigning each bird sound to a human personality, Coates ensures that I will never again wake up to the racket in our garden without straining to hear each bird's voice, wondering whether it is young or old, male or female, in a good mood or bad.

The last thing I want to do is jinx Marcus Coates, but if after this show he isn't at least nominated for the Turner Prize, I'm a wood pigeon.

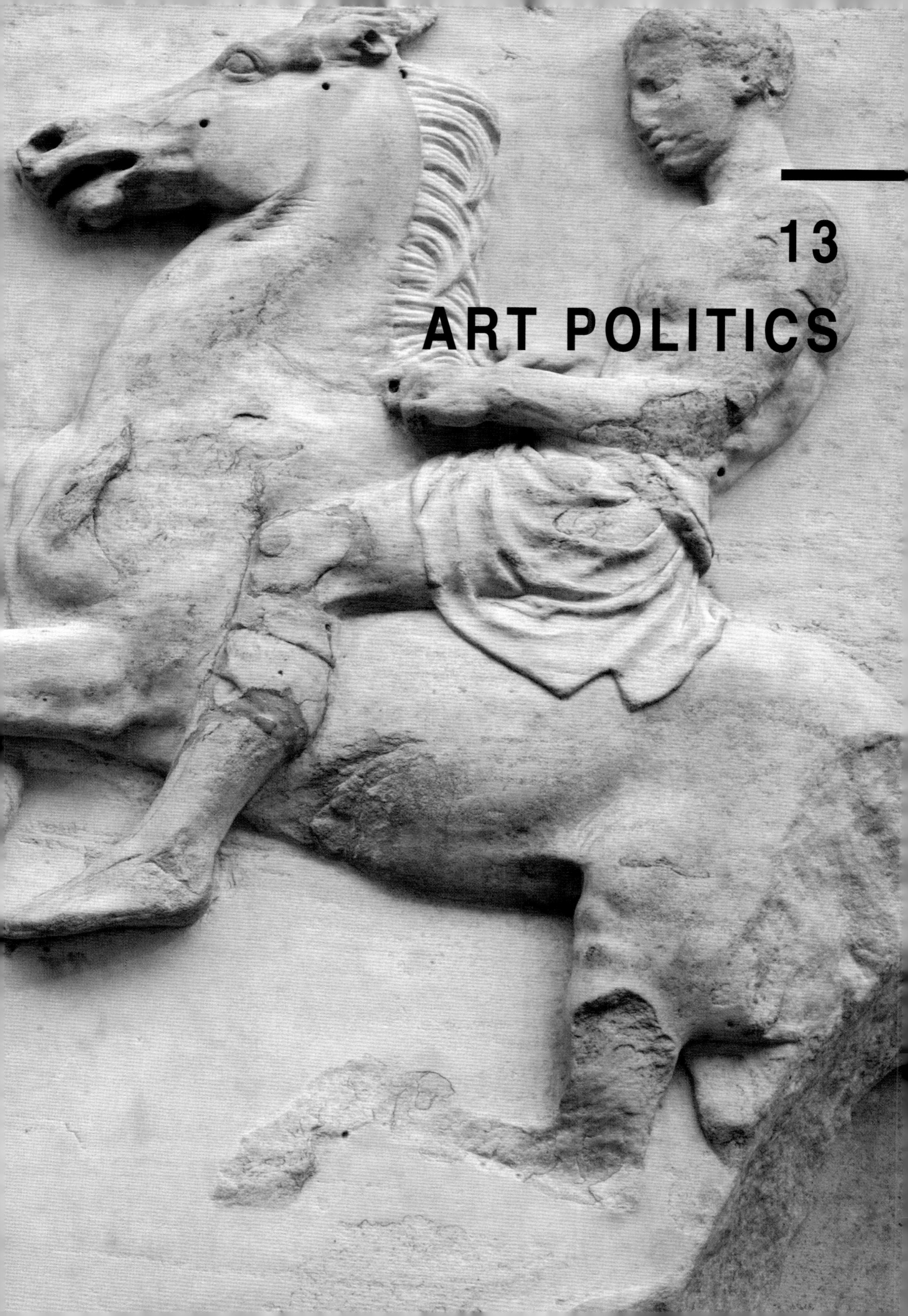

13
ART POLITICS

Tate Modern

Three months ago, the worst was over. The Swiss architects Herzog and de Meuron had transformed Sir Giles Gilbert Scott's Bankside power station into a pristine art gallery with plenty of space and light for showing contemporary art. When the Queen opens the new building tomorrow, London will acquire its most important museum since Edward VII opened the Tate Gallery at Millbank more than a hundred years ago.

Tate Modern is one of the most important galleries of twentieth-century art in the world, not because of the architecture but because of the art shown in it. All Sir Nicholas Serota had to do was to transport the permanent collection of twentieth-century painting and sculpture from across the river and, by applying the same high standards that he brought to display at the old building, create gallery after gallery of breathtaking beauty. With Serota in charge, it was unthinkable that the installation would be anything less than perfect.

I wish I could report that Tate Modern is a triumph, but I can't. Aesthetic presentation has been thrown to the winds in favour of a heavy-handed thematic installation and garrulous wall labels that demean the art and condescend to the visitor. This is the handiwork of careerist curators in love with the sound of their own theories. The art-speak of the polytechnic resounds throughout the building. And the maddening thing is that with a world-renowned collection and marvellous building, the Tate didn't need to follow the fashion for this kind of thing (in art-world lingo, it's called 'contextualisation'). It had the power to defy trends. Visitors would still have flocked to see it.

Though I must in fairness add that there are a number of galleries that do work visually, as well as a first-class loan exhibition, the first thing that Serota and Bankside's director, Lars Nittve, should do after the opening is to sit down, talk it over, and start again from scratch.

10 May 2000

Opening exhibition

Tate Modern, London

So what went wrong? Considering how uneven the Tate's collection of twentieth-century art is, a strictly chronological presentation would probably not have been the best solution to showing it. The idea of hanging the galleries thematically was not in itself unreasonable. The permanent collection is displayed on two floors in four different sections roughly corresponding to the categories of art established by the French Academy in the seventeenth century: landscape, still life, the nude, and history painting. Every so often we come across a gallery devoted to a single artist – Bacon, Riley, Auerbach, Cragg, Beuys. The success of each gallery varies wildly, depending on who was in charge of installing it.

Certainly in the more lugubrious galleries who wasn't in charge was Serota himself. His approach to displaying art has always been sensuous, not cerebral. Whatever you thought of his changing displays at Millbank, you had to concede that the galleries usually looked ravishing, and this was his own sensibility at work. The irony is that, on paper at least, the installation at Bankside appears to conform to Serota's views on museum installation. In his influential lecture *Experience or Interpretation: The Dilemma of Museums of Modern Art*, Serota argues for the presentation of contemporary art in clusters, overlapping and merging in what he calls 'zones of influence'.

An example he gives in his book is placing the white-on-white canvases of Robert Ryman next to a reflective metal floor-piece by Carl Andre, so playing up the similarities and highlighting the differences between two different kinds of minimalism. But he places the emphasis on the visual connections between the two artists, and advocates putting works of comparable aesthetic quality together. Is it possible that at Bankside the curators have taken Serota's basic idea, but misunderstood it? Lacking his eye, they have created galleries that reek of the lecture hall, each art-historical homily illustrated not with slides, but with real works of art. Whether or not the juxtapositions that these curators come up with make a beautiful or arresting display doesn't enter the equation.

And so, in the first gallery in the landscape section, one of Monet's paintings of water lilies at Giverny hangs opposite a floor-to-ceiling wall-piece by Richard Long, made with cascades of spattered mud which has been flung or dribbled on to the wall's white surface.

A long wall text explains this pairing by suggesting the many similarities between the two artists' approach to landscape. Legitimate though it is to make such a comparison, the curator did not care that the pastel blues and greens of the Monet absolutely kill the monochromatic Long, or that the scale and violence of the Long make the Monet look insignificant and saccharine. Even on its own terms, the gallery strikes me as specious: Long obviously made his painting in recent weeks, when he knew it was to hang opposite Monet. He therefore set out to create a work as like a Monet as possible in order to demonstrate that his work is like Monet's. So what, then, have we learned?

A third work by Long, a circle of red stone, sits on the gallery floor between the two, as though trying (and failing) to forge some visual connection between them. Just imagine for a moment that the wall label had simply mentioned Monet's importance for Long, and even emphasised the point by reproducing a photograph of the water lilies. Had Long been shown on his own, the gallery might have worked. Confronting a successful and well-displayed wall painting by Long is a visceral, sensuous experience, one that hits you in the solar plexus. At a moment like that, who the hell wants to have to think about Monet? But at every stage the curators have taken over, refusing to believe that the art is strong enough to speak for itself.

One of the most egregious moments occurs in a gallery in which Mattise's famous series of monumental bronze reliefs, the *Backs*, are shown opposite drawings of nudes by contemporary artist Marlene Dumas. It's not that the physical mass and moral weight of the Matisses utterly crush and destroy her feeble efforts (though they do), but that the lightweight art drags the serious art down. And how a curator could possibly show the Matisses along a side wall in a gallery that feels like a passageway between two more important spaces is incredible to me – but no more incredible than showing Francis Bacon in a gallery with no natural light, a gallery clearly intended to be used for drawings and photographs of documentary material.

Here's a test. Spot the odd one out in the following list: Picasso, Matisse, Taylor-Wood, Bonnard, Freud. It is not my intention to denigrate Sam Taylor-Wood, just to point out that when you place her video work, showing a naked man dancing to the sound of Samuel Barber's *Elegy*, next door to a gallery full of the greatest figure painters of the twentieth century, you don't create an interesting tension between old and new, you make it impossible to look at either without distraction. In this case, the sound of Barber's music is audible, like muzak, throughout this section of the museum, destroying your concentration just when you are trying to clear your mind to look at Picasso. But then, to make a comparison between such utterly different kinds of art is in itself mad, because the subject of each work (the nude) isn't the most important thing about it – it's how the artist works and the materials he or she uses.

For all I know Taylor-Wood's piece might have worked well in a room devoted to contemporary artists working in Britain. The thematic approach is great in theory. In practice it needs to be handled with a sensitivity Nittve and co. just don't have. What they do have is a lot to say about the art on view. Each gallery has a lengthy explanatory wall text, written in boilerplate curator-speak, so that the Tate is no longer a place of pleasurable discovery, but one where at every turn you are told what to think and how to respond.

At a certain point on my visit I went up to the third floor to see a loan exhibition called *Between Cinema and a Hard Place*. What a relief. No wall texts, only the name of the artist whose work was being shown in each gallery. The bliss. I realised how persecuted I had felt downstairs. There, I felt as though I had been trapped on a train with someone relentlessly yelling into his mobile phone for two hours. Now, suddenly there was silence and space to respond to the works on my own terms. What's more, it is a splendid show of the best in international contemporary art from Matthew Barney to Bruce Nauman, Gillian Wearing, Bill Viola, Christian Boltanksi and Cornelia Parker.

Am I being unfair? Well, yes, a little. There are some beautiful galleries in the permanent display – a really thrilling installation of Joseph Beuys's work, a gallery given over to Duchamp and Picabia (who really do work visually, as well as intellectually, together). Bridget Riley looks good. There's a superb room hung with paintings of modern interiors by Michael Craig-Martin, Patrick Caulfield and Roy Lichtenstein, and a strong gallery devoted to Tony Cragg.

As the president of the anti-Louise Bourgeois society, I can hardly
bring myself to comment on the three 30-foot-high steel towers with
viewing platforms that she has made for the huge turbine hall, or
on the equally large steel spider, which is inevitably entitled *Maman*
('Mama'). Vacuous, overblown, self-obsessed as always, Bourgeois
is the most overrated artist of our time. The fact that her work was
chosen to open the new Tate is the most depressing portent of all.

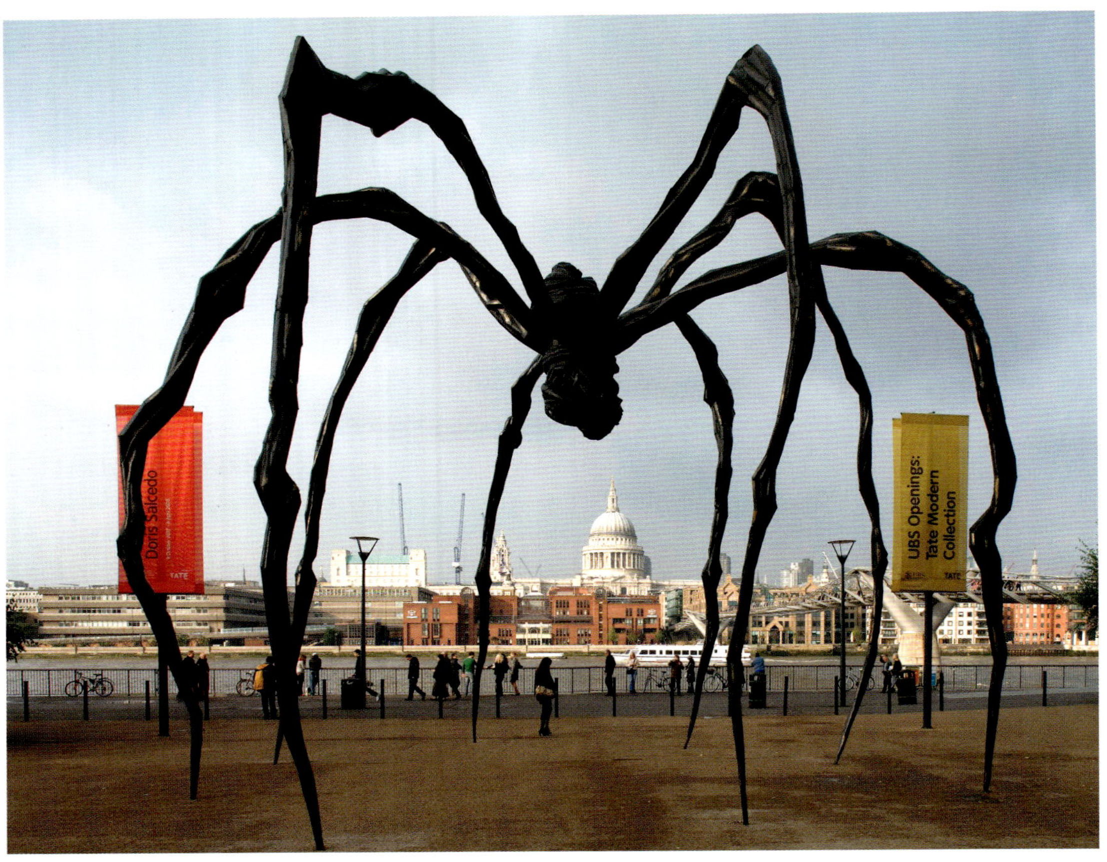

Louise Bourgeois
***Maman**, 1999*
Outside Tate Modern,
London

William Hogarth's *Sigismunda*

Why are practitioners of the new art history so unwilling to address
the subject of aesthetic quality? Although the organiser of Tate
Britain's *In Focus* exhibition on William Hogarth's *Sigismunda*,
Dr Marcia Pointon, has a lot to say in the catalogue about female
sexual desire and the evils of luxury consumption, at no point does
she discuss the picture as a work of art. If she did, she would have
to start by admitting that it isn't very good, at least not if you use
aesthetic criteria to judge the awkward composition, the unconvincing
anatomy, the uncertain depiction of space, the overworked paint
surface, the dark tonality and the lugubrious subject.

This is not my subjective judgement, but what you might call
execration by consensus. The patron who commissioned the picture
in 1758 refused to accept it; Hogarth's contemporaries mocked it; the
artist himself withdrew it from exhibition and then repainted large
areas of the canvas. What is more, plans to engrave it were dropped;
at Hogarth's death it remained unsold, and it has never been popular
with the public.

Hogarth painted *Sigismunda Mourning Over the Heart of Guiscardo,
Her Murdered Husband* late in his career, for a new and colossally rich
patron, Sir Richard Grosvenor. Impressed by *The Lady's Last Stake*, one
of Hogarth's high-spirited send-ups of contemporary manners and
morals, Grosvenor must have expected him to produce a modern
moral subject in the same lightly ribald vein. But he made the mistake
of leaving the subject of the new picture to the artist, who chose
a grim tale from Boccaccio's *Decameron* concerning Ghismonda,
daughter of King Tancred, who falls in love with Guiscardo, a page
at her father's court. Enraged by this mésalliance, the cruel king has
the boy killed and his heart sent to his daughter in a golden goblet.
Hogarth shows the distraught princess the moment after she has
received the grisly gift, but before she swallows the poison that will
end her life.

1 August 2001

Hogarth's *Sigismunda*
In Focus

Tate Britain, London

Anatomically, Hogarth's Sigismunda is a mess. Listing
dangerously towards the left-hand side of the picture, her impossibly
long right arm rests on her casket of jewels, but doesn't quite connect
to the head it is supposed to be supporting. Eyes swollen with tears,
lips parted and brow furrowed, Sigismunda's appearance is meant
to elicit our sympathy. But the effect of grief on a plain face is only
to make it even plainer. Likewise, as she morbidly draws the bloody
heart to her breast, we should feel a frisson of horror. But Hogarth's
ability to depict space is so tentative that it is impossible to tell how
far away from her body the vessel that holds the heart is, so we find
ourselves worrying that the goblet is simply tipping over. The
placement of a strategic hand and an artfully floating veil disguises
Hogarth's ineptitude in attaching Sigismunda's head and neck to her
shoulders. Unintentionally, he turns her into the stuff of comedy, an
ageing actress in an overheated melodrama.

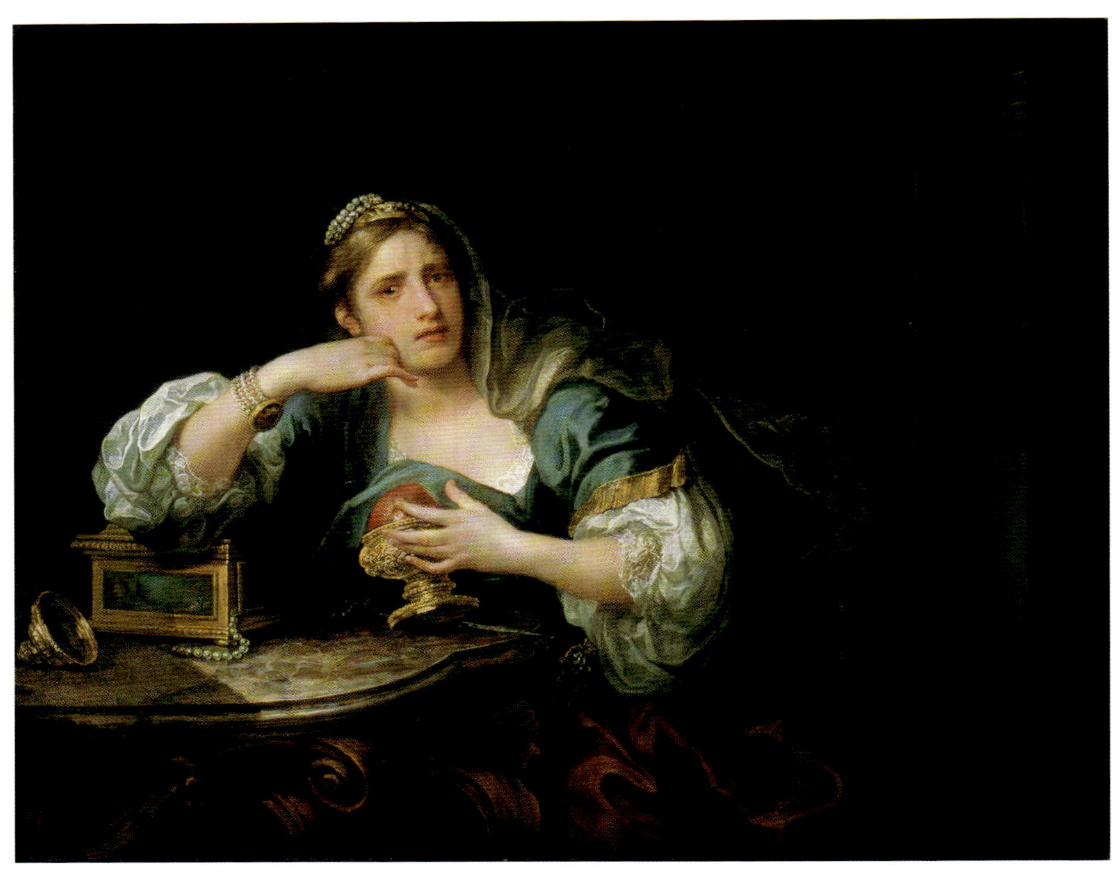

But a failed painting can make a fascinating exhibition, and the really interesting question is why an artist of genius painted such a terrible picture. What drew Hogarth to this particular subject? Why did he use a relatively old and (compared with the heroines in his other paintings) not particularly pretty model? What went wrong with the drawing and composition? Since Pointon couldn't care less, I'll try to suggest a few answers.

The place to start is with Hogarth's artistic training. Born in 1697, Hogarth entered the new Academy of Art in St Martin's Lane in 1720. Here he developed a system of visual mnemonics by which he would fix the image that he wished to remember in his mind's eye, then draw or paint it later in his studio. This way of working implies a considerable element of self-instruction, because it dispensed with the traditional academic practice of learning to draw by copying from plaster casts and from Old Masters. Indeed, Hogarth noisily rejected the teaching methods imposed in the previous century by Charles LeBrun at the Académie Royale in Paris, which he identified with the codification and embalming of art in sets of rules and regulations. But what Hogarth was against was academic classicism, not history painting itself, for in the later 1720s he attended the Covent Garden art school founded by a man he idolised, Sir James Thornhill, a painter trained in the tradition of the high Italian baroque.

This is the important part. In 1729, like Guiscardo, Hogarth eloped, with Thornhill's daughter Jane – and it is she, Mrs Hogarth, who sat for the figure of Sigismunda twenty years later. Here may lie one reason for Hogarth's attraction to an obscure subject which, he said, he had long wished to paint: it represented the tragic consequences of an illicit union not unlike his own with Jane. But Thornhill was no Tancred. He was soon reconciled to his new son-in-law, and was to instill in Hogarth the ambition to follow his own success by becoming a history painter.

But as a painter of what he called 'the grand stile of history', Hogarth was only fairly successful. Whereas his artistic education enabled him to paint portraits and genre subjects with an easy fluency, when it came to painting historical or religious subjects his lack of academic training left him without the ability to organise space, gesture and dramatic expression in a dignified and rational way. Sigismunda should be seen as the last in a series of failed history paintings, which include the murals at St Bartholomew's hospital in London, those in Lincoln's Inn Hall and the altarpiece for St Mary Redcliffe, Bristol – works that one contemporary called 'more than could be expected of [Hogarth]'.

Hogarth's portraits and genre paintings stand for all that was informal and anti-classical, unstuffy and fresh in English art. In his history paintings, however, he tended to emulate the stately baroque of Poussin or Carlo Maratta. *Sigismunda* is a pastiche in which we can detect elements of the Bolognese classicists Guido Reni and Domenichino, as well as the Florentine baroque painter Francesco Furini. In it, he is unsure of himself, and works against the grain to prove a point and to show that he was capable of equalling the Old Masters, whose works commanded such high prices among British collectors.

Now none of this interests Pointon. The author of *Strategies for Showing: Women, Possession and Representation in English Visual Culture 1665–1800* brings to her interpretation of the picture a deliriously inspired combination of Marxist and feminist art theory, culminating in her revelation that the string of pearls that spills from Sigismunda's jewel box is 'semen, which is here seen seeping away into the shadows, an . . . emblem of wasteful expenditure'.

What visitors to Tate Britain will make of the surrounding exhibition, which aims to contextualise the picture, is anybody's guess: bits of jewellery, prints and books are shown alongside the paintings, but in vitrines so badly lit that you literally can't see what is in them.

The Lure of the East

10 June 2008

The Lure of the East:
British Orientalist
Painting

Tate Britain, London

The first and greatest age of Orientalism in the visual arts started in France around the time of Napoleon's invasion of Egypt and peaked as the Romantic Movement swept through Europe. Works like Delacroix's *The Death of Sardanapalus* (1827) and *The Fanatics of Tangier* (1838) set precedents for later depictions of the East as a place given to sexual excess, wanton cruelty, mass murder and unbridled sensuality.

But as Tate Britain's *The Lure of the East: British Orientalist Painting* makes clear, on this side of the Channel the story was very different. From the seventeenth century onwards, British artists were happy to paint portraits of eccentric fellow countrymen and women who liked to dress up in oriental costume, but they didn't actually begin to visit the Middle East until the late 1830s. At the start of the period, a few exhibited sensationalist subject pictures, such as William Allan's *Slave Market, Constantinople* of 1838. Later, John Frederick Lewis would occasionally titillate the Victorian public with scenes purportedly showing scantily clad young women being introduced into the harem.

By and large, though, what is remarkable about the work in this show is how clear-sighted the British artistic response to the Arab world was. Unlike their French counterparts, the British did not generally impose their lurid fantasies on Eastern subject matter. You won't find a single British painting at Tate Britain showing a massacre, a beheading or a naked slave girl. Instead, you'll find descriptive and topographical paintings of a very high order, and David Roberts, Frederick Leighton and Edward Lear are all supremely accomplished artists. However, too often their Eastern landscapes and views of mosques and churches are more accurate than inspired.

By the end of the show, I felt as though I were turning the pages of an album filled with snapshots from other people's holidays. Individual British orientalist paintings may be exquisite, but the genre

as a whole is repetitive and dull. I'll take the full-blooded French
Romanticism any day.

Here are a few examples. Whereas Jean-Léon Gérôme is openly
lascivious in describing the nudity and degradation of the women
he shows in his *Slave Market at Cairo*, what is striking about William
Holman Hunt's full- length portrait *Afterglow in Egypt* is how careful
the British artist is to portray the handsome young woman as
personable, confident and healthy. Likewise, nothing could be more
dignified than David Wilkie's portraits of *Muhammad Ali Pasha of
Egypt* (1841) or *Sultan Abdul Mejid*, both of whom are shown not
as potentates lolling on cushions, but as modern heads of state seated
in chairs of European design.

However, the measured, nuanced, respectful approach of most
British orientalists to their subject matter is precisely what the
politically correct curators who organised this woefully misguided
exhibition can't stand. The very fact that a British artist was inspired
to paint a Middle Eastern subject automatically makes him a target
for their suspicion and scorn. And so we are told the Pre-Raphaelite
landscape painter Thomas Seddon went to the Holy Land because
he wanted to see the Bible land for himself. For this he is taken to
task in the catalogue as 'an enthusiastic Christian artist . . . intent on
remaking religious art for a modern Protestant audience'. But in his
landscape *Jerusalem and the Valley of Jehoshaphat* he painted every
pebble and blade of grass using exactly the hyper-realistic technique
he employed when painting the Swiss Alps. Where is there visual
evidence that his religious views inform these paintings? Surely the
whole point of the Pre-Raphaelite approach to landscape is that the
artist's commitment to 'truth to nature' is greater than any subjective
feelings he may have.

Those responsible for the catalogue haven't noticed that, if
anything, British artists tended to idealise the Arab world at the
expense of the European. John Frederick Lewis's virtuoso watercolour
A Frank Encampment in the Desert of Mount Sinai (1842) shows the
ridiculous Viscount Castlereagh dressed as a sheikh and stretched
out under an umbrella as though on the lawn of a country house in
Surrey. Surrounded by hunting dogs and dead game, he has obviously
come to the Near East for a bit of huntin' and shootin'.

Like a modern traveller on a luxury safari, he wanted to see

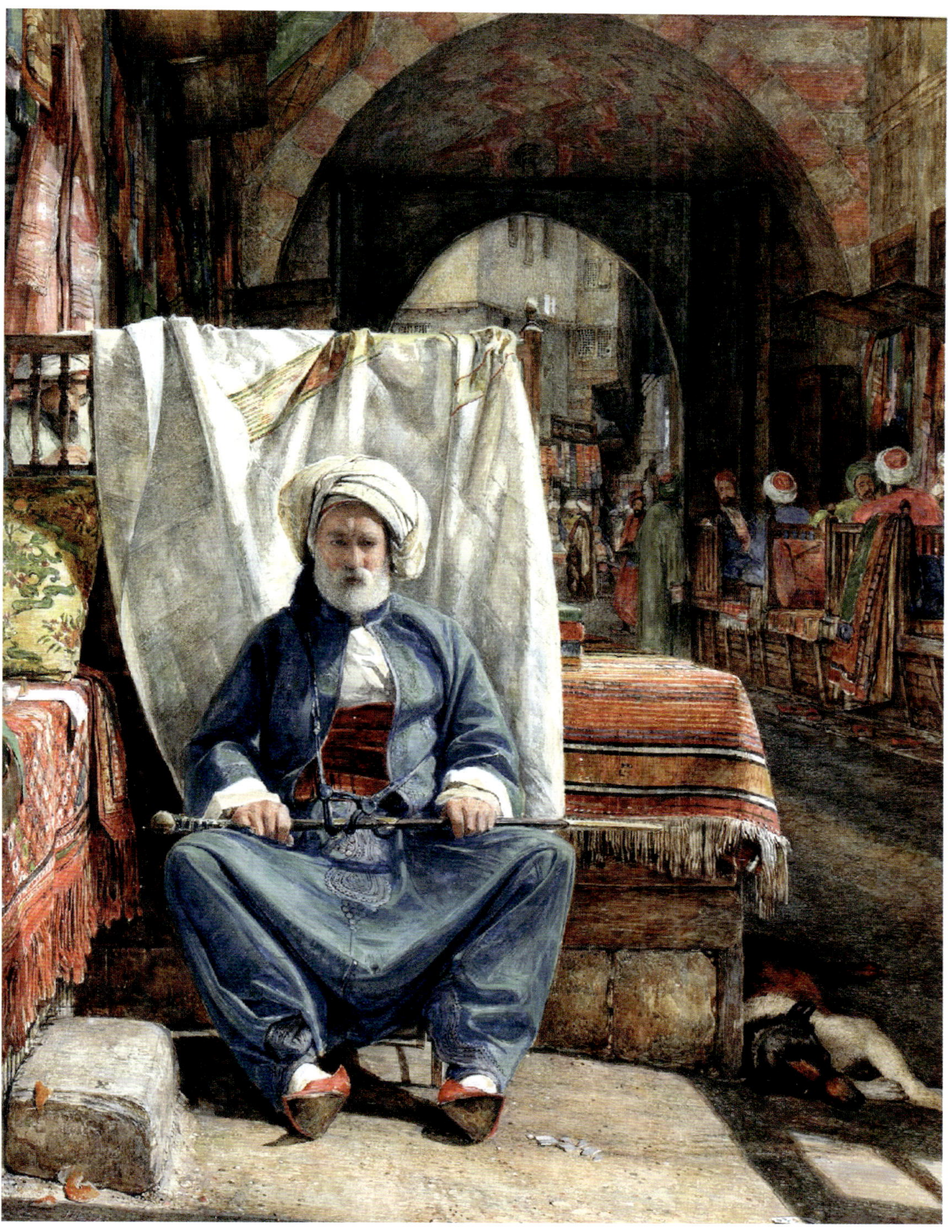

the desert without really leaving England, for he's brought English newspapers and books, a bottle of Harvey's sherry, and porcelain cups from which to drink his tea. Lewis shows the moment when a local sheikh approaches the camp of the effete European. Far from belittling the Arab, the artist contrasts his strength and dignity with the play-acting of the English gent. More than anything, Lewis finds the scene richly comical. Why is this not mentioned in the catalogue? Because it is at odds with the show's relentless tone of self-pity, aggrievement and victimhood. I see these pictures as perfect examples of the West's curiosity about the East. The organisers present them as by-products of colonial oppression.

In a near-hysterical and critically worthless essay in the catalogue, Rana Kabbani accuses British artists who worked in the Near East of being 'content to paint a static world of exquisite surface'. She is enraged that instead of the sublime landscapes, superb buildings and light-dappled interiors they did paint, these artists somehow forgot to show 'strikes, riots, rebellions, repressions and blockades, the impoverishment and famine; the communal punishments, hangings and massacres'. And – wait for it – guess who was responsible for these crimes? Right! All were 'marks of Britain's colonial moment in the Middle East'. Could someone please explain to Ms Kabbani that these paintings are by artists, not by investigative reporters working for BBC News?

I was just as amazed to see that the author of the introductory essay to the catalogue resurrects the controversial writings of Edward Said to belittle British artists for ignoring Islamic history in their paintings of the Holy Land. Does he also believe European artists working in, say, India or Japan had an obligation to include references to the entire history of that country in their work? Or do his strictures apply only when the region in question is the Middle East?

By all means go to this show to enjoy the many superb paintings and watercolours on view. But if you are tempted to fall for its specious arguments, get hold of a copy of *Defending the West*, Ibn Warraq's demolition of Said's misinterpretations of Western attitudes towards the Middle East – a distortion of historical truth all too faithfully reflected at Tate Britain.

Thomas Gainsborough

More than a decade ago, I spent many months cataloguing the
remarkable collection of paintings by Thomas Gainsborough owned
by the Philadelphia Museum of Art. This work entailed not only
hours in the British Library, but long days pursuing my researches
in local record offices trying to find material that would add to
our understanding of Gainsborough, his patrons and his art. It had
always been said, for example, that the museum's enchanting head-
and-shoulders portrait of Mrs Clement Tudway was painted in
Gainsborough's 'late Bath period' – but we had no idea precisely
when. One day in the Somerset Record Office, the archivist brought
me an enormous chest, filled to the brim with the uncatalogued
Tudway papers. With a sinking heart, I started to sift through the mass
of bills and receipts for wine, coal, candles and other household items.

I was convinced that I had a week's work in front of me, so
imagine my excitement when, after only a few hours, I reached down
and picked up from the pile Gainsborough's handwritten receipt for
payment on his portraits of Mr and Mrs Tudway: 'Bath Jul 2d. 1773 /
Rev.d of Clem: Tudway Esq. The sum of / seventy Pounds sixteen
Shillings, in full for / two Portraits (Viz. Himself & Mrs Tudway) /
and two Frames Burnish'd Gold, / Case& ec. – / Thos Gainsborough /
£70:16.' Now we had the date and the price of the portrait and even
knew that the frames were the originals selected by Gainsborough.

Then, looking through Mrs Tudway's few surviving papers,
I realised that her letters gave us a remarkably vivid impression of
her personality. Modest, gentle and religious, the person who wrote
these letters perfectly fitted the face of the lady in our portrait, a
plain woman with long nose and a sweet, shy smile who wore her
hair without powder, another indication of her lack of worldly
sophistication. Hardly an earth-shattering discovery, but it is through
this kind of research that historians add to our knowledge of the past.

23 October 2002

Thomas Gainsborough
1727–1788

Tate Britain

Another time, I was cataloguing one of Gainsborough's mature
landscapes. According to the then universally accepted view of
Gainsborough's working methods, his later landscapes were works of
the imagination. He simply did not paint real views from nature. But I
was struck by the fact that, since the picture's sale at Christie's in 1894,
the painting had always been called *A View Near King's Bromley-on-
Trent, Staffordshire*. The title was so specific that I decided to drive to
Staffordshire to see whether I could find the view. Sure enough, with
the help of members of the local historical society, I found the exact
spot where Gainsborough must have stood to view the tower of All
Saints' Church from the river bank at a distance of about half a mile
along the south bank, upstream. Such a view could be seen only from
the north terrace of the park of the manor at King's Bromley, in the
late 1760s owned by a man named Samuel Lane. We now knew that
Gainsborough had visited Stafford, a fact that had not been recorded,
and that he had a patron in Lane, of whom we had never heard. More
importantly, it had been proved that Gainsborough certainly did paint
'real views from nature'.

As you can see, I am proud of the work I put into *British Painting
in the Philadelphia Museum*. It was, therefore, with mounting irritation
that I began reading the catalogue of the Gainsborough exhibition
at Tate Britain, and discovered that all this information had been
incorporated into the catalogue entries without the slightest
acknowledgment to me. The Tate curators who had drawn so heavily
on my work, Martin Myrone and Diane Perkins, and Tate Britain
itself, have not even bothered to cite the Philadelphia catalogue in
the bibliography. This is not simply shoddy scholarship, it is close
to plagiarism. But, believe me, I am not so pompous as to devote
a whole article to the incident did I not think it has much wider
implications for what is happening to the once impeccable standards
of scholarship at Tate Britain.

To explain what I mean, let us now return to the portrait of Mrs
Tudway and examine the way in which Martin Myrone has used the
information available and in so doing distorted the way we see the
picture. After noting that Mrs Tudway is shown to be a modest
woman who does not wear powder in her hair, he adds: 'The picture
thus neatly avoids the imputation of excess that was concurrently [sic]
under so much satirical criticism in the 1760s and 1770s as Britain

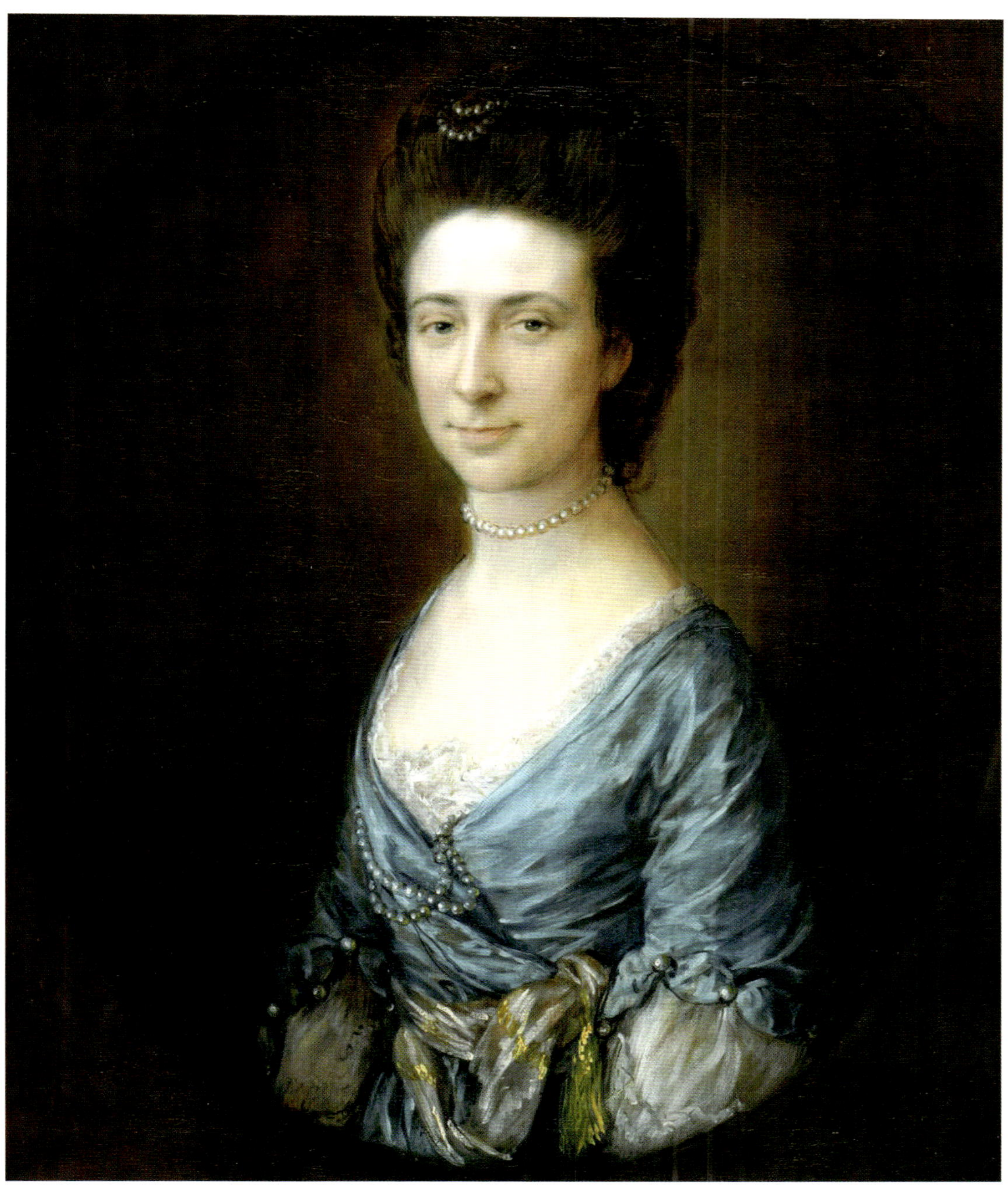

Thomas Gainsborough
**A Portrait of Mrs
Clement Tudway,**
1773
Philadelphia Museum
of Art

seemed to be overrun with luxuries and fashion underwritten by
the nation's imperial successes.' Poor Mrs Tudway! Had she dressed
more showily, Myrone would presumably have accused her of being
a typical imperialist of her age. As it is, she 'neatly avoids' that
imputation by dressing discreetly. But, since Myrone took the trouble
to use so much material from my original catalogue entry, why did he
not use the following sentence, quoted from a letter that the widowed
Mrs Tudway wrote to her nephew in 1821? 'I never was anxious for
great abundance, and my dear husband knew my retired disposition
– not ambitious of entering into high style of life, much less so now.'

Is the reason Myrone doesn't cite the letter because it offers a
straightforward explanation of the picture's appearance that does not
fit into the Marxist drivel he is spouting in the rest of the catalogue
entry? The intention seems to be to smear the sitter with the 'crime'
of imperialism, not to help us understand Gainsborough's portrait.
For, surely, what that portrait reveals is how sensitively Gainsborough
captured the personality of this simple woman, and with what
warmth and sympathy he responded to a person who had not
succumbed to the bonfire of vanities that was eighteenth-century
Bath.

In my original entry, I noted that her husband, the MP Clement
Tudway, in addition to family properties around Wells in Somerset,
managed extensive sugar plantations in Antigua. In Myrone's hands,
this information is twisted to become: 'The veneer of [Mrs Tudway's]
fashionable elegance rested ultimately on the economic exploitation
of men and women thousands of miles away.' But this is a travesty.
Art historians have a duty to place works of art in the context of their
time. Myrone is bringing a twentieth-century consciousness to the
interpretation of a portrait painted in 1773. It adds nothing to our
understanding of Gainsborough or of his art.

Likewise, in her entry on *A View near King's Bromley-on-Trent,
Staffordshire*, Diane Perkins implies that Gainsborough deliberately
turned his back on Samuel Lane's grand manor house to paint
publicly owned land, as though he had some objection to the
ownership of private property. This is pernicious nonsense. What
is important about the picture is that Gainsborough transformed
a very pretty local scene into a timeless, Arcadian idyll. In offering
such tendentious interpretations, Tate Britain is feeding visitors to this

exhibition with a distorted view of Gainsborough and the society in which he lived.

More than thirty years ago, John Berger looked at the wonderful double portrait of Mr and Mrs Andrews in the National Gallery and was outraged to see sitters who belonged to a land-owning class. Somehow, I had thought that that Marxist approach to criticism had been discredited long ago. But now Myrone goes further. He accuses Gainsborough of not showing labourers at work on the Andrews land. Apparently, had Gainsborough done so, he would have 'revealed the economic and social iniquities that allowed [Mr and Mrs Andrews] the leisure to pose for an artist'. What is more, 'the men and women who made that [wealth] possible through their labour are displaced from the picture'. Poor old Gainsborough can't win. Would things have been any better if he had shown labourers in the distance?

I have repeatedly criticised Tate Britain for the declining standards of its exhibitions. Travesties such as *The Victorian Nude* and *Thomas Girtin* seemed to me to have very little to do with artistic quality since, at times, the pictures on the walls were simply a pretext for allowing second-rate academics to disseminate tired feminist and Marxist theories about social history and sexual politics. Now, in the Gainsborough show, scholarship has so grotesquely broken free of academic standards that it is in free fall. Long, vacuous wall labels tell the visitor what to think and how to react to the pictures. The catalogue has virtually no scholarly substance.

Does it matter if the high standards of scholarship for which this country is world famous no longer apply at Tate Britain? After all, university lecturers use slides to show how works of art reflected social attitudes in eighteenth- and nineteenth-century Britain – and, if they do it well, it can be very stimulating. Why shouldn't Tate Britain do the same? The answer is that an exhibition is not a textbook and it is not a lecture. As the national collection of British art, Tate Britain's obligation is to allow great works of art to speak for themselves, to show the British school in such a way that visitors can respond to it in their own way at their own level. When exhibitions at Tate Britain are diminished by the imposition of a political agenda on the interpretation of the pictures, that should cause as much concern as when the Royal Opera or Royal Ballet aren't mounting world-class productions. What is happening there is a scandal that concerns us all.

British Iconoclasm

When some bright spark at Tate Britain came up with the idea of
doing a show about the history of iconoclasm in this country why
wasn't the plan strangled at birth? Was there no one around to point
out that the story of the dissolution of the monasteries has been told
so often in books like Eamon Duffy's *The Stripping of the Altars* that
there isn't a lot that's new to say? Even if it proved possible to update
the story to the present day, most of the visual material has long
been destroyed or defaced. Did anyone at Tate think to mention that
looking at photographs of works of art that no longer exist rarely
makes for a satisfactory gallery-going experience? And finally, did it
occur to the director to take the curator responsible for the section on
modern art aside and explain to her what the word 'iconoclasm' is
usually taken to mean? Obviously, the answer to all these questions
is 'no'. If you decide to visit *Art Under Attack* don't expect to see much
in the way of art, don't expect to learn anything new, and don't expect
to enjoy the experience.

The exhibition starts with the familiar story of the dissolution
of the monasteries under Henry VIII, then moves on to sacrilegious
annihilation of religious imagery by the government of Edward VI.
So effective was the order to 'utterly extinct and destroy' religious
images that the first gallery is relatively empty, apart from a sad
miscellany of mutilated fragments of sculpture, shards of stained
glass, and savagely defaced paintings – each and every one a
sickening reminder of how much of this country's visual culture was
lost during the Reformation. The deliberate destruction of any work
of art is distressing, but since the reformers focused on sacred images,
the sense of violation is even more acute. In front of a decapitated
Madonna or the viciously scratched face of Christ, your instinct is
to avert your eyes as you'd do in front of a mutilated corpse.

As it happens a mutilated corpse (or the representation of one) is
the most eloquent work of art in the entire show, a limestone figure of

1 October 2013

Art Under Attack:
Histories of British
Iconoclasm

Tate Britain, London

the dead Christ carved by a Netherlandish sculptor working in this country in the first quarter of the sixteenth century. No reproduction can begin to suggest the overwhelming power of the realistically carved torso and head of Christ's body *in transitu* (that is, during the period between his death on the Cross and the Resurrection when the flesh was subject to corruption like any other corpse). We look down not on a divine personage but on a human cadaver in the early stages of rigor mortis. After the reformers had hacked off the figure's right

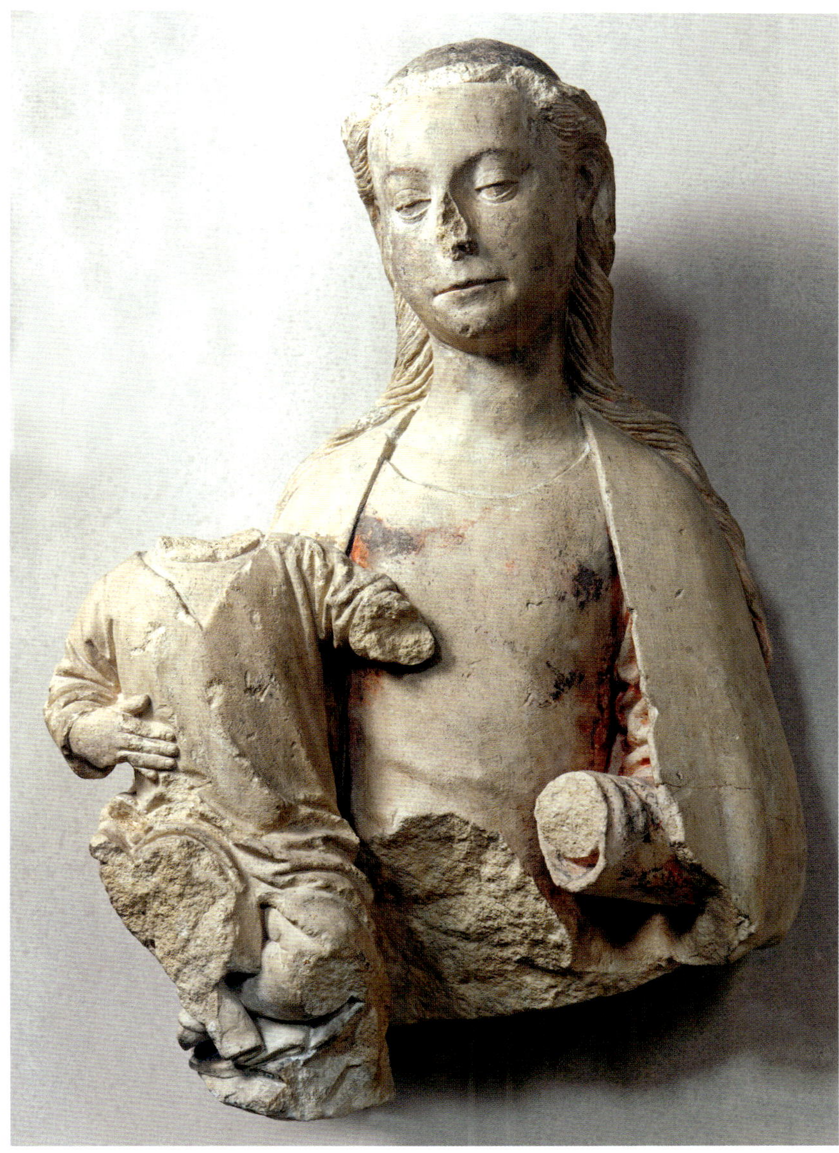

Anonymous
Madonna and Child,
15th century
Winchester Cathedral

arm, legs and feet they stopped their foul work. I'd like to believe that it is a tribute to the artist's skill that they could not bring themselves to smash a face that with its half-closed eyes and open mouth is so expressive of vulnerability, suffering and resignation.

Almost as eloquent is a mid-seventeenth century painting showing the stripped down interior of Canterbury Cathedral. At first you think that the worst is over because all the images have already been obliterated by Puritan zealots. Then with a sinking feeling in the pit of your stomach you spot the tiny figures high up in the clerestory of the nave, systematically smashing the remaining stained glass windows with pikes.

The exhibition then looks at a far less disturbing form of iconoclasm – the destruction of images for political reasons. Did any of us care when Saddam Hussein's statue was overturned by a mob in 2003? Of course not – because the Iraqis weren't destroying a work of art but a political symbol. We may regret the destruction by Irish nationalists of Grinling Gibbons's equestrian statue of King William III in 1926 or the loss of Nelson's monument in Dublin's O'Connell Street in 1966, but we can at least understand why they were targeted.

When Mary Richardson took a meat cleaver to Velázquez's *Rokeby Venus* in the National Gallery she did it on a 'free day', as if to emphasise that her purpose was to take the picture away from the British people of whatever age, sex or class until the demands of the suffragettes were met. Richardson, like all women who participated in the iconoclastic campaign of 1913–14, could have attacked a statue or portrait of an MP opposed to votes for women. Instead they mutilated pictures in public museums, often chosen at random. Richardson's fatuous words of self-justification – 'you can get another picture but you can't get another life' – reveal just how little she knew or cared about what she was trying to destroy. Her sole purpose was to draw attention to her cause. That her cause was a noble one is irrelevant.

This is why I read the catalogue essay on the suffragette campaign with incredulity. The author, whose degree is clearly not in art history but in gender studies, describes these iconoclastic acts 'not as vandalism against the nation but as vital contributions to the freedoms now perceived as inherent to British national identity'. She concludes by denying that these iconoclastic acts were about destruction but instead 'a creative process'. This pernicious drivel

amounts to an open invitation to any person or any group with
a grievance to target works of art hanging in national museums.
The next time the guards at Tate Britain encounter an axe-wielding
animal rights activist, a paint-hurling environmental campaigner, the
divorced father with a hammer in his hand, or the radical vegan with
a little knife, it will serve the gallery right if they decline to intervene
in what a publication by the gallery they work for describes as a
'creative process'.

Modern iconoclasts are motivated by a thirst for publicity that's
easily gratified by running amok in an art gallery. It all started in 1976
when a pompous ninny called Peter Stowell-Phillips splashed blue
food dye on Carl Andre's *Equivalent VIII* on the grounds that as a
taxpayer he objected to its purchase by Tate. Since then we've seen
attacks on the works of Damien Hirst, Mark Rothko, Anish Kapoor
and Tracey Emin, most of which were carried out by failed artists.
However they try to justify what they've done, their actions are
always selfish, always self-serving and never forgivable.

The subject of aesthetic vandalism is therefore an enormously
interesting one, which is why the section of the show I most looked
forward to was the last. Unfortunately this final section isn't about
what is normally meant by iconoclasm. It looks instead at artists who
have made art by destroying something as opposed to constructing it.
Examples include Robert Rauschenberg's erased drawing by Wilhelm
de Kooning and the moment when Michael Landy pulped an artwork
by Chris Ofili along with the rest of his possessions. Plenty of artists
including John Stezaker and Dinos and Jake Chapman alter inferior
artworks to create greater ones. But this isn't iconoclasm. And
what on earth does Raphael Montanez Ortiz's work have to do with
iconoclasm? The objects he destroyed were not works of art but chairs
and pianos. Long before this I began to lose faith in this exhibition,
which is poorly conceived and badly thought through. It certainly
raises a lot of questions, but then so would a book or symposium.
I guess I just like to look at things.

Renaissance

I have to admit that I failed to get to the end of the BBC2 series *Renaissance* when I sat down to watch the six episodes on preview tapes. I gave up after the fifth, overcome with a leaden sense that I had just been subjected to a marathon viewing of *The Travel Show* lightly dusted with a thin coating of colour-supplement culture. Yet again, the BBC has demonstrated that it is incapable of delivering a serious programme on the visual arts.

Their failure is particularly galling because the Renaissance should have made such a splendid subject for television. All you have to do is point your cameras at the art, hire someone who knows about the period to write the script, and you've got your audience by the lapels. But the BBC did not bother to ask a recognised authority on the Renaissance to act as a consultant on the series, as would have happened automatically had the programmes been about the Second World War or the British Empire.

Instead, it chose as writer and presenter Andrew Graham-Dixon, a journalist who once wrote a book on Howard Hodgkin, to lecture us all on a subject about which, by his own admission, he had no special knowledge. It is this breathtaking arrogance, this assumption that a TV personality can swot up in a year or two on a subject that scholars have devoted their lives to studying that gets my goat. That, and the fact that Graham-Dixon wasn't up to the job. I filled twenty pages of my notebook citing the scores of half-truths, inaccuracies and banalities he smugly trotted out in one programme after another. The BBC has ended up with a patchwork of half-digested ideas and commonplace observations put together in such a way that it leaves the viewer in a permanent state of bewilderment.

In episode one, for example, the Renaissance is presented not only as a revival of antiquity but as a survival of Byzantine art and culture. But even if you accept the view that the Renaissance was the

1 December 1999

Renaissance

BBC2 TV

culmination of artistic tendencies that took place in the late Middle Ages, you still have to explain why certain artists such as Duccio, Giotto and Masaccio differed from their predecessors and contemporaries, and why they are therefore regarded as the founders of a new tradition in Western painting. To achieve this, you cannot avoid detailed pictorial analysis, and this in turn means that the camera must linger on each image for more than a few seconds at a time. But the director can't seem to hold his camera still, jump-cutting from shots of skateboarders and street people to airplanes, speed boats, puppeteers and football players so frequently that it was as though he were determined to show us anything rather than to allow us to see the works of art.

As a result, the visual change in art that we call the Renaissance is never adequately explained. Instead, Graham-Dixon substitutes a glib prurience about works of art which both covers over his unfamiliarity with the period he is supposed to be celebrating, and betrays his contempt for the audience he is addressing. There are innumerable examples, but I was particularly appalled by his cheap shots at Botticelli's *Birth of Venus* where he discovers the 'male sexual principle' in the lovely figure of Zephyr, whose breath ('all that huffing and puffing') cools Venus, in whose hair and draperies we are invited to see both a vulva and a vagina 'penetrated by a leaf'. Now all this is fine if your aim is to titillate adolescents, but at no point is Botticelli's masterpiece discussed as a picture in which the artist creates illusion through his handling of space, volume, light, line and colour.

How is it possible for the presenter of a major programme on Renaissance art to say of Leonardo da Vinci's *Adoration of the Magi* that the Three Kings are 'reliving their own birth pangs', or 'we are uncertain [as to whether] the leading Magus is laying down his crown before Jesus, or scrambling to pick it up'. Such statements merely demonstrate Graham-Dixon's perfect ignorance both of Christian theology and iconography.

But then, he bluffs his way through Leonardo, just as he did through Botticelli. As Our Man in Italy, he reports that when employed by the Sforza court in Milan the artist was confronted for the first time by the uncertainties of a free market. In fact, as the show of Florentine art in the 1470s presently at the National Gallery demonstrates, precisely the opposite is true: it was the system of competing studios in Florence that made for a free market, enabling the Medicis to choose between the workshops of Botticelli, the brothers Pollaiuolo, or Leonardo's own master, Verrocchio. In Milan, Leonardo da Vinci was another court artist on the payroll of the Sforzas.

Oblivious to the possibility that viewers might enjoy looking at art simply as art, Graham-Dixon consistently uses great paintings to make simplistic historical points. For the sake of clarity I will concentrate on programme four, the nadir of the series, in which he discusses the art of Bramante, Raphael and Michelangelo as though their stupendous creations were no more than the visible manifestations of the spiritual decline of the Renaissance church.

Because there are male nudes on the Sistine ceiling, for example, Graham-Dixon presents that masterpiece as a visual embodiment of Catholic corruption. But surely the introduction of naked bodies into a sacred setting is no more decadent in sixteenth-century Rome than it was in thirteenth-century Pisa, when Giovanni Pisano carved nude male figures on the pulpit of the Baptistry. And by slyly equating Michelangelo's sensuous treatment of the nude with real abuses in the church, such as the sale of indulgences, Graham-Dixon implies that a work of art was somehow responsible for the Reformation. This is an approach to history worthy of *1066 and All That*.

But then, what Graham-Dixon has to say about the Reformation has all the subtlety of a comic book. When he contrasts the degenerate art and patronage of Rome to the lot of happy Protestants painting away north of the Alps, you have to remind yourself that the art he is belittling includes the church of St Peter's, the Sistine Chapel and the Stanza della Segnatura. Only rarely does Graham-Dixon have anything really original to say about the Renaissance, but here I have to hand it to him: this is the first time I've heard the art of Michelangelo and Raphael denigrated in favour of that of Lucas Cranach, Martin Luther's favourite painter. And I really was left speechless by a description of Raphael's fresco *The Disputation over the Holy Sacrament* as a 'cover-up' which 'prefigures the propaganda of Soviet Socialist Realism'. Graham-Dixon's complaint is that the work presents a picture of saints and theologians gathered together in the presence of the Holy Trinity to discuss the nature of the Eucharist,

*From **Renaissance**, BBC2 TV, 1999*

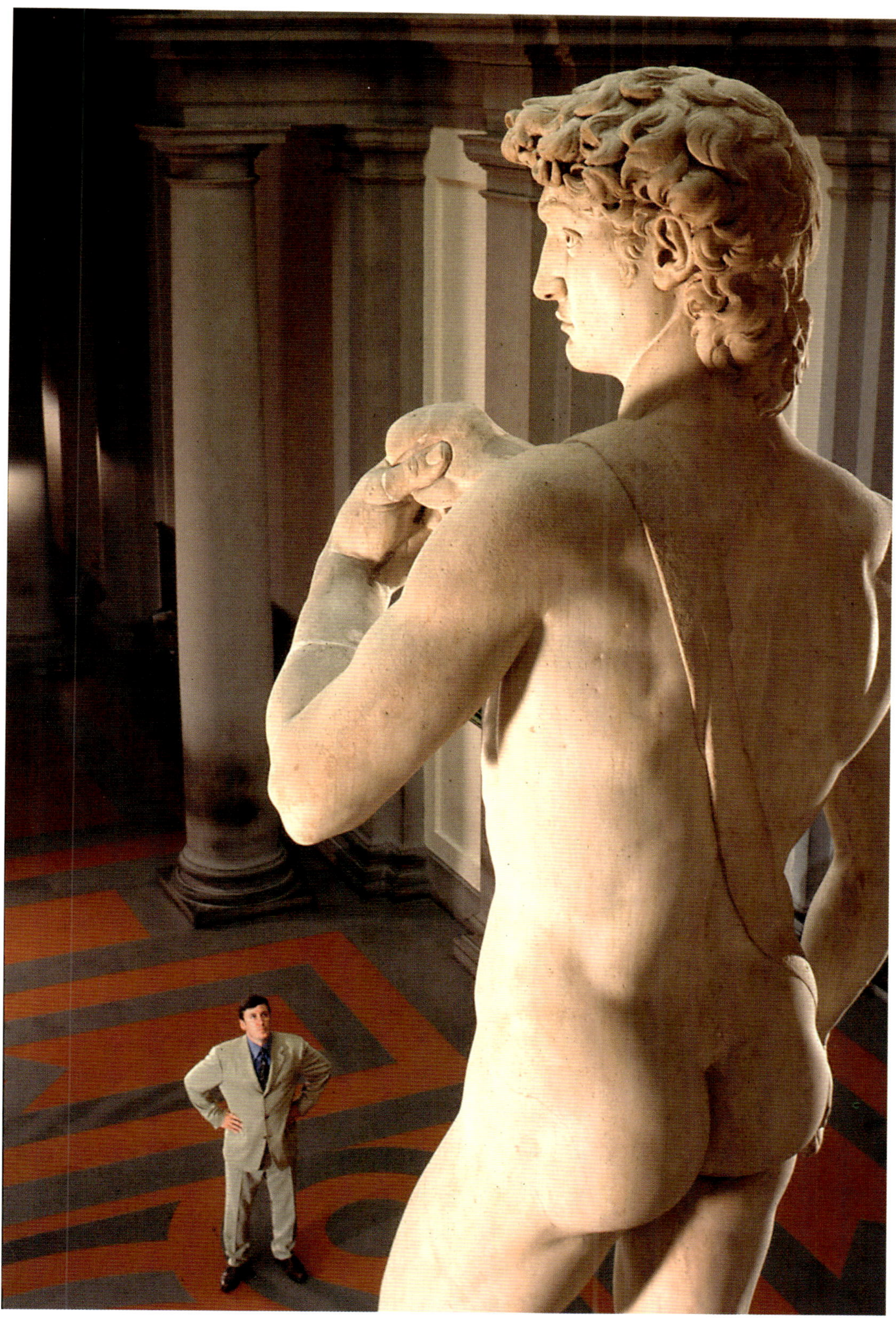

whereas in reality the Renaissance hurch did not encourage debate on matters of faith.

Misled by the title, Graham-Dixon seems to think that the picture is a 'dispute' in the modern sense of the word. In truth it shows a gathering together of the whole church, human and divine, to glorify one of the central mysteries of the faith, the reality of Christ's presence in the Eucharist. Far from being 'propaganda', it was painted for the pope's private apartments in the Vatican, an object of inspiration and meditation at the heart of the papacy. If Graham-Dixon can so wantonly misread one of the most sublime works of art ever painted, how can we trust the accuracy of even his most banal utterances?

And believe me, banal is what they are. Time and again he stands impassively in front of a work of art and delivers a made-for-TV soundbite which, after a moment's reflection, turns out to be meaningless. 'The Renaissance looked forward, as well as back.' Claptrap. 'The fifteenth century was a time of great change, but so was the century that preceded it.' Gosh. Donatello's *Mary Magdalene* he finds 'extremely disturbing' while Mantegna's *Camera degli Sposi* has for him 'psychological depth'. I could write this whole article again, with new examples.

Everyone connected with this travesty should be ashamed of themselves, but at the end it's Graham-Dixon who wrote the text and who has to take the blame. What is almost frightening to me is that he seems to have got away with it. With the honourable exception of Brian Sewell, such is the state of art education in this country that all the reviews I've read have been excellent.

The Elgin Marbles

Anyone can understand why a patriotic Greek might want the Elgin marbles returned to Athens. It is harder to fathom the motivation of British supporters of what, on the face of it, is a hopeless cause. Credulous, idealistic or simply out of touch with reality, many are romantics smitten with the idea that the marbles can somehow be 'returned' to the Parthenon, which is in fact a total ruin. Not perhaps realising that half of the Parthenon sculptures have been lost for ever, and that surviving sections are now in ten museums in eight countries, they imagine that, if only Britain would co-operate with Greece, the frieze could somehow be reconstructed.

Their activities have always seemed harmless enough, but, with the launch last week of a new campaign called 'The Marbles Reunited', led by Professor Anthony Snodgrass and supported by the politician Robin Cook, a new tactic is being employed to gain what the lobbyists want: spin. 'The Marbles Reunited' is not like previous campaigns. Orchestrated by a lavishly funded PR firm, it has not hesitated to use evasions and half-truths in an attempt to manipulate British public opinion on this issue.

To counter their obfuscation, let me begin with a very brief history of the controversy. Built between 447 and 438 BC, for a thousand years the Parthenon was used as a temple of the goddess Athena. When it became a Christian church in the fifth century, most of the east pediment was destroyed. After the Ottoman conquest of Athens in 1458, the Turks used it as a mosque and then as a powder magazine. In 1687, when the building took a direct hit from a Venetian canon, most of its interior walls were destroyed, bringing much of the frieze down with them. By the time Lord Elgin became ambassador to Istanbul in 1798, the Parthenon was a ruin, with Turkish soldiers using the marbles for target practice, and local people burning pieces of statues to make lime for mortar. Lord Elgin's purchase of the marbles

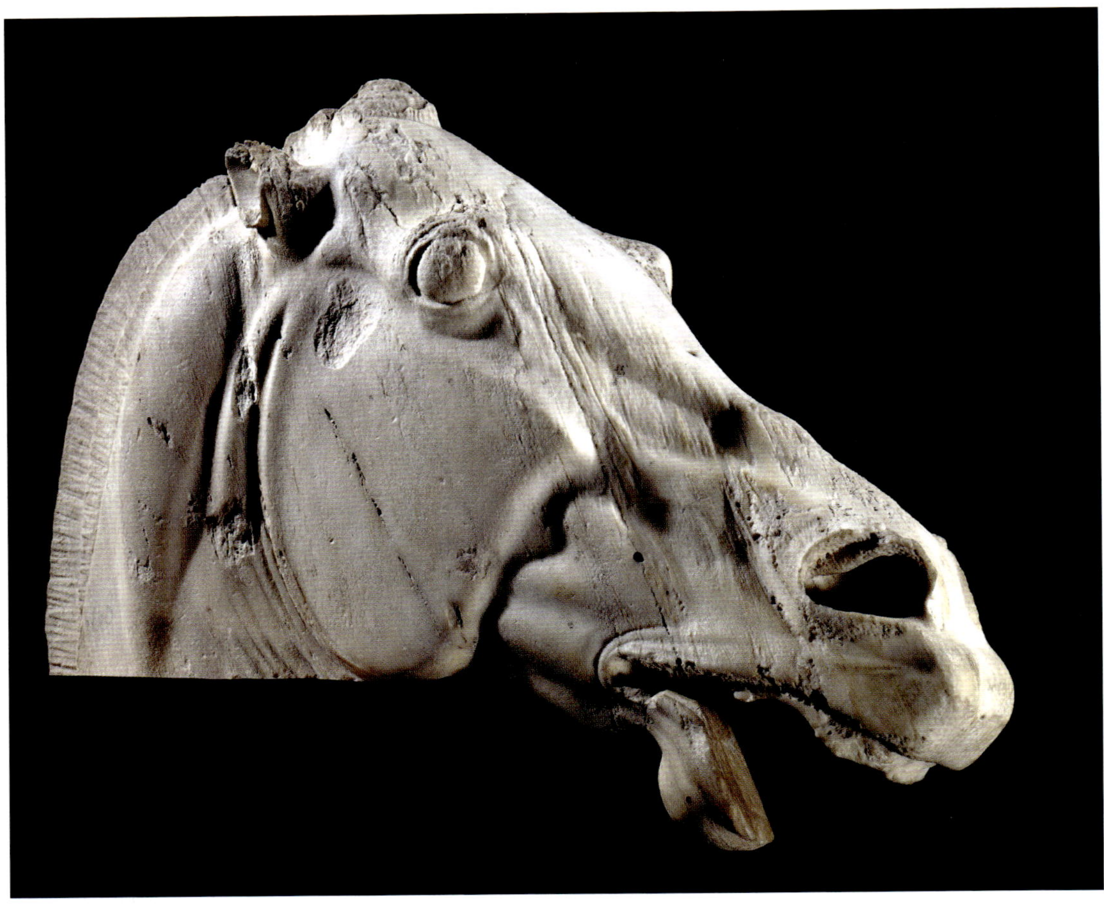

was motivated by the real risk to their survival if left *in situ*. He spent the colossal sum of £39,000 of his own money on the acquisition, transport to London and care of the marbles, and obtained documents from the Turkish government approving their removal from Greece. Since Parliament legally purchased the marbles from Lord Elgin in 1816, the British Museum's title to them is unassailable.

Last week, Mr Cook airily dismissed all this as an 'arcane dispute over legal title to the Parthenon Marbles', but he must know perfectly well that no court in Europe would question the legality of the BM's possession of them. And, even if it wished to, the British government could not simply transfer ownership of the marbles to another European state. Unlike in Greece, we operate an 'arm's length' policy, whereby the objects in our national museums belong in law not to parliament but to their trustees. This ensures that a government

Head of a horse, from
The Parthenon Marbles, *5th century BC*
British Museum, London

cannot sell works from our museums to raise revenue, or give them
away for short-term political advantage – which, as we shall see,
is precisely what Mr Cook proposes to do. What is more, were the
trustees of the BM to comply with such an outlandish scheme, they
would be in breach of their obligation to use the objects in their care
for the maximum public benefit.

Faced with this reality, the lobbyists working for 'The Marbles
Reunited' have now come up with what they call 'The Greek
Proposal' – that the marbles be 'loaned' to Athens but that Britain
would 'retain ownership' of them. In fact, the new formula is a
smokescreen. The Greeks are not asking for a loan in the ordinary
sense. They want the marbles to remain permanently in Athens.
They are now building a new museum to house them – on an
archaeological site so important for the study of Byzantine civilisation
that the Greek supreme court has twice declared its construction
illegal, only to be overruled by the government.

This is where the story gets ugly. With breathtaking cheek, the
PR company fighting the campaign in this country has conducted
a public opinion poll, which they claim shows that an impressive 73
per cent of the British people are in favour of returning the marbles to
Greece. But wait. Just look at how the survey formulates the crucial
question: 'Do you agree or disagree that the British Museum should
allow the Elgin Marbles to be reunited and displayed again in Athens,
Greece, where they come from?' What reasonable person would
not agree to such a proposal? No hint here that one of this country's
most important artistic treasures, works of art that have been seen by
visitors from all over the world and that have inspired British artists
and writers for two centuries, would be lost to us for ever.

Yet, brandishing the results of this dubious opinion poll in the
London *Evening Standard*, Mr Cook has the audacity to claim that it
'confirms public support for restoring the Marbles to Greece' and calls
on the trustees of the BM not to 'defy the wishes of the British people'
in this matter. Thank goodness that the duty of the BM's trustees is
not to follow opinion polls but to fulfil their fiduciary duty.

But the disingenuous methods used by the pollsters render the
survey's results utterly worthless. And the nauseating campaign
video, which has been sent to thousands of people, is an even more
outrageous travesty of the truth. To take a few examples, the term

used for the proposed permanent restitution of the marbles to Greece
is 'extended display' in Athens. It uses the words 'stolen by the
British' to describe Elgin's legitimate purchase of the marbles, and
characterises as 'plunder' the works of art he in fact saved. Our ill-
informed former foreign secretary even claims that Elgin 'dismantled
the Acropolis' in an 'act of vandalism'.

'The Greek Proposal' piously calls for the 'two-way traffic' of
antiquities between Greece and Great Britain – but only in exchange
for the marbles. Since the Greek government has ruled out any form
of compromise with the BM, it has made any serious discussion about
the marbles impossible. Their attitude is very different from that of the
Egyptians, who recently confirmed that they wish merely to borrow
the Rosetta Stone for a few months for the opening of a new national
museum.

What is more, the interest and significance of the Parthenon
marbles is actually enhanced by being displayed in the BM, where
4.6 million visitors a year can view them without cost. In Athens, the
surviving fragments of the Parthenon tell one story: that of the art and
culture of ancient Greece. In the BM, they tell many stories, and not
only about Greece but about the whole of Western civilisation and
its relationship to Eastern cultures. By walking a few steps from the
Duveen Galleries, where the marbles are so beautifully shown, for
example, we can see how profoundly the sculptors who carved them
were influenced by Assyrian, Persian and Egyptian art. Without
having to leave the building, we can see how much Western architects,
artists and sculptors learned from the Greeks. Surely it is the whole
purpose of great museums to show these appropriations. And, from
a purely British perspective, the marbles are particularly important
since our artists – among them William Blake, Edward Burne-Jones
and Frederic Leighton – owe so much to the presence of the marbles
in this country.

Finally, I come to the nastiest part of this new campaign, the
attempt to link the issue both to this summer's Olympic games in
Athens and to Britain's bid to host the games in 2012. The Olympics
are not supposed to be used for political ends. But the Greek
government is deliberately using the games for a political purpose
in a way that has not happened so blatantly since Berlin in 1936. In
his article in the *Evening Standard*, Mr Cook bared his teeth. Hand over

the marbles, he wrote, or 'every Olympic dignitary' will be 'shepherded by their Greek hosts around the new Acropolis Museum with a long blank wall where the Elgin Marbles should be'. Then, in a direct threat to the trustees of the BM, he warned: 'Nor would wise trustees want to risk being seen to undermine London's bid to host the Olympics.' In other words, in exchange for the possibility that London might host a few weeks of sporting events and so gain votes for the Labour party, he wants the trustees to give away one of the most glorious work of art in this country.

This whole campaign is sheer lunacy. If by some remote chance these people were to succeed in their aims, just think of the flood of claims for restitution of art back to Italy or the Netherlands. Our museums would be emptied within a decade.

Closer Examination:
Fakes, Mistakes and Discoveries

I've never understood why the public and press routinely treat forgers
as romantic rapscallions. Passing off a fake or a pastiche as authentic
may or may not be a crime committed for personal gain, but it is
always a form of slander. It diminishes the stature of an artist by
introducing inferior works into his or her canon, and it makes it
impossible for art historians to build a coherent picture of his artistic
personality. One consolation is that even if a forger manages to fool
the experts, it is rarely for very long. Never underestimate the power
of disinterested scholarship to confirm or overturn attributions. As the
Old Masters never stopped telling us, Time Unveils Truth.

Close Examination at the National Gallery looks at forty
problematic works from the collection – including outright forgeries,
misattributions, pastiches, copies, altered or over-restored paintings,
and works whose authenticity has wrongly been doubted. Curators
Ashok Roy and Marjorie E. Wieseman have taken on a huge
subject – the range of possibilities museum professionals take into
consideration when they investigate a picture's status and the variety
of technical procedures conservation scientists use to establish
authorship and date. The case histories they discuss have a single
common denominator. In whatever direction and to whatever
conclusion the combined disciplines of connoisseurship, science
and art history may lead, the study of any work of art begins with
a question: is the work by the artist to whom it is attributed?

A good example is an Italian painting on panel that the National
Gallery acquired in 1923 as the work of an artist in the circle of the
Italian fifteenth-century painter Melozzo da Forli. Today we find it
incredible that anyone was ever fooled by a picture that looks like it
was painted by a Surrealist follower of Salvador Dalí. But that is to
forget how little was known about Melozzo ninety years ago, and
how little could be done in the conservation lab to determine the date

29 June 2010

Close Examination:
Fakes, Mistakes and
Discoveries

National Gallery,
London

of pigments or wood panel. Even so, from the moment the picture was acquired, sceptics called its status into question. In 1960 a costume historian pointed out the many anachronisms in the clothing. When technological advances enabled the gallery to test the pigments they were found to be nineteenth-century.

Scientific evidence can be invaluable but it has to be used with caution and always in tandem with historical research. For example, Corot's ravishing *plein-air* sketch *The Roman Campagna with the Claudian Aqueduct* has always been dated to about 1826, soon after the artist's arrival in Rome. However, the green pigment called viridian that Corot used throughout the picture only became available to artists in the 1830s. The landscape wasn't a fake and for stylistic reasons couldn't have been painted later than the mid-1820s. All became clear when art historians did further research and discovered that the firm that sold artists' supplies to Corot in Paris started making the newly developed colour available to selected customers in the 1820s, long before it came into widespread use.

The flip side of a fake – but capable of doing equal violence to an artist's reputation – occurs when an authentic work is mistakenly labelled a forgery. Back in 1996 I well remember how distressing it was to read an article published in *The Sunday Telegraph* in which the former director of the Metropolitan Museum of Art, Thomas Hoving, declared that Uccello's lovely little canvas of *St George and the Dragon* was forged. The gallery therefore X-rayed the picture and tested paint samples, before concluding that it was a rare survival of a work by Uccello dating from the early 1470s. Hoving was irresponsible not because he questioned the attribution of a much-loved work, but because the old publicity hound went public without first asking the gallery to carry out a thorough scientific analysis of it.

Any crank can label a picture a fake or copy, but their opinions are worthless unless they can support them with tangible proof. One picture that's been smeared in this way is Raphael's *Madonna of the Pinks*. In this exhibition we are shown infrared photographs that reveal the presence both of major *pentimenti* (corrections) which a copyist would not need to make, and also of underdrawing in a hand comparable to Raphael's when he sketches on paper. The pigments and painting technique exactly match those the artist used in other works of about the same date.

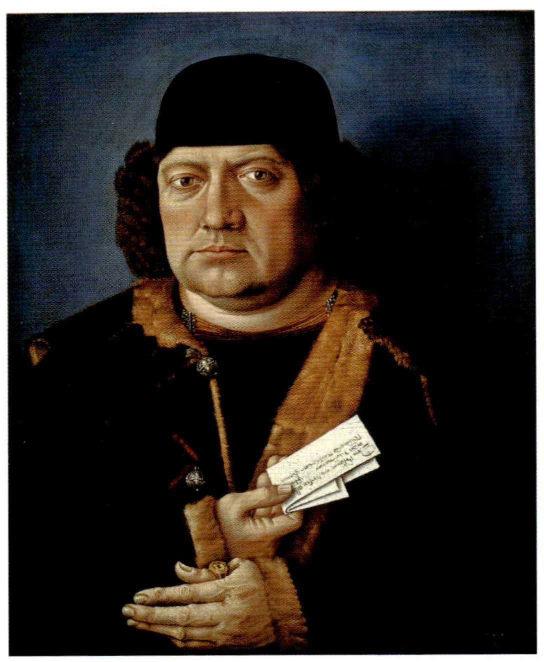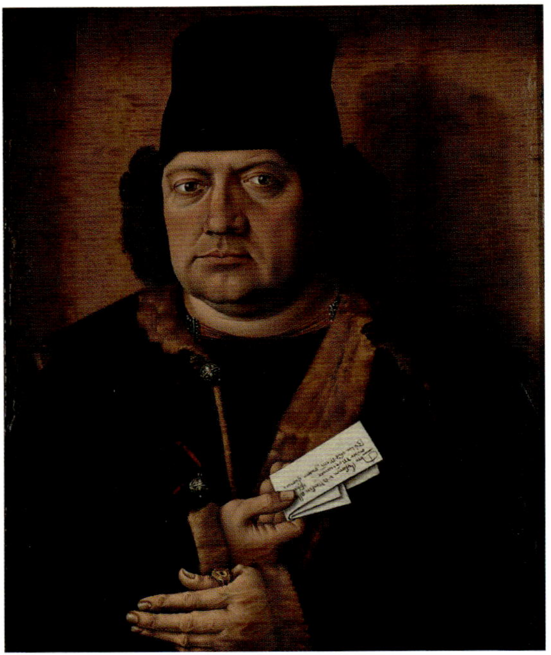

Conservation science is the glamorous part of making attributions, and the aspect of a museum's work that receives the most publicity. But it will never entirely supplant the human eye – or touch. When the Sainsbury Wing opened in 1990 the National Gallery acquired a small portrait on panel attributed to an unknown artist working in Germany in the mid-fifteenth century. The sitter is shown holding a letter in his hand which identifies him as Alexander Mornauer, town clerk in the Bavarian city of Landshut. At the time of purchase the painting showed the burgher against a plain, anti-naturalistic blue background, much as Hans Holbein was to do in the next century.

But the moment Ashok Roy ran his hand over the background's smooth surface, alarm bells rang. In the Renaissance, deep blue pigment was made by pulverising hard stone, which made the paint surface gritty to the touch. As Roy suspected, ensuing tests showed that the background had been painted over in the eighteenth century. Once it had been removed, the original picture was revealed to be typical for a work of about 1464–68, but not a proto-Holbein.

For all its pleasures, the show also has an unspoken agenda. It is a riposte to the mistaken belief that museums have anything to gain by hiding the true status of the art they own. As the downgrading in this show of Courbet's *Self Portrait* to the status of a posthumous copy after a picture in the Louvre shows, the opposite is the case: museums and galleries constantly question, revise, reattribute and re-date the works in their care. If they make a mistake, they acknowledge it. If a respected scholar reattributes a painting, the picture is re-labelled or taken off view. The press loves to publish stories and letters accusing museums of lurid cover-ups, usually originating from a very small number of amateurs who rarely know what they are talking about. But any curator or director will tell you that art museums have to deal in the truth, because if they lose credibility, they lose the reason for their existence.

I Look Back with Amazement

Late in 1986 I received a telephone call from Miriam Gross, arts editor
at *The Daily Telegraph*. She was calling out of the blue to ask whether
I'd be interested in writing for the paper as its chief art critic. Until
then I'd worked as a museum curator, freelance writer and exhibition
organiser. The idea of a career in journalism had never entered my
mind, but thank goodness I accepted. As I retire after almost thirty
years doing a job I loved, I look back with amazement at how different
the gallery and museum scene in this country is from the one I wrote
about back then.

Any notion I might have entertained that my new job would be
stress-free vanished within weeks. The problem was not how I wrote
but what I wrote about. Most of my reviews were unproblematic
because they dealt with Old Master and classic twentieth-century art.
But I also loved the challenge of reviewing contemporary art – and to
my surprise, this didn't always go down well with my employers.

My enjoyment of contemporary art had to do in part with my
background. As a graduate student studying art history in New York
at the age of twenty-two I fell in love with my first wife. Through Kate
and her family I became enthralled with the work of Jasper Johns, Cy
Twombly and Robert Rauschenberg and came into frequent contact
with them. In photos of our small wedding in 1970, they are all among
the guests – as were the gallerist Leo Castelli, architect Philip Johnson
and the future biographer of Picasso, John Richardson. Only later
did I come to realise how influential those experiences had been on
someone who might otherwise have been locked into the study of
eighteenth- and nineteenth-century art. To put it simply, they taught
me the value and importance of art, both old and new.

I took for granted my obligation as a critic to tell readers about the
art of my own time. That was naive. A deep mistrust of modern art
existed at every level of British society. Just as I was starting out in the

23 June 2015

late Eighties, early exhibitions at the Saatchi Gallery, the first years of the Turner Prize, and the appointment of Nicholas Serota as director of the Tate Gallery followed in quick succession. The effect was to ignite smouldering resentment into open hostility. There were many sources of art-rage, but any favourable comment about the Turner Prize, Twombly or Gilbert and George guaranteed outraged press coverage in the *Daily Mail*, *Sunday Telegraph* (when Peter Fuller was its critic), *The Spectator* and the *Evening Standard*.

But not in *The Daily Telegraph* – at least not from me. Without intending to, I made life difficult for successive editors who were torn between support for their critic and profound disagreement with what he was saying. The solution was to run quite a few strongly worded leaders disassociating the paper from those particular reviews. That was fair enough. I reasoned that as long as the paper continued to print my views, it was entitled to take a different line.

Outside of the organisation things were much more brutal. One art critic called on one of the Tate's principal sponsors to withdraw its financial support, simply because he did not approve of a new display. Then a few rightwing political columnists joined in the debate. Their pieces were contemptuous in a way I'd not experienced before. Only once did I feel that an attack was so personal – I was called a fool – it required a forceful public response if I was to retain the respect an art critic needs in order to write effectively.

On the other hand, there could have been no better time for a journalist to defend new art. An opinion piece I wrote stays in my mind. It was published on 26 February 1993. In it, I didn't say that all (or even most) modern art had merit – only that readers were being short-changed by reviewers who simply strung together adjectives like 'stupid', 'aimless' and 'rubbish' without feeling obliged to explain what the artist does, why he does it, and whether he succeeds or fails. I pointed out that they were getting away with it only because editors normally didn't take much interest in art. Had the same critics been writing about film, sport or the stock market they'd have been rumbled in a week.

That, of course, fuelled even more controversy, but this time something felt different. Never before or since did I receive so many letters of support. The artist Michael Craig–Martin put his finger on the reason when he wrote that 'to have published such an article

anywhere would have been helpful, but in the *Telegraph* was
profoundly so.' That was perceptive. A conservative newspaper
read by the establishment is the ideal platform from which to defend
tolerance, encourage curiosity and praise the virtue of keeping an
open mind. No one could have known then that over the next three
decades museums and galleries in this country would develop in
ways not seen since the mid-nineteenth century, or that in our own
time the entire country would embrace new art in the way it did.

I will always be grateful to those editors for allowing me to write
what I wanted. Because of their forbearance, *Telegraph* coverage of the
visual arts in the years leading up to the opening of Tate Modern in
2000 reflected the profound cultural changes taking place in Britain
in these years. In long reviews praising Richard Long, Anish Kapoor,
Tony Cragg, David Tremlett and Richard Deacon, or in our support
of video installations by Mark Wallinger, Douglas Gordon and Susan
Hiller, readers were given an alternative to the irrational prejudice
against new art expressed in some places. Those voices didn't stop
after 2000, but as the mood of the country changed they began to
sound more and more irrelevant.

I do not, however, overestimate the importance of the *Telegraph*'s
role. At best it amounted to a rearguard action in support of the
achievements of Serota, Julia Peyton-Jones at the Serpentine, and
James Lingwood of Artangel. Nor was it alone. Critics like Richard
Cork in *The Times* and Andrew Graham-Dixon when he was at *The
Independent* wrote eloquently about the same artists I did. Much more
important than any of us for changing hearts and minds were the
Unilever displays in the Turbine Hall at Tate Modern like Olafur
Eliasson's stupendous *The Weather Project* in 2003, where a giant sun
dominated the space, or Doris Salcedo's unforgettable *Shibboleth* in
2007, where the length of the floor was riven by a crack. By 1997 that
massive cultural shift was already well under way. Then, overnight,
New Labour made New Art acceptable. The *Telegraph*'s culture
skirmishes were over.

As for me personally, I don't by any means think I got all of it
right. But I have many more regrets about the artists I failed to
appreciate – Peter Doig is a good example – than the ones I now think
didn't deserve as much attention as I gave them, including quite a few
of the Young British Artists who came to prominence in the Nineties.

How would I like to be remembered? By reviews such as the one I wrote about the 2012 Turner Prize exhibition, when I saw the work of Elizabeth Price for the first time. After watching her video *The Woolworths Choir of 1979* – which combined dry-as-dust images from a textbook on Gothic architecture with newsreel footage taken in the aftermath of a tragic blaze in Manchester to create an unforgettable collage of sound, image and text – I remained in my seat and sat through it two more times. Then I went home and wrote that I'd just experienced 'twenty of the most exhilarating minutes I've ever spent in an art gallery'. That's the spirit in which I always wanted to write about all art – loud and clear and without hedging my bets. On my best days, that's what I hope I did.

And with that I'll take my leave, with sincere thanks to my editors and colleagues at the *Telegraph*, and to the kind readers who have written to me over the years, particularly Barbara Duce, my correspondent from Canterbury whose letters never failed to buck me up.

Picture credits

Pages 52, 57, 113 Royal Collection Trust/© HM Queen Elizabeth II 2016; 75 © RMN-Grand Palais (Musée du Louvre)/Gérard Blot; 77 © National Portrait Gallery, Smithsonian Institution; acquired as a gift to the nation through the generosity of the Donald W. Reynolds Foundation; 78, 203 © The Metropolitan Museum of Art/Art Resource/Scala, Florence; 83 © Rothschild Collection, Waddesdon; 93 bottom © Art Gallery of Ontario, 2016; 95 © Getty Images/Hulton Fine Art Collection; 103 Courtesy Courtauld Institute of Art; 107 © Cleveland Museum of Art; 109, 115 both, 170 left, 238, 243, 494 © Trustees of the Tate Gallery; 116, 235 © Royal Holloway, University of London/Bridgeman Images; 123 © National Gallery of Art, Washington DC; 125 Reproduction courtesy of the Museum Oskar Reinhart am Stadtgarten; 127 © INTERFOTO/Alamy Stock Photo; 129 © FineArt/Alamy Stock Photo; 139 © PARIS PIERCE /Alamy Stock Photo; 145 © The Metropolitan Museum of Art/Art Resource/Scala, Florence; 146 bottom © Musée d'Orsay/Scala, Florence; 157 © Christie's Images, London/Scala, Florence; 161 © Josse/Scala, Florence; 167 © Princeton University Art Museum/Art Resource NY/Scala, Florence; 170 right © RMN-Grand Palais/ Agence Bulloz; 172 © Artepics/Alamy Stock Photo; 189 © Heritage Image Partnership Ltd/Alamy Stock Photo; 194 © Göteborgs Konstmuseum; 205 © Digital Image Museum Associates/LACMA/Art Resource NY/Scala, Florence; 230, 232 © Bridgeman Images/Faringdon Collection, National Trust; 268–69 © Wellcome Library, London; 277, 281 top, 287, 288–89 © Succession H. Matisse/DACS 2016; 281 bottom, 303 © Succession Pablo Picasso/DACS 2016; 305 © Menil Collection, Houston/DACS; 307 © DACS/Scala Archives; 309 © 2016 Successió Miró/DACS/Museum of Modern Art, New York; 313 © 2016 ADAGP Paris/DACS, London; 319 © 2016 Metropolitan Museum of Art/Scala Archives; 325 © Herbert Gehr/The LIFE Picture Collection/Getty Images; 329 © Artepics/Alamy Stock Photo; 333, 335 © Estate of Arshile Gorky/DACS 2016; 340 © The Pollock-Krasner Foundation/ARS, NY/DACS, London 2016; 345 © Estate of Roy Lichtenstein/DACS 2016; 350, 351 Estate of Cy Twombly; 353, 358–59 © 2016 The Andy Warhol Foundation for the Visual Arts, Inc./Artists Rights Society (ARS), New York/DACS, London; 362 © DACS/ Museum of Fine Arts, Houston, Texas, USA/Museum purchase funded by the Agnes Cullen Arnold Endowment Fund/Bridgeman Images; 366 © 2016 Brice Marden/DACS, London; 372 © DACS/Trustees of the Tate Gallery; 372, 374 © DACS/Trustees of the Tate Gallery; 377 © DACS/Bruce Nauman; 391 © The Cecil Beaton Studio Archive at Sotheby's; 395, 396, 397 © Stanley Spencer Estate/Bridgeman Images Copyright Services; 401 © DACS; 403 Photo © Edward Quinn edwardquinn. com; 407 © Estate of Robin Ironside; 409 © Estate of Keith Vaughan/Fitzwilliam Museum, University of Cambridge/DACS; 412 © Succession Pablo Picasso/Trustees of the Tate Gallery/DACS 2016; 413 © The Estate of Francis Bacon 2016/DACS; 416 © Estate of Cecil Collins/Courtesy Offer Waterman Gallery, London; 423 © DACS/Bruce Nauman/ Photograph Fujitsuka Mitsumasa, Courtesy of Benesse Holdings, Inc.; 427 © Estate of On Kawara/David Zwirner Gallery, London; 431, 433 © Estate of Eva Hesse. Hauser & Wirth Zürich London; 437 © Mary Sue Ader-Andersen/DACS; 440 top © Jeff Wall/Trustees of the Tate Gallery; 443 © Gary Hill/photographs Dirk Bleicker, courtesy Gladstone Gallery, New York and Brussels; 446 © Francesco Clemente; 460 © Francis Alÿs; 467 © David Hockney, courtesy of the artist; 469 © Gilbert and George/Tate Images; 473 © Andy Goldsworthy, courtesy of the artist; 485 © Marcus Coates, courtesy of the artist and Kate MacGarry, London; 487 © Steve Vidler/Alamy Stock Photo; 492 LOOK Die Bildagentur der Fotografen GmbH/Alamy Stock Photo; 503 © Classicpaintings/Alamy Stock Photo; 507 © John Crook/With thanks to the Dean and Chapter of Winchester Cathedral; 522 both © Courtesy of the National Gallery, London.

All other images copyright the artists and/or other copyright holders where applicable. Every effort has been made to trace copyright holders and to obtain their permission for the use of copyright material. The publisher apologises for any errors or omissions in the above list and would be grateful if notified of any corrections that should be incorporated in future reprints or editions of this book.